HAMMOND, N. G. L. **A history of Macedonia. v. I: Historical geography and prehistory.** Oxford, 1972. 493p il map. 38.50. ISBN 0-19-814294-3

The first of a three-volume history of Macedonia which will undoubtedly remain for long the definitive work on that large part of ancient Greece whose kings were ultimately to conquer the world. The work is divided into two parts: the historical geography of Macedonia and the prehistory of Macedonia. There is no other previous work which for completeness and thoroughness of documentation can in any way compare with it. Hammond knows intimately and at firsthand every part of the region, having walked over most of it in the past four decades. Here is a perfect combination of the trained observer and the consummate scholar; the result is excellent. The second part is more of a desk job, a thorough assembling of all excavation results synthesized to give a running account of Macedonian prehistory from palaeolithic beginnings to the end of the Iron Age, about 550 B.C. Most important is the treatment of the contemporary prehistory of the neighboring regions of Albania and Yugoslavia together with that of Macedonia, for this has been sorely lacking in most other accounts. This, then, is Macedonia in its largest sense. A must for all Greek scholars.

CHOICE JULY/AUG. '73

History, Geography &
Travel

Ancient (Incl.
Archaeology)

A HISTORY OF
MACEDONIA

A HISTORY OF
MACEDONIA

VOLUME I

Historical geography and prehistory

N. G. L. HAMMOND
D.S.O., D.L., M.A., F.B.A.

Officer of the Royal Hellenic Order of the Phoenix
Professor of Greek in the University of Bristol
formerly Headmaster of Clifton College
and Fellow and Tutor of Clare College
Cambridge

OXFORD
AT THE CLARENDON PRESS
1972

Oxford University Press, Ely House, London W. 1

GLASGOW NEW YORK TORONTO MELBOURNE WELLINGTON
CAPE TOWN IBADAN NAIROBI DAR ES SALAAM LUSAKA ADDIS ABABA
DELHI BOMBAY CALCUTTA MADRAS KARACHI LAHORE DACCA
KUALA LUMPUR SINGAPORE HONG KONG TOKYO

© *Oxford University Press 1972*

*Printed in Great Britain
at the University Press, Oxford
by Vivian Ridler
Printer to the University*

TO
FRANK EZRA ADCOCK

PREFACE

I WAS still working on my book *Epirus* when the Clarendon Press invited me to undertake a history of Macedonia. It was clear to me that such a history was needed, and that if it was conceived on the same scale as my work on Epirus it would require two or three volumes. The project became feasible when G. T. Griffith kindly agreed to collaborate with me, and it received the blessing of Sir Frank Adcock, of whom we are both proud to have been pupils and friends. We express our gratitude to him for his continuous support and interest in our work by dedicating *The History of Macedonia* to his memory.

In the first part of this volume the foundation of historical geography is laid. The accounts of the early travellers have been very valuable—especially those of Heuzey, von Hahn, Delacoulonche, Leake, and Struck —and I have gained much from the work of C. F. Edson, F. Papazoglou, and D. Kanatsoulis. But in the long run autopsy counts for most. In December 1929 I was introduced to Macedonia by Walter Heurtley, then the leading authority on the region and a great walker. He began by taking T. C. Skeat and me up the great Haliacmon gorge from below Verria to Servia, the site of one of his excavations. We went later to Armenokhori and then worked in Salonica on prehistoric pottery from that site and from other sites. In 1930 I visited Kavalla, Philippi, and some places in eastern Thrace. In the course of my work in Epirus I crossed the Pindus range by more than one route and came down to Grevena. I walked from Konitsa via Slatina to Hrupista (Argos Orestikon) and Kastoria; and I crossed back from Florina over the Tsangon pass to Koritsa. I traversed parts of Western Macedonia at that time, and I went into Chalcidice to Poliyiros and Olynthus. In 1941 events took me through the British line in Macedonia as far as Florina and Kalliniki. In 1943 I lived for six winter weeks high up on Mt. Ossa, made a reconnaissance of the Tempe pass, traversed most of Lower Olympus, and moved through north-eastern Thessaly to Kalabaka. From May 1943 to January 1944 I was in charge of the Allied Military Mission in Macedonia, and I came to know very thoroughly and under primitive conditions Southern and Western Macedonia from the Pierian coast at the Haliacmon mouth and the Litokhoro–Katerini area as far inland as Kastoria and Ephtakhori. Voïon I knew village by village, and all the high routes of north-eastern Pindus, the Cambunian mountains, and the northern Pierian mountains. In 1968 the British Academy generously gave me a research grant which enabled me to travel through Greek

Macedonia as far east as Amphipolis and through Yugoslav Macedonia as far as Ochrid, Kitsevo, and Priština. I walked to some sites such as Tsepicovo, Trebenishte, Palatitsa, Palatianon, and Sut Burun. Thus my knowledge of Macedonia, though far less intimate and detailed than my knowledge of Epirus and southern Albania, seemed sufficient for a study of the historical geography of the region.

The prehistory of Macedonia itself owes most to Rey, Casson, and Heurtley, and it was Heurtley who organized and synthesized their knowledge in his invaluable book, *Prehistoric Macedonia*, published in 1939. Heurtley concerned himself little with literary evidence, matters of geography, and the setting of Macedonia in relation to adjacent territories, and he omitted the bronzes entirely in his treatment of Early Iron Age Macedonia. He was indeed writing a magnificent archaeological handbook of the area, as it was then known, and not a prehistory of the region. Since 1939 there have been extensive excavations in Greek Macedonia at Vergina, Pella, Olynthus, and many other sites, and in the adjacent territories of Albania, of Yugoslavia, and of northern Thessaly within Greece.

The body of evidence has increased hugely. It is almost entirely uncoordinated. Prendi at Malik in Albania, Grbić at Porodin in southern Yugoslavia, and Andronikos at Vergina in Southern Macedonia might have been excavating on separate planets. This is no discredit to them, because their concern has been with the accurate recording of particular excavations. What I have attempted here is a co-ordination of the evidence from Macedonia and from adjacent areas, and an interpretation of the prehistory of the region. It has proved a long and demanding task. My early preoccupation with the Dorian invasion had made it clear to me that Macedonia and Epirus held the key to the movements of the Greek-speaking peoples and indeed to those of other peoples too. This is inevitably so, since any movements overland into the Greek peninsula go perforce through one area or the other or through both. An essential preliminary to answering the question which J. L. Myres asked, 'Who were the Greeks?', has always seemed to me to be the study of Epirus and Macedonia together. At some points in the second part of this volume such a study is undertaken with the result, I think, that a new understanding may have been attained of the coming of the first Greeks, and of the movements of the Ionian-, Aeolian-, and Doric-speaking branches of the Greek people, the Phrygian peoples, and the Macedonians themselves. A study on this scale is at least a novelty.

I owe gratitude above all to my collaborator in this undertaking, G. T. Griffith, and to C. F. Edson, who has allowed me to draw upon his unrivalled knowledge of Macedonian inscriptions and topography. They have both read and commented on the first draft of the present volume.

The writing of it was made possible only by the generosity of the Institute for Advanced Study at Princeton, New Jersey, which made me a member for the spring term of 1968. I am grateful too to the University of Bristol, which granted me leave of absence for that term. At Princeton I owed much to the interest and the help of Homer and Dorothy Thompson, Stefan Foltiny, and Professor D. Rendić-Miočević. The Fulbright authorities kindly gave me a grant, and the British Academy a research award, which helped me to travel in Macedonia. In August 1968 the Institute for Macedonian Studies invited me to its Conference on Macedonia in Salonica. It was a most stimulating and heart-warming experience, for which I thank Mr. Ch. Frangistas and Professor B. Laourdas in particular. It enabled me to renew my friendship with Ph. Petsas, whom I first met in Epirus, and to make the acquaintance of M. Andronikos, Ch. Makaronas, D. Kanatsoulis, and other leading scholars of Macedonia. I express my gratitude to them all and especially to M. Andronikos who gave me a copy of his magnificent publication *Vergina*.

At the same time I express my gratitude to S. I. Dakaris for past and present help in Epirus; to Mrs. Vokotopoulou, who showed me some of her discoveries at Vitsa while they were still unpublished; to Frano Prendi for his kindness in sending me offprints of his reports of excavations in Albania; to Fanoula Papazoglou for sending me copies of her work on Macedonia; to Dragica Simovska for showing me round the museum at Monastir; and to Panagiotis Manos for taking me round the site at Palatianon. Miss Elizabeth Horton of the Institute for Advanced Study and Mrs. Janet Gliddon of the Classics Department in the University of Bristol have given me secretarial help with ungrudging cheerfulness, and I take the opportunity to thank all those in the Clarendon Press who have assisted in the production of the maps and line drawings. I drew the first draft of these myself.

In the spelling of personal names and place-names I have used the latinized forms when I refer to names of the classical and Hellenistic periods, and the anglicized forms of Albanian, Bulgarian, Greek, and Yugoslav names, mainly as they are given on the maps of the U.S. Army (scale 1 : 200,000). I have not aimed at complete consistency in the matter. For almost all place-names the reader will find in the Index a map-reference to a map in this book. Where it seemed desirable, I have given the earlier name as well as the name introduced by Metaxas for places in Greek Macedonia. Sometimes I have used a traditional name instead of a modern one; e.g. Monastir and not Bitola, Scodra and not Shkodër, Salonica and not Thessaloniki.

N. G. L. HAMMOND

The University of Bristol
September 1969

CONTENTS

Contents

LIST OF MAPS

LIST OF FIGURES

(pp. 444 ff.)

Note. The figures are not drawn to scale, and objects on each figure are not in scale with one another, unless it is stated otherwise

ABBREVIATIONS

are those listed in Liddell–Scott–Jones, *Lexicon*, ninth edition, except as follows:

AAA	*Annals of Archaeology and Anthropology* (Liverpool)
AD	Ἀρχαιολογικὸν Δελτίον
AE	Ἀρχαιολογικὴ Ἐφημερίς
AJA	*American Journal of Archaeology*
AM	*Athenische Mitteilungen*
AI	*Archaeologia Iugoslavica*
Alt-Ithaka	W. Dörpfeld, *Alt-Ithaka* (Munich, 1937)
Arch. Anz.	*Archäologischer Anzeiger* in *JDAI*
Arch. Reports	*Archaeological Reports*
Археология	Археология Българската акад. на науките, София
AS	*Anatolian Studies*
ASPR	*American School of Prehistoric Research Bulletin*
ATL	B. D. Meritt, H. T. Wade-Gery, and M. F. McGregor, *The Athenian Tribute Lists* (Harvard, 1939–53)
BCH	*Bulletin de correspondance hellénique*
BRGK	*Bericht der Römisch-Germanischen Kommission*
BS	*Balkan Studies*
BSA	*The Annual of the British School at Athens*
BUSS	*Buletin për shkencat shoqërore* (Tiranë)
BUST	*Buletin i Universitetit Shtetëror të Tiranës, Seria shkencat shoqërore* (Tiranë)
CAH[2]	*Cambridge Ancient History*[2], edited by I. E. S. Edwards, C. J. Gadd, and N. G. L. Hammond, in the form of fascicles
Carapanos	C. Carapanos, *Dodone et ses ruines* (Paris, 1878)
Casson, *Macedonia*	S. Casson, *Macedonia, Thrace and Illyria* (Oxford, 1926)
Childe, *Danube*	V. G. Childe, *The Danube in Prehistory* (Oxford, 1929)
Chronologie	H. Müller Karpe, *Beiträge zur Chronologie d. Urnenfelderzeit*, Röm.-German. Forsch. 22 (1959)
Comptes rendus	*Comptes rendus de l'Acad. d'inscriptions de belles lettres*
CP	*Classical Philology*
Cvijić	J. Cvijić, 'Grundlinien der Geographie und Geologie von Makedonien und Altserbien', in *Petermanns Mitteilungen*, *Ergänzungsheft* Nr. 162 (Gotha, 1908)
Delacoulonche	Delacoulonche, *Mémoire sur le berceau de la puissance macédonienne* (Paris, 1858)
Desborough, *PGP*	V. R. d'A. Desborough, *Protogeometric Pottery* (Oxford, 1952)

Desborough, *TLM*	V. R. d'A. Desborough, *The Last Mycenaeans and their Successors* (Oxford, 1964).
Dimitsas	M. G. Dimitsas, Ἡ Μακεδονία ἐν λίθοις φθεγγομένοις καὶ μνημείοις σωζομένοις (Athens, 1896)
Ebert	M. Ebert, *Reallexikon d. Vorgeschichte* (de Gruyter, 1924–32)
Ep. Chron.	Ἠπειρωτικὰ Χρονικά
Epirus	N. G. L. Hammond, *Epirus* (Oxford, 1967)
FGrH	F. Jacoby, *Fragmente der griechischen Historiker* (Berlin, 1923)
FHG	C. Müller, *Fragmenta Historicorum Graecorum* (Paris, 1841–70)
Gimbutas, *Bronze Age*	M. Gimbutas, *Bronze Age Cultures in Central and Eastern Europe* (The Hague, 1965)
Gimbutas, *Prehistory*	M. Gimbutas, *The Prehistory of Eastern Europe I* (Cambridge Mass., 1956)
Heuzey, *Ol.*	L. A. Heuzey, *Le Mont Olympe et l'Acarnanie* (Paris, 1860)
Heuzey–Daumet	L. A. Heuzey and L. Daumet, *Mission archéologique de Macédoine* (Paris, 1876)
HG²	N. G. L. Hammond, *A History of Greece to 322 B.C.*, second edition (Oxford, 1967)
IG Bulg.	G. Mihailov, *Inscriptiones Graecae in Bulgaria Repertae IV* (1966)
Jacobsthal	G. Jacobsthal, *Greek Pins and their connexions with Europe and Asia* (Oxford, 1956)
JDAI	*Jahrbuch des deutschen archäologischen Instituts*
JHS	*The Journal of Hellenic Studies*
JRS	*The Journal of Roman Studies*
Kanatsoulis	D. Kanatsoulis, Μακεδονικὴ Προσωπογραφία (Thessaloniki, 1955)
Kirrha	L. Dor, J. Jannoray, H. and M. van Effenterre, *Kirrha* (Paris, 1960)
Leake	W. M. Leake, *Travels in Northern Greece* (London, 1835)
Mak.	Μακεδονικά
MEE	Μεγάλη Ἑλληνικὴ Ἐγκυκλοπαιδεία
MP	*The Mediterranean Pilot IV⁷* (London, 1941).
Olynthus	D. M. Robinson, and others, *Excavations at Olynthus* (Baltimore, 1929–52)
PAE	Πρακτικὰ τῆς ἐν Ἀθήναις Ἀρχαιολογικῆς Ἑταιρείας
Papazoglou	F. Papazoglou, *Makedonski Gradovi u rimsko Doba* (Skopje, 1957)
PM	W. A. Heurtley, *Prehistoric Macedonia* (Cambridge, 1939)
PPS	*Proceedings of the Prehistoric Society*
Praschniker	C. Praschniker, *Muzakhia und Malakastra* (Vienna, 1920)
Praschniker–Schober	C. Praschniker and A. Schober, *Archäologische Forschungen in Albanien und Montenegro* (Vienna, 1919)
PTh	A. J. B. Wace and M. S. Thompson, *Prehistoric Thessaly* (Cambridge, 1912)

RE	Pauly–Wissowa, *Realencyclopädie*
REG	*Revue des études grecques*
Rey	L. Rey, 'Observations sur les premiers **habitats** de la Macédoine', in *BCH* 41–3
Riv. d. Alb.	*Rivista d'Albania* I–V (Milan, 1940–4)
SA	*Studia Albanica* (Tirana)
Schránil	J. Schránil, *Die Vorgeschichte Böhmens und Mährens* (Berlin, 1928)
SEG	*Supplementum Epigraphicum Graecum*
Snodgrass, *EGA*	A. M. Snodgrass, *Early Greek Armour* (Edinburgh, 1964)
Spomenik	Српска академија наука споменик (Belgrade)
StH	*Studime Historike* (Tiranë)
Struck I	A. Struck, 'Makedonische Fahrten I: Chalcidice', in *Zur Kunde der Balkan Halbinsel, Reise und Beobachtungen* 4 (Vienna, 1907)
Struck II	A. Struck, 'Makedonische Fahrten', ibid. no. 7 (1908)
Tozer	H. F. Tozer, *Researches in the Highlands of Turkey* (London, 1869)
Verdelis	N. M. Verdelis, Ὁ Πρωτογεωμετρικὸς Ῥυθμὸς τῆς Θεσσαλίας (Athens, 1958)
Vergina or *V*	M. Andronikos, ΒΕΡΓΙΝΑ I, τὸ νεκροταφεῖον τῶν τύμβων (Athens, 1969)
von Hahn, *Denkschriften*	J. G. von Hahn in *Denkschriften der kaiserlichen Akademie der Wissenschaften, Philosoph. histor. Klasse*
WMBH	*Wissenschaftliche Mitteilungen aus Bosnien und Hercegovina*
ZA	*Ziva Antika*

BIBLIOGRAPHIES of earlier writings will be found in Casson, *Macedonia*, and in *RE* s.v. Makedonia, and of more recent material in *PM*, in the periodicals *Mak.*, *BUSS*, *BUST*, *SA*, *StH*, *AI*, and *Starinar*, and in D. H. French, *Index of Prehistoric Sites in Central Macedonia and Catalogue of Sherd Material in the University of Thessaloniki* (Athens, 1967), 52–5. The last work, published in a limited number of copies for the University of Thessaloniki, has a very useful list of sites with a map reference for each site, a description of its topography, size and physical features, a note of visits to it, and bibliographical references.

PART ONE

THE HISTORICAL GEOGRAPHY
OF MACEDONIA

I

THE PHYSICAL FEATURES OF MACEDONIA

1. *A definition of Macedonia*

OUR first need is to define Macedonia not as a political area but as a geographical entity. It is true that the very name 'Macedonia' has a political connotation in that it originated in the conquering 'Macedones' of 650 B.C. and onwards. Moreover 'Macedonia' has acquired in the modern mind a Greek colouring, not only because we view the great age of the Macedonian State through Hellenic and Hellenistic spectacles, but also because the bulk of what was once the Macedonian State is situated today within the confines of the Greek National State. This is an accident of politics and not a consequence of geographical congruity. It has been well said that the Greek National State today is 'at once a Mediterranean State and a Macedonian State',[1] with Athens/Peiraeus as the focal point of the former and Salonica as the focal point of the latter. The essential truth is that Athens looks primarily to the Mediterranean Sea; Salonica looks primarily to a continental hinterland. The extent of Athenian involvement in the Mediterranean area has never been in doubt. The extent of Salonica's involvement in the hinterland has depended upon changing political conditions. Before the crumbling of the Turkish Empire in 1912–13, as indeed during most of the prehistoric period, Salonica and its predecessors had a catchment-area of trade which extended westwards to the Adriatic Sea, northwards to the Danube basin, and eastwards into the interior of Thrace. Now, since 1919, the frontiers of Albania, Yugoslavia, and Bulgaria, in some decades more often closed than open, have reduced the actual catchment-area of Salonica to a mere fraction of what it had been, with the inevitable consequence that Salonica and its present hinterland have become more dependent on the Greek peninsula than they have ever been. Thus, if we try to define Macedonia on political lines, we shall be chasing a chameleon through the centuries.

As a geographical entity Macedonia is best defined as the territory which is drained by the two great rivers, the Haliacmon and the Vardar, and their tributaries (see Map 1). The lowest reaches of the original rivers and of some of their tributaries were drowned by the Aegean Sea, when its waters entered what was then a great basin encircled by high

[1] M. I. Newbigin, *Southern Europe* (London, 1932), 397.

land and is now the plain of Salonica and the Thermaic Gulf. The Haliacmon has many tributaries in its upper and middle reaches and one considerable tributary in the south, the Moglenitsa; in addition, the rivers which flow from Pieria into the Gulf should be regarded as truncated tributaries of the Haliacmon river-system. The Vardar has as its main western tributaries the Tresca, the Babuna, the Cerna Reka, and as a truncated tributary, the Ludias. Its main eastern tributaries are the Pecinj and the Bregalnitsa, while its truncated tributaries are the Gallikos, the Vasilikos, and the rivers of Crousis.[1] The limits of Macedonia as so defined are set by the watersheds of its river-system and by the sea-coast. There are, however, some peripheral areas which are marginal to our definition, in that they do not drain directly either into the Macedonian river-system or into that of its neighbours. To the west Lake Prespa and Lake Little Prespa and to the east Lake Doiran and Lake Koronia are in this position. As they are closer to Macedonian centres of population than they are to Albanian or Bulgarian centres, they are best regarded as peripheral to Macedonia in a geographical sense. Lake Ochrid and Lake Malik adhere to the Albanian river-system. Lake Bolbe drains into the Strymonian Gulf, but being adjacent to Lake Koronia it is normally included in Macedonia. On the other hand, those parts of the Chalcidic peninsula which do not drain westwards into the Thermaic Gulf are outside Macedonia. To the south those districts which face southwards from the Cambunian range and westwards from Mt. Olympus belong not to Macedonia but to the Greek peninsula. For, geographically speaking, Macedonia is not a part of Greece. Philippson assumed this when his book *Die Griechischen Landschaften* began not with Macedonia but with Epirus and Thessaly.

The greater part of Macedonia is remote from the sea. Its affinities are inevitably with the continental land-mass of the Balkans and not with the maritime peninsulas of Greece and Italy. This is true even of the coastal plain and its port Salonica. They are the terminals of a system of land-communications and they have a maritime outlet; but they remain continental in character. The high hinterland and especially the Vardar valley, acting as a funnel, endows the coastal plain with a continental climate. The distinction between the continental climate and the Mediterranean climate, which the Greek peninsula (in a geographical sense) and the three prongs of Chalcidice enjoy, is most clearly seen in the figures for rainfall. Of the total rainfall at Salonica 21·6 per cent is

---

[1] The westernmost peninsula of Chalcidice is in part a low-lying extension of Crousis and in part has its hill-system draining southwards; at the same latitude the Peneus river enters the sea. The Gulf is shallow north of this latitude; it deepens as one goes southwards from this latitude. In view of this it is best to regard Pallene and the Peneus as part of a different drainage system and not as belonging to Macedonia in a geographical sense. The depths are given in Cvijić pl. 17. See Map 1.

in the three summer months and 52·6 per cent in the six winter months. Even at Corfu, which is the wettest place in Greece, only 3·9 per cent of its rainfall is in the three summer months, and 78·7 per cent is in the six winter months. The Macedonian regime in rainfall is east European and not at all Mediterranean.[1] It is better for most cereals, for horses, cattle, and sheep, and for continental fruits, but it is unsuitable for the olive and the fig. The summer is more heavy and torrid than in peninsular Greece; for the great heat in the plains is broken only by thunderstorms, which are frequent in the late summer. The winters are far more severe than they are in northern Greece. In Epirus, which is the coldest part of the Greek peninsula, there is often more snow than in Macedonia, but the temperature is rarely as low as it is in Macedonia. I spent the first part of the winter of 1943 at Pendalophon in Voïon and was much in the open. One realized the meaning of 'the cold which kills the birds'.

2. *Macedonia and her neighbours*

In relation to her neighbours Macedonia has a geographical character of her own (see Map 19). Thessaly rather than Southern Macedonia is the transitional zone between the Continent and the peninsula. Although its wide plains resemble the coastal plain of Macedonia, and although Mt. Ossa suffers from the freezing 'Vardaris' wind in the winter months, Thessaly is already bordering on the Mediterranean region, and Volos in the Gulf of Pagasae is fully Mediterranean in its climate and products, whereas Salonica is continental. The closest affinities between Macedonia and Thessaly are to be found in north-east Thessaly and especially in Perrhaebia, where the upland basin of Elassona resembles the upland basins of Macedonia.

Epirus and Macedonia stand back to back along the range of Mt. Pindus and Mt. Grammos. There is a strong similarity in fact between the western side of the upper Haliacmon valley and the eastern side of the upper Aous valley. In ancient terms Tymphaea and Orestis were akin to northern Molossis and Parauaea; so much so that Tymphaea was often reckoned to be politically in Epirus, and Orestis sometimes opted to move with the Epirotes. The reason for this similarity is that they share the advantages of the central Balkan ridge of greenstone, which has natural forests of great extent, rich Alpine pastures and long ridges running down towards the rivers Aous and Haliacmon respectively.[2] There is a further point of similarity. The plain of Ioannina, with Dodona

[1] M. I. Newbigin, op. cit. 348 f.
[2] I have walked for instance from Konitsa to Kastoria and noted the similarities; see my description in *Epirus*, 275 f.

on its edge, is a high lacustrine basin which is very like the basins of Kastoria, Lyncus, and Pelagonia. When the country of the Molossians extended from the plain of Ioannina to the borders of Parauaea and Orestis, there was a sense in which Molossis was linked with Western Macedonia as far north as Pelagonia inclusive. There the similarity ends. For Epirus consists mainly of strongly folded limestone ranges, between which the valleys are squeezed tighter and tighter as one moves from north to south. Macedonia consists mainly of open plains and widely spaced mountains.

Albania as a geographical entity, corresponding to the ancient Illyris, lies to the west of the Balkan watershed, and its rivers flow westwards into the Adriatic Sea. These are the Drin with its two arms, the White Drin coming from the north and the Black Drin flowing northwards out of Lake Ochrid; the Shkumbi rising in the Candavian mountains; and the Devoli, which, unlike the Shkumbi, cuts through the southern extensions of the ranges that enclose Lake Ochrid. For much of its length Albania is insulated from Macedonia by the lakeland belt of Ochrid, Prespa and Little Prespa; for at this point the Balkan range has a triple spine with lakes on either side of the central ridge, and the watersheds for Albania and for Macedonia are formed by the outer ridges (see Map 6). To the north of Lake Ochrid there is again a single watershed, but it is formed by a high and densely forested range.

A feature which Albania and Macedonia have in common is a large coastal plain. In Albania it is not continuous. It is split into two halves by the promontory on which Epidamnus stands, in the north the plain of Zadrimë and the Mati valley, and in the south the plain of Myzeqijë. The rivers inundate the lowlands in autumn and spring, and the plains are swampy and rich in pasture. They are less well cultivated than the coastal plain of Macedonia, but their potential productivity is probably as high. In climate too Albania is closer to Macedonia than to Epirus or Thessaly.

The coastal plains of Albania and Macedonia are the starting-places of the main routes which lead from the sea to the central Balkans. That was more apparent in the past, before the modern states of Albania and Yugoslavia were established. From the Gulf of the Drin, which extends from the Bojana (the outflow of the Lake of Scodra) to Durazzo, one route cuts across the bend of the river Drin via the headwaters of the Fand, a tributary of the river Mati, to Kukus at the confluence of the White Drin and the Black Drin. From Kukus it follows the general line of the White Drin valley and climbs to Prizren. Here one is already in the central Balkans. Passage is easy northwards across the great upland basin of Metohija to Peć, north-eastwards into the great upland basin of Kossovo where the Ibar rises, and eastwards to Kačanik on a tributary of the Vardar (see Map 1). This route was very important in the Middle Ages and in Turkish times.[1]

The best route from the Aegean Sea to the central Balkans starts from the coast of the Thermaic Gulf. It proceeds via Edessa, Monastir, Prilep, Skopje, and Kačanik to the watershed between the Vardar and the Danube. In the past this route was usually preferred to the more direct route up the Vardar valley, which has narrow defiles, especially at Demir Kapu. But whichever route is taken, one descends from the Kačanik pass into the upland basin of Kossovo. This basin is the focal point of the central Balkans.

The coastal plains of Albania and Macedonia are linked together by the fact that they are the terminals of the best routes across the Balkans from east to west, or from west to east. The best-known route is that followed by the Via Egnatia. Starting from Salonica in the coastal plain, it proceeds, like the road northwards to the central Balkans, through Edessa to Monastir. There it branches off to Ochrid, rounds the head of the lake, and follows the general line of the Shkumbi valley into the coastal plain of Albania. A less well-known route lies to the south of the Via Egnatia. It crosses the Balkan range from the upland basin of Florina to the upland basin of Koritsa by two passes; it is more direct, and it involves no greater difficulties. It too descends into the coastal plain of Albania.

There is one respect in which Macedonia was more closely connected with Albania, Epirus, and Thessaly in the past than it is today. When pastoral life was important in a relatively primitive economy the trans-humance of sheep was conducted on a very large scale. The flocks moved in April from the coastal plains to the alpine pastures and returned in the early autumn. For example, Cvijić mentioned 6,000 sheep, which pastured in the summer on Mt. Babuna above Prilep and in the winter in the plain of Thessaly. The chief areas for winter pastures were the coastal plains of Albania, Epirus, and Macedonia, and the plain of Thessaly. Where sheep-raising is on a small scale, transhumance can be practised within relatively shorter distances. Thus in the *Oedipus Tyrannus* the two shepherds moved their flocks from Corinth and from Thebes respectively to Mt. Cithaeron for six months.[2] But large-scale sheep-raising, as practised by the Vlachs in Turkish times, demanded the movement of flocks far inland from the coastal plains which I have mentioned. It was evidently this practice in Macedonia which inspired Theopompus, if he is the source behind Justin 8. 5, to draw a comparison between Philip II's movement of cities and the shepherds' movement of their flocks.[3] On the other hand, when agriculture becomes more intensive

---

[1] See Cvijić 22 f. and pl. 17.   [2] *O.T.* 1127 f.

[3] Justin 8. 5, 'Ut pecora pastores nunc in hibernos nunc in aestivos saltus traiciunt, sic ille

the areas of pasture in the coastal plains grow smaller and sheep-raising declines rapidly, as it has done in this century.

The division between Macedonia, as I have defined it, and central Yugoslavia is formed by the watershed between the Vardar and the Morava catchment-areas. The closest resemblances are on both sides of the Kačanik pass, because the very high upland plains of Kossovo to the north and Tetovo to the south are very similar. The Preševo pass[1] north-east of Skopje is easier and more open than the Kačanik pass, but there is less affinity between the valley of the Pecinj and the valley of the Morava. As one proceeds southwards the differences between central Yugoslavia and Macedonia become more marked.

The division between Macedonia and Bulgaria, or in ancient terms Thrace, is formed by the very high watershed between the Vardar and the Strymon catchment-areas (see Map 17).[2] The main difference between the two valleys is that the Vardar valley is generally wide and open, and the Strymon valley north of the Rupel defile is narrow and pinched between very high ranges, providing only a mediocre route inland on its left side. There are some resemblances. In the upper valley of the Strumitsa the basin of Radovište (257 square km in area) is similar to the basins of Doiran and of Tetovo. The swampy basin of the lower Strymon is similar to the delta of the Vardar in the coastal plain of Macedonia, and the Strymonian Gulf has much in common with the Thermaic Gulf. Chalcidice, however, is entirely different from Macedonia and from Thrace; for its climate and its products are Mediterranean.

3. *The structure of Macedonia*

The most distinctive feature of Macedonia is the changes of level which have resulted from the raising and the sinking of many parts of its land-surface at different periods in geological time. Such movements have occurred even within a zone of uniform type. For example, the basin of Ovče Polje south-east of Skopje and the basin of Skopje were once two parts of the bed of a neogenic lake, but the former is now considerably higher than the latter. Similar movements on a larger scale have caused the Haliacmon river and the Cerna Reka to adopt their present devious courses and have separated basins from their outlets, for example, Lake Ostrovo from the valley leading to Edessa. Most of these movements occurred very early. For instance the great basin which is now encircled

populos et urbes . . . transfert.' The point is worth stressing, because Kirsten has expressed doubts whether transhumance was practised in ancient times (*Die Griechischen Landschaften* (Frankfurt, 1950–9) 2. 1. 172).

[1] The pass is well described by Cvijić 45.

[2] Cvijić 46, 'Bulgarien ist von Mazedonien durch natürliche feste Grenzen getrennt. Das sind die grössten Gebirgsmassen der Balkanhalbinsel: Osgov, Rila und Rhodope.'

by the mountains of Southern Macedonia, Chalcidice, the northern Sporades and Mts. Pelion, Ossa, and Olympus was created at a time when the Aegean Sea did not exist. Later, when Aegean waters flowed into part of the basin, they created the Thermaic Gulf, engulfing the lower courses of the rivers, but they left the plain of Salonica as it now is.[1]

One consequence of such movements has been the creation of many fertile basins which contain diluvium (the sediment of early lakes), and alluvium (the sediment still accumulating), and in some cases standing water. These basins are the chief centres of production and of population, except when they are filled or almost filled with water.

The names of the main basins in Macedonia from north to south are as follows. In some cases their area has been recorded by Cvijić; I have placed his number of square kilometres in brackets after the name.

1. Tetovo or Polog (232).
2. Skopje on both sides of the Vardar (393).
3. Ovče Polje in the catchment area of the northern part of the Bregalnitsa (1,400).
4. Maleš, being the eastern catchment area of the Bregalnitsa.
5. Kočane on the middle course of the Bregalnitsa (40).
6. Pelagonia, from Prilep to Monastir (1,212).
7. Kavadarci (Tikveš), including the Vardar valley between the defiles of Veles and Demir Kapu and also the lower Rajetz valley (2,047).
8. Florina, being the catchment area of the Cerna Reka south of the Monastir gap.
9. Kastoria, extending with one interruption from Lake Kastoria to Grevena.
10. Ostrovo, extending from Lake Ostrovo to the Sarigol.
11. Kozani, extending to the southern side of the Haliacmon river.
12. Moglena, some 30 km long and mainly narrow.
13. Bojmija, a narrow basin between the two defiles of the lower Vardar.
14. Salonica, being the coastal plain from Salonica to below Edessa and Verria (1,715).
15. Langadha, extending from Lete to Lake Bolbe.
16. Sedhes, extending up the Vasilikos valley.
17. Pieria, being the eastern, gentle slopes facing the Thermaic Gulf, and extending from the edge of the central plain to Malathria (Dium).
18. The Vasilikos valley and delta.
19. Crousis and the northern part of Pallene, which are of the same formation precisely as the basin of Pieria.

There are similar basins on the periphery or just beyond the periphery of Macedonia in the basins of Poloskë; Koritsa (including Lake Malik); Ochrid (the land area being larger in the north than in the south); Prespa (the land area being in the north by Resen); Metohija between

---

[1] The deposits of the Salonica plain are not marine but sweet-water deposits. The sea is the intruder.

Prizren and Peć; Kossovo Polje with Pristina as its centre; Radovište in the upper Strumitsa; Petrić; Doiran; Butkova; Serres.

The basins in Macedonia have a variety of soils. Some have the dark black soil which is typical of the Fens in England (e.g. Pelagonia). Others have the sandy soil and the clays of earlier lakes (e.g. Tikveš). Others still have volcanic deposits, which are exceptionally fertile (e.g. near Kratovo in the Pecinj basin and in the Moglena basin). All these soils are very fertile.

The productivity of the basins depends mainly on the amount of water available for irrigation. In this respect Macedonia is particularly fortunate. The great majority of the mountain ranges on both sides of the Vardar catchment area are of a crystalline formation, which is rich in water. In contrast to the eroded and barren limestone ranges of western Greece, for instance in Epirus and the Megarid, the crystalline ranges of Macedonia are densely forested and conserve the rainfall. The great rivers which rise in them flow strongly throughout the year. There is ample water for the irrigation of the basins during the summer.

The great forests and the fine pastures of the mountain ranges, which are due to their fertile soil, the numerous springs, and the spread of rainfall over the year are a source of natural wealth to the country. Timber from inland can be floated down the rivers, as in Canada, and timber is also cut in the vicinity of the coast (e.g. in the Pierian mountains and on Mt. Khortiatis). There is a wide variety of timber. The most densely forested mountain of Southern Macedonia, Mt. Bermion, has beech, oak, chestnut, pine, hazel, whitethorn, cornel-cherry, and evergreen maquis, in which there are wild pig, red deer, and roedeer. The forests of northern Pindus, Grammos, and the ranges which enclose Macedonia on the north-west are of enormous extent and harbour the brown bear, as well as pig, deer, and wolves.

In geological terms Macedonia, as I have defined it, may be split into three sectors.[1] The first is the Pelagonian massif, which extends from the Šar Planina in the north down to the Pierian mountains in the south. It is the oldest part of Macedonia, having been largely consolidated before

---

[1] The best work on the geology of Macedonia as a whole is that of Cvijić. He gives a geological map on pl. 18, and I have taken the heights of towns above sea level from his pl. 17. His information is better for the northern and north-eastern areas than for the rest of Macedonia. For the Greek part of Macedonia there is the excellent 'Geological Map of Greece', issued by the Institute for Geology and Subsurface Research at Athens, Ministry of Coordination, 1954 (scale 1:500,000). The best geological map of Albania is that of E. Nowack, *Geolog. Karte von Albanien* 1:200,000 (Berlin, 1928). There is an outline of the geology of Greece in the 'Livre à la mémoire du Prof. Paul Fallot, consacré à l'évolution paléogéographique et structurale des domaines méditerranéens et alpins d'Europe' (1960–3) 2. 583 f., and this is translated in *Guide to the Geology and Culture of Greece*, a publication of the Petroleum Exploration Society of Libya, Seventh Annual Field Conference, 1965. I am grateful to Mr. I. H. Ford of Bristol University for telling me of this publication.

the Mesozoic era. The massif is wide and generally high. It is cut by the upper Vardar, the Tresca, the Cerna Reka, and the Haliacmon. The continuation of this massif forms the coastline of the Greek peninsula from Mt. Olympus through Mt. Ossa to Mt. Pelion and is continued in the mountains of Euboea and in Attica. As the Pelagonian massif is high, the basins within it are also high, being from 900 to 600 m above sea level. Thus Kastoria is 870 m above sea level, Kozani 708 m and Monastir 613 m. It is this area, that is to say Western or 'upper' Macedonia, which has most affinity with the eastern side of the Greek peninsula. Large limestone formations, which developed later, occur within the zone of the Pelagonian massif in the lower Tresca valley; in the lakeland area of Ochrid, Prespa, and Kastoria; on both sides of Lake Ostrovo; in Mt. Siniatsikon (west of Kozani); and in Mt. Olympus itself. These formations are similar to formations further south in the Greek peninsula.

The second sector is the sunken region of the Vardar trough. Thus Skopje is only 290 m and Kačanik 475 m above sea level. This sink is in fact longer in extent than the Vardar valley, because it extends northwards beyond the Kačanik pass (578 m high) into the Kossovo basin and southwards into the seabed of the Thermaic Gulf, where it is terminated finally by the mainly limestone ranges of which the northern Sporades are the peaks. Within this trough there are two zones of crystalline rock, one between Skopje and Titov Veles, and the other just below Veles; then there are outcrops of granite at Štip and below Gevgheli, and a limestone outcrop at Demir Kapu. The gorges of the Vardar river are provided by these rocks: the Taor defile between Skopje and Veles, the Veles defile south of the town, the gorge of Demir Kapu, and that of Gevgheli. The Vardar zone is particularly wide in the plain of Salonica and in the northern part of the Thermaic Gulf, where the sides only are above water. These sides—the eastern part of Pieria, and Crousis— consist of the same deposits, which are mostly freshwater deposits, such as sand, clay, marl, conglomerate, and gypsum. On the western rim of the Vardar trough in the latitude of the Salonica plain there is a lofty travertine terrace, on which stand three important cities, Verria, Naoussa, and Edessa (Vodhena). Travertine is a general term for a porous light-yellow rock, and the rock at Verria, Naoussa, and Edessa is a limestone tufa. It is very rich in water, and it is easily worked for building, as is apparent from the ancient walls of Edessa which are now being cleared by excavation. The Vardar zone is unique in this area; for no analogous formation is found in Albania, Thrace, and Greece.

The third zone is that of easternmost Macedonia, where one enters upon the western fringe of the Thracian mountains. These mountains consist mainly of crystalline and granite rocks. They are generally higher than the Macedonian mountains, and they form the largest mountainous zone in the Balkan peninsula. In this zone one may include the western side of Mt. Osogov, where the Pecinj and the Bregalnitsa rivers take their rise, and the western and southern faces of Mt. Plaskovitsa and Mt. Belasitsa. It is the southern extension of this system which forms the watershed between the Vardar and the Strymon rivers and runs on through central Chalcidice into the prongs of Sithonia and Acte.

These broad geological divisions are interesting historically, because they have some general implications. Thus Thrace in a geographical sense may be said geologically to include the eastern overhangers of the Vardar zone. These extend up to the narrows of the Vardar below Demir Kapu by Gradec and below Gevgheli; they come close to the plain on the east side of Kilkis and Salonica; and they form the two eastern prongs of Chalcidice. One can see some reason for the view of Hecataeus and Herodotus that Thrace extended up to the plain of Salonica. The Vardar zone has no affinities with Greece. Its attractions are most apparent to northerners who have come from the northern extension of the sink, that is from Metohija and from Kossovo, into the upper Vardar zone, or who wish to settle in that zone, as the Dardanii so often did. On the other hand, Western Macedonia leads geologically not into central Albania, which is mainly flysch country, nor into Epirus, which is mainly limestone country, but into north-eastern Greece. One can thus understand the tendency of western Macedonians to press into north-eastern Greece at many periods in prehistory and in history.

Within Macedonia itself the meeting-ground of three geological formations is in Pieria. Lowland eastern Pieria belongs to the Vardar trough. The northern Pierian mountains belong to the Pelagonian massif of upper Macedonia. And Mt. Olympus is attached rather to the Thessalian massif than to the Pelagonian massif. It is perhaps no accident that the breeding-ground of the Macedones before their expansion was precisely in the northern Pierian mountains; that they expanded first into the Vardar trough; and that they turned southwards to acquire Mt. Olympus and a foothold on the Thessalian massif.

4. *The resources and the population of Macedonia*

Macedonia is much richer than the Greek peninsula in minerals.[1] There is gold-bearing sand in almost all the rivers of Central and Eastern Macedonia, and especially near Kilkis. Gold is still being obtained from

[1] The minerals are shown on the 'Geological Map of Greece' mentioned in the preceding note, and they are summarized in *MEE* s.v. *Makedonia* and in the Supplementary Volume III, p. 603. Mining in Yugoslav Macedonia is shown on a map compiled by O. S. S. entitled 'Yugoslav Mining and Manufacturing' (map no. 1068, dated 1942); but it is far from complete. I have made use of O. Davies, *Roman Mines in Europe* (Oxford, 1935) 226 f., which is sometimes lacking in detail, and of Gazetteers which give ores under individual place-names.

the silt of the Gallikos river. There are traces of gold ore to the east of Lete, at two places south-east of Kilkis and at one place north of it, and in the mines of Stratoniki, which are near the coast of Chalcidice facing the Strymonian Gulf. There are traces of gold at Kratovo in north-east Macedonia and at Nigrita on the western side of the lower Strymon valley. Silver is found together with lead in the mountains between Ochrid and Resen, and there are old workings of silver and lead near Tetovo; lead is mined at Kratovo. Tin exists near Velmej in the Saletska valley north-east of Ochrid. Silver is found also in the upper valleys of the Pecinj river and the Bregalnitsa river at Kratovo, Lesnovo, and Zletovo. Copper ores have been discovered at Avdhella and Grevena in Tymphaea, north of Kastoria in Orestis, north-east of Verria, and north-east of Kilkis in Amphaxitis; and copper is mined at Kratovo.

Iron ores without chrome occur to the south-west of Florina in Lyncus; near Stratoniki in eastern Chalcidice; at Kratovo; and north of Skopje. Iron containing nickel and chrome, and also magnetic iron are found in the mountains of Pieria. There are rich mines of iron pyrites at Madem Lakkos in eastern Chalcidice.[1] It is found also on Mt. Paiko and in Moglena. Chrome is plentiful. It is mined in the areas of Kozani and of Mt. Bermion; at Elafina, Polidhendri, and Palatitsa in northern Pieria; near Naoussa; at Sedhes; in Chalcidice at Vavdhos; in two places north and west of Skopje; and in Pelagonia south-east of Prilep. There are beds of chromites also by Kastoria, Florina, Verria, and Edessa, and in Moglena.

Molybdenum, used for alloying steel, is mined at Mavrodhendron near Axioupolis, and is found elsewhere on Mt. Paiko and near Ptolemaïdha. Lignite comes from Pelagonia; from the country between Florina and Kozani via Ptolemaïdha; from Kastoria; and from near Skopje. Magnesite comes from several sites in Chalcidice, from south of Servia and from Edessa; zinc from Kratovo on the upper Pecinj and from Mt. Paiko; and asbestos from near Skopje, from Gevgheli, from Pozar in the Pella district, from Salonica, from near Servia, and from places in Chalcidice. Talc is mined near Salonica, and mica near Prilep. Bauxite is found on the mountain of Crousis, and antimony at a number of places, especially in East Macedonia. Fine marble, serpentine, and carnelian are available in Macedonia.

There are a number of mineral springs. Therme, the predecessor of Salonica, took its name from a hot spring; and there are hot springs at Sedhes and Langadha. Other mineral springs are near Kilkis; at Pozar in the Pella district; at Bania between Naoussa and Edessa; at two places in Chalcidice; at Xino Nero in western Eordaea; and at Štip and Katlanovo in north-eastern Macedonia. Xino Nero is alkaline; others are sulphurous.

[1] These famous mines were described in 1555 by the French traveller P. Bellon.

Of neighbouring areas three are very rich in mineral resources. The Metohija-Kossovo district produces gold, silver, lead, zinc, chrome, pyrites, magnesite, lignite, and coal. On the west side of the upper Strymon valley Kjustendil produced gold and silver in antiquity and in the seventeenth century, and it has deposits of copper, iron, and iron pyrites. Beyond the lower Strymon the district of Akhladhokori has gold, silver, lead, and iron pyrites, while Mt. Pangaeum yielded gold and silver in antiquity and it still has gold, copper, and iron pyrites.

The area under cultivation in Macedonia increased considerably between 1928 and 1958. The figures for Greek Macedonia alone were 4,216,236 stremmata in 1928 and 6,153,196 stremmata in 1958. Cereals were the main product; they were grown on 5,546,154 stremmata in Greek Macedonia in 1958. Beans, lentils, potatoes, melons, marrows, and other vegetables, and recently a great amount of apples, pears, and peaches, came next in importance. There are extensive vineyards in many parts of Macedonia and especially in the Kavadarci region. All parts of Macedonia are excellent for the breeding of cattle and sheep, and there are many herds of buffalo in the swampier plains. In Greek Macedonia alone the cattle in 1959 numbered some 500,000, being almost 40 per cent of the total for all Greece. Sheep in Greek Macedonia stood at over 2 million. Of these more than 250,000 belonged to the nomadic group which engages in transhumance. The forests in Greek Macedonia are chiefly on the mountains of Central Macedonia, covering 4,600,000 stremmata; next come those of West Macedonia, covering 1,180,000 stremmata; and those of East Macedonia in my sense of the term are particularly dense on Mt. Dysoron in Crestonia and Mt. Kholomos in Chalcidice. If we add the immense forests of north-western Macedonia and those on the mountains east of the upper Vardar valley, the proportion of forest which is in Central Macedonia becomes much smaller; nevertheless, it is this forest which has immediate commercial value through its proximity to the coast. The export of sawn timber from the coast of the Thermaic Gulf is conducted on a large scale. There are fisheries along the coast of the Gulf, and in the numerous lakes of Macedonia.

In prehistoric times there is no doubt that the forest cover extended into the plains, where the lignite beds are evidence of primaeval woods. Even in the fourth century B.C. the plain of Philippi was forested when Philip II was king of Macedon. The hunting of the aurochs and deer was practised then on horseback, which indicates that relatively level ground was still wooded. Neolithic settlements were made on lakes (e.g. at Kastoria), on river-banks (e.g. at Servia), on the edge of marshes (e.g. at Nea Nikomedeia), or on the coast (e.g. at Kritsana), and these sites were chosen presumably because the plains themselves were forested.

Pastoral life predominated and the transhumance of sheep was practised without hindrance. In consequence the settlements in the highlands of the central ranges became important (e.g. at Malik). Something similar happened in the Middle Ages, when the Vlachs of the highlands derived their wealth and their power from the transhumance of sheep. Agricultural life was restricted to comparatively small areas of the plain; for instance near the Cerna Reka by Porodin and Crnobuki in Pelagonia and in the parts of the coastal plain by Nea Nikomedeia and by Vardina. Already in the Neolithic Age houses were built with chestnut, oak, pine, and cedar. The settlers kept sheep, goats, cattle, and pigs, and the primary importance of sheep indicates that transhumance was practised on a considerable scale. Woollen clothing was worn, as by the Vlachs today. Two forms of wheat (*triticum durum* and *triticum turgidum*), barley, lentils, peas, and millet were grown in the vicinity of the settlements. Fishing was practised in the lakes. Clay, serpentine, and marble were used for making figurines which represent people, cattle, sheep, goats, pigs, frogs, lynxes, bears, dogs, and in the late Neolithic period at Porodin in Pelagonia, horses. Bones of deer and wild boar were found in the settlements. Water-birds and water-reptiles were imitated in the handles of altar-tables.

Thus the basic elements in the economy of Macedonia were already operative in the Neolithic period. Communications too had been established, both overland up the Vardar valley and westwards across the main Balkan range, and by sea to Greece, the islands and Asia Minor. The development of its economy since Neolithic times has fluctuated widely. One reason for the fluctuation is that the transhumance of sheep and intensive agriculture conflict with one another. The shepherd must have access to the plains for winter pasture, but the agriculturist resists the movement of the herds through his fields and regards the provision of pasture as a matter of minor importance. The shepherd obtains fodder from oak scrub, whereas the agriculturist prefers to clear the land of timber. Economic progress is on the side of the agriculturist in the plains, because they have such fertile soil and so many advantages of water and climate for the growing of cereals. Cultural progress is promoted also by the more settled life of the agriculturists, who live in villages and towns, whereas the shepherds live a semi-nomadic existence. A decisive step on the path of progress was taken by Philip II of Macedon, if we understand the speech of Alexander to the Macedonians at Opis in this context. 'Philip found you nomadic and poor, clothed as most of you were in sheep-skins, as you pastured your few sheep on the mountains, . . . and he gave you cloaks to wear instead of sheep-skins, brought you down from the mountains to live in the plains . . . made you inhabit cities and civilized you with good laws and customs.'[1] Deforestation, drainage, and

[1] Arrian, *Anabasis* 7. 9. 2.

irrigation of the plains made a rapid expansion of agriculture possible. The exploitation of Macedonia's mineral wealth and the development of commerce by land and by sea were part and parcel of a remarkable economic revolution, which occurred during Philip's reign.

A similar revolution has taken place in Macedonia since 1928, and it is still under way. The greatest changes within my experience, which runs intermittently from 1929 to 1968, have taken place in the coastal plain. Upper Macedonia is still developing rapidly, both in Greece and in Yugoslavia. Modern and antiquated methods exist side by side, for instance in the plain north of Lake Ochrid where state farms are the neighbours of Albanian-speaking villagers who use traditional methods. The contrast is as marked as it used to be in Palestine, when Jews and Arabs farmed adjacent land. There is no doubt that Macedonia, unlike Epirus, has a prosperous economic future.

The population of Macedonia has fluctuated very greatly, because it is keyed to the economic state of the country. In recent times the increase has been spectacular. The census returns are given by districts which do not always correspond with my definition of Macedonia as a geographical entity, but they give us a general picture.[1] Yugoslav Macedonia is divided into four regions: Bitola (Monastir), Skopje, Bregalnitsa (Štip), and Oblasti (Kitsevo-Tetovo). Bulgarian Macedonia consists of Okrăg and Petrić. Greek Macedonia, divided into twelve regions (*nomoi*), extends from Pieria to the Strymon valley and beyond as far as Serres, Kavalla, and in some contexts Drama. The general picture for Macedonia between 1928 and 1961 is an increase of almost 50 per cent from 2,365,111 to 3,544,791. This increase is due mainly to greater productivity, and it has proceeded almost *pari passu* in Yugoslav Macedonia and in Greek Macedonia.

We may divide Macedonia internally into Lower or 'coastal' Macedonia, using the terminology of Thucydides; Upper Macedonia including Pelagonia; and the Vardar region on both sides of the river above Demir Kapu. The first of these divisions had a population of 990,510 in 1961; the second had about 853,000; and the third about 847,000. If we think of Macedonia in the time of Philip II, these figures make us realize that the territory of the Macedones proper, when extended to Mt. Pangaeum, is likely to have carried a population which exceeded that of the Upper Macedonian cantons and that of the Paeonian territory in the Vardar valley above Antigonea.

The cantonal figures do not correspond precisely to ancient divisions, but again they give us a general idea. The figures for the cantons of 'coastal Macedonia' in the year 1961 are:

[1] Statistics are given in *MEE* s.v. *Makedonia,* in the Supplement Volume III, pp. 603 f., and in *Enciclopedia Italiana* s.v. *Macedonia.*

Pieria	97,505
Pella	133,128
Salonica	542,880
Emathia	114,150
Kilkis	102,847
Total	990,510

The preponderance of Salonica may not be entirely a result of modern urbanization. Ancient Mygdonia and Anthemus were certainly wealthy cantons, and the chief ports of Macedonia in most periods were on the east side of the Thermaic Gulf. Kilkis, which represents the ancient Amphaxitis and Crestonia, goes with Salonica. Thus the districts east of the Vardar give a total of 645,727. The districts west of the Vardar, being Pella and Emathia in the plain and Pieria outside the plain, had a population of 344,783, which is very much less. At the time of the Trojan War, for instance, the Paeones east of the river Axius were probably much more numerous and formidable than the peoples west of the river. The relatively small population of Pieria is interesting, when one recollects that the Macedones proper expanded from Pieria and eventually controlled the whole of 'coastal Macedonia'.

The figures for the districts of Upper Macedonia are as follows:

Kastoria	47,349
Florina	67,238
Kozani	190,607
Bitola (Monastir)	548,027
Total	853,221

Kastoria corresponds to the ancient Orestis and probably a part of Elimea. Florina corresponds to Lyncus. Kozani contains Eordaea and most of Elimea. The large size of Kozani's population in relation to Pieria, Orestis, and Lyncus makes it possible to understand the importance of Eordaea in the Early Iron Age. Bitola corresponds with Pelagonia, Derriopus, and the territory of the Brygi; the bulk of its very large population draws its livelihood from the great and fertile Pelagonian plain. Here too we can understand the strength and the importance of Pelagonia in the Neolithic period and in the Early Bronze Age.

The upper Vardar valley consists of Skopje, Bregalnitsa, and Oblasti. In this sense Skopje covers not only the Skopje basin but also the territory of the Argestaei west of the Vardar and the lands of the Paeonians in the north-eastern part of the valley. Skopje's population of 692,741 persons helps us to bear in mind that most of the Vardar valley is open country with long and fertile slopes, which supports a very large number of towns and villages.

The figures for districts which were normally outside Macedonia but which often affected her history are as follows:

Chalcidice	82,525
Serres	248,045
Kavalla	190,445
Drama about	160,000
Total	681,015

The figure for Serres reflects the great prosperity of the lower Strymon valley below the Rupel pass. Leake, commenting on its wealth and productivity, remarked that the plain of Serres was better cultivated than the plain of Salonica at the beginning of the nineteenth century.[1] The districts of Serres, Kavalla, and Drama possess greater mineral wealth than Macedonia proper, and Chalcidice is rich in timber, mines, and olives. The acquisition of these territories by Philip II of Macedon brought with it an access of population comparable to that of 'coastal Macedonia' east of the Axius river.

[1] Leake 3. 258 f.

II

THE NORTH-WESTERN AREAS

1. *The Via Egnatia between the Adriatic coast and Lychnidus*

FOR the western part of the Via Egnatia there is a large amount of literary evidence. A lost passage of Polybius[1] underlies the account in Strabo at C 322, which describes Apollonia as the western terminal. Strabo himself at C 327 gives Epidamnus (Dyrrachium) and Apollonia as the terminals in his phrase ἡ ᾽Εγνατία ὁδὸς ἐξ ᾽Επιδάμνου καὶ ᾽Απολλωνίας. The Epitome (fr. 10 of Strabo bk. 7) gives Dyrrachium. The Peutinger Table, which may be based on a Roman road map of the Antonine period, shows Dyrrachium as the terminal; so too does the account in the Antonine Itinerary 317. 7, composed in A.D. 211–17, on the basis of a Roman road map.[2] The second account in the Antonine Itinerary 329. 1 gives Aulon as the terminal, and the occurrence of the names 'Diocletianopolis' for Pella and 'Heraclia' for Perinthus dates this account to some time not long after A.D. 286;[3] so too Aulon is the western terminal in the Itinerarium Burdigalense, written by a traveller who followed the road in A.D. 333.[4]

With the possible exception of the Peutinger Table and the first account in the Antonine Itinerary the accounts are independent of one another, and we should expect them to corroborate one another. However, there are variations. These are of two kinds. Different places are named, because they were important at different times; for example, Apollonia was at first the more popular port, then Dyrrachium in the early empire, and then Aulon in the period around 286 to 333. In the same way names of places for staying the night or changing horses varied over the centuries. However, the road itself is unlikely to have changed; for once made, paved, and repaired from time to time its course and its milestones remained where they were, unless a landslide or the like

---

[1] Printed as Plb. 34. 12 but not a verbatim quotation.

[2] For a possible relationship between the maps underlying Peut. Tab. and It. Ant. see W. Kubitschek in *RE* 9. 2336 f. and 10. 2112 f. Dyrrachium is established as the western terminal on the Roman milestones dating to A.D. 107, 112, and 305–6 (see *BCH* 59 (1935) 408 and 403; and *BCH* 17 (1893) 635).

[3] So C. F. Edson, 'The Location of Cellae and the Route of the Via Egnatia', *CP* 46 (1951) 13 n. 22.

[4] The best edition of It. Ant. and It. Burd. is that of O. Cuntz, *Itineraria Romana* i (Leipzig 1929). Where I give variant readings, they are from his apparatus criticus.

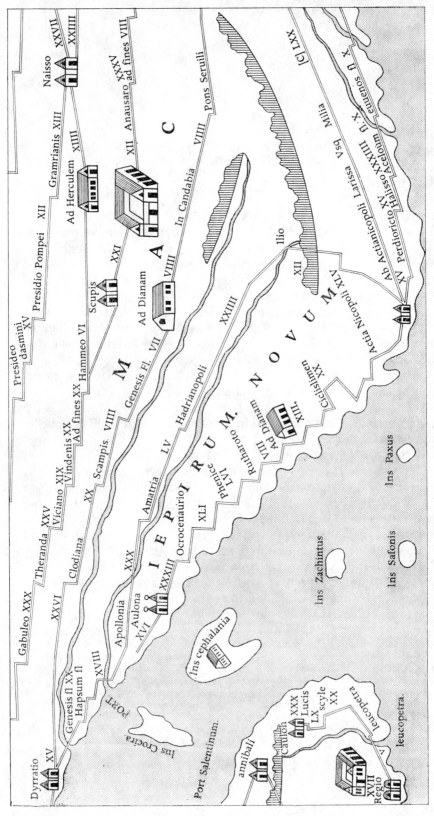

MAP 2. THE WESTERN PART OF THE VIA EGNATIA AND ADJACENT ROADS ON THE PEUTINGER TABLE

intervened.[1] The second type of variation arises in the reporting of distances by miles. Here one may count exclusively or inclusively. Let us say, for instance, that Stefanaphana, which is intermediate between Apollonia and Absos, is 18¼ miles from Apollonia and 12½ miles from Absos. The distance in terms of mile units may be counted as 30, or as 31, or as 32, if the distance from Apollonia to Stefanaphana is given as 19 and that from Stefanaphana to Absos as 13. Therefore, when we have one account giving a distance without intermediate stops, it is more likely to give the true distance in miles than one with several intermediate stops.

With these considerations in mind let us turn to the first stretches of the road, those from Dyrrachium to Clodiana and from Apollonia to Clodiana, from which point a single road, the Via Egnatia proper, ran eastwards. Strabo C 323, using Polybius, tells us in effect that Dyrrachium and Apollonia were equidistant from Clodiana in terms of miles (συμβαίνει δ᾽ ἀπὸ ἴσου διαστήματος συμπίπτειν εἰς τὴν αὐτὴν ὁδὸν τούς τ᾽ ἐκ τῆς Ἀπολλωνίας ὁρμηθέντας καὶ τοὺς ἐξ Ἐπιδάμνου). This equidistance was the distance in mile units, known from milestones.[2] The Peutinger Table (see Map 2) gives two figures, XV and XXVI, with a blank between them. K. Miller assumed that the first figure should be transferred to the lower line, and he therefore put Dyrrachium XXVI miles from Clodiana.[3] But he improved on this by emending XXVI to XXX. He then emended three figures in Ant. It. 329, namely in 329. 6 XXIIII to XIIII, in 329. 7 XXV to XV, and in 318. 1 XXXIII to XXX. Finally, he altered the total of figures in It. Burd. 608. 4–8 from 57 to 30. His golden number 30 was adopted by him as an average, a 'Mittelzahl'.[4] He then transferred his two pieces of 30 miles each to the ground and placed Clodiana at Peqin (see Map 3). He was apparently unaware that, though a crow can fly from Apollonia to Peqin covering 30 miles, a road cannot do so because the marshy plain of Myzeqijë intervenes. His method is also unjustifiable in theory; for if all the numbers are corrupt an average of them is an average of corruptions, and the basic assumption that all the numbers are corrupt sets an incomparable standard of distrust in the value of the entries.

I take the Peutinger Table to show that Dyrrachium was XV m.p.

---

[1] One should therefore agree with K. Miller, *Itineraria Romana* (Stuttgart, 1919) 518, in his view that in the case of the Via Egnatia (as well as elsewhere) the temptation to attribute differences of entries to differences of routes should be resisted.

[2] The western part at least of the Via Egnatia is likely to have been in use between 146 B.C., when Macedonia was made a Roman province, and the death of Polybius. *c.* 120 B.C. It was surveyed and marked with milestones before 120 B.C. (Str. C 322 βεβηματισμένη κατὰ μίλιον καὶ κατεστηλωμένη). [3] Op. cit. 519.

[4] Op. cit. 517. Praschniker 106–26 used different emendations; he decided first on the route (p. 112) and then altered some of the data. He did not himself know the Shkumbi valley from Rogozhinë to Elbasan, and he did not study the distances in the Itineraries for the road east of Elbasan.

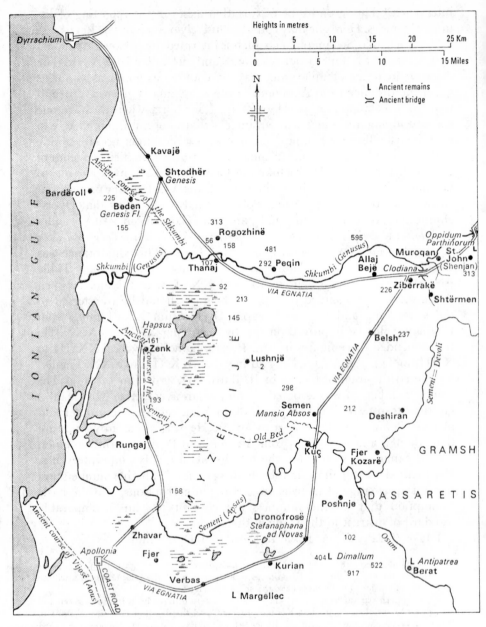

MAP 3. THE WESTERN PART OF CENTRAL ALBANIA

from a place not named. Its position is easily determined; for the road must have followed the edge of the rising ground by the plain, and XV m.p. being 22·2 km[1] brings us on the flat to Shtodhër. The next stage is XXVI m.p. But the total distance in m.p. units from Dyrrachium to Clodiana with stages of XV m.p. and XXVI m.p. may be 41, 42, or 43 m.p. on inclusive and exclusive reckonings. The manuscripts of It. Ant. 318. 1 give variant readings for the distance from Dyrrachium to Clodiana (without any intermediate station): 1 L gives XXIII, 2 L gives XXXIII, and B gives XLIII.[2] Of these the last fits the datum of the Peutinger Table and should be preferred. I take it then that Dyrrachium was 43 m.p. from Clodiana.

The direct route for the road after Shtodhër is to cross the Shkumbi river at Thanaj, follow the left (south) bank, and then proceed through Allaj Bejë (avoiding the narrows of the Shkumbi at this longitude). The distance from Dyrrachium XLIII m.p. is 63·7 km; if we take 62 km on the surface of the map to correspond to 63·7 km on the ground, we shall place Clodiana at a point between Allaj Bejë and Muroqan and just above Ziberrakë. As Leake suggested, the name Clodiana, which is a plural form in It. Ant. 329. 7, stands for Clodiana castra and was so named after Appius Claudius, the victorious commander of 168 B.C. The strategic importance of this situation is obvious.[3]

The evidence for the stretch from Apollonia to Clodiana is as follows:

It. Ant. 329. 5–6	It. Burd. 608. 2–8 (reversed for comparison)
Apollonia XXIIII Ad Novas	civitas Apollonia XVIII mutatio Stefanaphana
Ad Novas XXV Clodianis	mutatio Stefanaphana XII mansio Absos
	mansio Absos XIIII mansio Marusio
	mansio Marusio XIII mansio Clodiana[4]

---

[1] Reckoning a Roman mile at 1,482 m. My measurements are taken on the U.S. Army Maps 1 : 200,000 of Albania.

[2] The manuscripts known as L and B are of equal authority in the edition of O. Cuntz.

[3] Leake 3. 280. Appius Claudius having put his men for winter quarters into the towns of the Parthini, who occupied the middle and upper Shkumbi valley, called them together in spring 168 B.C. and pitched camp 'circa Genusum amnem' (Livy 43. 23. 6 and 44. 30. 10). There he was joined by Anicius who came from Apollonia 'triduo', within three days. On reaching the camp Anicius added to his army 2,200 men of the Parthini. It is clear from these passages that the camp was in the territory of the Parthini, that is either near Ziberrakë or further east, and not at Peqin (where Miller puts Clodiana), which was probably in the territory of Dyrrachium. In this position Clodiana controls the passage up the Shkumbi valley, the exit of the track from Tirana in the north (see Praschniker–Schober 47 f.), and also the easiest routes southwards to Apollonia and to Antipatrea (Berat); see my article in *JRS* 56 (1966) 43 for the last. My own travels in the Shkumbi valley area were by car from Dyrrachium to Tirana, on foot from Dyrrachium to Peqin in bitter March weather, by lorry from Peqin to Elbasan, on foot from Elbasan to Belsh, and on foot from Elbasan to Shenjan and Shtërmen. An episode at Venice in which King Zog's equerry was shot led to my being imprisoned for a day at Elbasan and getting away next day only by starting before dawn; it cut short my study of the environs of Elbasan.

[4] I have given the entries in this form instead of as in the original form, e.g. Apollonia XXV,

The total of 57 m.p. in It. Burd. is evidently too high, but the explanation is easy. Nowhere else in the European part of this Itinerary do we find two mansiones next to one another, and here we have three next to one another with quite short distances between. One must be deleted. The obvious victim is mansio Marusio; for Marusio is probably a corruption of mansio, and a repetition of mansio becoming Marusio may have led to a repetition of XIII, the text then becoming XIII and XIIII.[1] Fortunately there are external arguments to support this choice of victim. The Ravenna Geographer, who at some time between A.D. 660 and 700 made a list of towns from the contemporary itineraries, and the geographer Guido, who in A.D. 1119 made a similar list based on that of the Ravenna Geographer,[2] give Absos and Clodiana but not Marusio (Absos appearing as Apsum in Ra. 379. 1, as Absura in Ra. 206. 14, and as Apsum in Gu. 540. 2, and Clodiana as Gloditana in Ra. 206. 10). It is thus likely that there was no such place as Marusio. The entry 'mansio Marusio' with its number XIIII may therefore be deleted, and the total distance between Apollonia and Clodiana reduced to 43 m.p. This is also the correct number of miles, we have decided, between Dyrrachium and Clodiana. The stretches then were of the same length ἀπὸ ἴσου διαστήματος, as Strabo said, using Polybius. We are left with a different total in It. Ant. 329. 5–8, namely 49 m.p. This is not compatible with the other figures. Therefore one figure may be corrupt. If we read Apollonia to Ad Novas as XVIIII and not XXIIII, it will be close to the figure XVIII for Apollonia to Stefanaphana in It. Burd. and it will give an acceptable total of 44 miles.

In applying these distances to the terrain we should note that the route for a traveller setting out from Apollonia for Macedonia is not to Peqin and along the Shkumbi valley, as K. Miller supposed, but alongside the low ground where the Semeni river comes closest to the Shkumbi valley. Such a traveller has in any case to avoid the marshy Myzeqijë plain. The Via Egnatia then had to follow the eastern edge of the plain via Kurian and Dronofrosë. Indeed Dronofrosë is 26 or 27 km (XVIII to XVIIII m.p.) from Apollonia (Poyan) and we may place near Dronofrosë both Stefanaphana and Ad Novas, if we read XVIIII in It. Ant. 329. 6. This is below the ancient site which I have identified with Dimallum.[3]

Ad Novas XXIIII, Clodianis XXV, in which form the application of the distances to the places is less clear.

[1] A corruption arising from a repetition is found in It. Burd. 558. 2: mut. LXIII *bis positum, alterum del.* 2 P. Once the repetition had occurred and mansio been read as Marusio, the present version could have arisen.

[2] I quote these from the edition of M. Pinder and G. Parthey, *Ravennatis Anonymi Cosmographia et Guidonis Geographia* (Berlin, 1860) by the page and line numbers.

[3] *JRS* 68 (1968) 12 f. Another ancient site close to the road is at Margellec; see Praschniker–Schober 75 f. Praschniker saw definite remains of the road to the west of Verbas (the embanked road is illustrated on his p. 119 fig. 45) and again by Kumani, which is west of Kurian.

The road from Dronofrosë should run north to the best place for crossing
the Semeni river, that is between Kuç and Semen village where the
modern bridge is.[1] The distance from mutatio Stefanaphana at Dronofrosë over low-lying but dry ground to Semen village is some 18 km,
which fits the XII m.p. (17·7 km) to mansio Absos. The name Absos
is taken from the river Apsus, even as Semen is named after the modern
name of the Apsus. If we proceed from Semen through low rolling hills
via Belsh to Ziberrakë, we shall cover some 20 km, that is between XIII
and XIIII m.p. The junction then of the road from Dyrrachium and
the road from Apollonia may be placed near Ziberrakë.

To the south-east of Muroqan is Shenjan, the well-known monastery
of St. John. In 1932 I copied four inscriptions there and noted several
ancient blocks and sculptured fragments.[2] When I was walking from
Shenjan to Elbasan I found an ancient fortified site on the second spur
jutting towards the valley. It is some 2 km away from the monastery.
The acropolis wall, made of large blocks (e.g. $1·00 \times 0·50 \times 0·40$ m),
formed a circuit of some 400 metres, and an unusually wide ramp, some
10 metres wide, led up to the acropolis from the main hill behind. As
there is no other ancient site in the vicinity, it is the ancient counterpart
of Elbasan. The ramp carried a road, perhaps an offshoot of the Via
Egnatia. I have shown it on Map 3 as 'oppidum Parthinorum'.[3]

A little upstream from this site and 3 km below the bridge at Elbasan
there are the piers of a very large ancient bridge, some 300 m long,
spanning the Shkumbi river at a point where the usually wide bed is
somewhat confined by a spur of rock. The piers were built in Hellenistic
times, probably by Epirotes in the third century B.C. Praschniker noticed
later repairs to the piers and also on the south bank an ancient road,
cut in the rock, leading from the west towards the bridge. The piers, being
flat-topped, were designed to take wooden planking, removable presumably in time of spate.[4] Further down the valley and some 2 km south-
west of Muroqan Praschniker saw beside a Turkish bridge the remains
of a one-arched ancient bridge over a stream in a marsh. It was made of
'gussmauerwerk' (i.e. using a bituminous[5] cement) and he considered
it ancient, i.e. of Roman date. On both sides of it the line of a raised road
('Dammstrasse'), no longer in use, was visible for several hundred metres.

[1] Praschniker 122 fig. 46 shows the remains of large bridge piers in the Semeni by Kuç.
The material from that bridge had been used in building a (then) new bridge. These piers
may not be ancient, but they show that this was the best place for bridging the Semeni.
[2] *Epirus* 736–7; one of them is *CIL* iii. 617.
[3] Elbasan is built on almost flat ground, unsuitable for an ancient site. Praschniker–
Schober 48 f. have studied the medieval moated citadel most thoroughly, and they date one
part to after A.D. 300; they propose any time between 300 and 530 for the first fortification
of the site. My site is probably the Parthinian town mentioned by Caesar *BC* 3. 41. 1.
[4] Praschniker–Schober 59 f. and *Epirus* 235.
[5] For bitumen in this area see *Epirus* 231 f.

He judged the road to run in the one direction towards the Shkumbi bridge. As regards the other direction all he says is that he assumed that the road went towards Berat, but he found no further trace of such a road on his way to Berat. This is not surprising, for it is now clear that both bridges and the pieces of road beside them were parts of the Via Egnatia.[1]

We may turn back to the blank in the Peutinger Table between XV and XXVI (see Map 2). The name can be readily supplied from the list of 'civitates' given by the Ravenna Geographer 379. 2 and by Guido 540. 3: Alona (for Aulon), Apollonia, Apsum, Genesis, Durachium, and then Aulon, Appollonia, Apsum, Genesis. The name missing in Tab. Peut. is Genesis, situated at Shtodhër as we have seen, and named after the nearby river, as mansio Absos was named after the Apsus river. It has been observed that in antiquity the great rivers of Albania entered the sea further north than they do today. We know this to be true of the Vijosë (Aous) and the Drin (Drilo), and an old bed of the Semeni (Apsus) is marked on the modern map (see Map 3).[2] If Genesis was at Shtodhër, the Shkumbi (Genusus or Genesis) evidently entered the sea near Shtodhër. We may also explain the discontinued line on the Peutinger Table (see Map 2). The Table shows a coastal road coming up from Epirus to Aulon and, after the gap, continuing up the coast from Apollonia via Dyrrachium, a road which is not to be confused with the Via Egnatia. The entry XVI with the discontinued line above 'Aulona' is the distance needed to bring us over the seaward exit of the Artë Lagoon and along a track marked on a modern map via Poro to Poyan (Apollonia); on the surface of the map I make it some 23 km, corresponding to 16 Roman miles. The discontinued line, then, represents the road from Aulon to Apollonia.

The next entry is XVIII m.p. (26·6 km) from Apollonia to Hapsum fl. Leaving Apollonia and proceeding via Fjer on to the low but dry hillocks, one passes an old bed of the Semeni at 23 km near Rungaj. One should therefore mark the course of the Semeni (Apsus) c. A.D. 211–17 as running some 3 km further north. Continuing northwards from there for XX m.p. (29·6 km) to Genesis fl., one reaches the latitude

---

[1] Praschniker did not connect these bridges with the Via Egnatia because he thought, like K. Miller, that it ran from Apollonia to Rogozhinë and thence along the north side of the Shkumbi valley to Elbasan; in writing *Epirus* 235 n. 1 at a time when I had not studied the evidence for the road in full, I accepted the opinion of Praschniker and Miller. Praschniker (122) saw a few traces of *a* road between Kuç and Rogozhinë but nothing comparable to what he had seen between Kuç and Apollonia; moreover at Rogozhinë, where the Austrian army built a bridge 900 m long across the Shkumbi, no signs were found of any ancient or other bridge, and he suggested a ferry might have been used for the Via Egnatia there.

[2] For the Vijosë see *Epirus* 133, 493, Map 2 and Map 18, and *Archaeology* 14 (1961) 161; for the Drin see J. M. F. May in *JRS* 36 (1946) 54 f. As regards the Shkumbi K. Miller, op. cit. 517, deduced from the entry Genesis fl. in the Peutinger Table, an entry to which I come shortly that the river entered the sea much further to the north-west than now.

of Shtodhër, where we have already put the place Genusus on the evidence of the XV m.p. from Dyrrachium. *Circa* A.D. 211–17 the Shkumbi entered the sea north of Bardëroll. Thus the coast road from Epirus through Illyria met the Via Egnatia at Apollonia and at the place Genusus, from which it proceeded along a bit of the Via Egnatia to Dyrrachium. It is probable that in the delta area the great rivers Apsus and Genusus were crossed by ferry, as they were in 1932, when I was travelling in this part of Albania. In 48 B.C. Caesar ferried his army over the Shkumbi, evidently near Thanaj, the chief difficulty being the steep banks (*B.C.* 3. 75 ripis impeditis), and going south at speed in April he was impeded by the very deep rivers, until he entered Epirus (77 altissimis fluminibus atque impeditissimis itineribus). The author of the Peutinger Table found it difficult to show both the coastal road and the Via Egnatia on this part of his map, and this difficulty has led to some confusion.[1]

Strabo C 323, using Polybius, treated the two roads from Apollonia and from Dyrrachium to Clodiana as introductory. He makes the Via Egnatia start from this point and names the first section ἐπὶ Κανδαουίας. ἡ μὲν οὖν πᾶσα 'Εγνατία καλεῖται, ἡ δὲ πρώτη ἐπὶ Κανδαουίας λέγεται, ὄρους 'Ιλλυρικοῦ, διὰ Λυχνιδοῦ (MS. Λυχνιδίου) πόλεως καὶ Πυλῶνος τόπου ὁρίζοντος ἐν τῇ ὁδῷ τήν τε 'Ιλλυρίδα καὶ τὴν Μακεδονίαν. The second section is from there to Thessalonica: ἐκεῖθεν δ' ἐστὶ παρὰ Βαρνοῦντα διὰ 'Ηρακλείας καὶ Λυγκηστῶν καὶ 'Εορδῶν εἰς "Εδεσσαν καὶ Πέλλαν μέχρι Θεσσαλονικείας. The Illyrian mountain Candavia dominates the first section of the road, from the time when it enters the defile of the Shkumbi river above Elbasan near Polis i Vogel until it drops down to Lake Ochrid. In relation to the section ἐπὶ Κανδαουίας the name embraces both the region of the lakes by Lychnidus (Str. C 327 περὶ δὲ τὴν ἐπὶ Κανδαουίας ὁδὸν αἵ τε λίμναι εἰσὶν αἱ περὶ Λυχνιδόν), that is Lake Ochrid, Lake Malik, and Lake Prespa, and the headwaters of the rivers flowing into the Ionian Gulf (the Genusus, Apsus, and Aous) and even those of the Arachthus, Inachus, Achelous, and Euenus (καὶ ποταμοὶ οἵ τε εἰς τὸν 'Ιόνιον κόλπον ἐκπίπτοντες καὶ οἱ ἐπὶ τὰ νότια μέρη C 327). Thus the Candavian range is not only the great mountains through which the river Shkumbi cuts its course,[2] but also the mountain ridges which enclose the lakes and the

---

[1] See, for instance, K. Miller, op. cit. 519 and 560 together with figs. 161 and 179.

[2] The visual aspect of the Candavian range, as seen by the traveller looking east from Elbasan, is best described by J. G. von Hahn, *Denkschriften* 15 (1867) 2. 50 no. 3: 'Wenn man . . . gegen Osten blickt, so bietet sich dem Auge ein nicht minder eigenthümlicher Anblick auf eine Masse von sich in einander schiebenden Bergreihen dar, welche sämmtlich in nordsüdlicher Richtung streichen, von denen die hintere stets die vorgehende überragt und zwischen denen der Fluß sich durchzuwinden scheint. Hinter der Stadt erhebt sich ein völlig freistehender Hügelrücken, Malji Kraschtese genannt, rechts dahinter Malji Schuschitza, dahinter Malji Politzit, dahinter endlich Malji Mbelischtest, von der linken Seite zwischen durch Malji Gibaleschit und dahinter Malji Tschermenikese. Diese Gebirgsansicht bildet den westlichen Eingang zur alten Candavia, durch welche die römische Via Egnatia führt

southward-running range which includes Mt. Boïon and Mt. Pindus. The extent of the northern part of the Candavian range is clear from Caesar's narrative of the civil war in 48 B.C. Pompey marched from Dyrrachium to Macedonia 'through Candavia', and Caesar was afraid that in so doing he might catch by surprise the army of Domitius at

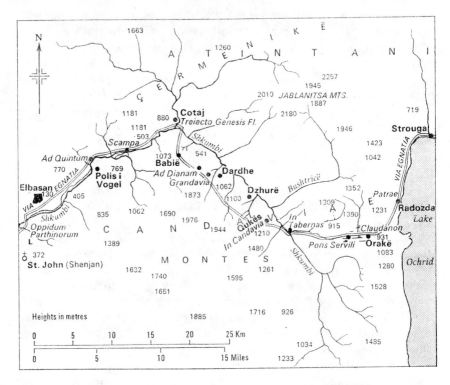

MAP 4. THE EASTERN PART OF CENTRAL ALBANIA

Heraclea (near Monastir) which lay 'under Candavia', that is under Mt. Peristeri, a north-easterly outlier of the Candavian range (Caesar *BC* 3. 79, Pompeius per Candaviam iter in Macedoniam expeditum habebat . . . Heracliam quae est subiecta Candaviae).

We are fortunate in having a fixed point in this long section. It had often been maintained that Lychnidus was on the site of Ochrid; and this was confirmed when a milestone of the Via Egnatia with the mark ΑΠΟ ΛΥΧΝΙΔΟΥ Η was found *in situ*[1] at Strouga. The 8 Roman miles (11·8 km) bring us exactly to Ochrid on the surface measurement of the

_____
[1] Heuzey–Daumet 344 = *CIL* iii. 711, 712.

map; the ground between is all flat. At the other end of the section we have now fixed Clodiana near Ziberrakë. For this section our difficulties do not arise from the entries in the Itineraries, which are remarkably consistent and mutually corroborative. I give them in two groups. The first group is in It. Ant.:

It. Ant. 318	It. Ant. 329
Clodiana XX Scampis	Clodiana XXII Scampis
Scampis XXVIII Tres Tabernas	Scampis XXX Tribus Tabernis
Tres Tabernas XXVII Licnido	Tribus Tabernis XXVII Lignido
(total m.p. 75)	(total m.p. 79)

It will be remembered that It. Ant. 318 refers to a time almost a hundred years earlier than It. Ant. 329, and that It. Ant. 329 gave the largest number of miles, 49 (or 44) m.p., from Apollonia to Clodiana. Whatever the reason may be,[1] the numbers of It. Ant. 329 are unusually high, and for general purposes we should regard It. Ant. 318 as more dependable with its total of 75 m.p., which is closer to the totals of the second group. The second group is more detailed:

Tab. Peut.	It. Burd. 608 (reversed for comparison)
Clodiana XX Scampis	mansio Clodiana XV mutatio Ad Quintum
	mutatio Ad Quintum VI mansio Hiscampis
Scampis VIIII Genesis fl.	mansio Hiscampis VIIII mutatio Treiecto
Genesis fl. VII Ad Dianam	mutatio Treiecto VIIII mansio Grandavia
Ad Dianam VIIII In Candavia	mansio Grandavia VIIII mutatio In Taber-
	nas
In Candavia VIIII Pons Ser-	mutatio In Tabernas VIIII mansio Clauda-
vili	non
	mansio Claudanon III mutatio Patras
Pons Servili XVIIII Lignido	mutatio Patras XII civitas Cledo
(total m.p. 73)	(total m.p. 72)

That these totals are credible is apparent from the fact that the modern road from the longitude of Clodiana to Ochrid, the ancient Lychnidus, is 108 km or 73 m.p.

The correspondence in the totals of m.p. in these Itineraries, which are independent of one another and are separated in time by more than a century, is in striking support of my contention that the numerical entries in these Itineraries for this section of the road are textually sound, that the Via Egnatia of A.D. 211–17 and the Via Egnatia of A.D. 333 followed the same route, and that the authors of Tab. Peut. and It.

---

[1] Inundations and landslides in mountainous country, such as recently (1960) destroyed villages in the northern Agrapha, might well carry away bridge piers, flood low-lying sectors, and demolish long strips of road; calamities of this kind might cause such an increase in mileage as we see in It. Ant. 329.

Burd. used a fairly similar method of counting, whether it was exclusive or inclusive. The variations between them in the naming of stations on the way may represent the personal preference of the authors, or different situations in A.D. 211–17 and in A.D. 333. There is of course no case for altering the individual entries, in order for instance to equate Pons Servili, XVIIII m.p. from Lychnidus, with the bridge at Strouga, which we know from the milestone was VIII m.p. from Lychnidus.[1]

When we look at all four Itineraries together, we may make the further point that in this case at least Kubitschek's theory of a common source for It. Ant. and Tab. Peut.[2] is rendered untenable by a comparison of the entries in Tab. Peut. for this stretch and for the preceding stretch with those of both It. Ant. 318 and It. Ant. 329, which are of course themselves of different dates from one another and not attributable to a common source either. The situation for the Via Egnatia as far east as Lychnidus at least is simpler than Kubitschek supposed. We have four independent Itineraries. When any two or more gave the same number of miles, they happened to use the same method of reckoning for the same actual distance. Similarities of distance, e.g. Clodiana XX Scampis in It. Ant. 318 and in Tab. Peut., or Scampis VIIII Genesis fl. in Tab. Peut. and Scampis VIIII Treiecto in It. Burd., or Tres Tabernas XXVII Licnido in It. Ant. 318 and Tribus Tabernis XXVII Lignido in It. Ant. 329, should not lead us to postulate an intricate web of common sources.

Our difficulties begin when we try to transfer the data of distances to the terrain. Since 1912, when Albania was created a sovereign state, communications with her neighbours have been spasmodic, and since 1912 the route from Elbasan to Ochrid has been little used and, so far as I know, has not been described. Under the Turkish Empire the route was in regular use. The accounts of that period which I have traced are those of travellers, interested indeed in ancient geography, but going on horseback with guides and attendants. This is a rather different matter from using wheeled transport, and it is not to be supposed that the route followed by these travellers was necessarily always that of the Via Egnatia. At the same time the terrain is so rough and difficult that their accounts will serve as a guide to the probable line of the route which the Via Egnatia may have taken. I therefore give a summary of the notes recorded by H. F. Tozer in 1861, by L. Heuzey and H. Daumet also in 1861, by von Spaun a year or two later, and by F. C. H. L. Pouqueville some fifty years earlier. They travelled in summer and from east to west,

---

[1] Even Heuzey and Daumet, the discoverers of the milestone, succumbed to the temptation of making this equation. Others have suggested equating Grandavia (It. Burd.) and Candavia (Tab. Peut.), but they are a few m.p. apart in the Itineraries.

[2] *RE* 10. 2118, die Gründe genügen mir um zu behaupten, daß das Itin. Ant. aus der gleichen Karte wie der Ravennas und die Tab. Peut. abgeleitet sei.

starting from Lychnidus with the advantage of being already some 2,000 feet above sea level.

Pouqueville[1] took an hour from Strouga to a point where he turned south-west into the defile of a stream falling into Lake Ochrid. He climbed up the course of this stream for an hour and then turned west to cross a narrow pass leading into a marshy basin. He crossed this basin on a paved 'chaussée' (a raised way) twelve feet wide; and this chaussée led to another defile, where he saw a river on his right. From the defile he entered a gorge in which a river was running, and he followed its sides for three hours. Thereafter 'the almost impracticable road' grew wider, and he descended to the valley of the Shkumbi river, here running from south to north. He followed its right bank until he came to a single-arched bridge. Crossing this he ascended to the village 'Cucuse'. On the steep ascent to this 'den of Tosk Albanians' he was riding along a chaussée four feet (?metres) wide and three-quarters of a league long. Tozer[2] seems to have taken the same route but the latter part of it in the dark; he spent the night at 'Kukus'. Heuzey and Daumet[3] in the same year took much the same route over the pass; they mention a ruined bridge in the basin where Pouqueville saw the paved chaussée twelve feet wide, and near it a khan (i.e. inn) of Domousova, and also a khan called Darna, evidently in the Shkumbi valley before ascending to the khan of 'Kukuss'. They describe the enormous walls of rock overhanging the defile just west of the basin which contains the khan of Domousova. Von Spaun[4] is brief but clear: he took three hours from Strouga to reach the east end of the plain of Domousova, that is the basin now called Fusha e Fododoshit, west of Orakë. One hour later he passed the khan of Brinjatz, and after a further two hours he reached 'Kjükes'.

Continuing from 'Cucuse' Pouqueville followed the general direction of the Shkumbi valley, running south-east to north-west, for three hours. He then turned leftwards into the mountains, striking west, and after more than three hours descended by 'a scabrous path' to the valley of the Shkumbi. Here he crossed the river on a three-arched stone bridge. He then followed the right bank to a fortified khan, crossed a torrent beyond the khan, and entered on a road 'eighteen feet wide which is cut in the rock, perpendicularly to the river, for the distance of half a league'. After this the gorge opened to give a view of a rich and cultivated plain. While the river swung away southwards, he rode on into Elbasan in an hour. On leaving Kukus Tozer 'spent the next day in winding along the steep mountain sides by an extremely rough track, in and out, and up and down, wherever the steep rocks left room for

---

[1] *Voyage dans la Grèce* (Paris, 1920) 3. 63 f.
[2] Tozer i. 203 f.   [3] Heuzey–Daumet 346.
[4] Quoted by J. G. von Hahn, loc. cit. (see p. 27 n. 2 above).

the path'. He stopped an hour out of Kukus for breakfast at the khan of
'Jura'. He evidently followed the general line of the Shkumbi valley
throughout, 'the road being carried for a considerable distance along
the heights far above the Shkumbi, penetrating from time to time into
the mountain-side to round a gorge, while in some places the slopes
below shelved away in a manner not seriously dangerous but such as to
require caution in passing'. He too took 'a steep and tortuous path' down
to the river and he noted the three-arched stone bridge. The account of
Heuzey and Daumet is very brief. On leaving Kukus they followed
a route at 'middle' height, flanked by precipices, as far as the three khans
of Babië, and beyond this they saw the slopes of red earth leading down
to the valley of the Shkumbi and towards Elbasan. They traversed part
of the route at night. Von Spaun took one hour from Kjükes to Dschura,
one hour thence to Darda, two hours thence to Babië khan, two hours
thence to the bridge of Hadji Bektari over the Shkumbi, and three more
hours to Elbasan.

With this background of detailed information we can apply the
measurements of distance given by the more detailed pair of Itineraries,
Tab. Peut. and It. Burd., as shown on p. 29 above (see Map 4). I con-
flate them here for convenience of reference: Clodiana XV Ad Quintum
V (VI) Scampis VIIII Genesis fl. = Treiecto VII Ad Dianam II
Grandavia VII In Candavia II In Tabernas VII Pons Servili II Claudanon III Patrae XII Lignido (Pons Servili XVIIII Lignido in Tab.
Peut. being a higher figure). The going is flat from Clodiana near Ziberrakë, as one crosses first the small bridge, then the great bridge over the
Shkumbi, and finally enters the gorge north-west of Polis i Vogel. The
distance on the map is 22 km, exactly XV m.p. Here then was mutatio
Ad Quintum (It. Burd.).[1] At this point Pouqueville had his first view of
the plain of Elbasan. We continue for V or VI m.p., i.e. some 8 km, to
mansio Scampa (Tab. Peut. and It. Burd.), which is still on the right
(north) bank of the river and about opposite the scabrous path mentioned
by Pouqueville. Its position is shown on Map 4. The Via Egnatia did
not take the scabrous path. It continued on the right bank of the river
for VIIII m.p. (13·3 km) to mutatio Treiecto (It. Burd.) or Genesis fl.
(Tab. Peut.).

As von Spaun remarked,[2] the difficulties of the journey start on leaving
the point which I have identified with Scampa. From that point I shall
take 3 km on the ground to be represented by 2 km on the map until
we reach the plain by Lake Ochrid. Proceeding then from Scampa for
13·3 km (8·5 km on the map), we put the crossing from the right bank
to the left bank of the Shkumbi at the sharp bend near Cotaj. This, then,

[1] The name may mean 'at the fifth milestone' from Scampa, which might well be 5¾ miles
from Scampa and so be entered as VI in the Itinerary.   [2] loc. cit.

is Treiecto or Genesis fl. Much the worst part of the route begins now and continues as far as Qukës. According to von Spaun the route runs above the villages of Babië and Dardhë and crosses a mountain ridge between Dzhurë and Qukës. Leaving Treiecto or Genesis fl. we climb for VII m.p. (10 km on the ground and 6·6 km on the map), to Ad Dianam[1] (Tab. Peut.), a high point above Babië. Two m.p. later we are at mansio Grandavia (It. Burd.),[2] and after a further VII m.p., we reach Qukës, the ancient 'In Candavia' (Tab. Peut.). Thus the Candavian pass proper runs from Babië to Qukës.[3]

We drop down 2 m.p. to mutatio In Tabernas (It. Burd.), crossing the river probably where the single-arched bridge is today, and we then ascend for VII m.p., which brings us to Pons Servili (Tab. Peut.), the ruined bridge in the western part of the basin west of Orakë. Two m.p. further on is Orakë itself, mansio Claudanon[4] (It. Burd.), just below the top of the pass which opens up the view of the lake. Then the descent for III m.p. to mutatio Patras.[5] Looking back, we can see that fresh horses were needed for the crossing of the 'Claudanon' pass and for the crossing of the Candavian pass; the mutationes Patras, In Tabernas, and Treiecto were in the correct places for the purpose. Continuing from Patrae on level ground we reach Lychnidus in XII m.p. 17·7 km, having passed on the way the milestone near Strouga which recorded VIII m.p. from Lychnidus. Finally the entry of the Tres Tabernae in It. Ant. 318, being XXVIII m.p. from Scampa, as compared with the aggregate of 27 m.p. from Scampa to In Tabernas in It. Burd. 608, suggests that they may be the same set of Tabernae. In Turkish times the nearby village of Qukës was regarded as the half-way halt between Elbasan and Ochrid; it was therefore natural for the Antonine Itinerary in giving only one halt to mention the Tres Tabernae rather than any other intermediate station.

[1] This Diana is the goddess of the mountain, the Diana Augusta Candavie(n)sis of the inscription found at Doclea by Praschniker–Schober 2.

[2] The traveller of Bordeaux naturally tends to turn the strange names into a more familiar Latin vernacular. Grandavia may be a corruption of Candavia; for we are indeed on the high part of the mountain, close to the shrine of Diana Candaviensis.

[3] This was seen to be the case by Praschniker–Schober 2–3, 'der gleichnamige Paß (Candaviensis), durch den die Via Egnatia führt, entspricht der 7 r.M. langen Strecke von Kjuks nach Babia Han'.

[4] As names are usually Latinized in It. Burd. and this is the only entry ending in -on, I infer that the o was long and in Greek would have been spelt Κλαυδανών. Such a name, like Πυλών between Lychnidus and Heraclea, fits a district and not a spot, and mansio Claudanon may have taken its name from the high basin and its northern extension; for the khan of Domousova at this spot is called after the valley-basin of Domousova, as appears from the map by H. Kiepert at the end of *Denkschriften* as cited p. 27 n. 2 above. In looking at the route of the Via Egnatia on Kiepert's map it must be remembered that neither Kiepert nor von Hahn had crossed the Candavian mountain.

[5] The suggestion by E. Polaschek in *RE* that Patras may be the Parthinian town Parthos (s.v. Parthini, 18. 4 (1949) 2038) is to be dismissed, because the names are not close enough and the exposed hillside here is no place for what sounds like the capital town of the Parthini.

D

We gain some insight into the difficulty of this part of the Via Egnatia from a fragment of the history of Malchus.[1] In A.D. 479 Theodoric, having forced the passes east of Lychnidus, ordered his main body, which consisted of those with the wagons and baggage-animals (τοῖς ἐπὶ τῶν ἁμαξῶν καὶ τοῖς ἄλλοις σκευοφόροις 250. 16) and the rearguard under Theodimund (ἐπὶ τῆς οὐραγίας), to come through the passes. He himself went ahead at speed, was repulsed at Lychnidus, captured 'Scampia' which the inhabitants abandoned, and got possession of Epidamnus. Meanwhile the two Roman commanders, Adamantius and Sabinianus, came up from Edessa to Lychnidus. Long-range negotiations broke down, although Theodoric sent Soas and others as hostages to Scampia, where they were ordered to wait, and Adamantius then set off by a most devious route, hitherto unused by cavalry, met Theodoric in the vicinity of Epidamnus, and offered him lands in Dardania. The matter, however, was not finally concluded.

While Adamantius was away, Sabinianus, still at Lychnidus, heard that the barbarians were going down at a slow rate from the Candavia (σχολαίτερον κατίασιν ἀπὸ τῆς Κανδαβείας 256. 14),[2] that is the main body with baggage-animals, most of the wagons, and the rearguard, among them Theodoric's brother Theodimund and their mother (οἵ τε σκευοφόροι αὐτῶν καὶ τῶν ἁμαξῶν αἱ πλείους καὶ οἱ ἐπὶ τῆς οὐραγίας 256. 14). Sabinianus seized his chance. Having sent some infantry ahead 'through the mountains' to seize the heights, he set out with his cavalry in the evening and at daybreak fell upon the Goths, who were already on their way. Theodimund and his mother, no doubt with their bodyguard, slipped away and escaped to the level ground (εἰς τὸ πεδίον, 257. 1), destroying the bridge which spanned a deep gorge (φάραγγι βαθείᾳ) and so cutting off not only their pursuers but also their own followers. The Roman infantry had now shown themselves on the peaks. A short battle ended in the capture of the wagons, about 2,000 in number, more than 5,000 prisoners, and much booty. On the way back to Lychnidus Sabinianus burnt some of the wagons on the mountain (ἐπὶ τῷ ὄρει), because it was a task to draw them through such precipitous country (διὰ κρημνῶν τοσούτων).

[1] Cited by the pages and lines of *Corpus Scriptorum Historiae Byzantianae* part i (ed. Niebuhr, Bonn, 1829).

[2] G. L. F. Tafel, *De via Romanorum militari Egnatia* (Tübingen, 1841) 7, misinterprets the situation in supposing that the Goths were returning towards Ochrid. A comparison of the two passages which I have quoted shows that Theodimund was commanding the same main body, which was slowly and painfully tagging along behind Theodoric; Theodimund will have been aware of the long-range negotiations of which the Goths sent to Scampia were a part, and he may have trusted in the good faith of the negotiators—unwisely. Malchus glosses over this by attributing the slowness of the Gothic main body to over-confidence (καταφρονήσαντες). They were in fact just short of the steep descent, the most hazardous part for wagons heavily loaded with loot. It was because Theodimund and his party were still on the Via Egnatia that Adamantius had taken such a devious route to meet Theodoric near Epidamnus.

This account has some points of topographical interest. As we have seen from the detailed itineraries, 'the Candavia' is the terrible stretch between Qukës and Babië, and the main body of the Goths with Theodimund was descending slowly from above Babië. It was some 38 m.p. (56·3 km) from Lychnidus to somewhere near Babië (that is, if we use the data of the Peutinger Table and put Ad Dianam above Babië). Because the distance was so great, Sabinianus sent off the infantry first through the mountains; then he and his cavalry force set off in the evening. The cavalry reached their objective as the sun rose (ἅμα τῇ ἡμέρᾳ). Sabinianus depended on the element of surprise. While the infantry could slip unobserved through the mountains by daylight, the cavalry had to use the Via Egnatia and therefore could not set out until the evening, lest their movements were seen and reported. With twelve hours available the cavalry covered the distance, but only just in time to surprise the Goths at dawn.

Another point of topographical interest is the bridge, close to the Candavia and spanning a deep gorge, which was a complete bar to pursuit once the bridge was destroyed. This bridge is evidently the bridge at Treiecto over the 'Genesis fl.', that is over the Shkumbi. The three-arched stone bridge at Hadji Bektari will not fit the bill, because its two central piers were set in a wide river bed, and because its situation is too far removed from Ochrid to make the night march of Sabinianus feasible.[1] On the other hand, the Shkumbi runs in gorges and defiles in its upper course, and a one-span bridge is possible in the vicinity of Cutaj.[2] The last point is that Theodimund on crossing the bridge got on to level ground (τὸ πεδίον). At Cutaj, where the river from Çermenikë joins the Shkumbi, the valleys are open and the ground is relatively level as compared with the descent from the Candavia.

[1] If the current view of Miller, Praschniker–Schober, von Hahn (op. cit. 156), Bürchner (*RE* 4. 1 (1900) 62) and many others is accepted and Clodiana is to be placed at Rogozhinë or at Peqin and Scampa at Elbasan, it follows from distances in the Itineraries when calculated from Clodiana and Scampa that the bridge which Theodimund destroyed was the bridge of Hadji Bektari above Polis i Vogel. The difficulty then arises that the distance from the hillside above that bridge to Lychnidus is excessive. In this connection the times given by von Spaun may be used, if we alter his three hours from Ochrid to Strouga to two hours which were enough for Tozer (Tozer 1. 195). From Ochrid von Spaun took nine hours to reach a point above Babië khan and twelve hours to a point above the bridge. Now the ground which von Spaun covered by daylight in nine hours might have been covered at night by the Roman cavalry force in the twelve hours between evening and dawn (ἀφ' ἑσπέρας . . . ἅμα τῇ ἡμέρᾳ). But if the scene of the action is moved three hours closer to Elbasan and the nine hours of von Spaun is consequently raised to twelve hours, the night march of Sabinianus and his cavalry passes the bounds of the credible.

[2] An interesting point is the ability of Theodimund and his followers to destroy the bridge so quickly; I think the only explanation is that the span was of removable wooden timbering, as I have argued was the case with the ancient bridge below Elbasan and that near Phoenice in Epirus (see *Epirus* 117 and 235).

As I have argued elsewhere,[1] the Parthini occupied the middle and upper Shkumbi valley, the Atintani the valleys and mountains of Çermenikë, and the Dassaretii the valleys of the middle and upper Semeni, which divides below Berat into two branches, the Devoli and the Osum (or Beratinos). This was true at least of Hellenistic and Roman times. As regards the eastern limit of the Parthini we know that Lychnidus was described as a town of the Dassaretii in 170 B.C., when the Roman commander, Appius Claudius, used it as his base (Livy 43. 9. 7, ad Lychnidum[2] Dassaretiorum consedit), and that in the following year Lucius Coelius sent an officer from Lychnidus to obtain hostages from the Parthini (Livy 43. 21. 3). It follows that the Parthini were the immediate neighbours to the west of the Roman base at Lychnidus. The Dassaretii themselves reached the area of the watershed not through the Shkumbi valley but through the Devoli valley, and it follows that their communications with Lychnidus ran from the region of Lake Malik through the country on either side of Lake Prespa. As occupants of the upper Shkumbi valley, the Parthini are likely to have extended as far as Claudanōn, which would form an appropriate frontier to their territory. In 170 B.C. the land just round the northern end of Lake Ochrid and the valuable fishery by the outlet[3] belonged to Lychnidus and the Dassaretii by right of Roman arms, if not by tradition, and its possession was more likely to be disputed by the tribe which held the upper Drin valley than by the Parthini. The Atintani who held Çermenikë[4] flanked the Parthini to the north; they occupied the valleys of the Jablanitsa mountains (see Map 4) and probably extended across the uppermost valley of the Drin (Drilon).

The Parthini and the Dassaretii are credited with a number of towns which are described as 'urbes' and as 'oppida' by the Roman writers.[5] The site near Shenjan is an example of a Parthinian town, and that at Kalaj

[1] *Epirus* 599 f.

[2] Ptol. 3. 13. 32. Δασ(σ)αρητίων Λυχνιδός and Schol. Λυχνιδών ἢ Ἀχρίδα (later Ochrida). Von Hahn, *Denkschriften* 16 (1867) 2. 162 no. 5, saw at Ochrid an inscription 'on a statue-base dedicated to Dryas, son of Caepion' with the name of 'the Dassaretii'. Heuzey–Daumet 340 identified the site of the fortifications of Lychnidus on a hill just north of Ochrid town, overlooking the lake; this is where the magnificent mosaics of the Byzantine site have been found. It accords with the first part of the description in Malchus 250 ἐπὶ ὀχυροῦ κειμένην καὶ πηγῶν ἔνδον πλήρη (I do not know about springs), and its position agrees with the data of the Roman Itineraries, as I have noted above. A fortified site, excavated by Unversagt (*Germania* 32 (1954) 19 f.), on a rocky hill-top above the monastery of St. Erasmus (St. Razmo on the Ochrid sheet, G4 of the English version of the Greek Staff Map 1:100,000), is unsuitable for identification with Lychnidus, because it has no deposit of settlement and it does not fit the distances given in the Roman Itineraries. The name Lychnidus appears in various forms in Greek and in Latin. Often the manuscripts of Livy give corrupt forms, e.g. V has 'lycidinum' here and 'lycidu' at 43. 21. 1.

[3] 'Struga is the headquarters of the fishery in consequence of the fish resorting at certain seasons to the outlet of the lake' (Tozer 1. 197).

[4] See *Epirus* 599 f.   [5] Livy 43. 23. 6 and Caesar *BC* 3. 41. 1.

e Irmajt or Kalaja Rrmait[1] of a Dassaretian town. Both are small in area
but well fortified. The entries in the Itineraries do not refer necessarily
to towns, which were often off the road on higher ground, and this is apparent from the rarity with which a civitas as opposed to a mansio and
a mutatio figures in the Bordeaux Itinerary. The name Scampa, which
appears in the Itineraries in the dative Scampis and in the latinizing
It. Burd. as Hiscampis,[2] is a neuter plural; it is a mansio and not a
civitas. It may be the name of a topographical feature; for the modern
name of the river Shkumbi is clearly the same word. I suggest that
Scampa was the Illyrian name of the river above Polis i Vogel, while in
its lower course it was called the Genusus, a name which spread inland
later with the Via Egnatia. Something similar has occurred with the
great river to the south, which in its lower course is the Semeni but in
its upper branches is the Devoli and the Osum.[3] The town 'Scampia',
which occurs in the history of Malchus, and the 'Scampina civitas' of
the *Conciliorum* is then the town of the Shkumbi, whether it lay above
Polis i Vogel or below it at Elbasan, and the 'Scampinus episcopus'
was the bishop of the Shkumbi valley.[4] The other names in the Itineraries
on which I have not commented seem to have no topographical significance.

2. *The Via Egnatia between Lychnidus and Heraclea, the lakeland district, and the routes leading from it*

The evidence of the Itineraries for the stretch from Lychnidus to
Heraclea is again very satisfactory. The totals are 45 m.p. in It. Ant. 318.
4–319. 1, 45 m.p. in It. Ant. 329. 10–330. 3, and 44 m.p. in It. Burd.
606. 9–607. 4; these Itineraries are all independent of one another,
as we have seen already, and their correspondence alone shows that their
distances are correct. Moreover, the distance on the modern road is
65 km, i.e. 44 m.p. In Tab. Peut. a name is missing, as we have seen was

[1] Excavated by F. Prendi and D. Budina with a report in *BUST* 1963. 4. 3–60; see *Epirus* 586, 723 n. 2, 733 n. 2; and in *JRS* 56 (1966) 43, and map on p. 40.
[2] In Greek inscriptions of Epirus and Illyris a sigma is often duplicated, because it was pronounced as a powerful sibilant, as in modern Albanian 'ska'. The strong initial 's' led the Bordeaux traveller to understand the word Scampis as Hiscampis.
[3] So too probably in Epirus with the Acheron and the Selleis; see *Epirus* 372.
[4] The form ending in -ia is attested in Malchus 250. 21 and 252. 10 (of A.D. 479) and *Conciliorum* 10. 514 (of A.D. 519), and it is probably more correct than the contracted form Σκάμπα in Hierocles 653. 2 (A.D. *c.* 533–5) and *Conciliorum* 10. 519. The inhabitants are Scampenses in *Not. Dign.* 9. 48. The place Σκαμπεῖς Ἐορδετῶν in Ptol. 3. 13. 26 is not to be confused with Scampia of the Parthini. The earliest signs of Elbasan becoming a fortified place (see p. 25 n. 3 above) are placed by Praschniker–Schober 57 f. in the wide bracket A.D. 300–530. It is likely that the original Scampia was in a stronger position inland of the Shkumbi defile of Polis i Vogel, but in the settled peace of the Empire people moved to a more exposed position at Elbasan.

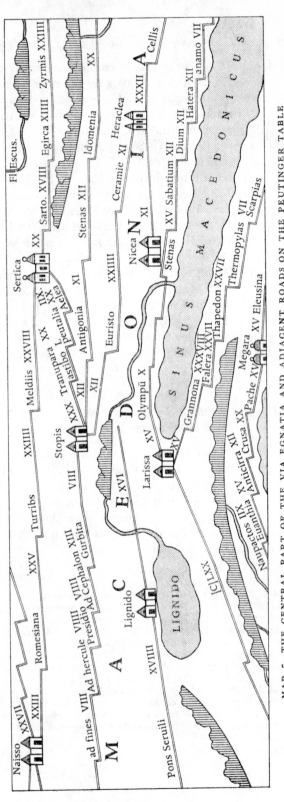

MAP 5. THE CENTRAL PART OF THE VIA EGNATIA AND ADJACENT ROADS ON THE PEUTINGER TABLE

the case between Dyrrachium and Clodiana (pp. 23 and 26 above), but this time the distance is also missing and the line is discontinued (see Map 5). One of the two entries of distance in Tab. Peut., Nicea XI m.p. to Heraclea, has the same number of m.p. as Nicia XI m.p. to Heraclea in It. Ant. 319. 1. I do not see any justification for K. Miller's alteration of an entry in It. Ant. 329. 10 from XXVII to XVII, which reduces that itinerary's total to 35 m.p.[1] Once again we must recognize that at different periods different authors chose to record different places on this busy road; and that we shall be mistaken if we follow Miller in supposing that Nicea, Castra, and Parembole are one and the same, or that they lie on two parallel pieces of road.[2] Following the same procedure as I employed for the stretch from Clodiana to Lychnidus we have the following sequence of stations:[3] Lychnidus 13 m.p. to mutatio Brucida (It. Burd.), 3 to blank (Tab. Peut.), 11 to Scirtiana (It. Ant. 329), 5 or 6 to mutatio Parembole or Castra, its Latin equivalent (It. Burd. being responsible for 5, and It. Ant. using Castra), 1 to Nicaea (It. Ant. 319 and Tab. Peut.), and 11 to civitas Heraclea (It. Ant. 319 and Tab. Peut.). There is a further entry in It. Burd. 607. 3 between civitas Cledo (i.e. Lychnidus) and mutatio Brucida: finis Macedoniae et Ephyri (i.e. Epiri). Now when Strabo, using Polybius, defined the first or Candavian part of the Via Egnatia, he mentioned the border between Macedonia and what in Polybius' day was Illyris: C 323, ἡ δὲ πρώτη ἐπὶ Κανδαουίας λέγεται, ὄρους Ἰλλυρικοῦ, διὰ Λυχνιδοῦ πόλεως καὶ Πυλῶνος τόπου ὁρίζοντος ἐν τῇ ὁδῷ τήν τε Ἰλλυρίδα καὶ τὴν Μακεδονίαν. While Lychnidus is a city, a civitas, Pylon is a τόπος, a district.[4] The word Πυλών is in form like

---

[1] *Itin. Romana* 520–1, followed by Fluss in *RE* 2. A. 1 (1921) 826; he makes these (to me) extraordinary changes in order to equate a couple of stations (here the missing one in Tab. Peut. with Scirtiana) without considering the repercussions of the changes on the totals or subsequent parts of the Itineraries.

[2] Op. cit. 521, 'Nicea, Nicia, Castra und Parambole müssen zum Teil identisch sein, zum Teil nahe beisammenliegen. Es führen hier 2 parallele Straßen.' For my criticism of the hypothesis of two parallel roads see p. 19 above. The Ravenna Geographer 196. 13 gives Heraclea, Nicea, Praesidium.

[3] The data of the Itineraries one by one are as follows:

Tab. Peut.	It. Ant. 318. 4–319. 1
Lignido XVI blank	Licnido XXXIIII (P XXIIII D XXXII)
— — Nicea	Nicia
Nicea XI Heraclea	Nicia XI (D XL) Heraclea

It. Ant. 329. 10–330. 3	It. Burd. 606. 9–607. 4
Lignido XXVII (P XXVIII) Scirtiana	civitas Cledo XIII mutatio Brucida
(D Scyrtiana)	finis Macedoniae et Ephyri
Scirtiana VI Castra	mutatio Brucida XVIIII mutatio Parambole
Castra XII Heraclea	mutatio Parambole XII civitas Heraclea

I have given the variant readings as indications of the types of corruption which arise in numbers.   [4] The distinction is stressed by the contrasting word τόπος.

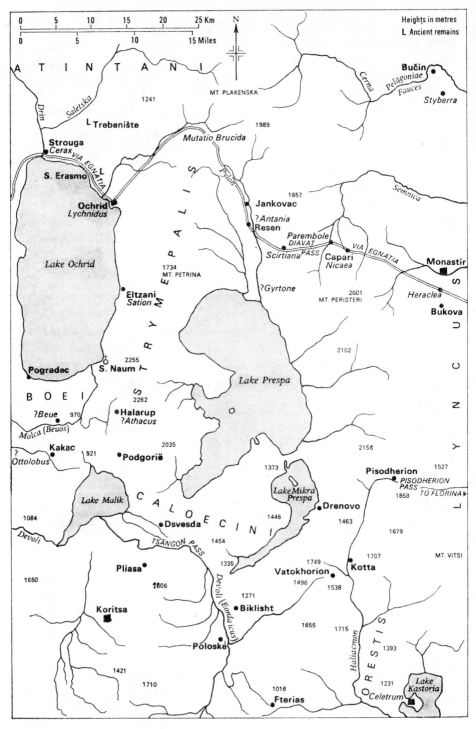

MAP 6. THE LAKELAND BETWEEN ILLYRIS AND MACEDONIA

Αὐλών and ἀνδρών 'the place of the channel' or 'the place of the men', and it means the place of the gate, the gateway. It is not used as a synonym for εἰσβολή, the normal word for an entry or pass. Pylon is placed by Strabo, using Polybius, between Lychnidus and Heraclea which he mentions next. It is possible in theory that the missing name XVI m.p. from Lychnidus in the Peutinger Table is Pylon and the missing number in the Peutinger Table is XVIII, that is from Pylon to Nicaea.

We must now apply our data to the ground between Lychnidus and Heraclea. Heraclea has been identified beyond doubt by Heuzey at a point 2 km south of Monastir towards Boukova, where there are traces of an acropolis on a hill.[1] The current excavations, which I visited in 1968, have revealed a part of the lower city on a gentle slope. Heuzey noted to the north of Monastir on the edge of the plain evidence of a Roman road in a chaussée, wider and paved with bigger stones than was usual on a Turkish road; if this was a Roman road it may have been one going northwards from Heraclea. The route from Lychnidus to Heraclea is not in doubt; for the passes are clearly defined. On Map 6 I have placed the individual stations at the appropriate intervals, as best I can in accordance with the data of the Itineraries. Taking von Hahn as our guide[2] we cross the plain from Lychnidus, and, turning gradually southwards, ascend the pass between Mt. Petrina and the Plakenska range to the north-east. The ascent through dense beech forest leads to an even ridge, which we follow to a guardhouse (now in ruins). This ridge marks the frontier between Ochrid and Resen. Von Hahn reached it from Ochrid in three hours, using 'the summer route'. As we descend through beech forest towards Resen, we pass along a flat-bottomed grassy coombe and then enter a very remarkable flat-bottomed coombe with steep sides, north of Izbiste. This coombe may well be described as a long gateway. I propose, then, to identify it with the τόπος Πυλών. The distances will now permit us to put mutatio Brucida at the site of the guardhouse 13 m.p. from Lychnidus, and Pylon 3 m.p. from mutatio Brucida, so that the blank in the Peutinger Table may be filled with the name Pylon.

As we have inferred from Strabo, the frontier between Illyris and Macedonia was drawn at Pylon in the time of Polybius, that is by the order of Rome. Centuries later, in A.D. 333, when the Bordeaux traveller

---

[1] Heuzey–Daumet 300. On the other hand, Leake 3. 282, having visited Florina but not Monastir, placed Heraclea at Florina, and his authority has led some to follow his identification, particularly Keramopoullos in *AE* 1932. 48 f. The current excavations at Boukova support Heuzey's view.

[2] *Denkschriften* 15 (1867) 2. 52 and 56. He calls the first part as far as Resen a 'summer route', and I take it that the Via Egnatia used this route summer and winter, as it would have had permanent bridges.

passed along the Via Egnatia, the frontier was not between Illyris and Macedonia, but between Epirus and Macedonia. It lay at that time not at Pylon but somewhere to the west of mutatio Brucida. On the other hand, the Ravenna Geographer[1] gives the stations Heraclea, Nicea, Praesidium, Fines. As Praesidium is the Latin translation of Parembole, and as Praesidium-Parembole was only 12 m.p. from Heraclea, it is most probable that the place Fines, 'the frontier', lay not very far west of Praesidium. The obvious place for his Fines is at the Diavat pass, as we shall see. Was this a frontier of the Macedonian period between Illyris and Macedonia, as the position of the Macedonian military camp Parembole might suggest, or a frontier between Epirus and Macedonia at some time during the Roman Empire but not in A.D. 333?

From the guardhouse, where we have put mutatio Brucida, there is a long descent (von Hahn took two hours) to Resen, which in Turkish times controlled the resources of the northern part of the Lake Prespa area. Leaving Resen we climb gradually for $1\frac{1}{4}$ hours to the first guard-house marking the frontier between Resen and Monastir. At this point we should place Scirtiana; for it is 27 m.p. (40 km) from Lychnidus, and Resen being 34 km from Ochrid on the modern road, we shall have covered another 6 km in the $1\frac{1}{4}$ hours. From here there is a gradual ascent for $1\frac{1}{4}$ hours to the watershed ridge between the basin of Resen and the plain of Monastir. Here there are a khan and the guardhouse of Diavat, reached in $2\frac{1}{2}$ hours from Resen. The pass of Diavat is very high and open as one crosses the ridge. It is in no sense a 'gateway'. The mountain-sides to the north and south alike are densely forested with beech and pine, and lower down with oak and apple-orchards on the Resen side.

On the eastern side of the pass the descent is much more steep as we turn the flank of Mt. Peristeri. We then enter a small plain between the two arms of the Rotska Reka. Here we should place Parembole, alias Castra and Praesidium (Ra. 196. 15), which was the Macedonian base for troops holding the pass of Diavat. The 'Fines' of the Ravenna Geographer should presumably be put at the Diavat pass. Nicea was a mile or so nearer to Heraclea. The name Νικαία may commemorate a victory over an enemy caught in this plain and attempting to escape over the steep narrow pass towards Illyria. From Nicaea, if we are aiming for Heraclea 2 km south of Monastir, we keep on the southern side of the plain and reach the site of Heraclea in some four hours from the guardhouse of Diavat.

Before we follow the Via Egnatia into Macedonia it is advisable to consider the country north and south of Ochrid and Resen. From Strouga

---

[1] The Ravenna Geographer 196. 13: it would be unwise to suppose that his 'Fines' is the same as the Bordeaux traveller's entry 'finis Macedoniae et Ephyri'.

on the northern shore of Lake Ochrid the Drin runs northwards, and its valley forms a reasonable route as far as Divra, ten hours away. The frontier between the district of Ochrid and the district of Divra in Turkish times was at a place four hours distant from Strouga near the confluence of the Jablanitsa stream with the Drin. Divra occupies a strong position and is the centre of several routes: one goes from Divra to Elbasan in eighteen hours, another to Guribarth in the upper Mati valley in eight hours, another to the middle Mati valley and thence to Scodra, another of an arduous kind high above the eastern side of the Drin and either alongside the White Drin towards Prisrend or following the great bend of the main river eventually to Scodra, and yet another eastwards up the Radika valley and over the hills to Kitsevo in eleven hours.[1]

Another route northwards from Ochrid reaches Kitsevo on a tributary of the Vardar in eleven hours of walking time. This was one of the routes I followed by car in 1968, so that the description is mine but the times are those of a walker. From Ochrid to Trebenishte in the corner of the great plain takes two hours, and then one enters the narrow valley of the Saletska, a considerable river. From this valley one turns up the valley of an eastern tributary and enters a fertile basin, which was at one time a lake bed. From this basin there is a long, gradual ascent through an open ride or coombe through the oak forest, and finally a steep climb to the top of a high ridge. An even steeper descent takes one down into a valley, itself high and of an Alpine character. Vrbjani lies to the west. From the valley there is a long, steep climb to a ridge even higher than the first. This ridge is eight hours from Ochrid. From it the descent is very steep to the village Popovec. We are now in the valley of the Velcka. One road goes westwards from here to Divra. We go eastwards through a narrow valley between steep, wooded slopes as far as Drugovo, and then enter the plateau of which Kitsevo is the capital. From the ridge to Kitsevo is three hours. All the high country between Trebenishte and Kitsevo and all the mountains to the north and to the east are densely forested with oak and beech, and it is likely that this has always been the case. The rich, open plain and the large farm-houses and farm-buildings of Trebenishte, wealthy in cereals, cattle, and pigs, provide a very striking contrast.

The border between the district of Ochrid and that of Kitsevo in Turkish times was by Vrbjani. It is likely that the ancient city of Uscana was at Kitsevo. In 170 B.C. Appius Claudius, whose orders were to protect (from Perseus) the peoples adjacent to Illyricum (Livy 43. 9. 6, ut accolas Illyrici tutaretur), stationed himself at Lychnidus with 4,000 Roman

---

[1] See J. G. von Hahn, op. cit. 40–4 for Divra and for some of these routes; the routes are shown very clearly in Kiepert's map at the end of the volume.

infantry and 8,000 allied troops. His orders and the position he adopted show that the Illyrians generally were allies of Rome and that at Lychnidus he was protecting the Dassaretii to the south and the peoples north of Lake Ochrid in the borderland between Illyris and Macedonia. Here he was approached by some citizens of Uscana, the chief city of the Penestae, which was controlled by a garrison of Cretan mercenaries in Macedonian pay, and he set out to take the city by surprise. He camped that day 12 miles from Uscana (i.e. near Vrbjani), started three hours before dawn, arrived in disorder, and was soundly defeated. As he had hoped to surprise Uscana, his camp 12 miles away was not in Penestian territory but in allied or at least friendly territory, so that the frontier of the Penestian territory was probably the high ridge just north of Vrbjani.

Later that year the Illyrian allies of Rome evidently succeeded where Claudius had failed; for in the winter, when Perseus wished to reduce the Illyrians nearest to his realm, because that people was affording Rome an access to Macedonia (Livy 43. 18. 3, aditum praebentibus Romano), he decided to attack Uscana, held by Romans and Illyrians. Bringing 12,000 infantry and 500 cavalry to Styberra in the Pelagonian plain (see p. 68 below), he marched to Uscana in three days, a reasonable time in winter conditions, and quickly captured the place. As his object was to wipe out the Roman bases in this area, he captured a number of forts, of which the garrisons included Roman troops, and in particular a city Oaeneum, which was on a route of passage over to the Labeates round Scodra (transitus ea est in Labeates, ubi Genthius regnabat, 43. 19. 3). Oaeneum lay by a river Artatus and a steep mountain. If Uscana is Kitsevo, the passage from there towards the Labeates is up the Velcka and over the hills into the Radika valley. Oaeneum then was in the upper Velcka valley and the river Artatus was the Velcka. He now blocked any Roman entry into the territory of the Penestae. He withdrew and sent envoys to Genthius by a route far to the north. He left garrisons in Uscana and in other fortresses. These repulsed a Roman attack based on Lychnidus, but later in 169 B.C. he withdrew his troops 'ex Penestarum gente' (Livy 43. 23. 7).

The territory of the Penestae probably comprised the long valley of the Velcka. It was bordered on the south and on the east by very steep, densely forested mountains, and its main outlets were towards Gostivar and Tetovo in the Vardar valley and towards Prilep in northern Pelagonia. Remote though it was, the territory of the Penestae had strategic importance. It provided one of the few passages from Illyris into Macedonia via Divra–Kitsevo–Prilep, and it provided the only alternative to the Vardar valley route for invaders from the north, the alternative being via Tetovo–Gostivar–Kitsevo–Prilep. The key point is Kitsevo, which we have identified with Uscana.[1] When the Romans held Uscana, there was a danger that they might bring Dardanians from the north as well as Illyrians from the west into Macedonia. Perseus therefore had good reason to make a major campaign in this strategic area. But it is most unlikely that he ever thought of fighting his way on through Divra and through the Mati valley to seek the doubtful embraces of Genthius.

There are three routes southward from Ochrid and Resen, of which those from Resen are particularly easy. The most westerly follows the east side of Lake Ochrid, where it is pinched in the south between the water and the mountain-side north of the monastery of San Naum, and then proceeds via Podgorië to Koritsa in twelve or more hours. The frontier between the district of Ochrid and that of Koritsa runs through Podgorië. The central route runs from Resen via Dsevsda and the western exit of the Tsangon pass to Koritsa in some twelve hours. The last route, keeping east of Lake Prespa, branches at Drenovo, so that one can go either via the east end of the Tsangon pass to Koritsa or in a SSE. direction to Kastoria.[2] This remarkable corridor, which holds the rich fisheries and the fertile soil of the lacustrine basins between the Illyrian watershed on the west and the Macedonian watershed on the east, is of the greatest strategic value for peoples invading from the south or from the north. This corridor was used in 217 B.C. by Scerdilaïdas coming southwards[3] and in 220 B.C. by Sulpicius going northwards. In the latter case, when Philip V of Macedon was in Lyncus, Sulpicius came unobserved as far as the river Bevus near Lyncus, which was probably

---

[1] The rival candidate for Uscana is Divra, favoured by Leake and Kiepert. The arguments against Divra are that it is too far away from the base of Perseus at Styberra in the Pelagonian plain and too open to attack from three sides by Romans and Illyrians; further, if Uscana is Divra, Perseus' advance from Divra towards the Labeates is either down the Drilon, which cannot be the Artatus, or else into the valley of the Mati, which would then be the Artatus; but either advance leaves his lines of communications open to attack from the main force of Romans and Illyrians based on Lychnidus. Yet Perseus was able to leave garrisons safely in Uscana and in other towns still further from Macedonia. Kitsevo seems to me to meet all the requirements. See the discussions by B. Saria in *RE* 9. A. 1 (1961) 1075; by F. Papazoglou 66 f., who identifies Uscana with Kitsevo; and by T. Tomovski in *ŽA* 12 (1963) 339 f., who identifies Uscana with Velmej in the upper Saleska valley and cites other articles by N. Vulić and P. Lisičar. There are difficulties in Livy's text which have sometimes distorted the issue; e.g. Livy 43. 9. 7 'accolas Illyrici' leads Weissenborn and Müller to suppose it means Illyrians in north Illyria living near Illyrians in south Illyria, whereas Livy 43. 10. 1 'Uscana oppidum finium imperiique Persei' has been taken to mean Uscana was in Macedonia; yet at 43. 20. 4 from Uscana 'Perseus in Macedoniam sese recipit' (Weissenborn's emendation 'finitimum imperio Persei' gives the required sense). Many suppose Livy to have produced a double account of a single attack by the Romans on Uscana: one in 43. 10 from an annalist and the other in 43. 21. 1 from Polybius. It is true they are from different sources, but that does not make them a doublet. In my opinion there were two attacks, one in 170 B.C. and one in 169 B.C., as Livy indicates.

[2] J. G. von Hahn, op. cit. 49, 55, and 56.

[3] See *Epirus* 606.

(see p. 64 below) the Molca river flowing from the south into Lake Ochrid.[1]

When the Romans made their first settlement of Macedonia in 167 B.C., the country was split into four autonomous self-contained regions without the right of commercium with one another. The fourth region consisted of three contiguous cantons—Pelagonia, Lyncestis, and Eordaea—and three adjacent districts, cold in climate, rough in terrain, and fringed by barbarian neighbours. The names of the districts are corrupt in the text of Livy 45. 30. 6–7: 'autincaniaestrymepalisetelimonites'. I have suggested elsewhere[2] that the first should be restored as Atintania and the second not as Tymphaea but as Strymepalis. The third is usually restored as Elimiotis, and this is likely to be correct. For, though Livy elsewhere uses Elimea for this district, the ethnic Ἐλειμιώτης is used of a third-century proxenus at Delphi,[3] and we can surmise that the form ἡ Ἐλειμιωτίς (sc. γῆ) may have been used in Livy's source. Moreover, Elimiotis is adjacent, on the one hand, to Eordaea and, on the other, to Tymphaea in Epirus, and it is also west of Mt. Bermium, so that it meets all requirements. I should then read the text of Livy as 'Atintania et Strymepalis et Eleimiotis', which has the same number of letters as the corrupt passage. By adding Atintania and Strymepalis—an otherwise unknown district—to the fourth tetrarchy Rome gave to it a greater strategic unity as well as the valuable fisheries and pastures. For I think that Atintania and Strymepalis stretched from Dzepi on the upper Drin in the north to Dzvesda or so in the south.[4]

Of the names on the Via Egnatia between Lychnidus and Heraclea we may connect Brucida with βροῦκος, a word for a locust, as we learn from a fragment of Theophrastus (fr. 174. 4).[5] Scirtiana, like Clodiana, has a Latin adjectival termination, and the stem may conceal the name of a Greek town. I suggest Κυρτώνη or Γυρτώνη, the 's' of Scirtiana having been added by a Latin speaker hearing, for example, τὸ πανδοκεῖον τῆς Γυρτώνης. If we are right Kyrtone or Gyrtone was the predecessor of Resen. There are two hitherto unexplained references to a Gyrtone.[6] One in Orph. *Argonautica* 146 reads thus:

---

[1] See *Epirus* 616, and more fully in *JRS* 56 (1966) 43; St. Byz. Βεύη, πόλις Μακεδονίας καὶ πρὸς αὐτῇ Βεῦος ποταμός.

[2] See *Epirus* 633.

[3] *BCH* 21 (1897) 112; see p. 120 n. 3 below. Arrian, *Anab.* 1. 7. 5, has the form Elimiotis.

[4] Rome had ceded Atintania to Macedonia on a previous occasion in 205 B.C. and it is described by St. Byz. as μοῖρα Μακεδονίας. The Dassaretii were given their freedom (see *BSA* 61 (1966) 253 n. 54); if Rome took away some of their recently acquired territory at the same time, it would be a typical example of Roman statecraft. Orestis was also given its freedom.

[5] 'The Thirsty Locust' would be a good name for an inn at such a height. The personal name 'Breukos' occurs on an ephebic inscription of Styberra (*AI* 4 (1963) 81).

[6] See Stählin in *RE* 7. 2 (1912) 2101: 'Von unklaren Zusammenhang [with Gyrtone in Thessaly] ist die Angabe des Ptolem. 13. 43 daß G in Stymphalia lag und das Beiwort ἁλιστεφές.'

Ἄλκωνος δὲ Φάληρος ἀπ' Αἰσήποιο ῥοάων
ἤλυθεν ὃς Γύρτωνος ἁλιστεφὲς ἔκτισεν ἄστυ,

and the other is in Ptol. 13. 43 Στυμφαλίας· Γυρτώνη. Neither passage suits Gyrtone near Larissa in the Thessalian plain, founded by a brother of Phlegyas, but they may fit a Gyrtone by Lake Prespa. According to Pape[1] the words Γυρτώνη and Κυρτώνη are closely related. This is probable, since γυρτόν is a milk-vessel in Epirotic dialect[2] and κύρτος, κύρτη, and κυρτίς are fisherman's baskets or lobster-pots (the shapes being similar); further, Hesychius gives κυρτεύς· ἁλιεύς, 'a fisherman'. Kyrtone or Gyrtone as a fisherman's village is well found on the shore of Lake Prespa. In addition we then have an explanation of the strange epithet ἁλιστεφές, because this area was famous for salting fish. Alcon, its founder's father, carries a name found in the Molossian royal house,[3] and the word Γυρτώνη may have Epirote affinities. The entry in Ptolemy is a single one, and Stymphalia may be a corruption of Strymepalis (or vice versa).[4]

3. The Via Egnatia between Heraclea and Thessalonica

The stretch of the Via Egnatia from Heraclea to Edessa, both fixed points, has been intensively studied by C. F. Edson, who has brought important epigraphical evidence to bear on the problem.[5] One difficulty is that the Peutinger Table in this stretch (see Map 5) has one or two successive entries which are impossible, namely XLV for Cellis to Edessa and XLV for Edessa to Pella; there is no hope of salvaging these entries.[6] Another difficulty is that It. Ant. 330 and It. Burd. have each a much higher total of miles than It. Ant. 319 for Heraclea to Edessa, and yet all three agree pretty well for the stretches Edessa to Pella and Pella to Thessalonica. But the greatest difficulty of all is that the total distance for Heraclea to Edessa in the detailed Bordeaux Itinerary is far higher than that of either of the accounts in the Antonine Itinerary. Whereas

---

[1] *Wörterbuch d. gr. Eigennamen* (1884) s.v.

[2] Hsch. ed. M. Schmidt 365. 32.   [3] See *Epirus* 797.

[4] Both in Livy and in Ptolemy the suggestion has been made that we should read 'Tymphaea'. But Tymphaea is too far south for the passage in Livy, and there is no explanation of the strange epithet, if it is referred to a Gyrtone in Tymphaea. For Tymphaea, see *Epirus passim*. Another suggestion, made by Fluss in *RE* 2. A. 1 (1921) 826, is that Scirtiana is to be connected with the Scirtones of Ptol. 2. 16(17). 8 or the Scirtii of St. Byz. s.v. *Skordiskoi*, but both are outside Macedonia and are associated respectively with the Pirustae and with Paeonia. As a personal name we have Γάιος Σκίρτιος Πρόκλος (? for Curtius) in an inscription from Styberra (*Comptes rendus* 1939 221A line 75) and Σκηρτιώ in one from Debresta northwest of Prilep (*Spomenik* 71 (1931) no. 404).

[5] *CP* 46 (1951) 1–16.

[6] K. Miller's suggestion that the first of the two may be possible 'auf Umweg ähnlich der Bahnlinie' does not allow for the difference between a graded line and a direct Roman road.

his predecessors rejected the Bordeaux Itinerary, Edson took its account to be correct. At the same time he rejected the evidence of the other three Itineraries; and he felt justified in doing so, because he followed Kubitschek (though with reservations) in supposing them to be derived from one single source.[1] This belief of Kubitschek seems to me to have been disproved by the data of the Itineraries at least for the stretch from the Adriatic coast up to Heraclea, and it gains little support for the stretch from Heraclea to Pella from the fact that there is not a single figure in common between these three accounts. I regard the three accounts as independent, and I am therefore not prepared to reject them.

I give the data of the Itineraries in the same form as hitherto and include variant readings where they occur;[2] and I have asterisked the two cases of XLV to show they are irredeemable.

It. Ant. 319. 1–320. 1	Tab. Peut.	It. Ant. 330. 3–7	It. Burd. 605–6 (reversed)
Heraclea–Cellis XXXIIII P XXIIII D XXIII	XXXII	XXXIII	H. XIII mut. Melitonus M. XIIII mut. Grande G. XIIII mans. Cellis
Cellis–Edessa XXVIII D XXVIIII	*XLV	XXXIII	C. XVI mut. Ad Duodecimum D. XII civ. Edissa
Edessa–Pella XXVIII D XXVIIII	*XLV	XXX Dioclitianopolis	E. XV mut. Scurio S. XV civ. Polli
Pella–Thessalonica XXVII	XXVII	XXVIIII	P. X mut. Gephira G. X mut. Ad Decimum Ad D. X civ. Thessalonica

If we work from Thessalonica, the four accounts at first are in reasonably close agreement, allowing for small differences due to inclusive reckoning and exclusive reckoning and to a time span of more than a century; those earlier in date (It. Ant. 319 and Tab. Peut.) giving 27 and 27, those later in date 29 and 30 for Thessalonica–Pella, again 28 or 29 and 30, 30 respectively for Pella–Edessa, and even (though it is only one of each period) 28 or 29 and 28 respectively for Edessa–Cellis. This suggests that, as has been the case so far, the entries are generally sound, and that, where similarities or approximate similarities of distance occur, they may be accepted as sound. It is true that corruption of any

[1] Op. cit. 9, 'the 32 to 34 Roman miles given by the Antonine Itinerary and the Peutinger Tables as the distance between Heraclea Lynci and Cellae must be dismissed as erroneous'. The reservations which he expressed in note 22 on p. 13 of his article as a correction were of much help to me in forming my views.

[2] It may be noted that MS. V, one of three which are derived from the archetype, is not available for the relevant part of It. Burd., indeed for 601 to 611.

one entry may have occurred in the transmission; however, this is not necessarily serious, if, as we think to be the case, the Itineraries do not go back to a single source which was itself liable to an initial and infecting corruption but are independent of one another. Thus for Edessa to Cellis I should accept the figure 28 as the correct figure (here one of It. Burd.'s two entries is guaranteed by the correspondence of the name Ad Duodecimum and of the entry XII), and regard both the XLV and the XXXIII as corrupt.

When we look at the examples of corruption which appear for this section of the road,[1] we see from the first column that an X may easily drop off, or a I as between XVIII and XVIIII; and from the next two columns that a cause of corruption is the repetition of a number. For XLV is a repetition of the preceding XLV, and XXXIII is a repetition of the preceding XXXIII. For Cellis to Heraclea we have approximate agreement for three accounts at 34, 32, and 33, and we notice in the entries of the fourth one, which yield a total of 41, that we have a repeated number XIIII. In accordance with our practice so far, I should regard the second XIIII as a corruption due to repetition, and either leave a blank for the entry 'mutatio Grande' to 'mansio Cellis', or propose IIII as more likely than any other figure to help a scribe to repeat XIIII. In the latter case the total is 31. So far then as our experience of the Itineraries since Dyrrachium and Apollonia goes, it appears that the numbers are correct except for a freak error in Tab. Peut. of XLV Cellis–Edessa and three cases of a repeated figure: XLV in Tab. Peut. for Edessa–Pella, XXXIII in It. Ant. 330 for Cellis–Edessa, and XIIII in It. Burd. for Grande–Cellis.

When we apply these data to the ground, beginning from Thessalonica and using the kilometres marked on the German copy of the Greek Staff Map, we proceed for X m.p. (14·8 km) to the crossroads at Anchialos (Inglis), which is therefore mutatio Ad Decimum (It. Burd.). The next piece, also of X m.p. (It. Burd.), making in all 29·6 km from Thessalonica, brings us to Nea Khalkhidon (Yialatsik) beside the Axios river, which is therefore mutatio Gephira, where the river was bridged. The distance of XVII m.p. from Thessalonica (It. Ant. 320 and Tab. Peut.) being 40 km brings us precisely to Nea Pella. It appears then that the other itineraries, It. Ant. 330 and It. Burd., have given too high a total figure for Pella–Thessalonica, the latter perhaps through inclusive reckoning. Continuing from Pella XV m.p. (It. Burd., 22·2 km) we reach the crossroads by Trifilli as mutatio Scurio, and another XV m.p. brings us to

---

[1] So far I have proposed only one case of corruption of a number, XXIIII being corrupt for XVIIII at It. Ant. 329. 6; as the numbers so far have been rather accurately transmitted, one needs to put forward an explanation if possible for the origin of corruptions and not just alter the entries to suit one's preference.

E

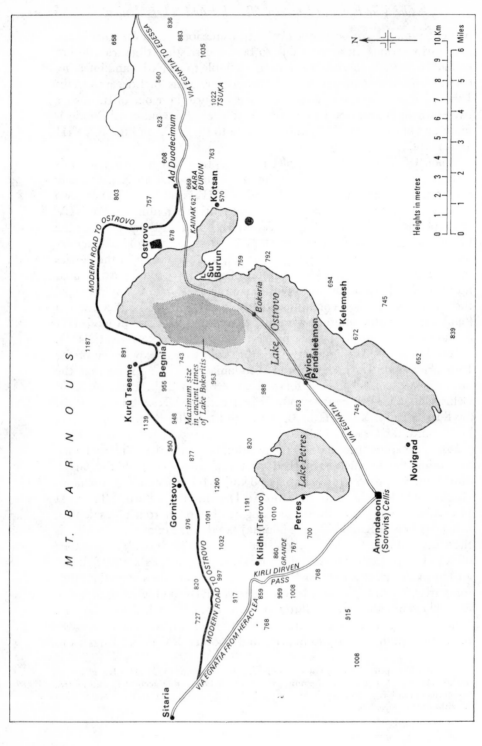

MAP 7. THE DISTRICT ROUND LAKE OSTROVO AND LAKE PETRES

Edessa, which being 83/4 km from Thessalonica is 43/4 km from Pella, that is XXIX to XXX m.p. from Pella (It. Ant. 319 and 330 and It. Burd.).

There is no doubt about the line of the road west of Edessa as far as a point north of Kara Burun, because it follows a well-defined pass (see Map 7). Taking then the entry of XII m.p. from Edessa to mutatio Ad Duodecimum (It. Burd.), that is 17·7 km, and transferring it to the modern road within this pass, we can place Ad Duodecimum at a point north of Kara Burun. After going through this point and the town of Arnissa the modern road runs north of the two lakes, Ostrovo and Petres; there it follows a long pass through the mountains, and finally enters the plain before Sitaria (Rosna). If this road is taken, the distance from Edessa to Heraclea, 2 km short of Monastir, is some 86 km (58 m.p.). When we add together the 28 m.p. for Edessa to Cellis (It. Ant. 319 and It. Burd.) and the 32, 33, or 34 m.p. for Cellis to Heraclea (Tab. Peut., It. Ant. 319, and It. Ant. 330), the total of 60, 61, or 62 m.p. = 88·9 to 91·8 km is too high; for the Roman road with its emphasis on the direct line is likely, if anything, to have been shorter and not some 3 to 6 km longer than the modern road. The Via Egnatia, then, did not follow the line of the modern road north of Lake Ostrovo and Lake Petres.[1]

Taking now the distances from Heraclea, avoiding the modern road between Sitaria and Arnissa, and going on through the alternative pass of Kirli Dirven, we reach after XIII m.p. (It. Burd, 19·2 km) Kato Kaliniki, beside which the Gusachia river is joined by the Florina (or Eleska) river; Kato Kaliniki then is mutatio Melitonus. As we pass through Sitaria (Rosna), we may note that a Roman milestone was built into a chapel there; it recorded a repair to the road 'from Dyrrachium', that is the Via Egnatia, in A.D. 305–6.[2] Another XIIII m.p. (It. Burd., 27 km) brings us into the Kirli Dirven pass below Klidhi; here then was mutatio Grande. If we go on to Amyndaeon (Sorovits), we shall be some 48 km (XXXII to XXXIII m.p.) from Heraclea; these are the figures in Tab. Peut. and It. Ant. 330 for Heraclea to Cellis. We should then place Cellis at Amyndaeon. A fragment of a Roman milestone in a house wall at Petres comes probably from the road between the Kirli Dirven pass and Amyndaeon.[3]

Edson's knowledge of the terrain and his application of the epigraphical evidence enabled him to prove that in A.D. 305–6 the Via Egnatia passed through the Kirli Dirven pass and ran south of Lake Petres. A Macedonian milestone, found *in situ* in the Kirli Dirven pass, which is

---

[1] Until Edson wrote his important article, all students of the Via Egnatia had supposed that it did run north of the lakes. The availability of accurate maps now makes it possible to show that this was not so, unless one alters some of the entries given by the Itineraries.

[2] Published by Dimitsas i. 268 and restored with full commentary by Edson, op. cit. 4–7.

[3] Pappadhakis in *Athena* 25 (1913) 432 no. 8; seen by Edson and published with commentary, op. cit. 7.

inscribed ἐγ Βοκερίας στάδιοι ἑκατόν, shows that in the third and possibly the fourth century B.C. a Macedonian military road passed along this route.[1] The Via Egnatia, which was built by the Romans as a military road and was still regarded as such by Cicero a century later (*Prov. Cons.* 2, via illa nostra, quae per Macedoniam est usque ad Hellespontum, militaris), is most likely to have controlled this pass, which has at all times been of great strategic importance.[2] A Roman milestone, recording a repair of the road in the years A.D. 305-6, was found 'outside the railway line' which runs from Amyndaeon to Ayios Pandeleëmon on the shore of Lake Ostrovo (it was subsequently taken to the nearby village of Novigrad).[3]

At this stage we are faced by a dilemma. If the Via Egnatia came to a point between Amyndaeon and Pandeleëmon, where did it go from there? The sides of the lake are too steep to carry a road, ancient or modern; indeed the construction of the railway along part of the western side was quite a feat of engineering. Could the Via Egnatia have gone through the valley which is now covered by the lake?

Mrs. Hasluck made a special study of Lake Ostrovo.[4] She showed that the level of the lake rose by some 15 m between 1903 and 1923; that a rocky area crowned by a broken minaret near Arnissa (Ostrovo) was exposed in 1903 and was covered in 1923; and that an inscription in Greek of *c.* A.D. 240 was visible there in 1903 on a massive limestone block, which, she argued, 'may be presumed to be in its original position'. She referred also to remains of the prehistoric period and of the ancient period which had been found at different times near the shore of the lake at Ayios Pandeleëmon (Pateli), Begnia, Kelemesh, and Novigrad. She concluded that for considerable stretches of time in those periods the level of the water had been much lower than in 1903. Such variations are not surprising since the lake was, until recently, drained only by swallets (some of which issue at Gougovo, 8 km to the east), and the level depended on the blocking or clearing of the swallets.

---

[1] Mrs. Hasluck describes the Macedonian milestone, which was published by Mordtmann in *AM* 18 (1893) 419, as 'found buried 2 m. deep in the ground at km. 170. 450 on the railway, i.e. half a kilometer south of the railway station of Tserovo in the wild defile called Kirli Dervan' (*Geographical Journal* 88 (1937) 454). See Edson, op. cit.

[2] Most recently in March 1941, when it was held by the advanced left flank of the British forces; I passed through it at that time and turned off at what I now realize is mutatio Melitonus to go to Florina, which was being evacuated by a Greek headquarters group.

[3] The Roman milestone was published by Giannopoulos in *BCH* 17 (1893) 635 with the note 'Novigrad en dehors de la ligne'.

[4] 'A historical sketch of the fluctuations of Lake Ostrovo in West Macedonia', *Geographical Journal* 87 (1936) 338 f.; and 'The archaeological history of Lake Ostrovo in West Macedonia', *Geographical Journal* 88 (1937) 448 f. with a chart of the depths, facing p. 451. The lake of Ioannina in Epirus is similarly drained by swallets; it seems not to have existed as a lake in ancient times, but it was probably there in the sixth century A.D. (see *Epirus* 39 and 185).

In 1952 a new situation arose; for a tunnel was cut to draw off water, and the level sank by 18 m, revealing once again the rocky area with the broken minaret. In 1968 I saw the massive limestone block. It has four dowel holes and is therefore not in its original position. Yet Mrs. Hasluck's general conclusion is valid. For there is no town site or agora appropriate for such a monumental piece on the exposed rocky area or in its vicinity, and the odds are that it came from a site which is today still under water. I visited a low islet, some 30 m by 30 m, which had appeared since 1952 between the rocky area and a promontory called Sut Burun. On this islet, called Ayios Nikolaos, I saw many pieces of tile and some bones, including a piece of a human skull. This islet was visible in 1899. Struck wrote in 1903 that he had opened graves there and had found a tombstone with a Latin inscription of the Roman period.[1] Here too we must conclude that the level of the water was considerably lower in the Roman period than it is today.

I must turn aside to discuss the fortification on Sut Burun, because Mrs. Hasluck based some of her arguments upon it. She seems to have thought of this fortification as enclosing on four sides an area used as a fortress and not for habitation; she argued that such a fortress was built to protect a road which could have run only in the valley which is now under water; and she thought the fortification was at latest of the Byzantine period and might be earlier. I visited the site in 1968. The water level was then some 18 m lower than at the time of her visit, and more could be seen. Sut Burun is a rather bare limestone ridge which descends in a series of diminishing heights to the lake, and the last of these heights, separated from its neighbour by a slight and narrow saddle, is fortified. The fortification consists of a single cross-wall, built at right angles to the line of the ridge and reaching down to the shore of the lake on either side *as the shore was in 1923*. Today there is an undefended stretch of shore on either side below the wall. Undoubtedly the wall was built when the water was at an unusually high level, such as existed in 1923. Further, there is no other fortification wall. The promontory jutting into the lake north of the cross-wall has no fortifications; here the defenders relied on the water of the lake and not on walls to protect them.

There are indications too that the promontory was inhabited; for there are many bits of tile and many pieces of walls, whether house walls or terrace walls. In other words the cross-wall was built to protect on the landward side a large village or a small town, situated there, in troubled times. In the recently exposed stretch of shore there are also tiles and remains of walls, some of which extend under the present surface of the

---

[1] For the Greek inscription on the massive limestone see J. H. Mordtmann, *AM* 18 (1893) 418, and Asima, *BCH* 17 (1893) 634. For the Latin inscription see A. Struck, *Globus* 83 no. 14 (1903) 217, and N. G. Pappadhakis in *Athena* 25 (1913) 434–5 no. 16.

water. The promontory in fact was still inhabited when the level of the lake sank and the cross-wall became ineffective as a defence; times were evidently less troubled. At the highest point a part of the wall and a rectangular tower have been exposed by peasants digging for treasure. They are built of small blocks, about one foot square, set in mortar. The lowest courses of the wall which descends on either side are made of larger stones, roughly faced on one side only and set in mortar. The wall is certainly not of the Greek or the Roman period; indeed it is likely to be late rather than early in the medieval period. To the north-west of Arnissa there is a ring of wall, said to be made of small stone set in mortar, on a rocky knoll above the shore of the lake; I saw it across the lake but did not visit it. I conclude that the fortification on Sut Burun has no bearing on the level of the lake in antiquity.[1]

The Via Egnatia, which we have brought as far as Amyndaeon, may have run through what is now a lake. The number of kilometres available from Cellis at Amyndaeon to Ad Duodecimum by Kara Burun is 23·7 = XVI m.p. (It. Burd.). Measuring on the surface of the 1 : 100,000 map via Ayios Pandeleëmon and keeping towards Sut Burun and up by Kaïnak to Ad Duodecimum I make it 20 km, which allows enough for the actual road with its climb up to Ad Duodecimum to have been 23·7 km = XVI m.p. in length. It is also possible now to deduce the maximum but not the minimum level of the lake during the period at least from *c.* 140 B.C. to A.D. 333; for the level then must have been 60 m lower than it is today to permit the passage of the road on a reasonably gradual slope below Sut Burun. I show on Map 7 the size of the lake at that level.

Strabo C 323, using Polybius, contrasted the Candavian section ending with the frontier between Illyris and Macedonia at Pylon with the succeeding section, which we have just considered. His summary of it is as follows: ἐκεῖθεν δ' ἐστὶ παρὰ Βαρνοῦντα διὰ Ἡρακλείας καὶ Λυγκηστῶν καὶ Ἐορδῶν εἰς Ἔδεσσαν καὶ Πέλλαν μέχρι Θεσσαλονικείας· μίλια δ' ἐστί, φησὶ Πολύβιος, ταῦτα διακόσια ἑξήκοντα ἑπτά. Whereas the road has run hitherto on the Candavian range (ἐπὶ Κανδαουίας), it now runs along the side of Mt. Barnous (παρὰ Βαρνοῦντα),[2] the great range of Kaïmatsala, now named Voras, which rises from the eastern side of the plain south of Monastir and extends as far east as the valley of the Vardar (Axius). Its finest peak, 2,521 m high, is north of Lake Ostrovo. In the first part of its course this range forms the frontier between Yugoslavia and Greece.

---

[1] Mrs. Hasluck discussed the fortification on Sut Burun in *The Geographical Journal* 88 (1937) 451 f. She thought that the uniform level of the remains of the walls was due to Basil the Bulgar-Slayer, but the absence of the stones of the upper courses is due rather to the villagers; in 1968 I saw the men of Arnissa removing blocks in the area by the minaret. The ring of wall to the north-west of Arnissa is mentioned by Keramopoullos in *AE* 1932. 194.

[2] Mistranslated as 'the road runs to Barnus' in the Loeb edition of Strabo 3. 295.

Strabo, using Polybius, here separates Heraclea from the Lyncestae, which suggests that the city was not in the area originally named as that of the Lyncestae (see further p. 59 below). The frontier between the Lyncestae and the Eordi may most reasonably be placed at the summit of the Kirli Dirven pass near Klidhi and at the corresponding place on the pass used by the modern road from Sitaria to Arnissa. As Edessa lies outside the territory of the Eordi, the eastern frontier of Eordaea may be put at the summit of the pass by mutatio Ad Duodecimum. The north-eastern frontier of Lyncus and the northern frontier of Eordaea were formed by the ridge of Mt. Barnous. Thereafter Strabo gives not tribes but cities—Edessa, Pella, and Thessalonica, the 'civitates' of the Bordeaux traveller.

'There are 267 miles up to this point', says Polybius. It is a verbatim quotation, and these miles are Polybian miles. We see the significance of this fact when we look back to the sentences before the summary description of the Via Egnatia. There Strabo tells us that the Polybian mile contained 8⅓ stades, whereas 'the majority of people', οἱ πολλοί, reckoned a mile at 8 stades. In order to convert 267 Polybian miles into the standard miles used by the majority, for instance by the compilers of Itineraries, we have to add stades to the extent of one-third of the number of Polybian miles (τὸ τρίτον τοῦ τῶν μιλίων ἀριθμοῦ), i.e. 89 stades = 11 standard miles. Thus 267 Polybian miles are 278 standard miles, the m.p. of the Itineraries.[1] The conclusions to which our study of the Itineraries and the terrain have led us so far in terms of standard miles are as follows: Dyrrachium or Apollonia to Clodiana 43 m.p.; Clodiana to Lychnidus 72 or 73 m.p.; Lychnidus to Heraclea 44 or 45 m.p.; Heraclea to Thessalonica 118 m.p. (made up of 33, 28, 30, and 27). Our total, then, is a bracketed one of 277 to 279 standard miles. The agreement between the two totals indicates that the text of Strabo is sound and that our calculations based on the Itineraries are on the right lines. Further encouragement may be derived from Pliny *HN* 3. 145, 'montes Candaviae a Dyrrachio LXXVIII m.p.', with a variant reading of LXXVIIII. Pliny's information was derived ultimately from the

[1] The difference between the Polybian mile and the standard mile of 8 stades (Plb. 3. 39. 8 κατὰ σταδίους ὀκτὼ διὰ 'Ρωμαίων; see F. W. Walbank, *Commentary on Polybius* I. 373) has been overlooked in this connection by Tafel, op. cit. 16, K. Miller, *Itin. Romana* 516 'diese Strasse hat eine Länge von 267 Meilen', and others. P. Pédech, *La méthode historique de Polybe* (Paris, 1964) 595, converts Polybius' 265 miles to 2,225 stades on the Polybian standard, but he is applying the result to the cartographical preconceptions of Polybius into which it does not fit—not surprisingly perhaps as it is an actual measurement. The statements of Pliny *HN* 4. 10 (17) § 36, that the distance from Dyrrachium to Thessalonica was CCXLV miles, and 4. 11 (18) § 42, that the distance from Dyrrachium to Philippi was CCCXXV, are not consistent with one another, since the Itineraries reckon the distance from Thessalonica to Philippi at 100 or 101 miles (see P. Collart in *BCH* 59 (1935) 405), or with the statement of Polybius, unless of course Pliny was using a sub-standard mile; even so his two figures are not proportionately acceptable.

milestones of the Via Egnatia. Our study of the Itineraries has led us
to figures of Dyrrachium to Clodiana 43, Clodiana to Scampis 20, and
Scampis to Ad Dianam, the goddess of the Candavian mountains, 16.
These figures give a total of 79 miles, LXXVIIII m.p.

The measurement recorded by Polybius for the road from Dyrrachium
to the Hebrus river (Str. C 322, μέχρι Κυψέλων καὶ Ἕβρου)[1] was in stades
(evidently 4,458 stades), in accordance with his usual custom, and Strabo
warned us that Polybius' conversion of those stades into miles was on an
unusual standard. It is just conceivable that Polybius first obtained the
distance in terms of standard miles from milestones, *if* the Via Egnatia
was already built;[2] that he then changed these miles into stadia and
reported the sum as 4,458 stadia; and that he changed the 4,458 stadia
back into miles by an unusual standard and reported the total in miles.
But it is more probable that knowing the length of the Macedonian road
which was marked by stadion-stones (probably in tens) he reported its
length in stades and added a note of the corresponding number of
miles.[3]

The stadion-stone from the Kirli Dirven pass inscribed ἐγ Βοκερίας
στάδιοι ἑκατόν is not the only testimony to the existence of such roads in
Macedonia. Three road markers, inscribed ὅρος τῆς ὁδοῦ, of which two
may be dated to the fourth or the third century B.C., have been found

---

[1] Oberhummer in *RE* 5 (1905) 1989 infers from Str. 329 fr. 10 and fr. 13 that the road
ended at Thessalonica, but it is illogical to pit the fragments of an epitome against the original
text and prefer the fragments.

[2] The general belief is that the Romans built the whole Via Egnatia soon after the creation
of the province of Macedonia in 148 B.C. However, it is based on inadequate grounds.
No Egnatius is known for the period between 146 and *c.* 120 B.C. from whom the road could
have taken its name. The suggestion that the road was named after the town Gnathia in
Apulia is highly improbable, not only because of Gnathia's unimportance but also because
the great roads were named after individuals. Of the known Egnatii in T. R. S. Broughton,
The Magistrates of the Roman Republic (New York, 1951) 2. 439, 490 and Supplement p. 23, the
senator mentioned in *SEG* 3. 451 of *c.* 170–160 B.C. is too early, but the father who disinherited
his son, then a senator, in 74 B.C. might be a suitable candidate for building the road at the
turn of the first century B.C. It was a military road, designed rather for armies defending the
civilized areas against the northern barbarians, as Cicero indicated in 56 B.C. (*Prov. Cons.* 2),
than for armies marching to Asia, and the period when the Scordisci broke into Macedonia,
the Cimbri were on the move further north, and consular armies were operating year after
year from bases in Macedonia is the time when we should expect the Roman army to have
built the road. This period extended from 119 to 106 B.C. at least and probably on to the turn
of the century (see *CAH* 9. 108 f.). I am inclined to believe that the whole Via Egnatia was
built in its Roman form in the decade 110 to 100 B.C. The stretch Apollonia to Lychnidus was
probably improved before 120 B.C.

[3] Philip II and Alexander had a survey service, and as they conquered new lands they
made roads and recorded their length in stades. Philip II reduced Illyris to beyond Scodra
(see Hammond, *BSA* 61 (1966) 244 f.), and he or Antipater is likely to have made a road as
far as Dyrrachium at least. In the other direction Alexander, if not Philip, extended the road
to the Hebrus at Cypsela, where the river was navigable. It ended there in the lifetime of
Polybius; that is why Str. C 322 fin., using Polybius, wrote of the road ending at Cypsela,
whereas in fact the Romans carried it on to the Hellespont (Cic. *Prov. Cons.* 2). Polybius
probably consulted Macedonian Itineraries, as we consult Roman Itineraries.

at Philippi and at Drama in eastern Macedonia.[1] The place Bokeria was on the road at a distance of 100 stades, i.e. 12½ m.p., from the scene of its discovery ½ km south of Klidhi railway station. As k and g were easily confused in western Macedonian pronunciation and spelling, as here ἐγ for ἐκ,[2] it is likely that Bokeria is the place from which the 'lacus Begorritis' of Livy 42. 53. 5 took its name. In that case, as there are no pockets to accommodate lakes in the plain north-west of Klidhi, Bokeria lay along the road towards Ad Duodecimum at a distance of 12½ m.p., that is 18·5 km, which places it half-way between Ayios Pandeleëmon and Sut Burun and south of the maximum level of the lake in ancient times (see Map 8). There was then a small lake here in 171 B.C. Its official name was 'Bokeritis' but the name has been transmitted as 'Begorritis'.[3] Perseus pitched camp by the lake in 171 B.C., having come at the head of 43,000 men, including 4,000 cavalry, from Citium via Edessa along the military road, which was suitable for the transportation of the siege-train and the commissariat. His horses found pasture and his men provisions in what was then a fertile and well-populated basin.

The names on the Bordeaux Itinerary are sometimes in the nominative, e.g. civitas Edissa or mutatio Gephira, sometimes in the dative, e.g. Lignido, and sometimes in a genitive, e.g. civitas Polli and mutatio Perpidis (i.e. Euripidis, as the next line 604. 7, shows) The first station after Heraclea, mutatio Melitonus, at the crossing of the Florina river, may well be the transliteration of a genitive Μελιτῶνος; in that case Μελιτών may be the name of the river, as the ending -ōn is usual in upper Macedonia (e.g. Erigon and Haliacmon).[4] The next mutatio, 'Grande', is in a rugged pass, and the mansio Grandavia of 607. 8 was also in such a pass; neither word is a transliteration or corruption of a Greek word, and they may be the Bordeaux traveller's own coin. 'Cellis' or 'mansio Cellis' might be explained as the ablative of 'Cellae', a name which occurs elsewhere in the Itineraries and simply means 'stores, granaries, etc.' in Latin. Here, however, 'Cellis' is almost certainly a place-name in the nominative, like Heraclea, Edessa, Pella, and Thessalonica in our Itineraries. If so, it is a transliteration of Κελλίς. A place-name of the same root, Κέλλιον, occurs on an inscription found in the area of the upper Devoli river.[5] 'Mutatio Scurio' has probably picked up its initial 's' from the Bordeaux traveller, as Scirtiana did. For this 'mutatio' is in the

---

[1] Cited and discussed by Edson, op. cit. 11 f.

[2] See Gyrtone and Kyrtone, p. 46 above, and in the Itineraries Lignido and Lychnido; it is the same in Epirus with names like Githana related to Kitium and Galaithos to Kelaithos.

[3] This was suggested by Mrs. Hasluck in *Geographical Journal* 88 (1937) 454; she put Bokeria at an ancient site near Kelemesh (Farangi). Edson, op. cit. 14, n. 55, regarded the identification as uncertain.

[4] Cf. St. Byz. Μελιτοῦσα πόλις Ἰλλυρίας, for the form of the word.

[5] *Athena* 25 (1913) 450 no. 54 = Kanatsoulis no. 491.

plain below an ancient site, which is identified with Κύρρος, or in Ptol.
3. 13. 9 Κυριός. Four m.p. short of Thessalonica a milestone inscribed in

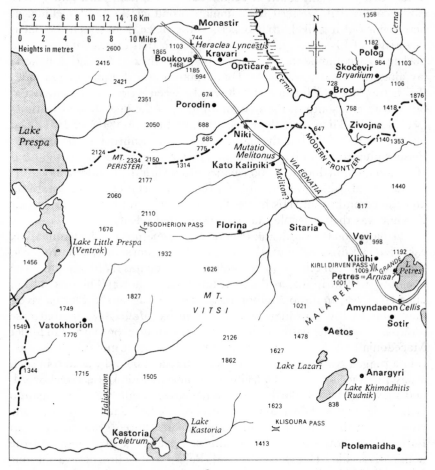

MAP 8. LYNCUS

A.D. 123–4 was reinscribed at some date between A.D. 317 and 324;[1]
it may have caught the eye of the Bordeaux traveller as he set out in
A.D. 333 on the long journey to Dyrrachium.

[1] Published by A. Dain, *Inscriptions grecques du Musée du Louvre* (Paris, 1933) 30 f. no. 24;
S. Lambrino, *Istros* i (1934) 157; P. Collart, *BCH* 59 (1935) 401. The suggestion that the
later inscription should be emended in two places to VIIII instead of IIII because it ends
with the Greek letter θ is not really acceptable; one cannot display an incorrect mileage on
a milestone and get away with it for long. The θ is surely an abbreviation for Thessalonica.
The earlier inscription has the abbreviation in Latin 'Thessal.' IIII θ should be left undisturbed on this overused stone. For a contrary view see Ch. I. Makaronas in *Studies presented
to D. M. Robinson* i (1951) 385 f.

4. Routes and Places in Lyncus, Pelagonia, and Derriopus

The Via Egnatia between Heraclea and mutatio Grande in the Kirli
Dirven pass crosses a wide plain in which the southern tributaries of the
Cerna Reka are gathered from the eastern slopes of Mt. Peristeri and of
Mt. Vitsi (Vernon) and from the western slopes of Mt. Kaïmatsala
(Voras); or in terms of Polybian geography, as reported by Strabo, from
the slopes of the Candavian range and from those of the Barnous range
(Maps 7, 8). The southern end of the plain is closed by the Mala Reka,
through which the Via Egnatia passed by the Kirli Dirven defile. As we
have seen from Polybius' description of the road, the Lyncestae occupied
the plain south of Heraclea (Str. C 323, διὰ 'Ηρακλείας καὶ Λυγκηστῶν).
Their frontiers were set on the west by the ridges of Mt. Peristeri and Mt.
Vitsi; on the south by the Mala Reka, where they marched with the
Eordi; and on the east by the slopes of Mt. Barnous. A northern frontier
was drawn by nature at the narrowing of the plain, more or less on the
line of the Yugoslav–Greek frontier, but it was an open frontier, hard to
defend. The possibility always existed of extending the territory of the
Lyncestae northwards through the gap to include Monastir and capture
the pass westwards towards Lychnidus. This possibility was realized by
Philip II, who subjugated all the peoples as far as Lake Lychnitis
(Ochrid).[1] It seems that he extended the territory of the Lyncestae,
'Lyncus', to include Monastir and the district of Resen. Nevertheless,
the tradition that the plain north of the gap had belonged to Pelagonia
persisted. It was a fact of geography, and that is probably why the city
of Heraclea, 2 km south of Monastir, appears in the codex Parisianus of
Ptol. 3. 12. 30 as Λυγκηστίδος 'Ηράκλεια ἡ Πελαγονία, and why in A.D.
553 the bishop was 'episcopus Heracleae Pelagoniae, Heracleae Pelagonensis'.

Pelagonia, sharing with πέλαγος the meaning of a flat expanse, derives
its name from the long, flat plain watered by the upper Cerna and its
tributaries. A natural frontier on the west is set by the ridges which
form the watershed between the Cerna, on the one hand, and the Saletska
and the Velcka, on the other hand, the valley of the latter being occupied
by the Penestae (see p. 44 above). To the north the tangled mass of
the high mountains of Golesnitsa separates the lower valley of the
Velcka from the lower valley of the Cerna, as both rivers swing in a
northerly direction and fall eventually into the Vardar. On the east the
mountains between the Golesnitsa massif and Mt. Barnous are pierced
in the north by the low pass of Pletvar east of Prilep leading into the
valley of the Rajetz, a tributary of the Cerna, and further south by the
Cerna itself.

[1] D.S. 16. 8. 1.

The plain is much dominated by the river Cerna, the ancient Erigon. Rising in the same mountains as the Saletska and the Velcka, the river flows eastwards, enters the plain at Bučin, flows southwards past Topol-čane as far as Brod, turns abruptly eastwards and then northwards, and enters the Vardar at Gradsko. The 'fauces Pelagoniae' of Livy 31. 34. 6, or the defile leading into the Pelagonian plain, 'fauces ad Pelagoniam' and 'angustiae quae ad Pelagoniam sunt' of Livy 31. 33. 3 and 31. 28. 6, is the gorge just above Bučin, 'les gorges de Boutchin par lesquelles l'ancien Érigon sort de la région montagneuse où il se forme'.[1] A short distance downstream from the gorge and on the right bank of the river an isolated hill was reported by Heuzey to be the site of an ancient city from which a number of inscriptions had been taken to the nearby village of Tsepicovo.[2] This site, as Heuzey remarked, was ideally situated to guard 'les débouchés de la rivière', and it lay at a point where Illyrians coming from Divra in the Drin valley via Kitsevo and Dardanians descending from the north into the Velcka valley were most likely to approach the Pelagonian plain.

The importance of the defile is clear from the operations of the Mace-donians and the Romans in 199 B.C. In the previous autumn the Romans had gained control of western Dassaretis[3] and had received offers of help from Pleuratus, the king of the Ardiaei, whose power extended into the area of Scodra and probably far up the Drin,[4] and from the Dardanian king, Bato. Sulpicius, the consul, who had under his command two legions, a small force of cavalry, an unknown number of elephants, and auxiliaries raised from Rome's allies in Illyria—a total force of some 30,000 men—, said he would use their help when he led his army forward into Macedonia. Philip V, who was aware of the danger from Pleuratus and Bato, had posted an army under his young son Perseus to occupy the defile leading into Pelagonia, that is above Bučin (see Map 9). In the spring of 199 B.C. Philip moved his main army into position. Livy does not tell us where he was, but we may assume that he occupied the camp above Heraclea called Parembole (see Map 6). He was well placed for supplies. He was within an eight-hour ride of Perseus at Bučin, so that they could quickly reinforce one another. He could send forces forward through Lychnidus and Atintanis, which he had held since 205 B.C., if not earlier, and keep a watch on the pass of Claudanon, which led into the upper valley of the Shkumbi. He was able also to send forces

---

[1] Heuzey–Daumet 314. Livy here uses Polybius and translates τὰ στενά; see Hammond, *JRS* 56 (1966) 54, for similar expressions used of the Aoi Stena.

[2] Heuzey–Daumet 314 f.; these and other inscriptions are discussed below, p. 87.

[3] For the operations in Dassaretis see my article in *JRS* 56 (1966) 42 f. In what follows I differ from previous interpretations of the campaign; they are well discussed by F. W. Walbank, *Philip V of Macedon* (Cambridge, 1940) 141 f. Heuzey–Daumet 302 f. and 323 f. has the best understanding of the topography.   [4] See Hammond, *BSA* 61 (1966) 245 f.

quickly southwards to Florina, whence a pass led into the upper valley of the Devoli. A position at Parembole gave Philip complete flexibility of movement.

The initiative lay with Sulpicius. He advanced through southern Dassaretis and established a fortified camp near the river Bevus, which is probably the river Molca flowing into the southern end of Lake Ochrid (see p. 45 above and Map 6).[1] He was now close to the border of Lyncus, being a day's march from the pass leading to Florina, or he could move northwards into the district of Resen; but he was still in Dassaretis, from which he was drawing his supplies (Livy 31. 33. 6, ad Lyncum stativa posuit prope flumen Bevum; inde frumentatum circa horrea Dassaretiorum mittebat).

Neither the consul nor the king knew where the other was. Their cavalry forces eventually made contact on one of the three routes which led northwards from the consul's camp (see p. 45 above). Philip moved first. Having recalled Perseus, he established a fortified camp on higher ground a little more than a mile from that of Sulpicius (Livy 31. 34. 7, paulo plus mille passus a castris Romanis tumulum propinquum Athaco[2] fossa ac vallo communivit). He now blocked the advance of Sulpicius northwards and prevented him from joining hands with the Illyrians and the Dardanians, should they materialize. Philip's position can be determined approximately as being on the hills by Halarup on the right bank of the eastern branch of the Molca river (see Map 6). His position had further advantages: his lines of supply from the Ochrid and Resen districts were short, and he could move either back to Heraclea or south-east via the Tsangon pass into Lyncus.

Philip had 2,000 cavalry and 20,000 infantry. Although stronger in cavalry, he was considerably weaker in infantry of the line than Sulpicius. Yet he had a marked advantage in being much more mobile. This was important to Philip, since he intended to avoid a pitched battle and to wear down the Romans in the hope of obtaining a reasonable peace. He manœuvred now as brilliantly as Caesar did later in Illyria. On the other hand, Sulpicius was troubled by the problem of supplies throughout the campaign.[3] Therefore he wished to force a pitched battle as soon as possible but not by attacking a fortified position. Philip soon made the situation of Sulpicius desperate; for he used his cavalry and light-armed troops to cut off the Roman foraging detachments. Sulpicius retired 8 miles and made a fortified camp at Ottolobus. Philip repeated the same tactics. But this time an engagement developed, and the king

---

[1] In *JRS* 56 (1966) 43 and n. 19 I have given reasons for Sulpicius' choice of route.

[2] A variant reading is 'Achaco' and the Milan edition of 1505 gave 'Areto'.

[3] For references to supplies see Livy 31. 33. 4 and 6; 31. 36. 5–7; 31. 38. 1; 31. 39. 3–4; and Plu. *Flam.* 4 τοῦ Φιλίππου φυγομαχοῦντος ἀπορήσῃ σιτίων.

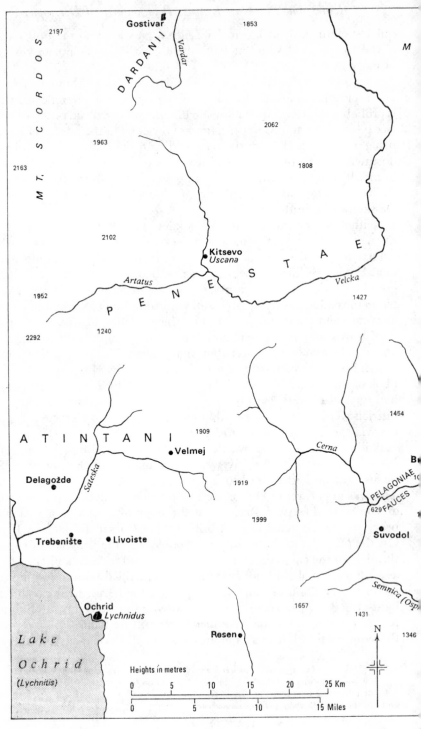

MAP 9. NORTH-WEST

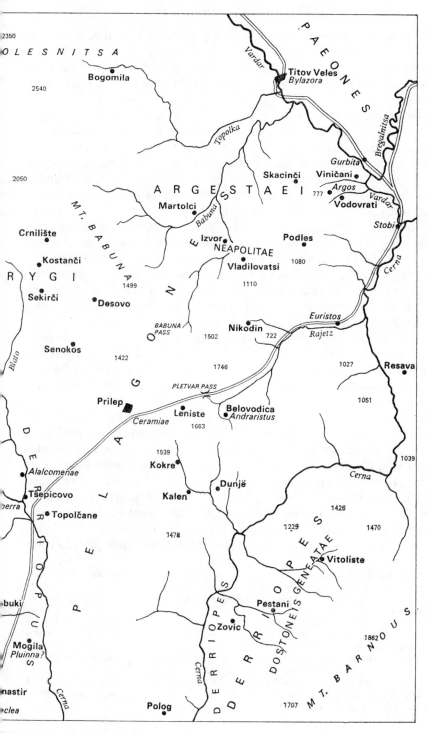

OLESNITSA

2350

2540

Bogomila

P A E O N E S

Vardar

Titov Veles
Bylazora

Topolka

Bregalnitsa

Gurbita

2050

Skacinči

Viničani

Argos

777

Vodovrati

Vardar

A R G E S S T A E I

Martolci

Babuna

Stobi

Crnilište

MT. BABUNA

Izvor

NEAPOLITAE

Podles

Cerna

Kostanči

1499

Vladilovatsi

1080

R Y G I

1110

Sekirči

Desovo

BABUNA
PASS

Nikodin

Euristos

1502

722

Rajetz

Blato

Senokos

1422

1746

1027

Resava

PLETVAR PASS

1051

Prilep

Leniste

1663

Ceramiae

Belovodica
Andraristus

1539

Kokre

1039

Alalcomenae

Dunjë

Cerna

Tsepicovo

Kalen

1426

berra

Topolčane

1229

1470

1478

GENEATAE

Vitoliste

buki

Pestani

Zovic

1862

Mogila
Pluinna?

1707

MT. BARNOUS

nastir

clea

Cerna

Polog

EDONIA AND ITS NEIGHBOURS

and his cavalrymen withdrew with difficulty through ground so swampy that horse and rider were sometimes sucked down in the deep mud of the swamp (Livy 31. 37. 8, in paludes quidam coniecti profundo limo cum ipsis equis hausti sunt; and 31. 37. 11, showing that the marshes were extensive).[1]

The ground which Livy describes so vividly was a large and boggy fen, not just soft going, and it was without doubt the area of Lake Malik. Ottolobus then was on the high ground west of the lake. The name, a distinctive one derived from 'eight peaks', is particularly appropriate to this area; for it contains a large number of isolated small hilltops between 1,055 m and 1,495 m high.[2] This identification enables us to confirm that the river Bevus, by which Sulpicius made his first camp, was the Molca. We hear also of a *polis* Beue from Stephanus Byzantinus: Βεύη, πόλις Μακεδονίας, καὶ πρὸς αὐτῇ Βεῦος ποταμός. τὸ ἐθνικὸν Βεναῖος. The attribution to Macedonia dates from a later time, when Macedonia extended down to the coast by Oricum, and we hear of a city of the Dassaretii which is evidently the same as Beue but pronounced without the initial β: Δασσαρητίων· Εὐία, Λυχνιδός, Ptol. 3. 13. 32.[3] The chief city in the large plain which contains Lake Malik is nowadays Koritsa (Korcë), but in the eighteenth century and earlier it was Moschopolis to the west of the lake. In Hellenistic times it was evidently north of the lake near the river Molca. We can now see why Sulpicius stopped where he did 'prope flumen Bevum'; for he was near the chief city of the region, from which he commandeered supplies.

Having lost 300 cavalry, Philip used one of Hannibal's tricks. He left camp fires burning and disappeared overnight on a route unsuitable for the heavy column of the Romans (Livy 31. 39. 2). As he had heard a report that Pleuratus and the Dardanians had set out with huge forces (Livy 31. 38. 7), he probably crossed the hills to Leskovec and returned to Heraclea with the intention of intercepting the Illyrian and Dardanian forces before they could make contact with the Romans. Sulpicius now made good his supplies, advanced up the corridor (probably to Lychnidus) and went on not over the pass to Heraclea[4] but to Styberra, where

---

[1] This vivid detail and others, such as the effect of seeing the wounds inflicted by swords of Spanish metal, show that Polybius got his account from eyewitnesses, perhaps while he was at Oricum waiting to be shipped off to exile in Italy in 167 B.C. Frankish knights and horses were similarly sucked down in the mud of Lake Copaïs.

[2] These heights are shown on a German Staff Map, 1:50,000, of this area, which I saw in the Map Room of the Firestone Library of Princeton University. The heights are west of Pirgu and Novasela (in the German spelling).

[3] The two places seem not to have been connected by commentators, e.g. in *RE* 3. 1 (1897) 375 s.v. Beue. For Moschopolis see Leake 1. 343 f.

[4] If he had attempted to do so, it is probable that Philip would have appeared and blocked him; and if he had gone via Heraclea, Livy is likely to have mentioned Heraclea as a better-known place than Styberra.

he brought in the grain from the fields of the Pelagonian plain (Livy 31. 39. 4, Stuberram deinde petit atque ex Pelagonia frumentum quod in agris erat convexit).[1] He presumably chose Styberra because he was expected to meet his Illyrian and Dardanian allies[2] on the way or at Styberra. The 'fauces Pelagoniae' were no longer defended.

At this point we must describe the terrain on the east side of the Pelagonian plain and work towards an identification of Styberra. When the Cerna leaves the plain and swings eastwards and then northwards, it enters wild country. Heuzey, the first European scholar to explore it, has left a vivid account of the deep ravines and tangled gorges, the rocky outcrops and pinnacles, and the paths high above the slippery slopes or overhanging the river enclosed in its narrow bed. Soon after leaving Brod he noticed a fortified acropolis by the river near Skočevir, and then another near Gounitsa. Further downsteam on passing Zovic the valley was open for a time, and up a lateral valley to the north he heard of the remains of a considerable ancient site at Dunjë. An inscription recording a dedication to 'Artemis Kunagos and the polis' was found at Kokre which lies on the route from Dunjë to Prilep, and this shows that there was a *polis* or state in this area.[3]

Below this open part of the valley of the Cerna there are a series of gorges, where the river cuts through a high northern outlier of the Barnous range.[4] When the river emerges on the other side, it is close to more open and cultivated hillsides. Here Heuzey visited a strongly fortified site, which he believed to be an ancient site, refortified in the Byzantine period. It is below the village Resava and above the right bank of the Cerna. A separate site nearby was not fortified and may have been a sanctuary. At Resava Heuzey copied four Greek inscriptions, one of which recorded a dedication to Ἡρακλῆς θεὸς μέγιστος. It came from the unfortified site.[5] From Resava the countryside is well cultivated as far as the junction of the Cerna with the Vardar below Gradsko. At the confluence, known as Smixi, he found a fortified site, not more than 500 m in circumference, with Byzantine and medieval

---

[1] Although Livy tries to score a point for Sulpicius in his remark 'ab consule non parabatur sed gerebatur iam bellum', it is clear that Sulpicius did not start at all until the fields offered some fodder for his men (Livy 31. 33. 4), and that in Pelagonia he was in time for the harvest in July or so.

[2] As Livy was concerned with the feats of Rome's regular troops and not of their associates, his silence here should not be taken to mean that they did not come. For later, at 31. 40. 10, he mentions the report 'equestris ad Ottolobum pugnae Dardanorumque et Pleurati cum Illyriis transitum in Macedoniam'.

[3] *Spomenik* 94 (1941–8) no. 354.

[4] Heuzey–Daumet 321 f., calling the district 'the Morihovo'. He was indignant with his guide, who did not take him down the Cerna far below Zovic but went to the north. The map shows the reason for the guide's action; for there is no track marked except one down in the gorge itself, usable only in dry summer weather.

[5] Ibid. 329 = *Spomenik* 71 (1931) no. 176.

fortifications but on the emplacement of an ancient town. An important inscription in the village-fountain of Sirkovo mentioned the municip(ium) Stobe(nsium), and Heuzey thus identified the site as Stobi.[1]

The direct route from Stobi to Pelagonia crosses a wide area of excellent arable land, and then enters an impressive defile of the Rajetz river, a tributary of the Cerna Reka. The gorge is pinched between precipices, into which a road has been cut on either side. There are further gorges higher up the river; indeed Heuzey's description of the valley as merely one long gorge is very apt. The motor road follows the slopes on the north side of the river. Here Heuzey saw two inscriptions, both cut in natural rock and presumably facing an ancient road. One is a dedication by a veteran of the Praetorian Guard to a snake honoured in these parts, and the other is a dedication made to Zeus Agoraeus in A.D. 167, situated on the edge of a dry ravine which was probably followed by 'la route antique'.[2] During the long climb one sees the fine crags of the limestone outcrop of Mt. Babuna to one's right, and the great mass of Mt. Kaïmatsala to the south, impressive with its limestone peaks between Alpine pastures above the line of coniferous forest and then very green in September with deciduous woods and some maquis on the lower slopes. The road enters a wide basin at a high altitude, and across it to the south one sees the large village of Belovodica, near which Heuzey visited the remains of a considerable but unfortified ancient city.[3] Above this basin the old road and the motor road higher up cross the ridge which links Mt. Kaïmatsala to Mt. Babuna. The pass is called the Pletvar pass. The ridge is uniformly high and open, so that any defence of Pelagonia in ancient times was sited lower down in the Rajetz valley and preferably at the first defile. The descent on the west side is gradual through orchards of fruit-trees and cultivated slopes with thickly wooded, green hills to the south and picturesque high crags to one's right. Below these lies Prilep, the Prilapos of Byzantine writers, to which the nearby medieval castle of Makro-kral belonged, and below Prilep one sees the flat fen-like upper plain of Pelagonia which is separated from the lower plain by the hill known as Dupen Kam.

On a spur north of Prilep towards the high crags, Heuzey visited the monastery of Treskavetz, where he found two altars with inscriptions recording dedications to Ἀπόλλων Ὀτευδανός and Ἀπόλλων Ἐτευδανίσκος, the latter dated by the Macedonian era to the year A.D. 114. A Turkish cemetery at Prilep was the source of a marble column fragment, seen by Heuzey at Monastir, which recorded in A.D. 730 the dedication of a colonnade by Φρόντων Διονυσίου Στυβερραῖος. Heuzey decided that

[1] Heuzey–Daumet 336 = *CIL* iii 629.
[2] Heuzey–Daumet 327 = *Spomenik* 71 (1931) no. 447.   [3] Ibid. 325.

Styberra was situated at Prilep.[1] But this is not in accord with the ancient evidence; for there is no reason to suppose that Sulpicius would have come to this side of the plain in 219 B.C. or that Perseus in operating against Uscana in 170–169 B.C. would have made his base here rather than on the west side of the plain. The column may have been brought to the cemetery from some distance, and there is evidence to show that 'Ceramie' and not Styberra was near or at Prilep.

The route we have followed from Stobi at the confluence of the Cerna and the Vardar to Prilep is the only possible route for the Roman road from Stobi to Heraclea. This road is recorded only in the Peutinger Table (see Map 5): Stopis XII Euristo XXIIII Ceramie XI Heraclea. As K. Miller saw,[2] the total distance is inadequate. He suggested that a place-name and a distance had dropped out between Ceramie and Heraclea, the meeting-place of three roads; and this is an acceptable hypothesis, as similar confusions occurred at Dyrrachium and at Apollonia, where three roads met (see pp. 21 and 26 above). The same hypothesis would apply at the Stobi end; but the individual distances suit Miller's supposition better. Starting from Stobi and using the kilometres of the modern road, as shown on the U.S. Army Map, we find that XII m.p. (17·7 km) brings us to a point above the cross-roads and near the first defile, that is to Euristo; that XXIIII m.p. (35·5 km) brings us to Ceramie at Prilep; and that XI m.p. (16·3 km) bring us to Dupen Kam by Topolčane. The modern road, which crosses the flat plain, bridges the Cerna here and proceeds to Monastir and Heraclea south of it in 27 km (XVIII m.p.). What of the missing place-name? Here the Ravenna Geographer 196. 10 f. comes to our aid by giving the names on this route in sequence: Euriston, Ceramie, Istubera, Heraclea, Nicea, Praesidium, Fines. As the others are in order, we may accept Istubera, i.e. Styberra, as the missing place-name.

At the time of the Roman Empire to which the Ravenna Geographer refers there is no doubt that Styberra was at Tsepicovo. I walked from Topolčane to Tsepicovo, part of the way being on a straight stretch of wide road on a slight embankment, which is probably the line of the Roman road. One skirts the south side of Dupen Kam and reaches the ancient site which faces westwards and lies on the lowest slope between Trojkrsti and Tsepicovo. One of the inscriptions which were found during the excavation of the site began with the words Στυβερραίων ἡ πόλις.[3] The site lacks any natural defences, and I saw no evidence of a circuit-wall.

---

[1] Ibid. 317. The inscriptions to Apollo are in *Spomenik* 71 (1931) no. 490 and no. 491 and another, no. 489, to Apollo Oteudanikos; others found there include a dedication to Artemis Ephesia ἡ ἐν Κολοβαίσῃ in *Spomenik* 77 (1934) no. 58.

[2] K. Miller, *Itin. Romana* 578 and 580 with maps 162 and 177.

[3] *Spomenik* 71 (1931) no. 501. Styberra was put at Tsepicovo by B. Saria in *RE* 9. A. 1 (1961) 1075 and nearby at Srpci by Miller.

The choice of this site for Roman Styberra was evidently related to the crossings of the two rivers, the Blato and the Cerna, which unite to the south of Tsepicovo. Whereas the modern road crosses their combined waters within flood banks in the plain below Topolčane, and the railway does likewise in the plain below Trojkrsti, the Roman road crossed the Blato just west of Tsepicovo, where it flows between Dupen Kam and a small outcrop in the plain. It then made a separate crossing of the Cerna. This crossing was probably near Bučin; for in von Hahn's travels[1] there is a note that the comfortable route from Prilep to Diavat Han (north-west of Heraclea; see p. 42 above) crossed the Cerna at Bučin. From the vicinity of Bučin the Roman road then followed the western side of the plain to Heraclea. The distance from Styberra to Heraclea was XVIII m.p. (27 km), and this distance is correct from Tsepicovo. The missing entry in the Peutinger Table may be restored then as 'Stubera XVIII' or 'Istubera XVIII'. The stretch of paved chaussée which Heuzey saw north of Monastir at the foot of the hills by the plain was evidently a piece of the Roman road on the way from Styberra to Heraclea.[2]

On the other hand, the Macedonian city of Styberra was probably not at Tsepicovo but at Bučinsko Kale, a defensible site on the right bank of the Cerna and closer than Tsepicovo to the gorge through which the Cerna enters the plain. This site too has been excavated; it was an important town of the classical and the Hellenistic periods, and there is little doubt that Heuzey and Daumet were correct in placing Macedonian Styberra at Bučinsko Kale. Strabo C 327 supports this identification: πρότερον μὲν οὖν καὶ πόλεις ἦσαν ἐν τοῖς ἔθνεσι τούτοις . . . καὶ ἐπὶ τῷ Ἐρίγωνι πᾶσαι αἱ τῶν Δευριόπων πόλεις ᾤκηντο, ὧν τὸ Βρυάνιον καὶ Ἀλαλκομεναὶ καὶ Στύβαρα. For 'formerly', that is in Macedonian times, Styberra was on the Erigon river, that is the Cerna river, whereas Roman Styberra at Tsepicovo was beside the crossing of the Blato river.

We now see that when Perseus was placed at the 'fauces Pelagoniae' he was based on Macedonian Styberra; that Sulpicius entered Pelagonia at Styberra through the undefended defile; and that Perseus operated from Styberra against Uscana, which was at Kitsevo. Further, Styberra was probably the richest market in the Pelagonian plain, because Perseus brought his thousands of prisoners and his loot to Styberra and sold them there. A happy confirmation that Styberra was a chief city of the district emerges from the inscriptions said to have been found at the site near

---

[1] In *Denkschriften* 15 (1867) 2. 57 'die bequeme Strasse über Diawat Han kreuzt bei Wuschtrin die Tscherna'. Heuzey–Daumet 314 used a bridge by Topolčane. A note of excavations at Bučin is in *Svornik* 1961–6, the report of the Skopje Museum, which I have not seen.

[2] Heuzey–Daumet 300: 'les vestiges d'une vieille chaussée, plus large et pavée de plus grandes pierres que ne sont ordinairement les routes turques'.

Bučin and seen at Tsepicovo. In them the acts of a council convened by οἱ ἐν Δερριόπῳ πολειτάρχαι in the principates of Nerva, Trajan, and Hadrian are recorded.[1] The phrase ἐν Δερριόπῳ recalls that of Livy 39. 53. 14, translating a phrase of Polybius: 'oppidum in Deuriopo (MSS. Derriopo) condere instituit—Paeoniae ea regio est—prope Erigonum fluvium, qui ex Illyrico per Paeoniam[2] fluens in Axium amnem editur haud procul Stobis,[3] vetere urbe; novam urbem Perseida . . . appellari iussit.' In the inscription and in the text of Livy using Polybius Derriopos is the name of a 'regio', a district. So it is also in the following passages of Strabo:

C 326 πρὸς δὲ τούτοις Λυγκησταί τε καὶ ἡ Δευρίοπος καὶ ἡ τριπολῖτις Πελαγονία, and C 327 ὁ δὲ ᾽Ερίγων πολλὰ δεξάμενος ῥεύματα ἐκ τῶν ᾽Ιλλυρικῶν ὀρῶν καὶ Λυγκηστῶν καὶ Βρύγων καὶ Δερριόπων καὶ Πελαγόνων (Corais for πλειόνων) εἰς τὸν ᾽Αξιὸν ἐκδίδωσι. πρότερον μὲν οὖν καὶ πόλεις ἦσαν ἐν τοῖς ἔθνεσι τούτοις· τριπολῖτις γοῦν ἡ Πελαγονία ἐλέγετο ἧς καὶ ᾽Αζωρος ἦν, καὶ ἐπὶ τῷ ᾽Ερίγωνι πᾶσαι αἱ τῶν Δευριόπων πόλεις ᾤκηντο, ὧν τὸ Βρυάνιον καὶ ᾽Αλαλκομεναὶ καὶ Στύβαρα.

Derriopus, a better-attested form than Deuriopos, is then not a city any more than Pelagonia is a city in the phrase of Livy 'fauces Pelagoniae'.[4] The district Derriopus adjoined Illyrian territory, namely that of the Penestae, who were called 'Penestae Illyrii . . . bellicosum genus', when Pleuratus sent them to serve in the Macedonian army (Livy 44. 11. 7); as 2,000 were engaged in the defence of Cassandrea, they were a large tribe. Livy and Strabo both say that the Erigon rose in the 'Illyrian mountains', and this perhaps implies that the Penestae held the head of the valley, and that the frontier of Derriopus was not much above the defile by Styberra. Sulpicius, then, first entered Macedonia at Styberra, and we may assume that on the way he had made a rendezvous with the

---

[1] Heuzey–Daumet 315.

[2] A. Schaefer in *N. Jahrbuch* (1876) 368 emended Paeoniam to Pelagoniam. The emendation should be rejected because it makes the river Erigon flow *through* Pelagonia, which is inconsistent with the cities of the Derriopes being ἐπὶ τῷ ᾽Ερίγωνι (Str. C 327).

[3] I take it that 'haud procul Stobis' defines the confluence of the Erigon and the Axius, and the word order is arranged to produce the juxtaposition of 'vetere urbe' and 'novam urbem'. I do not agree with the proposition in Weissenborn and Müller 'daß die Lage der Stadt dreifach bestimmt ist: in *Deuriopo, prope Erigonum, haud procul Stobis*', if for no other reason than that the area round Stobi is attributed to Paeonia or Pelagonia and not to Deuriopos.

[4] In Livy 39. 53. 14 derriopo, derrhiopo, and derchiopo are in the manuscripts and Deuriopo is due to Sigonius; the inscription should have settled the matter in favour of Derriopo. St. Byz. Δουρίοπος, πόλις Μακεδονίας. Στράβων ἑβδόμῃ. οὕτως ἡ χώρα. In quoting Strabo as his source, Stephanus may reveal his own error, as the two mentions in Bk. 7 are both of the district; yet as the book is incomplete, it is possible that he may be correct. Except for this mention in St. Byz., there is no evidence for the existence of a city of this name. Those who have thought there was such a city have usually made a false deduction from the inscription (e.g. Philippson in *RE* 5. 1 (1903) 280); Heuzey voiced a warning against such a deduction (Heuzey–Daumet 316 f.). Weissenborn and Müller on Livy 31. 28. 5, and 31. 33. 3 believe Pelagonia is a city but at 31. 34. 6 and 31. 39. 4 a district; I doubt such ambivalence within a dozen chapters.

Illyrians and Dardanians. The territory Derriopus is clearly related to the river, as all its cities are said to have been beside it. As it is already a large river when it enters the plain, it forms a natural frontier with the Pelagones. Derriopus then was the district west and south of the river, Styberra being at that time on the right bank. This is supported by an inscription[1] built into the church wall of Bela Tsarkva, which is on the right bank of the river Blato just above its confluence with the Cerna. For the inscription records the building of an altar ἐν Ἀλκομενᾶ, and this name is evidently a κώμη or *mahalas* of the city Alalcomenae given by Str. C 327.

The limits of Derriopus to the west may be set at the ridge between Demir Hissar and Suvodol. When I travelled on the motor road from Kitsevo to Monastir, I was struck by the difficulty of the country north of Demir Hissar; for the ridge south of Kitsevo is very steep and high, and it is covered in a dense forest of beech and oak, and on the south side of the ridge there are very narrow valleys, for instance at Dolenci. At Demir Hissar itself one is surrounded by thickly wooded hills. This country probably belonged to the Penestae. To the south of Demir Hissar there is a flat plain by Suvodol, and on crossing an oak-clad ridge one descends through a wide valley with arable slopes, which merges into the main Pelagonian plain just north of Monastir. It is likely then that the country to the south of Demir Hissar goes with the main plain, and that it belonged to the Derriopes. This receives some support from three inscriptions in Greek found at Suvodol (*Spomenik* 98 (1941–8) no. 58). They record the dedication of slaves to Θεᾷ Πασικράτᾳ, and two of them are dated by the Macedonian era, one to the month of Dios in A.D. 286 and the other to A.D. 307. An inscription in Greek comes from Dragomantsi, a village south of Suvodol (ibid. no. 60). These inscriptions are appropriate to the territory of the Derriopes and not to that of the Penestae. The richest part of Derriopus was the plain west of the Cerna Reka, which is well watered by the tributaries flowing from the western hills. These tributaries run now within high flood banks. When their waters were uncontrolled, they turned part of the plain into a swamp.

The Cerna Reka makes a great bend by Brod and flows north-eastwards into the difficult country known as the Morihovo. There the Derriopes held both sides of the river valley. This is apparent from the campaign of Sulpicius and Philip. When Sulpicius left Styberra, he had no idea where Philip was. He advanced to Pluinna, a place of unknown position. Having gleaned the fields near Styberra, he was presumably heading southwards and aimed to enter Lyncus. Philip meanwhile was in a fortified camp near Bryanium. As Bryanium was on the Erigon

---

[1] *Spomenik* 71 (1931) no. 339, giving an improved text of Dimitsas no. 262. Another with the same name in *Spomenik* as no. 342, also from Bela Tsarkva.

(Str. C 327) and yet was hidden from the Romans, it lay downstream from Brod. It may be identified with Heuzey's site near Skočevir. As the Romans walked into the trap, Philip emerged by minor roads ('trans-versis limitibus') and threw the Romans into a sudden panic; for they were in danger of being taken in the flank, while in column of march. They withdrew hastily from Pluinna and pitched camp near the river Osphagus. Philip then took up a position not far away, and fortified the bank of the Erigon with a rampart (Livy 31. 39. 4–6).

In these manœuvres Philip's aim was clearly to deter the Romans from advancing and entering Lyncus through the Monastir gap. As the Romans were still north of the gap, the river Osphagus was the river Semnica, and Pluinna, obeying the rule of Derriopan cities, was by the river near Trnovo; a fine funerary relief of pre-Hellenistic date from Crnobuki in the Semnica valley may be from the site of Pluinna ($\mathcal{Z}A$ 7 (1957) 252 f. = *Spomenik* 98. 26). As the Cerna may have changed its bed since 219 B.C., we do not know how narrow the passage was between the river and the hillsides at the point threatened by Philip. His rampart was presumably on the left bank, as he had no wish for a set battle.

Sulpicius was now in as awkward a situation as he had been in at Ottolobus (see p. 61 above). He had little room in which to forage. Retreat was undesirable, and advance was dangerous with Philip on his flank and later on his tail. If Sulpicius had had Roman troops only, he might have been forced to retreat. But by now the Dardanians and the Illyrians of Pleuratus were with him (cf. Livy 31. 40. 10), and it was probably they who managed to dislodge Philip from his fortified position. Livy does not dwell upon the situation of Sulpicius or mention the pre-sence of the Dardanians and the Illyrians. He moves on to the withdrawal by Philip, for which he advances an absurd reason: 'inde satis comperto Eordaeam petituros Romanos, ad occupandas angustias, ne superare hostes artis faucibus inclusum aditum possent, praecessit' (31. 39. 7).[1] As he arrived in time to fortify the pass of Kirli Dirven, he had probably slipped away once again during the night, unobserved. The distance was 53 km (36 m.p.). We shall return to the campaign in connection with the topography of the areas south of the Via Egnatia (see p. 105 below).

The Pelagones held the plain east of the river and the hills to the east.[2] One of the three cities of Strabo's $\Pi \epsilon \lambda \alpha \gamma o \nu i \alpha \ \tau \rho \iota \pi o \lambda \hat{\iota} \tau \iota s$[3] was at Belovodica. Its name was perhaps Andraristus; for Ptol. 3. 13. 34 mentions only

---

[1] The abruptness of the connection shows that Livy has omitted a piece of Polybius' account, probably because it did no special credit to Roman arms. For the presence of Dardanians and Illyrians, see p. 65 n. 2 above.

[2] Rejecting Schaefer's emendation (see p. 69 n. 2 above), which would make the Erigon flow *through* Pelagonia. See below, p. 75 n. 4.

[3] Str. C 326 and 327 and St. Byz. s.v. Tripolis.

Andraristus and Stobi as cities of the Pelagones, and Andraristus was therefore probably close to the Roman road, as is the ancient site at Belovodica. Another city was Azorus, the only one named by Strabo (C 327). As Stobi was Paeonian in Strabo's time, the third city may have been Pissaeum, although Plb. 5. 108. 1 calls it a 'polisma'. As it was sacked by Scerdilaïdas the Illyrian, it was probably in north-west Pelagonia.[1] The frontier of Pelagonia marched with that of the Derriopes on the south-west, south, and south-east, and with that of the Illyrian Penestae of the Velcka valley on the north-west. To the east a frontier was most readily defended at the defile above the confluence of the Rajetz and the Cerna near the station 'Euristo' on the Roman road (see further p. 76 below).

The Brygi remain for consideration. Strabo C 326 (quoted above) said that the Erigon drew its waters from their territory also, and we should therefore put them at the northern end of the plain in the valleys of the Golesnitsa range. Here their western neighbours were the Illyrian Penestae of the lower Velcka valley. Such a situation suits the entry of St. Byz. s.v. Βρύξ· τὸ ἔθνος καὶ Βρῦγαι. τοῦ Βρῦξ τὸ θηλυκὸν Βρυγὶς καὶ Βρυγηὶς ὡς Καδμηίς. εἰσὶ δὲ Μακεδονικὸν ἔθνος προσεχὲς 'Ιλλυριοῖς. Ps.-Scymnus 434 and 437 places them 'above' the Enchelei and Lake Lychnitis. One of their cities was Κύδραι (Str. C 327). Another was probably either Βρυγίας or Βρύγιον; for St. Byz. gives both as cities of Macedonia. It is likely that only one of two so similarly named cities was in one district and that the other belonged to one of the other groups of Brygi in Macedonia. Funerary reliefs and Greek inscriptions, dated by the Macedonian era to A.D. 81 and 94, have been found in the northern part of the plain at Kostanči, Crnilište, and Sekirči. One records a dedication to Zeus Agoraeus.[2] The prevalence of Greek shows that the population then was neither Illyrian nor Dardanian, but considered itself Macedonian.

In this part of Macedonia we are faced by the fact that the limits of the districts changed with the expansion of their inhabitants, the policy of the Macedonian kings, and the administrative reforms of the Roman and the Byzantine governments. Heraclea is a case in point. The district in which Heraclea was founded was surely part of the great plain of Pelagonia until such time as Arrhabaeus or Philip II subjugated the people up to Lychnidus and incorporated the valley above Heraclea into Lyncus. This seems the most probable explanation of the description of Heraclea as in Lyncestis, admittedly very late, in Ptol. 3. 12. 30

---

[1] G. Zippel, *Die römische Herrschaft in Illyrien* (Leipzig, 1877) 61 and F. W. Walbank, *Commentary on Polybius* 1. 632 transfer it to Lyncus, thus putting it further from the Illyrians.

[2] *Spomenik* 98 (1941–8) nos. 355, 378, 379, 384–6; a Greek inscription from Leniste between Prilep and the Pletvar pass comes from Pelagonian territory.

Λυγκηστίδος· Ἡράκλεια, in Hierocles, *Synecdemus* Ἡράκλεια Λύγκου and Const. Porph. *Them.* 2. 49 Ἡράκλεια Λάκκου and Λαούκου which are clearly corruptions of Λύγκου. The addition to the entry in Ptolemy of the words ἡ Πελαγονία in the Cod. Paris. Coislin. is perhaps a reminder that it was in the Pelagonian plain rather than a statement that Pelagonia was an alternative name.[1] Pelagonia itself has a strange history as the name or supposed name of a town. It first appears in Livy 45. 29. 9 as capital of the fourth division or tetrarchy into which Macedonia was divided by Rome in 167 B.C. It has been suggested that Livy's Pelagonia was Heraclea renamed for political reasons by Rome. But this is unlikely. In *CIL* vi 2382 b 8 and b 9 we have two soldiers of the Praetorian Guard of A.D. 177 who come one from Pelagonia and the other from Heraclea. Also Heraclea Lyncou and Pelagonia both appear in Hierocles and in Const. Porph. *Them.* 2. 50, and, what is more, in different subdivisions of Macedonia. As Heraclea Lyncou is in the subdivision containing Eordaea and Cellae, and as Pelagonia is in that containing Stobi, it is clear that Pelagonia was towards Stobi and so in the central or eastern part of the great plain. If this Pelagonia is Livy's city Pelagonia, then Pelagonia was distant from Heraclea. But Livy's city Pelagonia may be an impostor, as we shall see.

The division of Macedonia into tetrarchies is given by Livy 45. 29 and by Diodorus 31. 8. 8, both being based on a lost passage of Polybius. The first three divisions are described with rivers as boundaries from east to west, and the third is bounded in both Livy and Diodorus by the Axius and the Peneus, that is the lowest reach of the Peneus.[2] The orientation is distorted from our point of view; for we might say north-east to south instead of east to west. The third division is described further as limited by a mountain on the north, that is in terms of our orientation on the west. The name of the mountain is given as Bora in the standard texts of Livy; but the name is in fact obtained by two emendations of corrupt texts. One is 'ad septentrionem Bora mons' for 'absentenonemboramons'; and the other is 'trans Boram montem' for 'transdorsummontem'.[3] The emendations may be set against the text of Diodorus, which is not disputed.[4] The corresponding phrases are κατὰ δ' ἄρκτον τὸ

---

[1] Malchus 246. 19, referring to A.D. 479, calls Heraclea just ἡ Ἡράκλεια ἡ ἐν Μακεδονίᾳ. The Bishop was episcopus Heracleae Pelagoniae and Heracleae Pelagonensis in A.D. 553, and the meaning of Cinnamos (ed. Bonne) 127 ἐν Ἡρακλείᾳ . . . τῇ Μυσῶν ἦν Πελαγονίαν τινι γλώττῃ κατακολουθοῦντες Ῥωμαῖοι νῦν ὀνομάζουσιν may well be that the Romaei of A.D. 1118 called the town Heraclea Pelagonia. Later still, when the name Heraclea was replaced by Bitolia, the bishop's title was the Metropolites of 'Bitolia and Pelagonia', where Bitolia is the town and Pelagonia the district.

[2] Weissenborn, Müller, Heusinger, and Schlesinger are needlessly worried by the mention of the Peneus. Pieria was included in Macedonia and its western limit for Polybius (and southern limit for us) was well defined by the last reach of the river.

[3] I give the corrupt texts from Weissenborn and Müller's edition.

[4] Dindorf gives no variant readings in his edition of George Syncellus p. 510, where the fragment of Diodorus is preserved.

λεγόμενον Βέρνον ὄρος and ὑπὲρ τὸ Βέρνον ὄρος συνάπτει τῇ Ἠπείρῳ. It is
at once apparent that the second emendation has little palaeographical
probability since DORSUM and BORAM are not readily confused, and above
all that it has no justification, because 'trans dorsum montis' is the counterpart of ὑπὲρ τὸ ... ὄρος and is a good Livian expression.[1] The emendation
which is made to include 'Boram' is gratuitous. Now we have to choose
between Bora occurring once and Bernon occurring twice. The choice
is complicated by the fact that we have names already for many Macedonian mountains, but we have no Bora and no Bernon. The nearest
known names are Barnous for Bora and Bermion for Bernon. Now
Bermion is better than Barnous as an emendation of 'boramons', on the
supposition either that 'bermion' was misread initially as 'ber mons' or
that 'bermion mons' was telescoped into 'berimons'. And in Diodorus
Βέρμιον is a better emendation of Βέρνον than Βαρνοῦς would be. I conclude then that the mountain mentioned in the passage of Polybius on
which Livy and Diodorus drew was Mt. Bermion.[2]

Geographically, provided we remember to reorientate ourselves, there
is no possible doubt. The mountain on the west of the third division is
Mt. Bermion. Beyond it, i.e. west and north-west of it, are the districts
which Livy in the following chapter (45. 30. 6) attributed to the fourth
division: Eordaea, Lyncus, Pelagonia, and Atintania, Strymepalis, and
Elimiotis (these three being restored).[3] On the other hand, if Mt. Barnous
is preferred (and the mythical 'Bora mons' is usually substituted for Mt.
Barnous), three of these districts are south of Mt. Barnous and two are
north, a state of affairs not consonant with the statements that this fourth
division was 'trans dorsum montis' and ὑπὲρ τὸ ὄρος. The fourth division
was in fact a solid block of country. It included the strategic corridor, and
it bordered on the Illyrian Penestae, the Parthini and the Dassaretii, and
on the Epirote area of Parauaea, which consisted of Kolonië and Danglli.[4]
It was 'una parte confinis Illyrico, altera Epiro' (Livy 45. 29. 9) and
συνάπτει τῇ Ἠπείρῳ καὶ τοῖς κατὰ τὴν Ἰλλυρίδα τόποις (Diod. Sic. 31. 8. 8).

Livy names 'capita regionum, ubi concilia fierent' and names the caput
of the fourth division 'Pelagonia' (45. 29. 9). Diodorus puts it in the form
ἡγοῦντο δὲ καὶ πόλεις τέσσαρες τῶν αὐτῶν τεσσάρων μέρων ... καὶ τοῦ τετάρτου
Πελαγονία, the other three being Amphipolis, Thessalonica, and Pella.
But here a fragment of Strabo, recording the division of Macedonia and

---

[1] Livy uses 'dorsum' to mean 'the ridge of a range' in several passages, e.g. 36. 15. 6 Apennini
dorso Italia dividitur; 41. 18. 9 iugum quod eos montes perpetuo dorso inter se iungit; and
44. 4. 4 iugum montis in angustum dorsum cuneatum. Having given the name of the mountain three lines above, Livy does not here repeat it.

[2] Str. 7 fr. 25 gives the form as τὸ Βέρμιον ὄρος and fr. 26 places Beroea on its lowest slopes.
I take it that Livy transliterated Βέρμιον as Bermion, keeping the termination -on as for
instance in Orchomenon at 32. 5. 4.

[3] For these restorations see p. 46 above and *Epirus* 633.   [4] See *Epirus* 634.

based probably on Polybius, allocates the administrative responsibility to Amphipolis, Thessalonica, Pella, and 'the Pelagones': τὸ μὲν προσένειμεν Ἀμφιπόλει . . . τὸ δὲ Πελαγόσι (7 fr. 47). The purpose of the Romans was not to create 'capital cities' in any modern sense but to delegate the government of each tetrarchy to an already existing competent body. In three of the tetrarchies there were large and fully developed cities—'municipia' in Roman terminology—, and the Boule or Concilium of each city, perhaps reinforced by delegates from elsewhere, was named as the competent body.[1] Diodorus expresses the situation most clearly: 'the command (administrative control) of the four divisions was vested in four *poleis*'. In the case of the fourth division, where large and fully developed cities on a comparable scale did not exist, Rome placed the powers of administrative control in ἡ πόλις τῶν Πελαγόνων,[2] that is the Pelagonian tribal state, which was described by Livy and by Diodorus more succinctly as 'Pelagonia'. And we have the inscription of imperial times to remind us that οἱ ἐν Δερριόπῳ πολειτάρχαι were officials of the tribal state of the Derriopes (see p. 69 above). I believe, then, that Pelagonia in Livy[3] is never an urban centre but always a region or a tribal state, and that a city called Pelagonia first appears for certain in Hierocles *Synecdemus*, which was composed *c.* A.D. 527,[4] when urban centres had developed in these regions.

[1] We had a similar situation in 1945 when Germany was divided into zones and it was necessary to find local bodies capable of administrative tasks; in the western zone, where I served in military government, the city authority of Hannover was given powers extending over the whole province in autumn 1945. The Control Commission laid down guiding lines for such authorities, analogous to the 'leges Macedoniae' of Livy 45. 31. 1 and 45. 32. 7. It is not clear from Livy 45. 32. 2 how the synedroi were chosen, except that they had to be taken from de-royalized Macedonians.

[2] I suggest this form of words because it was used of the tribal states of the Chaones, for example (see *Epirus* 539), and of the Argestaei (*ŽA* 3 (1953) 222).

[3] The references in Livy are 26. 25. 3 and 4; 31. 28. 5; 31. 33. 3; 31. 39. 4; 45. 29. 9.

[4] E. Honigmann ed. 641. 5 and p. 1 for the date of composition. The fact that Ptol. 3. 13. 4 mentions only Stobi and Andraristus as cities of the Pelagones suggests that Pelagonia as a city was created later than the time of Ptolemy (*fl.* A.D. 139). F. Papazoglou discusses the problem of Heraclea and Pelagonia very fully in *ŽA* 4 (1954) 308–45. She thinks that Pelagonia appears as a town in Zosimus i. 43, describing the raids of the Goths in A.D. 268, τὰ περὶ Δόβηρον καὶ Πελαγωνίαν ἐληίζοντο πάντα χωρία. This is possible but not certain, because περί can be used of an area, as it is in the preceding chapter, i. 42 περὶ τὸν Τύραν ποταμόν. She distinguished Heraclea and Pelagonia as two separate entities, but we differ in that she believes Pelagonia to have been a city in Hellenistic or early Roman times. For example, she finds a city Pelagonia in Str. 7 fr. 20 ὁ Ἐρίγων . . . ἐκ Τρικλάρων ῥέων δι' Ὀρεστῶν καὶ τῆς Πελλαίας ἐν ἀριστέρᾳ ἀφιεὶς τὴν πόλιν καὶ συμβάλλων τῷ Ἀξιῷ by emending the passage to read ὁ Ἐρίγων . . . ἐξ Ἰλλυριῶν ῥέων διὰ Λυγκηστῶν καὶ τῆς Πελαγονίας . . . The emendations are bold indeed. If a city is to be found on the left of the Erigon where it joins the Axius, that city is Stobi; and the ultimate source for any such emended text might be a passage in Polybius which underlies Livy 39. 53. 15 Erigonum . . . qui ex Illyrico per Paeoniam [emended by Schaefer to 'Pelagoniam'] fluens in Axium amnem editur haud procul Stobis, vetere urbe. Again, she supposes that Pelagonia in inscriptions refers to a town and not to the tribal state of the Pelagones or to their territory. There are, however, a number of such inscriptions (e.g.

Before and at the time of the division of Macedonia the lowest reach of the Erigon river was in Paeonia. For Livy 33. 19. 3, referring in 197 B.C., uses the words 'circa Stobos Paeoniae', and again at 40. 21. 1 in 181 B.C., and at 45. 29. 13 in 167 B.C., just after the division, 'Stobos Paeoniae'. Stobi, being on the left bank of the Erigon and on the right bank of the Vardar, must have had territory extending up that bank of the Cerna, probably as far as the defile (see p. 66 above). This deduction gains support from the statements in Livy 45. 29. 8 and Diodorus 31. 8. 8 that parts of Paeonia west of the Axius were included in the third tetrarchy, and in Livy 45. 29. 13 that the third tetrarchy brought salt to Stobi, which was therefore inside it, whereas Pelagonia was included in the fourth tetrarchy.[1] It is probable then that the boundary between the two tetrarchies was at the defile near which the Euristo of the Peutinger Table lay.

Atintania was one of the areas added to the fourth division. As I mentioned above (p. 36), the territory of the Atintani was mainly in the district of Çermenikë west and east of the high Jablanitsa range, and it is probable that it extended eastwards into the valley of the Saletska river, because the Atintani were allies of Rome and Appius Claudius was in friendly territory in this valley (see p. 44 above and Maps 4 and 9). As described by Polyaenus 4. 11. 4, Atintanis was on the eastern flank of Illyris (κώμας ὑψηλὰς κειμένας ἐπὶ τῶν ὁρίων Ἰλλυρίδος καὶ Ἀτιντανίδος). It can have been only the eastern part of Atintanis that was included in the fourth tetrarchy, because the incorporation of the whole territory would have created a considerable salient into Illyris. It was probably the same part of Atintanis which was ceded to Philip V with the consent of the Senate in 205 B.C. There were then Atintani in Illyris and Atintani in Macedonia after the setting up of the tetrarchies.

This throws light upon an inscription which was found in the district of Monastir.[2] It records an order, probably in the latter half of the second

CIL iii 2017, 3530, 7325; CIL vi 2382 *b* 8; viii 2865), all of Roman soldiers, and they are more likely to have come from a district than from a single town.

[1] Livy 39. 53. 15 is thoroughly confused, probably because Livy abbreviated his source, Polybius. It is true perhaps that the Erigon passed through Paeonia as it joined the Axius, but it looks from Livy's words as if its main course was through Paeonia: 'Erigonum flumen, qui ex Illyrico per Paeoniam fluens in Axium amnem editur'. In the first part of the sentence 'oppidum in Derriopo condere instituit—Paeoniae ea regio est—prope Erigonum flumen' the aside looks like a mistaken addition made by Livy to the text he was adapting. An inscription (CIL iii 630 = 7325) found in the bank of the Erigon not far from Stobi towards Monastir in the district Morihovo commemorates a veteran of 'Pelago(nia)' but it does not help us to fix the limits of Pelagonia precisely. It may be inferred from the entry in Ptolemy that Stobi was in the administrative zone of the Pelagones *c.* A.D. 139; but Roman soldiers distinguished between Pelagonia and Stobi, as one Praetorian Guardsman came from Stobi in A.D. 174 and another from Pelagonia in A.D. 177 (CIL vi 2382 *a* 25 and *b* 8).

[2] BCH 21 (1897) 161 f. = *Spomenik* 77 (1934) p. 32. The stone had been found in a vineyard and was sent to Monastir. It carries two inscriptions, of which the later one recording a service by an official of τῆς πόλεως καὶ τοῦ Λυγκηστῶν ἔθνους suggests that it was set up at

century A.D., that the expenses of repairing the roads should be borne two-thirds by wealthy citizens of Heraclea and one-third by τῶν ἐν Μακεδονίᾳ ὄντων Ἀντανῶν. As the Antani are mentioned twice in this inscription, the name is doubly secure. It is probable that these Antani were a free tribal community, through whose territory some of the roads ran. The town Antania occurs in Hierocles *Synecdemus* 639 2a immediately after Heraclea Lyncou, and it was clearly the chief town of the Antani *c.* A.D. 527, just as Pelagonia was then the chief town of the Pelagones. A record of the Antani in Macedonia may be present in an inscription on the side of an Ionic capital which was copied by Dimitsas. It was found in the garden of the Bishop at Monastir.[1] The inscription, 'partly mutilated' (ἐν μέρει ἠκρωτηριασμένη), begins thus according to Dimitsas and von Hahn:

AY..ANTANO.....EKATHCΔIO

We should perhaps read some name like A[ΛYC]ANTANO[C], the second word being either an ethnic 'Antanos' or the genitive of 'Antas', a name which occurs in an inscription from Belo Crkva, and explain the inscription as recording the dedication of a manumitted person to Hecate Hodios.

I take it then that the Antani were a constituent tribe of the group of tribes called Atintani, and that some of them were in Illyris and some were in Macedonia to the north of Lychnidus and Heraclea. N. Vulić published an inscription, found at Stobi, which has the words δέμονες Ἀντανο[ί] beneath representations of Dionysus, Pan, Demeter, and a satyr on a marble relief; and L. Robert saw that these represent the gods of the Antani.[2] The entry in St. Byz. Ἀτιντανία μοῖρα Μακεδονίας is probably derived from the time of the Roman period, as is the entry Βεύη πόλις Μακεδονίας, a town previously in Dassaretis (see p. 64 above).

The Romans created the fourth tetrarchy with some consideration of past services but chiefly with an eye to military defence, since they stationed soldiers on the outer frontiers (Diodorus 31. 8. 9 ἐν δὲ τοῖς

Heraclea itself; and the subject of the earlier one supports this suggestion. The personal name Ἄντας occurs on an inscription from Tsepicovo (*Comptes rendus* 1939. 221 B line 32).

[1] Dimitsas no. 228 and von Hahn, *Denkschriften* 16 (1867) 2. 165 no. 18. Republished by A. J. B. Wace and A. M. Woodward in *BSA* 18 (1911–12) 174 no. 13; they were less confident of Dimitsas's readings, but the independent version read by von Hahn supports Dimitsas. Although ἁ τὸν Ἀντανῶν πόλις Ἑκάτη ὁδίο would fit the space, it is too late in date for the use of ἁ instead of ἡ. I am most grateful to C. F. Edson for help with this inscription. For the name Antas see *Comptes rendus* 1939. 221 B line 32 Ἄντας Ἀδαίου, and for Alys see Dimitsas, no. 261 line 19.

[2] *REG* 47 (1934) 31 f. = *Spomenik* 75 (1933) no. 79. He discusses there the inscription ordering the repair of the roads and gives references to the earlier literature on it. He places the Antani between Heraclea and Stobi and, like Rostovtzeff, thinks that they were not free but 'attributed' to Heraclea. He does not mention the inscription to Hecate in this connection.

ἐσχάτοις τῆς Μακεδονίας τόποις διὰ τὰς τῶν περικειμένων ἔθνων ἐπιβουλὰς κατέστησαν στρατιώτας. Orestis, which had joined the Roman side early in the second century B.C., was a separate and free community outside the tetrarchy. The Dassaretii, helpful to Rome on many occasions, also received their freedom.[1] The Pelagones, who may have helped Sulpicius in 199 B.C., were given special powers in the tetrarchy. But for the defence of the western frontier of the tetrarchy Rome took over the important corridor, running at least from Beve and probably from the Koritsa basin inclusive in the south to the southern frontier of the Penestae; this corridor included the Tsangon pass, the area north of Lake Ochrid through which the Via Egnatia later passed, and the country northwards which lies between the Drin and the western limits of Derriopus.[2] It was an extremely prudent decision by Rome.

5. *Western Paeonia and its Illyrian neighbours*

For the Paeonians Stobi was an all-important centre of communications (see Map 9). For they held territory down the Vardar as far as the great defile of Demir Kapu (see p. 174 below), up the Vardar as far at least as Titov Veles, and across the Vardar from Stobi up the valley of the Bregalnitsa, which gave fairly easy access to their lands in the upper Strumitsa. Stobi thus became the centre of four roads in the Roman road-system. One came from Thessalonica through the defile of Demir Kapu,[3] on the north-west side of which Antigonus Gonatas had founded the city of Antigonea. Another, as we have seen, from Heraclea. Another from Tranupara, the modern Kratovo, and Astibus, now Istib, or Štip, in the Bregalnitsa valley.[4] And the fourth from Bylazora, now Titov Veles, with a station Gurbita on the Peutinger Table or Cubita in the Ravenna Geographer (205. 17) VIII m.p. before Stobi, that is at Nogaevci on the left bank.[5] In 181 B.C. Philip V used Stobi as a good mustering point for the Macedonian forces, when he wished to march into the territory of the Maedi (Livy 40. 21. 1). From the Paeonian point of view this part of their territory on the Axius lay between

---

[1] Pliny *HN* 4. 3 Epiros . . . a tergo suo Dassaretas supra dictos [3. 145], liberam gentem. For the distinction between these Dassaretae and the Dassaretii, between the Ardiaei and the Dardani in Strabo C 316 and C 318, see my article in *BSA* 61 (1966) 251 in opposition to the view of F. Papazoglou in *Historia* 14 (1965) 175 n. 120.

[2] When Macedonia became a province in 146 B.C., it seems that other provisions were made and the frontier was brought back to the district called Pylon (Str. C 323; see p. 39 above).

[3] Str. 7. fr. 4 mentions the entry through Gortynium and Stobi to Paeonia.

[4] K. Miller, *Itin. Romana* 850.

[5] Ibid. 572. T. Tomovski in *ŽA* 11 (1961) 123 tries to unravel the confusion in the Peutinger Table north of this point.

two great defiles, that of Demir Kapu and that just at and below Titov Veles.

Titov Veles, the ancient Bylazora, spans the upstream end of the long defile and blocks passage southwards. Its own position is strong and readily defended, and in addition some way upstream there is another defile, which the modern road avoids by climbing high up the mountain-side. The holders of Bylazora cover also the entry into the long western tributaries of the Vardar which rise in the Babuna range and lead to a pass into the Pelagonian plain. Starting from Titov Veles one crosses two ridges to enter the Babuna valley and then follows it, until the valley becomes a rocky defile, now six hours distant from Titov Veles. There is a climb of another $2\frac{3}{4}$ hours before one reaches the top of the Babuna pass, which was guarded by a watch-house in Turkish times. The descent to the edge of the Pelagonian plain at Prilep takes $4\frac{1}{2}$ hours.[1] The district between the Golesnitsa ridge and the Rajetz valley has yielded many inscriptions in Greek. They come from villages in the Topolka valley (e.g. Bogomila), the Babuna valley (e.g. Martolci and Izvor), and the north side of the lower Rajetz valley (e.g. Nikodin). It appears from the inscriptions that the occupants of this area formed the community of the Argestaei, ἡ τῶν Ἀργεσταίων πόλις. Inscriptions recording its decisions come from two southern villages, Skacinči, south-west of Veles,[2] and Vodovrati, south of Veles,[3] and two from Prilep, to which they may have been brought over the Babuna pass or the Pletvar pass. Gratitude is expressed in one to the proconsul Junius (Rufinus), governor of Macedonia in A.D. 192 τὸν κτίστην καὶ πάτρωνα,[4] in another to the Emperor Galienus, and in another to a *prostates* for his services. Another inscription, found in the village of Vladilovatsi in the Babuna valley, records a decision by Νεαπολειτῶν τὸ κοινόν in the year A.D. 152, dated by the Macedonian era.[5] It is likely that we have here a large tribal community or *polis*,[6] and within it smaller *koina* of which one was Νεαπολειτῶν τὸ κοινόν. There are also a number of inscriptions and funerary reliefs, depicting figures with interesting details of dress, especially that of the women, who wore heavy woollen clothes and cloaks;[7] two of the reliefs were made by a local artist by the name of Dionysius Dioscouridou,

---

[1] J. G. von Hahn, *Denkschriften* 11 (1861) 2. 183 f.

[2] *Spomenik* 71 (1931) no. 88. Three are published together in *ŽA* 14 (1965) 118 f. *Spomenik* 98 (1941–8) no. 363 (at Prilep).   [3] *ŽA* 3 (1953) 223 f.

[4] I take κτίστης here to stand for 'restitutor' in the sense that Cicero was called κτίστης τῆς πατρίδος in Plu. *Cic.* 22.

[5] *Spomenik* 71 (1931) no. 63, using the koppa in the dating.

[6] B. Josifovska in *ŽA* 3 (1953) 223 thinks of a city and believes it may have been situated within the area of Skacinči, Vodovrati, and Viničani; for the use of *polis* for a tribal community see p. 75 n. 2 above.

[7] *ŽA* 3 (1953) 234 and 226; in the former the cloak is similar to the Vlach's 'kapa'. Other stelai from the area in *ŽA* 13 (1964) 162 no. 4 and 16 (1966) 411.

the latter name being very common in these parts.[1] The inscriptions are all in Greek and the names are Greek, whereas across the Vardar in the neighbourhood of Veles more use is made of Latin and of Thracian names. It is possible that the Argestaei were, at least in origin, a constituent tribe of the Pelagones rather than of the Paeones.[2] For at most times of the year the Vardar is difficult to cross, and the Argestaean territory was easily defended against attack from the eastern side of the Vardar.[3]

It has been suggested that Argestaeus is the ethnic of a city called Argos. This is not so, because Stephanus Byzantinus in enumerating eleven cities of that name adds the sentence: τὸ ἐθνικὸν πασῶν Ἀργεῖος. On the other hand, there is or may be some connection between Argestaeus and Argos, because the Argestaeus campus in Orestis was close to Argos Oresticum (see p. 110 below). It is probable that in Orestis and in this area the tribe, the Argestaei, was earlier than the foundation of a town. There are three mentions of an Argos which cannot be Argos Oresticum. Stephanus gives in his list πόλις . . . ἑβδόμη κατὰ Μακεδονίαν· ὀγδόη Ἄργος Ὀρέστιον (Ὀρεστικόν AV). The seventh Argos is 'by, near, at the edge of Macedonia', if κατά has the same meaning as it has a few sentences later in πεδίον κατὰ θάλατταν. The second mention is in Hierocles, *Synecdemus* 641. 3, where 'Argos' comes immediately after Stobi in the second division of Macedonia. The third mention is in an inscription honouring Marcus Annius in 117 B.C. which will be discussed later (see p. 184).

There was then an Argos hereabouts. There is much to be said for identifying it with a site at Vidin near Vodovrati (see Map 9), which has been examined and reported on by B. Josifovska-Dragojevic in *ŽA* 14 (1965) 117 f. The tribal name Argestaei is similar in form to one in Epirus: St. Byz. Αἰγεσταῖοι οἱ Θεσπρωτοί.

In 217 B.C. Philip V took possession of Bylazora and made it secure. Polybius describes the city as all too conveniently placed in regard to the routes of entry from Dardanian territory into Macedonia (5. 97. 1), that is down the Vardar valley into Central Macedonia or over the hills

---

[1] For instance, in inscriptions from the Kavadar area in *ŽA* 3 (1953) 240, *Spomenik* 71 (1931) no. 144, *Spomenik* 75 (1933) 33 and no. 140; from the Veles area *Spomenik* 71 (1931) nos. 53, 89; from the Gradsko (Stobi) area *Spomenik* 71 (1931) nos. 104, 631, and *Spomenik* 77 (1934) no. 20; from Prilep *Spomenik* 75 (1933) nos. 191, 428; and from Tsepicovo (Styberra) *Comptes rendus* (1939) 221 A line 40. Further occurrences in *Spomenik* 98 (1941–8) nos. 118, 140, 348, 354, 388 line 39. Mestrios and Selene are common names in the inscriptions of the Babuna area.   [2] See further p. 88 below.

[3] Their territory is strongly demarcated by the long ridge of Mt. Golesnitsa running down to the Vardar on the north (this ridge formed the frontier between Veles and Skopje in Turkish times), by the great defile of the Vardar on the east, the ridge above the Rajetz valley on the south, and the Babuna range towards Prilep. The Roman road probably followed the left bank of the Vardar from Stobi to Skopje, as did the Turkish road from Veles to Skopje (J. G. von Hahn, *Denkschriften* 11 (1861) 2. 180).

by the Babuna pass or the Pletvar pass into Pelagonia. His control of
Bylazora certainly closed the main entry and made invasion difficult.
It has sometimes been assumed that Bylazora was at that time on the
frontier of Dardanian territory.[1] But this is most unlikely. If it is on the
site of Veles, it is on the exposed side of the defile. It is true that there are
narrows of the Vardar also some way upstream from Veles, but they
are more easily by-passed. As it was 'the greatest city of Paeonia' in
217 B.C., it is almost certain to have been nearer the centre rather than
on the periphery of the Paeonian lands in the Vardar valley. The clearest
indications of the extent of Paeonian territory come from passages in
Strabo, where he is representing the view of Polybius[2] that the Balkan
peninsula is a triangle, based on the head of the Adriatic and the Ister
(Danube), and divided into two by the line of the Illyrian, the Paeonian,
and the Thracian mountains (C 313). The mountains are described as
being parallel to the Ister 'in a sense' ($\tau\rho\acute{o}\pi o\nu$ $\tau\iota\nu a$). They are in fact (1) the
high chain from north Albania to Šar Planina, the 'Illyrian' mountains,
(2) the Zrna Gora and the Kosjak Planina, the 'Paeonian' mountains,
and (3) the great range of Rhodope and Haemus, the 'Thracian'
mountains. 'Paeonia', as he puts it, 'is in the middle and it is all high,
with Rhodope confining it on the Thracian side, and with the Illyrian
parts on the other side towards the north, namely the territory of the
Autariatae and the Dardanian land'. This description does not fit, if
we put the northern frontier of Paeonia at Bylazora; for Paeonia has to
extend to the latitude of the Šar Planina.

In the passage which we have just quoted, Strabo's orientation differs
somewhat from our own: his north is our north-west. It is the same
in Str. 7 fr. 4: Paeonia is 'south' of the Autariatae, Dardanii, and
Ardiaei, where we should say south-east, and Paeonia is 'west' of the
Thracian mountains and 'north' of the Macedonians, where we should
say south-west and north-west respectively. Livy's description of Mt.
Scordus (the Mt. Scardon of Plb. 28. 8. 3 and Ptol. 3. 13. 18, whence the
Axius rises), which is derived from Polybius, gives a similar picture. The
Oriundes rising in Mt. Scordus is the White Drin and Mt. Scordus is
the Šar Planina, 'longe altissimus regionis eius, ab oriente Dardanicam
subiectam habet, a meridie Macedoniam, ab occasu Illyricum' (44. 31. 5
under the year 168 B.C.).

---

[1] This springs partly from the belief that Philip captured Bylazora from the Dardanians,
but Polybius does not say so. In using the middle form $\kappa a\tau\epsilon\lambda\acute{a}\beta\epsilon\tau o$ (cf. A. Mauersberger,
Polybios Lexicon s.v.) he is emphasizing that Philip took it for himself and fortified it, words
which would apply if it was a Paeonian town. The proximity of a frontier is put more strongly
by Walbank, *Philip V of Macedon* 63: 'Bylazora, a town in Paeonia commanding the pass over
into Dardania'.

[2] See the analysis of Polybius' theories in P. Pédech, *La Méthode historique de Polybe* (Paris,
1964), especially p. 595.

The relationship of all these Illyrian peoples to Paeonia is not clear. We can see from Str. C 323 that the mountains north of the Via Egnatia are the Illyrian mountains, and that the tribes (not named here by Strabo) living in them extended up to Macedonia (on my placing of them, these tribes were the Parthini, the Atintani, and the Penestae) and up to the Paeonians. The Dardanian territory is described at C 316 as touching on the Macedonian tribes and the Paeonian tribes to its south, i.e. our south-east; and this entails the extension of Dardanian territory into the western headwaters of the Vardar, that is into the region of Tetovo, in order to bring it close to the territory of the Macedonian Brygi (see p. 72 above). And this extension agrees with the statement in the same chapter that the Drilon (Drin) is navigable towards the east, i.e. our north-east as far as the Dardanian territory; for the upper waters of the White Drin rising in the area of Prizren must then have been in Dardanian territory. It is possible that at one time the Dardanian power reached down the White Drin as far as Kukës, the point of confluence with the Black Drin. But that extension was probably from the seventh to the fifth century B.C. (see pp. 422 and 427 below). In Hellenistic times the power of the Dardanii had retired from the White Drin. For the power of the Ardiaei came down to Scodra and extended some distance up both the Black Drin and the White Drin. The Autariatae lay further north and between the Ardiaei and the Dardanii.[1] The Autariatae also expanded in the Hellenistic period both at the expense of the Ardiaei and also northwards to the Danube. Each of the three was a group of Illyrian tribes, and each conquered or combined itself with other Illyrian tribes.[2] The map of power changed not infrequently, but it was the Dardanian group which menaced most the Paeonians and the Macedonians.[3]

In Paeonia north of Bylazora the most important centre of communications is the ancient Scupi, at the north end of Skopje town. The acropolis, of which great blocks are incorporated in the castle, lies on the end of a high ridge overhanging a bend of the river. It commands an amazing view of the Šar Planina and of Zrna Gora with the dip of the Kačanik pass between them; and, on the west, the flank of the Šar Planina and Mt. Golesnitsa with the marked gap between them which gives access to Tetovo. Scupi is situated above the confluence of the Pecinj river with the Vardar, and below the confluence of the Lepenac with the Vardar, which turns westwards into the Tetovo area. The two main routes from Paeonia northwards into the Danube basin follow the lines of these two rivers, the Pecinj and the Lepenac, and Scupi controls the district from

---

[1] This may be the meaning of the confused passage in Str. C 316. The Autariatae were at war with the Paeonians in 310 B.C. (D.S. 20. 19. 1); the scale of operations was very large.

[2] See Plb. 2. 6. 4, where Teuta recalled Scerdilaïdas from Epirus, because some of the Illyrians had revolted from the Ardiaei to join the Dardanians.

[3] I have discussed the position of the Illyrian tribes more fully in *BSA* 61 (1966) 239–53.

which they start. Thus the Roman road from Thessalonica up the Vardar via Stobi branched at Scupi.

The left-hand road follows the Lepenac valley, which today is enclosed between hills at first rather bare and then covered with scrub. The valley opens out at Krekapak. It then becomes steep-sided, and is a regular defile with almost sheer sides just before one reaches the pretty town of Kačanik. This defile is known as the Kačanik pass. It is 475 m above sea level. Above Kačanik one enters a vast and very fertile tableland of deep and stoneless soil, peaty or pinkish, which extends to the foot of the mountains on either side and runs unbroken from Kačanik to Pristina. This great tableland was certainly the heart of Dardania. From it one sees the high tops of the Šar Planina (Mt. Scordus) to the west, and the gap in the mountains above Peć. The river Sitnica rises between Uroševac and Lipljan on the northern side of the watershed; it flows below Pristina and enters the Ibar, which is a tributary of the Morava. The right-hand road from Scupi goes up the valley of the Pecinj, turns north at Kumanovo, and crosses the high open watershed of Preševo, 426 m above sea level, to descend into the upper valley of the Morava; this road goes down the valley to Niš, the ancient Naissus.[1] The fork between the left-hand road and the right-hand road is filled by the Paeonian mountain, the Zrna Gora or Black Mountain.

The northern boundary of Paeonia lay probably at the narrows of the Lepenac below Kačanik and at the watershed north of Kumanovo. The Dardanii occupied the territories north of these two passes. They also held the high and fertile basin between Tetovo and Gostivar on the uppermost Vardar, an area which is most easily entered from the tableland north of Kačanik. On many occasions the Dardanii broke through the Kačanik pass or the pass of Preševo and entered the Vardar valley by Scupi. But they were also able to by-pass this sector; for they could descend from the Tetovo–Gostivar basin into the lands of the Penestae at Kitsevo and proceed from there either into Pelagonia or into the corridor containing the lakes of Ochrid and Prespa.[2] Nor were they the only danger. For the Illyrians coming eastwards from Prizren into the Kačanik pass or entering Tetovo were able to follow the same route southwards.[3] In an attempt to discourage both peoples from invading Paeonia and

---

[1] See K. Miller, *Itin. Romana* 493, 555 f., where map 176 is a reconstruction of the Peutinger Table, and map 177. The routes are clear but there is much confusion in the details of the Peutinger Table. Miroslava Marcovic argues in *ŽA* 10 (1960) 249 f. that the Roman road split into two not at Scupi but at Viciano, north of the Kačanik pass. For the watershed of Preševo see Cvijič 28 f. and 90 f., who notes that it was little used in the Middle Ages, the route through the Kačanik pass being preferred.

[2] For example, the actions of Scerdilaïdas in 217 B.C. (Plb. 5. 108); see *Epirus* 606 f.

[3] The Macedonians always dreaded a combination of the Illyrians and the Dardanians. It is remarkable that Philip V managed to deal with this combination and the Romans as well in 199 B.C.

Macedonia a great area was devastated by the Macedonians, in order to make entry difficult for the Dardanians into Macedonia and into Illyria (and vice versa).[1] This area 'Illyris Deserta' was probably somewhere between Prizrend and Uroševac; for the messengers who were sent by Perseus to Genthius in 169 B.C. passed 'above Mt. Scardos', i.e. over the Kačanik pass, and then through Illyris Deserta.[2]

The position of the Paeonians athwart the main route south of Dardania and between the hammers of the Illyrians and Dardanians and the anvil of Macedonia was a most unenviable one. Time and again they suffered heavily, and not only from these neighbours, but also from the Thracians on the east and from the Gauls who poured down from the north under Brennus and Acichorius in 279 B.C. At some time in the latter part of the third century the Dardanians occupied Paeonia; for at the time of the Roman partition of Macedonia in 167 B.C., they claimed that Paeonia had been theirs (Livy 45. 29. 12). Aemilius Paulus refused to give them Paeonia, on the ground that the Paeonians had been subjects of Perseus and were now liberated; and as Perseus had been able to send his messengers to Genthius via Kačanik in 169 B.C., when he was at war with the Dardanians, the Paeonians subject to Perseus in 169 B.C. extended into the Paeonian mountains by Kačanik. The second tetrarchy of Macedonia was bounded on the west by the upper Axius, that is by the stretch of the river from north of Stobi (for Stobi itself belonged to the third tetrarchy, as Livy 45. 29. 13 shows) to Scupi at least, where the Axius turns westwards.[3] Here, as on the western frontier of the fourth tetrarchy, Rome established a defensible line on which she placed troops (D.S. 31. 8. 9), to the disappointment of those who had helped her to defeat Macedon. But the Roman settlement was not maintained. The northern peoples broke into Paeonia and Macedonia repeatedly during the next hundred years. When we reach the geography of Ptolemy (*fl.* A.D. 139), Scupi is in Dardania, Stobi is in the sphere of the Pelagones, and the Paeonian area lies to the east.[4] This situation was probably the consequence of many centuries of attrition.

---

[1] Plb. 28. 8. 3 and Livy 43. 20. 1.

[2] For a discussion of its position see my article in *BSA* 61 (1966) 250.

[3] Diodorus 31. 8. 8, ἀπὸ δὲ δυσμῶν ὁ καλούμενος Ἄξιὸς ποταμὸς καὶ οἱ παρακείμενοι αὐτῷ ὅπτοι, and Livy 45. 29. 7, ab occasuque Axius terminaret fluvius, additis Paeonibus, qui prope Axium flumen ad regionem orientis colerent. These passages indicate that above Veles at any rate the Paeones did not have territory west of the river (that area belonging to the Brygi and then further north to the Penestae) or above Scupi in that part of the river which runs westt nto Tetovo.

[4] Ptol. 3. 9. 6; 3. 13. 28; and 3. 13. 34. So also in Hierocles *Synecdemus* 641. 2 and 655. 8. It was left to Diocletian to form a province of Dardania at the end of the third century. In the data of the Peutinger Table for the stations Stobi VIII Gurbita XIII Adcephalon VIIII Praesidio VIIII the total of 39 m.p. is still short of Scupi, because the distance on the modern road from Gradsko (Stobi) to Skopje is 67 km = 45 m.p. The individual data as far as Praesidio may be correct. If Gurbita is placed at Nogaevci (p. 78 above), Adcephalon comes

6. Tribal organization in North-Western Macedonia

Most of the evidence which we have for the organization of the north-western peoples comes from inscriptions dating from the time of the Roman Empire. This evidence is indicative of long-surviving institutions and not of new developments due to the pax Romana, such as the formation of urban centres. It is therefore of great importance for our understanding of the conditions which prevailed at the time of the Macedonian Empire and indeed before the expansion of the Macedonian state. Let me give an example.

Παῦλος Καιλίδιος Φρόντων ἀγορανομήσας, πρεσβεύσας εἰς Δελφοὺς ἐπὶ τὸ-Πύθιον, ἀργύριον ἐπιδοὺς τῇ πόλι εἰς σείτου ἀγορασίαν, σεῖτον ἐν σπάνει παραν πωλήσας, γυμνασιαρχήσας ἐκ τῶν ἰδίων, εἰκόνων ἀναθέσεως καὶ ἀνδριάντων ἀξιωθεὶς ὑπὸ τοῦ βουλευτηρίου διὰ δόγματος ταμιεύων καὶ πολιταρχῶν, γυμνασι-άρχης ἀποδεδει(γ)μ(έ)νος καὶ τῆς πόλεως καὶ τοῦ Λυγκηστῶν ἔθνους καὶ υἱὸς πόλεως διὰ δογμάτων, τὴν στήλην ἀνέθηκεν ἐκ τῶν ἰδίω(ν).

In this inscription of the second century A.D., of which the report came from Monastir,[1] Paulus Caelidius Fronto included in the record of his career his election to serve as a *gymnasiarches* both of the city (of Heraclea) and of the tribe of the Lyncestae, γυμνασιάρχης ἀποδεδειγμένος καὶ τῆς πόλεως καὶ τοῦ Λυγκηστῶν ἔθνους. As such, Fronto was to hold not just one office either in the polis of the Lyncestae or in a polis comprising two parts, viz. the polis and the ethnos, but two separate offices: he was to be *gymnasiarches* of the city of Heraclea, and he was to be *gymnasiarches* of the tribal state of the Lyncestae, in the same way that a man may be an alderman of London and a Member of Parliament.[2] Heraclea may have enjoyed some degree of self-government since *c.* 350 B.C., if Philip II

near Basino Selo and Praesidio comes just north of Letevci at the very head of the pass from which one descends towards Skopje. The head of the pass may well have marked a frontier either of the Antonine period or of an earlier period, so that 'guard-post' would be an appropriate name for the halt Praesidio on the Roman road.

[1] Published by P. Perdrizet in *BCH* 21 (1897) 161 f., giving a better text than Dimitsas no. 248. It is not known where the stone was found.

[2] Perdrizet, Dimitsas p. 273, and M. Holleaux, *Études d'épigraphie et d'histoire grecques* (Paris, 1938) i. 272, speak of Heraclea being the capital of the Lyncestae, which tends to obscure the issue that they are separate entities, although they may overlap geographically. Fronto, writing from Dyrrachium, was no doubt a native of Heraclea serving in the Roman army or administration. He gives a list of offices he had held in Heraclea—agoranomos, presbeus to Delphi, tamieus, politarches, and gymnasiarches—and then reaches the climax by *repeating* his office as gymnasiarches of Heraclea and stressing that he had in addition been gymnasiarches of the ethnos of Lyncestae. He was a Lyncestes himself, and it was a greater honour to have held office in the larger organization. Incidentally Heraclea is not likely to have been 'capital of the Lyncestae', because it was a relatively late foundation and because no one of the many inscriptions copied there records an act of the Lyncestae. F. Papazoglou in *ŽA* 9 (1959) 164 draws the same distinction between Heraclea and the Lyncestae, but she thinks Heraclea was the administrative centre of both and later absorbed the whole of Lyncus.

was its founder as seems probable, but the Lyncestae had been a tribal state long before that.[1] In Thuc. 2. 99. 3 the Lyncestae are one of the ἔθνη with their own kings, and in Ps.-Scymnus 621 we have ἔθνος τῶν Λυγκηστῶν.

The tribal state of the Lyncestae which elected Fronto as its *gymnasiarches* is only one of many such tribal states in north-western Macedonia and indeed in adjacent territories to the west. On the stone which recorded the career of Fronto we have an edict of the second century A.D. which ordered two payments to be levied, one from the rich citizens of Heraclea and the other from τῶν ἐν Μακεδονίᾳ ὄντων Ἀντανῶν. Here again we see a contrast between the city Heraclea and the tribal state οἱ Ἀντανοί.[2] The Antani appear in Hierocles, *Synecdemus* 639. 2, in the entry 'Antania', whether this is the title of a tribal state's district or of a tribal capital in the sixth century A.D.[3] Next we have three inscriptions which record acts of the tribal state οἱ Δασσαρήτιοι:

1. *Spomenik* 71 (1931) no. 263 = Dimitsas no. 330 on a large stone before the door of the school in Ochrid = von Hahn, *Denkschriften* 16 (1867) 2. 160, having seen it in the garden of the Bishop of Ochrid at

---

[1] Thuc. 2. 99. 2.

[2] Perdrizet thought the Antani to be contractors, Holleaux to be the Atintanes of Epirus, and L. Robert in *REG* 47 (1934) 35 to be a tribe between Heraclea and Stobi. Holleaux and Robert supposed the letter to be addressed to the Lyncestae. As they print τηι [?πολει], and as we have on the same stone καὶ τῆς πόλεως καὶ τοῦ Λυγκηστῶν ἔθνους in contrast with one another, their supposition is most unlikely to be sound, because the addressees should then be the citizens of ἡ πόλις, that is Heraclea. They also suppose the Antani to have been administratively attached or subordinate to the Lyncestae, but this does not follow from the inscription, since it is the author and not ἡ πόλις which orders the Antani to make a contribution. M. Rostovtzeff, *Social and Economic History of the Roman Empire* (vol. 2² (Oxford, 1957) 651, 'it is therefore probable that the city of Heraclea included in her territory the country of the Lynkesti, who were not citizens of the city, one part of the tribe of the Atintani being attached to the city in the same way as the Carni and Catali were attached to Tergeste', seems to me to be wide of the mark.

[3] Antania, being named Antania Gemindos or Gemindou, is perhaps more likely to be a town than a tribal district. As it is mentioned immediately after Heraclea Lyncou, as the stones recording the dedication to Hecate and the order about the repair of the roads were seen first at Monastir, and as the order was made apparently to the Heracleotes and involved 'the Antani in Macedonia', these Antani were near Heraclea, had in their territory two roads or more (ὁδούς in the plural), and had members of the same tribe living outside Macedonia. The Antani were thus on the edge of Macedonia, i.e. to the west of Heraclea, and the Via Egnatia and offshoots of it are north-west of Heraclea. The boundary between this division of Macedonia and Epirus Nova in the sixth century A.D. lay east of Lychnidus, which was in Epirus Nova (Hierocles 653. 8), and it was probably where it had been in A.D. 333 when the Bordeaux traveller passed through the frontier between 'mutatio Brucida' and Lychnidus (It. Burd. 607. 3). I am inclined, therefore, to put the Antani in the valleys by and above Resen, the frontier at 'mutatio Brucida' on the Petrina pass, and the related Antani across the border north of 'mutatio Brucida'. If so, Antania would have been in an equivalent position to Resen. Epirus was created a province probably not long before the date of the order involving the Antani. 'Gemindou' was presumably added to Antania, as 'Lyncou' was added to Heraclea, in order to distinguish it from a like-named place; so the district Gemindus may be the district of Resen.

Monastir; and Heuzey–Daumet 140, dating it to the third century A.D. [Δ]ασσαρήτιοι Δρύαντα Κα[ι]πίωνος [τὸ]ν προστάτην [π]ρεσβεύσαντα [πρὸς] τὸν κύριον α[ὐτ]οκράτορα.

2. *Spomenik* 75 (1933) no. 177 βουλὴ καὶ] δῆμος ['Ιουλ. Πτολε]μαῖον ἀρε[τῆς ἕνεκα].

3. *ŽA* 6 (1956) 166 f., found in the church of St. Sophia at Ochrid, ἀγαθῇ τύχῃ. τὸν μέγιστον καὶ θ[ει]ότατον αὐτοκρά[τ]ορα Μάρκον Ἀντώνιον Γορδιανὸν εὐσεβῆ εὐτυχῆ σεβαστὸν Δασσαρήτιοι.

From the second of these inscriptions we see that the tribal state had its magistrates, council, and assembly (*demos*) of enfranchised members, and from nos. 1 and 3 that it sent an envoy to an emperor and honoured an emperor. The Dassaretii, a large tribal state with constituent tribes and with territory extending from the lakes to Berat, was a free state and not, of course, attributed to the town Lychnidus. In the third century A.D., if not earlier, the officials and the assembly met at Lychnidus at least on occasion; for the town then lay within their territory, as it had done in 170 B.C. ('ad Lychnidum Dassaretiorum', Livy 43. 9. 7). The Lychnidii themselves had their own officials and passed their decrees, as we see from an inscription found in the ruined church of St. Barbara in Ochrid.[1]

ΑΓΑΘΗΤΥΧΗ
ΛΥΧΝΕΙΔΙωΝ
ΟΑΤϹΑΙΡΟΥ
ΟΥΑΡΗ Τ

Whether we restore the beginning of the third line as [ΗΠ]ΟΛΙϹ viz. ἡ πόλις or not, we see Lychnidus acting here as a polis similar to the polis Heraclea.

A similar situation presents itself in Derriopus. The Council, having been convened by τῶν ... ἐν Δερριόπῳ πολιταρχῶν, takes a decision to honour M. Vettius Philo. As we have seen (p. 69 above), Derriopus is not a city but a district inhabited by the Derriopes, and the politarchs in Derriopus are the officials of the tribal state ἡ πόλις τῶν Δερριόπων. Dimitsas reported that this stone and many other inscribed stones had been brought to Tsepicovo from a site on the other side of the river Cerna, where he said there were remains of an ancient city.[2] Recently another stone was found, built into the wall of a church at Tsepicovo and

[1] Dimitsas no. 342 and F. Papazoglou in *ŽA* 9 (1959) 167 on the Dassaretii with an administrative centre at Lychnidus.

[2] As it is repeatedly said that Styberra was at Tsepicovo, it is wise to quote the words of Dimitsas on no. 258 p. 302: εἰς τὸ χωρίον ὅμως τοῦτο μετηνέχθη ἡ πλὰξ ἐκ τοῦ παρὰ τὴν δεξιὰν ὄχθην τοῦ ποταμοῦ ἀνυψουμένου γηλόφου ἔνθα κατὰ τὴν διαβεβαίωσιν τῶν χωρικῶν ὑπῆρχεν ἀρχαία πόλις. A metrical inscription from Tsepicovo, published in *AI* 4 (1963) 82, ends with the words δήμῳ μάρτυρι Δερριόπων.

doubtless brought originally from the site across the river. The inscription on this stone begins Στυβερραίων ἡ πόλις and records the honouring of a benefactor of Styberra: Στυβερραίων ἡ πόλις καὶ οἱ συνπραγματευόμενοι 'Ρωμαῖοι Ἀρχέπολιν Ἀπολλοδώρου τὸν εὐεργέτην.[1] It is thus clear that Styberra happened to be the place at which the Council of the Derriopes met at least on occasion, and that the Styberraei themselves formed a separate community capable of passing decisions to honour a benefactor on the authority of ἡ Στυβερραίων βουλὴ καὶ ὁ δῆμος (*AI* 4 (1963) 79). We may note that the acts of the Dassaretii were not dated, but that those of the Council of the Derriopes were dated by the Macedonian era to A.D. 95. Inscriptions from Tsepicovo, from Zivojna, east of Monastir, and from Vitoliste in the Morihovo are dated also by the Macedonian era (*BCH* 47 (1923) 291 and 282; *AI* 4 (1963) 77 and 81; *Spomenik* 75 (1933) no. 20 = *ŽA* 8 (1958) 305 f.). The Derriopes and the Styberraei among them counted themselves to be Macedonians.

The Pelagones also were a tribal state. They appear in Ps.-Scymnus 621 as ἔθνος τὸ τῶν Πελαγόνων. The tribal state was judged by Rome in 167 B.C. to be capable of administering the fourth tetrarchy (see p. 75 above). If a man was described as 'Pelagon' or 'from Pelagonia', this was enough to indicate his membership of this tribal state, whether in the fourth century B.C. (Tod, *GHI* 14 Μενέλαος Πελαγών) or in the fourth century A.D.[2]

Within these tribal states of the Lyncestae, the Dassaretii, the Antani, the Derriopes, and the Pelagones there were smaller units. Such units were the Heracleotae, the Lychnidii, and the Styberraei, who lived mainly in an urban centre. Other units were smaller tribal groups. Thus within the large tribal state of the Pelagones we find ἡ τῶν Ἀργεσταίων πόλις, which passed its own decrees and honoured a Roman proconsul (see p. 79 above); and probably within the community of the Argestaei we find a small community paying its devotion to Hera Νεαπολειτῶν τὸ κοινὸν "Ηραν θεὸν ἔτους ηρϛ'.[3] In this case the dating by the Macedonian era to A.D. 150 shows that the Neapoleitae considered themselves to be Macedonians and so were Pelagonians and not Paeonians. Within the tribal state of the Derriopi an inscription was found by Kazarow in the church of Pestani, south of the Cerna and south-east of Dunjë, which recorded a vote of gratitude by Δοστωνέω[ν] τὸ κοινόν. Another inscription, this time in Latin and dating to A.D. 120, was found at Vitoliste, nowadays the chief place in the Morihovo district. This records the laying of boundary-markers between the Geneatae (possibly Ceneatae) and

[1] *Spomenik* 71 (1931) no. 501, where the rho is the error of the printer and not of the inscription; N. Vulic in *Mélanges G. Glotz* (1932) 875.

[2] *CIL* iii 2017, 3530, 7325; viii 2865; vi 2382 b 8; *BCH* 47 (1923) 275.

[3] *Spomenik* 71 (1931) no. 63; where it is given as ἦραν θεόν. The inscription is from Vladilovatsi near the Babuna pass.

another group whose name ended in -xini. It seems likely that here too we have small communities of a tribal kind rather than of an urban character.[1]

A smaller community still is the κώμη. The acts of such a community are recorded in Greek inscriptions found at Suvodol in western Derriopus (*Spomenik* 98 (1941–8) no. 58; see p. 70 above). Another is mentioned in an inscription found at Bela Tsarkva, a village to the north of Tsepicovo, where it was built into a church wall. It is dated by the Macedonian era to A.D. 192. It records a gift of money to τῇ Ἀλκομεναίων κώμῃ, ταῖς φυλαῖς, and arranges for the four tribes to make sacrifices on the same day, one to Zeus Agoraeus and Hera in the agora and the other three 'at the altar in Alcomena (ἐν Ἀλκομενᾶ) which the donor had made and inscribed and Octavius(?) had delighted in'.[2] Alcomena is a *kome*, a corporate group of persons known as the Alcomenaei, and there can be no doubt that it is one of several *komai* which made up Alalcomenae,[3] one of the cities of the Derriopes (Str. 7 C 327 αἱ τῶν Δευριόπων πόλεις . . . ὧν τὸ Βρυάνιον καὶ Ἀλαλκομεναὶ καὶ Στύβαρα); or the Derriopan cities were on the Erigon, and Bela Tsarkva is beside the northern branch of the Cerna, the Blato. The four tribes in the *kome* are presumably those of the polis of the Alalcomenaei, and they presumably existed in all the constituent *komai*. The ephebic inscription which was found also at Bela Tsarkva begins with the words ἀλειφούσης τῆς πόλεως (not τῆς κώμης), and the polis is probably

[1] *BCH* 47 (1923) no. 277, the inscription from Vitoliste. In the phrase '[in]ter Geneata[s et . . . . .]xinos' the Geneatae come first as the record is placed in their territory; so too in *BSA* 17 (1910–11) 195 where the Dolichani come first and the stele is set up in their agora. The Gentianus who dealt with the dispute was active also in the district of the Battynaei (see p. 114 below); he was *censitor Macedoniae (Prosopogr. Imp. Rom.* 3. 301 no. 56). *BCH* 47 (1923) no. 277, the inscription from Pestani = *Spomenik* 71 (1931) no. 437. F. Papazoglou, giving the place of discovery as Kokre in *ŽA* 9 (1959) 167, whereas Kazarow says he saw it in the wall at Pestani, says that the koinon of the Dostoneis may be part of a tribal system but that the koinon of the Neapolitae cannot be. I do not see the force of the distinction she draws, because a group of new members can be adopted into a tribal system.

[2] *Spomenik* 71 (1931) no. 339, and another inscription, no. 342, on the same topic but with variations. Dimitsas no. 262 with details of its discovery and N. Vulic, loc. cit. *Spomenik* reads ΤΟΚΤΑ . . ΟΣ and Dimitsas . . . . ΤΑΙΡ . . CT. From the illustration in *Spomenik* Dimitsas has too many letters, and it looks as if ΟΚΤΑΒΙΟC is a probable reading; Gn. Octavius settled disputes among the Macedonians in 164–163 B.C., and G. Octavius was a famous governor of Macedonia in 60 B.C. Either may have done some special service to Alcomena, or it may be another, more recent, Octavius.

[3] F. Papazoglou in *ŽA* 9 (1959) 167 takes Alcomena to be Alcomenae, but there is no room on the stone for the change of reading from Ἀλκομενᾶ to Ἀλκομεναῖς. The name of the polis in Strabo's codices is Alcomenae, and this form is given in most of the codices of St. Byz. s.v. *Alkomenai*; but Kramer and Meineke in their editions believe the name to have been Alalcomenae. The distinction which is important is the distinction between the *kome* in the singular and the *polis* in the plural. The *kome* Alcomena as part of a *polis* Alalcomenae may be compared to the Antani being part of the larger tribe, the Atintani; the syncopation is similar in each case. For an official κ]ωμαρχῶν see *Spomenik* 71 (1931) no. 265 = von Hahn, *Denkschriften* 16 (1867) 2. 162 no. 4 = Heuzey–Daumet 341 on a stone seen at Ochrid.

Alalcomenae.[1] The inscription is dated by the Macedonian era to
A.D. 121. We may visualize here a polis of the early Dorian type,[2] such
as Sparta was in the time of Thucydides, οὔτε ξυνοικισθείσης πόλεως . . .
κατὰ κώμας δὲ τῷ παλαιῷ τῆς Ἑλλάδος τρόπῳ οἰκισθείσης (Thuc. 1. 10. 2).

This structure of large tribal groups, containing lesser tribal groups,
and forming into political units of ἔθνος, φυλή, πόλις, κώμη, and κοινόν,
is one which we should regard in central and southern Greece as typical
of the archaic period. Was it indigenous in these remote north-western
territories or was it imposed by Macedonian or Roman rulers? All
historical parallels suggest that it was indigenous, a survival of a system
congenial to the peoples of this high and mountainous terrain and
as old as the time of their first arrival. The *ethnos* and the *komai* were
already in Lyncus in the fifth century (Thuc. 2. 99. 2 and 4. 124. 4). If
the structure is Greek, it may not be exclusively Greek; for all we know,
the Illyrian Penestae or the Dardanii may have had similar institutions.
But there is another point of distinction, not only the use of Greek speech
but the very high proportion of Greek names. The ephebic lists found
at Tsepicovo, being evidently those of the Styberraei, and those of the
ephebarchus and the ephebes found at Bela Tsarkva, being probably those
of the Alalcomenaei, contain a great many names.[3] These are almost
to a man Greek names; the exceptions are some Latin names, due no
doubt to legionary fathers, and an occasional Illyrian or Thracian name,
such as Epicadus, Beithys, Sitas, and Cetriporis. If the Derriopes were in
fact Illyrians or Thracians in descent, it is impossible to account for the
purity of their Greek speech and for the almost complete dominance of
Greek names, especially as the occasional one which is admitted cannot
be regarded as substantial evidence of Illyrian or Thracian survival. It
seems clear that these people were Greek by descent; that is they bore
the marks of institutions, language, and nomenclature which distinguished
the Hellenic tribes from their neighbours, and they were Greek in this
sense before they became Macedonian in a political sense.

The closest parallels to the origin and situation of the Derriopes, Pelagones, and the others are to be seen in the tribes of Epirus, which were
also neighbours of Illyrians. There we have the same tribal structures in
large groups, e.g. Molossi or Chaones, and numerous small tribes making
up a large group but each having its own *koinon*;[4] the same use of Greek
language and the same dominance of Greek nomenclature, both seen from
inscriptions of 370–368 B.C.[5] and neither attributable to the extension

---

[1] *Spomenik* 71 (1931) 343 = Dimitsas 261. The money came from M. Vettius Philo, the
benefactor of the Derriopes, and the stone came from Bela Tsarkva.

[2] See *HG*² 97–107.

[3] *Comptes rendus* 1939. 221 (of the years A.D. 74, 87, 90, and 107); *Spomenik* 71 (1931) no.
343 = Dimitsas no. 261 (of the year A.D. 121); and *AI* 4 (1963) 81 f.

[4] See *Epirus* 531 f. and 536 f.   [5] Ibid. 525 f.

of Macedonian rule. But, more than this, we have a close similarity in the formation of the ethnics of north-western Macedonia and of Epirus: Lyncestae, Dolenestae and (in Epirus) Hyncestae, Ethnestae, Orestae; Derriopes and Hellopes; Alcomenaei and Eurymenaei; Argestaei and Aegestaei; Limnaei and Larisaei; Combreatae, Geneatae, (?) Maleiatae and Oriatae, Phylatae, Edonesatae; Pelagones and Chaones, Amymones, Sylliones. The names of the Derriopan cities are also comparable to those in Epirus: Styberra (Strabo's Stybara) to Kemara (modern Himarrë), Alalcomenae to Eurymenae, Bryanium to Bryanium, Pluinna to Gitana.[1] These analogies are so close that we have no reason to doubt the ancient tradition in Str. 7 C 326 and 9 C 434 that the Pelagones, Elimiotae, and Orestae, and in general the inland tribes bordering on the Illyrian mountains (οἱ ὑπερκείμενοι καὶ συνάπτοντες τοῖς Ἰλλυρικοῖς ὄρεσι) were Epirotic tribes. I shall discuss later the origin and significance of Strabo's statements. They rest upon observations of ethnic relationships rather than of a way of life; for Strabo goes on in C 326 fin. to say that 'some' (indicating a different source) call the whole area up to Corcyra 'Macedonia' because of similarities of tonsure, dialect, and dress (the *chlamys*).

While we have the geography of the north-western area in mind, it is desirable to note the extent of Strabo's statement in C 326. The Illyrian mountains begin for him in book 7 to the north of the Via Egnatia, and the traveller has on his right 'the Epirotic tribes' (C 323); in general these tribes lying inland[2] and bordering on the Illyrian mountains occupy rough country, and some of them are 'close to the Macedonians rather' (than to ? central Epirus), whereupon Orestias is mentioned (C 326). But the Illyrian tribes are interspersed there, that is those tribes by the south part of the (Illyrian) mountain range and those inland of the Ionian Gulf; for the Bylliones and Taulantii (being inland of the Ionian Gulf) and the Parthini and the Brygi (being at the southern end of the Illyrian range, i.e. where the Shkumbi cuts through it) live inland of Epidamnus and Apollonia. After a short digression he adds apparently to his list of 'the Epirotic tribes' the Lyncestae, Derriopus, Pelagonia, the Eordi, Elimea, and Eratyra. And at the end of the chapter he explains, as he does also at C 434, that as a result of imperialism the Epirotes close to the

---

[1] For the Epirote names see the *Onomastikon Epeirotikon* in *Epirus* 795 f. Many more ethnics are known from Epirus, where the inscriptions are much earlier. In Macedonia the tribal ethnic was little used under the Empire; for Limnaei see *Spomenik* 98 (1941–8) no. 388 line 33; for Combreatae and Dolenestae see *Comptes rendus* 1939. 221A lines 79 and 80 of the year A.D. 87 and *Spomenik* 98 (1941–8) no. 388; for Geneatae *BCH* 47 (1923) 277; for ?Maleiatae Papazoglou 178. For the Triklares or Triklari of Str. 7 fr. 20 compare the Kares and Talares in Epirus. Petsas suggests in *AE* 1961. 19 that Mariniaeus may be an ethnic; Epirus has Tiaeus.

[2] ὑπερκείμενοι is mistranslated in the Loeb edition; it means lying inland, as is clear from the expressions in the same chapter τὰ ὑπὲρ τοῦ Ἰονίου κόλπου ... and τῆς Ἐπιδάμνου ... ὑπεροικοῦσι and πλὴν ὀλίγων τῶν ὑπὲρ τοῦ Ἰονίου κόλπου.

Macedonians became part of their domains and indeed all except a few inland of the Ionian Gulf (C 326 fin. πλὴν ὀλίγων τῶν ὑπὲρ τοῦ Ἰονίου κόλπου). Now if his list of the interspersed Illyrian tribes is complete, it means that the Dassaretii, the Amantes, the Parauaei, and the Chaones are regarded by him as Epirotic, and of these the few close to Macedonia and inland of the Ionian Gulf who escaped Macedonia's clutches were the Dassaretii and the Parauaei. There are also independent reasons for supposing these two peoples to have been in some sense Epirotic; for *FGrH* 1 (Hecataeus) F 103 describes the Dexari—those after whom the district Dassaretis was named—as a Chaonian tribe living under Mt. Amyron, which is the great mountain behind Berat, Mt. Tomor; and *FGrH* 265 (Rhianus) F 19 attributes the Parauaei to Epirus as a Thesprotian tribe.[1] I conclude then that the Dassaretii were a Greek-speaking people of the so-called Epirotic group, akin to the Lyncestae and the Orestae, for instance, and to the more southerly tribes of the Chaones.[2]

[1] For these two peoples see *Epirus* 451 and 701.

[2] Because the territory west of Macedonia and north of Epirus was known generally as Illyris and later was part of the Roman province of Illyricum, there has been a tendency to regard all peoples in it, except those of Apollonia and Dyrrachium, as Illyrians.

III

THE WESTERN AND THE SOUTHERN AREAS

1. *Lychnis and Dassaretis*

WHILE the district round Lychnidus had great strategic value, it was also extremely rich in its own right. The pasture, the arable land, and the fisheries supported a very large population, as we see for instance from Procopius *Anecd.* 18. 42 (ed. Haury) Λυχνιδόν τε τὴν ἐν 'Ηπειρώταις καὶ Κόρινθον, αἳ δὴ πολυανθρωπόταται ἐκ παλαιοῦ ἦσαν. Greek tradition associated the descendants of Cadmus and Hermione with a powerful dynasty of the Encheleae or Enchelei, 'the eel-men', so called perhaps from their control of the northern end of Lake Lychnitis, where the fisheries are finest, and also with the foundation of Lychnidus, which proved to be the strongest city in the area of the lakes.[1] In a corrupt passage of Str. C 326, which I have discussed elsewhere,[2] it appears that an Illyrian or Thracian royal house, called the Peresadyes, joined that of the Encheleae and increased its power; and this gains some support from the tradition that a city Harpyia among the Encheleae had been founded by the charioteer of Amphiaraus, called Bato, a dynastic name in the royal house of the Dardanii.[3] Such a fusion of royal houses and strong tribes as these traditions suggest may account for the astonishing wealth of the royal graves found at Trebenishte and dating to the late sixth century B.C.

One feature of these graves was the abundance of silver, and this and other reasons led me to suggest that the silver mines of Damastium, which Strabo mentioned in the previous sentence at C 326, were in fact in the realm of this dynasty and were 'situated probably to the north of Lake Ochrid'.[4] In reading *Živa Antika* 3 (1953) 261 I came across a sentence which seems to indicate the whereabouts of at least one of τὰ ἀργυρεῖα τὰ ἐν Δαμαστίῳ: 'in iis enim partibus ad viam quae hodie ab oppido

---

[1] Str. C 326; Ps.-Scymnus 436; *Anth. Pal.* 7. 697, Λυχνιδὸν ἦν Φοῖνιξ Κάδμος ἔδειμε πόλιν.

[2] *Epirus* 466 f.

[3] St. Byz. s.v. Harpyia. Ps.-Scymnus 431 f. mentions a tradition of Diomedes' death on an island nearby, perhaps the island in Lake Prespa. One may compare the death of Ali Pasha on the island of Ioannina Lake.

[4] *Epirus* 438 f., 466, 541; J. M. F. May, *The Coinage of Damastium* (Oxford, 1939) 28, placed Damastium northwards of Lake Ochrid. I have not found 'Starski dol' on a map but it must be near Istok, where Wace reported 'remains of antiquity'; see *BSA* 18 (1911–12) 176. Silver mines in the Ochrid Sanjak were reported by Haci Halfa in the seventeenth century, and O. Davies, *Roman Mines in Europe* 239 reported Turkish workings at Gümüş Çeşme, which he places north-west of Resen in his Map VI.

Ohrid ad Resan ducit, prope "Starski dol" et "Raleica" novissimis temporibus officinae antiquissimae, quae ad effodiendum ac elaborandum plumbum cum argento pertinent, inventae sunt.' As the author, P. Lisičar, maintains, the mines of Damastium lay not only to the east but also to the north of Lake Ochrid; for if they had been only by Starski dol, the mines would have been called those of Lychnidus. There is also a mention by T. Tomovski in *ŽA* 12 (1963) 341 of finding tin at an ancient site near Velmej in the Saletska valley north of Ochrid (see Map 6).

In the late sixth century the Encheleae must have ruled the area of the lakes. Their neighbours to the south-west were the Dexari, a Chaonian tribe, as we learn from Hecataeus *FGrH* 1 F 103 = St. Byz. s.v. Δεξάροι· ἔθνος Χαόνων τοῖς Ἐγχελέαις προσεχεῖς. Ἑκαταῖος Εὐρώπῃ. ὑπὸ Ἄμυρον ὄρος οἴκουν. It is clear that the Dexari gave their name to the territory Dassaretis, and that Mt. Amyron is the beautiful Mt. Tomor, the central feature of Dassaretis. We hear no more of the Dexari, probably a group of tribes which lost its cohesion, and the name Dassaretii seems to have been used later to describe the peoples of an area of varying extent. The Encheleae survived but only as one of several tribes in the area of the lakes, such as the Caloecini and the Boei. They are mentioned by Polybius with the west Greek form of ethnic as 'Enchelanes' in the sentences τῶν δὲ περὶ τὴν Λυχνιδίαν λίμνην Ἐγχελᾶνας, Κέρακα, Σατίωνα, Βοιούς, τῆς δὲ Καλοικίνων χώρας Βαντίαν, ἔτι δὲ τῶν καλουμένων Πισαντίνων Ὀργησσόν (5. 108. 8).[1] As we have already seen, the Enchelanes were at the north end of the lake and the Boei were at the south end;[2] Cerax, a form of κέρας (Hsch. s.v.), which is used of the branch of a river, is probably to be placed beside the Drilon where it emerges from the lake, that is near Strouga, itself a Bulgarian word 'désignant les émissaires naturels servant de décharge au lac'.[3] Sation may then be placed near Eltzani, where it is separated from the Boei by the narrows between the mountain and the shore (see p. 45 above).[4] If Polybius is mentioning the peoples and towns in a north-to-south order, as in the first sentence I have quoted, we should place the Caloecini south of the Boei. The

---

[1] The general view is that there were towns called Enchelanae and Boioi, but the forms are rather improbable. The most important town to secure was Lychnidus (cf. Livy 27. 32. 9 for its importance), and I take it to be included under the tribe of the Enchelanes. For the variant spellings of tribes in the north-west see *Epirus* 703 and note St. Byz. Δασσαρῆται giving also Δασσαρηνοί, Δασσαρήτιοι, and Δασσαρητῖνος. By an oversight I left Enchelanae as a town in *Epirus* 606; elsewhere I had changed it to the tribe.

[2] I take it that the town Beue and the river Beuos were in the territory of the Boei, and that the words are different spellings of the same root.

[3] Heuzey–Daumet 345.

[4] J. V. A. Fine, 'Macedon, Illyria and Rome, 220–219 B.C.', in *JRS* 26 (1936) 26 and map facing it, places these tribes and towns on the west side of the Lake Ochrid and further south; but the west side is steep and without villages south of the Lin promontory. He follows Leake and Geyer in this; Kiepert put Sation and the Boei on the east side.

Pisantini were probably in western Dassaretis as their town Orgessus is likely to be the Orgyssus of Livy 31. 27. 2.[1]

Dassaretis was made up of the valleys and mountain-sides of the two branches of the Semeni (Apsus), which flow on either side of Mt. Tomor and are united inland of Kuç. The southern branch, the Osum, rises in the wild and little-known district of Danglli. Here Dassaretis is co-terminous with Chaonia and Parauaea, both areas attributed usually to Epirus.[2] The northern branch, the Devoli, rises on the western face of the mountain ridge which is the southern continuation of Mt. Peristeri; its headwaters are divided by this ridge from the headwaters of the Erigon above Florina and from the headwaters of the Haliacmon above Kastoria (see Map 10). The river then cuts through the range which further north divides Lake Prespa from Lake Ochrid; this break-through is known as the Tsangon pass. Its waters form Lake Malik in the basin of Koritsa, out of which it flows and enters a long defile through the continuation of the range dividing Lake Ochrid from the headwaters of the Shkumbi. It cuts deeply through a broad belt of mountains to emerge into the district of Gramsh and flows north-west until it turns south-west to join the Osum. Its upper course has opened important routes of entry from Epirus and South Illyris into Macedonia, both into Lyncus at Florina and into Orestis at Kastoria.

The inhabitants of the upper basin, probably that of Koritsa, were named Eordetae by Ptol. 3. 13. 26, who credits them with three cities, Skampeis,[3] Deboma (or Diboma), and Daulia. The Eordaicus river of Arr. *Anab.* 1. 5. 5 should then be identified with the upper part of the Devoli. St. Byz. s.v. Ἄμυρος says that the Amyroi were also called Eordi, and these Amyri-Eordi should probably be connected with Mt. Amyron = Mt. Tomor (see p. 92 above) and situated east of Mt. Tomor. The two towns of Dassaretis, Creonium and Gerous, which Plb. 5. 108. 8 mentions as having been secured by Philip V against Scerdilaïdas, were probably in north-western Dassaretis. The other towns which are known to us were probably in central and western Dassaretis, Antipatrea at Berat being the strongest and most important.[4]

The extent of Dassaretis eastwards and northwards varied with political conditions. When the Encheleae were strong and bordered on the Dexari, the former are likely to have held the strategic corridor of the lakes. In the latter part of the fifth century, when the Bacchiad kings of the Lyncestae were powerful[5] and developed a force of hoplites (Thuc. 4. 124. 3),

[1] The connection ἔτι δέ suggests that Polybius has made an addition, and the Pisantini may be in Dassaretis and not necessarily close to the Caloecini.

[2] For the evidence in support of this see my article in *JRS* 56 (1966) 53–4 and *Epirus* 677 f.

[3] This town should not be confused with Scampia, a city of the Parthini.

[4] For these towns see my article in *JRS* 58 (1968).

[5] On this dynasty see *BSA* 61 (1966) 243.

they are likely to have expanded westwards and may have controlled the area round Lychnidus. In the fourth century Bardylis, king of the Dardanians in all probability,[1] used this corridor repeatedly to invade Epirus and Macedonia, and the first action of Philip II after defeating Bardylis was to take from him the area around Lake Lychnitis (D. S. 16. 8. 1). In the conflicts which followed between his successors, the Molossian kings and the Illyrian dynasts it is unlikely that the peoples of the corridor were independent for long, and it was only with the intervention of the Romans that the possibility of the Dassaretii acquiring the area round Lychnidus became feasible.

In the first settlement made by Rome in 228 B.C., when the Parthini and the Atintani became allies of Rome, Macedonia held Lychnidus, in which there was a Macedonian garrison in 208 B.C. (Livy 27. 32. 9), but Dassaretis seems to have been independent.[2] When Scerdilaïdas overran Dassaretis, Philip intervened and added it to his realm. In the operations of the Second Macedonian War Dassaretis is described as marching with the borders of Lyncus and Orestis; for Sulpicius passed from Orestis 'in Dassaretios' and Flamininus was advised to go διὰ τῆς Δασσαρητίδος κατὰ Λύγκον,[3] that is through the Tsangon and Pisodherion passes. After the Second Macedonian War the Orestae of Macedonia were made autonomous and Lychnis (probably the area round the northern part of Lake Lychnitis) and Parthos (perhaps some Parthinian territory in the upper Shkumbi valley) were given to Pleuratus the Illyrian.[4] But by 170 B.C., when the Illyrians and the Dassaretii had asked for help against their neighbour, Macedonia, and had been reinforced with Roman

---

[1] On the identification of his kingdom, which has been much disputed, see my article in *BSA* 61 (1966) 239 f. and especially p. 252, and for a contrary view F. Papazoglou in *Historia* 14 (1965) 143–79.

[2] See my article in *JRS* 58 (1968).

[3] Livy 31. 40. 4; Plu. *Flam.* 4. 1 and Livy 32. 9. 9, per Dassaretios potius Lyncumque (the district and not a town as Weissenborn and Müller ad loc. suggest).

[4] Plb. 18. 47. 12, ἔδωκαν δὲ καὶ τῷ Πλευράτῳ Λυχνίδα καὶ Πάρθον, οὔσας μὲν Ἰλλυρίδας, ὑπὸ Φιλίππου δὲ ταττομένας and Livy 33. 34. 10, Pleurato Lychnidus et Parthini dati; Illyriorum utraque gens sub dicione Philippi fuerant. In Plb. 5. 108. 8 ἡ Λυχνιδία λίμνη implies that Polybius called the lake after the city Λυχνιδός, which occurs in Str. C 323 init. who was using Polybius. There should be no doubt that, if Polybius had meant to say that the town 'Lychnidos' was given to Pleuratus, he would have said not 'Lychnis' but 'Lychnidos'. Now the lake was known also as ἡ Λυχνῖτις λίμνη (Ps.-Scymnus 431; D.S. 16. 8. 1, using Ephorus; and Vibius Sequester *Geog. Lat. Min.* 148), a word derived from 'Lychnis' and not from 'Lychnidos'. Lychnis then was the area from which the lake took its name; and an inhabitant of the area was Λυχνίτης, a form given by St. Byz. Livy mistranslates, either carelessly, or intentionally in order to give a place-name more familiar to a Roman audience. So too ἡ Πάρθος, being also feminine as the participles show, may well be a district; and, being clearly adjacent to Lychnis, was in the upper Shkumbi valley, where towns of any consequence must have been hard to find. Again Livy mistranslates, but his meaning is clear, if exaggerated; and his addition of 'utraque gens' indicates that more than the citizens of any two towns were involved. For these much-discussed passages see the entries in *RE* 18. 4 (1949) 2037 f. by Polaschek and *RE* 13. 2 (1927) 2112 by Fluss.

troops (Livy 42. 36. 9), Lychnidus was no longer in the hands of Pleuratus but was already 'Lychnidus Dassaretiorum' (Livy 43. 9. 7).[1] When the partition of Macedonia took place, the area of the lakes was probably incorporated in the fourth tetrarchy (see pp. 46 and 74 above); but with the formation of the province in 148 B.C. and the withdrawal of the frontier between Illyris and Macedonia to Pylon (Str. C 323, using Polybius), Lychnidus and the corridor were probably given to the Dassaretii. For they were made a 'gens libera' now or later[2] (Pliny *HN* 3. 145) and we find them recording their acts at Lychnidus under the empire (see p. 87 above).

In Map 10 I have shown the limits of Dassaretis for the period before 170 B.C., taking as its western frontier the watershed of the Osum river from Mt. Shpiragrit to its sources at Qarishtë, as its northern frontier the watershed of the Candavian range, as its eastern frontier the watershed of the upper Devoli, and as its southern frontier a line roughly from Qarishtë to Mt. Lofka.[3] This area, though relatively poor, is very large and breeds a sturdy type of Albanian Tosk mountaineer, and it was much strengthened economically by the addition of Lychnidus and the lakes. It had plenty of small towns or 'vici' and 'castella', as Livy 27. 32. 6 and 42. 36. 9 calls them, but there were cities only in the area of the lakes, apart from the Macedonian foundation, Antipatrea. So far as our evidence goes, the Dassaretii were of Chaonian stock, that is of the Epirotic group, and Greek-speaking in the time of the Roman Empire. The strategic significance of their country was that two routes ran through it, one from the north through the corridor of the lakes down via the modern Leskoviq into Epirus and the other from Apollonia to the basin of Kastoria, whence one could turn towards either Lychnidus or Lyncus or Orestis.

The best description of the route from Kastoria to Berat through Dassaretis is that of Leake.[4] Going north at first from Kastoria, that is from Celetrum in Orestis, into the Haliacmon valley (see Map 6), he climbed over 'a low ridge' by Vatokhorion and descended into the basin containing the headwaters of the Devoli, and on to Biklisht, which he reached after 5 hours and 40 minutes. The low ridge is the watershed between the Haliacmon and the Devoli, the ancient frontier between Dassaretis and

---

[1] This passage may be due to an annalist and not Polybius; Rome is likely to have found the Dassaretii more reliable than Pleuratus.

[2] Caesar *BC* 3. 35 and Str. C 326 refer to part of Macedonia being 'free', and the freedom of the Dassaretii may have been granted at the same time. The arrangements made by Augustus (Str. C 840) seem to have left Lychnidus with the Dassaretii.

[3] Its neighbours were to the west Apolloniatis, to the north the Parthini, to the east the Boei and other people of the northern Kastoria basin and then Lyncus and Orestis, and to the south Chaonia and Parauaea; for its relations to the last two see *Epirus* 679 f. and Hammond, *JRS* 56 (1966) 53 f.

[4] Leake 1. 332 f., on horseback in wet weather in September 1805.

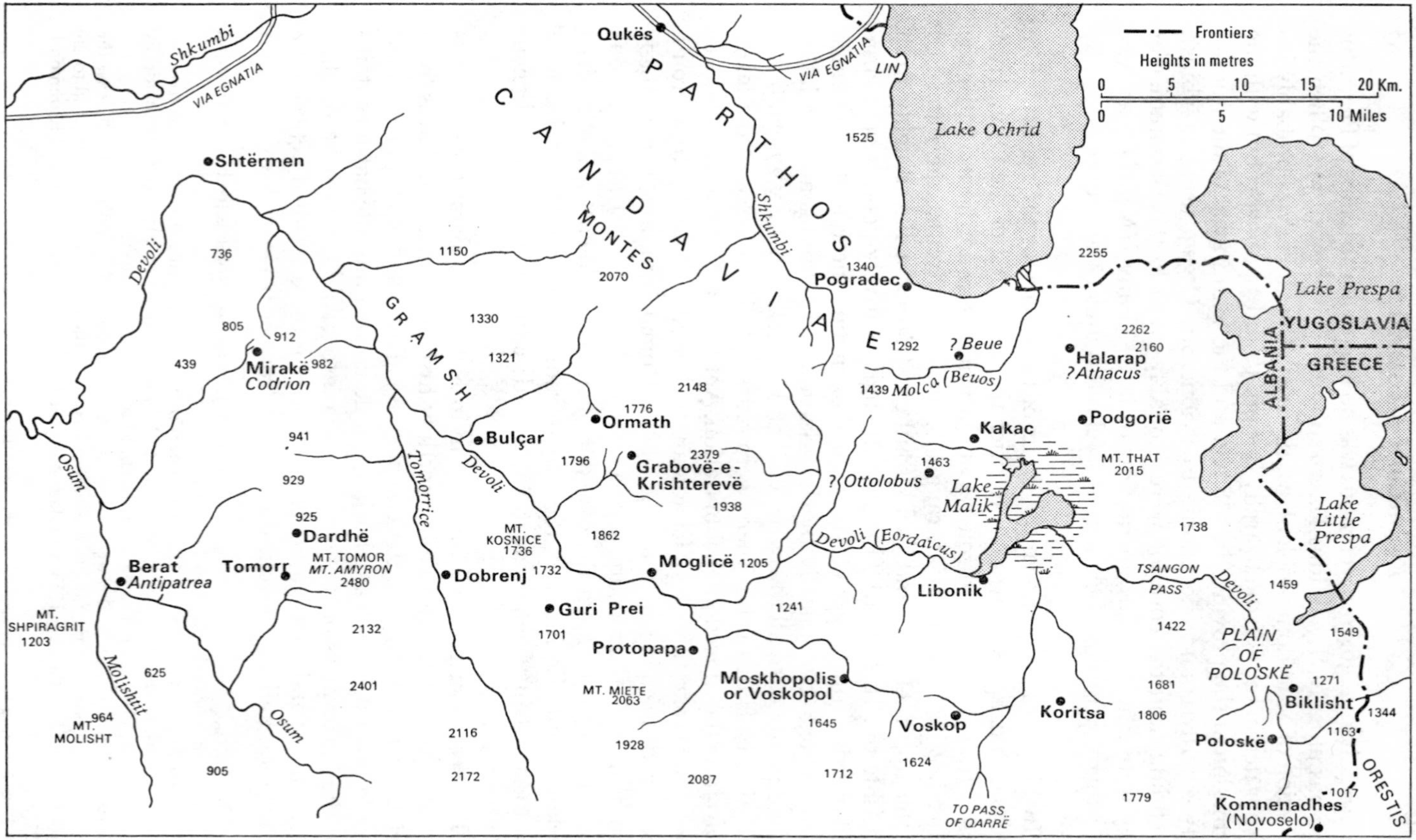

MAP 10. DASSARETIS

Macedonia. The traveller who goes from Florina in the ancient canton of Lyncus to Biklisht has to climb over a pass by Pisodherion, between the range of Mt. Peristeri and the range of Mt. Vitsi, in order to enter the Haliacmon valley, and then to cross the watershed over the same low ridge by Vatokhorion. Continuing from Biklisht, Leake reached in two hours the narrowest part of the Pass of Tsangon, which 'is not as strong as it is narrow' since 'the river occupies all the space'. 'The hills which border it on either side [are] not very abrupt, but they soon become steep and lofty, and the great rocky summit to the north ... is a suitable link to the chain formed by the great summits Ghrammos, Russotari and Smolika.'[1] Here Leake mentions a bridge, and one evidently has to cross the river to get through the pass. The remarkable feature of the pass is the unparalleled cleft in the main range, which southwards runs generally at a high altitude dividing the waters of the Haliacmon and the Peneus from those of the Aous and the Arachthus. The cleft is a natural gateway, exploited by the river Devoli, which rises further to the east than the Drin, Shkumbi, or Vijosë. In another two hours Leake reached Koritsa in the southern part of the plain, whereas an ancient traveller might have crossed the plain nearer Lake Malik.

From Koritsa Leake took the Turkish road well to the south of the defiles of the Devoli, crossed the ridge above Moskhopolis (a very considerable town *c.* 1700) and followed a tributary of the Devoli to Protopapa, which he reached in some eight hours of riding from Koritsa. At this point the roads divide. One track crosses the Devoli, climbs over a pass in the mountain of Moglicë west of Grabovë-e-Krishterevë and returns to the Devoli at Bulçar in the district of Gramsh; from Bulçar one can either descend down the valley to Shtërmen in the sink between the Devoli and the Shkumbi or turn westwards through the hill country to reach the lowest part of the Osum, before it joins the Devoli. The other track, which Leake took, is a shorter but much more arduous route to Berat. Leaving Protopapa he had a 4½ hours' climb up to the high ridge between Mt. Kosnicë and Mt. Mietë at Guri Prei ('the cut rock'), descended to reach the Tomorricë river by Dobrenj in another seven hours, and climbed in 3¾ hours to the very high village of Tomorr, half an hour south of which he reported a 'Hellenic fortification'. From this eyrie below the northern peak of Mt. Tomor he descended to the valley of the Osum and followed it through the defile above Berat to reach the castle, which is the site of Antipatrea[2], in some five hours from Tomorr.

[1] Leake 1. 335.

[2] Its magnificent situation commanding the gorge of the Osum is described by Leake 1. 360 f., and its identification with Antipatrea, 'in faucibus angustis sitam urbem' (Livy 31. 27. 2), is certain. See T. S. Hughes, *Travels in Sicily, Greece and Albania* (London, 1820) 2. 383; C. Patsch, *Sandschak von Berat* (Vienna, 1904) 125 f., and for the remains of the ancient walls see *SA* 1964. 1. 184.

The army of Sulpicius, with cavalry and elephants, will have taken the longer but easier and also more populated route through the district of Gramsh.[1] In the previous autumn his camp had been on the Apsus near Kuç, and he had captured and destroyed Antipatrea, killing all adult males, and he had then placed a garrison in Codrion, which had capitulated. A fortified site, Kalaja Rrmait near Mirakë, which guards the entry into the district of Gramsh, is probably to be identified with Codrion.[2] In 199 B.C. he marched through Codrion and took the less difficult route to the basin of Koritsa, where he camped at its north end by the river Bevus (the Molca, see pp. 61 ff. above).

Later in the same year he crossed from Celetrum in Orestis to the territory of the Dassaretii, that is over the low ridge by Vatokhorion, and captured by storm a city called Pelium. He left a strong garrison in this city because it was conveniently placed for making attacks into Macedonia (nam et sita opportune urbs erat ad impetus in Macedoniam faciendos, Livy 31. 40. 5). It is clear that Sulpicius had not already passed Pelium, a strong place held by Macedonians, on his way through Dassaretis to reach the basin of Kastoria and encamp near the river Bevus. Therefore Pelium was not on the west side of the basin of Koritsa but between that basin and the low ridge by Vatokhorion. This is also obvious from the fact that, wherever one is in the basin of Koritsa, one cannot deliver attacks on Macedonia unless one holds the Tsangon pass. It is then probable that Pelium lay either at the pass or to the south-east of it.[3]

When Alexander heard in 335 B.C. that Cleitus had captured Pelium and that Glaucias the Taulantian king was on the way to join Cleitus or had already done so (Arr. *Anab.* 1. 5. 1 and 5), he came from the direction of Paeonia along the Erigon (the Cerna) and marched for Pelium. He came, that is, through the Monastir gap, marched via Florina over the pass, went down the Haliacmon and up over the low ridge into the basin which contains the headwaters of the Devoli. He was now in Illyria (Arr. 1. 10. 3; Plu. *Alex.* 11. 3; D.S. 17. 8. 1). The purpose of Cleitus, the king of the Dardanians, and of Glaucias, the king of the Taulantians, whose capital was in the vicinity of Tiranë,[4] had been to invade and devastate Macedonia in the absence of Alexander and the Macedonian field-army. The Dardanians had come down the corridor from

---

[1] For these operations see my article in *JRS* 56 (1966) 42 f. For Kalaja Rrmait see *Riv. d. Alb.* 3. 157 and *BUST* 1963. 4. 3 ff. with illustrations of the walls; its excavators, F. Prendi and D. Budina, identify it with Codrion.

[2] This route was blocked by the Greek line in the winter of 1940–1, running from Pogradec to Grabovë-e-Krishterevë, which commands the pass of Moglicë, and then from Grabovë to Dobrenj on the Tomorricë, cutting through Leake's route, and then southwards to Fratar just east of Këlcyrë. See A. Papagos, *The Battle of Greece, 1940–1941* (Athens, 1949) 290.

[3] A. J. B. Wace in *BSA* 18 (1911–12) 168 put it 'probably near the Vlach village of Pliasa' on the east side of the plain of Koritsa, just south-west of the entry to the Tsangon pass.

[4] For the kingdoms of Cleitus and Glaucias see my article in *BSA* 61 (1966) 243 f.

the north and were awaiting the arrival of the Illyrians. Pelium was a good rendezvous. It was also an important place to hold, in order to keep the line of withdrawal open after a successful raid. Their aim was in fact to do what the Dardanians did later, in 208 B.C., when they came through by Lychnidus and entered Orestis (Livy 27. 32. 9–33. 1). But Alexander anticipated them and caught Cleitus alone at Pelium. He camped by the Eordaicus, that is the Devoli, and confined the enemy within the city.

Next day Glaucias arrived with a large force. The tables were turned on Alexander. He could no longer attack the city. The Illyrians held the hillsides. They endangered his cavalry and his baggage animals when they went to be watered and to get pasture in the plain, i.e. in the small plain of Poloskë; and they could make it impossible to graze the horses at night. He managed to rescue the baggage animals when they were attacked on that day. But his position was untenable, and he had to withdraw in the face of superior numbers holding the hills with light cavalry, javelin-men, slingers, and some heavy infantry. His own strength lay in his heavy cavalry and in his phalanx. As Arrian puts it: 'they seemed to have cut off Alexander on difficult ground' (1. 5. 11). It follows, I think, that Alexander was cut off from withdrawing into Macedonia over the pass by which he had come. Pelium then was on the east side of the small plain of Poloskë, the Illyrians held the hillsides leading to the pass of Vatokhorion, and Alexander, being able to fight his way out best on level ground, had to withdraw through the Tsangon pass into the wide plain of Koritsa, where his army could obtain pasture and supplies and his heavy cavalry could keep the Dardanians and the Illyrians at bay.[1]

Arrian's description of the narrows through which Alexander had to withdraw (1. 5. 12) fits the Tsangon pass admirably. 'These narrows were on the one hand confined by the river; on the other hand the mountain was very high, and there were cliffs on the side of the mountain; so that the army could not pass through even four abreast.' It is probable that the very high mountain is that which Leake described on the north side of the pass, namely Mt. That, and that the narrowest point was where the river itself had to be crossed. At this stage of its course the Devoli could still be forded and Alexander's archers could fire standing in it, but I doubt if that would have been possible below the outlet from Lake Malik. It would seem then that Pelium should be sought on the eastern hillsides of the plain of Poloskë.[2]

---

[1] W. W. Tarn, *Alexander the Great* (Cambridge, 1948) 1. 6, 'Alexander was not strong enough to fight on two fronts', seems to think Alexander lay between the army of Glaucias and that of Cleitus, but Arrian's narrative makes it clear that they had combined and were holding the heights as well as the town (1. 5. 11).

[2] If Pelium is placed on the side of the plain of Koritsa, the following difficulties arise. The plain is 35 km long and 15 km wide at the middle, so that the enemy could not have held τὰ

The route from the Myzeqijë plain through Dassaretis into Macedonia was used later by the Romans, when Philip V met the Roman commander Baebius, based on Apollonia (Livy 35. 24. 7), in Dassaretis and their joint forces moved south into Thessaly (Livy 36. 10. 10 and 13. 1). When the Normans advanced from Dyrrachium, the emperor Alexis occupied the area north of the Tsangon pass in order to prevent their passage into Macedonia (Anna Comnena, *Alex*. 5. 13). The route from Epirus to Kastoria and so northwards to Lychnidus or eastwards to Macedonia presents no serious difficulties, once the river Aous has been crossed at Mesoyefira; one climbs up to Leskoviq and then winds round spurs and across ravines to enter the small but fertile basin of Ersekë, from which one crosses Mt. Lofka by the pass of Qarrë and descends into the plain of Kastoria. This pass marked the frontier between Dassaretis and Parauaea. There are also lesser routes from Ersekë leading through Mt. Grammos, e.g. by Grammos village, into Orestis. The army of the First Crusade, which had wintered in the Drin valley of Epirus, probably took the main route via Leskoviq and Koritsa to Kastoria, and then went on into Pelagonia and down to the Vardar at Stobi (*Gesta Francorum* 1. 3). It was used in reverse by Dardanians under Bardylis, and probably by Perseus in 170 B.C. when he was at first unable to cross the Aous (Plb. 27. 16. 3).[1]

2. *Lyncus*

Lyncus is a relatively small canton (see Map 8). On the west it is bounded by the Peristeri range and Mt. Vitsi, between which the pass of Pisodherion leads into Dassaretis; on the north by the open plain between Mt. Peristeri and the outliers of Mt. Barnous; on the east by a ridge running down from Mt. Barnous;[2] and on the south by a ridge running down eastwards from Mt. Vitsi and continuing in the Mala Reka, through which the Kirli Dirven pass leads into Eordaea. The plain of Lyncus is very well watered by the numerous southern tributaries of the Cerna which rise in the surrounding mountains, and the mountains provide good pasture and timber, especially Mt. Vitsi. Within the canton, as I

κύκλῳ ὄρη τοῦ πεδίου (Arr. 1. 5. 9); Alexander has to withdraw on to more favourable level ground, in order to avoid attacks from the cavalry and light-armed infantry and graze his horses, and he has to be within range of a night-attack on the enemy camp, but there is no such level area outside the Koritsa plain itself; and there is no outlet from the Koritsa plain, other than the Tsangon pass, which combines a river and a narrow pass except that west of Lake Malik leading into a maze of mountains and defiles.

[1] I have described this route in *Epirus* 275 (see map 12 on p. 259); and for Perseus see *Epirus* 280.

[2] To the east of Vevi (Banitsa), where the intoxicating mineral waters of Arist. *Meteor*. 2. 3 and other authors περὶ Λύγκον, are to be found (Leake 3. 318).

have described it, there appears never to have been a town of any considerable size in antiquity. As we have seen (p. 85 above), an inscription shows that in the second century A.D. the Lyncestae were still a tribal state, τὸ Λυγκηστῶν ἔθνος, and we may imagine that they still lived in the *komai* or villages (τὰς τοῦ Ἀρραβαίου κώμας) which were the only objectives left to Perdiccas to destroy, when the defeated Lyncestae took to the heights (Thuc. 4. 124. 4).[1] The excavation conducted by Keramopoullos near Florina, the largest town of the canton today, tends to confirm this; for the site proved to have been a village without a walled enceinte.[2] The contrast with the neighbouring cantons of Derriopus and Pelagonia is at first sight surprising.[3]

Despite its small size and lack of towns 'the Lyncestae' were by far the strongest tribal state in these parts in the second half at least of the fifth century. Their strength is associated with the establishment of a royal house *c.* 450 B.C.,[4] which was not native to Lyncus but claimed descent from the Bacchiadae, the clan which had ruled at Corinth until their expulsion *c.* 657 B.C., when they established themselves in Corcyra. It is probable that the Bacchiadae now in question had become dynasts in Illyria and that they imposed themselves on the Lyncestae, either by force of conquest[5] or by a dynastic marriage, rather as the Illyrian Perisadyes may have amalgamated with the royal house of the Encheleae (see p. 93 above). For we can best explain the great strength of the Lyncestae at this period if Arrhabaeus ruled not only over Lyncus but also over the area of Resen or Ochrid, so that the territory of Lyncus went up to Monastir and the Diavat pass. Some supposition of the kind is needed to account for the fact that Arrhabaeus was able to face the army of Perdiccas supported by the troops of Brasidas and by Brasidas'

---

[1] οἱ δὲ λοιποὶ διαφυγόντες πρὸς τὰ μετέωρα ἡσύχαζον. . . . ὁ Περδίκκας ἐβούλετο προϊέναι ἐπὶ τὰς τοῦ Ἀρραβαίου κώμας. The royal seat may well have been in a *kome*, but the expression here probably means 'the villages of Arrhabaeus' realm', as Thucydides uses ἡ Ἀρραβαίου for his territory (4. 124. 2 and 127. 2).

[2] *PAE* 1931. 55 f.

[3] Attempts have been made to find a city in Lyncus. Heraclea was held by Keramopoullos to have been at his site near Florina, but this is ruled out by the evidence of the Itineraries alone. St. Byz., Λύγκος· πόλις Ἠπείρου. Στράβων ἑβδόμῃ, is clearly a misunderstanding of Str. 7 C 326 fin. τὰ περὶ Λύγκον (Meineke for Λυγκηστόν), and little faith can be put in Hesychius 996. 13 (ed. Ritschl)? Λυγκαίη· πόλις Μακεδονίας. The *argumentum ex silentio* is fairly strong because the Via Egnatia and numerous armies of which historians have left their accounts passed through Lyncus.

[4] For the approximate date see my account of the stemma of the Lyncestid house in *BSA* 61 (1966) 243.

[5] If the reference in Thuc. 4. 126. 2 is specifically intended to apply to Arrhabaeus, he gained his position in Lyncus by force of arms (τῷ μαχόμενοι κρατεῖν). For I agree here with the view of A. W. Gomme, *A Historical Commentary on Thucydides* (Oxford, 1956) 3. 614, that Brasidas is alluding to the enemy in saying that the few command the many, when they have acquired τὴν δυναστείαν. It may well describe what Arrhabaeus had done, since Thucydides is likely to have known the origins of his position.

Chalcidian allies, that he disposed of comparable forces of cavalry and of hoplite infantry, and that the Illyrians who came up joined him and not Perdiccas.

The two adventures of Brasidas in this region enable us to see that the Kirli Dirven pass was ἡ ἐσβολὴ τῆς Λύγκου. On the first occasion, when he was ἐπὶ τῇ ἐσβολῇ τῆς Λύγκου, i.e. before invading the territory of Arrhabaeus, Brasidas came to terms with him (Thuc. 4. 83. 2). On the second occasion Perdiccas, Brasidas, and the Chalcidians entered Lyncus unopposed with 3,000 Greek hoplites, almost 1,000 cavalry and the full force of Macedonian infantry, and in the ensuing battle in a plain between two hills, where Arrhabaeus offered battle, they defeated the Lyncestae but did not pursue them on to high ground. When the Illyrians arrived and joined Arrhabaeus, and when the Macedonians fled during the night, Brasidas withdrew in good order across the plain, but the main force of Arrhabaeus rushed ahead to occupy τὴν ἐσβολήν, ἥ ἐστι μεταξὺ δυοῖν λόφοιν στενὴ ἐς τὴν Ἀρραβαίου, . . . εἰδότες οὐκ οὖσαν ἄλλην τῷ Βρασίδᾳ ἀναχώρησιν (4. 127. 2).[1] On approaching the entry to the pass Brasidas kept moving. He had given orders in advance to his special corps of 300 men to charge up the ridge on one side of the pass and dislodge the enemy. This they did at full speed, capturing the top of the ridge; meanwhile the main body was fighting its way up after them, and when they too reached the ridge the whole force began to move along the high ground (τῶν μετεώρων 4. 128. 3), parallel to the pass and above the enemy.[2] By this brilliant move, the initial charge and capture of the ridge being very similar to the tactic of Alexander at the Tsangon pass (Arr. Anab. 1. 6. 5), Brasidas escaped encirclement and destruction. The enemy no longer pursued him; for they had lost their

---

[1] C. F. Edson in CP 46 (1951) 4 and n. 29 showed that the one route of entry and exit from Lyncus was the Kirli Dirven pass. Gomme, op. cit. 617, recognizes the weight of Edson's judgement but expresses some doubts in favour of the route taken by the modern road. It is clear from the narrative of Thucydides that Thucydides believed there to be only one route and that this route was used first up to the border of Lyncus (4. 83. 2), then in invading the territory of Arrhabaeus, which at this point at any rate was Lyncus (4. 124. 1 and 2), and finally in retreating to the pass which led into (and out of) the territory of Arrhabaeus (4. 127. 2). On the first occasion the army is likely to have taken the route which offers pasture and supplies, i.e. to the south of the lakes as they then were (see p. 54 above). On the last occasion Brasidas had to keep as much as possible ἐν τῇ εὐρυχωρίᾳ (4. 127. 2), and he did so by taking the Kirli Dirven pass, beyond which he was again on flat ground south of the lakes. If he had followed the route of the modern road, as Gomme thinks possible, Brasidas would have gone into the defiles of the mountains and been at the mercy of the light-armed Illyrians.

[2] This tactic was particularly appropriate to the Kirli Dirven pass, which, as Gomme loc. cit. says, is a 'narrow, though not lofty, pass'. Edson loc. cit. remarks that 'Thucydides 4. 127. 2 precisely describes the western exit from the defile'. Coming from Lyncus, Brasidas did not enter the defile at all, or rather the pass which becomes a defile; he kept on the high ground instead. I have translated λόφος as 'ridge' rather than 'hill' which suggests (to me) an isolated hill; Livy 31. 39. 14 has the appropriate translation of Polybius in his 'in iugum collis', which describes the same place more or less as Thucydides was describing.

chance and Brasidas was already at the border (4. 128. 2 νομίζοντες καὶ ἐν μεθορίοις εἶναι αὐτοὺς ἤδη καὶ διαπεφευγέναι).

A similar situation faced Sulpicius and his Illyrian and Dardanian allies in 199 B.C., when Philip V slipped ahead and fortified the pass from Lyncus into Eordaea (see p. 71 above). Then the pass itself was wooded, and there was abundant timber in the vicinity (Livy 31. 39. 10, erant pleraeque silvestria circa). A Roman force with their shields locked together in a 'testudo' formation delivered a frontal attack down the entry of the pass; at the same time another force which had reached the ridge on one side by a circuitous route drove the Macedonians from their strongposts. Thus the pass of Kirli Dirven was carried with less of a struggle than had been anticipated by the Romans. In a speech attributed to Flamininus by Polybius (18. 23. 3; cf. Livy 33. 8. 5) the Romans are praised for driving the Macedonians from the high ground at the pass leading into Eordaea; for it was the turning movement that was decisive and not the frontal attack.

Both these operations are easily envisaged when one travels through Lyncus and the Kirli Dirven pass. The plain east of Florina is at first mainly level; then ridges develop to the south-west and the north-east, and these make gently rolling country. As one approaches the head of the Kirli Dirven pass, the plain narrows. The road through the pass follows a narrow, winding, and waterless coomb between steep hills. The Lyncus end of the pass is appreciably higher than the Eordaea end, and as one descends towards Eordaea the hills on either side become higher in relation to the road. As one enters the pass from the Lyncus plain, there is on either side of the road a ridge thinly covered with maquis. The top of the right-hand ridge (on the west side) is some 250 feet above the level of the road within the pass; but if one ascends the ridge from the Lyncus plain, the ascent is less high and not particularly steep, although rough. The top of the ridge is fairly level, narrow, and straight, and if one follows the line of the top one cuts across the curving bend of the road in the pass below. In other words, the line of the ridge-top in relation to the curve of the road is roughly that of a diameter to a semicircle. On the other hand, the left-hand ridge (on the east side) runs on the outer side of the bend and its top is longer than that of the right-hand ridge. It is thus likely that Brasidas captured the right-hand ridge at the entry to the pass, and that his men followed the hills on the west of the pass, presenting their shielded side to any attack launched from the road below. On the other hand, the Romans delivering a frontal attack down the coomb were stopped by the Macedonians, who held fortified positions within the coomb and on its steep sides. The Roman turning force which reached the ridge lower down the pass must have been unseen by the Macedonians during its march. It probably took a route east of the pass and near Lake Petres.

3. Eordaea

Though Thucydides calls it Eordia, other writers give Eordaea.[1] It is bounded on the north by Mt. Barnous; on the west by the watershed towards Lyncus; on the east by Mt. Bermium; and on the SSW. by the watershed of the Haliacmon river. This canton is entirely ringed round by mountains and hills, and the only drainage is by underground swallets. The levels of the three considerable lakes and the two small lakes which it contains vary with the clearing and the blocking of the swallets, as we have seen especially in the case of Lake Ostrovo, which was much smaller in antiquity (see p. 54 above). The passes which lead out of Eordaea are those of Kirli Dirven to the west and of Kara Burun to the east, both used by the Via Egnatia (see p. 51 above); a wide passage east of Kozani from the marshy plain of Sarigol over a long low saddle into the Haliacmon valley (see Map 11); a narrow defile, called the Klisoura of Siatista, leading again into the Haliacmon valley; and a short but steep pass over the southern end of Mt. Vitsi via Klisoura village to Lake Kastoria. The land around the lakes and in the small plains is very fertile and excellent cereals are grown round Ptolemaïdha and in the Sarigol. It is potentially a powerful canton, but there is little mention of it in our literary sources and few inscriptions have been found in it.

Of the three known towns we have already determined the position of Cellis and Bokeria (see pp. 51ff. above). Arnisa was reached by Brasidas on the day of his withdrawal from Lyncus over the Kirli Dirven pass, and it was the first place he came to in the kingdom of Perdiccas (Thuc. 4. 128. 3, αὐθημερὸν ἀφικνεῖται ἐς Ἄρνισαν πρῶτον τῆς Περδίκκου ἀρχῆς). Leake placed Arnisa 'in the vale of Ostrovo',[2] and others have identified Arnisa with Ostrovo itself, which is now officially 'Arnissa'. This identification is not compatible with Thucydides' description of the campaign which ended with Brasidas' arrival at Arnisa.

An essential feature of the flight of the Macedonians was that it began immediately after nightfall (Thuc. 4. 125. 1, νυκτός τ᾽ ἐπιγενομένης . . . εὐθὺς . . . ἐχώρουν ἐπ᾽ οἴκου). It was midday at least when the main force of Arrhabaeus went ahead to occupy the pass of Kirli Dirven and caught up with the tail-end of the fleeing Macedonians (τοὺς φεύγοντας τῶν Μακεδόνων, 4. 127. 2). In the afternoon Brasidas' troops, having got into Eordaea, seized some ox-drawn wagons (ζεύγεσιν . . . βοεικοῖς) which the fleeing Macedonians were using on the road. Such a wagon travels at some 2 miles an hour,[3] and the oxen had been at it off and on for some

---

[1] Thuc. 2. 99. 5; Eordaea in Plb. 18. 23. 3 and St. Byz. s.v. for instance. 'Ordaea' occurs in St. Byz. as a separate entry and in some manuscripts of Pliny *HN* 4. 34.

[2] Leake 3. 315; *RE* 3. 1 (1897) 315.

[3] In 1941, when the Greek troops stationed at Florina retreated in some haste to the Kirli Dirven pass after hearing of the German approach towards the Monastir gap, some of them

eighteen hours. As the Macedonians were fleeing for their lives, we can hardly suppose that in this length of time they had covered less than 30 miles. With this yardstick to apply we can fix the approximate position of the battle which had occurred some days earlier.

Perdiccas and Brasidas, having entered Lyncus unopposed, must have advanced across the wide plain, hoping to join hands with the expected Illyrians, ἀνθρώπων μαχίμων (4. 125. 1), and destroy the Lyncestae (see Map 8). But Arrhabaeus had already chosen a position in which to offer battle. His infantry occupied a hill (or ridge) above flat ground, beyond which was another hill (or ridge), and after the battle his infantry got on to high ground immediately without being pursued (4. 124. 3 ἐχόντων τῶν μὲν πεζῶν λόφον ἑκατέρωθεν, πεδίου δὲ τοῦ μέσου ὄντος . . . πρὸς τὰ μετέωρα). Such a place is to be found not in the central part of the plain of Lyncus, which is more or less flat, but on the west side or the east side of the plain, where the mountains rise fairly sharply. The choice between the west side and the east side is determined by the coming of the Illyrians, which was not seen by Perdiccas and Brasidas, and resulted in their joining Arrhabaeus. In other words, the Illyrians did not cross the open plain to reach Arrhabaeus on its east side. Arrhabaeus then was on the west side of the plain. Now the Illyrians were to be expected from the north-west, and the aim of Arrhabaeus must have been to place himself between the Illyrians and Perdiccas.[1] The pass which the Illyrians might be expected to use, and which in fact they probably did use in coming unobserved by Perdiccas and Brasidas, was the pass of Diavat (see p. 42 above). I take it then that Arrhabaeus held a position on the rising ground just north-west of Monastir at the entrance to the valley which leads up to the Diavat pass (see Map 6). After the action he stayed on higher ground perhaps further up the valley and nearer the pass. When he heard of the approach of the Illyrians, he was able by virtue of his position to offer them either a battle in the pass or employment and pay in his own service. They chose the latter.

Meanwhile Perdiccas and Brasidas, sitting in the plain near Monastir, had begun quarrelling again. Perdiccas wanted to go forward to the villages of Arrhabaeus (προϊέναι ἐπὶ τὰς τοῦ Ἀρραβαίου κώμας)[2]—as we might say to his capital—which must have lain in what we have called Derriopus. Brasidas wanted to retreat, particularly as the Illyrians were

were using ox-drawn wagons, as I noted at the time. I have also ridden on one after an all-night operation in Pieria; it was very slow and comfortless.

[1] Philip V was later faced by the same problem of placing himself between the Illyrians and the Romans (see p. 64 above).

[2] The distinction should be observed between ἡ Ἀρραβαίου sc. γῆ at 4. 127. 2 and this phrase. We have noted that there were *komai* in Derriopus (see p. 89 above); there were also *komai* in Atintanis (Polyaen. 4. 11. 4); and a 'komarchon' in or near Lychnidus (*Spomenik* 71 (1931) no. 265). His capital may have been in either district, but, if I am right in my siting of the battle, Perdiccas meant to go northwards into Derriopus in the first instance.

not turning up. When they did, panic ensued among the Macedonians and Brasidas was faced at dawn with a situation from which he extricated himself only by superb leadership and tactical skill. He had 27 Roman miles to cover across the plain from the site of the later Heraclea to the 'Grande' of the Via Egnatia in the Kirli Dirven pass (see p. 51 above). Moving in a square formation with the light-armed in the centre and fighting a rearguard action with his special corps, he must have taken nine or ten hours to reach the pass and another hour to get through it on to level Eordaean soil. It is unreasonable to suppose that that very same day (αὐθημερόν) he marched his men to Ostrovo, a matter of another 20-odd Roman miles.[1]

Arnisa, then, must be placed close to the Eordaean frontier at the Kirli Dirven pass, not on the road but either at Sotir or at Petres. I have chosen the latter as a probable identification (see Map 7).[2] The name is recorded in this form only by Thucydides. Two mentions of it are probably concealed in the corrupt form Larissa. The first is in Hierocles, *Synecdemus* 638. 11, where the list of places runs in the general direction of the Via Egnatia from east to west: Edessa, Kellae, Almopia, Larissa, Heraclea Lyncou. Apart from the tribal district Almopia, which is off the road, we have stations on or near the Via Egnatia. The emendation of Larissa to Arnissa, proposed by Tomaschek, should therefore be accepted.[3] The other mention seems to have escaped emendation.[4] Jordanes, *Getica* 56. 286, describing the Gothic invasion under Thiudimer and Theodoric, who had captured Naissus, Ulpiana, and Stobi, says that from Stobi Theodoric captured some inaccessible places of Illyricum and then took and occupied by right of war 'Eracleam et Larissam civitates Thessaliae'. At this stage Thiudimer the king came from Naissus (Niš) to Thessalonica, but finding its defences strong he came to terms with the Roman governor, who gave the Goths places to inhabit, namely 'Cerru, Pellas, Europa, Mediana, Petina, Bereu et alia quae Sium vocatur'.[5]

---

[1] The word αὐθημερόν, reminding us of ἅμα τῇ ἕῳ at 125. 2, underlines this remarkable feat of arms. Thucydides had to be selective in the military episodes he chose to describe. He included this one as an example of Brasidas' professional skill, meriting the inclusion of a speech underlining the value of disciplined courage; moreover, it involved μέρος τι τῶν βαρβάρων (1. 1. 2), and eyewitnesses were available to him soon after the event. He wrote it up for the history of the Archidamian War, which I think he completed before the end of the Peace of Nicias (I give reasons in *CQ* 34 (1940) 146 f.).

[2] The water of a lake has an almost irresistible attraction for footsore troops, when the heat of the day is over.

[3] In *Ztschr. f. oesterr. Gymn.* 18 (1867) 717, cited by E. Honigmann ad loc.

[4] At least in the standard edition by Mommsen in Monumenta Germaniae Historica 5 (1882) 132. The attempt by C. Müller and Tomaschek to transfer Ptolemy 3. 13. 20 Ταυλαν-τίων· Ἄρνισσα to the Eordaean Arnissa is totally misplaced (*RE* 2. 1 (1895) 1206).

[5] For Bereu compare Berua in an inscription from Scupi (*ŽA* 6 (1956) 402). The same group of names appears with variations of forms in the Ravenna Geographer 197. 1–6 as a group of cities not far from Thessalonica: Ceras, Europa, Mediana, Petina, Bireum,

Shortly afterwards Thiudimer died 'in civitate Cerras'. It is clear from this account that Theodoric did not go into Thessaly but that, having acquired Heraclea and 'Larissa', that is Arnisa, by right of war, and having threatened Thessalonica, Thiudimer was given territory which he had already traversed to the east of Arnisa : Cerru = Cyrrus, Pellas = Pella, Europa = Europus (north-east of Pella), Mediana = Methone, Petina = Pydna, Bereu = Beroea and Sium = Dium.

The inhabitants of this canton called themselves Eordi. They formed a tribal state. Thus Str. C 323 using Polybius describes the Via Egnatia as passing through the Eordi (διὰ Ἡρακλείας καὶ Λυγκηστῶν καὶ Ἐορδῶν εἰς Ἔδεσσαν) and he describes the district by the tribe in C 326 (Λυγκησταί τε καὶ ἡ Δερρίοπος καὶ ἡ τριπολῖτις Πελαγονία καὶ Ἐορδοί). They are not, however, in his list of Epirotic tribes at C 434, and this is in accordance with Thucydides' implication that the Macedonians repeopled this district, from which they had expelled the remnants of the original Eordi (2. 99. 5). The tribal district was called ἡ Ἐορδαία (Plb. 18. 23. 3). Dimitsas and others[1] have thought that there was a city Eordaea, which was the capital of the canton, but in each case the name seems to be that of the tribal district. Thus in Hierocles, *Synecdemus* we have names of districts : Eordaea, Almopia, and Pelagonia; and Constantine Porphyrogenitus, who goes back to the same original source, gives Berroea, Ἐορδαῖοι, Edessa (*Them.* 2. 49). Pliny *HN* 4. 34 has Scydra, (E)ordaea, Mieza, and *HN* 4. 35 ab hoc amne (sc. Axio) Paeoniae gentes, Paraxiaei, Eordenses, Almopi; but Pliny is referring probably to a tribe and a place near the Axius and not to the present canton (see p. 164 below).

Although it is historically an obscure canton, it contained the important royal Macedonian road, which later became the Via Egnatia, and two branches from it leading southwards, one through the pass of Siatista to Grevena, whence routes radiate into Epirus and Thessaly, the other through the Sarigol to Servia, whence one proceeds over the pass of Volustana into Perrhaebia and Thessaly. When Alexander marched from the vicinity of Pelium (see p. 101 above) 'along Eordaea, Elimiotis and the high ground of Tymphaea and Perrhaebia'[2] to Pelinna in Thessaly on his way to Thebes, he went probably via south Eordaea through the Siatista gap into Elimiotis, up to Grevena and then via Mavreli and Dheskati, where the ridge belonged in part to Tymphaea and in part to

Quesium. He seems to have taken this group from Jordanes, omitting Pellas and reading 'quae Sium' as 'Quesium'.

[1] Dimitsas 1. 243 and Oberhummer in *RE* 5. 2 (1905) 2656.

[2] Arr. *Anab.* 1. 7. 5 ἄγων δὴ παρὰ τὴν Ἐορδαίαν τε καὶ τὴν Ἐλιμιῶτιν καὶ παρὰ τὰ τῆς Στυμφαίας καὶ Παραυαίας ἄκρα. Here ΠΑΡΑΥΑΙΑΣ has to be emended to ΠΕΡΑΙΒΙΑΣ in order to make sense, as Parauaea is west of Pindus (see Hammond, *Epirus* 679 f.). The route through Mavreli and Dheskati is along the ridge of the mountain range, which belonged in part to Tymphaea and in part to Perrhaebia.

Perrhaebia, and so came down to Pelinna. When Perseus marched with the full Macedonian army from Lake Bekoritis into 'Elimea by the river Haliacmon' in one day (Livy 42. 53. 5), he passed over the low saddle below the Sarigol, and took the Volustana pass into the Perrhaebian Tripolitis. In the Roman partition of Macedonia, the Eordaei were allotted to the fourth tetrarchy (Livy 45. 30. 6), which comprised the cantons west of Mt. Bermium.

4. *Orestis*

The canton of Orestis is set in the upper valley of the Haliacmon river (see Maps 6 and 11). Near the river's source the pass of Vatokhorion leads into Dassaretis and the pass of Pisodherion leads into Lyncus (see p. 99 above). A little further downstream the river is joined by the tributary which flows from the large Lake of Kastoria. At this latitude there is the pass by Klisoura village into Eordaea on the east (see p. 106 above), and there are two routes towards the west, running beside the valley of a long tributary which rises on Mt. Grammos; the one on the northern side passes through Nestorion (Nestram) and round the northern end of Mt. Grammos into the plain of Ersekë, belonging to Parauaea (see p. 102 above), and the other on the southern side passes round the southern end of Mt. Grammos via Kotili and Khrisi to Konitsa in Molossis.[1] The journey along the latter route took me 20½ hours of walking in fine July weather, and its particular value is that it usually remains open during the winter, unlike most passes over the Grammos–Pindus range. It was probably used by Perseus in 170 B.C. when he attempted to kidnap a Roman consul.[2] The limit of Orestis downstream is set by the march of Alexander when he passed from Eordaea to Elimiotis through the pass of Siatista (see p. 109 above). The probable boundary just north of the exit of this pass is set by the watershed between the Pramoritsa river and the Grevenitikos river. The most fertile land in the canton is round Lake Kastoria and in the wide valley by and below the lake, but the greater part of the canton lies on the long and fertile ridges which run down from the heights of Mt. Grammos and north-east Pindus. In Turkish times these ridges carried as many as a hundred villages according to Leake.[3] The canton, then known as Anaselitsa, corresponded fairly closely with the ancient canton of Orestis.

The centre of the canton is in the plain near Kastoria. This plain is evidently the 'Argestaeus campus' of Livy 27. 33. 1, into which the Dardanii descended when they invaded Orestis from Dassaretis in 208 B.C.

[1] See *Epirus* 683.
[2] The route is described in *Epirus* 276, and the attempt of Perseus ibid. 280.
[3] I. 321. He gives an excellent account of the area, pp. 316 ff.

It is from the village of Armenokhorion in this plain that an inscription recording a decision by τὸ κοινὸν Ὀρεστῶν came to Hrupista (now called Argos Orestikon), which is a mile or so to the south of Armenokhorion. In this inscription the tribal state of the Oresti, being analogous to the tribal states of the Pelagones, Derriopes, Lyncestae, and Dassaretii, makes a dedication to a Roman emperor, either Claudius or Nero.[1] The centre at which it met and recorded its decisions is likely to have been Argos Oresticum, which advanced the claim that Orestes, the son of Agamemnon, had held this territory, named it Orestias, and founded the city under the name 'Argos Oresticum'.[2]

The earliest mention of the Orestae is in Hecataeus (*FGrH* 1 F 107 = St. Byz. s.v.) Ὀρέσται· Μολοσσικὸν ἔθνος. Ἑκαταῖος Εὐρώπῃ.[3] Here Hecataeus was distinguishing a Molossian tribe from a Macedonian tribe, and it is probable that the label had political connotations (see p. 439 below). The Orestae appear next in 429 B.C., when 1,000 men served in the expedition against Stratus (Thuc. 2. 80. 6). In the list which Thucydides gives the Orestae come between the Parauaei and the thousand Macedones sent by Perdiccas. They are regarded by Thucydides as an independent state; for at the discretion of their king, Antiochus, their men served with the Parauaean contingent under the Parauaean king, Oroedus. They were not included in the Macedonian state, which Thucydides defined carefully in a later chapter of the same book (2. 99; see p. 436 below). In Thuc. 2. 80. 6 'the Orestae' are a tribal state, ruled by a monarchy which had the right to command and to delegate command of the military forces of the state. At an unknown date the Orestae were absorbed into the Macedonian state, but the tradition of their association with the Molossians and Epirus survived in Strabo's references to them as an Epirotic tribe (7 C 326 and 9 C 434). Their tribal territory was known as Orestis, and they claimed that it had taken the name from Orestes himself or from a like-named son.[4] The tribe was called equally Orestae and Orestoi,[5] and the ethnic Ὀρεστὸς Μολοσός occurs c. 164 B.C. at Dodona (*Ep. Chron.* 1935. 248).

Within the canton of Orestis, as we have defined it, there are two inscriptions which indicate that there were, as we should expect, a number

[1] A. J. B. Wace and A. M. Woodward, *BSA* 18 (1911–12) 179 no. 23 and N. Pappadhakis, *Athena* 25 (1913) 440 no. 27, whcse different reading enables him to attribute the dedication to the Emperor Claudius. See F. Papazoglou in *ŽA* 9 (1959) 163 f.

[2] Str. 7 C 326; Appian *Syr.* 63 Ἄργος τὸ ἐν Ὀρεστείᾳ, ὅθεν οἱ Ἀργεάδαι Μακεδόνες. St. Byz. s.v. *Argos* has Argos Orestion or Argos Orestikon in a corrupt passage.

[3] See *Epirus* 462, resisting the view of F. Jacoby in his commentary that the Orestae lived between Ambracia and Argos Amphilochicum.

[4] Str. 7 C 326 and *FGrH* 774 (Theagenes) F 10. The form Orestias = ἡ Ὀρεστιὰς γῆ is a natural variant, even as one finds Lyncus and Lyncestis. So too Oresteia and Orestia.

[5] For such variants among the Epirotic tribes see *Epirus* 703 and Onomasticon there, p. 811.

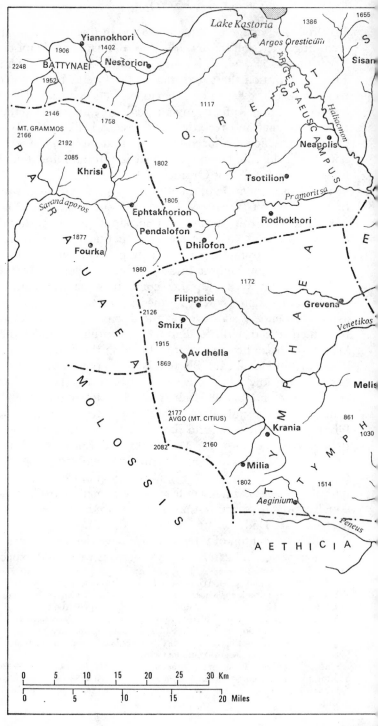

MAP II. SOUTH

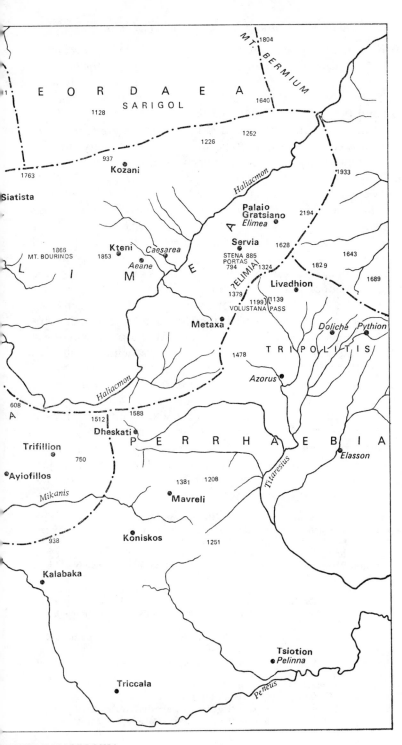

E O R D A E A

SARIGOL

MT. BERMIUM

1804
1640
1128
1252
1226
937
1763
Kozani
1933

Siatista

Haliacmon

Palaio
Gratsiano   2194
Elimea

A

Kteni   Caesarea   Servia   1628
1866   1853   STENA 885   1643
MT. BOURINOS   Aeane   PORTAS   1324   1829
794   1689
L   I   E   PELIMIAI   Livadhion
M   1379   1199)(1139
VOLUSTANA PASS

Metaxa   Doliche   Pythion

1478   T R I P O L I T I S

Haliacmon   Azorus

608
A   1588
1512   Dheskati   P E R R H A E B I A
Trifillion   750   Elasson
Ayiofillos   1381   1208   Titaresius
Mikanis   Mavreli

Koniskos   1251
938

Kalabaka

Tsiotion
Pelinna

Triccala   Peneus

WESTERN MACEDONIA

142943   I

of small tribes, each forming its own state or *polis*. The first was reported by Leake to be in the monastery of Sisanion at the head of the valley of a tributary rising on the east side of the Haliacmon valley. It gives a list of *ephebi* with the names of the officials, the *archon tou gymnasiou* and the *ephebarchon*, and the date by the Macedonian era is probably A.D. 146.[1] The name of the *polis* is not given; and in this valley, as in those west of the upper Axius (p. 88 above), we have to deal not with a city but with a small tribal community. This community was evidently one of those which made up 'the Orestae'. The other inscription, dated to A.D. 143/4 by the era peculiar to Orestis, comes from Dranitsevo, four hours from Kastoria up the river of Nestorion and on the NNE. side of Mt. Grammos.[2] It begins with the words ἐκκλησίας ἀγομένης ὑπὸ τοῦ . . .αττυναίων πολειτάρχου Ἀλεξάνδρου τοῦ Λεωνίδα, who appears again at the end of the inscription as ὁ πολιτάρχης. The convening of the assembly by the politarch is analogous to the convening of the Bouleuterion by the politarchs 'in Derriopos' (see p. 87 above). We are again dealing not with a city[3] in these remote valleys but with a tribal community, an *ethnos* which was able to negotiate with the Roman governor of the province διὰ τῶν πρεσβευτῶν τοῦ ἔθνους (line 32). At the place where the community (ἡ πολιτεία)[4] met, there was an *agora* in which its resolutions were displayed (l. 35). The resolution was concerned with the encroachment by members of the Roman province on the land of the community for pasture, stake-cutting, and passage through it, and it proposed to limit the use of the land to the members of the community except only within the provision made for members of the province by the order of Gentianus and excepting only the Oresti who had fixed the (agreed) price for grazing.[5] Thus we have here a community which is subject to rulings made by the Roman governor; which is in some sense outside the Roman province; and which is distinct from the Oresti.[6]

[1] Leake 1. 318 and inscription no. 3 at the end of the volume. He had it from a copy made by the Bishop of Siatista. Duchesne published it as no. 134 from another copy made by one Sarropoulos. See Dimitsas, who publishes the best version as his no. 216. The date as given by Leake is too early for the Latinized forms of some names.

[2] So on the British version of the Greek map; or perhaps Kranokhori, as given by F. Papazoglou in *ŽA* 9 (1959) 163 and *MG* 350. The best publication of the inscription is by A. M. Woodward in *JHS* 33 (1913) 337 f., from a copy by A. J. B. Wace; other versions are in *Arch. Zeit.* 38 (1880) 159 and Dimitsas no 217; for the date see F. W. Walbank, *Philip* 163 n. 2.   [3] Woodward, for instance, uses the term 'city' in his commentary.

[4] In lines 10 and 30.

[5] Line 22 μόνοις δὲ ἀνεῖσθαι τὴν γῆν τοῖς ἀποτετειμημένοις 'Ορέστοις. It is possible that ἀποτιμᾶσθαι in the middle here has a general meaning rather than the particular one of 'establishing a claim by mortgage', as Woodward ad loc. The word ἀνεῖσθαι is technical to grazing rights (cf. Isoc. 14. 31 and L–S–Jᵒ ἀνίημι ii. 6).

[6] I see no justification in the text for the statement of F. Papazoglou in *ŽA* 9 (1959) 164 n. 4 that the *koinon* of the Oresti is called '*ethnos*' in this inscription line 45. The *ethnos* is the community which passes the resolution; the Oresti are individuals who have acquired a right of pasture. Woodward p. 344 did not perhaps see the distinction clearly either. M. Rostovtzeff

This document might almost have been drawn up today; for it deals with the problems of the mountain villages in letting out summer pastures, permitting the passage of flocks, and the cutting of timber by the shepherds who bring their flocks from the lowland winter pastures, nowadays Vlachs from the Salonica plain and local Greek shepherds from lower down the Haliacmon valley.[1] The name of the community which owned the land was restored by A. M. Woodward as τον ['Eρ]αττυναίων with reference to the Eratyra of Str. C 326. He thought of Eratyra as a city; but Strabo talks of the Epirotic tribes and gives either a tribe or a district in the sentence πρὸς δὲ τούτοις Λυγκησταί τε καὶ ἡ Δερρίοπος καὶ ἡ τρι-πολῖτις Πελαγονία καὶ Ἐορδοὶ καὶ Ἐλίμεια καὶ Ἐράτυρα. As he had already mentioned also the Molossi, the Orestae, and the Tymphaei, we can look for Strabo's Eratyra only in the region between Molossis, Orestis, and Tymphaea, so that the actual position on Mt. Grammos fits the bill precisely. If Strabo's word Eratyra is emended to Eratyna, the ethnic Erattynaei is what we should expect.[2] Tempting as Woodward's restoration is, we must abandon it in favour of the reading made by C. F. Edson and confirmed by others, namely Βαττυναίων, a word otherwise unknown.

Of the sixty-or-so names in the inscription 'a large proportion', as Woodward says, 'are of Greek origin'. A few are foreign: Pleuratus for example, and a probable variant of it in another inscription from the same district, 'Preuradus',[3] and Epicadus are names of Illyrian affinity. The same is true of the ephebic inscription from Sisanion. Thus we find here communities which are Greek in terms of political institutions, nomenclature, and language. These communities, according to the tradition preserved in Strabo, were of Epirotic stock. There seems no reason to reject this tradition, now that we have seen communities of the same kind from the Pelagones in the north through the Derriopi, Lyncestae, and Dassaretii to these tribes which border immediately upon the Parauaei, the Molossi, and the Tymphaei. It is to be noted that these Epirotic tribes straddle the mountainous spine of the Balkan peninsula at latitudes at which villages can be occupied throughout the year. Further north Mt. Scordus presents a great mass of very high and often

---

Social and Economic History of the Roman Empire[2] (Oxford, 1957) 2. 651 sees that the Oresti are 'a third category', but his suggestion that 'the Oresti were members of a tribe attached to the city' is as much out of touch with the geographical situation as his picture of the provincials being 'Roman landowners' on this remote mountain-side. The Gentianus who made the order was active also in the Morihovo; see p. 89, n. 1 above.

[1] See *Epirus* 25 for the hiring of pastures today.

[2] So Mt. Amyron and the Amyraei (Steph. Byz. s.v.). Pappadhakis read [Λ]απιναιων in *Athena* 25 (1913) 462, and C. F. Edson read Βαττυναιων which is supported by Ch. Makaronas in *Mak.* 2 (1944–52) 644. This last reading is adopted by F. Papazoglou in *ZA* 9 (1959) 164 n. 4. Perhaps 'Eratyra' in Strabo is a corruption of 'Batyra'.

[3] From Tshuka, five hours west of Kastoria; Wace and Woodward in *BSA* 18 (1911–12) 180 no. 25.

barren mountain, which cannot be inhabited at all in winter; and further south the Pindus range widens into a broad belt of very high country which again is not habitable in the winter. But as one walks from Orestis into Epirus there is no continuous high ridge or natural frontier which separates the two areas.[1] Villages tend rather to group together. Those of the Battynaei are an example in antiquity, and the Kastanokhoria round Pendalofon are an example today.[2]

Apart from Argos Orestikon the only town certainly known to us in Orestis[3] is Celetrum. In 199 B.C. Sulpicius ravaged Eordaea, then withdrew into Elimea, and thence invading Orestis threatened Celetrum. Livy describes its situation (31. 40. 1–2): 'Oppidum in paene insula situm; lacus moenia cingit; angustis faucibus unum ex continenti iter est.' There is no doubt that this is Kastoria. It was described in very similar terms by Procopius, *Aed.* 4. 3, when Celetrum was called Diocletianoupolis and the lake was called Kastoria, and by Anna Comnena, *Alex.* 6. 1, when the Emperor Alexis laid siege to the place in 1085. The site is likely to have been occupied from the earliest times. It was from Celetrum that Sulpicius proceeded up the Haliacmon valley to cross over the pass of Vatokhorion into Dassaretis (see p. 100 above). Whereas the modern map shows the river of Nestorion as the Haliacmon, Ptolemy gives the river above the latitude of Kastoria as the Haliacmon; for he says it rises in the Candavian mountain range (3. 18. 10). There is the same distinction in Strabo between the Candavian range, which links up with the Illyrian mountains, and the Poïon or Boïon range, which links up with the Greek mountains of Corax and Parnassus. Strabo defines Orestis as a large area in which the Poïon range starts; around it, he says, live the Orestae and the Tymphaei (C 329, fr. 6), and at a river's source lived the Triclari or Triclares, probably a constituent tribe of the Orestae(fr. 20, where there is some confusion; see p. 143 below).

5. *Elimea*

Elimea is bounded, as we have seen, by the general line of the watershed between the Pramoritsa river and the Grevenitikos river (with Siatista belonging to Elimea) on the side of Orestis, and by the pass of Siatista and the low saddle of Sarigol towards Eordaea (see Map 11)

[1] I walked extensively in this area in the latter part of 1943, and crossed the watershed easily and often between Avgerinos and Ephtakhorion, Pendalofon and Zouzouli, and again Dhilofon and Filippaioi.

[2] For these 'chestnut villages', so named from the sweet chestnut (from which they made bread in the war) see *Epirus* 276.

[3] St. Byz. s.v. Ὀρεστία, πόλις ἐν Ὀρέσταις, ἐν ὄρει ὑπερκειμένῳ τῆς Μακεδονικῆς γῆς ἐξ ἧς Πτολεμαῖος ὁ Λάγου. Some suspicion attaches to this, because Arr. *Anab.* 6. 28. 4 says that Ptolemy was an Eordaean, and that Perdiccas came from Orestis. If there was such a city, it may have lain near the village Klisoura.

Down the Haliacmon it is bounded by the great gorge which the Haliacmon cuts as it passes between Mt. Bermium and the Pierian mountains. Its frontiers are in doubt only towards the south, that is towards Perrhaebia and Tymphaea. Here the long range forming the southern watershed of the Haliacmon river was called the 'montes Cambunii' by Livy 42. 53. 6, when he was describing the march of the Macedonian field-army under Perseus through Eordaea and Elimea into the Perrhaebian Tripolitis, consisting of the three towns Azorus, Pythoüs, and Doliche and their territories. As Perseus had no reason to expect resistance, he will have crossed the Cambunian mountains by the easiest pass, that of Volustana, which he held in force two years later (Livy 44. 2. 10 Volustana ipsi vocant).

The climb from Servia on the Macedonian side is steep but fairly short, if one takes the direct route on foot and not the winding motor road.[1] The ascent is at first up a mountain-side of flysch formation, flanked by almost precipitous walls of limestone which face the Haliacmon valley. Passing through the gap between them, which is known as the Stena Portas, one then ascends steeply and reaches the watershed at a point where the ridge is flanked by higher summits of 1379 m and 1324 m. The pass known as the Stena Sarandaporou or the Volustana Pass now begins; for one follows the narrow stream-bed of the Sarandaporos flowing southwards between Mt. Koka (1199 m) and Mt. Vigla (1139 m). If one takes the watershed as the natural frontier between Macedonia and Perrhaebia, then the Macedonian side is eminently defensible at Stena Portas and above it, and the Perrhaebian side is easily defensible at Stena Sarandaporou. If, however, the Macedonians held both Stena Portas and Stena Sarandaporou, they then had a complete stranglehold on the passage from Perrhaebia into Macedonia. On the other hand, the descent from the Stena Sarandaporou into Perrhaebia is gradual and open, as one follows the side of a high tilted plain, deeply scarred by river valleys. Then there are steep climbs and long descents, as one moves across the grain of the country into the flat and elevated plain of Elassona, very similar in appearance to a plain of Upper Macedonia. Leaving the plain and passing through Dhomenikon one enters the valley of the Titaresius, which becomes narrow and defensible at and below Dhamasi. Here a strongly defensible frontier may be drawn between Perrhaebia and the low-lying Thessalian plain.

In determining the boundary between Elimea and the Perrhaebian Tripolitis we are guided by an inscription found and published by A. J. B. Wace and M. S. Thompson. The stone bearing the inscription was in

---

[1] I have walked from Servia to Elassona, and I have also been by bus, which takes a different route via Metaxa. The best maps are the Greek Staff Map, 1:100,000, sheets E6 (Kozani) and Z6 (Trikkala).

a ruined church of Ayia Triadha about half-way down from the head of the pass to Elassona and in the middle of the tilted plain. It records the judgement of an arbitrator appointed by the Emperor Trajan in A.D. 101 to settle a dispute between the Dolichani and the Elemiotae, and it orders the disputants to abide by the royal ruling made by Amyntas, the father of Philip, and recorded on a stele in the forum of the Dolichani ('definitioni regiae factae ab Amynta Philippi patr⟨a⟩e').[1] We may accept the identifications made by Leake[2] and by Wace of Doliche with Kastri (now Dolikhi), of Azorus with Vouvala, and of Pythium with Selos (now Pithion). The details of the royal ruling provided for the division of a plain called Pronom[ae] between the disputants, but it is uncertain whether this plain is that round the village of Metaxa, as Wace suggests, or the part of the sloping plain south-west of Livadhion which would secure to Macedon the land south of the narrow gate of the Volustana pass. Apart from this plain the frontier is defined as running 'per summa iuga', that is along the watershed between the Haliacmon river and the Sarandaporos river, the ancient Titaresius, which is a tributary of the Peneus. At one time at least in the third century Macedonia annexed the Perrhaebian Tripolitis, to judge from the definition of a *proxenus* at Delphi as Μακεδὼν Ἐλειμιώτης ἐκ Πυθείου (*BCH* 2 (1897) 112).

We have already mentioned the march of Alexander from Pelium in Dassaretis to Pelinna in Thessaly (p. 109 above): ἄγων δὴ παρὰ τὴν Ἐορδαίαν τε καὶ τὴν Ἐλιμιῶτιν καὶ παρὰ τὰ τῆς Στυμφαίας καὶ Περαιβίας (for MS. Παραναίας) ἄκρα ἑβδομαῖος ἀφικνεῖται εἰς Πέλινναν τῆς Θετταλίας. Tymphaea, a canton of Epirus, lay on the east side of north Pindus and must have included areas habitable in winter, that is well below the level of Smixi and Avdhella (see Map 11).[3] The present-day centre of this area is Grevena, and it is therefore likely to have been within Tymphaea. The watershed formed by the Cambunian mountains provides a good route from Grevena through Melissi and Trifillion to Dheskati, and I imagine that Alexander used this route, passing from Tymphaean into Perrhaebian territory just west of Dheskati, and then came down by the tributary of the Titaresius and over the last hills to Pelinna near Tsiotion.[4] If he had aimed to enter Thessaly at Kalabaka and go on to Tricca, he would have taken the direct route from Grevena to Khani Murgani in some twelve hours.

[1] The inscription is published in *BSA* 17 (1910–11) 193 f. It was cut on a stele by someone whose knowledge of Latin was sketchy, and his spelling even of 'Elemiotae' is not necessarily correct.

[2] Leake 3. 341 f.

[3] For Tymphaea see *Epirus* 680 f. For the level at which there is evidence of ancient habitation, see ibid. 256 f. and 267.

[4] I was familiar with the route from Grevena to Dheskati in 1943. It is likely that Tymphaea included in its territory the part of the Khasia area in which the Murganis (Micanis) river rises. For the site of Pelinna see F. Stählin in *RE* 19. 1 (1937) 327.

The canton of Elimea has excellent land on both sides of the Haliacmon, as it makes its full bend round Mt. Bourinos, and it was one of the
richer and more powerful kingdoms of Upper Macedonia. According to
Str. 7 C 326 and 9 C 434 its inhabitants were of Epirotic stock and were
later absorbed into the Macedonian state. They formed one of the tribal
states named by Thuc. 2. 99. 2 as subject to Perdiccas but maintaining
their own royal houses. We should probably refer to this royal house the
tradition of descent from Elymus or Elymas, king of the Tyrreni, who is
said to have settled in this area and founded its two cities, Aeane and
Elimia (St. Byz. s.vv.). A variant of Elymus is Helenus, the Trojan seer,
who is said to have founded Ilium in Macedonia (St. Byz. s.v.); and
this Helenus is firmly seated in the traditions of the royal house of the
Chaonians.[1] It would seem that this branch of the Epirotic peoples drew
on the same set of traditions as their cousins in Chaonia. Towards the
end of the fifth century the Macedonian royal house intermarried with
that of Elimea,[2] and it rapidly became Macedonized. The city Aeane,
supposedly founded by Aeanus, son of Elymus, was first identified by
Heuzey, who copied two inscriptions in a monastery and a church of
Kaliani; they gave the name of the city as 'Aeane' and 'Eane'.[3] There
were probably two sites. One is on an isolated hill near Kteni and has the
remains of a wall-circuit, 'en petit appareil hellénique, encore rude et
grossier'; and the other is at Kaliane, an open town, which Heuzey
considered had never been walled. The former was probably the earlier
city, to which the tradition of Elymus was attached, and the latter became
the Macedonian town.

In 1959 D. Kanatsoulis published two inscriptions from Kaliani, in
which Ἐλημιω[τ]ῶν τὸ κοινόν paid honour to Antoninus Pius and to
Marcus Aurelius.[4] At this time Aeane was the place where, at least on
occasion, the tribal state of the Elimiotae met and carried its resolutions.
Once again we see the survival of a tribal state in Upper Macedonia in
the second century A.D.; for the Elimiotae meeting at Aeane cannot be
just the citizens of a city 'Elimia' but are the tribesmen of the region
Elimea. The city Elimia recorded by Stephanus Byzantinus is found in
a form closer to that of its traditional founder in Ptol. 3. 13. 21 as
Ἐλυμιωτῶν (ἢ Ἐλιμιωτῶν)· Ἔλυμα (ἢ Ἔλυμαι). Livy 43. 21. 5 mentions

---

[1] See *Epirus passim* and esp. 412f.

[2] Arist. *Politics* 5. 8. 11.

[3] Heuzey–Daumet 285 f. = Dimitsas nos. 213 and 214. The place-name occurs perhaps
in an inscription of the third century A.D. in the form Αἰανή (*ZA* 14 (1965) 114) from Pisiča
in the neighbourhood of Štip. *Anth. Pal.* 7. 390 has the form Αἰανέη, and the list of Delphic
Theorodokoi has the form Αἰανέα, which is, I think mistakenly, supposed by Plassart to stand
for Αἴνεια on the Thermaic Gulf (*BCH* 45 (1921) 18, iii 75).

[4] Μακεδονικὸν Ἡμερολόγιον 1959. 209 f. nos. 1 and 2 = *SEG* 17 (1960) 83 nos. 313 and
314; see also F. Papazoglou in *ZA* 9 (1959) 163.

that Perseus purified his army 'circa Elimeam', that is 'in the neighbour-hood of Elimea', which makes for more precision if Elimea is the town rather than the province, before he undertook his daring winter cam-paign in 169 B.C. He purified his army, one imagines, when he was about to leave Macedonia, and on this occasion he did so before entering Perrhaebia as he went up to the Volustana pass.[1] Elimea then should be on the south side of the Haliacmon. The only other mention of the city is in Plu. *Aemilius* 9. 3, where Hostilius is said to have failed to force his way (into Macedonia) κατὰ τὰς 'Ελιμίας, 'by the Elimiae'. The account of Hostilius' attempt has not survived; but Livy 44. 2. 6 refers to an action of Hostilius on the route 'per Cambunios montes', and this is evidently the route which a few sections later (44. 2. 10) Perseus sent a large force to defend: 'iugum Cambuniorum montium—Volustana ipsi vocant'. We should then expect Elimiae to have been just on the Mace-donian side of the Volustana pass. Here Wace described an ancient site at Palaiogratsiano, with a small acropolis and with pithos burials 'perhaps of the Early Iron Age'. He proposed to identify it with the city Elimea, and I accept his identification as the most likely one.[2] It is possible that 'Ελίμιαι is the name of the heights above the town Elimea, Elyma, or Elemea.[3]

An inscription which was found in the central square of Kozani on a stone re-used in Byzantine times reads κ]ατα το δο[ξαν τη β]ουλη και [τω δημω and F. Papazoglou has proposed a restoration for the next words: τω]ν Μαλει[ατων.[4] The inscription is of the second century A.D. and records the resolution of an autonomous community within the *koinon* of the Elimiotae. We have seen the same phenomenon in the tribal states of the Pelagones, the Derriopi, the Dassaretii, the Orestae, and the Lyncestae, where greater and smaller units within the tribal state carry their own resolutions, whether those units are primarily of an urban

---

[1] For the route taken by Perseus see *Epirus* 281; from the Volustana pass Perseus probably used the Dheskati–Melissi route towards Grevena.

[2] *BSA* 17 (1910–11) 201, as against Heuzey, Kiepert, and Dimitsas, who thought it to be Phylacae in Pieria. Wace did not make use of the literary evidence in connection with the identification of Elimea. I am not convinced by the argument of F. Papazoglou in *ZA* 9 (1959) 168 that there was no such city ('il n'y a pas eu de cité du nom d'Élimée'), because we are dealing with the authority not of Strabo alone but of the source behind the tradition of Elymus; Plu. *Aemilius* 9. 3 should be added to the passages she considers.

[3] Compare Olpe and Olpae, and Idomene and Idomenae in Amphilochia and my explanation of them in *BSA* 37 (1940) 134 and 139. There is variation in the spelling also of the district, X. *HG* 5. 2. 38 τὸν 'Ελιμίας ἄρχοντα and Arist. *Pol.* 5. 8. 11 'Ελίμεια, and of the ethnic 'Ελειμιώτης (*BCH* 21 (1897) 112) or 'Ελιμιώτης (St. Byz.), ἡ 'Ελιμιωτίς sc. γῆ (Arr. *Anab.* 1. 7. 5) and ἡ 'Ελιμιωτὶς στρατιά (D.S. 17. 57. 2), in addition to the variants quoted in my text.

[4] Published by Ch. I. Makaronas in *AE* 1936, *Chronica* 10 with a sketch of the stone which suggests that there may not be room for two letters before the first *mu* as suggested by F. Papazoglou in *MG* 178. By a strange chance an inscription apparently with the personal names Μαλεία and Μαλει[ῳ] has recently been found on an island in Lake Little Prespa (*AD* 21 (1966) 2. 355).

character such as Lychnidus and Heraclea or of a tribal character such as the Geneatae or the Argestaei or the (?) Maleiatae. This thoroughgoing and living tribal structure in these cantons of Upper Macedonia in the second century A.D. does not fit at all into the general picture which M. Rostovtzeff, for instance, paints of the provinces. 'Thus the Empire in the second century presented more than ever the appearance of a vast federation of city-states. Each city had its local self-government. . . . Over the cities stood a strong central government which managed affairs of state . . . the head of this central government was the emperor.'[1] Here the tribal *koinon* administers the territories of its members, and the lesser units, whether lesser tribes, *komai*, or towns, are subsumed within the tribal state. So far as the evidence goes, there is no indication that the lands of the tribal *koina* were attributed to any town or city of Upper Macedonia.[2]

We have already seen in this structure the survival of a strongly rooted tribal system, which stretched far back into the past. It is likely to have been a deliberate part of Rome's policy to provide the conditions under which it continued to flourish. The period of partition and the series of invasions which followed the creation of the province may have shaped Rome's policy in the matter—a policy entirely different from that pursued for instance in Epirus, where tribal life seems to have died out. In the partition there was one difference between the fourth tetrarchy and the others, that the tribal state, the Pelagones, and not a city was given some responsibility in the administration of the tetrarchy (Str. 7 fr. 47 and p. 75 above). Another difference was that alongside the fourth tetrarchy there were two tribal states, the Orestae who had been within the Macedonian state for two centuries at least, and the Dassaretii, who had been only intermittently within the Macedonian state. The Orestae had been proclaimed a *gens libera* by Rome in 196 B.C. (Livy 33. 34. 6, Orestis—Macedonum ea gens est—quod primi ab rege defecissent, suae leges redditae), and in 167 B.C. they were not included in any of the tetrarchies. The Dassaretii fared likewise in 167 B.C. We find both of them described later by Pliny as *liberae gentes* (*HN* 4. 3 and 4. 35), and their freedom may have been continuous since 167 B.C. It is probable that the Orestae and the Dassaretii served Rome well in the troubled times when Macedonia was invaded and that Rome decided to extend the area of 'liberae gentes'. At any rate at some unknown date some special grant of

---

[1] *The Social and Economic History of the Roman Empire*[2], 1. 135 f.

[2] It is on this point that I disagree with the view of Rostovtzeff, op. cit. 2. 651, that 'the city of Heraclea included in her territory the country of the Lyncesti, who were not citizens of the city, one part of the tribe of the Atintani being attached to the city in the same way as the Carni and Catali were attached to Tergeste'; and that 'the Oresti were members of a tribe attached to the city'. He is arguing here from the general to the particular without noticing the particular conditions in north-western Macedonia.

freedom was made to 'that part of the Roman province which was called free' (Caesar *BC* 3. 34. 4). Str. 7 C 326 fin. defined the free part rather in parenthesis when he said that 'the area round Lyncus, Pelagonia, Orestias, and Elimea used to be called Upper Macedonia, and was called free by later people' (καὶ δὴ καὶ τὰ περὶ Λύγκον καὶ Πελαγονίαν καὶ Ὀρεστιάδα καὶ Ἐλίμειαν τὴν ἄνω Μακεδονίαν ἐκάλουν, οἱ δ' ὕστερον καὶ ἐλευθέραν). It is probable that this is not an exclusive list and that we should add Derriopus, Eratyra, and the Eordi; for Strabo had lumped them together a few sentences earlier, and we know from inscriptions that Derriopus and the Battynaei, who may have been in Eratyra, were on the same free footing as the others.[1]

If we try to define the freedom of these cantons, we may guess that it took several forms. There was an absence of Roman colonies, the more marked as they existed at Dyrrachium, Pella, Stobi, and Scupi, and 'the Romans' do not appear in local inscriptions except as joining in the business (συμπραγματευόμενοι).[2] The tribal *koina* and the lesser *koina* were to a great extent self-governing, and they seem to have had direct access to the governor of the province and even to the emperor. In so far as a co-ordination of the tribal states was needed, it was evidently performed by a body of delegates who were called οἱ σύνεδροι τῶν Μακεδόνων[3] and

[1] The limits both of the fourth tetrarchy and of the free part of Macedonia are a matter of some controversy. As regards the fourth tetrarchy Tymphaea has usually been included, because Tymphaea or Tymphaeis is restored in the corrupt passage in Livy 45. 30. 6. Geyer in *RE* 14. 1 (1928) 764 and F. Papazoglou *MG* 348 add Parauaea, although it does not figure in the sources. Geyer's inclusion of it is based on a misunderstanding, I think, of Strabo's remark that in making the four tetrarchies Paulus linked the Epirotic tribes with Macedonia (7 fr. 47 συνάψας τῇ Μακεδονίᾳ καὶ τὰ Ἠπειρωτικὰ ἔθνη); for Strabo is referring to the Epirotic tribes, named in C 326 and C 434, who fell under the power of Macedon and then of Rome (C 327 init.), i.e. the areas of Lyncus, Pelagonia, Orestias, Elimea, etc. and not areas which were part of the Epirote League or geographically nearer to Epirus. As regards the free part of Macedonia its limits towards Thessaly and Epirus are set by the statement of Caesar *BC* 3. 36. 3, that the Haliacmon divided Macedonia from Thessaly—that is not the course but the basin of the river (cf. Str. 7 fr. 15 where the Peneus and its tributary the Titaresius similarly divide Thessaly from Macedonia),—and by the statement of Str. 7 fr. 12, which refers probably to his own time, that the Haliacmon was the boundary of Upper Macedonia. F. Papazoglou has Eordaea in the fourth tetrarchy but not in the free part of Macedonia, because she believes it not to have been in Upper Macedonia. She bases her view on Thuc. 2. 99. 5, where the conquests of Alexander I and his ancestors are briefly described, but there is no reason to suppose that these conquests were made only in Lower Macedonia (a part of Paeonia ἄνωθεν is included in these conquests). The arrangements made by Augustus (Str. 17 C 840) seem to have left the free part of Macedonia unaffected. In the latter part of the second century A.D. Lychnidus was in the province of Macedonia (*CIL* ix 1602 stat(ionem) provinc(iae) M[ace]doniae Lychnidu[m] percepit).

[2] For instance in *ŽA* 9 (1959) 287 ἡ πόλις καὶ οἱ συνπραγματευόμενοι Ῥωμαῖοι from Marvinci east of the Morihovo. For Scupi see B. Josifovska in *ŽA* 6 (1956) 277; and *ŽA* 13 (1964) 155; *Spomenik* 77 (1934) no. 63; 71 (1931) nos. 528 and 556.

[3] They are seen at work in two inscriptions which Ali Pasha reported to Leake as coming from a site near Monastir, evidently that of Heraclea near Bukova, as Dimitsas says (i. 258). First published in Leake 3. 319 f. = Dimitsas nos. 218 and 221, and probably of the second century A.D. Μακεδόνων οἱ σύνεδροι and ἀγαθῇ τύχῃ τὸ κοινὸν τῶν Μακεδόνων. The 'Makedoniarkhai'

acted within what was in the main the fourth tetrarchy, probably with the addition of Orestis. These arrangements enabled this group of freedom-loving peoples to preserve their self-respect, and they benefited the Roman Empire by serving in the Roman army and later in the armies of the Eastern Roman Empire.[1]

6. *Pieria*

When one lives and travels in Upper Macedonia, one's horizon is dominated by mountain ranges and particularly by the towering mass of Mt. Olympus, snow-clad to its feet in winter. One is aware only of land masses. It is a memorable experience to cross the northern outlier of Mt. Olympus and suddenly to look down upon the sea, stretching as far as the eye can see.[2] Down there lies 'Macedonia by the sea', ἡ παρὰ θάλασσαν Μακεδονία of Thuc. 2. 99. 3, a more evocative phrase than the more usual 'Lower Macedonia', ἡ κάτω Μακεδονία (Hdt. 7. 173. 1 and Thuc. 2. 99. 1), as opposed to Upper Macedonia, ἡ ἄνω Μακεδονία (Hdt. 7. 173. 4). The easiest route for those coming from the west to the Pierian plain is through the Perrhaebian Tripolitis via Livadhion or Doliche over the ridge of Mt. Titarium[3] and down to Petra, so called from an isolated and conspicuous rock, which is close to the edge of the plain. An alternative but more difficult route, keeping closer to the north face of Mt. Olympus, runs from Pythium to Kokkinoplos and down to Petra.[4] It is these two routes which Perseus endeavoured to close to the Romans in 168 B.C., when he sent 5,000 Macedonians to garrison Pythium and Petra (Livy 44. 32. 9), the Roman army being based on Thessaly.

The plain of Katerini forms the centre of Pieria (see Map 12). To the south the plain tapers down till it reaches the river Peneus, where it emerges from the vale of Tempe, the five-mile-long defile,[5] which at one point can be held easily by ten armed men in the picturesque words of Livy (44. 6. 11, et media et angustissima valles . . . quam vel decem armatis tueri facile est). North of Katerini the plain merges into the foothills of long valleys running down from the spur of the Pierian

of these councils are found in a family commemorated at Tsepicovo (*ŽA* 3 (1953) 216) and in another case at Marvinci, east of the Morihovo, in what was the third tetrarchy (*ŽA* 14 (1965) 137). For the continued existence of the tetrarchies or *merides* see J. A. O. Larsen in *CP* 40 (1945) 65 f. and C. F. Edson in *CP* 41 (1946) 107.

[1] See the conclusions expressed by F. Papazoglou in her excellent study of the regional *koina* of Upper Macedonia in *ŽA* 9 (1959) 170–1.

[2] We crossed the Tripolitis one night in 1943 and were on the ridge of Mt. Titarium by dawn, and then had the view of the sea.

[3] Str. 7 fr. 14 and 9 C 441 συμφυὲς τῷ Ὀλύμπῳ. The Titaresius river, the later Europus, flows from Mt. Titarium.

[4] Leake 3. 337 and Heuzey, *Ol.* 145 f. with map facing p. 9.

[5] Str. 7 fr. 14 and Livy 44. 6. 8, probably taking the distance from the milestones of the Roman road.

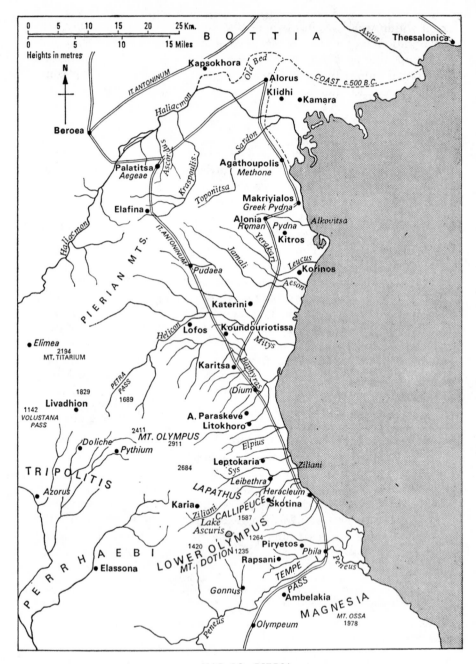

MAP 12. PIERIA

mountains, which forms the watershed between the Haliacmon valley and the plain. There is a special beauty in the Pierian mountains; they have very rich meadows and pastures and the most magnificent forests high up, and the valleys facing east and south-east are open to the sun and the sea and enjoy a more temperate climate than even the most low-lying parts of Upper Macedonia.

The ancient counterpart of Katerini was Dium. Leake inferred from the remains of a stadium and a theatre in the flat plain below Malathria that the site was that of Dium, and his inference was confirmed by Heuzey's discovery there of two Latin inscriptions appropriate to a Roman colony.[1] Leake describes the many copious springs of water which change the stream into a river at Dium, and he describes the landing-place for small boats at the outflow of the river into the sea. In ancient times the river, called the Baphyras, was navigable up to Dium at least (Paus. 9. 30. 8, Βαφύρας κάτεισιν εἰς θάλασσαν ναυσίπορος), and it formed below Dium a wide pool which was not artificial but part of a marsh extending to its mouth, to judge from a phrase in Livy 44. 6. 15, 'ostium late restagnans Baphyri amnis'. Thus Dium was a port. It appears as such in the *Periplous* of Ps.-Scylax 66.

We have a measurement from the coast to Dium in Str. 7 fr. 17, which states that Dium was not on the shore of the Thermaic Gulf, but almost 7 stades away. This measurement is likely to have been made by someone going by water up the river. Livy, drawing on Polybius, reckoned the distance from the sea to the roots of the mountain 'at a little more than a Roman mile', which we may take to equal some 10 stades. Half of that distance, he says, was taken up by the pool of the Baphyras river. His reckoning puts the distance from the coast to Dium at some 5 stades. It is clearly a reckoning of distance as the crow flies. Thus his 5 stades as the crow flies and Strabo's 7 stades as a ship sails are compatible with one another.[2] Such was the situation in 169 B.C., the year of which Livy was writing. Today the coast is not 5 stades, which equal 1 km, but 3 km from Dium. The advance of the coast since 169 B.C. is due to alluvial deposits made mainly by the Baphyras. The river itself has changed its course. It now enters the sea further north than it did in 169 B.C.[3]

Livy's statement puts the distance from the east side of Dium town to the roots of the mountain at some 5 stades. On a modern map this distance brings one to the 100-m contour. On the ground one sees the flat plain of Dium, then the gradually rising slopes, and at several kilometres' distance the steeply rising mountain-side. There is a kernel of truth in

[1] Leake 3. 409 f. and Heuzey–Daumet 267 f.

[2] Leake 3. 411 dismissed the data of Livy on the ground that he was 'not correct', and he thought Pausanias 'to have had a more correct idea of the distance'; but they were not in fact measuring the same things.

[3] See my article in *JHS* 88 (1968) 22 for similar changes in the Bay of Marathon.

Livy's description but it is hardly the whole truth. The description is given by Livy when he is castigating Perseus for failing to hold against the Romans the narrow passage between Dium and the mountain-side. In this context the description is less than fair to Perseus. Such unfairness to Perseus is not unique in Livy's account, which was based on that of Polybius.

With Dium as a fixed point, we can check the data for the road from Larissa via Dium and Beroea to Thessalonica. They are given by the Itinerarium Antoninum which was composed in A.D. 211–17 as 'Larissa XXIIII Dio XVIIII (XXVIIII *D*) Pudaia (Pudata *L*) XVII Berea LI Thessalia'.[1] The distance from Larissa to Dium is in fact some 50 km = 34/5 m.p., so that we should alter the XXIIII to read 'Larissa XXXIIII Dio'. If we take the more direct route from Dium to Beroea (Verria), that is along the foothills below Elafina, where there are clear signs of the broad cutting of an ancient road on the slopes,[2] it is some 53 km on the map = 36 m.p., which is in accordance with the XVIIII + XVII = 36 m.p. of the itinerary. The line of the modern road from Verria to Salonica across the plain to Nea Khalkidhon is 75 km = 50/1 m.p., which agrees with the itinerary.

I have dealt with this matter now because it has something to contribute to the topography round Dium. Pausanias tells us that the Macedonians who inhabit Pieria under the mountain and the city of Dium say Orpheus met his death there at the hands of women.

'As you go from Dium on the road towards the mountain, when you have advanced twenty stades, you find a pillar on your right and a monument on it, a stone hydria, containing the bones of Orpheus, so the locals say. There is also a river Helicon; when you go on up to 75 stades, the water from this river disappears underground. After an interval of some 22 stades the water comes up again, and, when it has taken the name Baphyras instead of Helicon, it enters the sea.' (9. 30. 7)

Heuzey noted an unusually well-preserved, cone-shaped tumulus near the village of Karitsa (evidently on the Olympus side of the village), which he thought corresponded precisely with the first distance given by Pausanias. It is indeed to be expected that the grave of the heroic Orpheus lay under a mound, as did the graves of the traditional heroes,

---

[1] It. Ant. 328. 1–5. As Miller in *Itin. Romana* 573 f. is concerned primarily with the confused state of the Peutinger Table, he does not give much attention to the It. Ant. I discuss the Peutinger Table below on p. 131. For the type of corruption which I have here suggested, XXXIIII becoming XXIIII, see p. 49 above.

[2] I was based on Elafina for some weeks in 1943 and knew the tracks well between Elafina and Litokhoro. Pudaea, then, is near Kato Milia. I differ here from Edson in *CP* 50 (1955) 175 who equates Pudaea with Pydna and has to emend the figures. Since writing this note I have been told that a new motor road has been made from Katerini to Verria through Elafina.

and that the pillar as described by Pausanias was, as Heuzey said, set upon the tumulus.[1] The next stage, that is the 75 stades from Dium along the same line of the road, brings us to the river Petriotikos, the first considerable river on our way. This river, then, is the Helicon. It must have entered a swallet or disappeared underground in ancient times somewhere near the village of Lofos, and was believed to re-emerge some 4½ km away to the south, that is where the Baphyras does receive a *kefalovrisi* below Koundouriotissa.[2] From there the Baphyras flowed south, was reinforced by the copious springs by Dium, and turned from there to the sea. Now the road which Pausanias' informants told him went from Dium 'towards the mountain' was evidently one on which stades or miles convertible into stades were marked.[3] It was in fact the Roman road of the Antonine Itinerary and from Dium it went not to Pydna on the coast but towards the mountain, that is up into the hills by Lofos and over the ridge of the Pierian mountains, as we have inferred from the distances given by the Antonine Itinerary.

The next entry after Dium in Ps.-Scylax is Pydna πόλις Ἑλληνίς. By the village of Alonia, south-west of Makriyialos, an inscribed slab was found by chance (τυχαίως) which recorded a meeting of worshippers θεοῦ Διὸς ὑψίστου held ἐν Πύδνῃ in the year A.D. 250.[4] Before this was discovered C. F. Edson had published three remarkable inscriptions,[5] all metrical and all commemorating Aeacidae descended from Olympias, the mother of Alexander the Great, who was killed at Pydna by the relatives of her own victims (D. S. 19. 51. 5). One of the inscriptions mentions the tomb of Olympias, beside which apparently the Aeacids were buried. These inscriptions should be from monuments in or close to Pydna. The stone which Edson was the first to publish was found by a villager ploughing a field beneath the kastro of Makriyialos; the second, published by G. P. Oikonomos,[6] was discovered in a private house at Makriyialos and was said to have been found in Makriyialos; and the third was seen by Heuzey at the village of Kitros, a village south-east of

---

[1] Heuzey–Daumet 270.

[2] There are a number of these strong *kefalovrisia*, fed by the waters of Mt. Olympus. The map also shows several streams disappearing underground into the plain north of Dium, a phenomenon not uncommon in Greece.

[3] Leake 3. 411 and Heuzey op. cit. miss the force of τὴν ἐπὶ τὸ ὄρος sc. ὁδόν, and translate the sense as being so many stades from Dium towards the mountain, i.e. Olympus; but this is impossible, Olympus being so much closer to Dium than a distance of 75 stades. There were three roads from Dium, one south down the plain to Tempe, one along the coast to Pydna, and the third north towards the mountain-side of the Pierian mountains. It is this last road which is ἡ ἐπὶ τὸ ὄρος. Moreover, if one goes 75 stades to the south, as Leake, Heuzey, and recently Kotzias suggest, the story of the swallet and the *kefalovrisi* cannot be applied to the Baphyras river.

[4] *Mak.* 2 (1941–52) 625.

[5] 'The Tomb of Olympias', in *Hesperia* 18 (1949) 78 f., a most interesting and illuminating article.   [6] Oikonomos, *Ep.* no. 65.

Alonia.[1] It would appear from the places of discovery that the kastro of Makriyialos is an ancient site with a settlement in the fields below it, and that there was another site on the Kitros side of Alonia, at least in the third century A.D., which called itself Pydna.[2] The places are some 5 km = 25 stades apart. This fits in with the statement of Diodorus 13. 49. 2, that Archelaus transferred Pydna to a site some 20 stades from the sea, with the intention presumably of creating a town more easily defended against attack from the sea and not of suspending the use of Pydna maritima, if we may so call the original 'Greek city'.

We may notice here the difference between Dium, a Macedonian town, and Pydna, a Greek city. Dium was not large, even in 169 B.C.; it was built in the plain, exceptionally well fortified, conspicuous for its public buildings, of which some lay outside the walls, and linked to the sea by a navigable river.[3] Pydna, on the other hand, was on the coast, situated on a defensible hill, controlling its own hinterland and forming an independent state.[4] When Archelaus captured Greek Pydna and moved it inland, he was refounding it as a Macedonian town, safer perhaps from attack by any sea power and more at the mercy of the Macedonian king.

We have seen at Dium that the coast has advanced since antiquity, and it is likely that the same thing has happened to the coast at Makriyialos and south of it. Here the river Alkovitsa, which rises above Alonia, has deposited much alluvium on the coast and has probably changed its outlet into the sea since antiquity. It is therefore impossible now to find the site of Pydna's harbour without excavation, but the fortifiable hill is evidently the kastro which Edson described and tentatively identified with the acropolis of Greek Pydna, 'an elevation 56 m high directly on the coast due east of the village.'[5] The harbour will probably have been on the south side of the acropolis, and it may have had the advantages now

---

[1] Heuzey, *Ol.* 164 and 482 no. 40.

[2] The stones seen in the villages of Alonia and Kitros are less indicative of a precise location than the two or perhaps three found in the ground, namely Edson's first stone from Makriyialos dating to *c.* 50 B.C., that found near Alonia dating to A.D. 250, and perhaps that said to have been found in Makriyialos dating to the second century B.C.

[3] Livy 44. 7. 3, urbem . . . non magnam, ita exornatam publicis locis et multitudine statuarum munitamque egregie and 44. 6. 15, partem planitiae aut Iovis templum aut oppidum tenet. For the site see Leake 3. 409 f. and Heuzey–Daumet 266, 'l'enceinte antique laissait voir bien à découvert sa belle ligne d'assises en marbre blanc et les profondeurs de son double fossé'.

[4] It is clear from Polyaenus 4. 11. 2 that a penteconter could row up to the walls of the city, and from D.S. 19. 50. 4 that a quinquereme could be launched from the city, when it was under siege on the landward side. Theramenes helped from the seaward side, when Archelaus was besieging Pydna on the landward side. (D.S. 13. 49. 1). It is doubtful whether any precision can be attached to the remarks of the Scholiast on D. *Olynth.* i. 12 Πύδνα τὸ νῦν Κίτρος, as his next remark is Ποτιδαία ἡ νῦν Βυρροία; or to Str. 7 fr. 22 (*epit. ed.*) Πύδνα ἡ νῦν Κίτρος καλεῖται. Heuzey put the Greek city of Pydna by Cape Atheridha further to the south, but this lacks ancient remains; see Edson, loc. cit.

[5] *Hesperia* 18 (1949) 84–5.

possessed by Neon Elevtherokhorion, which offers good landing and 'good shelter for small craft in all weathers'. The harbour of Pydna was used by a large part of Xerxes' fleet (D. S. 11. 12. 3). The distance by sea from Pydna to Stomium, the earlier mouth of the river Peneus, is given by Str. 7 fr. 36; the actual distance is some 65 km = 325 stades, which suits the 320 stades of Strabo, if Kramer's alteration of the text from 120 to 320 is accepted.[1]

The next city on the coast was Μεθώνη πόλις Ἑλληνίς (Ps.-Scylax 66) at a distance of 40 stades = 8 km from Pydna, that is by sea (Str. 7 fr. 20), and this distance brings us to the plain north of Nea Agathoupolis, a plain which has resulted from the alluvial deposits made by the river Toponitsa and perhaps more recently by the river Haliacmon. It seems likely that Methone should be located tentatively in this area, its harbour by the then mouth of the Toponitsa having become silted up.[2] The river Toponitsa may be the ancient Sardon river, if that form rather than Sandanus is correct.[3] The situation is in very fertile country and at the end of the longest outlier of the Pierian mountains, an appropriate place for an early Eretrian colony.

Livy provides the names of some of the lesser rivers of Pieria: the Elpeüs, which he says is 5 m.p. south of Dium, and so is the river south of Litokhoro (44. 8. 5); the Mitys, which he says is a day north of Dium for a foraging expedition, probably the Mavroneri (44. 7. 4); thence, after an advance to a town Agassae, another day's march for a foraging expedition, while Perseus lay at Pydna, to the river Ascordus, perhaps the river of Palatitsa (44. 7. 5–6, and 45. 27. 1).[4] Plutarch provides the names of two rivers in the plain before Pydna on which the battle of Pydna was fought. This is the plain by Korinos. The Romans and the Macedonians both drew water before the battle from a river which ran knee-deep in late summer (Livy 44. 40. 8). Plutarch says two not very deep rivers ran through the plain, the Aeson and the Leucus (*Aem.* 16. 5),

---

[1] The change is ρ' to τ'. The quotation is from *MP* 4. 218.

[2] As Pydna has usually been placed with Heuzey at Cape Atheridha, Methone has been placed south of Nea Agathoupolis at Elevtherokhori, where there is no trace of ancient remains, as Lenk remarks in *RE* 15. 2 (1932) 1385.

[3] There are two traditions of the circumstances in which Philip lost an eye at the siege of Methone. Of these that in Theopompus (*FGrH* 115 F 52) is to be preferred, but the mention of a river by Methone in the sensational account of Duris (*FGrH* 76 F 36), narrated also by Callisthenes (*FGrH* 124 F 57, which Jacoby regarded as not genuine), should not be dismissed as wrong, since the account was plausible only if a river was available.

[4] The consul was desperate for supplies. He was able to move freely in the hilly country and he could do so without provoking Perseus at Pydna. He was probably unwilling to descend into the main plain of Macedonia, in case Perseus should come out and hold the ridge by Elafina against his return. The Elpeüs should not be confused with the Enipeus of Plb. 5. 99, which is in Thessaly, as it is by Weissenborn–Müller on Livy 44. 8. 5; the form Ἐλπιός occurs in Zonaras 9. 23 and in the Y codices of Plb. 29. 4. 4; and it is similar to Πηνειός. Another river on this coast was the Μέλης where the head of Orpheus was found (*Orphicorum Fragmenta* no. 115, ed. Kern).

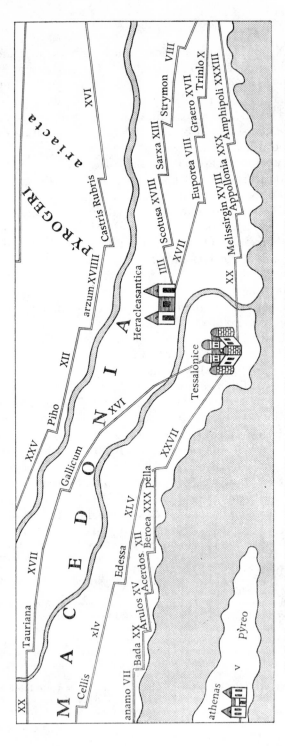

MAP 13. THE EASTERN PART OF THE VIA EGNATIA AND ADJACENT ROADS ON THE PEUTINGER TABLE.

and that the Leucus was still red with blood when the Romans crossed it on the day after the battle (21. 3). These rivers may then be identified, the Leucus with the Yerakari, and the Aeson with the river south of it.

The river 'Acerdos' appears in the Roman Itineraries. As we have seen, the Antonine Itinerary took a direct road from Dium to Beroea and from Beroea to Thessalonica. The Peutinger Table certainly takes a different route; for it omits the Pudaea and the Pella of the Antonine Itinerary and has many more stations from Dium to Beroea (see Map 13). We have in fact four lists of stations for this other route (I give them all in the same order, from Thessalonica to Larissa):

Ravenna Geog. 194. 14	Ravenna Geog. 373. 6	Guidonis Geog. 536. 2	Peutinger Table	
Thesalonici	Thesalonici	Thessalonici	Tessalonice	XXVII
Pella	Pella	Pella	Pella	XXX
Beroea	Beroea	Beroea	Beroea	XII
Acerdos	Acerdos	Archelos	Acerdos	XV
Arulos		Arulos	Arulos	XX
Bata	Bada	Bada	Bada	VII
Anamon	Anamon	Anamon	Anamo	XII
Imera		Imera	Hatera	XII
Diume	Dium	Dium	Dium	XII
Sabatum	Sabation	Sabacium	Sabatium	XV
Stenas	Stenas	Senas	Stenas	X
Thuris	Turiste	Thuriste		
	Tenos	Tenos		
	Lubion	Lumbion		
Olimpius	Olympium	Olipyon	Olympū	XV
	Larissa	Larisa	Larissa	

As we shall see, there are some difficulties in the figures of miles on the Peutinger Table. These have led to the supposition that the author of the Peutinger Table has conflated two roads and made one fictitious road out of two separate sets of names and figures. Miller thought those two roads went from Beroea to Larissa, one via Servia and Elassona and the other via Dium; Edson has proposed a more probable variant, that one road went inland via Pella and Beroea and the other, later road went along the coast of the Gulf. But the preliminary supposition does not seem to me to be acceptable. In a road map which is designed for use and is in use, a conflated road cannot survive: a conflation of the road from Bristol to London with the road from Southampton to London would be of little help even to the most astute motorist. The Roman road maps of the imperial period were designed for use, and they cannot have contained conflated roads. Our Peutinger Table is a copy of such a Roman road map. It follows that, if what we have in the Peutinger Table is a conflation, then that conflation is due not to the Roman road map but to the copyist himself who made our copy. In other words, the conflated version is unique; it exists only in our one surviving copy. But the entries of the Ravenna Geographer and of the Geographia Guidonis show that this is not so; for they have between them all the same stations and all in the same order. I conclude then that we are dealing with one road which is common to the Peutinger Table, the Ravenna Geographer, and the Geographia of Guido, and this road was a real road and not a farrago of two roads.[1]

At first the distances are satisfactory (see Map 14). The entry XXVII m.p. to Pella = Nea Pella is in order (see p. 49 above); and the distance of XXX m.p. = 44·4 km from Pella to Beroea is correct, if we keep just below Yiannitsa and branch off before Kariotissa to go via Esovalta, Yimna, Zervokhori, Yiannisa, and Tourkokhori to Beroea. And the entry of 12 m.p. = 17·7 km from Beroea to Acerdos brings us to the river of Palatitsa, which we have tentatively identified as Livy's river Ascordus. The problems arise with the following entries. In the first place it is probable that we have to do with a road along the coast, such as there was on the west side of the peninsula,[2] and that we should see the chief towns on this part of the coast, Alorus[3] and Pydna,[4] in the next two names Arulos and Bada (P and B being often interchanged). Our first task is to determine the position of Alorus.

As one advances from the south into the main plain, the Haliacmon enters the sea and then the Ludias comes next, the latter being navigable as far as the Lake of Pella and Pella itself. The Haliacmon and Alorus seem to be similarly related. For Ps.-Scylax 66, using καί to mark a new stage, ends one group with Dium, Pydna, Methone, and then continues: καὶ Ἁλιάκμων ποταμός, Ἄλωρος, πόλις· καὶ ποταμὸς Λυδίας, Πέλλα πό λις (καὶ βασίλειον ἐν αὐτῇ καὶ ἀναπλοῦς ἐς αὐτὴν ἀνὰ τὸν Λυδίαν), Ἀξιὸς ποταμός, Ἐχέδωρος ποταμός, Θέρμη πόλις, Αἴνεια Ἑλληνίς, Παλλήνη ἄκρα μακρὰ εἰς τὸ πέλαγος ἀνατείνουσα· καὶ πόλεις αἵδε ἐν τῇ Παλλήνῃ Ἑλληνίδες. As he is giving a periplous for a mariner, he mentions first the mouth of the river (of which the discoloured outflow shows far out to sea) and then the place on its bank or delta, e.g. Alorus and Pella; but the mention does

---

[1] K. Miller, *Itin. Roman.* 494–5, figs. 148–50, 573–5, figs. 183–5. As Edson in *CP* 50 (1955) 189 n. 127 remarks of Miller's reconstruction, 'his attempt at a reconstruction of this route as exhibited in his sketch map No. 184 on col. 575 amounts to a *reductio ad absurdum*'. Edson has a full discussion of the evidence and the terrain in *CP* 50 (1955) 178 f. As regards the relationship between the Peutinger Table and the other two sources, he writes that the Ravenna Geographer copied his lists of place-names from an earlier version of the map now represented by the Table [perhaps two versions, different from one another, as his two lists vary from one another not only in the spelling of names], and that the Geographia of Guido preserves a transcript of part of an earlier copy of the Cosmographer than is represented by the extant manuscripts.

[2] See p. 26 above for the coastal sector from Aulon to Dyrrachium, and *Epirus* 690 f. and Map 18 for the roads in Epirus.

[3] So Miller, op. cit. 574.   [4] Jordanes, *Getica* 56. 287 has the form 'Petina'.

not indicate on which bank the place is situated. On this point Pliny *HN* 4. 34 gives us the information we need, because he is describing the coastal sector from a landsman's viewpoint: 'in ora Heraclea, flumen Apilas, oppida Pydna, Aloros, amnis Haliacmon . . . mox in ora Ichnae, fluvius Axius.' It is clear then that Alorus is to be sought on the south bank of the river Haliacmon at a place where the delta was still navigable. This is also necessary if the Arulos of the itinerary is Alorus, because the Haliacmon in the plain was certainly unbridgeable and the road would therefore stay south of the river.

The other mentions of Alorus are in passages based on Strabo's lost chapters of book 7. In fr. 20, preserved in the *Epitome Vaticana*, we have a sentence which is clearly the same as one in St. Byz. s.v.: fr. 20 ἔστι δὲ ὁ Ἄλωρος τὸ μυχαίτατον τοῦ Θερμαίου κόλπου, and St. Byz. Ἄλωρος, πόλις Μακεδονίας· ἔστι δὲ τὸ μυχαίτατον τοῦ Θερμαίου κόλπου· τὸ ἐθνικὸν Ἀλωρίτης καὶ Ἀλωρῖτις.[1] The sense in which Alorus was the most recessed part of the Thermaic Gulf is made clear by fr. 22, where Strabo defines the coast called 'Pieria' from Dium to the outflow of the Haliacmon as the northward-facing coast of the Gulf (τὸ ἀπὸ τούτου (sc. Δίου) ἡ πρὸς βορρᾶν τοῦ κόλπου παραλία). In modern orientation his north is our NW. (see p. 81); the most recessed part of the Thermaic Gulf is that which extends furthest towards the west. We are told in fr. 20 and in fr. 22, preserved in the *Epitome edita*, that Methone was 40 stades from Pydna and 70 stades from Alorus; as this information is conveyed in each case after the statement that Pella was 120 stades' sail up the Ludias, the stades give the distances by water. If we apply 70 stades = 14 km to the map from the plain north of Nea Agathoupolis, where we put Methone, and go outside the edge of the hills, we reach the vicinity of Trikkala. If Alorus was here, it was the most westerly place on the shore of the Gulf to anyone sailing up from the south. We shall assume that the Haliacmon then took the course of the northernmost of its old beds (see Map 15), and that the plain had not then developed just north of what is now the lowest reach of the river.

We have two further distances to apply: Acerdos XV m.p. = 22·2 km to Alorus, and Alorus XX = 29·6 km to Bada = Roman Pydna = Alonia. All three requirements are met if we put Alorus near Trikkala[2] and make Acerdos the river Ascordus by Palatitsa.[3] One result of this

---

[1] In Meineke's edition of St. Byz. the suggestion is made of adding κατά before τὸ μυχαίτατον. Evidently he had not noticed the passage in Strabo. The form of the superlative is unusual. Strabo and St. Byz. may have taken it from a common source; or the latter may have taken it from the former.

[2] Leake 3. 436, followed by Miller, loc. cit., put Alorus at Paleokhora, a little south-west of Trikkala, but on quite different reasoning; see too F. Papazoglou *MG* 123 and map 3 at the end.

[3] The Haliacmon was probably bridged above Verria and the road divided before it crossed the Pierian mountains, one branch going to Alorus and the other direct to Dium.

conclusion is a clearer idea of the southern part of the central plain. Alorus, a Macedonian and not a Greek town, was on low ground, and in this respect it resembled Dium; and it too was beside a navigable river.

The next stage from Bada = Roman Pydna = Alonia to Dium is 28 km = 19 m.p., if we go via Karitsa on the Baphyras. It is necessary to change the entries in the Peutinger Table, which are open to suspicion as we have three XIIs in a row. In place of Bada VII Anamo XII Hatera XII Dium one may suggest Bada VII = 10·3 km to Anamo = Gannokhora on the Jamali river, Anamo X = 14·8 km to Karitsa on the Baphyras = Hatera, and Hatera II Dium.[1]

If we proceed now from Larissa towards Dium, we know that the Roman road followed the right bank of the Peneus through the Vale of Tempe, because at some places there is room only on this side. Remains of the road have indeed been seen on this side by Leake, and an inscription commemorating the work of L. Cassius Longinus, a legate of Julius Caesar, is cut on a rock on the south side, which indicates that the road there was on the south side. The river was crossed by Leake only after he had gone through the pass. This was probably where it was crossed in antiquity, whether by a bridge or by a ferry, as the river was then navigable to above that point.[2] Starting from Larissa and keeping south of the river, we reach in XV m.p. = 22·2 km a point north-east of Makrikhori, where there may have been an Olympeum or shrine to the god of Mt. Olympus before one entered the five-mile-long defile.[3] From the Olympeum to the crossing over the Peneus is some 15 km = X m.p. In the list of stations Lubion and Lumbion, which appear in two of them, seem to be faulty repetitions of Olympium. Tenus or Tenos may be the river Peneus, of which the crossing is shown after the X m.p. stretch on the Peutinger Table, and Thuris, if a corruption of Turris, may be a guardpost by the river. The station Stenae is then at the approach to this end of the pass.[4] Between Stenae and Dium we have some 36 km = XXIV or XXV m.p., so that it is necessary to change the data of the

[1] As Edson points out in *CP* 50 (1955) 181, the name is probably Anamōn and is likely to be that of a river; I take it to be the name of the river Jamali. Hatera is perhaps the place at which the river Baphyras was reached; the Itharis of Mela 2. 3. 35 may be a form of the same place-name. The river itself appears as Φαρύβου ἢ Βαφύρου in Ptol. 3. 15.

[2] Leake 3. 390 f. gives a good account; the inscription is *CIL* iii 588. The passage was certainly improved by the Romans, and its earlier condition may be that described by Livy 44. 6. 8 (using Polybius), when there was hardly room for a pack-horse (exiguum iumento onusto iter est). Pliny *HN* 4. 30, Penius . . . dimidio eius spatii navigabilis.

[3] Livy 44. 6. 8 and Pliny *HN* 4. 31 give the distance as 5 miles, which equal Strabo's 40 stades (7 fr. 14). The milestone giving 19 miles from the city (Larissa) was found near Baba village (now called Tembi), which is south of the river at the entry to the pass (*CIL* iii 7362); it was not necessarily *in situ* in the village.

[4] A milestone giving 27 miles 'a civitate' (*CIL* iii 14206. 32 and 33) came from a ruined church near Vurlami, a village by the east end of the Tempe pass; the distance is probably taken from Larissa.

Table, Dium XII (for the third time running) Sabatium XV Stenas, into say Dium X Sabatium XV Stenas. If so, Sabatium may be placed at the river Ziliani. The changes which we have suggested in the figures of the Table are thus limited to the triple entry of XII, which becomes Anamo X Hatera II Dium X Sabatium.

To the north of the Vale of Tempe there is a narrow passage between Mt. Olympus and the sea at Platamona, where a Byzantine fort, built on a rock above a gorge, holds a commanding position. Heuzey identified the site with that of Heracleum 'media regione inter Dium Tempeque in rupe amni imminente positum' (Livy 44. 8. 9), and he found slight remains of an ancient wall there.[1] The stream in the gorge may then be the Apilas river of Pliny *HN* 4. 34. Phila, a town founded by Demetrius II ἐπὶ τοῦ Πηνειοῦ (St. Byz. s.v.), was about 5 m.p. from Heracleum (Livy 44. 8. 9); it should be placed in the plain below Piryetos on the north bank and at the most northerly point of the course of the river, which is here navigable.[2] This Macedonian town resembles Dium and Alorus in its position. Leibethra lay between Heracleum and Dium in Livy 44. 5. 12 and 45. 6. 5 and in the list of places for the Delphic Theorodokoi (*BCH* 45 (1921) 17 iii 53). It was near the torrent Sys, which flows from Mt. Olympus and once destroyed the walls of the town (Paus. 9. 30. 11). The name τὰ Λείβηθρα (Str. 7 fr. 18) means the wet or pouring places, and Heuzey compared with it the name Kanalia given by the people of Leptokaria to the four torrents which issue from Mt. Olympus and form the Ziliani river. Heuzey therefore placed the town south of Leptokaria by the Ziliani river. Leake placed it further north near Litokhoro.[3] Heuzey's position may be preferred because the territory of Leibethra was distinct from that of Dium (Paus. 9. 30. 11 fin. ἐς τὴν ἑαυτῶν) and also from that of Heracleum; the district of Litokhoro will have belonged to Dium, and a roughly midway position between Litokhoro and Platamona is therefore preferable. The crags, the memorial of Orpheus, and the spring with which the place was associated in Orphic legend, afford no certain clue to its location.[4] Pimpleia was another centre of Orphic legend. It was a constituent *kome* of Dium, and

[1] Heuzey, *Ol.* 88 f., following Leake 3. 403 and 421; this identification is accepted by Oberhummer in *RE* s.v. Leake 3. 406 identified Pliny's river Apilas with the Ziliani river north of Platamona. The neuter form of the name, Heracleum, occurs also in Plu. *Aem.* 15. 4, whereas St. Byz. has a feminine form; an inscription seen by Leake (3. 427) may refer to this 'Heraclea'.

[2] Heuzey, *Ol.* 80 f. found some inscriptions and capitals at the village of Piryetos and seems to have been inclined to place Phila where the village is; Leake 3. 422 placed Phila on the left bank of the river, which is in accordance with the evidence of St. Byz., but near its mouth, which was too far south (see Map 12) to conform with Livy's datum of 5 miles from Heracleum.

[3] Heuzey, *Ol.* 93 f.; Leake 3. 422.

[4] Paus. 9. 30. 5; *Orphicorum Fragmenta* (ed. Kern) F 342; Lycophr., *Alex.* 273 and Tzetz. ad loc.; Pliny *HN* 4. 9 (attributed to Magnesia); Str. 10 C 471.

it seems to have rivalled Leibethra in offering the same Orphic features of crags, a spring, a memorial of Orpheus, and the Muses.[1] The rivalry between Pimpleia and Leibethra is clear from the story told to Pausanias by his Larissaean friend. As its connection in legend seems to be with the river Baphyras, Pimpleia may be placed on the mountain-side west of the river Baphyras.[2]

In 1951 Mr. Kotzias reported some ancient remains which he had found in this region.[3] I have already given the inferences which I draw from the literary evidence, because I do not accept all his deductions from the remains.[4] The important thing is that he has found the site of Leibethra (or of one of its *komai*, if it had *komai*) at the very place where Heuzey inferred it would be. He was drawn to this place by a report of some tombs, which he opened. They were lined and covered with un-worked slabs, and they contained bones and nothing else, even when they were demonstrably unplundered; he dated them to the Geometric period, but this type of cist-tomb is common and undatable. In seeking signs of a settlement near the tombs he came across a small hill, 120 m long and 40 m wide, with a torrent-bed on either side and the Ziliani river at its foot, and on this hill there were pieces of dry wall about 1·50 m wide and 2·30 m high. He excavated inside the walled area and found sherds of 'Hellenistic pottery' and some bronze coins. The photographs of the hill and the wall suggest a small and poorly fortified site of the Hellenistic period, the successor probably of an earlier site occupied in the archaic period, to which the story of Pausanias' friend from Larissa may have been attached. The literary evidence, the meaning of the name τὰ Λείβηθρα, and the finding of this Hellenistic site in the fork between three of the spouting torrents lead me to locate Leibethra at this place. One of the two torrent-beds, and not the Ziliani river, which is below the hill, is the Sys.[5] Mr. Kotzias found also a similar but larger-topped

---

[1] Str. 7 frs. 17 and 18; 10 C 471 (in the form Πίμπλα, perhaps the mountain); Ap. Rhod. 1. 24; Lycophr., *Alex.* 409; Hsch. s.v. Πίπλειαι· αἱ Μοῦσαι ἐν τῷ Μακεδονικῷ Ὀλύμπῳ, ἀπὸ κρήνης Πιπλείας.

[2] See p. 126 above for Orpheus and the Baphyras; and Lycophr. *Alex.* 273

Νύμφαισιν αἳ φίλαντο Βηφόρου γάνος
Λιβηθρίην θ᾽ ὕπερθε Πιμπλείας σκοπήν.

Leake 3. 423 placed Pimpleia at Litokhoro. The group of similar names in Boeotia (Paus. 9. 34. 4) includes Petra, which implies a position north of Dium, if the group is derived from Pieria.   [3] N. Ch. Kotzias in *AE* 1948/9 [1951], *Chronica* 25–40.

[4] Kotzias p. 26 maintains that there was a city called Pieris, but Pieris is simply a variant name for the district Pieria. His argument, that the *agalma* of Orpheus in Pieris and the *xoanon* of Orpheus near Leibethra are not one statue which broke into a sweat before Alexander set off for Asia but two separate statues in separate towns, is not at all convincing; for Arr. *Anab.* 1. 11. 2 and Plu. *Alex.* 14. 5 are referring to the same incident, and *agalma* is a general term which includes the specific term *xoanon*.

[5] Kotzias calls the torrents the Griva and the Kavourolakka; only the former is shown on the U.S.A. map 1:250,000, and I have marked it as the Sys. The disaster at Lynmouth in Devon in 1952 reminds one of the effect of a cloudburst above a torrent-bed leading to a town.

hill with torrents on three sides and even scantier remains of a wall; this hill is situated near Ayia Paraskeve, between Litokhoro and Dium.[1] It was evidently a *kome* of Dium, but there is no special reason to make it Pimpleia, and there is the disadvantage that it is south of Dium and of the Baphyras river.

The southern boundary of Pieria was normally the river Peneus, Heracleum being the first city of Macedonia in Ps.-Scylax 66 and Phila having that honour later, while Homolium, south of the mouth of the river, was in Magnesia. Whichever power was the stronger held the Vale of Tempe and the villages just north of it; for the pass can be turned through them, if one takes the track from Rapsani to Dereli, the ancient Gonnus, a city of the Perrhaebi. The southern part of Mt. Olympus is now called Lower Olympus. Its ancient name was Mt. Dotion; it is described by Lycophron *Alex.* 409 and Tzetzes ad loc. as marking the boundary of Greece, because it is itself in Macedonia, being contiguous with the Leibethrioi, and it creates the pass or gates (i.e. of Tempe). Lower Olympus forms the watershed of the Peneus river, but there are ways over it which lead into the high shelf or plateau under the bastions of High Olympus.[2] This high shelf or plateau supplies the headwaters of the river of Leibethra, the Ziliani; it has a pocket which contains a lake or swamp called Nezerou, the ancient Lake Ascuris (Livy 44. 2. 11), and it supports several villages, of which the chief is Karia. The Macedonians are likely to have claimed both the lake and the basin of the upper Ziliani river as the hinterland of Leibethra, while the Perrhaebians held the western part of both Lower Olympus and High Olympus. In 169 B.C. the consul Marcius Philippus marched from Pharsalus into Perrhaebia and camped between Azorus and Doliche (see Map 12). Here he was close to the cross-roads (Livy 44. 2. 7, *prope divortium itinerum*): he could take the Volustana pass into Elimea, or the Petra pass into the Pierian plain north of Dium, or turn back on to the high shelf between High Olympus and Lower Olympus, from which he could come down either into the Tempe pass or via Rapsani to Phila.

By camping where he did, the consul made Perseus divide his forces. One group held the Volustana pass. Perseus, being based on Dium, had under his own control a group which held the Petra pass.[3] And a third group held a strong-point above Lake Ascuris, which commanded the

[1] Ibid., p. 34; pieces of wall are shown in figs. 3 and 4, and the hill of Leibethra in fig. 2.

[2] I used one of these ways in March 1943, going at night from Ambelakia on Mt. Ossa across the river in the Tempe pass and climbing up over the pass of Lower Olympus on to the high shelf. After some days at Karia we moved high up round the west flank of Olympus and later crossed the Tripolitis to near Vouvala (Azorus). Lake Ascuris has been drained; there is a picture of it as a lake in Tozer 1. 40.

[3] Livy does not mention this point, which is in fact an obvious one; he was no doubt abbreviating the account of Polybius. Perseus had his headquarters—his castra stativa—at Dium. The garrisoning of Pythoüs and Petra in 168 B.C. is mentioned by Livy (44. 32. 9).

pass leading from the high shelf over Lower Olympus towards Rapsani. The consul moved with his whole army against the third group, but despite all his efforts he could not force the passage over the ridge of Lower Olympus which lies between Lake Ascuris and Rapsani. Rather than return as he had come, he put his army into reverse and descended on a desperate track above the tributaries of the Ziliani river and then via Skotina, making collapsible runways for his elephants and coming out in the end between Leibethra and Heracleum (Livy 44. 5. 12). The district in which the Macedonian strong-point lay was called Lapathus, and the track down to the plain between Leibethra and Heracleum passed through Callipeuce.[1] In 168 B.C. Scipio Nasica carried the Petra pass and came into the plain north of Dium (Plu. *Aem.* 15. 1).

When Perseus was defeated in the plain before Pydna, he set out with his cavalry for Pella (Livy 44. 42. 2). He took the 'via militaris', that is the Macedonian Royal road, into the Pierian forest (Livy 44. 43. 1, ad Pieriam silvam via militari . . . fugit), and some members of the royal entourage ('regius comitatus') stopped off at Beroea (Livy 44. 45. 2). It is clear from this that the 'via militaris' did not go along the coast into the central plain by Alorus, but went inland into the forests of the Pierian mountains and thence across the Haliacmon and up to Beroea, just as the later Roman road from Dium to Pella did (see p. 126 above). Aemilius Paulus will have taken the same 'via militaris', when he marched in two days from Pydna to Pella, a distance of some 44 m.p. The natural boundary of Pieria towards the north is the watershed of, or the lower slopes above, the river Haliacmon, so that for instance Alorus was in Bottiaea, whereas Pydna was in Pieria (Str. 7 frs. 20 and 22), but the actual boundary changed with circumstances, as the next chapter will show.

In Pieria there is no sign of an organization by tribal groups, such as we have seen in Upper Macedonia, either in Macedonian or in Roman times. The original Pieres had been exterminated or expelled to beyond the river Strymon (Thuc. 2. 99. 3). The name survived as that of the district Pieria and as that of a city Pierium or Pieria on the borderland between Macedonia and Thessaly. It was this city which the army of Ramphias reached in winter 422–421 B.C., when the Thessalians evidently held the Vale of Tempe (Thuc. 5. 13. 1), and the citizens of it were called the 'Pierotae'. Under the Macedonian kingdom the people of Pieria

---

[1] 'Lapathus' is probably the basin from which the upper Ziliani river and the Lake Ascuris drew their waters. It is possible that the Ziliani river was called the Lapathus, and that the 'Sabatum' of the Peutinger Table, which is at the crossing of the river (see p. 135 above), is a corruption of 'Lapathum'. At least this is less far-fetched than Heuzey's suggestion that Sabatum is a corruption of Sabazius, an epithet of Dionysus transferred to Orpheus and given as the name of a station on the road. Leake 3. 350 f. described the district of Lapathus and reported an ancient fortress 'on the ridge to the westward of Rapsani'; but he had not seen it himself.

were the Macedonians, and the individual cities, whether Macedonian or Greek, had their own boundaries.[1] Under Roman government Pieria was in the third tetrarchy, of which Pella was the administrative centre, and in later times, when Dium was 'colonia Julia Augusta Diensis', its territory comprised in effect the whole of ancient Pieria south of the watershed of the Haliacmon river.[2]

---

[1] The city Pieria is given by St. Byz. s.v. and by the *Suda* s.v. *Kriton*; the former gives the ethnic Pieriotes, the latter calls Kriton 'Pieriotes' = *FGrH* 277 T 1, and the ethnic occurs in the feminine form 'Peieriotis' in *IG* xii Suppl. no. 80 of the second century A.D. Hesychius s.v. helps to locate the Pierium of Thucydides, which is probably the same city, at the southern end of the Olympus range. The personal name Πειερίων occurs on an inscription in Delacoulonche, p. 114. The ethnics in Pieria are those of towns: Heracleotae, Leibethrii, Diastae, etc. The Aeginium of Livy 44. 46. 3 and 45. 27. 2 is not in Pieria, as Heuzey–Daumet 271 and others have supposed, but in Tymphaea (see *Epirus* 681); the Aeginium of Pliny *HN* 4. 33 is a conjecture based on Strabo's Αἰγίνιον Τυμφαίων (C 327), but the original reading should be retained: 'in regione quae Pieria appellabatur e nemore Aegidium (Aegydium *AFa*)'. The name Aegydium is probably the correct form, being a diminutive of Aegys, which is the name of a town, for instance, in Laconia. As Pliny ranks it with Aegeae and Beroea, Aegydium must have been an important city. The Acesae of St. Byz. is probably the Agassae of Livy 44. 7. 5 (where *V* has acassam) and 45. 27. 1 (where *M* has etcassas), but different from the Acesamenae of St. Byz. (some manuscripts giving a double sigma), which had its own tradition of having been founded by a king in Pieria, that is in the pre-Macedonian era.

[2] The extent of its territory is known from *CIL* iii 591, setting the frontier between Oloosson and Dium on the high shelf below High Olympus near Konispoli, where there is the watershed between the Ziliani and a tributary of the Titaresius, and from other inscriptions cited by Heuzey–Daumet 271.

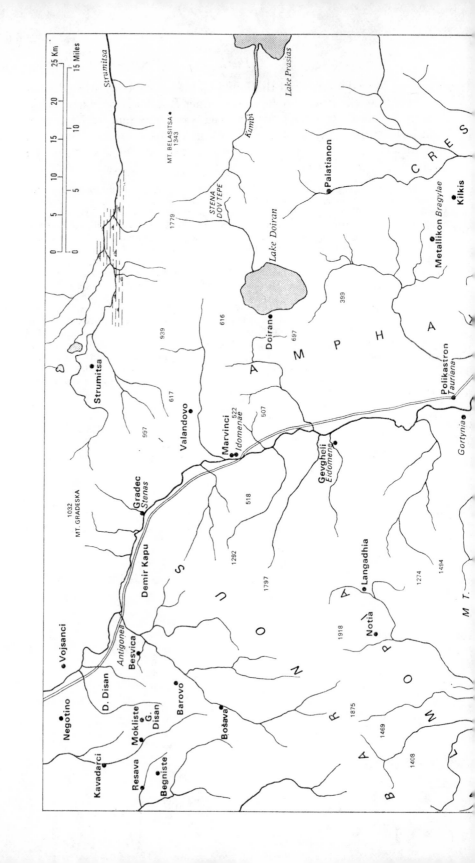

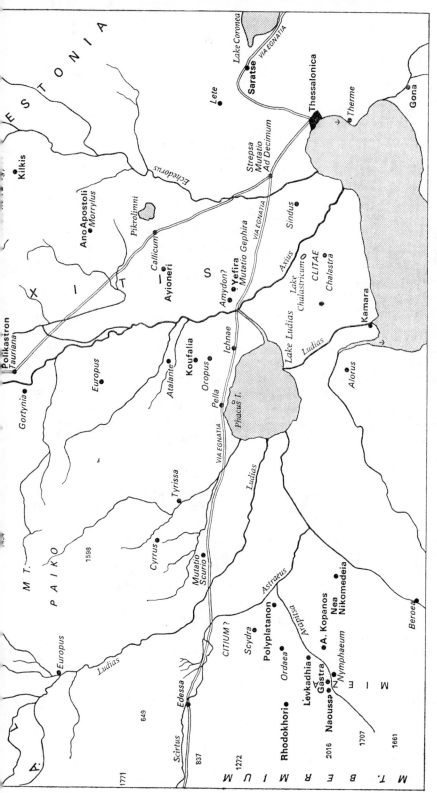

MAP 14. THE CENTRAL PLAIN AND THE MIDDLE VARDAR VALLEY *circa* 356 B.C. (HEIGHTS IN METRES).

IV

THE CENTRAL PLAIN AND ITS
HINTERLAND WEST OF THE AXIUS

1. *The Central Plain*

THE central plain of Lower Macedonia has been created by the alluvial deposits of the rivers which flow into the Thermaic Gulf (see Map 14). As the platform of silt has gradually spread and encroached upon the waters of the Gulf, the rivers themselves have repeatedly had to change their courses. The process is admirably described by Anna Comnena.

What happens in every large river is this: when a considerable embankment has been raised by the deposit they bring down, then they flow to a lower level, and forsaking as it were their first bed, leave it quite dry and bereft of water, and fill the new bed they now traverse with rushing streams. Between two such channels of the Bardarius, one the old gully, the other the newly formed passage, lay a piece of ground, and when that clever strategist, Alexius, my father, saw it, he pitched his camp there, since the two channels were not more than three stades distant from one another (*Alex.* 1. 7. 3, translated by E. A. S. Dawes).

A modern map shows old beds of the Haliacmon and the Axius which are still visible. A similar development has taken place, for instance, on the shore of the Ionian Gulf, where the Drin, the Mati, the Shkumbi, the Semeni, and the Vijosë have brought alluvium down to the sea; and again on the north shore of the Ambraciote Gulf, where the Arachthus and the Louros have done likewise.[1]

The chief rivers which enter the central plain are the Haliacmon, the Ludias which rises in the district of Moglena, the Axius, and the Echedorus which rises above Kilkis. These rivers are identified beyond doubt by Hdt. 7. 124 and 127. 1. There is one other river which enters the plain, that below Edessa. The part of this river above Edessa was called the Scirtus by Procopius (*Arc.* 18. 38; *Aed.* 2. 7. 2); he reports that the river destroyed much of Edessa, and that Justinian made a new channel for it through the town. Below Edessa the river is joined by several short but considerable streams at Skidhra and then flows into the plain. It is

---

[1] For these rivers see J. M. F. May in *JRS* 36 (1946) 55 f.; *Epirus* 133 and 138; and above, p. 26.

probable that the lower part of this river was called the Astraeus; for Aelian, in describing the Macedonian form of fly-fishing for the dappled trout (apparently with a mock dragon-fly), says that it was practised in a river, called the Astraeus, 'flowing between Beroea and Thessalonica'. Leake suggested that Aelian's Astraeus was the Haliacmon under another name, but the Haliacmon does not flow between Beroea and Thessalonica.[1] The Astraeus and its upper tributary, the Skirtos or 'leaper', would certainly be an excellent river for trout. In its lower course it may have been joined by the stream of Beroea; and if so, its nymph Astraea had good reason to be chosen as the nurse of the lady Beroe (Nonn. *D.* 41. 212 f.).

The part of book 7 in which Strabo described the rivers of the Thermaic Gulf is lost. We have three confused fragments in which mention is made of a river Erigon. The confusion begins in fr. 20 from the *Epitome Vaticana* and in fr. 22 from the *Epitome edita*, which both give 'after Dium' the outlets of the Haliacmon, then Pydna, Methone, Alorus, the Erigon river, and the Ludias. It is clear that the Haliacmon has got misplaced between Dium and Pydna and that its proper place between Alorus and the Ludias has been given to the Erigon. We may then dismiss the Erigon here as an interloper. But it also appears twice as a tributary of the Axius, not where it belongs, in Lyncus, Pelagonia, and Paeonia, but in the central plain: in fr. 20 'leaving the city (Pella) on the left and joining the Axius'; and in fr. 23 from the *Epitome edita* 'the Axius dividing Bottiaea from Amphaxitis and receiving the Erigon river flows into the sea between Chalastra and Therme'. Now this confluence with the Axius is only possible if the Erigon jumped over the Ludias river, which in the same fragments comes between the Erigon and the Axius and itself flows into the sea. The junction of the Erigon with the Axius by Stobi has evidently been totally misplaced by the epitomizers.

We can, however, extract some points of interest from the fragments. The description of the supposititious Erigon in fr. 20 should be given to the Haliacmon 'flowing from the (territory of the) Triclari (or Triclares) through the (territory of the) Orestae and through the territory of Pella, leaving the city on the left', and this description, though much abbreviated and incomplete, is likely to have been true of Strabo's time, when Pella, like Dium, had a very extensive territory.[2] Secondly, the river Ludias forms a lake of the same name and then flows from it into the sea; its course is navigable for 120 stades, that is up to Pella, a city enlarged by Philip, which stands on an ἄκρα in the lake (frs. 20 and 22;

---

[1] Leake 3. 293 and 468. The phrase 'between Beroea and Thessalonica' probably means that the ancient road between the towns crossed the river.

[2] For a different interpretation of this passage by F. Papazoglou see p. 75 n. 4 above; the Loeb edition, p. 340 n. 2, gives a summary view of the difficulties.

cf. fr. 23 init.). Thirdly, an offshoot of the Axius flows into Lake Ludias (frs. 20 and 23, both using the word ἀπόσπασμα); the Axius enters the sea 'between Chalastra and Therme' (frs. 20 and 23); the mouth of the Axius is 20 stades from that of the Echedorus; and the latter is 40 stades from Thessalonica (fr. 21 from the *Epitome Vaticana*).

If we take the last point first, the distances show that the Echedorus entered the sea where the Axius does today, and that the Axius entered the sea about half-way between the two outlets it has today. This information dates from a time after the foundation of Thessalonica by Cassander. The outlet of the Axius 'between Chalastra and Therme' is to be dated before the foundation of Thessalonica, which displaced Therme in importance and was closer to Chalastra, and after the time of Herodotus, when Chalastra as well as Therme was to the east of the outlet of the Axius (Hdt. 7. 123. 3). As a change of course is normally caused by the accumulation of heavy deposits below the point of entry into the plain, a new bed can have been formed without destroying Chalastra. As regards an arm of the Axius flowing into Lake Ludias, this is possible, particularly in times of flood.

The lake itself has been drained, and the channels which carry the water off give a general idea only of the lie of the land. But we can see from the descriptions of travellers that the Lake of Yiannitsa, as it was then called, underwent some change between 1800 and 1870. In December 1806 Leake described the lake as occupying the plain 'in great part' and the rivers Ludias and Axius as forming 'a joint stream . . . navigable into the lake, and probably up to Pella, as it was in ancient times'. His map at the end of his volume iii shows the extent of the lake at high level and at low level, and the Ludias joining the Axius a few kilometres above the point where the Axius entered the sea. In late August 1869 Tozer saw from Yiannitsa 'a dull green marsh and beyond it a lake which is not visible from the plain' with an outflow into the Axius 'just before that river flows into the sea'; but he knew nothing of a navigable channel into the lake, which had evidently become much blocked with silt.[1]

In the time of Herodotus the Ludias joined the Haliacmon, not the Axius (Hdt. 7. 127. 1, ἐς τὠυτὸ ῥέεθρον τὸ ὕδωρ συμμίσγοντες); and we can see that this is likely to have occurred only when the Haliacmon flowed north-eastwards into the plain for some distance and the Ludias flowed towards the Haliacmon rather than towards the Axius, as on Map 15. Now Herodotus says that the Echedorus entered the sea alongside the swamp which was 'by the river Axius' (Hdt. 7. 124, ἐξίει παρὰ τὸ ἕλος τὸ ἐπ᾽ Ἀξιῷ ποταμῷ). This swamp is something different from the string of little lagoons which occur all along the delta and are valuable especially for salt and for fish,[2] and it was evidently a considerable swamp,

---

[1] Leake 3. 436; Tozer 1. 155.   [2] Leake, ibid.

separating the mouth of the Axius from that of the Echedorus but fed
by the Axius. It bears no relation to the Lake of Yiannitsa. Indeed it is
very interesting and striking, when one thinks of it, that he does not
mention any lake in the region occupied until recently by the Lake of
Yiannitsa. The natural explanation is that there was not one there in
the first half of the fifth century.

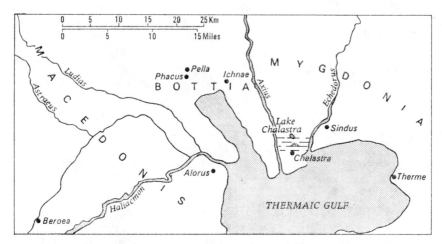

MAP 15. THE THERMAIC GULF, *circa* 600–450 B.C.

In 1938 Oberhummer described the Lake of Yiannitsa as being 5
square km in extent within some 90 square km of swamp and as being
3 m deep and 4 m above sea level.[1] In antiquity the level of the sea in the
Mediterranean was some 5 feet lower than it is today, and this means
that the high flood level in the central plain, e.g. in the vicinity of
Alorus, was 5 feet lower and that the rivers had that much more fall.[2]
But even so it seems that the Lake of Yiannitsa did not lie in a deep hollow
or basin, being only 3 m deep, but was created by the waters of a river
and the accumulation of silt round it and below it. There is then no *a
priori* reason to assume that a lake existed there in the first half of the fifth
century. Indeed such a swamp or lake as there was at that time lay
between the beds of the Axius and the Echedorus, as they approached
the sea.

The courses of the rivers in the first half of the fifth century are known
to us: those of the Haliacmon and the Ludias from the position of Alorus
on the Haliacmon's south bank and from Herodotus' statement that
their waters joined before entering the sea; and those of the Axius and

---

[1] *RE* 19. 1 (1937) 343.
[2] For the evidence on this matter, see my article on the battle of Salamis in *JHS* 76 (1956)
35 and *Epirus*, index under 'Sea-level, changes of'.

Echedorus from his statements that Therme, Sindus, and Chalastra were east of the Axius, and that a marsh lay between their lower courses. We can now understand his further statement that the strip of Bottiaeis *beside the sea*, which the two towns, Ichnae and Pella, held to the west of the river Axius, was a narrow area (Hdt. 7. 123. 3, Βοττιαιίδα, τῆς ἔχουσι τὸ παρὰ θάλασσαν, στεινὸν χωρίον, πόλιες ῎Ιχναι τε καὶ Πέλλα). For it is apparent that a narrow arm of the sea ran up between the mouth of the joint Haliacmon–Ludias and the mouths of the Axius and the Echedorus as far as the territory of Ichnae and Pella. I have shown on Map 15 the approximate shape of the Gulf at that time.[1] One can see readily that the Athenians and their allies in 432 B.C., in marching from Pydna to the vicinity of Potidaea, had to proceed to Beroea and then round the head of the Gulf (Thuc. 1. 62. 4),[2] and that Thucydides was speaking almost literally when he referred to territory reaching from inland 'down to Pella and the sea' (2. 99. 4, ἄνωθεν μέχρι Πέλλης καὶ θαλάσσης).

The division of the central plain into districts was certainly related to the courses of the rivers, which were serious obstacles and could not be bridged in the delta.

Thus the Axius provided a clear line of demarcation in the plain. To Hecataeus the country east of the Axius was Thrace,[3] and he therefore attributed the first three cities or peoples east of the Axius to Thrace— namely, Chalastra, Therme, and the Sindonaei (*FGrH* 1 F 146 and F 147). To Herodotus the country east of the Axius in the plain was Mygdonia (no doubt known to Hecataeus as a canton of Thrace), and he attributed the same three cities or peoples to Mygdonia (Hdt. 7. 123. 3). The country west of the Axius in the plain was stated by Herodotus to be Bottiaeis (7. 123. 3 τὸν Ἀξιὸν ποταμόν, ὃς οὐρίζει χώρην τὴν Μυγδονίην τε καὶ Βοττιαιίδα), and it is likely that he was here too in agreement with Hecataeus. The next line of demarcation in the plain is provided by what Herodotus calls the joint waters of the Ludias and the Haliacmon, that is, in our terminology, by the Haliacmon below the point of con- fluence of the Ludias. We should note that Herodotus is writing only of the coastal sector and not, for instance, of the Ludias above its confluence with the Haliacmon, because he is describing the encampment of Xerxes' forces along the coastal belt of the Thermaic Gulf. The passage runs as follows: ἐπέσχε δὲ ὁ στρατὸς αὐτοῦ στρατοπεδευόμενος τὴν παρὰ θάλασσαν χώρην τοσήνδε, ἀρξάμενος ἀπὸ Θέρμης πόλιος καὶ τῆς Μυγδονίης μέχρι

---

[1] Oberhummer, loc. cit., reproduces the maps of A. Struck for the shape of the Thermaic Gulf at various periods and remarks that they are far-fetched; Edson in *CP* 50 (1955) 187 n. 77 supports Oberhummer's comments. Struck's map for the fifth century does not show Alorus as the most westerly point of the Gulf, or a narrow strip by the sea for Ichnae and Pella. I have therefore not thought it necessary to deal with his arguments in detail.

[2] This campaign is discussed below, p. 183.

[3] See C. F. Edson in *CP* 50 (1955) 171 on Hecataeus' definition of Thrace.

Λυδίεω τε ποταμοῦ καὶ Ἁλιάκμονος, οἳ οὐρίζουσι γῆν τὴν Βοττιαιίδα τε καὶ Μακεδονίδα, ἐς τὠυτὸ ῥέεθρον τὸ ὕδωρ συμμίσγοντες (127). Thus in the coastal part of the plain Bottiaeis extended from the Axius to the Haliacmon, and Macedonis commenced south of the Haliacmon below its confluence with the Ludias, as those rivers ran *c.* 500 B.C. (see Map 15). The district Macedonis, which included 'the Makedonikon mountain', lay between this part of the Haliacmon river and Pieria, which evidently began for Herodotus close to Mt. Olympus (Hdt. 7. 131). It was peopled by Macedones living in this coastal sector and also by Macedones living inland on 'the Makedonikon mountain' (Hdt. 7. 128. 1 Μακεδόνων τῶν κατύπερθε οἰκημένων and 7. 131). This district was evidently the home-land in a special sense of the Macedones at this time.[1]

Two other fragments of Hecataeus are relevant to the central plain. In one mention is made of the river Ludias in the form Loidias: F 145, Λοιδίας ... ὅτι δὲ τῆς Μακεδονίας ἔστι ποταμός, ἄλλοι τε ἱστοροῦσι καὶ Ἑκαταῖος ἐν Περιόδῳ Γῆς. The second fragment is more interesting: F 144, *à propos* the word φακός, meaning a lentil, Ἑκαταῖος· πρὸς μὲν νότον Παωλος καὶ Φάκος. We meet Φάκος later as the name of an isolated rise below Pella, which had to be enlarged by an artificial embankment, in order to support the fortified keep, in which the Macedonian kings, probably from Philip II onwards, kept their treasury and their prisoners; even when it was so built up, it was surrounded by swamp.[2] The fact that Hecataeus mentions Phacus indicates that it was *not* then a small rise in a swamp, but rather that it was the central feature of a town, similar to Chalastra or Therme. The expression πρὸς μὲν νότον probably means south of the Axius river according to Hecataeus' orientation, and the adjacent name read as Παωλᾶ by Epimer and as Παῶλος by Cramer is more likely to be Pella, perhaps spelt Πάλλα, than Pactolus, Tmolus, and Alorus, which have been suggested.[3] In F 146 there is an additional state-ment, which I think is from Hecataeus, that there was a lake of the same name as Chalastra.[4] This lake, ἡ λίμνη Χαλάστρα or Χαλαστραία is to be distinguished from the swamp by the Axius (Hdt. 7. 124, τὸ ἕλος τὸ ἐπ᾽ Ἀξιῷ ποταμῷ).

Our next body of information comes from Ps.-Scylax, whose work refers to the state of affairs obtaining probably in 380–360 B.C. and cer-tainly not later than 356 B.C., and from Ps.-Scymnus, whose information

[1] Herodotus uses 'Macedonis' here alone; otherwise he has 'Macedonia' but in a much wider sense (e.g. at 5. 17. 2 and 7. 185. 2).

[2] The description is from Livy 44. 46. 6.

[3] The opposite inference is usually drawn from Hecataeus' mention of Phacus, e.g. by Edson in *CP* 50 (1955) 188 n. 91. For the use of πρὸς νότον in Hecataeus compare F 171 Τριζοί· ἔθνος πρὸς νότον τοῦ Ἴστρου. Ἑκαταῖος Εὐρώπῃ. For suggested restorations see Jacoby ad loc. and Edson, ibid., n. 88; Hecataeus has Χαλάστρη and Herodotus has Χαλέστρη, so that the use of an alpha for an epsilon by Hecataeus giving Πάλλα is not improbable.

[4] Compare Hecataeus F 159 ἐν δὲ λίμνη Μάρις, ἐν δὲ Μαρώνεια πόλις.

is of the years just before 356 B.C.[1] We have already noted that Ps.-Scylax uses καί to connect his groups, and that his first group is καὶ Ἁλιάκμων ποταμός, Ἄλωρος πόλις, indicating to the mariner sailing from the south that he strikes the outflow of the Haliacmon and that the town Alorus lies on its bank (on its south bank as we have seen, p. 133 above). The next group is καὶ ποταμὸς Λυδίας, Πέλλα πόλις (καὶ βασίλειον ἐν αὐτῇ καὶ ἀναπλοῦς ἐς αὐτὴν ἀνὰ τὸν Λυδίαν), Ἀξιὸς ποταμός, Ἐχέδωρος ποταμός, Θέρμη πόλις. Ps.-Scymnus 624–5 adds one significant point, that of the many towns in the interior (ἐν τῇ μεσογείῳ)[2] the most distinguished are Pella and Beroea, whereas on the coast (ἐν παραλίᾳ) there are Thessalonica and Pydna.

It is clear that a radical change has taken place. There are now four and not three rivers entering the Gulf, because the Ludias no longer flows into the Haliacmon. Pella is on the bank of the Ludias, it is reached by sailing up the Ludias, and the distance up the river is such that the city is said to lie in the interior. It contains the royal residence;[3] and as we know from Xen. *HG* 5. 2. 13, it was already in 383 B.C. the greatest city in the realm. The radical change in the central plain has evidently come about through further deposits of silt, made by the rivers on both sides, which finally closed the arm of the sea. The major part in this change was certainly played by the Axius, the creator of the sixth-to-fifth-century marsh and lake near Chalastra; but the separation of the Ludias from the Haliacmon was probably due to the Haliacmon deposit blocking the point of confluence with the Ludias and diverting it eastwards in its lower course.

There is reason to believe that the Lake of Ludias existed in the time of Philip II. We know from Ps.-Scylax that the Ludias was navigable then as far as Pella, and this occurred at other times when there was a lake below Yiannitsa. Aristotle was twitted with preferring to live 'in the outflow of slime' (Plu. *Moralia* 603 c, βορβόρου ἐν προχοαῖς) rather than in the Academy, when he was with Philip and Alexander. Plutarch explains the words by saying that there was a river Borborus near Pella, but it is more likely (as Delacoulonche, p. 120 n. 3, observed) that the allusion is to the muddy waters by Phacus, due perhaps to the inflowing arm of the Axius. Moreover, Archestratus, a contemporary of Aristotle, mentioned the chromis fish of Pella, which supposes a lake or some open water by Pella (Athen. 7. 328). The description of Pella and the lake which is preserved in Str. fr. 20 (from the *Epitome Vaticana*) seems to be made with reference to the time of Philip, who, having been brought

---

[1] For these dates see my arguments in *Epirus* 511 f. and 515 f.

[2] Pliny *HN* 4. 34 makes the same distinction: 'in ora ... oppida Pydna, Aloros ... intus ... Pella colonia.'

[3] The expression refers not to a palace but to the administrative centre of the Macedonian Kingdom.

up there (i.e. when it was already the capital), enlarged the city, which was situated on a headland in the lake.[1] At that time, too, if our inference is correct, the lake was filled by an arm of the Axius (αὐτὴν δὲ πληροῖ τοῦ Ἀξιοῦ τι ἀπόσπασμα). Such an arm evidently represents an earlier bed of the Axius. In this earlier bed the Axius will have contributed to the creation of the lake and of the navigation channel to the sea, followed by the Ludias. The subsequent filling or replenishing of the lake will have occurred when the Axius was in flood. Such a process is indicated by Livy's mention of the 'restagnantes amnes' in relation to Pella: 44. 46. 5, 'cingunt paludes inexsuperabilis altitudinis aestate et hieme, quas restagnantes faciunt amnes'.[2] In the same fragment from the *Epitome Vaticana* the Axius enters the sea between Chalastra and Therme. This change from the situation which existed in the time of Herodotus is likely also to have come about before 356 B.C.

After 356 B.C. the situation seems to have been held on fairly constant lines. This was due not to chance but to man's control of the rivers. Theophrastus, who was born between 372 and 369 B.C., and studied the plants of the plain of Philippi, says that when the Thracians occupied the plain it was full of trees and water, and that changes had come about, because the whole area round Philippi and Crenides had been drained and dried up. This great work of drainage and reclamation was due to Philip II, who took the plain from the Thracians in 356 B.C.[3] There is no doubt that in the time of Philip the Macedonians had devised means also of controlling the flooding of the central plain of Macedonia, and that these means were maintained by his successors. Our last piece of evidence, from fr. 22 of the *Epitome edita*, that the voyage up the Ludias to Pella was one of 120 stades = some 24 km, represents the maximum distance in the time of Philip; it shows us roughly where the coast of the Gulf ran at that time.[4] In Map 16 I have given an indication of the probable shape of the Gulf *c.* 356 B.C.[5]

[1] The description refers to Pella, the subject of the sentence ἔχει δὲ ἄκραν ἐν λίμνῃ τῇ καλουμένῃ Λουδίᾳ, and not to the fortified keep on a small island in the lake. Analogies are provided by the site of Ioannina on a promontory running into the lake and the island in the lake, on which Ali Pasha took his pleasures and met his death (see *Epirus* 167 for the site).

[2] Livy is referring not to the absolute depth of the lake but to the fact that troops could not wade through it to attack the walls of Pella. Livy describes the delta of the Baphyras in similar terms: 44. 6. 15, ostium late restagnans Baphyri amnis.

[3] One imagines Theophrastus did most of his field-work in the 340s and 330s, and one has to allow an interval of time after the drainage for the new flora and trees to become established. Aelian *VH* 4. 19 states that Theophrastus was honoured by Philip II. He was probably with Aristotle in Macedonia, when Aristotle was teaching Alexander in the late 340s.

[4] The distance today is 26 km as the crow flies and 34 km if one follows the sinuosities of the modern drainage channel from the site of the old lake. On the same basis Pella was about 18 km from the sea at the mouth of the Ludias as the crow flew.

[5] It is very probable that something similar happened with the Drilon and Lake Labeatis (the lake of Scodra). Strabo C 326 says that one could sail up the Drilon as far as Dardanian territory, a statement which is likely to have come from Hecataeus, who underlies the

Of the cities on the coast of the plain Therme is the most easterly in Herodotus' account of the fleet of Xerxes sailing into the Thermaic Gulf. On passing Aenea (situated on Cape Karaburnu), which was the last city in 'the Crossaean territory', the fleet entered 'the Gulf itself' and the territorial waters of Mygdonia (Hdt. 7. 123. 3) and came to Therme, which was thus the first city Xerxes reached in Mygdonia. Sindus and Chalastra came between Therme and the area round the river Axius (7. 179, Θέρμης πόλιος, 7. 123. 3 and 7. 124. 1). The Gulf took its name from Therme,

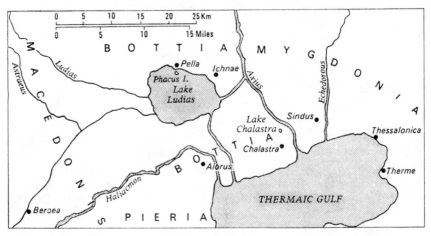

MAP 16. THE THERMIC GULF *circa* 356 B.C.

presumably therefore a port on the coast, and Therme took its name from hot springs. Such springs exist still at Loutra Sedhes, some 8 km inland of the coast which lies between Cape Karaburnu and the Cape of Little Karaburnu, a coast which is exposed to 'a strong current from the Axios river, which sweeps across the bay southward of Cape Mikro Karaburnu ... this current sometimes attains a rate of 2½ knots'.[1] The distance of these springs inland and the unsuitability of the coast between the Karaburnu Capes rule out an identification of Therme with Loutra Sedhes.[2]

description of Illyris in Strabo (see *Epirus* 468). Such a voyage was probably up through Lake Labeatis, formed by the great outflow of the Drilon. At a later date the Drilon or Oriundes, as it was also called, did not enter the lake, and the outflow of Lake Labeatis, using the bed cut originally by the Drilon, was called the Barbanna (Livy 44. 30. 3), which remained navigable (44. 31. 10). The Drin returned into the bed of the outflow, now called the Bojana, as recently as 1859 as a result of two years of abnormal floods (A. Baldacci, *Itinerari Albanesi, 1892–1902* (Florence, 1917) 292).

[1] *MP* 4. 221. 6.

[2] More exactly with a site of the classical period north-east of Sedhes, but my arguments turn on the position of the hot springs and the suitability of the coast. C. Edson in *CP* 42 (1947) 100 f. adduces other arguments too against the identification, which was proposed by E. Oberhummer in *RE* 5 A 2 (1934) 2391 and adopted in *ATL* 1. 546.

Hot springs are known to have existed at Thessalonica in the seventh century A.D. The town is on a part of the coast which is not exposed to the current from the Axius, and a quay south-east of the modern harbour provides sailing-craft with shelter from the dangerous south-westerly winds and the strong northerly winds.[1] This piece of coast, called Kalamaria, seems the most appropriate place for the harbour of Therme. The town may have been not on the strand itself but on higher, defensible ground, and the most convenient height is on the Cape of Little Karaburnu. Excavation has shown that both sites were of importance from the Early Iron Age onwards.[2] We may conclude, then, with some confidence that Therme was on the eastern side of the bay, its harbour at Kalamaria and its citadel on the northern side of Little Karaburnu.[3]

The position of Sindus is known only from Herodotus' statement that it lay between Therme and Chalastra; the exact site has yet to be discovered.[4] Chalastra was famed for a lake, fed by a spring, which yielded nitre, an ancient equivalent of soap. Such a lake with nitre was recorded by one Hadschi Chalfa as being near a village Aschik, north-west of Salonica.[5] Unfortunately the village does not appear on a modern map. The lake may be the small one shown between the two arms of the Axius on the U.S.A. map 1:250,000 (see Map 14). Chalastra was a city in its own right (Plu. *Alex.* 49. 2) with a strong place for defence (D. S. 30. 4), and it appears as an 'oppidum' on the coast in Pliny (*HN* 4. 36), who gives a full description of the nitrous lake, situated in a district called Clitae, and of its 'nitrum Chalestricum' (*HN* 31. 107 f.).[6] The most likely site for Chalastra is Koulakia (now Khalastra), just above the modern high-flood level, because habitable sites are rare in this part of the delta.

[1] *MP* 4. 223. 23.
[2] See p. 327 below and in particular K. A. Romaios in *Mak.* 1 (1940) 1–7, and *AD* 20 (1965) 2. 411.
[3] I owe much to the work of C. F. Edson cited above, although we come to a slightly different conclusion, as he regards the old city of Salonica as the most probable site. The fact that Pliny *HN* 4. 36 distinguishes between the sectors of the upper Thermaic Gulf and gives both Thessalonice and Therme leads me to keep the sites apart ('medioque litoris flexu Thessalonice . . . Therme in Thermaico sinu'); Procopius, *Aed.* 4. 4. 3, includes a Therma in the list of places fortified by Justinian, and St. Byz. s.v. gives only one city Therme, which suggests that it is the same old Therme under different management.
[4] See C. F. Edson, op. cit. 105, who argues decisively against the tentative proposal in *ATL* 1. 548 to equate Sindus and Sinus.
[5] Cited by E. Oberhummer in *RE* 3. 2 (1899) 2038 and Struck, p. 8. The latter thinks the reference is to the modern Pikrolimni, but this lake is rather north than north-west of Salonica.
[6] Among the writers who refer to this lake is St. Byz. s.v. *Chalastra*, where the reading λίμνη is better attested than λιμήν. He quotes Hecataeus on Therme and Chalastre = F 146, and I have suggested on p. 147 above that the mention of the homonymous lake comes also from Hecataeus. At the end of the entry St. Byz. quotes an unnamed author for the name of the lake producing λίτρον, an early form of the later word νίτρον. This early form indicates that he was continuing to quote Hecataeus, although the sentences in St. Byz. have got out of order or lack some connecting words.

Its position gives us a clue to the ancient coastline.[1] It is now 7 km inland. Procopius (*Aed.* 4. 3. 28) gives a glowing account of the fertility of the plain watered by the Echedorus, which he calls the 'Rhekhias'.

The position of Ichnae is not far from Pella, since these two cities held the coastal strip, 'a narrow area', of Bottiaeis. It was west of the Axius, being in Bottiaeis and not in Mygdonia (Hdt. 7. 123. 3). The fact that Pliny *HN* 4. 35, taking places on the coast first and peoples or places inland second, puts Ichnae on the coast next to the mouth of the Axius ('mox in ora Ichnae, fluvius Axius'), indicates that he was using an early periplous, indeed such a work as Hecataeus, *Periodos Ges*. As Herodotus was naming places from east to west, Ichnae was east of Pella. Being by this piece of coast in the sixth to fifth century means that Ichnae was on the edge of the plain. An inscription first recorded by A. Struck in *AM* 27 (1902) 309 has as the sixth line of a broken-topped stone 'I]χναιων δη[. The stone had been found on the left bank of the Axius near Koufalia, and Struck's suggestion that it was concerned with some agreement between the Ichnaei[2] and their neighbours across the Axius is a possible one. Koufalia is not far from the point where the Axius enters the plain. The best position for Ichnae is in the vicinity of Nea Khalkidhon.

The recent excavations of Pella have determined the exact position of the enlarged Pella of Philip II. The city was on both sides of the modern road at the 38th km and it extended a long way inland to two gently rising hills, of which that to the west is thought by the excavators to have been the acropolis. The buildings with the famous mosaics are just beside the road, and from them one can see the mound known as Phacus lower down in what was the ancient lake-bed. The city was built on arable land, low-lying and slightly undulating, and it lacks any natural defences. Roman Pella was on a different site, at least on the evidence of the excavations so far, and it lay probably by the spring known as 'the baths of Alexander' towards Nea Pella.[3] Before the conquest of this area by the Macedonians, according to a tradition preserved by Stephanus Byzantinus s.v. *Pella*, the site of Pella was occupied under the name Bounomus or Bounomea, and it took the name Pella from the Macedonian founder 'Pellas'.

---

[1] Hecataeus (*FGrH* 1 F 146) places Chalastra *on* the coast of the Gulf: ἐν δ' αὐτῷ Θέρμη πόλις. ἐν δὲ Χαλάστρῃ. So too does Hdt. 7. 124, as the naval part of the expeditionary force camped on the coast by Chalastra and the other cities. Struck, p. 6, noted that Koulakia, then some 3 km inland, had been on the coast within living memory.

[2] St. Byz. s.v. gives this ethnic; the ethnic 'Ιχναῖος occurs on an inscription in Athens (*IG* iii 2. 2500). The list of Delphic *Theorodokoi* has ἐν 'Ιχναις (*BCH* 45 (1921) 17, iii 63). St. Byz. reports that Eratosthenes gave the name of the city as Achnae.

[3] P. Petsas in *Archaeology* 17 (1964) 75–84, where the nature of the site is seen from figs. 1, 4, and 16. On p. 75 he refers to 'the remains of a Roman wall' near the spring. 'The baths of Alexander' are probably those mentioned by Machon (third century B.C.) in Athenaeus 8. 348 e.

The site is strategically placed at the centre of the main routes through
Lower Macedonia. It commands the route from west to east which runs
between the foot of Mt. Paiko and what was still the coast in the early
fifth century and became a swampy part of the coastal plain. To this
route there is no alternative until one reaches the latitude of Stobi, and
then the route is much more difficult of access from the west and from
the east (see p. 66 above). At the same time it stands close to the route
from south to north which runs west of the Axius river. No other route
west of the Axius was available to the inhabitants of Lower Macedonia,
except the devious route through Eordaea, Lyncus, and Pelagonia to
Stobi. Moreover, the route northwards through the great gorge of the
Axius at Demir Kapu is on the west side of the river, so that inhabitants
of Lower Macedonia east of the Axius had to cross over to the right
bank in order to use the route. The best crossing of the lower Axius is
just to the east of Pella and Ichnae. Here is the ford which was used by
the army of Xerxes (Aesch. *Persae* 493), and here is the site of the bridge
which was used by the Macedonian kings and by travellers on the Via
Egnatia. Add to this the advantages of a land-locked all-weather harbour,
and one can see why Archelaus adopted Pella as his capital.

The district to which Pella belonged in terms of the divisions given by
Herodotus was Bottiaeis (7. 123. 3). Strabo too is aware of the early
connotations of Bottiaeis as a district of Macedonia, so called from Cretan
settlers led by Botton (in what we should call the Late Bronze Age), and
he attributed Alorus and Pella in Lower Macedonia to the Bottiaeis
of the Cretan settlers.[1] It is likely that Strabo drew this information
from a source used also by Herodotus. But Thucydides, using pre-
conquest terms, attributed Pella to what had been 'Paeonia' and not to
what had been 'Bottia' (2. 99. 3–4) ; and then, using contemporary terms
in describing the course of Sitalces' invasion from a northerly direction,
he says that Sitalces went into Macedonia to the left of (i.e. east of)
Pella and Cyrrus and not inland of (i.e. west and north-west of) Pella and
Cyrrus into Bottiaea and Pieria, the consequence being that Sitalces
ravaged Mygdonia, Grestonia, and Anthemus (2. 100. 4). It is thus clear
that already in the fifth century Bottia or Bottiaeis (ἡ Βοττιαΐς sc. γῆ)
was a term of shifting meaning. In the time of the Roman Empire the
term Bottiaeis seems to have been replaced by the term Emathia.[2]
Strabo himself said that Emathia was the previous name of what was
then Macedonia, and added that there was also a city by the sea called
Emathia (7 fr. 11). Ptol. 3. 13. 9 attributed eleven cities, including Pella,

[1] Str. C 279, C 282, and C 329 frs. 11, 20, and 22. The *Epitome Vaticana* preserves frs. 11 and
20, while the *Epitome Edita* preserves the one relevant sentence of fr. 22 which closely resembles one in fr. 20.

[2] Tiles and waterpipes have been found at Pella with the letters *HMA*, short probably for
Ἠμα(θίας) (*BS* 4. 157 f.).

to Emathia, and he evidently used the term 'Emathia' to cover all Lower Macedonia west of the Axius river with the exception of Pieria.

As regards Pieria we have already noted the discrepancy between Herodotus and Thucydides, the former placing Macedonia between Bottiaeis and Pieria, and the latter placing Bottiaea and Pieria alongside one another as representing τὴν ἄλλην Μακεδονίαν, which Sitalces did not invade (2. 100. 4). The explanation is no doubt that the nomenclature of these regions changed with changing circumstances between *c*. 500 B.C., if, as we suppose, Herodotus was drawing on Hecataeus, and 429 B.C., when Sitalces invaded Macedonia. When the term Macedonis was abandoned, the meaning of Bottiaeis was evidently extended by some writers to include an area south of the Haliacmon river. For two fragments of Strabo (7 frs. 20 and 22) state that (at an unspecified time) Alorus was considered a Bottiaic city and Pydna a Pieric city.[1] It seems probable that the watershed south of the Haliacmon had become for them the frontier between Bottiaeis and Pieria. Other writers extended the meaning of Pieria to include Alorus and other towns in Pieria, evidently making the Haliacmon the frontier.

There are three cities which were apparently situated between the watershed and the Haliacmon river: Alorus, Vallae, and Phylacae. For Pliny *HN* 4. 10. 33, proceeding round the plain from Alorus to Pella, gave after Alorus 'Vallaei, Phylacaei', and Ptolemy placed both Vallae and Phylacae in Pieria. The situation of Alorus is clearly expressed by Pliny's words 'in ora . . . Aloros, amnis Haliacmon, intus Aloritae'. The city was on the bank of the river near its mouth, and the territory of the inhabitants extended on to the low ridge inland (intus), which forms the watershed on the south side of the river. It is very probable that Vallae and Phylacae were also down in the plain between the foothills and the river, because the plain was much more extensive then than it is today, since the river then had a more northerly course (see above, p. 133). If so, these three cities were in the same sort of position as Dium, Macedonian Pydna, Pella, Chalastra, Sindus, and Therme. Vallae appears in Greek as Οὔαλλαι in Ptol. 3. 13. 40 and as Βάλλα in St. Byz. s.v. The form which is most Macedonian is Βάλλα, because a number of Macedonian names begin with beta and none with the diphthong ου. Balla and Pella, particularly if it was sometimes spelt as Palla (see p. 147 above), are almost interchangeable, even as B and P were interchangeable. It is not unlikely that in their conquest of the central plain east of the Haliacmon river the Macedones named their new town Pella after their old town Balla. The other notice of Vallae is St. Byz. Βάλλα,

---

[1] The *Epitome Vaticana* and the *Epitome Edita* both have this sentence with the forms 'Bottaic' and 'Pieric'. The former includes the word νομίζουσιν, which implies a departure from what might have been expected. The subject of the verb remains unknown.

πόλις Μακεδονίας ὡς Πέλλα. ὁ πολίτης Βαλλαῖος. Θεαγένης ἐν Μακεδονίᾳ (*FGrH* 774 F 3) "Βαλλαίους μεταγαγὼν εἰς τὸν νῦν λεγόμενον Πύθιον τόπον". I shall discuss later the date of the transfer of Balla's population to Pythion. The only mentions of Phylacae in a literary source are in Pliny and Ptolemy. Neither place is mentioned in any inscription. Their total disappearance is understandable if they were close to the Haliacmon, before the river changed its course and flowed closer to the foothills.

Those who have studied the topography of Macedonia have usually placed Balla at Palatitsa, which is not far from the entry of the Haliacmon into the plain (see Map 12). They are then faced with the difficulty that the order in Pliny—Alorus, Vallaei, Phylacae—requires Phylacae to be east of Palatitsa, and that there is not room for another large city in the available space. On the whole it seems best to place Balla and Phylacae on or near the south bank of the Haliacmon river, some distance out into the plain in classical times.[1]

It remains to consider the site at Palatitsa, which is entirely different in character from the cities in the plain. Here Heuzey reported and then excavated the remains of some remarkably fine public buildings of the Hellenistic period, one of which he and subsequent excavators have called 'the palace'. These buildings stand on a small plateau some 150 m above the plain, over which they have an extensive view. On a steep-sided hill rising high above this plateau there was a well-fortified acropolis. In Heuzey's day there were pieces of circuit-walls with round towers descending from this acropolis towards either side of the plateau, but these walls down to their foundations were constructed with cement and thus were not of the Hellenistic period. As remains of a town of late antiquity, probably of the late Roman Empire, extend from below the plateau to the edge of the plain, it is apparent that these fortifications were built in late antiquity. However, at the very top of the acropolis there was a gate 'en grand appareil', which was of the Hellenistic period at the latest.[2] It seems most likely that the acropolis was fortified at that time; that the walls were deliberately razed, presumably by the Romans; and that this gate alone was left standing. Subsequent excavation and exploration have shown that the area north of 'the palace' was occupied

---

[1] In this I run contrary to the opinions of Heuzey–Daumet 180 f., C. F. Edson in *CP* 50 (1955) 182, and E. Oberhummer in *RE* 2. 2 (1896) 2829 (B. Saria in *RE* 8 A 1 (1955) 278 adds little to Oberhummer's article), who have tentatively proposed to identify the Palatitsa site with Balla. E. Oberhummer in *RE* 20. 1 (1941) 980 gives the identifications proposed for Phylacae, namely Paliogratsiano above Servia—but this is in Elimea and probably is Elyma (see p. 120 above)—or at Karabunar north-east of Servia which is also in Elimea; see Heuzey, *Ol.* 218 f., and Dimitsas pp. 173 f. Heuzey refers to an inscription, seen by Delacoulonche, which gave in a list of victors in the games at Beroea one Parmenion son of Glaucias 'Phylacéen', but this is no guide to a particular location for Phylacae.

[2] For the description of the site see Heuzey, *Ol.* 189 f., and Heuzey–Daumet 175 f. and Plan C in the volume of plates.

by a considerable settlement dating from the Early Iron Age and extending below 'the palace' in Hellenistic times.

When approaching the small plateau from the village of Palatitsa, that is from the east, Heuzey noted a long embankment of earth in a straight line (some 500 m in length on his Plan C), 'like an earthwork or a narrow raised way', which led to two piers, made of small stone without cement and therefore of the Hellenistic period at the latest; the piers were on either side of a small ravine and being flat-topped and not arching were intended to carry planking.[1] It is almost certain that we have here the remains of a Macedonian road. Moreover, Heuzey mentioned also a path climbing up from the gate at the top of the acropolis, which led to a high passage in the Pierian mountains called the pass of Galakto.[2] It is likely that the gate 'en grand appareil' was left standing to mark the entry of a road, perhaps the via militaris, built by the Macedonians (Livy 44. 43. 1) and maintained by the Romans, which came direct from the Pierian plain of Dium into the first city overlooking the centre of the Macedonian kingdom (see pp. 126 and 138 above).

The strategic importance of this city is obvious. It controlled both routes of entry into Pieria—one over the hills and the other along the coast—and the approach to the crossing of the Haliacmon river, which gives the entry into the central plain. Its cultural and political importance has been revealed by the extensive excavations below the ancient town of a vast cemetery of some three hundred tumuli, and by the opening of a fine early-Hellenistic built tomb. The latter is unique in containing a magnificent marble throne, which, in Macedonia, can only have been that of a Macedonian king.

I turn aside now to consider the position of Aegeae, the early capital of the Macedonian state, where the kings were buried. The scholars who have considered the matter have maintained, I think without exception, that Aegeae was at Vodena (now named Edessa); that Edessa was at Vodena; and that the city there was called throughout the Macedonian period both Aegeae and Edessa.[3] A moment's reflection on the complications caused by having two official names for a capital city makes one pause. When one looks at the evidence, it is clear that the supposition is built on sand. Only one author says that a city Edessa was re-named 'Aegeae': Justin 7. 1. 7, 'Caranus . . . urbem Edessam . . . Aegeas, populum Aegeadas vocavit'. He is talking of the legendary founder of the royal house, Caranus, capturing his first city and changing its name to 'Aegeae' after the goats ($\alpha \hat{\iota} \gamma \epsilon \varsigma$) which helped him to gain the victory.

[1] This bridge is described in Heuzey–Daumet 226. For similar bridges and the use of planking in Epirus see *Epirus* 235 f. and the index.

[2] Heuzey–Daumet 179.

[3] So F. Geyer in *RE* 14. 1 (1928) 657 'Aigai = Edessa . . . allgemein an die Stelle des h. Wodena gesetzt', and the same view is expressed in *Der kleine Pauly* (1967).

The point of the story is that the change took place. Justin is giving the origin of the current name 'Aegeae'; it is this origin which involves mention of a long-forgotten name from the distant past, 'Edessa'. It is erroneous to suppose that this Edessa of the dim past had anything to do with the famous fourth-century city Edessa, situated in its strategic position at Vodena. Neither Justin nor any other ancient author suggests that this was so.

The ancient evidence makes it clear that Aegeae and Edessa were two separate cities in the fourth century B.C. Persons and money came officially from each city: Μακεδὼν ἐξ Αἰγειᾶν in an inscription of c. 300 B.C. (Ditt. Syll³. 269 L) and money ἐξ Ἐδέσσας in an inscription of the late fourth century B.C. The latter is an inscription, which records contributions from cities of Thessaly and Macedonia to Argos (IG iv 617 line 15). For southern Macedonia the relevant part of the texts runs ἐξ ..γεαν θθθ Αιγ.......... εξ Εδεσσας θθθ Αιγιν. Foucart restored ἐξ Αἰγεᾶν, and no other plausible restoration has been suggested. The field is restricted for the restorer, because the contribution being as large as that of Edessa means that it came from a city as wealthy and as important as Edessa. In 274 B.C. the Gauls in the service of Pyrrhus sacked the tombs of the Macedonian kings at Aegeae. Plutarch has left a description in which the coming of Pyrrhus to Edessa is mentioned twice (Plu. Pyrrh. 10. 2 and 12. 6) and then comes the capture of Aegeae (26. 6). In Plutarch's mind Aegeae is certainly not Edessa. Ptol. 3. 13. 39 gives as the last cities of Emathia in his list Αἴδεσσα, Βέρροια, Αἰγαιά, Πέλλα, and not only that but he gives different co-ordinates for each of the four cities. Pliny too gives both cities: at HN 4. 33 'Aegae in quo sepeliri mos reges' and at HN 6. 216 'Thessalonice, Pella, Edesus, Beroea'. These pieces of evidence show beyond a doubt that Aegeae was a city in its own right and that it was not Edessa.

The question now is where Aegeae lay. We have a few clues. The most important is in Theophrastus, who had personal knowledge of Macedonia. In discussing the fact that a strong wind in high country sometimes creates a back-current carrying low clouds towards the wind, he remarked that this happened περὶ Αἰγειὰς τῆς Μακεδονίας with a strong north wind striking the high country of Olympus, failing to surmount it, and so bringing the lower clouds back (De Ventis 27). These words mean that Aegeae was north of Olympus (not Bermium) and relatively low down, and that the country behind Aegeae and towards Olympus was steep. Aegeae was in Emathia in Ptolemy's list, which means at least that it faced the central plain. In 359 B.C., when the Athenian fleet lay at Methone, Argaeus and a force of mercenaries made an abortive strike at Aegeae and were intercepted on the way back. It appears that we should place Aegeae at Palatitsa. Such a situation suits the conditions required by the combined evidence of Theophrastus and Ptolemy, since it is more reasonable to extend the name Olympus to the whole range than to extend Emathia into the mountains of Pieria. It makes the action of Argaeus intelligible, because Aegeae is then within striking distance of Methone and the return journey is feasible within a day. It is in accordance with the restored text of *IG* iv 617, because in a list of names moving from Thessaly into Macedonia Aegeae precedes Edessa. It is situated on a Macedonian military road, and the deliberate destruction of its fortifications as those of a royal city was probably carried out by the Romans after their victory in the battle of Pydna. I propose therefore to identify Aegeae with the site at Palatitsa.

We may now revert to the transfer of Balla's population to Pythion. The words of Theagenes indicate a wholesale transplantation of the inhabitants and the abandonment of Balla. In the case of a city of Macedones this is likely to have been due to a natural disaster such as inundation, rather than to civic disobedience or political expediency. The choice of Pythion in Perrhaebia must have been due to policy at a time when Macedon had acquired Perrhaebia. The time may have been *c.* 275–250 B.C., when Pythion was in Macedonian hands, as we know from the presence at Delphi of a Macedonian *proxenus* Μακεδὼν Ἐλειμιώτης ἐκ Πυθείου.[1]

In his list of the peoples and the places of the central plain Pliny does not mention Aegeae or Beroea; for he had just named Aegae and Beroea in the previous section (*HN* 4. 33). Beroea had traditions of a pre-Macedonian founder and a Macedonian founder (St. Byz. s.v.), the former called Pheron, which illustrates the common interchange of phi and beta, and the latter Beres, whose son Olganos is attested in an inscription on a marble bust.[2] A river at Beroea was named after him and this is probably the river of Beroea itself. Beroea commanded the crossing of the Haliacmon and so the entry from Pieria into the upper part of the central plain. An important route runs inland from Beroea. It is arduous but unique in that it provides a way between two almost impassable barriers, the Haliacmon gorge and the mass of Mt. Bermium. On leaving Beroea one ascends the valley of Beroea's river, the Tripotamos, through orchards of fruit-trees at first and then through a thick

---

[1] *BCH* 21 (1897) 112, where P. Perdrizet gives an excellent commentary. The possession of Pythium and the Perrhaebian Tripolitis changed hands frequently, and it is most likely that the Pythian district of Theagenes is the one normally reckoned to be in the Perrhaebian Tripolitis. It was quite in line with the policy of Philip II, for instance, to transplant a population to a position which controlled an important entry into Pieria. It is probably this Pythium to which St. Byz. s.v. Πύθιον ... καὶ Μακεδονίας Πύθιον ἐν ᾧ καὶ τὰ Πύθια ἐπιτελεῖται refers as 'Macedonian'. He gives three such places but not one in Perrhaebia.

[2] St. Byz. s.v. *Beroea* and s.v. *Mieza*, where Beres has two daughters of those names and a son Olganos. For the bust see *Mak.* 2 (1941–52) 633 and *BCH* 71/2 (1947–8) 438; it was found near Ano Kopanos, east of Naoussa.

forest of oak and sweet chestnut. This long ascent brings one to the top of a ridge, and from it one descends to a magnificent spring, the Zoodokos Pege. Another climb over a high limestone ridge running down from Mt. Bermium and a descent with views of the long, high, forested Pierian range across the gorge of the Haliacmon bring one to Polimilon. From here a narrow, waterless coomb gives an easy passage to Ayios Theodoros and to the cantons of Eordaea and Elimea. From Beroea one road led round the edge of the plain to Pella, and another road, at least in the third century A.D., led across the plain south of Lake Ludias to Ichnae.

Beroea was a city of the greatest importance to military commanders, whether a Pyrrhus or a Pompey, and of great prosperity and size. The modern city is on the ancient site. It has yielded a rich harvest of inscriptions. Those found most recently mention a daughter of Cassander, and Philip V, son of Demetrius.[1] In its position Beroea resembles Naoussa and Edessa, for it is high above the plain and commands a wide view. But it is dominated more closely by the mountains. Mt. Bermium looms above it and the high Pierian peak by Palaiogratsiano is seen beyond a cleft, below which lies the Haliacmon gorge. A striking feature of the view over the plain is the curving rim formed by the Pierian range, very high above the gorge and then descending gradually towards the mouth of the Haliacmon.

Some three miles north of Beroea, by the village Metochi, an inscription dated to A.D. 189 by the Macedonian era records a manumission, a dedication to Ἄρτεμις Διγαία Βλαγανῖτις, and a shrine ἐν Βλαγάνοις.[2] There is no mention in our literary sources of such a place or of such epithets for Artemis.

Next to the Phylacaei in Pliny's list are the Cyrrestae. Their city, Cyrrus, was the one in which Alexander planned to dedicate a temple to Athena (D. S. 18. 5, reading Κύρρῳ for Κύρνῳ).[3] Here Perseus sacrificed in 171 B.C. to Athena Alcidemus (Livy 42. 51. 2). One of its citizens, Andronicus, built the Tower of the Winds in Athens, and the Cyrrus and Cyrrestae of Seleucid Syria were named after those of Macedonia. Thucydides linked it with Pella (2. 100. 4) in a context which indicates that it was west of Pella, and its position at Paleokastro, now named

---

[1] See E. Oberhummer in *RE* 3. 1 (1897) 304 for literary references to the city, which appears in the forms Beroea, Berroea, Beroeë, and Beroe in Greek and in various forms in Latin inscriptions. In Ps.-Scymnus 625 it ranks with Pella, and in Lucian, *Lucius* 34 it is πόλις μεγάλη καὶ πολυάνθρωπος. For the latest inscriptions see J. M. R. Cormack in *BSA* 58 (1963) 24 f. and Ph. Petsas in *Mak.* 6 (1967) 318.   [2] *Arch. Anz.* 55 (1940) 277.

[3] The emendation is justified by St. Byz. s.v. *Cyrrus καὶ Κυρρεστὶς ἡ Ἀθηνᾶ*, which indicates the cult in Macedonian Cyrrus, whether or not it was adopted by the Cyrrus in Syria. The Loeb edition regards the emendation as unnecessary, but no Cyrnus is known in Macedonia, where the word meant 'a bastard' (Hsch. s.v.). Cyrrus is one of the few recognizable names in Procopius' list of forts in Macedonia; it is in the form Cyrrou (*Aed.* 4. 4). It occurs as Cerru in Jordanes, *Getica* 56. 286.

Kirros, is indicated also by the 'mutatio Scurio' on the Via Egnatia (see p. 57 above). The next people in Pliny's list are the Tyrissaei, with variant readings Thyrisei, Thyresei, and Thyryssaei, and Ptol. 3. 13. 39 gives the city Τύρισσα. It lies between Cyrrus and Pella, and it may be placed perhaps at Palaion north-west of Yiannitsa.

The peoples of the central plain were thus organized in relation to the cities which lay on its periphery west of the Axius and on its coast line east of the Axius. Their wealth was derived from the fine crops grown on alluvial soil with an abundance of water available for irrigation, from the excellent pastures in swampy districts which are essential for horses and cattle on low ground, from the spring and autumn grass for sheep, and from the fisheries and the salt pans of the coastal lagoons. For the full exploitation of the natural resources of the plain there was need of intelligent agriculture, good stock-breeding, control of flooding, and well-organized irrigation. Immense strides in these matters have been taken in the last forty years, and the productivity of the plain has increased beyond recognition. I have suggested that in the reign of Philip II the Macedonians had a high degree of skill in drainage and irrigation and agriculture, which converted the plain of Philippi from a marshy forest into fertile agricultural land. One imagines that the central plain was at that time intensively cultivated by men and women who walked as far as 20 km from the cities to their fields in the plain and lived in the fields at the busiest seasons. The climate was healthy, and malaria was as yet unknown. The Vettii, as Livy called the Bottiaei or men of the plain, were a 'gens bellicosa', as the Roman wars had proved, and in time of peace they were 'impigri cultores' and their land boasted the 'nobiles urbes Edessam et Beroeam et Pellam' (Livy 45. 30. 5).

There is an interesting ruin in the plain which was seen by Delacoulonche and by Struck some 3 km east of Klidhi and some 5 km inland from the coast. Delacoulonche described one of the central arches of a bridge, which ran parallel to the shore and consisted of eight to ten arches, with a total length which he estimated at some 190 m. This arch alone survived. The arch is formed of single courses of well-cut stones, semicircular in shape, and 6·52 m above the present ground level. However, as the soil is now up to the point where the arch begins to engage on the piers, its original height above any water was considerably greater. The length of the span at ground level is 17·14 m, and the width of the top which carried the roadway is 5·73 m. The bridge between the arches was made of large stones and of stones of various sizes set in cement ('une maçonnerie de blocage'), together with some brick to support the paving of the road. The lowest courses were regular but of varying heights. The villagers having removed many stones, he was able to see in the villages some large stones, 1·80 × 0·62 × 0·59 m, which he was told came from the piers.

Struck found signs of thirteen arches, diminishing in size from the centre outwards down to an aperture 1·50 m wide.

Delacoulonche said that the bridge was obviously Roman; Struck judged it to be of Late Roman construction on the basis of its plan; Dimitsas, who had not seen it, claimed that it was a Macedonian bridge repaired in the Roman period. The closest parallel in the central plain is a bridge described and illustrated by Struck. In it too the arch was formed by single courses of well-cut stones, and the rest was made of rough stone and tiles; it was a much smaller bridge, the central opening being 2·30 m wide and the roadway 3·60 m wide, but the plan and the technique were very similar. This bridge was at Saridscha below Nea Khalkidhon, and it too stood on what is now dry ground. Struck dated it to the late Middle Ages. So far as one can judge from the descriptions by Delacoulonche and Struck, the bridge near Klidhi should be dated to the later period of the Roman Empire.[1]

In the Hellenistic period bridges were built across some rivers with wide beds. I have already mentioned the bridge some 300 m long over the Shkumbi river (see p. 25 above), and Ampelius described a bridge 1,000 feet long as 'pons magnus columnatus duplex', which crossed the marsh of the Acheron river. The technique was fundamentally different from that of the Roman type of bridge. A wide and rocky bed was chosen, within which the water could be diverted in summer and separate piers could then be built on rock-cut foundations. The piers were linked by wooden beams, which carried the roadway and could be removed in time of flood or war. In this type of bridge the strength of the bridge lay in each individual pier and not in the total mass of the solid masonry of a Roman bridge. As we have seen from the data of the Itineraries, in the first half of the third century A.D. the Haliacmon was crossed between Verria and Palatitsa where the bed is wide and rocky, and the Axius was crossed at Yefira, probably at a place—such as that used by a bridge built before 1860—where there were two islands in the river bed.[2] The main Roman road, which appears in the Peutinger Table, used those points of crossing and also kept inland of Lake Ludias. The road described in the Itinerarium Antoninum used these crossings too; but

---

[1] Delacoulonche, 'Mémoire sur le berceau de la puissance macédonienne' in *Archives des missions scientifiques* 8 (1867) 672 with a sketch of the arch, and Struck ii 11 and 17. Commented on most recently by C. Edson in *CP* 50 (1955) 179 and by Mrs. Karamanoli-Siganidou (*AD* 18 (1963) 2. 233 with Plates 266 a and b), who does not refer to any earlier literature.

[2] For the Acheron bridge see *Epirus* 66 and 235. In an interesting study of Greek bridges in *Archeologia* 11 (1959/60) 128–41 (in Polish with a summary in French) S. Parnicki-Pudelko says that in Greek times bridges of masonry were built with true arches, with false arches and with pillars on which beams were laid horizontally. I owe this reference to Professor Homer Thompson; I was not aware of the article when I wrote about the bridges in Epirus and Albania. Struck ii 93 refers to the wooden bridge before 1860.

it ran across the plain to Nea Khalkidhon near Ichnae and used a bridge over the outflow of Lake Ludias (see p. 126 above, and Maps 12 and 14). It is this outflow which could be most readily controlled; it was probably deep, since it was navigable, and between embankments. On the 1 : 100,000 map the ruined bridge by Klidhi is shown as 'the bridge of Alexander'. It is on the right bank of the present canal which drains what was, until recently, the Lake of Yiannitsa. I conclude that the bridge at Klidhi spanned the outflow of the lake at the time of the later Roman Empire.

The bridging of the Haliacmon and the Vardar in the delta area, which consists of accumulated silt, is a most difficult task. One would imagine it to have been beyond the powers of ancient engineers, but there is one piece of evidence which suggests that it may have been achieved. In 1078 when the Emperor Alexis expected Basilakios to invade Macedonia from Thessaly, he encamped between two arms of the Axius near Khalastra and intended to hold the western arm, in which the river was flowing (Anna Comn., *Alex.* 1. 8 and Nic. Bryenn. 4. 18). But Basilakios and his army of 10,000 men did not take 'the direct route' (καταλιπὼν τὴν εὐθεῖαν ὁδόν). Instead he went by an inland route, crossed the Gallikos river, and attacked the camp from the east. It is clear from these operations that 'the direct route' which Alexis intended to block was a coastal road which came through the delta area of the Axius. If so, the arch at Klidhi belonged to that coastal road, and there were presumably either bridges or efficient ferries over the Haliacmon and the Axius. The creation of such a coastal road in the central plain has been discussed by C. F. Edson, who has shown good reason to attribute it to the turn of the third century, when a new system of imperial defence was being developed. One of its effects, as he has shown, was to reduce Beroea, hitherto always one of the three greatest cities of Lower Macedonia, 'to the status of a minor provincial town'.[1]

2. *The hinterland of the central plain west of the Axius*

The mountains and the valleys which surround the central plain (see Map 14) played an important part in its defence and in its economy. We have already commented on the strong position which Aegeae and Beroea held on the approaches to the plain, and we have seen that Edessa commanded the route of the Via Egnatia. For Lower Macedonia west of the Axius the mountains form a continuous shield. The Haliacmon breaks through in an impassable gorge between the Pierian Mountains and Mt. Bermium. The saddle between Mt. Bermium and Mt. Barnous, over which the Via Egnatia runs, is narrow and easily defended. The

[1] *CP* 50 (1955) 180.

range of Mt. Barnous is cut through by the Axius in a long and pre-cipitous defile, the Demir Kapu, which is even narrower than the Vale of Tempe. The mountain sides and the valleys provide excellent summer pasture for sheep and cattle, timber of all kinds, stone, nuts, fruit, wine, and vegetables, and the constant flow of water which irrigated all parts of the plain. They also maintain a very considerable population of shep-herds, woodcutters, and villagers, who grow their own cereals.

Some towns derive their strength from being set on the edge of the hinterland. Naoussa is a good example. Set on a high terrace, like Edessa, it enjoys an abundance of water throughout the year, and it has many dependent villages, most of which are nearer to the plain. As excavations have shown, it is on the site of a city of the Roman period. Dimitsas reported remains of an ancient settlement south of Naoussa, and the finding of tombs and coins of Cassander in the hill villages on that side of Naoussa. The chief site is at Gastra, just east of Naoussa, where Delacoulonche recognized an acropolis and below it the emplacement of an ancient city. There have been many discoveries of built tombs and architectural fragments in different places below Naoussa towards the plain, culminating in the magnificent Macedonian tomb of Levkadhia, north-east of Naoussa, which was excavated by Ph. Petsas.[1] It is known from the list of Delphic *Theorodokoi*, dated between 190 and 180 B.C.,[2] that the chief place between Beroea and Edessa was then Mieza, spelt Meza in the inscription at Delphi but known as Mieza in St. Byz. s.v. and Myeza in Ptol. 3. 13. 9.

The city was famous for the nearby Nymphaeum, where Aristotle taught Alexander (Plu. *Alex.* 7. 3), and for a cave, in which there were stalactites 'pendentes in ipsis camaris' (Pliny *HN* 31. 30); and as a Nymphaeum and a cave were so often closely associated with one another, it is probable that this was so at Mieza. A cave at Palio-Sotira, an hour south of Naoussa, which was reported by Delacoulonche, Struck, and Dimitsas to contain stalactites, has been blown up since then in quarrying operations.[3] Petsas found no sherds at Palio-Sotira, but he has recently discovered at Izvoria, east of Naoussa, three caves, of which the largest has stalactites, and a large area in which the rock has been cut perpendicularly. What may have been a quarry originally seems to have been made attractive by careful cutting of the rock, and in a trial trench inside the area he found roof-tiles of good style and early Hellenistic date.[4] The caves too had been improved by cutting of the rock, and in the side of the largest cave a niche had been cut. It seems most likely

[1] Ph. Petsas, Ὁ τάφος τῶν Λευκαδίων (Athens, 1966), with a map of the district, which shows the position of Gastra = Delacoulonche 98 f.

[2] *BCH* 45 (1921) 17 iii 59.   [3] Dimitsas 91 and Petsas, op. cit. 10.

[4] *Ergon* 1965 [1966], 21–8, with illustrations of the site and caves; also *Mak.* 6 (1967) 33 and pl. 50. I had the great pleasure of visiting the site and caves with Dr. Petsas in 1968.

that this area is the Nymphaeum and the so-called 'School of Aristotle'. The site of the Macedonian city Mieza may then be at Gastra. The city claimed to be named after its founder Mieza, daughter of Beres, son of Macedon; but there are indications of a pre-Macedonian history in the name Strymonium for the city and the name Strymonus for the district. These two names are rather awkwardly attached to the legend of Beres in St. Byz. s.v. *Mieza* = *FGrH* 774 (Theagenes) F 7.[1] It is evident that Mieza, both as the name of a district and as the name of a city, succeeded a compound of the root Strymon. One of Alexander's trierarchs, Peucestes, has the ethnic Μιεζεύς (Arr. *Ind.* 18. 6).[2]

It is clear from the numerous tombs which have been found on the side of the plain that there were other inhabited sites besides Mieza. The remains of an ancient bridge in the form of two bridgeheads on the banks of the Arapitsa just south of Levkadhia and another ancient bridgehead just east of Levkadhia indicate that there were, as we might expect, a number of roads in this area. The two bridgeheads may well lie on a road linking Beroea to Edessa.[3] A bust bearing the name Ὄλγανος was found near Ano Kopanos;[4] as he is a son of Beres and a river god, the bust was probably associated with a Nymphaeum there. Pliny *HN* 4. 34 mentions Ordaea between Mieza and Scydra, and Stephanus Byzantinus also has an entry Ὀρδαία, πόλις Μακεδονίας. τὸ ἐθνικὸν Ὀρδοί. λέγονται καὶ Ὀρδαῖοι, ὡς Νίκανδρος.[5] This town is to be placed probably near Episkopi, which has yielded two inscriptions in honour of Artemis Agrotera Γαζωρεῖτις and Artemis Γαζωρία.[6] Scydra is given by Pliny

---

[1] Jacoby in *FGrH* emends the text, but even so the attachment is awkward. I prefer the unamended text, punctuating as follows: Μίεζαν, Βέροιαν, Ὄλγανον ἀφ' οὗ ποταμὸς ἐπώνυμος· καὶ πόλις Βέροια καὶ τόπος Στρύμονος.

[2] St. Byz. gives two forms of ethnic, Μιεζεύς, which is likely to be that of a district, and Μιεζαῖος, which is likely to be that of a town.

[3] A fragmentary milestone of the early fourth century A.D., marking a distance of one mile by the letter 'A', was found at 'Rizari' which is presumably Rizo, north of Episkopi; this is evidence of a road from Beroea to Edessa, not of the Via Egnatia leading from Edessa as is supposed in *BCH* 76 (1952) 228, *JHS* 72 (1952) 102 and *Mak.* 6 (1967) 308. Ph. Petsas, op. cit. 4 n. 3 and map facing p. 16, items 5 and 21. Petsas associates the tombs and the bridges with the main road from Pella to Beroea, which he takes through Mieza (pp. 16–17); but I am inclined to put the main road of the Peutinger Table further to the east (see p. 132 above). Delacoulonche p. 101 noted another ancient bridge by the Arapitsa, east of Naoussa.

[4] *Mak.* 2 (1941–52) 633; Petsas, op. cit. 10 and 12.

[5] In the next section Pliny gives the Eordenses, where he has a list of peoples, and St. Byz. has an entry Ἐορδαῖαι δύο χῶραι Μυγδονίας [καὶ Μακεδονίας], where the addition is needed as he continues εἰσὶ καὶ ἄλλαι δύο. It seems somewhat captious to add an 'E' to Ordaea in Pliny and censure him for mentioning both Eordaea and Eordenses—the more so as a city Eordaea did not exist and Pliny was giving the names of cities; or/and to add an 'E' to St. Byz. Ὀρδαία and censure him for repeating an entry, admittedly a different one the second time. Yet this is usually done.

[6] St. Byz. s.v. Γάζωρος mentions this cult-title of Artemis; one city Gazorus was near Amphipolis (Ptol. 3. 13. 31). I cannot make anything of another cult-title 'Baoureitis' in the former of the two inscriptions. For the inscriptions see Dimitsas no. 125 and no. 126; he

HN 4. 34 after Ordaea, and by Ptol. 3. 13. 39 after Mieza; St. Byz. s.v. Σκύδρα· Μακεδονικὴ πόλις. ὡς Θεαγένης ἐν Μακεδονικοῖς (*FGrH* 774 F 4), τὸ ἐθνικὸν Σκυδραῖος. Its position is known from an inscription, seen at Arseni, which records the purchase of a boy by a man of Scydra from another man of Scydra before witnesses from the same city.[1] It is not the Skidhra (Vertekop) shown on the Staff Map, but a village some 5 km NNE. of Episkopi.

Leake wrote enthusiastically of Edessa's 'lofty, salubrious and strong position, at the entrance of a pass which was the most important in the kingdom, as leading from the maritime provinces into Upper Macedonia'. From Edessa one looks out over the plain to Salonica and Mt. Khortiatis, and from the pass above the town one sees Mt. Vitsi, the neighbour of Kastoria and Florina. The name Edessa was derived from the Phrygian word for water, 'vedu', just as its recent name 'Vodhena' was derived from the Bulgarian word for water; for the river Scirtus, 'the leaper', comes down to the town in a series of waterfalls.[2] Edessa has a place in the tradition about the Abantes, who returned from the Trojan War to the Bay of Oricum and then came through Illyria to Edessa and founded a city Euboea in that neighbourhood,[3] probably at the site on an isolated hill in the marshy plain north-east of Agras, which was noted by Delacoulonche. The city has yielded relatively few inscriptions.[4] Excavations conducted by Ph. Petsas have recently revealed a part of the city walls, including a monumental towered gateway, with a circular courtyard, through which the road passed. The face of the large ashlar blocks is roughish with a smooth bevelled strip at the edges. When Dr. Petsas showed me the walls in 1968 I was reminded of the fourth-century gateway and the masonry of Messene, which were known most probably to Philip II. The site itself lies below the modern town on sloping ground, and the walls are covered by a deep deposit of silt and stones, which have been brought down by the cascading streams of the Scirtus and other water-courses.

Its central position in Macedonia west of the Axius made Edessa a natural mustering-point for the Macedonian army. In 217 B.C. Philip V,

---

assumes this worship to have been in Scydra, but I see no special reason for thinking that the stones came to Episkopi from Arseni, the site of Scydra. For recent comment on the inscriptions see F. Bömer in *Akad. d. Wissensch. u.d. Lit.; Abhandlungen d. Geistes-u. sozialwiss. Klasse* (1960) 1. 92 f.

[1] Dimitsas no. 126, found in the village Arseni by Delacoulonche; cf. Struck ii 56. Published again in *SEG* 2. 396.

[2] Leake 3. 271 f. He describes the streams passing through the streets and even through houses, and it was this which caused the disaster, described by Procopius, *Arc.* 18. 38, when the Scirtus came down in flood.

[3] See *Epirus* 384–5; Str. 10. 1. 15, C 449; St. Byz. s.v. *Euboea*. Delacoulonche p. 85. In 1968 there was much standing water in the plain.

[4] See *Mak.* 2 (1941–52) 636 f.; 6 (1967) 308; *BSA* 58 (1963) 24 f.

having raised the forces of Bottia and Amphaxitis, met the troops from Upper Macedonia at Edessa, and marched from Edessa to Larissa, which he reached on the sixth day (Plb. 5. 97. 3–4). In 171 B.C. Perseus mustered all his forces at the city of Citium. He pitched camp before the city and reviewed his 43,000 men in the plain (Livy 42. 51. 3), and from there he marched via Edessa and Lake Begorritis into the Perrhaebian Tripolitis, which he entered on the third day. The position of Citium has not been identified, but it lay down in the plain below Edessa, perhaps between Episkopi and Skidhra.[1]

In his enumeration of peoples Pliny *HN* 4. 35 gives 'Eordenses, Almopi, Pelagones', and this suggests that the Almopi are to be placed on the southern flank of the Barnous range, north of which lay the Pelagones (including the Derriopi) in the valley of the Erigon. Consequently the district Almopia is best identified with the upper basin of the Ludias river, from which paths lead over the mountain into the Morihovo (see pp. 65 and 70 above). This basin, known now as Moglena, is set among high mountains and experiences a hard winter, but the alluvial soil of the basin is well watered and very fertile, while the mountain-sides provide timber and pasture. Indeed in 1863 it was considered the most fertile district of Macedonia, famous for its red peppers, silk, and three crops a year, and it supported fifty-four villages. It is a natural refuge, easily approachable only from the south. In 1863 it was said to contain a Bulgarian population, two groups of Vlachs with special dialects, and Yuruks, ruled for long by chiefs drawn from the royal house of the Yuruks who once conquered Macedonia.[2] In antiquity the invading Macedonians drove out the Almopes and peopled it themselves (Thuc. 2. 99. 5).

The Almopes had their own pre-Macedonian traditions of descent from an eponymous ancestor, a son of Poseidon and Helle; and, like the peoples of Aeane and Elyma, they claimed a connection with the legend of Aeneas and with that of the Tyrseni (St. Byz. s.v. *Almopia*; Lycophr. *Alex.* 1238). The name of the district is found in Hierocles, *Synecdemus* 638. 10 and in Const. Porphyr. *Them.* 49. 17. As it is mentioned after 'Cellae' or 'Celle' and in the former before 'Larissa', viz. Arnisa, it is likely that it included the mountain-side west of the Ludias basin. Ptol. 3. 13. 24 credits the Almopes with three cities, Horma, Europus, and Apsalus. Of these Europus was on the Ludias river, which 'flowed through it' (Pliny *HN* 4. 34). It should probably be identified with the only site

[1] Dimitsas 91 f. and others proposed to put Citium at Naoussa; see Ph. Petsas, op. cit. 5 f. for the literature on the subject. Livy's statement shows that the city was not up above the plain, e.g. at Naoussa, but in the plain itself; a review of so large a force is more impressive on flat ground than on a hillside, and Livy's 'in campo' refers to the central plain.

[2] See the description in von Hahn, *Denkschriften* 16 (1867) 2. 72–4; Moglena derives from the Bulgarian word for mist, 'mogla'.

which is reported to have been walled, on a hill north of Slatino (now Khrisi), beside which flows the Moglenitsa, that is the Ludias. Europus in this position controlled one entry into the basin from the south (see Map 14). Remains have been reported at other villages, but there is no evidence for placing Horma and Apsalus.[1]

The eastern border of Almopia is formed by the fine mountain Paiko, of which the ridge runs roughly north and south, parallel to the course of the Axius; where Mt. Paiko joins Mt. Barnous, there is a high pass from Almopia into the Axius valley.[2] The strip of land between Mt. Paiko and the Axius river from the defile of Demir Kapu down to Ichnae seems to have been part of Bottiaea; for the Axius was the eastern boundary of Bottiaea (Hdt. 7. 123. 3), and the Macedonians had conquered and acquired the narrow strip of Paeonia by the Axius river from inland (ἄνωθεν) as far as Pella (Thuc. 2. 99. 4). It is described also as part of Emathia by Ptolemy (3. 13. 39); for the cities Europus, Idomene, and Gordenia, which he includes in his list of Emathian cities, were in this strip of land. The district Amphaxitis lay on the east side of this part of the Axius river; for the central plain east of the Axius lay in Mygdonia. This seems to be clear from Str. 7 fr. 23 (from the *Epitome edita*), where he moves from south to north: τὴν δὲ λίμνην (of Pella) πληροῖ τοῦ Ἀξιοῦ τι ποταμοῦ ἀπόσπασμα. εἶτα ὁ Ἀξιὸς διαιρῶν τήν τε Βοττιαίαν καὶ τὴν Ἀμφαξῖτιν γῆν, καὶ παραλαβὼν τὸν Ἐρίγωνα. It was then above Pella and the lake that the Axius divided Bottiaea from Amphaxitis. The word Amphaxitis has a slight ambiguity, because as a preposition of place ἀμφί can mean 'on both sides of' or just 'by', as in the phrase ἀμφ' ἅλα 'by the sea'. Here it means 'by the Axius'. In the same way in Str. 7 fr. 11 the Paeones lived 'by the Axius (περὶ τὸν Ἀξιόν) in the land called for that reason Amphaxitis'.[3] By the time of Ptolemy (*fl.* A.D. 139) the word seems to have been used in an extended sense, but that need not concern us here.[4]

The strip of land between the mountain-sides of Paiko and Barnous and the Axius river is not only very fertile and well watered, but when Pella was the capital and a leading port of Macedonia it formed the main

---

[1] Pliny's Rhoedias is a variant form of Loedias. For the hill north of Slatino see von Hahn, op. cit. 73, Delacoulonche in *Revue des sociétés savantes* 4 (1853) 710, and Kougeas in *Hellenica* 5 (1932) 7 n. 8; inscriptions published by Duchesne = Dimitsas nos. 290–3, one being a dedication to Heracles Kallinikos from a village Goltzousani, north of Edessa; early Christian remains in *Mak.* 6 (1967) 308 and *AD* 17 (1961–2) 2. 258.

[2] Von Hahn, op. cit. 75 reported a track leading from Notia, then the chief Vlach village, through this pass.

[3] Kramer and Meineke insert a τά before περὶ τὸν Ἀξιὸν ποταμὸν καὶ τὴν καλουμένην διὰ τοῦτο Ἀμφαξῖτιν; but it is unnecessary, because the understood verb ἐνέμοντο can be used absolutely. Here both constructions are used.

[4] Amphaxitis has got into the text twice: at 3. 13. 10, where it clearly does not belong, and at 3. 13. 14, where it is used for the delta of the Axius and the Echedorus. By that time the word may not have been in current use. The two articles in *RE* 1. 2 (1894) 1884 and *RE* 14. 1 (1928) 650 make rather heavy weather of Amphaxitis.

route of passage for merchandise and for travellers northwards into Paeonia. In Roman times the main road from Thessalonica ran east of the Axius as far as Idomenae, but even then the Axius was used to float timber and produce down to the plain, and the direct land-route to Pella was much in use. For these reasons there were several important cities in this strip of Bottiaea.

The position of Europus has been determined approximately by the finding of an inscription in the school building of the village Asiklar, now called Europos.[1] In the inscription Εὐρωπαίων ἡ πόλις pays tribute to the Roman proconsul M. Minucius Rufus for his victory over the Galatae, Scordistae, Bessi, and the other Thracians in a war of 110–108 B.C. As there are large blocks of worked stone in the village of Asiklar, the acropolis of the city may not have been far from the village, but it has not been located precisely. The Europaei appear in an inscription which recorded subscriptions made to the Asclepieum at Epidaurus late in the fourth century B.C. (*IG* iv no. 617 line 17), and a Delphic *proxenus* in an inscription was 'Machatas Sabattaras Europaeus Macedon' late in the fourth century B.C. (*BCH* 20 (1896) 473 = *GDI* 2745). The ethnic agrees with that given by St. Byz. s.v. *Europos* and by *EM* 397. 47 for Europus, 'a city of Macedonia'.[2] The city of Europus claimed as its founder Europus, son of Macedon and Oreithyia, daughter of Cecrops,[3] and this reflects the Macedonian conquest of the strip of land which had belonged to Paeonia (Thuc. 2. 99. 4). It remained an important city under the empire, being mentioned by Pliny *HN* 4. 34 as 'Europus ad Axium' and figuring in Hierocles, *Synecdemus* 638. 4 and Const. Porphyr. *Them.* 2. 49 next to Pella and also in Ptolemy's list of cities of Emathia (3. 13. 39).

It has been suggested that the city Europus may be the same as the city Oropus.[4] This is not the opinion of the lexicographers, who quote the ethnic Oropios as an analogy to, and not as an alternative for, the ethnic Europios. This form of the ethnic was used by cities called Europus but situated elsewhere than in Macedonia. In addition St. Byz. gives to Macedon two sons, Europus and Oropus, each being the eponym of his city. Oropus is attested in the list of Delphic *Theorodokoi c.* 190–180 B.C. (*BCH* 45 (1921) 16 iii 62 ἐν Ὠρώπωι Παράμονος), where it comes between Pella and Ichnae, and in a Delphic manumission of 194 B.C. (*GDI* 2082 lines 2–3 τὸ γένος Μακέταν ἐξ Ὠρώπου). Oropus was one of the Macedonian names used for cities in Syria (App. *Syr.* 57). As Europus and Oropus are attested in inscriptions, it is unlikely that they are variant

[1] S. B. Kougeas in *Hellenica* 5 (1932) 5 f.
[2] The entries of St. Byz. and *EM* are almost identical, whether derived from one another or from a common source. Macedones Europaei are mentioned in *AE* 1912. 82 of the late third century B.C. and Arvanitopoulos, *Catalogue des stèles* (Athens, 1928) no. 127.
[3] St. Byz. s.v. *Europos*.
[4] For instance in *RE* 6 (1909) 1309 and 18. 1 (1939) 1175.

spellings of one and the same place. It is therefore better to regard Oropus as a separate city.[1]

The location of Europus at Asiklar helps us to understand Sitalces' invasion of Macedonia from a north-easterly direction (see Map 14). His army marched from Doberus (in the vicinity of the upper Strumitsa) into Philip's former kingdom (which therefore included the Amphaxitis), captured Eidomene by storm, won over Gortynia and Atalante and some other places by negotiation, and failed to take Europus. This was the first stage of the invasion (introduced by πρῶτον μέν), and the next stage was to turn into the areas east of Pella and Cyrrus (see p. 153 above). Thus Thucydides is giving the steps of the campaign in geographical sequence. Eidomene, the most northerly or north-easterly of these places, may have claimed as its founder or namesake an Eidomene, daughter of Pheres, a local form perhaps of Beres, son of Macedon (Apollod. 1. 96; St. Byz. s.v. *Beroia*). Its position is indicated by Str. 7, fr. 36, from the *Epitome Vaticana*, when he talks of Parorbelia containing Callipolis and other cities 'on the channel running from Eidomene' (κατὰ τὸν αὐλῶνα τὸν ἀπὸ Εἰδομένης). This channel is the long sink, starting to the north of the most southerly of the defiles through which the Axius passes, i.e. the defile between Gevgheli and Axioupolis, and running eastwards to the Strymon valley. We should then expect Eidomene to be in the vicinity of Gevgheli. This position is in accordance with another passage in Str. C 389, if we accept the almost certain restoration by Kramer: ἐντεῦ[θεν ἐπ' ᾽Ιστρον δι' Εἰδομ]ένης καὶ Στόβων καὶ Δαρδανίων. Strabo is here deriving his account from Artemidorus (*fl.* 104–101 B.C.), who was himself developing statements made by Polybius. This passage suggests that Eidomene was a main station on the Macedonian route to the Danube valley, a route which in the time of Polybius ran from Pella and followed the right bank of the river perhaps to above Gevgheli. It is probably this city which appears in Hierocles, *Synecdemus* 639. 4–5, as 'Idomene' next to 'Doberus', and in Const. Porphyr. *Them.* 2. 49 as 'Hedomene' next to 'Diobourus'.

Idomenae appears first in the list of Delphic *Theorodokoi* of 190–180 B.C.; it comes between Thessalonica and Astrea (*BCH* 45 (1921) 17 iii 68). Pliny mentions the Idomenenses next to the Doberi (*HN* 4. 35). It lay on the Roman road from Thessalonica to the Danube valley; it appears on the Peutinger Table and in the Ravenna Geographer as 'Idomenia', a mis-spelling perhaps of Idomenai. We are faced again with the question whether Idomenae is to be identified with Eidomene (as is the general opinion) or whether Idomenae and Eidomene are separate places, like

---

[1] Epirus had both a Europus with the ethnic Europios and an Oropus; see *Epirus*, Onomastikon 803 and 817. I am at variance here with C. F. Edson in *CP* 50 (1955) 174 and A. Plassart in *BCH* 45 (1921) 54 n. 7.

their counterparts of similar name in Amphilochia, where they are
associated with a pass.[1] Stephanus Byzantinus gives us a lead. For he
gives two entries, Εἰδομένη with an ethnic Eidomenios, and Ἰδομεναί
with an ethnic Idomenios, and he calls each of them a πόλις Μακεδονίας.
I therefore think it probable that we have to deal with two cities, Eidomene on the right bank of the river and on the Macedonian road alongside the Axius, and Idomenae, which became important when the Roman
road system was developed.

The location of one city has been fixed by the work of B. Josifovska, who
first found an inscription in a house wall in the village of Marvinci. It had
come from immediately south of the village, from Isar Kale, which is the
emplacement of an ancient site. It recorded a decree by ἡ πόλις καὶ οἱ
συνπραγματευόμενοι Ῥωμαῖοι in honour of Publius Memmius Regulus,
the governor of the (united) province of Macedonia, Moesia, and
Achaea in A.D. 35–44; the decree was carried in a year between A.D. 41
and 44.[2] Later she found at Isar Kale some architectural members from
a temple with a dedicatory inscription, dated by the Macedonian era
to A.D.181, which may refer to a repair rather than to an original
construction. As a piece of a large male statue was found there, she has
conjectured that the temple was a temple of Heracles. The inscription
runs thus:

> 12 letters] μακεδονιαρχῶν τὸν ναὸν τῇ πατρίδι
> ?συ]ν παντὶ τῷ κόσμῳ τῷ θκτ΄ ἔτει

The dedicator was a Macedoniarch of τὸ κοινὸν τῶν Μακεδόνων, whether
he served in the second or in the third tetrarchy or division of Macedonia.
An inscription from Greciste, just south of Isar Kale, mentions a πολιτάρχης.[3] It is clear that an important city lay at Isar Kale, either Eidomene or, as Josifovska has proposed, Idomenae.[4] The site is on the left
bank of the river and north of the long sink, the αὐλών of Strabo, which
leads to the Strymon valley. It is therefore appropriate to Idomenae and
not to Eidomene, which is more likely to be further south by Gevgheli
on the right bank. This conclusion will receive some support when we
consider the distances given in the Peutinger Table.

Gortynia is south of Eidomene (Thuc. 2. 100. 3). Its position is related
to the passes into Macedonia by Str. 7. fr 4 (from the *Epitome Vaticana*):
ἡ δὲ Παιονία . . . πρὸς ἄρκτον δ' ὑπέρκειται τοῖς Μακεδόσιν, διὰ Γορτυνίου πόλεως
καὶ Στόβων ἔχουσα τὰς εἰσβολὰς ἐπὶ τὰ πρὸς [spatium decem fere literis sufficiens

---

[1] See my remarks in *BSA* 37 (1940) 139, where there is a similar case of Olpe and Olpae.
[2] *ZA* 9 (1959) 285 f.   [3] *Spomenik* 98 (1941–8) no. 100 line 18.
[3] *ZA* 14 (1965) 137 f. She has published also an inscription from the base which carried
a draped female statue; this came from Isar Kale and it recorded that the artist was Adymus
son of Evandrus 'Beroiaios', who was evidently related to an artist Evandrus Evandrou of
Beroea who figures elsewhere in Macedonia (see Kanatsoulis no. 481).

vacuum] δι 'ὧν ὁ Ἀξιὸς ῥέων δυσείσβολον ποιεῖ τὴν Μακεδονίαν ἐκ τῆς Παιονίας, ὡς ὁ Πηνειὸς διὰ τῶν Τεμπῶν φερόμενος ἀπὸ τῆς Ἑλλάδος αὐτὴν ἐρυμνοῖ.

Paeonia lies inland of and to the north of the Macedonians, and it contains the passes through the city of Gortynius and through Stobi into the area towards[. . .]; for the Axius flowing through these passes makes Macedonia hard to invade from Paeonia, as the Peneus coursing through the (Vale of) Tempe strengthens Macedonia in regard to Greece.[1]

There are in fact three defiles of the Axius: one just south of Titov Veles (Bylazora), the second called Demir Kapu between Klisura and Miravci, and the third between Dhogani and Axioupolis. Of these the first is in Paeonia; the other two form the defences of Macedonia, and they are defined, the more southerly in relation to Gortynius and the more northerly in relation to Stobi. In other words Gortynius was near Axioupolis. The first city in Bottiaea, Gortynia had a name which was consonant with the tradition that the Bottiaei came from Crete.[2] Pliny *HN* 4. 34 has the plural form Gordyniae, and St. Byz. gives Γορδυνία, πόλις Μακεδονίας. τὸ ἐθνικὸν Γορδυνιάτης. Ptol. 3. 13. 39 includes Γορδηνία in his list of the cities of Emathia, where it comes after Idomene and before Edessa.

Atalante is south of Gortynia, as we interpret Thuc. 2. 100. 3. It is probable that Atalante is the same city as Allante, of which the Allantenses are given in Pliny's list of peoples (*HN* 4. 35), and on which St. Byz. has the following entry: Ἀλλάντη, πόλις Μακεδονίας καὶ Ἀρκαδίας. Θεόπομπος δ' ἐν πρώτῳ Φιλιππικῶν (*FGrH* 115 F 33) Ἀλλάντιον αὐτὴν εἶπε. τὸ ἐθνικὸν Ἀλλάντιος ὡς Παλλάντιος. In the Delphic list of *Theorodokoi* there are *theorodokoi* in Pella, Oropus, Ichnae, ἐν Ἀλλ[α]ντειωι, and Thessalonica, which suggests that Allanteion is close to the plain. The people of the city have been restored after Edessa and before the Europaei in the list of subscribers on the inscription at Argos: *IG* iv (1902) no. 617 line 17 Ἀταλα]νταῖοι or Ἀλλα]νταῖοι, the ethnic in -aei being typically Macedonian.[3] One should therefore place Atalante or Allante, for anyone coming from the west, after Ichnae and south of Europus, that is in the territory of Athiras or of Koufalia. The huge army of Sitalces is likely to have swept down both banks of the Axius. In Amphaxitis, where it was moving through Philip's former realm, it was evidently welcomed;

[1] For the lacuna Kramer suggested τὴν Πέλλαν, but I prefer τὴν Βοττίαν (cf. fr. 11a) or τὴν Ἠμαθίαν (cf. fr. 11), which are ten letters long. The argument of the passage suggests that the Macedonians held the passes, and this makes me propose ἔχουσι for ἔχουσα. But the sense is clear. The period to which the passage refers is not known; but it may well refer to Strabo's own time, when the tetrarchies were in existence and the boundary between Macedonia and Paeonia was at or just north of Stobi (Livy 45. 29. 13; see p. 76 above).

[2] This tradition is discussed below, pp. 296 ff. The suggestion made by Ph. Petsas in *AE* 1961. 19, that the name is perhaps derived from Gordias, father of Midas the Phrygian, is interesting but unlikely, as the iota has disappeared.

[3] The ethnic in St. Byz. is probably that of the Arcadian Allante.

and on the right bank it captured or won over by negotiation all the chief cities except Europus. The whole force then assembled on the left bank at Yefira and began the second stage of the campaign, during which it ravaged Mygdonia, Grestonia, and Anthemus.

I am including in this section the area between Stobi and the great defile of Demir Kapu, because it was often held by the Macedonians and because it is an integral part of the main road from the central plain northwards to Paeonia and the Danube valley. The evidence for the road is in the Peutinger Table (see Map 5). The stations given there are Stobi, Antigonea, Stenas, Idomenia, Tauriana, Gallicum, and Thessalonica. The Ravenna Geographer 196. 3–7 (I invert the order) has Asigonea, Stenas, Idomenia, Tauriana, and Callicum. Here his Asigonea is a malformation of Antigonea, and his Callicum may be nearer the true name than the Peutinger Table's Gallicum, although the modern name of the Echedorus, the 'Gallikos', has evidently been derived from the latter's form of the station. The distances on the Peutinger Table are all accepted by Miller as sound.[1]

Beginning with XVI m.p. = 23·7 km from Thessalonica to Gallicum (see Map 14), we reach a point between Ayioneri and the Bitter Lake (Pikrolimni). Thence XVII m.p. = 25·2 km to Tauriana at Polikastron. Thence XX m.p. = 29·6 km to Idomenia at the railway station just north of Prdejci. The name Idomenia is evidently Idomenae (see p. 169 above), and is probably taken from the two almost equally high hills either side of the river (518 m and 522 m).[2] Thence XII m.p. = 17·7 km to Stenas at Gradec below the Demir Kapu defile. Thence XI m.p. = 16·3 km to Antigonea at Banja, north of the defile. Up to this point the Table shows two river crossings, one between Thessalonica and Gallicum, that is over the Echedorus, and the other between Tauriana and Idomenia, that is over the Axius from the left bank to the right bank, probably at Idomenae. The distance from Banja to Stobi is some 25 km = XVII m.p.; but the Peutinger Table here gives XII m.p. It is best to suppose that in fitting three roads to Stobi on this side of the Table (see Map 5) the copyist has put XII twice by error. We should then emend XII to XVII. I differ from Leake and Miller in my view of the line taken by the road between Gallicum and Stenas; for they make it run via Lake Doiran.[3] Their route is some 10 km = some VII m.p. longer, and it involves altering one or more entries in the Peutinger Table. I discuss the matter on pp. 177 ff. below. The triangle of territory which lies between Banja, Stobi, and Kavadarci is a part of Upper Macedonia in its climate

---

[1] Miller, *Itin. Romana* 494–5 figs. 148/150, and 571–3 and fig. 162.

[2] The two hills Idomenae in Amphilochia are similarly situated with a pass between them; see *BSA* 37 (1940) 139. Hierocles, *Synecdemus* 639. 5, has Idomene, and Const. Porphyr. *Them.* 49 has Hedomene.

[3] Leake 3. 440 and map at the end of his volume 4. Miller, loc. cit.

and situation. Tozer, travelling southwards in 1865, noticed that there were dwarf plane-trees by Banja and luxuriant plane-trees below the Demir Kapu defile; for 'they appear at once to have entered on a different temperature'. But it is of the greatest strategic importance to Lower Macedonia; for whoever holds this triangle controls the two main routes into Macedonia, that is through Pelagonia and through the Demir Kapu. As Tozer puts it, the Demir Kapu is 'a passage between steep walls of rock, through which the river forces its way in a series of rapids'. The path lies on the right (the southern) bank. Tozer noticed that the rock had been cut in one place to admit the road, and that 'in parts the road is supported on masonry, room being just left for it between the cliffs and the river, over which it hangs'. Tozer reckoned the defile to be about a quarter of a mile long between 'grand abrupt precipices' from 500 to 700 feet high, but von Hahn stepped it out and made it 1,030 metres. The river flows into the pass through a gate between two towering precipices of limestone rock, and the pass downstream is still narrow as far as Gradec, below which the valley begins to open out. Quite a small force could hold the Demir Kapu, and there are no alternative routes over the mountains on either side.[1]

Heuzey was the first to describe the district of Kavadarci (Tikvetch), which he entered from the side of the Cerna river, the ancient Erigon. He visited an important site below Resava and a nearby sanctuary (see p. 65 above), from which he reported some inscriptions.[2] Since then a very large number of inscriptions, almost without exception in Greek, have been found in the villages of the district; I have noted some 120, of which only 7 are in Latin.[3] The contrast is very marked on the east side of the Axius, as one goes further north; for the proportions are almost reversed. It is also noticeable that 'Makedon' occurs not infrequently as a personal name, which suggests that one is on the frontier of the Macedonian Greek-speaking population.[4] The inscriptions come from a wide spread of villages; in addition to Resava, Kavadarci, and Negotin, I have noted inscriptions from Demir Kapu, Dono Disan, Gorin Disan, Vatasa, Begniste, Marena, Mokliste, Mokreni, Sadevi, Barovo, Besvica, Bošava, Drenovo, Lenište, Manastirce, Tremnik, and Ovovo. On the other hand, only two inscriptions seem to have been

---

[1] Tozer, I. 379 f. Von Hahn, *Denkschriften* 16 (1867) 2. 63 noticed more evidence of the rock being cut to admit the road, both within the Demir Kapu and below it, than Tozer did. Today the skilfully engineered motor road follows the left bank and pierces the northern bastion of the Demir Kapu with a long tunnel.

[2] Heuzey–Daumet 329 f.

[3] *Spomenik* 71 (1931) 60 f.; 75 (1933) 33 f.; 77 (1934) nos. 24–6; 98 (1941–8) 107 f.; *ŽA* 3 (1953) 239; *ŽA* 13 (1964) 157 f. no. 3; *ŽA* 16 (1966) 411 no. 4. The earlier inscriptions are in Dimitsas nos. 304 f. and von Hahn nos. 36–40 in op. cit. 160–1.

[4] In *Spomenik* 71 (1931) no. 176, no. 177, no. 178; 75 (1933) no. 108 and no. 128. Kanatsoulis has two cases, of which one comes from Derriopus.

reported from just east of the river, at Vojsanci and Zarovets. On a hill near the former there were signs of an ancient settlement and a fragment of a life-size male statue in marble and a relief showing an eagle.

It is clear that we have to do here with a considerable plantation of Macedonians, distinct from the tribal communities of the Derriopi in the Morihovo (see p. 88 above) and from the Roman colony at Stobi. Whenever the main plantation was made, Antigonus Gonatas founded in this area the city Antigonea; and Antigonea is the only city between Stobi and Europus mentioned by Pliny *HN* 4. 34. As Tarn said, 'it no doubt commanded the entrance to the "Iron Gates", the pass . . . which gave access from Paeonia to Macedonia'.[1] It is in fact at the northern entrance to the pass that an inscription beginning ἡ πόλις Νουμήνιον was found in the wall of a church Ayia Paraskeve at Demir Kapu.[2] As Antigonea was the chief *polis* in this district, it lay probably in the vicinity of Banja, where the data of the Peutinger Table have led us to expect it.[3] The actual site has still to be identified.

Excavations by Yugoslav archaeologists have been very successful in the neighbourhood of Demir Kapu. There is a prehistoric site at Krečane, an interesting burial of the Sub-Mycenaean period between Demir Kapu and the road to Budur Čiflik, and a settlement at Manastir with imported Attic Red-Figure pottery, dating from the late fifth century B.C. There are tombs of the fifth and the fourth centuries and house-walls of squared masonry, 0·45 m to 0·50 m thick. The Roman site is by Bošava. The two peaks, Markove Kale and Ramniste (413 m and 489 m high respectively), which tower over the narrow entry to the defile, are both fortified. The fort on Markove Kale, north of the river, has a quadrangular tower, built of largish well-squared blocks, as well as an enceinte, and the excavators attribute it to the earliest period of the fifth-century settlement. On the south side of the river at the northern end of the defile by Manastir the ruts of an ancient road have been traced in the rock; the ruts are 10 cm wide and 1·25 m apart.[4]

The possession of the district of Kavadarci was certainly disputed between Paeonia and Macedonia. In terms of prior occupation it belonged to Paeonia, but in 167 B.C. it was largely peopled by Macedonians. The Roman policy in the settlement of Macedonia was to call it Paeonia,

---

[1] W. W. Tarn, *Antigonos Gonatas* (Oxford, 1913) 321.

[2] Von Hahn, loc. cit. no. 38; Dimitsas no. 307; *Spomenik* 71 (1931) no. 229; *ŽA* 2 (1952) 262 f.; *ŽA* 5 (1955) 140 f., using other bits of the inscription for the reading 'Noumenion'.

[3] Heuzey–Daumet 333 resisted the proposal to put Antigonea near Resava; it is too far removed from the pass. Heuzey suggested that Perseis was built at Tekvitch by Philip V, but it is doubtful if Resava–Tekvitch was in Derriopus (Livy 39. 53. 14 oppidum in Deuriopo condere instituit). A Roman milestone was found near the right river bank close to the entrance to the defile from the north; von Hahn, loc. cit. 161 no. 39 = Dimitsas no. 309.

[4] *AI* 5 (1964) has a brief report of the excavations of 1947–52; *Starinar* 12 (1961) 229 f. for the burial; ibid. 222 f. for the fortifications and the road.

but to put it in the third tetrarchy of Macedonia (Livy 45. 29. 8; see p. 76 above). If the Macedonians of the Roman period were to defend themselves against attack from the north, this was a sound solution to the problem. Stobi was included in the third tetrarchy. Its population is likely to have been mainly Paeonian, and it was rapidly Romanized; when it became a Roman colony, its territory was mainly on the eastern side of the river; and in the fourth century it became the capital of Macedonia Salutaris. It has yielded many inscriptions of the Roman period, which show that it was then a Greek type of city with a Jewish group in the community and with cults drawn from many parts of the Roman world.[1] The excavations have revealed much of its layout.

[1] The following list is far from complete: *Spomenik* 71 (1931) nos. 100 f.; nos. 636 f.; 75 (1933) nos. 40 f. (12 Latin, 25 Greek); 77 (1934) nos. 17 f.; nos. 71 f.; *ŽA* 3 (1953) 223 f. and 239; 12 (1962) 315. Heuzey–Daumet 333 drew attention to the Amazon representing Stobi and the two Nymphs representing the Axius and the Erigon on Roman coins, and in *ŽA* 12 (1962) 315 a relief is published showing three 'Hydrophoroi Nymphai'. There are worships of Thea Nemesis, Artemis Ephesia, Bacchus, Heracles, Daemones Antani, Zeus Olympius, Artemis, Apollo Soter, Apollo Clarius, Dioscuri, Cabiri, and Theae Daemones. A Roman soldier is from Stobi in *CIL* vi 2382 a 25, but there are far fewer of them from Stobi than from Pelagonia.

V

THE HINTERLAND OF THE PLAIN EAST OF THE AXIUS

1. *Amphaxitis*

THE rich agricultural area on the east side of the Axius is separated from the central plain by two low hills, between which the Echedorus flows, and from the long sink or channel in which Lake Doiran lies by a low mountain range (see Map 14). In the western part of the area there were until recently two considerable lakes, Lake Ardzani in the north below the prehistoric site Chauchitsa, and Lake Amatovo near Anthofiton. It is possible that these lakes did not exist either in prehistoric times or in antiquity.[1] The eastern part of the area is watered by the Echedorus and its tributaries, which rise in the Krusha Balkan, now Mt. Krousia and Mt. Kara Dag, forming a watershed with the Strymon. The whole area was divided into two ancient cantons, Amphaxitis by the Axius and Crestonia being the basin of the upper Echedorus; the boundary between them was probably the watershed of the Echedorus. The population of Amphaxitis may have been mainly Paeonian in the Macedonian period, because Thucydides does not mention any expulsion of the inhabitants when the Macedonians took control (2. 99. 6), and because its Paeonian connection is recorded by Str. 7 fr. 11.

Casson placed at the village of Amatovo the site of Amydon, from which 'Pyraechmes brought the Paeones of the curving bow to Troy, from the wide-flowing Axius' (*Il.* 2. 848). He did so partly because of 'the existence of a very fine spring in Amatovo village—the only one in the neighbourhood'.[2] There are two separable aspects of the problem. The first is the interpretation of the next line in the *Iliad*, (the reading was disputed in antiquity) : Ἀξιοῦ, οὗ κάλλιστον ὕδωρ ἐπικίδναται αἶαν. If we take this the standard reading, 'the fairest water of the Axius spreads over the land' is a phrase which well describes the flooding of the 'wide-flowing'

---

[1] Casson, *Macedonia*, figs. 31 and 32 facing p. 124 has views showing Lake Ardzani as an extensive sheet of water, and his map on p. 123 shows that Lake Amatovo was even larger. The largest concentration of prehistoric mounds in Macedonia is in this district; they are large and often sited on the Axius side of the plain. This indicates that the plain was arable and not mainly under water.

[2] Ibid. p. 46.

Axius over the central plain. And this is the meaning also of *Iliad* 21. 158, a line omitted in some manuscripts: Ἀξιοῦ, οὗ κάλλιστον ὕδωρ ἐπὶ γαῖαν ἵησιν. The alternative version of *Iliad* 2. 849 which has a different meaning is: Ἀξιοῦ, ᾧ κάλλιστον ὕδωρ ἐπικίδναται Αἴης. Here Aea is interpreted as a spring, whose fairest water spreads over the Axius; Str. 7 frs. 21, 23, and 23a argued in favour of this reading, that the Axius is a muddy stream and the clear water of the spring Aea spreads over the surface of the river. The same argument appears in the Scholia to *Iliad* 21. 158 (ed. Dindorf 4. 261) and to *Odyssey*. 11 239 (ed. Dindorf 2. 493), citing Eudoxus in its favour (*fl.* 366 B.C.). Of the two readings the former is surely to be preferred; for the verb is not appropriate to clear water mingling with muddy water, and the width of the river (500 feet in the Demir Kapu)[1] makes the idea peculiarly inapposite. As regards Casson's identification it may be added that the spring at Amatovo does not gush into the river Axius at all.

The second question is whether the site of Amydon was known. Str. 7 fr. 20, having drawn from an author later than Herodotus in saying that the Axius issued between Chalastra and Therme, goes on to remark that there lies by the river a strong place now called Abydon, which Homer called Amydon, and that it was razed by 'the Argeadae', a term used of the conquering Macedonians, as in fr. 11. It may well be, then, that the site was known, that it was destroyed, and that it was reoccupied later; for St. Byz. not only cites an Abydon from Strabo by name together with the line of the *Iliad* emended to ἐξ Ἀβυδῶνος but also has an entry Ἀμυδών, πόλις Παιονίας. τὸ ἐθνικὸν Ἀμυδώνιος ὡς Καλυδὼν Καλυδώνιος; and the Scholia to *Iliad* 16. 288 (ed. Dindorf 6. 180) report that there was a fort 'of the Macedones' by the Axius called Amydon. Once the controversy started about the reading in Homer, a spring Aea was produced at Amydon; already at the turn of the fifth century B.C. the epic poet Antimachus referred to a spring of this name in Macedonia.[1] The upshot of this is that Amydon may have been placed correctly in Paeonia, that is on the left bank of the Axius in Amphaxitis, which was traditionally Paeonian, but the grounds for placing it at Amatovo seem inadequate. A more likely site for a capital of Lower Macedonia is Vardarophtsa. It was a most important place in the Late Bronze Age, it has a fine spring (if a spring is called for by the Homeric passage), and the river is easily fordable in some seasons just by Vardarophtsa, as Heurtley remarked (*PM* 36 and see p. 237 below).

The position of Tauriana is disputed. It is mentioned only in the

---

[1] Cited in St. Byz. s.v. *Aia*. Mimnermus fr. 17 (Bergk) mentioned the Paeones being brought to Troy, and Aristotle fr. 640 (Rose) 47 had the Trojan Catalogue in mind; the Amytron of Hesychius, to which Hirschfeld in *RE* 1. 2 (1894) 1990 refers, seems to be irrelevant.

Peutinger Table and by the Ravenna Geographer[1] in connection with the Roman road. As I have shown (p. 172 above), the number of miles recorded in the Peutinger Table leads me to place Tauriana at Polikastron and not, as Leake, Miller and others have supposed, at Doiran, which would involve changing the number or numbers of the Peutinger Table. I imagine that Leake, Miller, and others were led towards Doiran partly by the purely superficial resemblance to our ears of Tauriana and Doiran and partly by the existence of the two large lakes of Ardzani and Amatovo in Turkish times. On the other hand, the large number of prehistoric sites and later of Macedonian cities in Amphaxitis suggests that these large lakes did not exist at that time. Now that these lakes have been entirely drained, the motor road from Thessalonica follows the direct and easy route via Polikastron to Evzoni and Gevgheli. This route runs through a rolling countryside which is all arable and open. On the other hand the route to Doiran keeps mainly to the foothills on the east side of the plain, climbs over a pass at Laotomeion, crosses two rivers, and enters the plain of Kilkis. On leaving the plain it enters open arable rolling country with flocks of turkeys, makes a long, gradual ascent through hills which become less fertile and then barren, and crosses a fairly narrow pass which suddenly reveals a view of the beautiful Lake Doiran. Having travelled on both routes, I am sure that the route by Polikastron is much the better one for the Roman road and that Polikastron should be identified with Tauriana in accordance with the data of the Peutinger Table. If I am correct, it indicates that Lake Ardzani at least did not exist in Roman times.

Casson noted during the First World War that a direct route was in use and that there was a causeway on it which led from the hamlet of Galavantsi to Chauchitsa. This causeway, he thought, 'in all probability lies on the ancient route'. He described the route as a track 'from Gevgheli to Chauchitsa, and thence straight across the Ardzani marshes to Salonica in almost a straight line', and he noted the existence of three classical sites on the route, at Kalabak and Jenesh and close to Sarigeul. As I have argued above (see p. 172), the distances on the Peutinger Table show that a direct route was used for the Roman road running up the Vardar valley. Casson's observations lend strong support. In Amphaxitis, as in the western part of the plain, there were certainly other roads, and a piece of one has been noted which may have led into the Doiran basin from Amphaxitis.[2]

---

[1] Tauriana has hitherto been identified with Doiran. As I have shown, this identification is not consistent with the evidence of the Peutinger Table, and the superficial similarity in sound to an English ear of Tauriana and Doiran is nothing to rest a theory upon.

[2] *BSA* 24. 3 f. and fig. 1 ; Casson, *Macedonia* 152 f. and Map 10, although he confuses the issue when he takes his route on a detour via Kilkis. In *BSA* 23. 60 and fig. 2 the supposed Roman road running north-eastwards to Avret Hissar and from there eastwards up the

A city of the Morrylii is known from two inscriptions. One on a stone in the Salonica Museum is a dedication to Asclepius, Hygieia, and 'Morrylii'.[1] The other was found at Ano Apostoli, just on the western side of the watershed of the Echedorus, and it records a decision by the polis of (the) Morrylii (δεδόχθαι τῇ Μορρυλίων πόλει) to honour a man and place the *stele* in the most conspicuous place in the Asclepieum. Two Hellenistic statues of Asclepius and Epione were found, and the foundations of a large building were discovered on the nearby hill, on which the city Morrylus or Morrylae was built.[2] The city Μόρυλλος appears in Ptol. 3. 13. 38 as one of three cities in Paraxia, which is evidently his form of the Amphaxitis of Polybius and Strabo (see p. 176 above).

At the village of Metallikon, further north and on the same side of the watershed, a dedication to the emperor Hadrian and the empress Sabina was inscribed on a base, the dedicators being Βραγυλίων ἡ βουλὴ καὶ ἡ πόλις καὶ ἡ πολιτεία.[3] This city figures as Bragylae in the list of Delphic *Theorodokoi* of 190–180 B.C.; the order is Idomenae, Astrea (both further north), Bragylae, Characoma, Leta, Aeanea. It appears also in Hierocles, *Synecdemus* 639. 6 and in Const. Porphyr. *Them*. 2. 49 in the form 'Bragylus'; it comes between Idomene and Primana. In both cases the directions in naming places seems to be south-eastwards. The Gallicum of the Peutinger Table or Callicum of the Ravenna Geographer which we have placed between Ayioneri and the Pikrolimni (see p. 172 above) is likely also to have been in Amphaxitis. As Ptolemy names two other cities besides Morrylus in Paraxia, that is Χαῖται and Ἀντιγόνη ψαφαρά, this canton was well endowed with cities.

2. *Crestonia*

Crestonia is one of the districts where the Macedonians gained control but did not eject the inhabitants (Thuc. 2. 99. 6), and we may infer from this that Crestonia lay some way back from the central plain (Maps 14 and 17). As Herodotus describes the Echedorus as rising among

Zensko valley cannot be a part of the main road from Thessalonica up the Vardar valley; it evidently crossed the main road and went towards Serres.

[1] *Rev. Phil.* 1939. 145.

[2] *AD* 17 (1961–2) 2. 207; *BCH* 86 (1962) 815; *REG* 77 (1964) 186; Panagiotes Manos in *Aristoteles* 55 (Florina, 1966) 57 f. Mr. Manos, the local Ephor of Antiquities, kindly showed me the stone from Ano Apostoli and the statues in the Apotheke at Kilkis.

[3] *AJA* 57 (1953) 286; *SEG* xi (1955) no. 349; *REG* 72 (1959) 100. In the last of these F. Papazoglou discusses the meaning of ἡ πολίτεια and concludes that it is 'le territoire municipal', so that the honours are done by the Council, the people of the city, and the people of the city's territory. Her case rests largely upon other instances, particularly at Pautalia (see G. Mihailov, *Inscriptiones Graecae in Bulgaria Repertae* iv (1966) no. 2236 lines 122 f.), and it seems likely that she has seen a distinction between the physical city and the territory of the group, which may have been drawn by Paeonians rather than by Macedonians in the narrower sense.

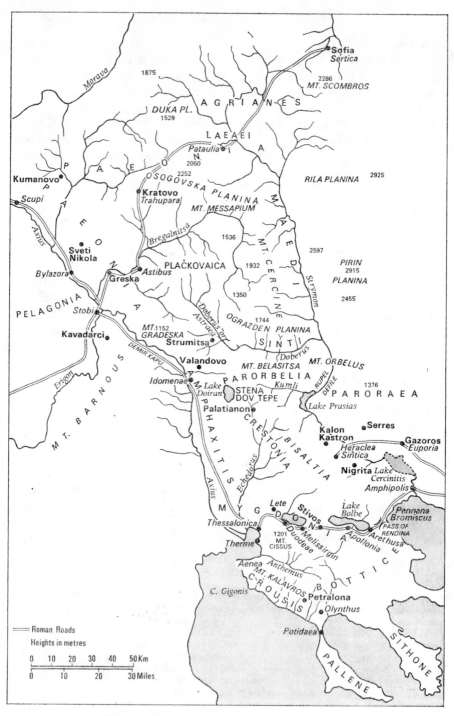

MAP 17. AREAS EAST OF THE RIVER AXIUS.

the Crestonaei and flowing through Mygdonia (7. 124 and 7. 127. 2), we should draw the line between Crestonia and Mygdonia somewhere about Kriston and Potamia. The Crestonian territory, which marched with that of the Bisaltae (Hdt. 8. 116. 1), consisted of a fertile basin by Kilkis which produced a rich harvest of figs, grapes, and olives,[1] and of a much larger area of high land affording pasture and timber on the sides of the Krusha Balkan. It is thus a canton which bears some similarity to Almopia as an area of refuge, withdrawn from the main plain of Lower Macedonia. The Thracian tribe which lived 'above' or to the north of the Crestonaei excited the interest of Herodotus (5. 3. 2. and 5. 5); for the men being polygamous, whenever a man died, the wife who was publicly judged to be his best beloved was killed and buried with him to the chagrin of the slighted wives.

The Crestonaei were probably not regarded as Thracian by Herodotus; nor were they mentioned by him among the speakers of the Pelasgic tongue in a list which included the people of Creston in the Athos peninsula (Hdt. 1. 57; see p. 192 below). The name was probably indigenous, being inherited from an earlier people. The worship of a god Candaon, whom the Greeks equated with Ares,[2] and the all-night vigil within the precinct of Dionysus for a flash of fire which would portend a good season,[3] may indicate that descendants of the earlier population persisted under the name Grastones[4] and claimed descent from one Grastus (St. Byz. s.v. *Grestonia*).

Small finds have been made at several sites in the canton (for instance an inscribed altar of the Roman period at Creston south of Kilkis), and the main site is at Palatianon (Saraïli),[5] north of Kilkis, where a statue of a young Dionysus wearing a panther skin and beside a tree-trunk with a snake around it[6] has been found in association with a funerary heroön and a hypocaust. Four statues, two intact,[7] and the names of the dead survive from the heroön; three were children of Patraüs, a name of the Paeonian royal house. The identity of the site is not known. If it is the famous temenos of Dionysus, there should be an emission of petroleum

---

[1] Theopompus (*FGrH* 115, F 237) in Athen. 3. 77 d. He speaks of the good luck of Philip II, for whom the figs, vines and olives bore fruit in the spring in Bisaltia, Amphipolis, and 'Grastonia of Macedonia', which distinguishes this Crestonia from that in the Athos peninsula.

[2] Lycophr. *Alex.* 937; the comment of Tzetzes ad loc. shows that he took this Crestone to be the one in Thrace and not that in Chalcidice.

[3] Arist. *Mir.* 122, distinguishing this 'Crastonia' by adding 'beside Bisaltia'.

[4] Hecataeus (*FGrH* 1 F 153) has the ethnic Krestones; this form, like Grestones, is unusual. Pindar fr. 309 and Herodotus have Krestonaioi.

[5] *AD* 16 (1960) 2. 212; 17 (1961–2) 2. 207; *BCH* 85 (1961) 812; 86 (1962) 815; *REG* 76 (1963) 149; Manos, op. cit. 58 f. (Palatianon) and 61 f. (small finds).

[6] Lycophr. *Alex.* 499 mentions the lethal bite of the adder of Crestone; this may be connected with a local myth of Dionysus.

[7] Illustrated in *BCH* 85 (1961) 812 figs. 1 and 2.

gas in the vicinity; for this would best explain the phenomenon, reported by Aristotle, that the birds and animals died within a particular area of it.[1]

I visited the site in 1968. It is on an isolated hill called Tórtseli, and there are remains of houses on its two tops and on the eastern slopes of the hill. A trial trench had been dug. This showed that the walls were of small stone set in mortar, and that an outer circuit-wall was of similar construction with larger stones. The local Ephor, Panagiotes Manos, told me that material of the third century B.C. had been found during the digging of the trench. The hillside is fairly steep but not precipitous; it is covered with soil but contains some rock, and I saw a number of large ancient blocks. The inhabited area within the circuit-wall seems to have been some 450 m by 100 m. The hill is strategically placed to the east of the modern road, and from it one has an extensive view westwards over the Axius, southwards to the plain of Thessalonica, and northwards to the pass leading into the Doiran area and the great mountain range beyond. The land by Palatianon is very fertile. The house remains and the circuit-wall are evidently medieval in date, but it seems to have been a Macedonian city in the Hellenistic and Roman periods. Its name is not known. Panagiotes Manos told me that there is a similar site on a flat-topped hill to the ESE. of Palatianon. It is visible from Tórtseli hill.

The mountainous part of Crestonia and its neighbouring canton Bisaltia were and are thickly forested. It was good country for hunting; here the camels of Xerxes' army were attacked by lions at night (Hdt. 6. 125), and the hares were double-livered.[2] The frontier between the two cantons is likely to have run along the watershed of the Strymon valley. Here the best pass is west of Mt. Krousia and is commanded by the site at Palatianon.

3. *Mygdonia*

The canton south of Crestonia was Mygdonia, which extended from the lower Axius in the central plain (Hdt. 7. 123. 3) through the long sink containing Lake Koronia and Lake Bolbe to the pass of Rendina, from which one descends to the sea. Here again the soil of the plain and of the sides of the long narrow sink is very fertile, and there was good pasture and much timber in the foothills and the ranges to the north and the south. The Macedonians acquired this territory as far as the Strymon, driving out a part of the previous occupants, the Edoni (Thuc. 2. 99. 4). The memory of some earlier rulers of this area lingered on in the traditions that the name Mygdones was most properly applied to people by Lake Bolbe (Str. 7. fr. 36), and that Mygdonia took its name

---

[1] Arist. *Mir.* 122. See *Epirus* 39 and 707 for the place Aornus in Thesprotia which had similar properties.   [2] Arist., loc. cit.

from one Mygdon,[1] whose son Grastus was the eponym of Grestonia or Crestonia and was the father of the girl Tirse, after whom a city of Mygdonia, Tirsae, was named, and of other girls, who gave rise to the name of a Macedonian city, Parthenopolis.[2] The Macedonian cities in that part of the central plain which belonged to Mygdonia were Chalastra, Sindus, and Therme (see p. 146 above), and Ptolemy 3. 13. 36 attributes to Mygdonis ten cities, which do not include any I have mentioned.

Strepsa was mentioned as 'a city of Thrace' in Hellanicus, *Persica*, book II (*FGrH* 4 F 61), a statement repeated in the *Suda* s.v., and it was therefore probably on the route of the army of Xerxes. As it was 'a city of Macedonia' in St. Byz. s.v., it was evidently situated in the area acquired by Macedon after 480 B.C., that is between the Axius and the Strymon. Aristophanes, *Georgoi* fr. 123 (ed. Edmonds) referred to the Strepsaei and to Hermes Strepsaeus 'the cross-eyed' in 424 B.C., a year in which military operations suggest that Strepsa was near the coast or near Chalcidice. In the disturbed period after the death of Alexander II 'Anthemus, Therma, Strepsa, and some other places' were captured by Pausanias, operating with a Greek force against Eurydice (Aeschines 2. 27), and the geographical sequence should put Strepsa on the route from Therma towards the capital at Pella. We therefore need a site with at least fifth-century remains north-west of Therme and at a cross-roads, if the name Strepsa is meaningful. Such a site is at Inglis (now Nea Ankhialos), at the cross-roads where one road from Therme turns off into the valley of the Echedorus and the other continues to Pella (see Map 14); there is no other 'cross-roads site' until Yefira. At Inglis imported pottery from Greece of the Protogeometric and Geometric periods, Early Iron Age pottery, and signs of bronze-working have been found during an excavation connected with road works (*AD* 20 (1965) 2. 421). We may provisionally put Strepsa at Inglis.

In 432 B.C., when the Athenians already held Therme and were besieging Pydna, they made a treaty of necessity, not of goodwill, with Perdiccas, and hastened back overland via Beroea towards Potidaea. At this point the text of Thuc. 1. 61. 4 reads καὶ ἀφικόμενοι ἐς Βέροιαν κἀκεῖθεν ἐπιστρέψαντες καὶ πειράσαντες πρῶτον τοῦ χωρίου καὶ οὐχ ἑλόντες ἐπορεύοντο κατὰ γῆν πρὸς τὴν Ποτείδαιαν. It is clear that the place the Athenians tried and failed to take cannot be Beroea, which they had already passed (κἀκεῖθεν), and it was therefore a place between

---

[1] I agree with the comment of E. Oberhummer in *RE* 16. 1 (1933) 998 on the derivation of Mygdonia from the Greek word μύχος, suggested by Tomaschek in *Thraker* (Vienna, 1893) 1. 33 f., as 'sehr fragwürdig'. St. Byz. ends his entry under Mygdonia with an aspirated form Μυχθονία.

[2] See St. Byz. s.vv. *Grestonia, Parthenopolis,* and *Tirsae,* and *FGrH* 774 (Theagenes) F 12 and F 13.

Beroea and Therme; for they already held Therme. As the treaty with Perdiccas was one of necessity and not likely to last, the Athenians could only hope to capture *and hold* a place near Therme (for a place inland such as Pella would soon be recaptured by Perdiccas). The most likely place then is Strepsa at Inglis. Pluygers made the following emendation with no topographical considerations in mind: ἀφικόμενοι ἐς Βέροιαν κἀκεῖθεν ἐπὶ Στρέψαν καὶ πειράσαντες τοῦ χωρίου κτλ. His emendation provides a suitable sense, although it may be doubted whether Thucydides wrote ἐς and ἐπὶ in such close proximity. At the same time one may wonder whether, having made a treaty with Perdiccas, the Athenians wished to disrupt it at once by attacking a Macedonian city. It is indeed more likely that Strepsa was one of the states which had been under Athens' control and had revolted together with the Chalcidians, Bottiaeans, and Potidaea. Here the Tribute Lists come to our aid; for Strepsa paid 1 talent each year from 454/3 to 433/2 (probably continuously) and was evidently in revolt in 432 B.C., the year in which the Athenians tried to capture it. At that time Strepsa was probably closer to the coast than it is today (see p. 146 above).

The most important of the inland cities of Mygdonia was Lete, which derived its name from a shrine of Leto and issued a silver coinage in the name of 'Letaei' *c.* 500–480 B.C.[1] Its location at Aïvat, now named Liti, was determined by the discovery of inscriptions there. It commanded the road which leads over the north-western spur of Mt. Khortiatis to Therme; indeed Thessalonica had a 'Letaean gate', through which the road entered the city.[2] Lete itself was the centre from which roads led to the central plain through the valley of the Echedorus, over the southern part of Mt. Kara Dag to Serres in the Strymon valley, and down the sink south of the lakes to the pass of Rendina. The city was thus in an excellent position to control the current of trade which flowed from the interior to the port of Therme on the Thermaic Gulf.

The inscriptions show that the city had a full range of magistrates: politarchae, bouleutae, tamias, agoranomi, grammateus, architecton, and ὁ μέγας γυμνασίαρχος of the ephebi.[3] The most interesting of them is a decision of the council and the demos of the Letaei (δεδόχθαι Ληταίων τῆι βουλῆι καὶ τῶι δήμωι)[4] to honour the Roman Quaestor, Marcus Annius, in the year 117 B.C. (dated by the Macedonian era), for his victories over the forces first of the Gauls and then of the Gauls and the Maedi. The inscription records that the Gauls, having superior forces,

---

[1] St. Byz. s.v. = *FGrH* 774 (Theagenes) F 6. Head, *Historia Numorum* (Oxford, 1887) 176 f.   [2] Jo. Camen. 41.

[3] Dimitsas nos. 675–80; *Mak.* 2 (1941–52) 616 f.; *Mak.* 6 (1967) 304; *Mon. Piot.* 46. 90. The funerary reliefs and two inscriptions are illustrated in *Mak.* 2 pls. 11–14.

[4] Published first by Duchesne in *Rev. Arch.* 29 (1875) 6 f. = Dimitsas no. 675. Annius was commended also for his earlier consideration for the interests of the city of Lete.

marched into the district by Argos (line 11, εἰς τοὺς κατὰ Ἄργος τόπους), and that the Roman governor, Sextus Pompeius, went out against them with his own troops, suffered defeat, and was killed. The Argos in question is evidently the Argos near Stobi (see p. 80 above). Marcus Annius then came up with his force and defeated the Gauls; he then called into his camp the garrison troops who were in advanced positions (line 19 τῶν τε ἐν τοῖς προκειμένοις τόποις φρουρῶν). A few days later the Gallic cavalry returned in greater numbers together with the forces of Tipas, a dynast of the Maedi, whereupon Annius defeated them decisively. The Maedi probably came down the Bregalnitsa valley from Istib (see p. 78 above); for when Philip V planned to attack the Maedi, he set off from Stobi (Livy 40. 21. 1).[1] We gain also an insight into the Roman arrangements for defending the province: there were garrisons in advanced positions north of Argos, probably placed to threaten the route beside the Axius, and there were evidently two Roman armies stationed in different places, which formed the strategic reserve and were ready to move to a threatened point. The inscription refers to ἐπ[ακτ]οὺς στρατιώτας ἐπὶ συμμαχίαν παρὰ Μακεδόνων, whom Annius did not call away from their work. It appears then that the Roman troops acted as garrison troops in the advanced positions, and that they are the soldiers who, under the Roman settlement of 167 B.C., were posted ἐν τοῖς ἐσχάτοις τῆς Μακεδονίας τόποις διὰ τὰς τῶν παρακειμένων ἐθνῶν ἐπιβουλάς (D.S. 31. 9). The Macedonian militia could also be called upon in an emergency.

In the village of Liti a district is called the gate of Thessalonica, or Derveni, and it is here that the papyrus of the late fourth century B.C. was found which contained a commentary on an Orphic hymn.[2] Lete was named as one of the cities in the interior by Pliny *HN* 4. 36 and as one of the cities of Mygdonis by Ptol. 3. 13. 36; and it was the seat of a bishop, at first by itself and then in conjunction with Rendina.[3] Inscriptions have been found at Dhrimos (Dhremiglava), north-west of Liti towards the valley of the Echedorus, and one of them records a decree by ἡ πόλις in honour of the emperor Vespasian.[4] It is beside the saddle through which one enters the long sink from the Echedorus valley and it may perhaps be Characoma, a name appropriate to a defended place at a strategic point, since Characoma comes between Bragylae and Leta in the list of Delphic *Theorodokoi* of 190–180 B.C.[5] A 'Macedonian' tomb of the third century B.C. has been examined at Laïna, a village just south-east

---

[1] Duchesne thought the word ἄργος meant the central plain of Macedonia, and Dimitsas saw that it was a proper name and referred it to Argos Oresticum; but one cannot see how the Maedi would have reached that Argos in a few days. [2] *AD* 18 (1963) 2. 193 f.

[3] G. Parthey, *Hieroclis Synecdemus et Notitiae Graecae Episcopatuum* (Berlin, 1866) Notit. 2. 133; 10. 329; and 3. 207.

[4] Dimitsas 681–4. [5] *BCH* 45 (1921) 18 iii 72.

of Liti.[1] At Zagliverion, the chief town south of the lakes, a funerary relief with an inscription of the late Hellenistic period suggests that it is the site of one of the Mygdonian cities. And south of Kalamoto there is the site of a considerable city which has yielded inscriptions honouring Andronicus 'the great Gymnasiarch' and making a dedication to Hermes, and many pieces of large stone buildings, one being a shrine.[2] At the east end of the long sink St. Byz. s.v. Βόλβαι . . . ἔστι καὶ Βόλβη πόλις καὶ λίμνη. τὸ ἐθνικὸν Βολβαῖος refers to what is now called Lake Besikia (Volvi); for in describing the march of Brasidas from Arnae in Chalcidice to Amphipolis Thucydides mentions his arrival in the evening at 'the aulon' and Bromiscus, where Lake Bolbe issues into the sea (4. 103. 1). The word aulon is used of a long sink, as in Strabo (see p. 169 above), and the name Aulon is appropriate here for the channel or coomb which forms the pass of Rendina. The coomb has not been cut by the stream which issues from Lake Bolbe but is earlier in origin. The sides are steep and rocky and partly covered with scrub, and the bottom is as narrow as a hundred yards in places. So narrow a pass was easily defended. It formed a defensible frontier for Mygdonia towards the east.

Thuc. 2. 99. 5 says that when the Eordi were driven out of Eordia by the Macedonians, most of them were destroyed but a small part of them settled at Physca. This city was mentioned by Theagenes (*FGrH* 774 F 15 = St. Byz. s.v.) as Physcus, a city of Macedonia, and by Ptol. 3. 13. 36 as Physcae, a city of Mygdonis. It was probably in a remote part of the canton, perhaps in the hills north of the lakes; for the co-ordinates given by Ptolemy for this city put it apart from the other cities of Mygdonia.

4. Crousis

While Therme is in Mygdonia, Aenea is the first city in Crousis in Herodotus' description of the voyage of Xerxes' fleet (Hdt. 7. 123. 2–3). The position of Aenea on Cape Karaburnu is determined by Ps.-Scymnus 627, who calls the cape 'Aeneia', and by Livy 44. 10. 7, who in reporting the naval operations of Gaius Marcius in 169 B.C. remarked that it was 15 m.p. = 22·2 km from Thessalonica, which is a correct measurement to the Cape by sea.[3] Livy adds that it is situated opposite Pydna, thus marking the entry to the Gulf, and in fertile soil. Ps.-Scylax 66 named it a Greek city between Therme and Cape Pallene, and its Greekness is supported by its early coinage, which began before 500 B.C. The people of Aenea made the claim, which is publicized on their earliest coinage,

---

[1] *Mak.* 2 (1941–52) 620; the same tomb as that described in *BSA* 13 (1918–19) 14 f.
[2] *Mak.* 2 (1941–52) 620 (Zagliverion). *AD* 17 (1961–2) 2. 206; *BCH* 86 (1962) 814; *REG* 77 (1964) no. 252 (Kalamoto).   [3] See C. F. Edson in *CP* 42 (1947) 88 f.

that their founder was Aeneas; this tradition was narrated by Hellanicus (*FGrH* 4 F 31 fin.), who brought Aeneas to the peninsula of Pallene and 'the Cruseaean tribe', and in a garbled version by Conon (*FGrH* 26 F 1. 46), who named the Thermaic Gulf but confused Aenea and Aenus. At Aenea a state sacrifice was made annually to Aeneas as the founder (Livy 40. 4. 9), probably at the temple of Aphrodite (D.H. 1. 49. 4). The city figures in the Tribute Lists, the list of Epidaurian *Theorodokoi* and the list of Delphian *Theorodokoi*, the last being after the inclusion of part of its population in Cassander's Thessalonica.[1] The Cape is a 'cliffy bluff of tableland', a useful landmark on this low coast, and it has a small stone pier half a mile to the south and some salt-pans.[2] The prosperity of Aenea indicates that in antiquity it was a port. Tombs of the classical period have recently been found on the south side of the Cape.[3]

A conspicuous landmark to anyone entering the inner part of the Thermaic Gulf or the central plain of Macedonia is the sharp peak of Mt. Khortiatis, which even today is thickly wooded. It lies immediately to the east of Thessalonica. In antiquity, it seems not to have belonged to Mygdonia but to have been a separate mountain, Mt. Cissus, famous for its forests and its game.[4] Str. 7 frs. 21 and 24 gives a list of cities from which Cassander made his enlarged Thessalonica, the names in fr. 21 apart from Apollonia being probably in a west-to-east order: Chalastra, Therme, Garescus (perhaps at Sedhes;[5] see p. 150 n. 2 above), Aenea, and Cissus, which should be inland towards Mt. Khortiatis. A fortified acropolis on the very top of the mountain has been excavated by G. Bakalakis, who was able to date its construction to the middle of the fourth century B.C. by the pottery at the base of the walls; the circumference is some 600 m, the walls are 2 m thick, with blocks of local stone, e.g. $1·00 \times 0·30$ m, and there are remains of houses of the period, as well as of some Byzantine buildings. The view embraces the Thermaic Gulf, Mygdonia, and Anthemus. It is probably the acropolis of Cissus, the town itself being lower down the mountain.[6]

While Aenea was a Greek city in Crousis, the Crousaei or Crossaei were an *ethnos*, a tribal group, and they may have been related to the

[1] *ATL* 1. 220 f. and 464 f.; *IG* iv². 1. 94, 1b line 10; *BCH* 45 (1921) 18 iii 75 in the form Αἰανέα, a mistake for Αἰνέα, which is the earlier form of the name; Str. 7 fr. 21 and fr. 24.

[2] *MP* 219. 46.

[3] Lycophr. *Alex.* 1236–7 and C. F. Edson, loc. cit.; X. *Cyn.* 11. 1; Nic. *Ther.* 804.

[4] For an ancient site here see *BSA* 20 (1913–14) 131. C. F. Edson in *CP* 42 (1947) 89 argues decisively against the proposal in *ATL* 1. 464 f. to elevate the 'cliffy bluff' of Karaburnu into Mt. Cissus.

[5] Between Nea Michanonia and the Cape; *BCH* 77 (1953) 224 and 78 (1954) 141.

[6] *Mak.* 3 (1953–5) 353 f.; among the finds were stamped amphora-handles of Rhodian and Thasian manufacture and arrow-heads. Bakalakis does not suggest its identification with Cissus, but it is hard to see what other name an inhabited site on Mt. Cissus would have had. He notes that the traditional location of Cissus at the village Khortiatou (e.g. Dimitsas 640) is not acceptable, as he found no ancient remains there.

pre-Macedonian inhabitants of Mygdonia, since St. Byz. s.v. *Krousis* derives
them from Crousis, son of Mygdon, and calls Crousis a part of Mygdonia.[1]
Their territory begins south of the Sedhes plain, where there is an abrupt
break in the nature of the country. The break is most noticeable if one
is coming from the south. Crousis is a long and wide area of rich arable
land, with light-coloured grey and pink soils; cereals, cotton, grapes, and
olives are among its products. It lies between the sea and the distant
mountains, which thrust out long, gradually descending ridges with water-
courses between them. As one goes north-westwards, the land becomes
higher and has deeper watercourses, until finally it comes to an abrupt
end overhanging the flat Sedhes plain in a series of heavily eroded bluffs
with steep sides, which are of a distinctive light-brown colour. The last
part of this sloping tableland was called Rhaecalus. It is associated with
Mt. Cissus by the scholiast to Lycophron 1236, and it was here 'by the
Thermaic Gulf' that the Athenian Pisistratus 'synoecised the district
called Rhaecalus' (Arist. *Ath. Pol.* 15. 2).

Hdt. 7. 123. 3 names six cities of the Crousaei from south to north as
the Persian fleet sailed past them: Lipaxus, Combrea, Lisae, Gigonus,
Campsa, Smila, and then Aenea. Of these Gigonus is the place where the
Athenians and their allies camped, when they were on their way by
land and by sea from Pydna to Potidaea in 432 B.C. (Thuc. 1. 61. 5),
and it figures in the Tribute Lists (*ATL* 1. 146 and 540). The *Etymo-
logicum Magnum* s.v. *Gigon* and s.v. *Gigonis* gives the former as a title of
Dionysus and the latter as a cape between Macedonia and Pallene.
Cape Gigonis then is Cape Epanomi.[2] It is very low with a rocky bank
at its extremity, and anchorage can be had on either side of it; as the
Athenian fleet of 70 triremes made it their naval base in 432 B.C., the
coast may then have been more deeply indented on either side.[3]

St. Byz. has the entry Γίγωνος, πόλις Θράκης προσεχὴς τῇ Παλλήνῃ.
ὁ πολίτης Γιγώνιος. ἀπὸ Γίγωνος τοῦ Αἰθιόπων βασιλέως ὃν ἥττησε Διόνυσος.
Ἀρτεμίδωρος δ' ὁ Ἐφέσιος (*FGrH* 438 F) Γιγωνίδα ταύτην φησίν. There
is a possibility that Stephanus' source here is Hecataeus.[4] For Stephanus
has two entries cited by name from Hecataeus: (1) Λίπαξος, πόλις
Θράκης. Ἑκαταῖος (*FGrH* 1 F 148). τὸ ἐθνικὸν Λιπάξιος. (2) Σμίλα, πόλις
Θράκης. Ἑκαταῖος Εὐρώπῃ "μετὰ δὲ Σμίλα πόλις". τὸ ἐθνικὸν Σμιλαῖος.
(F 149). In addition he has an entry under Aisa: Αἶσα πόλις Θράκης

---

[1] It has been suggested that St. Byz. s.v. *Brousis* refers to Crousis; but this is unlikely,
because St. Byz. derives the Brousi from Brousos, son of Emathius. Brousis should be a district
west of the Axius river.

[2] *ATL* 1. 540 proposes to put Cape Gigonis ten miles further south at a place marked
Antigonia, but *The Mediterranean Pilot* knows of no cape or anchorage there.

[3] *MP* 218. 16. In antiquity, when the sea level was some five feet lower, the narrow rocky
bank running SSW. of the cape will have offered better shelter.

[4] *ATL* 1. 540 n. 1 suggests that the source was Herodotus, but Herodotus says nothing of
Gigon and Dionysus.

προσεχὴς τῇ Παλλήνῃ. Αἰσαῖος ὡς Αἶα Αἰαῖος. The similarities in the citations of these cities as cities 'of Thrace', and in the use of προσεχής (as in F 93 and 95, for instance) indicate that the Aisa entry comes also from Hecataeus. It thus becomes apparent not only that Stephanus used Hecataeus for Gigonus, Lipaxus, Smila, and Aisa, but also that Herodotus drew from Hecataeus his list of Lipaxus, Combrea, Lisae, Gigonus, Campsa, and Smila. The question then arises whether *ΑΙΣΑ* or *ΑΙΣΑΙ* is the correct form. Hecataeus probably had Aisa, as Stephanus arranged his names alphabetically and therefore looked closely at the initial letter. The matter is decided by the Tribute Lists, in which 'Haisa' appears next to Gigonus (*ATL* 1. 146). Herodotus, then, or his copyist was at fault. Stephanus has also the entry Κάψα, πόλις Χαλκιδικῆς χώρας κατὰ Παλλήνην, ὁμοροῦσα τῷ Θερμαίῳ κόλπῳ. ὁ πολίτης Καψαῖος. This citation is not similar in form to the others and so may come from a different source;[1] but it is probable that the Campsa of Herodotus and the Capsa of Stephanus are the same place. Smila appears as Smilla in the Tribute Lists. The two inaccuracies in Herodotus make me prefer Capsa to Campsa.[2]

It is interesting that the Crousaei were able to maintain themselves as an independent group between the Greek cities Aenea and Potidaea. They fought as peltasts in 429 B.C. (Thuc. 2. 79. 4), and they may have had timber to export from Mt. Kalavros, from which many streams irrigated their coastal land.[3] The frontier with Kithas or Skithai is likely to have been where a spur of the mountain runs southwards, east of Nea Sillata. It is just to the east of Nea Sillata that the existence of a city from early archaic times has been inferred from the discovery of

---

[1] These entries are discussed in *ATL* 1. 540. The alterations equating Aisa with Lisai, and Campsa with Capsa, were already proposed in Meineke's edition of Stephanus and Hude's edition of Herodotus.

[2] The suggestions in *ATL* 1. 502 and 541 f., that Cissus should be included under the cities of the Crousaei, that it should be equated with the 'Kithas' of the Tribute Lists, and that Kithas should also be included under those cities, do not seem to be justified. For Cissus is associated with Mt. Cissus, which is much too far north for the territory of the Crousaei (on the location of Mt. Cissus see C. F. Edson in *CP* 42 (1947) 89 f.); and neither Cissus nor Kithas are included in Herodotus' list of the cities of the Crousaei next to the Thermaic Gulf. Kithas then is not a city of the Crousaei, and it is very probably the Skithai of Stephanus: Σκίθαι, πόλις Θράκης πλησίον Ποτιδαίας. ὁ πολίτης Σκιθαῖος, ὥς φησι Θεόπομπος. The expression 'near Potidaea' is more precise than Herodotus' description of the cities in Crousaean territory as being 'next to Pallene and bordering on the Thermaic Gulf'. Skithai or Kithas, then, was south of Crousaea. The list in *ATL* 1. 146, Syme (in the Dodecanese), Tyndaei (unknown), Kithas, Smilla, Gigonos, Haisa, Bysbikos (in the Hellespont) is not then in a dependable order from north to south, except in the case of Smilla, Gigonos, and Haisa.

[3] A 'Macedonian' tomb of the second half of the second century B.C. has been excavated at Mesemeri, in the coastal plain east of Cape Epanomi (*Mak.* 2 (1941–52) 621), whence earlier finds have been reported (*BCH* 76 (1952) 228). A finely built 'Macedonian' tomb, as yet unpublished, was found near Trilofon, north-east of Cape Epanomi, and has points of resemblance in construction and contents with the rich tombs at Sedhes (see p. 190 below). It is mentioned in *AE* 1937, 868 f.

some fifty inhumations in cist graves, made of slabs. Almost all the tombs had been robbed, but gold jewellery and fine pottery were found.[1]

5. *Anthemus*

Anthemus is described by Hesychius s.v. as the name of a city, a district, and a river, and it provided a squadron of the Companion Cavalry of Alexander (Hsch. s.v. *Anthemousia* and Arr. *Anab.* 2. 9. 3). The city Anthemus was included by Pliny *HN* 4. 36 among the cities of the Chalcidic peninsula, and its proximity to the Chalcidians is indicated by the fact that Philip II ceded Anthemus to the Olynthian League (D. 6. 20). At the same time it was close to Therme, as Aeschines 2. 27 relates that the pretender Pausanias seized Anthemus, Therme, Strepsa, and some other places, and it was adjacent to and south of Mygdonia, because Sitalces coming from the lower Axius and leaving Pella on his left ravaged Mygdonia, Crestonia, and Anthemus (Thuc. 2. 100. 4). The only district and river which fulfil these conditions are the valley and the hinterland of the Vasilikotikos river, which runs between Mt. Khortiatis in the north and Mt. Kalavros in the south and issues into the Thermaic Gulf between Therme and Aenea.[2] This small but rich land with its coastal plain and wooded hinterland was acquired by the Macedonians when they conquered Crestonia and Mygdonia (Thuc. 2. 99. 6). The inhabitants were not expelled. We have already noted that Pisistratus formed a settlement in the district Rhaecalus; his son Hippias was offered Anthemus by Amyntas (Hdt. 5. 94. 1). It looks as if the Macedonian kings regarded Anthemus in a rather particular sense as a crown possession, and Demosthenes remarked that all kings of Macedonia had claimed it, until Philip ceded it to the Olynthians (D. 6. 20).

A fragmentary inscription of the fourth century B.C. has been found a quarter of an hour north-east of Vasilika, which commands the entry into the upper valley of the river,[3] and the city of Anthemus may be placed tentatively at Vasilika by the river Anthemus. Down in the plain at Sedhes a number of very rich tombs were found in 1938. A masonry tomb in the shape of a small sarcophagus, laid beneath a large pyre, contained a gold olive-wreath, and in the ashes of the pyre there were pieces of the same wreath, a gold necklace, remains of a bronze vessel, a bronze mirror, and clay figurines; the tomb, of a Thracian type, is

---

[1] Ph. Papadopoulos in *AD* 19 (1964) 1. 84–112. She considers it to be probably a city of Bottice.

[2] So too C. F. Edson in *CP* 42 (1947) 91 n. 28; Desdevises, *Géographie ancienne de la Macédoine* (Paris, 1862) 360; and Dimitsas 604. For other identifications see *RE* 1. 2 (1894) 2369 and I. Papastavrou, *Mak. Pol.* 33.   [3] *Mak.* 2 (1941–52) 621.

dated to the late fifth century B.C. Nearby there were three built tombs. A small tomb in the shape of a truncated pyramid had been robbed. So too had a large and finely built 'Macedonian' tomb, famous locally for its gold contents, and all that was found was an iron sword and a drinking-cup outside the door of the tomb. The third was intact, another large and finely built 'Macedonian' tomb with a roof of wood, lined inside with an embroidered cloth of many colours, with decorated walls and with a brick-built bed for the corpse. On the bed and the floor were a gold wreath with a gold frontlet of exquisite workmanship, a gold necklace, three pairs of gold brooches, a pair of gold ear-rings, a gold finger-ring, a number of thin gold plaques showing Apollo, Demeter, Persephone, the Muses, and Eros, a gold coin as Charon's obol, a wrought silver bowl, four gilt-bronze wreathes, a bronze cup, a bronze mirror, small bronze rings and nails, and various fine objects of iron, bone, crystal, alabaster, and clay, and a honey-cake as an offering set before a bone statuette of Persephone. This tomb gives us an idea of the wealth and the beliefs of a rich family in Anthemus towards the end of the fourth century B.C.[1]

6. *Areas adjacent to Macedonia on the East*

At the head of the fertile valley of the river Anthemus one crosses a high belt of country with deep, twisting valleys and with wooded slopes, on which there is a mixture of large trees and garigue. It is a natural frontier area. Having crossed it one descends into the high basin of the river now called the Olinthios. In the centre of the basin is Poliyiros, a prosperous town, backed by a magnificent amphitheatre of densely wooded mountains, which form the range known as Mt. Holomon. Poliyiros faces seawards and enjoys a particularly fine climate. The descent to the coast is at first steep between wooded hillsides and then gradual, as one emerges into a long and wide rolling area, which is planted with olive trees far apart and grows cereals in the spaces between them. This southward-facing area enjoys the advantages of the Mediterranean climate and of a fertile and well-watered soil. It was the refuge of the Bottiaei when they were driven out of Bottia by the Macedonians; they named their new land Bottice, but they retained the name Bottiaei themselves. Like their neighbours, the Crousaei and the Chalcidians, they were conscripted to serve with the army of Xerxes, but in the following winter their city Olynthus was taken by Artabazus and given to the Chalcidians (Hdt. 7. 185. 2 and 8. 127, the latter passage referring to their earlier expulsion from Bottia). Their relations in war and in peace were mainly with the Chalcidians and the Athenians in the fifth

---

[1] N. Ch. Kotzias in *AE* 1937. 866 f. with good illustrations.

century, when their cities formed a federation but kept a considerable degree of independence.[1] In the fourth century they were absorbed by the powerful Chalcidian League and then by the Macedonian state. Their prosperity is shown by their coinage and by their provision of cavalry in a joint squadron with Amphipolis in the Macedonian army (Arr. *Anab.* 1. 2. 5).

The Greek cities of the peninsulas of Chalcidice were remote from Macedonia. They lived in the world of seafaring, which was entirely alien to the land-loving Macedonians; they had a culture and a political form which stemmed from an entirely different background; and they were familiar with a sophisticated kind of capitalism, which was unknown to the Macedonians until Philip and Alexander led them into a wider world. In so far as Greek cities influenced the development of Lower Macedonia, Pydna and Methone and Aenea played a more important part than the Chalcidian cities, until the Chalcidian League was powerful enough to intervene in Macedonia. Another reason for this remoteness from the Macedonian point of view was that the centre of the Macedonian kingdom was far away by land at Aegeae and then Pella, and two independent peoples, the Crousaei and the Bottiaei, lay as a buffer between the Macedonian plain and the Chalcidian cities.

The most easterly peninsula, Acte then and Athos now, was a refuge for a variety of peoples, whose native language was not Greek, but who had acquired Greek. They were called βάρβαροι δίγλωσσοι by Thucydides and later writers, and they lived in small settlements or 'polismata'. Herodotus mentions Tyrseni and Crestoniatae (1. 57); Thucydides people of the stocks of the Tyrseni, the Bisaltae, the Crestones, and the Edones (4. 109. 4); and Diodorus, perhaps abbreviating his source, ὄχλον βαρβάρων διγλώττων Βισαλτικόν (12. 68. 5). They were the flotsam and jetsam of many migrations and invasions.

The district which lay to the east of Crestonia and Mygdonia, as I have defined them, that is the district beyond the range of Kara Dag and Mt. Kerdillion, was called Bisaltia. In describing the Macedonian conquest of the central plain and beyond it Thucydides indicates that the Macedonians had acquired Bisaltia and had advanced as far as the Strymon, driving out the Edones (2. 99. 4).[2] The latter were in fact on

---

[1] See *IG* i². 90 = Tod, *GHI* no. 68 and A. W. Gomme, *Historical Commentary on Thucydides* 1. 207; the boundary stone published by B. D. Meritt in *AJA* 27 (1923) 334 f. = *SEG* 2 no. 408 shows that *c.* 400 B.C. the Bottiaei held the interior from just south of Vromosirtis; this suggests that at that time Potidaea held the coastal strip to its north-east up to the territory of the Crousaei or up to that of the Scithaei, if Scithae lay on the coast between them.

[2] The text of Thuc. 2. 99. 4 may be confused in the transmission; in this chapter he gives in the past tense the stages of the Macedonian conquest and in the present tense the current situation of 429 B.C. Thus the Macedonians drove the Bottiaei out and the latter now live next to the Chalcidians (2. 99. 3); again they drove out the Eordi and some of the latter are settled by Physca (2. 99. 5). In between these statements we have 2. 99. 4 τῆς δὲ Παιονίας παρὰ

the east bank of the Strymon in 480 B.C. (Hdt. 7. 110 and 114. 1), and they were there in proximity to another people who had been victims of Macedonian aggression, the Pieres, driven out of Pieria and settled east of the Strymon on the southern side of Mt. Pangaeum (Thuc. 2. 99. 3; Hdt. 7. 112). Herodotus, writing of the invasion of Xerxes, included in the geographical term Bisaltia the coast west of the mouth of the Strymon and the land above that coast (7. 115. 2); and he mentioned 'the Thracian king of the Bisaltae and of the Crestonian territory', which shows that the areas of Bisaltia and Crestonia were adjacent (8. 116. 1). At that time the Bisaltae were strong. There is no indication that the Macedonians then held any land east of the pass of Rendina. In later times the term Bisaltia was used to indicate the area inland and not the coastal plain between the Strymon and the pass of Rendina. Thus in Str. 7 fr. 36 Bisaltia begins 'inland of Amphipolis', it extends up to Heraclea, and the river Strymon 'flows between the Bisaltae and the Odomantes'.

The basin of the Strymon river between the Rupel gorge and the defile by Amphipolis has altered much in recent times with the vagaries of the river, of which the earlier beds are shown on many modern maps, and with the draining of the basin and particularly the disappearance of the great lake above Amphipolis. In Turkish times there were two lakes, one large and shallow above Amphipolis called Lake Takhinos, and another of considerable extent and also shallow at the northern end of the plain, called Lake Butkova. The plain itself is the old bed of a huge diluvial lake. We know from Thuc. 4. 108. 1 and from Mela 2. 2. 30 that the former of the two lakes was large in ancient times.[1] As Alexander marched 'past Lake Cercinitis en route for Amphipolis and the outflow of the Strymon' (Arr. *Anab.* 1. 11. 3),[2] Lake Cercinitis was evidently Lake Takhinos.

The northern lake is almost certain to have existed, because it is a legacy of the old diluvial lake, and it is always fed by the Strymon in flood and by the river Kumli. When Megabazus carried off the peoples of the Strymonian plain and sent them to Darius, his victims included

τὸν Ἀξιὸν ποταμὸν στενήν τινα καθήκουσαν ἄνωθεν μέχρι Πέλλης καὶ θαλάσσης ἐκτήσαντο, καὶ πέραν Ἀξιοῦ μέχρι Στρυμόνος τὴν Μυγδονίαν καλουμένην Ἤδωνας ἐξελάσαντες νέμονται. Here the stages of conquest in the past tense are clear with the contrast of παρὰ τὸν Ἀξιόν . . . μέχρι Πέλλης and πέραν Ἀξιοῦ μέχρι Στρυμόνος and with the expulsion of the Edones; but νέμονται in the present tense is left in the air, and one wonders whether, when the text was written, Thucydides said that the conquest was up to the Strymon at the expense of the Edones and (in a separate sentence) that the Macedonians now hold the so-called Mygdonia.

[1] Thuc. 4. 108. 1 ἄνωθεν μὲν μεγάλης οὔσης ἐπὶ πολὺ λίμνης τοῦ ποταμοῦ. Mela 2. 2. 30 'Strymon . . . non longe a mare lacum fecit'.

[2] Alexander may have mustered his forces near Eidomene. He marched through the Doiran district eastwards into the middle Strymon valley; for if he had used the very narrow pass of Rendina, he would not have gone beside Lake Cercinitis.

the Siriopaeones, associated with Sirrae, the modern Serres, and the Paeonians 'up to Lake Prasias', but those by Lake Prasias itself escaped him (Hdt. 5. 15. 3 and 5. 16). As the territory of the Siriopaeones was presumably the plain between Lake Cercinitis and Sirrae, the Paeonians up to Lake Prasias are those north-west of Serres, and we may equate Lake Prasias with Lake Butkova. This lake, being shallow and variable in extent, is suitable for the pile-dwellings of the villagers, who got the poles for their piles from Mt. Orbelus (Hdt. 5. 16), north of Lake Butkovo.[1] In any case the plain between the two lakes was held by Paeonian tribes and not by the Bisaltae, who lived in the hill country bordering Crestonia and Mygdonia.

When Megabazus had captured and deported his Paeonians, he sent envoys to Amyntas, king of Macedon. 'The journey is quite short', says Herodotus, 'from Lake Prasias to Macedonia. For first of all next to the lake is the mine worked by Alexander I, and after the mine a mountain called Mt. Dysoron, on crossing which one is in Macedonia' (5. 17. 2). The short route from Lake Prasias is up the Kumli valley, over a northern spur of Mt. Krousia through a pass called the Stena Dov Tepe, and so into the basin containing Lake Doiran, from which there is access to Amphaxitis by two routes. It appears from the account of Herodotus that Doiran was already in Macedonia and that Mt. Krousia was Mt. Dysoron.

We are now able to consider the main routes from the east into Macedonia. We may begin by discounting the modern road which runs direct over Mt. Dysoron from Kalon Kastron to Liti; for this crosses high country, which was heavily forested in antiquity and was infested with lions and wild oxen (aurochs), as we learn from Herodotus. There were two routes in antiquity: one from the coast of the Strymon plain through the very narrow and easily defended pass of Rendina to Lake Bolbe, and the other from Lake Prasias up the wide Kumli valley and through the Stena Dov Tepe into the area of Doiran. When Xerxes had come with his army and his fleet to the coastal plain, he himself marched constructing 'the inland part of the route . . . through Paeonian territory' (Hdt. 7. 124 τὴν μεσόγαιαν τάμνων τῆς ὁδοῦ . . . διὰ τῆς Παιονικῆς).[2] He thus went up the Strymon valley, then north of Bisaltian

---

[1] For a discussion of the position of Lake Prasias with notes of earlier literature see B. Saria in *RE* 22. 2 (1954) 1698. He places L. Prasias at L. Doiran. This lake, however, is relatively deep ('er hat eine Tiefe von rund 10 m.') and so generally unsuitable for villages built on piles; it is shallow at one side but the villages must have been well out in the lake to escape capture. Moreover Lake Doiran is far from the Strymon valley and nearer the Axius, whereas the Paeonians whom Darius wanted were living by the Strymon (Hdt. 5. 13. 2 ἡ Παιονίη ἐπὶ τῷ Στρυμόνι ποταμῷ πεπολισμένη). The village on piles in what was Lake Malik before it was drained is an interesting analogy, because the lake there was shallow (see p. 229 below).

[2] Artabazus returned on the inland route after his defeat at Plataea (Hdt. 9. 89. 4). How and Wells ad loc. hesitate about the meaning of the phrase; the inland part of the road is

territory up the Kumli valley, and came down via Palatianon into the valley of the Echedorus. In so doing he passed through Paeonian territory in the Strymon valley and in the Kumli valley (ἐπορεύετο δὲ διὰ τῆς Παιονικῆς καὶ Κρηστωνικῆς ἐπὶ ποταμὸν 'Εχείδωρον), and it was in this stage of the march that he recruited some Paeonians (Hdt. 7. 185. 2). The king of the Bisaltae took evasive action (Hdt. 8. 116). In 429 B.C. when Sitalces had ravaged Chalcidice, Bottice, Anthemus, Mygdonia, and Crestonia, he went home at speed (Thuc. 2. 100. 4– 2. 101. 6) without ravaging Bisaltia, and he therefore went either past Lake Prasias or along the route by which he had come. When Alexander marched past Lake Cercinitis on his way to the Hellespont, he had come down the Kumli valley and the Strymon valley; he had probably collected his army in Amphaxitis.

Our knowledge of the southern route through the pass of Rendina is derived mainly from the data of the Via Egnatia. The figures are excellent. Of eighteen entries for stages between Thessalonica and Amphipolis there is only one variant reading each for two entries, both in It. Ant. (330. 7 and 8), where *D* gives XXXI for the true XXXVI and XXII for the true XXXII; both variant readings are of the type noted above (see p. 49). We have an isolated entry in It. Ant. 328. 6 of XX m.p. which is the same on the Peutinger Table and in It. Ant. 320. 2. I give the data, omitting the isolated entry and reversing the order of It. Burd.[1]

Tab. Peut.	It. Ant. 320	It. Ant. 330. 7 f.	It. Burd. 604–5
Thess.: Melissirgin XX	XX	{ XXXVI	Thess.: mut. Duodea XIIII
M.: Apollonia XVIII	XVII		Duo.: mut. Heracleus XI
			H.: mans. Apollonia XI
			A.: mut. Peripidis X
			P.: mut. Pennana X
A.: Amphipolis XXX	XXX	XXXII	P.: Amphipolis XIII

The Bordeaux traveller gives more stations, as in the western part of the Via Egnatia. His first total, 36 m.p. from Thessalonica to Apollonia, agrees exactly with It. Ant. 330. 7, is 1 m.p. short of It. Ant. 320 and 2 m.p. short of the Table; these differences may be due to inclusive and exclusive reckonings (see p. 21 above). His second total, 33 m.p. from Apollonia to Amphipolis, agrees well enough with the 32 of It. Ant. 330, but both exceed the agreed figure of 30 m.p. of It. Ant. 320 and the Table. Measuring the distances in km on the modern road on the 1:250,000

contrasted with the route nearer the coast, and the description of the march makes the meaning clear. For τέμνειν see p. 209 below.

[1] See Miller, *Itin. Romana* 495 fig. 149 and 522 fig. 163.

map, we have 14 m.p. = 20·7 km to Ayios Vasilios (Duodea); 6 m.p. = 8·9 km to Yerakarou (Melissirgin); 5 m.p. = 7·4 km to short of Stivos (Heracleustibus); 11 m.p. = 16·3 km to the river Kois (Apollonia); 10 m.p. = 14·8 km to the western entry of the pass of Rendina (Peripidis); 10 m.p. = 14·8 km to the river Tashli (Pennana). As these are all suitable staging points, we are left with the 10 m.p. of the Table and of It. Ant. 320 = 14·8 km to the site of Amphipolis on the modern road over the Strymon. It is possible that the Strymon bridge was down and a detour was required to cross the river when the other two figures were recorded.

Of the names of the stations Duodea is at the fourteenth milestone and cannot therefore be a mistake for Duodeca or Duodecimum, as O. Cuntz suggests; it is presumably Duodeae, perhaps a shrine of Demeter and Persephone. Heracleustibus is evidently 'Heracles' footstep', like the hoofmark of Pegasus. Apollonia is the Apollonia Mygdonidos of Ptol. 3. 13. 36, mentioned after Lete,[1] and Pliny *HN* 4. 38, 'recedentes a mari Apollonia, Arethusa'. Peripidis is explained by the Bordeaux traveller as the grave of the poet Euripides, and Ammianus Marcellinus 27. 4. 8, having mentioned the pass of Acontisma (further east), continues: 'cui proxima Arethusa cursualis est statio in qua visitur Euripidis sepulcrum, tragoediarum sublimitate conspicui'. Arethusa is mentioned in Ps.-Scylax as a Greek city, being back from the coast (Pliny *HN* 4. 38) before 'Lake Bolbe' as one comes from the south-west, and therefore on its south side, and in Str. 7 fr. 36 as near Lake Bolbe (πρὸς δὲ τῇ λίμνῃ τῇ Βόλβῃ Ἀρέθουσα). Arethusa was independent in joining the Second Athenian Confederacy (*IG* 2² 43. 82) and in being on the list of Epidaurian *Theorodokoi* (*IG* iv² 1. 94. 1b); and in the last third of the fourth century citizens of Arethusa are described as [ἀπὸ Θρ]αίκης[2] and as Μακεδών (*Syll.*³ 268 G and K). Bromiscus was by the outflow of Lake Bolbe into the sea, mentioned after the Aulon (Thuc. 4. 103. 1) and therefore on its north side, as Brasidas was coming from the south; a Macedonian city, it has been identified with an ancient site on a small hill on the north bank of the outflow into the sea.[3] The last name, Pennana, is probably that of the river Tashli, especially if the 'pinna', a type of oyster, was found at its mouth.

The most important city on the west bank of the middle Strymon was Heraclea Sintica. The whole territory of the Bisaltae and the city Heraclea Sintica, although west of the Strymon (Livy 45. 29. 6; D.S. 31. 8. 8), were included in the first tetrarchy in 167 B.C. Of this tetrarchy

---

[1] But not that of Ps.-Scylax 66, who is giving coastal cities and defines the (Chalcidian) Apollonia as a Greek city, *pace* Miller, loc. cit.

[2] So also St. Byz. Ἀρέθουσα, πόλις . . . Θράκης.

[3] St. Byz. has Βορμίσκος, χωρίον Μακεδονίας ἐν ᾧ κυνοσπάρακτος γέγονεν Εὐριπίδης. The site was noted first by Struck I 74 f.

Amphipolis was the capital. As Bisaltia comprised the hill country adjacent to Crestonia (see p. 193 above), it is to be concluded that Sintica in which Heraclea lay[1] was between Bisaltia and the Strymon; and since Sintica was a suitable area for a moderate force of Roman infantry and cavalry based on Amphipolis to ravage in 168 B.C. (Livy 44. 46. 2), it was in the plain not too far from Amphipolis and so south of the Rupel defile. Ptol. 3. 13. 30 gives Sintica three cities, Tristolos, 'Paroikopolis' (in later records 'Parthikopolis')[2] and Heraclea. The Peutinger Table gives a road from Philippi to Heraclea 'santica' (which Miller needlessly assumed was from Amphipolis),[3] of which the course is clear from the data of distances; for they require a crossing of the Strymon between the two lakes, Prasias and Cercinitis. Going 10 m.p. = 14·8 km from Philippi we come to a big water-source west of Kalabaki (Trinlo); thence 17 m.p. = 25 km to short of Mesorrakhi (Graero), whence one sees the Strymonian plain; thence 8 m.p. = 11·8 km to a little west of Gazorus (Euporia); and thence 17 m.p. = 25 km to Kalon Kastron or with a detour round the lake to Veryi. The latter situation is the more probable, as it is more central in the plain and controls a narrow passage between the hills and the present small lake. A hoard of coins, hidden c. 250–200 B.C., two statues, and a dedication to Zeus Hypsistus have recently been found at Veryi.[4]

When the Macedonians seized this plain called Sintica, they dispossessed not Sintian but Paeonian tribes, such as those mentioned in Hdt. 5. 15–17. The Sinti, after whom the plain was named, were further inland. As regards the peoples above the Rupel defile of the Strymon we learn from Thuc. 2. 96 that the river rose on Mt. Scombrus and flowed through the Agrianes and the Laeaei, a Paeonian tribe; and that Sitalces, on leaving his empire, which extended to the Strymon river (2. 96. 3), and on passing next through an uninhabited mountain, Mt. Cercine, which is the boundary between the Sinti and the Paeonians, had the Paeones on his right and the Sinti and Maedi on his left (2. 98. 2). This mountain is evidently the long range of Mt. Ograzden, which forms the watershed between the Strymon and the upper Bregalnitsa, so that Sitalces came down this mountain range into the Strumitsa valley. Str. 7 fr. 36 (ὁ Στρυμών . . . ἐξ Ἀγριάνων γὰρ διὰ Μαίδων (for MS. Μέδων) καὶ Σιντῶν ἐς τὰ μεταξὺ Βισαλτῶν καὶ Ὀδομάντων ἐκπίπτει) shows that the Sinti held the part of the Strymon valley just above the Rupel defile

---

[1] D.S. 31. 8. 8 Βισαλτία πᾶσα μετὰ τῆς ἐν τῇ Σιντικῇ Ἡρακλείας and Livy 42. 51. 7 Heraclea ex Sintis.

[2] Hierocles, *Synecdemus* 639. 8 ed. Honigmann, who gives references. Paroikopolis, Tristolos (probably), and Heraclea appear on map XI of *C. Ptolemaei Geographiae* pt. 2.

[3] Miller, *Itin. Romana* 495 fig. 149 and 522 fig. 163. The Ravenna Geographer 195. 16 f. gives the names Trillon, Greron, Arason, Euporia, and Eraclia Xantica.

[4] *BCH* 81 (1957) 497 and 606.

and that the Maedi were north of the Sinti. Thus when Philip V set out to attack the Maedi in 181 B.C., he set out not from Amphaxitis but from Stobi; his course lay up the lower valley of the Bregalnitsa, where later the Roman road ran from Stobi to Astibus (see p. 78 above). The Sinti then held a part of the Strymon valley and also the fertile lower valley of the Strumitsa. Somewhere here lay their chief city, Sintia; it is mentioned by St. Byz. s.v. as a πόλις Μακεδονίας.[1] Arist. *Mir.* 115 and St. Byz. say that a river Pontus, flowing among the Sinti, had remarkable properties. It was perhaps a tributary of the Strumitsa. In map no. XI of *C. Ptolemaei Geographiae* pt. 2 there are both Heraclea Sintice near the Strymon and Sintice nearer to the Axius river. This supports the distinction I have drawn between Heraclea Sintice and the district Sintica.

The earliest mention of Mt. Orbelus is in Hdt. 5. 16. 2, when he says that the people of the pile-villages in Lake Prasias got their stakes from Mt. Orbelus. The closest source was certainly Mt. Belasitsa, the range running east and west on both sides of the Rupel gorge of the Strymon. The identification of Mt. Orbelus with this range fits the march of Alexander the Great from Macedonia to the river Nestus, 'keeping Philippi and Mt. Orbelus on his left' (Arr. *Anab.* 1. 1. 5). It is clear from the ancient geographers that the name was used also in a much wider sense for the group of mountains between the Axius and the Strymon which extends from the Belasitsa range to the watershed of the Danube valley. When Str. C 313 pictured Macedonia and Thrace together as forming a parallelogram, bounded on the west by the Adriatic Sea and on the east by the Hebrus river, he took the Via Egnatia as the south side of the parallelogram and the line of the Illyrian, Paeonian, and Thracian mountains as the north side. He names the mountains of that imaginary straight line in book 7 fr. 10 as Bertiscus (Montenegro),[2] Scardus (Šar Planina), Orbelus, Rhodope, and Haemus. Of these the first two are Illyrian mountains, the last two are Thracian mountains, and Orbelus represents the Paeonian group from Zrna Gora and Kosjak Planina in the north (see p. 81 above) to Mt. Belasitsa in the south. Ptolemy has a similar usage: Orbelus separates Upper Moesia in the

---

[1] Citing Eudoxus (*FGrH* 79) πόλις Μακεδονίας πρὸς τῇ Θράκῃ, to be distinguished from a like-named city on the Dardanian frontier of Macedonia (Livy 26. 25. 3). For Greek inscriptions from the lower Strumitsa see G. Mihailov, *Inscriptiones Graecae in Bulgaria Repertae* iv (1966) 277 f.

[2] This mountain appears also in Ptol. 3. 13. 19, where it has very nearly the same co-ordinates as the river 'Ereigon', which flowed ἀπὸ τῶν ὑπὸ τὴν Δαλματίαν. The mountain's name is not on the maps, but 'Ereigon' appears as 'Reichon' flowing into the 'Dreilon' river on map no. VI of *C. Ptolemaei Geographiae* pt. 2. This river is the White Drin, and its north-western sources are in Montenegro, which is, as in Strabo, Mt. Bertiscus. This is not understood by E. Oberhummer in *RE* 3. 1 (1897) 318. The 'Chrestomathia ex Strabonis Lib. VII' in *GGM* 2. 575 has the Drilon rising from Mt. Bertiscus; it is in fact the White Drin which does so and not the Black Drin, which issues from Lake Ochrid.

Danube valley from Macedonia, and it also separates Thrace from Upper Moesia and from Macedonia (3. 10. 1 and 3. 11. 1). And again in Pliny *HN* 4. 35 and Mela 2. 2. 2 Orbelus appears together with Rhodope and Haemus as a mountainous massif. The situation is clear in Ptolemy's map no. XI, in which Mt. Orbelus is pierced by the river Strymon above Heraclea Sintica and Mt. Orbelus is also shown extending far northwards.[1]

This double use of Mt. Orbelus is relevant when we consider the identification of the district Orbelia, also called Parorbelia. Ptol. 3. 20. 25, giving the inland cities of Macedonia by districts, places Orbelia with one city, Garescus, after Almopia; and the proximity is borne out by the map of Ptolemy no. XI, in which the cities of Almopia appear west of the Axius and Garescus appears east of it. The entry 'Orbelia' on the map is south of the long range of Mt. Orbelus. The other clue to its position is in Str. 7 fr. 36, a fragment from the *Epitome Vaticana*, which has been abbreviated to the point of obscurity. As the Bisaltae are mentioned immediately before and immediately after the passage I am about to quote, I take it that οἷς resumes the Bisaltae and not the Agrianes.

ὑπὲρ δὲ τῆς Ἀμφιπόλεως Βισάλται καὶ μέχρι πόλεως Ἡρακλείας, ἔχοντες αὐλῶνα εὔκαρπον, ὃν διαιρεῖ ὁ Στρυμὼν ὡρμημένος ἐκ τῶν περὶ Ῥοδόπην Ἀγριάνων· οἷς παράκειται τῆς Μακεδονίας ἡ Παρορβηλία (for MS. γαρορβηλια) ἐν μεσογαίᾳ ἔχουσα κατὰ τὸν αὐλῶνα τὸν ἀπὸ Εἰδομένης Καλλίπολιν, Ὀρθόπολιν, Φιλιππούπολιν, Γαρησκόν.

If it is correct that οἷς resumes the Bisaltae, then Parorbelia 'lying beside' the Bisaltae of the district inland of Amphipolis to Heraclea must be the southern slopes of Mt. Belasitsa, which we have identified with Mt. Orbelus proper. It comprised the area between Neon Petritsi on the Strymon river and the border of Amphaxitis (see p. 176 above). Str. 7 fr. 36 in speaking of the valley or sink, the 'aulon leading from Eidomene', relates the district Parorbelia to Eidomene as a more central place in Macedonia and refers in fact to a belt of relatively low-lying land, through which Alexander probably came in his march to the east. Of the cities mentioned by Strabo, Ptolemy has Garescus only, which I should put at the western end of Parorbelia with Philippoupolis, Orthopolis, and Callipolis reaching as far as Neon Petritsi, cities founded probably by Philip II and his successors.[2]

---

[1] In map no. X, Mt. Orbelus appears between Scupi and Pautalia.

[2] To the east of the Rupel defile the southern side of the mountain range was called Paroreia (Livy 39. 27. 10 and 42. 51. 5). Its peoples were Paeonian in race. One of the cities in Parorbelia, perhaps Garescus, was a little north of Stari Doiran on the west side of the present lake, where an ancient site has yielded two Greek inscriptions (*Spomenik* 71 (1931) no. 114; 77 (1934) no. 23). G. Mihailov, *Inscriptiones Graecae in Bulgaria Repertae* iv (1966) 277, and others place Parorbelia and its town in the lower Strumitsa and identify the river Strumitsa with the ancient river 'Pontos'.

The district Parorbelia is in fact a distinctive area. One enters it suddenly through a narrow pass from Crestonia (p. 182 above) and sees Lake Doiran under the towering mass of Mt. Belasitsa. The lake is at the western end of a flat, wide valley which is extremely fertile. On the west of Lake Doiran the hills are fairly low; on the east the valley rises very gradually to an almost imperceptible watershed at the so-called pass of Dov Tepe. To the north Mt. Belasitsa forms a continuous wall of great height, bare and precipitous at the top and then clad with coniferous forest, deciduous forest, and maquis. To the south the hills change into the high range of Mt. Dysoron, clad in forest from top to bottom, and split by deep, narrow valleys. The descent eastwards from the watershed is gradual, at first over boulder-strewn, flattish land sloping down from the roots of Mt. Belasitsa, and then through the wide and fertile valley of the Kumli river, which affords pasture for herds of cattle and horses and grows much maize. The descent to the Strymon is a steady one, and by Neon Petritsi the river is divided into two arms, which makes the bridging of its waters less difficult. During the long descent Mt. Belasitsa dominates the scene on the north, and the ranges continue to the east beyond the Strymon but at a less impressive altitude.

There is a natural gap in the mountain ring of eastern Macedonia between the easternmost part of the Barnous range, Mt. Gradeska, and the westernmost part of the Orbelus range, Mt. Belasitsa, and it is through this break that the modern road runs from Amphaxitis or from Lake Doiran into the Strumitsa valley. It by-passes both the defile of Demir Kapu and the defile of the Rupel gorge. Sitalces came through this gap, when he invaded Macedonia 'from the top' and took Eidomene (Thuc. 2. 100. 3). The area just north of this gap is the upper valley of the river Strumitsa, a very fertile and rather swampy basin. As Sitalces passed through Mt. Cercine (see p. 197 above), which was then the boundary of the Sinti on the east and the Paeonians on the west, he descended into Doberus of Paeonia, which lay thus to his west; in fact he came into the bend of the Strumitsa valley and here his forces prepared for action (Thuc. 2. 98. 2 ἐς Δόβηρον τὴν Παιονικήν[1] and 2. 99. 1). His intention was to invade Lower Macedonia 'from the top' (2. 99. 1 κατὰ κορυφήν), and from Doberus he did invade (2. 100. 3). The district Doberus is then that just north of Valandovo. This position is supported by the remark in Str. 7 fr. 36 that, as you go north from Heraclea (Sintica) and as you go towards the defile of the Strymon, while you keep the river to your right, you have Paeonia and the area 'round the Doberus' to your left (ἐκ μὲν τῶν εὐωνύμων ἐστὶν ἡ Παιονία καὶ τὰ περὶ τὸν

---

[1] There was another Doberus, east of the Strymon (Hdt. 7. 113. 1) and north of Mt. Pangaeum, where the Doberes lived, perhaps having been expelled by the Paeonians from what became Paeonian Doberus.

Δόβηρον). In A.D. 268 the Scythians, who had invaded Lower Macedonia, 'withdrew into the interior and as they went they ravaged the areas of Doberus and Pelagonia, every single place' (Zosimus 1. 43, εἰς τὴν μεσόγαιαν ἀναβάντες τὰ περὶ Δόβηρον καὶ Πελαγονίαν ἐληΐζοντο πάντα χωρία). They preferred the wider route via Valandovo into Doberus; they then crossed the Axius north of the Demir Kapu and so entered Pelagonia.

Whereas Thucydides uses the feminine gender for Doberus at 2. 98. 2, 99. 1, and 100. 3, which is appropriate to a district or to a city, Strabo has the masculine in fr. 36 and this gender indicates a mountain or a river. The latter is probably what is meant; for the area of the Doberus river, being the Strumitsa river, is more fully on one's left in passing the defile of the Strymon. The city (or the community)[1] of Doberus is mentioned by St. Byz. s.v. Δόβηρος, πόλις Παιονίας. οἱ πολῖται Δόβηρες, and Thucydides probably wrote of its territory as the marshalling point of Sitalces' army. It lay probably near where the town Strumitsa is today. An epigram of Addaeus tells how Peucestes on horseback killed a wild bull which came out of a dell of Doberus (*Anth. Pal.* 9. 300, Loeb ed.) ;[2] this suggests a district of the same name. There is no doubt that when Macedon became strong, she occupied this territory, just as she occupied the district of Kavadarci north of the Demir Kapu.

It seems likely that she planted near Doberus a Macedonian city called Astraeum and named the district that of the Astraei. In Ptol. 3. 13. 27 there are three inland cities of Macedonia attributed to the Astraei or to Astraea :[3] Aestraeum, Deborus, and Alorus.[4] The co-ordinates of the first two are very close, and their proximity to one another is clear from St. Byz. s.v. Ἄστραια, πόλις Ἰλλυρίας.[5] Ἁδριανὸς Ἀλεξανδριάδος α′ "οἱ δ᾽ ἔχον Ἀστραιάν τε Δόβηρά τε" (v.ll. Δόβηράν τε, Δόβηρόν τε), and from Pliny *HN* 4. 35, who cites the Doberi between the Idomenenses and the Astraeenses (v.ll. Aestrienses and Estrienses). 'Astrea' comes after Idomenae and before Bragylae in the list of Delphic *Theorodokoi* of 190–180 B.C. (*BCH* 45 (1921) 17 iii 69). In Hierocles, *Synecdemus*, Doberus and Idomene are next to one another in the first Macedonia, and Aestraeum, coming after Stobi and Argos and before Pelagonia, is in the second Macedonia (639. 4 and 641. 4). It appears then that Astraeum was north of Idomene and north or north-west of Doberus and specially

[1] St. Byz. uses *polis* sometimes not for an urban city but for a state or community.
[2] See Hdt. 7. 126. 1 and Arist. *Mir.* 842ᵇ33, for wild oxen in Crestonia and Paeonia, probably of the extinct species *Bos Urus*, known as the aurochs.
[3] The reading of the manuscripts in Ptolemy is overwritten and not clear.
[4] Both Aestraeum and Alorus were probably named after features of Lower Macedonia, namely the river Astraeus and the city Alorus on the west side of the central plain. The Deborus of Ptolemy is a slip for Doberus.
[5] A mistake by Stephanus Byzantinus for 'Macedonias' or 'Paeonias'.

situated to control the entry towards the district of Doberus. Such a position would accord with the story of the poisoning of Demetrius, who was moved from Astraeum in Paeonia to Heraclea (by Monastir).[1]

To the north of the upper Strumitsa valley the territory on the east side of the Axius valley was Paeonian up to the watershed with the Strymon's western tributaries and then up to the river itself. For Thuc. 2. 96. 3 placed the Agrianes, a Paeonian tribe,[2] at its headwaters, and then another Paeonian tribe, the Laeaei, on the upper Strymon river above the Maedi, a Thracian people, who were in the Strymon valley to the north of the Sinti and extended far into Thrace (Str. C 318). The Paeonian enclave in the Strymon valley held the main entry from the upper Strymon valley to the valley of the Axius, namely the entry from Kjustendil, the ancient Pautalia,[3] which in 429 B.C. was in the hands of the Laeaei but under the rule of Sitalces.

In 335 B.C. when Alexander marched 'towards the Agrianes and the Paeones' (Arr. *Anab.* 1. 5. 1), he must have taken the route through Pautalia, then in Paeonian hands. At that time the mountain Messapium, which is named by Arist. *HA* 630ª20 as marking the boundary between Paeonian and Maedian territory, may be identified with the Osogovska Planina. The route from Stobi to Pautalia was followed by the Roman road which is shown on the Peutinger Table with defective numbers. Its course, however, is fairly clear: up the Bregalnitsa[4] valley to Istib, the ancient Astibus, thence over a watershed to Kratovo, the ancient Tranupara, and through high country to Pautalia, situated in a high and very fertile valley of the Strymon, which had great mineral wealth.[5] In Roman times a powerful Thracian tribe, the Dantheletae, held Pautalia as well as much territory in Thrace.[6] In this area the

---

[1] It was probably Heraclea Lyncestis, as a citizen of Styberra helped to stifle Demetrius, and as Perseus had been sent to Amphipolis to have an alibi (Livy 40. 24. 3–7).

[2] In Thuc. 2. 96. 3 the Agrianes were a Paeonian tribe subject to Sitalces; they appear in St. Byz. s.v. *Agriai* in a number of ethnic forms, and they became so strong that they were sometimes contrasted with the Paeonian tribes, as in the epigram cited by Stephanus.

[3] See G. Mihailov, *Inscriptiones Graecae in Bulgaria Repertae* iv (1966) 113 f.

[4] K. Miller, *Itin. Romana* 579 and fig. 186. See the excellent account of Pautalia by C. M. Danoff in *RE* Suppl. 9 (1962) 800 f.

[5] The Bregalnitsa was probably the river Astycus of Polyaenus 4. 12. 2, in which Ariston, having been brought by Lysimachus from Thrace, i.e. along the Pautalia route, was given the royal bath. It is probable that the capital of the Paeonian royal house was in the area of Astibus. The mineral wealth of the Pautalia region accounts for the ability of the Laeaei to issue coinage (Head, *Historia Numorum* 202).

[6] Pautalia, so named from its hot springs, was founded as a city of a Greek type by Hadrian; it was the centre from which roads radiated to Amphipolis, Stobi, Naissus (Nis), Serdica (Sofia), and Philippoupolis on the upper Hebrus. The Dantheletae were on the right bank of the Strymon in Pliny *HN* 4. 40, and they held territory extending far to the east (Livy 39. 53. 12; Str. C 318). In A.D. 479, when the Goths were at Heraclea Lyncou, an attempt was made to settle them at Pautalia by the pass into Thrace (Malchus 247. 9 f. οὐ πολὺ δὲ ἀπέχουσα τῶν εἰσβολῶν τῆς Θρᾴκης).

Paeonians acted as a buffer between Macedonia and the powerful peoples of Thrace, and in course of time they were worn down.

7. *Systems of organization in the areas east of the Axius*

As the Macedonian kings acquired territories east of the Axius, they kept some of the existing territorial names, whether they expelled the native peoples or not, such as Mygdonia, Crestonia, Bisaltia, Anthemus, and Bottice. In other territories they coined new names, such as Amphaxitis, Astraea, and Parorbelia. The districts were individual units for such administrative purposes as the raising of troops and the collection of taxes; for we may infer the latter from the fact that the Macedones Amphaxii issued coinage in their own name before and after the Roman conquest.[1] But the Macedonians resident in these districts described themselves not by the district but by the city to which they belonged. In the second half of the fourth century B.C. we have Μακεδόνες ἐκ Πέλλης, an Ἀρεθούσιος Μακεδών (*BCH* 21 (1897) 105 and 107), and a Μακεδὼν ὄνομα Λίμνος ἐκ Χαλαίστρας (Plu. *Alex.* 49. 2). It is thus clear that the city was the centre of their social life and a part of their political definition. Tribal differentiation among the Macedonians resident in these districts seems to have been totally lacking. A man is a Macedonian as an acknowledged subject of the King of Macedon; he lives in a city and uses its ethnic; and he resides in a district of the Macedonian kingdom.

The position was different where the native peoples remained in strength. When Thucydides had described the expulsion in whole or in part of certain peoples, he went on to mention also 'the other *ethne*' whom the Macedonians conquered and still control: 'Anthemus, Grestonia, and Bisaltia' (2. 99. 6 ἐκράτησαν δὲ καὶ τῶν ἄλλων ἐθνῶν . . . ἃ καὶ νῦν ἔτι ἔχουσι, τόν τε Ἀνθεμοῦντα καὶ Γρηστωνίαν καὶ Βισαλτίαν). The Bisaltae certainly remained an *ethnos*. They claimed to be descended from Bisaltes, son of the Sun and the Earth, and to have been ruled by Rhesus who fought in the Trojan War.[2] By virtue of being a tribe, they retained their individuality as a people even under the Roman Empire; for Pliny *HN* 4. 38 refers to the 'gens Bisaltae'. In the same way the fugitives who settled east of the Strymon—Bisaltae, Pieres, and Edoni alike—continued to be tribal groups. It is probable that the Crestonaei did likewise, although precise evidence is lacking. The Crousaei and the Bottiaei of Bottice developed many cities of their own, but they too maintained their corporate individuality through a tribal tradition.

With the exception of the Chalcidian city-states, the peoples who were subsequently brought within the ambit of Macedonian power remained

---

[1] Head, *Historia Numorum* 242.   [2] St. Byz. s.v. *Bisaltia* and Str. 7 fr. 36.

entirely tribal in their organization. Some of these were Thracian and others were Paeonian in a generic sense, but each tribe was fundamentally autonomous and individual. Thus the Maedi and the Sinti were separate Thracian tribes, although they might be made subject for a time to an Odrysian or a Macedonian king; and this was true also of the Paeonian tribes, such as the Agrianes and the Laeaei. A number of Paeonian tribes might combine and form a Paeonian state, but they remained individual tribes within the state. Thus when Pliny writes of the people in the Paeonian territory alongside the river Axius, he speaks of 'Paeoniae gentes' and not of 'gens Paeones' (*HN* 4. 35).

The Paeonian area has yielded few inscriptions. The first group comes from the line followed by the Roman road from Stobi to Pautalia: one in Latin from Grecka, two in Latin and one in Greek from villages near Istib, the ancient Astibus, and four in Greek and two in Latin from Kratovo, the ancient Tranupara.[1] In a fertile valley north-east of Veles, which is named after the town Sveti Nikola, there are some eleven inscriptions in Greek; some of these are dated to the second and third centuries A.D. by the Macedonian era, one mentions the office of *prytaneus*, and the names are mainly Roman but some are Greek, notably Adaeus and Aeneas.[2] Villages north of Veles on the east side of the Vardar have produced four Latin inscriptions.[3] The district of Skopje, including a western tributary of the Vardar, has yielded a crop of twenty-seven Latin inscriptions, one Greek inscription, and one odd inscription partly in Latin and partly in Greek.[4] The valley of Kumanovo, north-east of Skopje, has a record of five Latin inscriptions and one Greek inscription.[5] When we compare the inscriptions of the Paeonian area at first east of the Vardar and then on both sides of the Vardar by Skopje with the great number of Greek inscriptions, many dated by the Macedonian era, on the west side of the Vardar from the Kavadarci district to the Babuna river (see p. 173 and p. 79 above), we may make the deduction that the Paeonians were not given to the writing of Greek but tended rather to use Latin as an adopted language. It follows from this that the Paeonian tribes were not Greek-speaking. On the other hand there are pockets which indicate the survival of Greek-speaking groups. The most notable is that at Sveti Nikola. Here we may see the survival of a Macedonian colony, in which the Macedonian era was still used in the third century A.D. The occurrence of a few Greek inscriptions on the route from Stobi to Pautalia may be a sign that here too some Macedonian colonies had been planted in the period of the Macedonian kingdom.

[1] *Spomenik* 71 (1931) 198; 75 (1933) 155 f.; 98 (1941–8) 90; *ZA* 14 (1965) 115.
[2] *Spomenik* 98 (1941–8) 395 f.   [3] Ibid. 80 f.
[4] Ibid. 418 f.; *ZA* 4 (1954) 366 f.; 6 (1956) 277 f.; 13 (1964) 157.
[5] *Spomenik* 71 (1931) 200 f.; 77 (1934) 28 f.

VI

A GEOGRAPHICAL SUMMARY OF THE MACEDONIAN AREA

THE heart of Macedonia is the central plain. It has several advantages which are not shared by the inland cantons. The annual flooding of the plain, which is indicated in Homer's description of the 'wide flowing Axius sending his waters over the land' (*Il.* 21. 157–8), deposits a layer of silt, in which seeds germinate without tillage or cultivation. In very early times this led to the raising of crops, as in other deltaic areas. We can visualize the conditions from Struck's description of the central plain as it was under Turkish control, when agriculture had reverted to the most primitive methods. The Gallikos river was 250 to 300 m wide where it entered the plain, and in rainy periods it overflowed and spread for miles; the Vardar (Axius) was 350 m wide on entering the plain, and in flood-time it created a great lake; and the Vistritsa (Haliacmon) caused even more sudden and extensive floods. In 1907 the flood waters of the Vardar and the Vistritsa joined and the plain became a vast lake, leaving silt everywhere and creating new channels as the waters subsided.[1]

When more advanced methods of agriculture, irrigation, and flood control are employed, the central plain is immensely productive of cereals, a crop of wheat being followed sometimes in the same season by a crop of maize. The change between 1930 and 1960, for instance, is amazing.[2] Another characteristic of the plain which is common to primitive and more advanced stages of development is the provision of spring and autumn pastures for vast numbers of sheep, which feed in the summer on the highlands of Macedonia; for the transhumance of sheep, which is due to climatic conditions, has always been practised and is practised today, although in a diminishing degree as the amount of arable land increases.[3] In classical times it appears that the central plain and its hillsides grew the olive; for it was a sign of Philip II's good fortune that olive trees bore in the spring in Crestonia.[4] Thus the central plain was able to provide the peoples of the inland cantons with olives and olive-oil,

[1] Struck II 9, 12, and 24 f.
[2] The following figures are taken from the *MEE*.
[3] For the transhumance of sheep in Macedonia see Justin 8. 5 'ut pecora pastores nunc in hibernos, nunc in aestivos saltus traiciunt'; and in Boeotia Sophocles, *O.T.* 1133 f.
[4] Athenaeus 3. 77 d = *FGrH* 115 (Theopompus) F 237.

the salt which is needed for animals as well as humans, fish caught in huge numbers off the delta, and the early and late pasture for sheep.

On the other hand, the central plain has no immediate need of the produce of the inland cantons. It has magnificent pasture in swampy land for horses and cattle, an abundance of animal products, and pasture and timber on its own surrounding mountains. It is only when a great central power is organized in Macedonia that the trade of Upper Macedonia and Lower Macedonia is integrated and geared to the maritime trade of the eastern Mediterranean. In primitive times the face of Macedonia was not turned towards the sea. It has no ports on the deltaic coast, which is made treacherous by shifting banks.[1] The harbours which can serve the central plain are at its extremities, Methone in the west and Therme in the east, and the development of ports up navigable rivers was probably a later phenomenon and not associated with seafaring by Macedonians of the central plain.

The prosperity of various parts of the central plain and of its immediate hinterland was proverbial in ancient as in Turkish times: the gardens of Midas, the peppers of Almopia, the population of Beroea, the waters of Edessa, are characteristic examples. Procopius praised the smoothly running drinkable waters of the Echedorus, which flows 'through good and deep-soiled land' and reaches the sea where 'the land is low, the cornfields are numerous and the swamp has good pasture'. Leake sang the praises of the Kalamaria, the district of the ancient Therme, as most suitable for the winter pasture of cattle and sheep, and as producing grain of superior quality, wool, honey, wax, silk, and timber of elm, chestnut, and oak.[2] The amount of good timber close to the coast was a particularly valuable asset in ancient times; the forests of Pieria close to Methone and Pydna were as famous as those on Mt. Cissus behind Therme.[3]

Although one speaks of the central plain, it is important to remember that it is not a single unit but an area split into three segments by rivers which are generally impassable. In the time described by Herodotus the first segment was Macedonis bounded on the north by the line of the joint Ludias–Haliacmon, then entering the sea further to the east than the Haliacmon does today. The second was Bottiaeis, between the Ludias–Haliacmon and the Axius, with a hinterland including the slopes of Mt. Paiko. The third was Mygdonia, east of the Axius and extending into the basin of Lake Bolbe. Each of these segments had its own hinterland of fine timber and summer pastures, and each had its own access to the fisheries, salt-pans, and harbours of the coast, Pella and Ichnae being then near the sea. There was no compelling reason for these segments to

---

[1] *MP* 220; mirages also lead to accidents on this coast.

[2] Procopius, *Aed.* 4. 3. 27; Leake 3. 163.   [3] Livy 44. 43. 1; Tod, *GHI* nos. 91 and 111.

combine under a single administration; indeed in Thessaly, where the divisions of the central plain are much weaker, the combination of the whole under one power was a rare occurrence.

When the central plain and its immediate hinterland are under the control of a single power, it is at once obvious that the landward approaches to it are remarkably few and easily defended. For the area west of the Axius there are only two entries, the passage of the Haliacmon between Palatitsa and Beroea and the long, narrow pass from Ostrovo to Edessa. In the central area the defiles of Demir Kapu and of Gevgheli form a double obstacle to an intruder coming down the Vardar valley; but here there is an alternative passage, the easiest entry into central Macedonia, over the hills above Valandovo. In the eastern area the pass of Dov Tepe is backed by another beside Palatianon, and the pass of Rendina is steep-sided and easily held. The easiest access to any side of the plain is from the south. Perseus contested this access, when he positioned his army in the plain before Pydna. A second line of defence, and a much stronger one, was on the line of the Haliacmon river, contesting the passage between Palatitsa and Beroea.

The cantons of Upper Macedonia are large by Greek standards. Pelagonia, for instance, is slightly bigger than Arcadia. The cantons are similar to one another in having lakes or swamps, an abundance of water, pasture, and timber, and a hard continental climate. They are cut off from one another by mountains and defiles, except that Pelagonia has easy access on the south to Lyncus, and Elimea has easy access on the north to Eordaea and on the west to Orestis. There are no geographical or economic reasons which suggest that they were likely to combine with one another or with the central plain. Convenience rather than necessity led them to turn to the central plain for winter pasture, olives, salt, and seaborne commodities; for these things could be obtained also from the coast of Illyris or northern Epirus. It is not therefore surprising that they remained virtually independent of Macedonian power in the central plain until well into the fourth century B.C.

Even today one-fifth of the surface of Greek Macedonia is under forest.[1] The proportion is considerably higher, if the cantons of Upper Macedonia are considered apart from the central plain. In the Neolithic period there is no doubt that the whole of Upper Macedonia, mountains and plains alike, was heavily forested especially with oak, pine, edible chestnut, and, at high altitudes, beech. When Philip II cut down the natural forest and drained the plain of Philippi, some of the trees could be girdled only by four men with their arms extended.[2] The same thing

---

[1] *MEE* 605.
[2] Theophrastus *CP* 5. 14. 6, of the plain of Philippi, 'totus enim campus arboribus aquisque erat refertus'.

MAP 18. THE WESTERN PASSES LEADING INTO MACEDONIA.

is likely to have been true of Upper Macedonia at that time; for Alexander reminded the Macedonians that until the reforms of Philip II most of them lived in goat-hair cloaks and herded sheep upon the mountains (Arr. *Anab.* 7. 9. 2). Hunting was an essential form of livelihood. Game of all sorts, including bear, boar, wild ox, and deer, was so abundant that lions, leopards, panthers, and wildcat (lynxes) preyed upon them. Herodotus mentions their presence on Mt. Dysoron, and Xenophon on the Pindus range and Mt. Cissus 'inland of Macedonia'.[1] In classical and Hellenistic times the larger animals, especially the wild ox, were hunted by men on horseback with the javelin or the lance, as we learn from Macedonian mosaics and reliefs, from Xenophon, and from the Anthology.[2] When Archelaus made straight roads he 'cut' a track through the forest (ὁδοὺς εὐθείας ἔτεμε), as Xerxes had done by Mt. Pangaeum and inland of the Bisaltae, and as Sitalces had done on Mt. Cercine (τεμὼν τὴν ὕλην).[3] Upper Macedonia was famous not only for its forests, pastures, and wild animals but also for the lakes which are very rich in fish. There was indeed such an abundance of fish that they were fed to horses and cattle at Lake Prasias in Paeonia and in Thrace.[4]

The outer cantons of Upper Macedonia are fenced off from their neighbours by mountains, through which there are few passes except on the side facing Epirus. The Volustana pass offers the only entry from Perrhaebia into Elimea. The great expanse of mountainous country which comprises the Cambunian mountains, northern Pindus, and the Grammus range provides summer pastures and hunting-grounds for the peoples of northern Epirus and western Macedonia alike. Str. C 327 init. mentioned that some writers found such similarities in the customs of the two peoples that they called the whole area as far as Corcyra 'Macedonia'. Even in modern times these peoples intermarry and have many customs in common.[5] In relation to the west Orestis and Lyncus are in a strong position; for only one pass, the Tsangon pass, gives access from the plain of Koritsa to the small plain of Pelium, whence one pass leads into Orestis and one into Lyncus (see Map 18). Pelagonia has four passes to hold: the Diavat pass, leading from Lake Ochrid; the 'Pelagoniae fauces', leading from the Illyrian Penestae; the Babuna pass, leading from Bylazora in the Vardar valley; and the two narrows of the Rajetz valley,

---

[1] Hdt. 7. 125–6 and X. *Cyn.* 11, where τὸν Κίττον τὸν ὑπὲρ τῆς Μακεδονίας 'the Cittus inland of Macedonia', cannot be the Cissos near Therme, namely Mt. Khortiatis, but is perhaps 'Kitios' in the main Balkan chain. The 'montes Lyncon' and the district 'Lyncus' were named presumably after the wildcat. Aelian *NA* 7. 3 describes the wild ox as Paeonian.

[2] X. *Cyn.* 11 and *AP* 9. 300. *Spomenik* 98 (1941–8) no. 106 from Janjevo shows a man on foot killing a wild ox in the hunt.

[3] Thuc. 2. 100. 2; Hdt. 7. 115. 3 and 131; Thuc. 2. 98. 1.

[4] Hdt. 5. 16. 4; Athen. 345 e; Aelian *NA* 7. 30, remarking that cattle would eat only live fish.

[5] See *Epirus* 276.

leading from Stobi and culminating in the Pletvar pass. Although they had these natural defences, any one canton acting alone was liable to be overrun, as history showed, and as Alexander pointed out in his speech to the Macedonians (Arr. *Anab.* 7. 9. 2). When the cantons combined with the central plain, the greater Macedonian state was in a remarkably strong position to resist invasion from the west, as the Romans found.

On her other frontiers Macedonia was also fortunate. Pieria provided her with a means of enfilading Perrhaebia through the Petra pass. This pass and the Vale of Tempe could both be held by small forces, if invasion threatened from the south. On her south-eastern flank central Macedonia was defended by a mountain range, and her possession of Anthemus closed the entry from the region of Chalcidice. On her eastern flank she could improve her defences by advancing to the Strymon river, which was difficult for an army to cross, and by holding the Rupel defile against the Thracians further north. If she looked outside the boundaries of the greater Macedonian state, Paeonia was of the greatest value to her; for the Paeonians were able to hold the pass of Kačanik, leading from the Danube valley into the upper Vardar valley, and the pass of Tranupara, leading from Pautalia in the Strymon valley to the middle Vardar valley. At first too the Paeonians held the upper Strumitsa valley, from which there was the entry by Valandovo into central Macedonia.

The natural defences of central Macedonia and of the greater Macedonian state alike played a large part in the independence of the Macedonian people. For Macedonia stood squarely upon the chief routes through the Balkan peninsula from north to south and from east to west, and she had as her neighbours powerful and warlike peoples who pressed hard upon her frontiers. She could be by-passed only on her western flank, where the Dardanians and the Illyrians could gain access to the corridor beside Lakes Ochrid, Prespa, and Malik. On that side too there was an area which was in many ways similar to Macedonia. For central Albania has a large and well-watered coastal plain, facing the Ionian Sea, and a mountainous hinterland through which there are very few passes. To invaders coming from the north central Albania and central Macedonia offer the same attractions in fertile land, abundant pasture, and good hunting; and they enjoy a climate which is intermediate between that of continental Europe and that of the Mediterranean lands.

Finally, it is important to emphasize the un-Greek nature of the Macedonian terrain. The great plains, flat and fen-like, which are extremely fertile when properly drained and irrigated, and the wide areas of arable sloping ground above the plains (e.g. in Anthemus and Amphaxitis) or between the coast and the mountains (e.g. in Pieria and Crousis) are entirely different from the small plains and rocky slopes most parts of the Greek peninsula. The mountains too are in general higher and form more continuous ranges. They rise very steeply from the plains and lowlands. They are clad with forests, in which the glades are rich in grass and ferns or bracken. The limestone mountains which are so characteristic of peninsular Greece are found mainly in southern Macedonia, and it is the districts of Olympus and Lower Olympus which make one feel close to the Greek peninsula. The climate too is very different, being much colder in the long-lasting winter and having a more oppressive heat in the summer. The three peninsulas of Chalcidice belong in their physiognomy and their climate not to the Macedonian world but to the Aegean basin.

PART TWO

THE PREHISTORY OF
MACEDONIA

COMPARATIVE CHRONOLOGY OF THE PERIOD
c. 6300–1900 B.C.

Thessaly	Albania	S. Macedonia	Pelagonia	Vardar valley north of Demir Kapu	S. Thrace
Proto-Sesklo		N. Nikomedeia I			
Pre-Sesklo		N. Nikomedeia II	Starčevo settlements	Starčevo settlements at Vršnik and Zelenikovo	Karanovo I
Sesklo		Servia I ,,	,,	,,	
Dhimini I	Malik I	,,	,,	,,	,,
(Arapi) II	Malik IIa	Vardina etc., Servia IIa, N. Nikomedeia III and E	Porodin group	Vršnik II–III	Karanovo II, Drama, Paradimi, etc.
(Otzaki) III	,,	,,	,,	,,	,,
(Classic) IV	,,	,,	,,	,,	Karanovo III
Larissa	,,	Servia IIb	,,	Vršnik IV	,,
Rachmani	,,	Kritsana I–II Servia IIb	Crnobuki group	,,	End of Paradimi, etc.
E.H. I	Malik IIb	Kritsana III Servia IIb	,,	Vinča-Plocnik	Karanovo IV
II	,,	Kritsana IV–V Servia IIb, Vardarophtsa	,,		
III	Malik IIb Malik IIIa	Kritsana VI Armenokhori	Crnobuki ends		
M.H.	Malik IIIa	Armenokhori ends	Bukri		

This chronological table does not claim to be more than a rough guide. It is based upon the following works in particular: W. A. Heurtley, *PM* (1939); V. Milojčić, *Chronologie d. jungeren Steinzeit Mittel- und Südösteuropas* (1949); M. Garašanin, *39 BRGK* (1958) 110 f. and also in *AI* 1 (1954), 3 (1959), 4 (1963); D. Srejovic ibid. 4 (1963); D. H. French, *AS* 11 (1961) 99 f. I have reproduced Milojčić's division of the Dhimini phase into four stages. Although it is unlikely that it applies either throughout Thessaly or beyond Thessaly in its entirety (see S. S. Weinberg in *CAH*[3] 1. i (1970) 607), there are particular points at Malik especially, where comparisons can be made, for instance with the Arapi stage of the Dhimini culture.

VII

THE REMAINS OF THE PALAEOLITHIC AND NEOLITHIC PERIODS, AND SOME ETHNOLOGICAL CONSIDERATIONS

THE only objects of the Palaeolithic period yet found in Macedonia are a skull of Neanderthal type and bones of cave bear and deer in a cave near Petralona in eastern Crousis (see Map 19), and a hand-axe of Acheulean type near the Haliacmon river at Palaiokastron, south of Siatista.[1] These are dated to the Middle Palaeolithic period. The axe may be 100,000 years old. Large deposits of this period have been discovered in Thessaly, and on the west side of the peninsula at places inland of Buthrotum, at Pandanassa in southern Epirus, and in Elis, while occasional finds have been made near Ioannina, in the Kalamas valley at Goumani, in the valley of the Aous at Apollonia and Byllis, and between the Aous valley and the valley of the Shushicë at Vajzë.[2] All these areas, and perhaps the western zones particularly, provided excellent hunting in wooded country.

Early Neolithic settlements in Northern Macedonia, dated c. 6200 to c. 5000 B.C., are marked first by the culture of Starčevo, and then by its successor the culture of Vinča. Both developed near Belgrade in the central Danube basin. The settlements of the Starčevo culture in Northern Macedonia were in two separate groups, each of which followed its own line of development thereafter. One was mainly on the eastern side of the upper Vardar valley and on its eastern tributaries with principal sites at Vršnik near Štip in the Bregalnitsa valley (the earliest in the group) and at Zelenikovo near Skopje in the Vardar valley.[3] The other group appeared at several sites in Pelagonia, reaching as far south as Mogila and Optičare near Monastir.[4] The next development was part of a general intrusion into the Balkans of a culture which spread out from Beyce Sultan in Asia Minor. It followed at least three main routes. The one

---

[1] *L'Anthropologie* 1961. 438 f.; *Antiquity* 38 (1964) 54.

[2] For finds in Greek Epirus see *AD* 20 (1965) 2. 361 and for those in Albanian Epirus see *Epirus* 289 with references; for other parts of Greece see S. S. Weinberg in *CAH*³ 1. i (1970) 557 f.

[3] M. Garašanin, 'Zur Chronologie des makedonischen Neolithikums' in *AI* 3 (1959) 1 f., giving references to the earlier literature. Other sites are Slatina and Tarinci.

[4] Ibid., with p. 4 n. 12. Other finds at Grgur Tumba, Alinci, Markovo Kale, and Crnobuki.

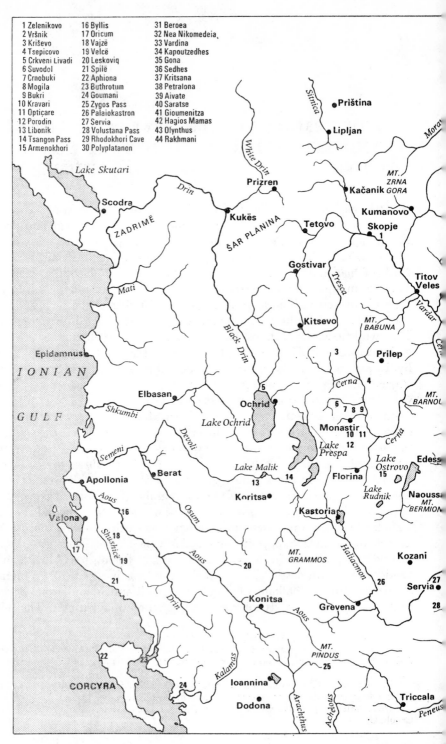

1 Zelenikovo
2 Vršnik
3 Kriševo
4 Tsepicovo
5 Crkveni Livadi
6 Suvodol
7 Crnobuki
8 Mogila
9 Bukri
10 Kravari
11 Opticare
12 Porodin
13 Libonik
14 Tsangon Pass
15 Armenokhori
16 Byllis
17 Oricum
18 Vajzë
19 Velcë
20 Leskoviq
21 Spilë
22 Aphiona
23 Buthrotum
24 Goumani
25 Zygos Pass
26 Palaiokastron
27 Servia
28 Volustana Pass
29 Rhodokhori Cave
30 Polyplatanon
31 Beroea
32 Nea Nikomedeia
33 Vardina
34 Kapoutzedhes
35 Gona
36 Sedhes
37 Kritsana
38 Petralona
39 Aivate
40 Saratse
41 Gioumenitza
42 Hagios Mamas
43 Olynthus
44 Rakhmani

MAP 19. PALAEOLITHI

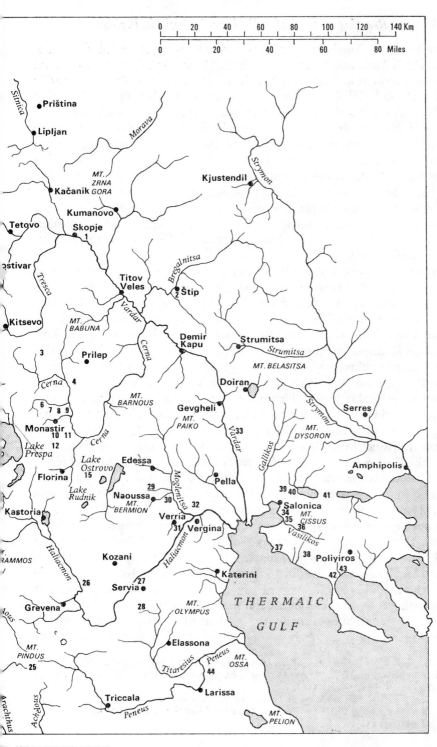

Sitnica ·Priština

·Lipljan

Morava

Kjustendil

Strymon

MT.
ZRNA
Kačanik *GORA*

Kumanovo

Tetovo

stivar **Skopje**
  1

Tresca

**Titov
Veles**

Bregalnitsa

2 **Štip**

Kitsevo

MT.
BABUNA

Vardar

**Demir
Kapu**

Strumitsa

Strumitsa

MT. BELASITSA

3 **Prilep**

Cerna

Doiran

Cerna 4

6
7 8 9

MT.
BARNOUS

Gevgheli
MT.
PAIKO

33

Strymon

Serres

Monastir
  10 11

Cerna

MT.
DYSORON

*Lake
Prespa* 12

*Lake
Ostrovo* **Edessa**
*Lake
Rudnik* 15

Vardar

Pella

Gallikos

Amphipolis

39 40
41

29

Florina

Naoussa   30
MT.
BERMION 32

Moglenitsa

Salonica
34 MT.
35 *CISSUS*
36

Kastoria

Verria
31 **Vergina**

Vasilikos

Kozani

Haliacmon

37

38 **Poliyiros**

42 43

RAMMOS

26

27
Servia ·

28

Katerini

Grevena

MT.
OLYMPUS

THERMAIC
GULF

aus

MT.
PINDUS

25

Elassona

Peneus MT.
OSSA

Titaresius 44

Arachthus

Triccala

Peneus

Larissa

MT.
PELION

D NEOLITHIC SITES.

which affected Northern Macedonia seems to have proceeded via Komo-
tini, Dikili Tash, and Drama in southern Thrace, and then to have turned
up the Strymon and reached Vršnik, creating there a Middle Neolithic
stage (Vršnik III–IV), from *c.* 4000 B.C. onwards.[1] The invigorating
effects of this mixed culture spread northwards from Vršnik, but failed
to penetrate the strong Vinča culture in the Kossovo area north of the
watershed between the Vardar and the Danube. In the meeting of these
two cultures, one originating from the Danube valley and the other
from Asia Minor, we can certainly see the meeting and perhaps the fusion
of two ethnic groups on the eastern side of the Vardar valley and its
tributaries; for the imposition of the second cultural element cannot
have been due simply to transmission through trade at this early stage
of evolution. Meanwhile the Starčevo group in Pelagonia seems to have
been undisturbed.

While the carriers of the Beyce Sultan culture used copper as well as
stone for tools and weapons, the first intrusion of more developed metal-
working techniques came from the upper Morava valley into the
Kumanovo valley of Northern Macedonia,[2] using the pass east of Mt.
Zrna Gora. The same techniques appeared probably later in the Kossovo area, displaced the Vinča culture, and established the so-called
Predionica culture. Meanwhile the group of settlements in Pelagonia
stood aside from this development in the Vardar valley, and created a
longlasting local culture, which passed through two phases, named after
Porodin and Crnobuki (see pp. 223 f. for a description). The second phase
began late in the Late Neolithic Age.[3] The settlements in Pelagonia remained distinct from those of the Vardar valley, even as the Pelagones
and the Derriopes of the Iron Age remained distinct from the Paeonians.
Their contacts were rather with the south, as we shall see. Very late in the
Late Neolithic period the area of the upper Vardar valley and the area
of Pelagonia were both attacked from the north by destructive invaders,
who came from the upper Morava valley, bringing with them the Bubanj-
Hum Ib culture. These invaders may have followed both the Vardar
valley and the Tresca valley, like the Dardanians many centuries later,
and their settlements are found not only at Skopsko Kale near Skopje
but also at Bakarno Gumno near Tsepicovo and at Suvodol, NNW. of
Monastir.[4] It seems that they did not succeed in occupying the Pelagonian
plain for long. Subsequently the settlements in and near Pelagonia
were marked by a local variety of the Macedonian Early Bronze

---

[1] D. Srejovic, 'Versuch einer historischen Wertung der Vinča-Gruppe' in *AI* 4 (1963) 7
with most helpful maps; D. H. French, 'Late Chalcolithic pottery in north-west Turkey and
the Aegean' in *AS* 11 (1961) 114 f.
[2] *AI* 4 (1963) 13. The sites are at Tabanovce and Nadpadina.
[3] *AI* 3 (1959) 2; *39 BRGK* (1958) 114 f.; *Arheološki Vestnik* 4. 1 (1953) 75 f.
[4] *AI* 4 (1963) 14.

Age civilization, which established itself particularly at Bukri and Kravari.[1]

In Southern Macedonia the only settlement so far known of the Early Neolithic Age is on the edge of the central plain at Nea Nikomedeia, NNE. of Beroea, which was then on the edge of a marshy lake or an inlet of the sea, and which in the fourth century B.C. was near Lake Ludias. At the outset its culture was simply an offshoot of the Proto-Sesklo culture of Thessaly, but it reached an unusually high level of architectural skill and artistic ability. Four separate houses, 8 × 8 m to 8 × 11 m, with one or more rooms, were built round a large house, 12 × 12 m, divided into three parts, which contained cult objects, such as steatopygous female figurines of clay, large axes of serpentine (a volcanic stone found in northern Pindus), and gourd-shaped vessels; the people wove textiles mainly of wool, used flint-bladed tools and clay seals, and made beautiful figurines of frogs in green serpentine and of sheep and goats in clay. Some pots had human faces moulded below the rim. A carbon-14 dating for the first stage of the settlement is 6220±150, but affinities with Proto-Sesklo culture suggest rather a date early in the sixth millennium. The community grew wheat, barley, lentils and peas, and kept sheep and goats, as well as pigs and cattle, which were of secondary importance.[2] In a later stage of the Early Neolithic period a pottery of a totally different kind appears at Nea Nikomedeia; this is a so-called 'impressed' ware, in which jags or ridges and incised dots were made on monochrome pots by techniques known as 'Barbotine' and 'Cardium'. In the last phase of the Early Neolithic Age, which further south is called the Pre-Sesklo period, this pottery spread thickly into northern Thessaly and thinly into southern Thessaly. The source of the 'impressed' ware is to be found in the north, where it is characteristic of the Starčevo–Vinča group.[3] It is likely then that the appearance of this ware at Nea Nikomedeia and its advance into northern Thessaly represent extensions of the peoples who had settled with this culture in Pelagonia. As yet no intermediate site is known between Optičare and Nea Nikomedeia, but it is reasonable to assume that most parts of Macedonia, and especially the west side of the coastal plain, were thinly populated by this time.

In Southern Macedonia the Middle Neolithic Age (*c.* 5000–4000 B.C.) brought great changes. The settlement at Nea Nikomedeia came to an end, and the Early Neolithic peoples of northern Thessaly were expelled,

[1] Ibid. 15 and *39 BRGK* 123, based on unpublished material in the museum at Monastir.
[2] For Nea Nikomedeia see Rodden in *PPS* 28 (1962) 267 f., *AD* 17 (1961–2) 2. 231 f., *AD* 19 (1964 [1967]) 2. 368, and S. S. Weinberg in *CAH*³ 1. i (1970) 577 f. The cattle too may have been domesticated.
[3] For the impressed ware in Thessaly and its northern origin, see V. Milojčić in *Jahrb. d. röm-german. Zentralmuseum* 6 (1959) 1–56, and Weinberg, loc. cit. 585 f. For an incised sherd of Starčevo type found in the Pre-Sesklo layer at Sesklo see D. R. Theochares in *Ergon* 1962. 44.

or exterminated, or absorbed by new peoples, who came from Anatolia and established the culture known as 'Thessalian A' or 'Sesklo'.[1] In the latter part of the period an offshoot of this culture was planted below Servia on the south bank of the river Haliacmon, at the very point where the road from the Volustana pass now crosses the river. In the first of the five successive settlements of Servia I in the Middle Neolithic Age there was a ditch, 2·35 m deep with one vertical side and one steeply sloping side, made probably to keep human enemies out rather than domestic animals in, but it was soon filled in and houses spread beyond it. The houses were rectangular with wooden frames, of which the uprights were of chestnut and the rafters were of oak and pine, and the walls were made of wattle and daub, some resting on a foundation-line of stones.[2] It is likely that the site was chosen with defence in mind against the Middle Neolithic inhabitants of Macedonia, of whom we have specific evidence only further north in Pelagonia.

The Late Neolithic Age (*c.* 4000–2800 B.C.) is of particular importance from the point of view of Macedonia, because in the course of it and especially in its last phase there is clear evidence of northern influences and of northern peoples entering Thessaly. In this period several settlements are known in Southern and Central Macedonia. At the beginning of the period the fifth settlement at Servia I was burnt, and it was occupied by newcomers. Their settlement is known as Servia IIa. They brought with them an incised ware consisting of shallow handleless bowls; the polished surface was decorated with incised reduplicated parallel lines, filled with whitish material or with clay, which formed bands, loops, chevrons, zigzags, or fillets, and the lines were often produced by a series of discontinuous strokes.[3] They created, probably through contact with the earlier people, a number of wares which became characteristic of the Late Neolithic Age in other settlements in Macedonia and in some cases in Thessaly. The old mound at Nea Nikomedeia was occupied again, and the top of it was encircled with a ditch some 1·50 m deep, similar to that of the first settlement at Servia. Another settlement grew up nearby at what may be called Nea Nikomedeia East. Two other sites have been found north and east of Naoussa: one deep inside a cave at Rhodokhori was probably used for burials, and the other is a settlement mound in the plain by Polyplatanon.[4]

Otherwise the settlements in Southern Macedonia which are known are all east of the river Axius. Their geographical position makes me doubt Heurtley's supposition that peoples spread eastwards from the

[1] *CAH*[3] I. i (1970) 589 f.
[2] *PM* 43 f. with a picture of the site as fig. 43. This was the earliest known site in Macedonia even when Mylonas wrote in *Mak.* 1 (1940) 261.
[3] *PM* 66 and figs. 8 and 9.
[4] R. J. Rodden, *BS* 5 (1964) 116 f.

Haliacmon valley;[1] for when the Argead Macedonians did so, they sited their towns mainly on the west side of the Axius. Of the Southern Macedonian sites one is at Vardina near Aspros on the left bank of the Axius in Amphaxitis. Then there are several places where Late Neolithic sherds probably indicate settlements: at Sedhes south-east of Therme, at Kapoutzedhes east of Therme, at Aïvate near Lete, at Saratse between Lete and Lake Koronia, and at Gioumenitsa (now Stivos) between Lake Koronia and Lake Bolbe. There are also three settlements on the Chalcidic peninsula: at Kritsana on the coast of Crousis, at Hagios Mamas just south-west of Olynthus, and at Olynthus itself.[2] These sites were all close to fertile and sometimes swampy land, but they were also on main routes and well placed for communication with the coast and with sea trade.

The significance of these sites should not be judged by their smallness. In many periods in Macedonia, indeed as late as the sixth or fifth centuries B.C., sites even of this size are lacking, although we know that the country was inhabited. The explanation is that the bulk of the population was engaged in a pastoral way of life, augmented by hunting and fishing, and their huts, like those of the Vlachs even today, left little trace for the archaeologist.[3] The settlements of the Neolithic Age represent an agricultural way of life in communities which settled at one spot for many centuries, engaged in trade of a primitive kind, were capable of defending themselves, and produced fine pottery and tools and weapons. They were the nuclei round which the pastoral peoples of the district formed a cluster, and they were able to generate aggressive power. The pattern of settlements in Southern Macedonia in the Late Neolithic Age is indicative of the channels through which the interchange of ideas and goods and the movement of peoples occurred between Macedonia and the south, particularly Thessaly. The sites round Therme and Olynthus obviously contributed to the former, and we may suspect that when peoples began to move into Thessaly they did so mainly from the area of Servia through the Volustana pass.

The districts west of Macedonia have an important place in the picture of the Neolithic Age which is gradually emerging. Here the chief site is at Libonik on the edge of what was until recently Lake Malik, at an

[1] *PM* 110. Heurtley thought of the central plain as hitherto uninhabited; for Nea Nikomedeia had not been discovered and little was known of Northern Macedonia.

[2] *PM* 7 f., under the descriptions of the individual settlements; some of the sites were known from surface finds made in the First World War. D. H. French (*AS* 11 (1961) 100) visited and confirmed the two sites at Gioumenitsa and published pottery from there, pp. 108 f. The sites at Akropotamos, just east of the Strymon near the coast, and at Polystylo, further inland towards Drama, are predominantly Thessalian in their culture, a fact which reflects the dominant position of Thessaly in sea-borne trade (*PAE* 1938. 103 f.).

[3] Thus in central Epirus there is no site larger than a group of huts until the fourth century B.C.

altitude of 850 m.[1] I refer to it hereafter as 'Malik'. At the beginning of the first settlement a two-roomed rectangular house was found; each room had a hearth, square in shape with rounded corners, the walls were of wattle and daub on a frame of timber, and the floor of beaten earth and stones was laid on a platform of wood, evidently to keep above the damp. Some clay hearths were incised and decorated, probably for religious purposes. The settlers had a wide range of painted pottery. It has strong links with that of Thessaly but also contains northern characteristics, such as the so-called crusted ware.[2] Some pottery of the same kind has been found at Velcë between the Aous and the Shushicë valleys, and there it is associated with incised and impressed wares, which have a northern origin.[3] The first settlement at Malik, Malik I, is probably contemporary with the first stage at Dhimini.

The second settlement at Malik, Malik II, was built on piles, mainly of oak, and was surrounded by a double palisade of cut stakes.[4] Copper celts, such as were used in constructing this pile settlement, have been found in the debris.[5] The settlement is very large by Neolithic standards, and very rich and varied in its inventory. Its contacts are very wide. There are objects which are either imitations of objects from or have themselves come from Krivodol in Bulgaria, Salcuta in western Romania, Dikili Tash in Greek Thrace (Fig. 3*b* cylinder seals), Lengyel in Hungary, and Butmir and Kakanj in Bosnia.[6] Its closest affinities are, however, with Servia II, itself in contact with Northern Thessaly, and secondarily with the culture of the Porodin group in Pelagonia (Fig. 3*e* altar-tables).[7]

---

[1] The preliminary report was in *SA* 1964. 1, and I gave a summary of it with my comments in my article in *BSA* 62 (1967) 102 f. The full report is in *SA* 1966. 1. 255 f., and there is a subsidiary report on further excavations in *SA* 1967. 1. 140 f. The excellent reporting of the excavations is due to Professor Frano Prendi, who has been very kind in sending me offprints. There are two levels in Malik I.   [2] *SA* 1966. 1. 267.

[3] *Epirus* 290–5; Prendi in *SA* 1966. 1. 269. Both give references to the original publication by D. Mustilli.   [4] *SA* 1966. 1. 257.

[5] *SA* 1964. 1. pl. 1, 18 and 19 (reproduced in *BSA* 62 (1967) pl. 21) and *SA* 1966. 1. pl. 111*d*. These are of the types A 4 a and A 4 b of J. Deshayes, *Les Outils de bronze de l'Indus au Danube* (Paris, 1960) 55 and typology p. 12. Copper is found in Albania, but was not worked as early as this.

[6] Lids of mushroom shape and of conical beehive shape in the case of Krivodol, saddle-shaped weights in the case of Salcuta, pierced cylinders with similar decoration in the case of Dikili Tash, milk-jugs in the case of Lengyel; Prendi does not specify in the case of the Bosnian sites. I saw an unpublished saddle-shaped weight from Tsiplevets in Pelagonia in the museum at Monastir in 1968.

[7] When I wrote my article for *BSA* 62 (1967), I had only the preliminary report of Malik in *SA* 1964. 1. 91–5. The settlement at the start was dated by the excavators to 'énéolithique', but on the evidence then available I wrote 'there is an overwhelming similarity in the techniques and designs of decorative motives at Libonik and in Macedonia, especially at Servia, predominantly in the Macedonian Late Neolithic period'. I am very happy to find Professor Prendi of the same mind in his full report in *SA* 1966. 1. 272. 'Si ces contacts de la civilisation énéolithique de Maliq avec ceux de la Macédoine orientale sont exprimés dans les seules identités des éléments particuliers, ces liens sont évidents avec les régions de la Macédoine centrale et notamment occidentale (aussi bien représentée à Servia), dans la concordance

To the south-west of Macedonia it seems on the present evidence that central Epirus was only sparsely inhabited in the Neolithic Age.[1] But there was a considerable area of Neolithic settlement in the vicinity of the Gulf of Valona. The most important excavated site is at Velcë. This site is several hours inland on a route which runs from the Gulf via Kanina to the central Aous valley; it seems to have been analogous to the site at Ploçë which lay on the same route in Hellenistic times and in Roman times.[2] At Velcë there is an incised ware with spiralling grooves, punched holes in parallel lines, and hatched bands meeting at an acute angle, which is related fairly closely to the incised wares of Servia II and Malik IIa and less closely to those of Molfetta in Apulia, of Nisos at Aphiona in Corcyra, and of Ayios Sotiros in the Nidhri plain in Leucas. Of the painted pottery at Velcë one ware is like the painted ware of Malik I. The other wares are very closely related to the wares associated with maritime trade which ran from Corinth along the west coast, e.g. via Astakos to the Gulf of Valona and to Molfetta in Apulia.[3] Here then at Velcë we have an inter-cultural site, as it were, analogous to that at Malik. Neolithic pottery has been found at several sites on the southern side of the Gulf of Valona, where the shelter from rough seas is best and where Oricum in classical times was the chief harbour; at Spilë below Himarë on the Acroceraunian coast, facing the open sea; and also near Buthrotum opposite Corcyra.[4]

In north-west Macedonia the plains of Pelagonia and northern Lyncus were thickly inhabited in the Middle and Late Neolithic periods. Heurtley divided the numerous mounds, which mark the sites of considerable villages by the standards of the time, into three groups: those between Kriševo and Monastir, those near and south of Monastir to the Greek frontier, and those south of them. Crnobuki belongs to the first group, Porodin to the second, and Armenokhori to the third.[5] The mounds stand on very slight rises in the plain beside the river and its swampy basin (like

étroite et très significative des principaux indices de leur physionomie culturelle: la poterie lustrée, plusieurs formes non seulement standard mais aussi assez spécialisées dans les techniques de fabrication et le caractère décoratif linéaire et spiralé de leurs motifs, les formes des outils, l'idoloplastique et plusieurs autres articles d'usage quotidien ou de culte, tels les phallos, les pintadères etc.' He dates the start of Malik IIa later than I do (as in all the excavations in Albania) and he puts it at the end of Larissa and at the time of Servia II 2 in Milojčić's chronology, *SA* 1966. 1. 273.

[1] *Epirus* 312. E. S. Higgs in *PPS* 33 (1967) 7 reports the discovery of a Neolithic site at the north end of the Ioannina basin.
[2] *Epirus* maps 9 and 13. Kanina was important at the time of Venetian thalassocracy.
[3] Ibid. 290 f. and 294 f., with references to the publications by D. Mustilli. When the preliminary report of Malik was published, I noted in *Epirus* (p. 295 n. 1) that there was a relationship between Velcë and Malik; this is confirmed by the fuller publication, and Frano Prendi has independently seen this (*SA* 1966. 1. 269) but not the connections of Velcë with Molfetta, Astakos, Aphiona, and Leucas.
[4] *Epirus* 290 and 312.
[5] *PM* 57; *ASPR* 10 (1934) 51 f.

the later cities of the Derriopes). The Porodin mound, some 190 m by 190 m, which was excavated in 1953–4, showed a closely built village of some thirty houses, each of two or more rooms. The floor of packed clay was laid on wooden beams. The walls, carried by upright posts and half-posts, sometimes packed in stone at the foot, were formed of clay plaster up to 0·40 m thick; the walls, about 1·60 to 1·70 m high, had a jagged top to take the ceiling rafters. Windows were sometimes round and some-times in the shape of an inverted T. The roof was pitched and reached a height of some 3·30 m; it was (presumably) supported by a post set in the middle of the house. Sometimes each room had a hearth; some-times a hearth was set only in a room opposite the door of entry, when a partition wall separated that room from one or more rooms on one's left on entry. The ground plans of the excavated houses were usually trapezoidal. House-models show also a long narrow rectangular house and a square house. In the house-models the aperture at the top of the roof was round; it may have had a chimney pot, and post-holes round one of the hearths suggest some sort of a chimney or flue. Outside the houses there were other hearths, rubbish-pits, and round grain-storage pits.

The house-models seem to represent, one a sacred house or temple (Fig. 1*a*), and the other a secular house. The clay figurines are of standing and sitting male and female figures, some of which wear a crown, unless it is a form of hair-style (Fig. 1*e*), and of various animals: sheep, horses, pigs, bulls and cows, lynxes, bears, and perhaps dogs (Fig. 2). Some plastic handles on pots are anthropomorphic, and upright plastic handles on altar-tables represent water-birds and water-reptiles (Fig. 1*b*). There are numerous clay altar-tables, three-footed and four-footed; one is throne-shaped, and a miniature one has a face moulded below the rim (Fig. 1*f*). Weapons and tools in stone are celts of most kinds, including flat celts, polishers, pounders, and arrow-heads; in flint are saws and blades; and in clay are sling bullets, ovoid and spherical. The main cereal was a wheat (*triticum turgidum*), and there was evidence of woven cloth and reed-matting.[1]

The beginning of the Porodin culture can be safely correlated with the Arapi stage of the Late Neolithic Age in Thessaly.[2] Its end is more difficult to date. The excavators placed its end towards the end of the Late Neolithic Age, apparently in the Larissa stage of Thessaly, and this fits in with M. Garašanin's belief that the Crnobuki group began in the

---

[1] I summarize from M. Grbić, *Porodin* (Bitolj, 1960), which is in Serbian with a German summary. See also M. Garašanin in *39 BRGK* (1958) 114 f. I saw some of the material in the museum at Monastir. The shapes of the houses are different from those of the house-models of the Neolithic/Copper Age site at Kodjadermen in north-east Bulgaria (*Bull. de la Soc. Archéol. Bulgare* 6 (1916)). Similar altar-tables have been found in Layers I and III at Karanovo in a 'tell'; see Археология, 6. 3 (1964) 62.   [2] *AI* 3 (1959) 3.

Rakhmani stage of Thessaly.[1] The Porodin culture ended, when the site at Porodin was burnt and abandoned. It is possible that the destruction was due to an early wave of the Bubanj-Hum I people;[2] but, if so, they did not displace the bulk of the population. For the Crnobuki culture, which followed on that of Porodin, had a strong relationship with it.[3]

When we turn to ethnological considerations in the Neolithic Age, we are often dealing with first settlers or perhaps with a second wave of settlers, and some very broad deductions can be made from the archaeological evidence.

1. Nea Nikomedeia I and at a later period Servia I were settled by people who not only had a Thessalian type of culture but were of the same stock as the then inhabitants of Thessaly, who had come from Anatolia. The first settlement at Malik, later than that at Servia, was probably made jointly by people of that stock and by people of the next group.

2. The incised and impressed wares of Nea Nikomedeia II were introduced by new settlers (the site had been uninhabited for a time) with a different culture. Their ancestors had come from the north. For they belonged to the same general stock as the first settlers of Pelagonia and the Vardar valley, a stock which had its origins in the middle Danube valley round Starčevo. If we judge them by their pottery, peoples of the same stock came later to Servia II,[4] Malik II,[5] and Velcë.[6] It seems then that the expanding wedge of country which begins in the north with Pelagonia and the Vardar valley by Skopje and extends down to the Gulf of Valona in the west and the Strumitsa valley in the east was occupied in general by peoples who had derived from the Danube valley.

3. There was at least one intrusion, and there may well have been more intrusions, from the east into Macedonia; but the one which we can see came via Drama and went perhaps up the Strymon and Strumitsa to Vršnik, where the fusion of peoples produced a new culture.[7] Here

---

[1] *Porodin* 108 f.; *AI* 3 (1959) 3.

[2] This may be implied in M. Garašanin's chronological chart in *AI* 3 (1959) pl. 1. J. Todorovic in *AI* 4 (1963) pl. 6 is in line with this suggestion in terms of chronology.

[3] *AI* 3 (1959) 2.

[4] *PM* 66, writing of Servia II, Heurtley says 'only one kind, the Incised, seems to owe nothing to the old local tradition, but rather to represent the ideas of the newcomers as to what shape a pot should be or how it should be decorated'.

[5] *SA* 1966. 1. 258 'le système ornemental (of Malik IIa) . . . offre différentes techniques. Outre la poterie peinte, une place importante occupe désormais celle à l'incision, celle à incrustation, en plastique, ou bien la poterie à techniques combinées de décoration, ce qui prouve de la meilleure façon leur caractère contemporain.'   [6] *Epirus* 295.

[7] *AI* 4 (1963) 8 'anderseits verfolgt eine abzweigende Strömung die thrakische Küste (Paradimi, Drama). Sie ist auch dem Weg über die Struma (Dikili Tash) in nördlicher Richtung zu verfolgen und findet durch das Strumica-Tal einen leichten Weg nach Ostmakedonien (Vršnik III–IV). Auf diesen Hauptwegen stößt die anatolisch-chalkolitische

we have an intrusion which derived ultimately from Anatolia. There was another intrusion, this time from the north, which occupied the Kumanovo valley.

4. Influences from the south take two forms. We can see that sites such as Nea Nikomedeia I and Kritsana probably received settlers from the south, and in particular from Thessaly, by sea rather than by lan,d just as Astakos or Himarë or the Gulf of Valona may have received some settlers from Greece by sea. When Servia I was founded, we can see that the Thessalian peoples extended their territory up to the south bank of the Haliacmon, at least in that area. But in Servia II, those peoples were pushed back by northerners,[1] and in the ensuing ebb and flow it seems that the Late Neolithic Age saw more northerners entering Thessaly than southerners entering Macedonia by land.[2]

Within this general picture we can see that Pelagonia is an important centre-piece. If Garašanin and Grbić are correct, and in my opinion the available evidence is strong in their favour,[3] there was an uninterrupted development in Pelagonia throughout the Neolithic Age from the first Starčevo culture to the Porodin culture and then to the Crnobuki culture, a development which came about through evolution in contact with the influences of trade and not through the irruption of an intruding culture.[4] It seems probable that the peoples of Starčevo origin held this

Welle überall auf die Kulturgruppen des älteren Neolithikums um in Fühlung mit letzteren die primären Zentren der mittelneolithischen Kulturen zu schaffen.' I follow M. Garašanin in his chronology for Vršnik II–III as opposed to that of Srejovic, cited here; see Garašanin in *AI* 3 (1959) 2 and plate i.

[1] *PM* 116 'Childe has already detected the affinities of Starčevo and Dimeni; had he known the pottery from Olynthus he would, I think, have been still more impressed by their virtual identity . . . . In view of all the analogies the case for a Danubian origin of the Servian Late Neolithic culture is, at least, respectable.' See also S. S. Weinberg, supporting Heurtley on the last point, in *CAH*³ I. i (1970) 607 f.

[2] This is what we should expect, because at no period in history have peoples situated in the happy climate of Greece moved in large numbers into the hinterland of Macedonia or Epirus with their continental climate. Settlement of Greeks on coastal belts which enjoy the Mediterranean climate is an entirely different matter. All arguments from historical analogy and geographical probability militate against the view that peoples from the Greek peninsula occupied Macedonia in the Neolithic or any other Age.

[3] Some of the material from Pelagonia and the Vardar valley is still unpublished, but Garašanin and Grbić have studied this material in the museums of Monastir and Skopje.

[4] M. Garašanin in *AI* 3 (1959) 2 on the relationship of the Porodin group and the Crnobuki group, and 3 on the evolution in Pelagonia: 'als älteste Erscheinung ist wohl auch hier die Starčevo-Gruppe zu vermerken, die von der mit Arapi und makedonischen Spätneolithikum zusammenhängenden Porodin-Gruppe abgelöst wird. Auf diese folgt schließlich noch die Crnobuki-Gruppe, wobei allerdings der zeitliche Ansatz des Überganges zwischen beiden letzten vorläufig nicht näher zu ermitteln ist.' Also in *39 BRGK* 109–10 and 119 'daher ist es wohl wahrscheinlich, daß die Crnobuki-Gruppe eine späte Entwicklungstufe der Porodiner Gruppe darstellt'. M. Grbić, *Porodin* (Bitolj, 1960) 109 concludes his report of the excavations with these sentences. 'Auf Grund obiger Ausführungen ist die Herkunft der Porodiner Gruppe in allgemein balkanischen Starčevo-Komplex zu suchen, wo sie zeitlich und inhaltlich eine Sonderstellung einnimmt. Inhaltlich ist dies die einzige gut ausgeprägte Retention auf der Balkan, welche bei ihre spät- oder end-neolithischen Zeitstellung noch keine Einflüsse

area (even as the occupants of this area did for at least a millennium from 500 B.C. onwards), and in addition that Pelagonia and perhaps other cantons of Upper Macedonia to the south of Pelagonia gave off waves of settlers who played some part in the creation of Nea Nikomedeia III, Servia II, Malik II, and Velcë. By contrast the areas of the Vardar valley were subject to intrusions of peoples, and already in the Late Neolithic Age they were occupied by a mixture of peoples of different stocks. With regard to central Albania in the Neolithic Age we are in a state of ignorance; but its terrain is so similar to that of Central Macedonia that it is almost certain that it was already inhabited.

The currents of trade in the Neolithic Age have to be distinguished from the movements of peoples. For it is as true of this Age as it is, for instance, of the period 750–350 B.C. in Greece, that many changes in pottery and in other classes of object may occur without involving changes or even shifts of population. Thus the spread of Thessalian Neolithic potteries is not to be interpreted as the spread of Thessalian peoples. The fact is that throughout the Neolithic Age Thessaly held a dominant position in fine pottery and in the trade associated with it. As far as the southern Balkan area was concerned, Thessaly was the chief centre o export and import. Goods were certainly carried from and to Thessaly by ships which used the harbours of the Thermaic Gulf and Chalcidice, and we have seen that such sites as Nea Nikomedeia and Sedhes and Olynthus were suitably placed for maritime trade. Trade overland between Thessaly and Pelagonia seems to have been channelled mainly along the best natural route; that is through Elimea via Servia, Eordaea, and Lyncus. When we consider not local trade but inter-cultural trade between the Near East, Sicily, and the Danube valley, for instance, we find not only that Thessaly is again an important area of exchange, but also that Malik and to a lesser degree both Servia and Velcë are inter-cultural centres. The explanation of this phenomenon is to be found in the use of a direct overland route from Thessaly and from the Thermaic Gulf to the Adriatic coast in preference to the long and sometimes hazardous voyage by sea round the tips of the Peloponnese.

As far as Thessaly is concerned, there are two routes overland to the west. The more southerly is over the high Zygos pass to Central Epirus and then along the valleys of the Drin and the Aous to the Gulf of Valona. This route was probably not used for trade in the Neolithic Age, when Central Epirus was very sparsely inhabited; indeed it was rarely used for trade at any time. The other route is to Servia; then up the

---

der frühen Metallzeit aufweist.' Garašanin distrusts the theory of a 'Retention' and shows the effect of influences from the south. D. Srejovic in *AI* 4 (1963) 14, of the Crnobuki group, 'auch diesmal von inneren Bewegungen auf den Balkan die Rede sein muß'. It is possible that the final stage of the Porodin group overlaps the Crnobuki culture.

Haliacmon valley to Kastoria and Koritsa; and thence to the Gulf of Valona via Leskoviq and the Aous valley. This route was much in use in the eleventh and twelfth centuries A.D.[1] It affords the easiest crossing of the Balkan range (see p. 7 above). There are again two routes from Macedonia to the west, and of these that through Koritsa is easier than that through Ochrid.

It is clear from the evidence at Malik that in the Late Neolithic Age the route through the Balkan range via Malik was much in use for goods which came from ports on the Thermaic Gulf and from Thessaly via Servia, and also for goods which came from across the Ionian Gulf and down the Adriatic Sea to the Gulf of Valona. The importance of maritime trade in the western seas is shown by the Neolithic sites on the north-west coast of Greece and by the Molfetta culture in Apulia. Even more striking is the evidence from Hvar. The rich deposits in the cave of Grabak show that the island was a centre of trade in the Late Neolithic Age, and had contacts with the north and with much of the Mediterranean area.[2] Hvar was a main station on the route by sea between the Gulf of Valona and the head of the Adriatic Sea, whence there was an overland passage to Hungary and the Danube valley.

The excavator, G. Novak, has emphasized that at Hvar there were direct imports of Sesklo–Dhimini B 3 B ware from Thessaly and that there are many analogies between the painted pottery of Hvar and that of Macedonia and Chalcidice. As he remarks, 'nor can there be cast a doubt upon the analogy between the painted pottery of Hvar and the Macedonian Neolithic'.[3] As Macedonian Neolithic pottery is not found at sites on the east coast of Greece, it is certain that Macedonian pottery and its contents were not carried by sea round the Peloponnese in competition with more valuable freight, but reached Hvar on the overland route which led to the Adriatic coast.

---

[1] For these routes see *Epirus* 38 and 367. In the first Crusade the army went from the coast to 'Andronopolis' (Drinopolis in the Drin valley in Epirus) and then to Kastoria (via Koritsa), and Bohemund moved from Kastoria to Larissa (*Gesta Francorum* i. 3; Anna Comnena, *Alex.* 5. 5. 1 fin. and 5. 7. 3 fin.). The twelfth-century Arab geographer Idrisi gives the route from Lablôna (Valona) to Adhernobôlî (Drinopolis) in two days; thence over Mt. Timora to Qastoria (Kastoria) in two or three days; thence to Tarofiniqua (unidentified) in three days; thence to Larsa (Larissa) in one day, and on to the Gulf of Volo. See also p. 209 above.

[2] G. Novak, *Prethistorijski Hvar* (Zagreb, 1955), with an English summary, and in *AI* 3 (1959) 11 f., 'Problems and chronology of the finds in the cave of Grabak'. In the former work on p. 320 he wrote as follows. 'The pottery found in the cave of Grabak points to the wide Mediterranean; it likewise points to connections with the Ionian and Tyrrhenian Seas, with the Aegean and its coasts, with Cyprus, Syria and Egypt, either directly or indirectly, but always by way of the sea.' This last sentence was written before the excavation at Malik. As an example of trade from the Aegean via Hvar to Hungary we may mention the shell, *spondylus gaederopus*, native to the Aegean and imported into central Europe; large amounts of the shell were found at Hvar (*AI* 3. 34). Some have been found at Rhodokhori, and examples of the pendants which they formed are in clay in Malik IIa (see *BS* 5 (1964) 117 and pl. 8a, and *SA* 1966. 1. 260 and pl. 3f).   [3] G. Novak in *AI* 3 (1959) 32.

The identification of the founders of the various settlements at Malik is of particular importance, because they were more gifted than their neighbours. In the first settlement, which was quite small, the culture was predominantly Thessalian, but there were already some northern traits. One of these was the occurrence of 'crusted' ware, and in particular the application of crusted paint to pots which were of Dhimini B 3 B shape and to 'clock-tower' stands with lozenge-shaped windows of the same period.[1] Crusted paint is used elsewhere only later: in the Porodin and Crnobuki groups (less often in the latter),[2] at Nea Nikomedeia III,[3] Servia II,[4] Kapoutzedhes,[5] Kritsana,[6] and perhaps at Rhodokhori cave.[7] A further and indeed surprising thing is that crusted paint, both red and white, was used both with and without incision in Malik I. Some of the settlers of Malik I must have brought the technique with them from central Europe.[8] Another northern feature was the construction of the village on a platform of timber joists. This technique was used in the Neolithic culture, for instance, of the Swiss lakes;[9] it is found also at Porodin.

The large settlement known as Malik IIa, which was built at some interval of time after the end of Malik I, was constructed on piles by newcomers, who had an abundance of copper tools and especially copper flat celts (both the so-called 'shoe-last' celts and the 'Flachbeile') and copper fish-hooks (Fig. 3a). Frano Prendi notes that the ends of the piles show clearly the employment of metal tools.[10] Pile-dwelling villages of the Danordic culture in the Neolithic Age are found in the Mondsee in Austria (in this region copper was smelted, and flat celts and fish-hooks of copper were in use) ;[11] in the Swiss lakes ;[12] and in north-west Yugoslavia at Ljubljana (formerly Laibach), just to the north-east of Trieste at

[1] *SA* 1966. 1. 256–7 and 268 pl. 1, 12, a clock-tower as in Tsountas, *Dimini and Sesklo* (Athens, 1908) 223 f. and pl. 30. Resemblances to pottery from Dhimitra and Dikili Tash in western Thrace are probably due to influences emanating from a common source, namely Thessaly. See *SA* 1966. 1, pl. 2; Casson, *Macedonia* 116 fig. 29a; D. H. French in *Praehist. Ztschr.* 42 (1964) 34 fig. 3.

[2] *AI* 3 (1959) 2 and *39 BRGK* 115 for Porodin; *AI* ibid., *39 BRGK* 119 and pl. 25. 4, and *Arheološki Vestnik* 4. 1 (1953) 91 for Crnobuki; *ASPR* 10 (1934) 51 for the Pelagonian area generally.

[3] *BS* 5 (1964) 116 with pl. 5b.   [4] *PM* 148 fig. 14 (i) *f*, fig. 22, and fig. 27k.

[5] *PM* 74.   [6] *PM* 75.   [7] *BS* 5 (1964) 116.

[8] S. S. Weinberg in *CAH*[3] 1. i (1970) 607 f. 'crusted wares in Thrace and Macedonia of the Late Neolithic period are of European derivation'; so also Delavoye in *BCH* 73 (1949–51) 73 f., M. Garašanin in *39 BRGK* 18 f. and V. Milojčić, *Hauptergebnisse der deutschen Ausgrabungen in Thessalien* (1960) 25 f. It appears in Thessaly on G I g and G I d wares of the Larissa culture. For crusted ware in Hungary at Polgar, for instance, see Childe, *Danube* 76.

[9] Childe, *Danube* 162.

[10] *SA* 1966. 1. 257 f.; p. 270 'cela est indiqué non seulement par la foule d'objets en cuivre, dégagés à partir des sediments les plus anciens de cette couche, mais également chez les pilotis du palafitte, dont les bouts expriment parfaitement les traces de l'usage d'outils metalliques'.

[11] Childe, *Danube* 126.   [12] Ibid. 161 f.

the head of the Adriatic Sea (here flat celts of copper, with straight sides, were in use).[1] Thus the three most striking innovations at Malik IIa— the use of copper, hitherto unknown in the area, the special kind of celt, and the construction on piles—are all explained if we derive the settlers from central Europe, probably from the vicinity of Ljubljana.[2] Although common at the outset at Malik II, the copper celt was very rare elsewhere: there are only two at Sesklo,[3] and they do not occur in Macedonia for many centuries. Imitations of the flat celt were made in stone in Pelagonia both in the Porodin culture and in the Crnobuki culture, at Servia I, and at Zerelia in Thessaly.[4]

A settlement on piles was found on the east side of Lake Kastoria. Keramopoullos counted some 500 stakes. He extracted one from the clay bed and found it to be of cedar. It had been driven in with its bark on and upside down, and the tip had been sharpened apparently with an axe. He found obsidian blades of grey colour and of reddish colour and a black nucleus of obsidian, a great many stone tools made locally, and signs of a metal blade on some worked hardstone. He was surprised to find signs of metalworking in such a Neolithic setting. The settlement on piles had been destroyed by fire. Similar settlements have been reported in Lake Prespa and in Lake Rudnik, and at Crkveni Livadi by Vraniste, that is by the Drin's outflow from the north end of Lake Ochrid.[5] The settlements at Kastoria and Malik lie upon the route from Thessaly via the Haliacmon valley and the Tsangon pass to the Adriatic coast.

Another settlement on piles formed the lowest layer at Gona, a site which is situated on the east side of the Thermaic Gulf by Therme. In this settlement a flat celt of copper was found. It is of a later type than those at Malik. Heurtley dated the earliest settlement at Gona to the Macedonian Early Bronze Age and the copper celt to the Middle Bronze Age.[6] The lowest stratum of a mound near the marshy outflow of the Vasilikos river into the Thermaic Gulf was found to rest on wooden

---

[1] Childe, *Danube* 209. Also at Donja Dolina on the Save; see *WMBH* 9.

[2] This is supported by other features of Malik IIa, especially the use of incised and impressed ornament, knobs, and diminutive handles (*SA* 1966. 1. 257 f. and pls. 4, 7, 13, 14), all of which are characteristic of Ljubljana (Childe, *Danube* 209). The view of J. Deshayes, *Les Outils de bronze de l'Indus au Danube* 55 that this type of celt spread from the east to Bulgaria may be true in a primary sense, but the Danube valley is a centre of dispersion too. Frano Prendi does not consider the origin of the settlers.

[3] Tsountas, *Dimini and Sesklo* 351 f. figs. 292 and 293, one example each of type A 4 a and A 4 b (see p. 225 n. 5 above). Some copper may have been obtained at Kastoria (see Map 1).

[4] For Pelagonia see *39 BRGK* 117 and 119, and *ASPR* 10 (1934) 52; for Servia I see *PM* 138 fig. 6a = pl. iv; for Zerelia see *PTh* 164 fig. iiic. There may be one from Akropotamos (*PAE* 1938. 108 fig. 5 no. 11).

[5] *PAE* 1938. 58 f.; *JHS* 59 (1939) 200; Kazarow, *Beitr. zur Kulturgesch. d. alten Thraker* (Vienna, 1916) 26; *Arch. Anz.* 1940. 279 and 1942. 187; *Starinar* vii–viii (1956–7) 234.

[6] Rey in *BCH* 41–3 (1917–19) 146 f.; *PM* 23. The celt is illustrated in Rey p. 244, and in *PM* 213 fig. 83*y*; its copper content in *PM* 254.

piles (*BSA* 23. 27). Herodotus 5. 16 describes the way in which a settlement on piles in Lake Prasias was maintained and extended. Many
centuries separate Malik from Gona, and many more separate Gona from
Lake Prasias; but the way of life is so unusual that we may see in these
settlements the movements of a people who became in the end a fragment
confined perhaps to Lake Prasias. Herodotus seems to have regarded the
pile-dwellers of Lake Prasias as a tribe of 'Paeonians'.[1]

At Malik it seems that the pile-dwelling settlers had a relatively
short run. For the settlement was completely burnt, piles were no longer
used to extend the area of habitation, and copper seems to have become
scarce. The next settlement of Malik IIa was built on the debris.[2] The
same thing happened to Servia I; it was completely burnt and Servia II
rose upon the debris.[3] It looks as if some powerful and artistically gifted
people seized these two places on the overland trade route and created
the unusually high civilization known as Malik IIa and Servia II. The
links between Malik IIa and Servia II are very close not only in pottery
of many kinds but also in the types of stone celt,[4] the phalli (Fig. 3*c*),[5]
the pintaderas (Fig. 3*b*),[6] and the figurines (Fig. 3 *d* and *f*).[7] These do not
occur elsewhere in Macedonia, except for some pintaderas in the Porodin
culture of Pelagonia. They are all included in Heurtley's list of elements
which are of a Danubian source.[8] There are two burials at Servia II,
which we shall consider in detail later. Part of a zoomorphic incised
vase was found in the crook of one skeleton's arm.[9] This type of vase
and this type of decoration are in Heurtley's list of northern elements.
They suggest a Danubian origin for the invaders. Heurtley knew of only
one other zoomorphic vase in the whole area south and east of Servia,

---

[1] The genitive Παιόνων in 5. 15. 3 seems to go also with the first sentence of 5. 16. 1.

[2] *SA* 1966. 1. 257. I differ here from Frano Prendi in the interpretation of what occurred.
He thinks floods ceased to occur (it is not clear why); the settlers then ceased to use a 'difficult
and costly form of construction' (but the reasons actuating them in the first place might well
have operated again); and there was no change of population. He regards the burning of the
whole settlement as accidental; but this is unlikely in a settlement built over standing water.

[3] *PM* 52 f.

[4] *PM* pl. 9, 33*a*; *SA* 1966. 1. pl. 3*b* for celts. The links in pottery include the unusual
'White on Pink' style (*SA* 1966. 1. 259 and *PM* 74). Heurtley dated it to the Late Neolithic
Age and D. H. French in *Praehist. Ztschr.* 42 (1964) 42 has proposed the Early Neolithic Age.
The examples at Malik support Heurtley's dating.

[5] *PM* 165 fig. 35 *t* and *u*; *SA* pl. 10*b* with two types. They are found also in Danordic
cultures (Childe, *Danube* 129).

[6] *PM* 165 fig. 35*r* and *s*; *SA* pl. 10*d*. Some of the designs on the Malik pintaderas are the
same as those on pintaderas from Salmanovo in north-east Bulgaria, which R. Popov
attributed to the Neolithic period (*Bull. de la soc. archéol. bulgare* 4 (1914) 152 fig. 110); animal
figurines and what appears to be the leg of a zoomorphic pot were also found there. Similar
pintaderas come from layers II and VI of a 'tell' excavated near Karanovo in central Bulgaria; see Археология, Sofia, 6. 3 (1964) 62.

[7] *PM* pl. 9, 34*g* and *SA* pl. 10*a* lower line; *PM* pl. 10, 7*i* and *SA* pl. 10 top line.

[8] *PM* 115–16; Grbić, *Porodin* pl. 25.

[9] *PM* 55, and 140 fig. 9*i*. It is to be seen in the museum at Salonica.

namely one at Olynthus. Zoomorphic vases occur in the Porodin culture of Pelagonia and are a feature of Malik IIa.[1]

The first settlers of Malik II, armed with their copper celts and accustomed to pile-dwellings, probably came from the north along the corridor of the lakes; for they kept to the west of Pelagonia, and they reached the corridor perhaps through Kitsevo, like the Dardani later (see p. 83 above). Their successors, who destroyed the first settlement of Malik II, are likely to have come by the same route. For neither group has left any trace of its passage either in Pelagonia and northern Lyncus, which form the area of the Porodin and Crnobuki cultures, or in Central Macedonia, which affords the only route of entry from the east. As we have seen, Malik II was the central station on the overland route joining the north-west corner of the Aegean and the Gulf of Valona. It was also the richest and most influential centre of civilization in the area which is now called Central Albania and Macedonia.[2] The people of Malik and their kindred controlled on the east side of the Balkan range the Haliacmon valley as far at least as Servia, and on the west side the area between the Aous and the Apsus (Semeni) or the Genusus (Shkumbi); for the flocks of sheep, which were a part of their wealth, must have had their winter pastures in the coastal plain which was later controlled by a Greek colony, Apollonia.[3] Towards the end of the Greek Late Neolithic Age when peoples of northern stock entered northern Thessaly, it is evident that they were peoples of the Malik type and culture.[4]

[1] *PM* 162 no. 160 = *Olynthus* I figs. 35–7. For Porodin see fig. 2, 2 here = Grbić, op. cit. pl. 32, 2 with mouth in the back, and cf. pl. 28; and for Malik IIa *SA* 1966. 1. 258 'comme formes communes et caractéristiques . . . les vases zoomorphes à embouchure dans le dos', and pl. 5, 31. See further p. 244 n. 3 below. We may add to the points which we have already mentioned the clay figurines of humans and of animals or birds of Malik II (see fig. 3d here, and *SA* pl. 10a and c). Some of the human figurines are made with the head and body separate, a technique which is found in the Crnobuki group (*AI* 3 (1959) 2; *39 BRGK* 119 and pl. 25. 2; *Arheološki Vestnik* 4. 1 (1953) 83 fig. 8 and 86 fig. 12; cf. *ASPR* 10 (1934) 52), and at Polyplatanon (*BS* 5 (1964) 117 and pl. 7g). In 1968 I saw three human figurines of Malik types from Tsiplevets in Pelagonia (unpublished in Monastir Museum). Also the numerous three- and four-legged altars of Malik II (see fig. 3e here, and *SA* 260 and pl. 10h), which were found at Servia II in the ashes above the earlier burial (*PM* 79 and 150 no. 91), in the Porodin group (see fig. 1b and f here, and Grbić, op. cit. pl. 21 and pls. 26–8), at Armenokhori in Lyncus (*PM* 76), as almost the only shape in an incised ware at Olynthus (*PM* 161 no. 148 = *Olynthus* i figs. 62b and 63), and at Akropotamos and Polystylo (*PAE* 1938. 104 and 111); they are common in the Vinča culture further north (Childe, *Danube* 28 and 70).

[2] The most recent analogy to an important centre near Lake Malik is that of the Vlach city Moskhopolis (see p. 64 above); it traded overland through the corridor of the lakes and the pass above Kačanik with the Danube valley. In the case of Malik the main routes were to the coasts, but the overland route to the Danube valley may also have been used for trade.

[3] See p. 7 and p. 15 above, and Leake 1. 343.

[4] It is outside the scope of this chapter to detail the evidence of northern influences in Thessaly at different stages in the Late Neolithic Age. The infusion of these influences and of peoples from the north was a gradual process over a long period of time from Dhimini I to Rakhmani in Milojčić's refined chronology. It is too simple to talk as he does (*Chronologie* 45)

At the time when the Early Bronze Age began in Greece and the Neolithic Age was continuing in Macedonia, we may summarize the position in the north as follows. (1) In northern Thessaly, particularly as shown at Rakhmani[1] between Mt. Ossa and the river Peneus, there was already a fusion of peoples of Anatolian origins and peoples of the Servia–Malik group. (2) The upper and middle Haliacmon valley as far downstream as Servia was in the hands of an able and aggressive group of peoples, defined by the settlements Servia II and Malik IIa, who had come ultimately from the Danube valley; this group of peoples held also the southern part of Central Albania, roughly from Velcë to the Shkumbi valley. They were in touch with the seafaring peoples of the Adriatic Sea, both those based on Apulia and those trading up the coasts of Albania and of Yugoslavia via Hvar to the head of the Adriatic Sea. (3) The next group of people, if we may so call them, held Pelagonia and Lyncus; they had come originally from the Central Danube area, bringing the Starčevo culture and being affected by its successor, the Vinča culture, but they had developed their own cultures, which we call the Porodin culture and the Crnobuki culture. (4) In the Vardar valley north of the Demir Kapu there was a fusion of different peoples, deriving mainly from the Danube valley and in part from Anatolia, who created the Vršnik culture. (5) Of Pieria we have no information. (6) In the central plain of Macedonia the population at the end of the Late Neolithic Age was probably very mixed. There were elements from Early Neolithic Thessaly, Chalcolithic pile-dwelling settlers, early Starčevo settlers, settlers from the middle Vardar valley, e.g. at Vardina, and peoples of northern and eastern origin in Mygdonia and Chalcidice, where they had contact with the sea-faring peoples of the Aegean; indeed some sites such as Kritsana may have been colonies founded by the seafarers. It is from this background that the first Greek-speaking peoples began to enter what was to be called Greece, perhaps in the final centuries of the Early Bronze Age and certainly in the opening century of the Middle Bronze Age.

of the Dhimini folk 'passing through Macedonia' ('Zu dieser Zeit, viz. Mittelneolithikum, werden auch die Dimini-Leute Makedonien durchzogen haben'); for the Dhimini cultures arose from a fusion of techniques, the population of Thessaly was a fusion of different peoples, and Macedonia was far from being an open field for passage. It is enough for our purpose here to quote S. S. Weinberg in *CAH*[3] I. i (1970) 608: 'The varieties of culture present in different parts of Greece in the latter half of the fourth millennium B.C. . . . are indications both of the arrival of new peoples from east and north and of the beginning of a new way of life.'

[1] At Rakhmani itself one may notice in *PTh* 32 f. crusted wares, 41 f. and fig. 25 figurines with separate heads, 42 f. and fig. 26 *a* and *f* flat celts or chisels of stone—all mentioned above as characteristic of Malik and Servia—p. 43 sling bullets typical of Porodin and Crnobuki in Pelagonia, p. 42 and fig. 27*g* bone spoons (cf. at Malik in *SA* 1966. 1 pl. 3*c*), and an interesting fiddle-shaped flat stone or 'waisted pebble-axe' in fig. 27*h*, which is exactly the same as one of Malik II (ibid. pl. 10*a* 1 = fig. 4*i* here) and like one of Servia I and one of Servia II (*PM* pl. iv, 6*k* and pl. ix, 33*m*).

VIII

THE REMAINS OF THE TIME CONTEMPORARY WITH THE EARLY HELLADIC PERIOD, AND THE COMING OF THE KURGAN PEOPLE TO MACEDONIA AND ALBANIA

THE Early Helladic period, with which the Macedonian Late Neolithic Age overlapped to different extents in different places, was marked by a great change, which affected at first only Southern Macedonia. In terms of culture the whole of the coastal sector and the central plain was fundamentally reorientated. In the Late Neolithic Age of Greece, as we have seen, these areas had been in such close contact with Thessaly and the South, that Kritsana, Olynthus, and Akropotamos, for instance, had been little more than offshoots of Thessalian culture. But in the Early Helladic period these sites had contact only with the culture of Troy and north-western Asia Minor, so much so that at Kritsana, where four settlements of this period were excavated, only one piece of pottery from Greece was found and that in the last phase, that is in E.H. III in terms of Greek chronology.[1] If I may borrow a phrase used by S. S. Weinberg, this area of Macedonia was 'placed firmly in the Near Eastern cultural area'.[2] Something similar occurred throughout the whole of the eastern side of Greece and the Cyclades, but with this difference that in Southern Macedonia there was a marked decline in cultural standards, a lack of inventiveness, an isolation, and indeed a stagnation. Thus although the use of bronze and the invention of the wheel in making pottery were known, neither is much in evidence, and only two pieces of obsidian, imported from Melos, were found in the four settlements at Kritsana, and those in the earlier ones.[3]

Such a change can have come about only through the arrival in Southern Macedonia of a new people or peoples who were singularly unenterprising and had little use for seafaring and maritime trade. They seem to have spread from the eastern side of the central plain, Kritsana[4]

---

[1] *PM* 121 and J. L. Caskey in *CAH*³ I. ii (1971) 774.

[2] *CAH*³ I. i (1970) 608.

[3] *PM* 79 f. and 121.

[4] This is of little significance, as the settlement consisted of less than a dozen houses (*PM* 21).

in Crousis being the earliest site with their culture yet known, followed by Hagios Mamas and Molyvopyrgo, a new site (both near Olynthus which was abandoned). At Stivos there were some E.B.A. sherds and then the settlement came to an end.[1] Another early and new site is at Saratse, between Lete and Lake Koronia. Then come two new sites in Amphaxitis, both on the east side of the Axius, at Vardarophtsa and at Kilindir.[2] These two sites are of strategic importance. Vardarophtsa is near the southern end of the escarpment on which Vardina stands; it is close to a fine spring; and it commands the crossing of the Vardar at a point where it is easily forded in summer. Kilindir commands the entry into the central plain from the district of Lake Doiran; it stands on the north edge of a low escarpment beside a river flowing from Lake Doiran.[3] The earliest dwellings in both sites were wattle-and-daub huts; stone and timber were not employed either here or at Saratse or Molvopyrgo. Mud-brick, the only building material found at Molvopyrgo, came later to Vardarophtsa, where brick platforms were made to carry houses, which had some timber posts in the walls. The newcomers were able to drill holes in their stone celts, which were usually smaller in size than those of the Neolithic Age, and the perforated celt, making a better tool or weapon, spread throughout Macedonia. They could work metal: pieces of slag of gold, obtained from the Echedorus river, and of copper have been found, for instance, at Saratse. Yet most of their weapons and tools—arrow-heads, knives, and saws—were of flint or chert. They had few bone or horn implements, few figurines and few ornaments; characteristic of them are the anchor-shaped hooks of clay which were found in the first E.B.A. settlement at Kritsana and at Saratse (as in Fig. 4*a*).[4]

It seems clear that the newcomers prevailed by force of numbers; for their cultural standard was lower, and the only superior weapons they seem to have had were perforated stone celts, used as axes, and perhaps some copper knives. They drove the earlier people away from sites like Olynthus and Aivate, which were abandoned, and they superseded them at other sites such as Kritsana and Sedhes.[5] A pile-dwelling settlement made at Gona in the Early Bronze Age may be an exception to the general displacement of earlier peoples, if these pile-dwellers, as seems probable, were descended from the group of peoples whose settlements

---

[1] *AS* 11 (1961) 111.

[2] *PM* 110 with the footnotes, followed by *CAH*[3] 1. ii (1971) 774.

[3] *PM* 36 with a picture of the site and 31.

[4] I am drawing throughout on the descriptions in *PM*. For the hooks see *PM* 203 fig. 67 *g*, *i*, and *j*.

[5] The process was probably gradual. For instance at Vardina the last level of settlement contained a mixture of Neolithic pottery and a little E.B.A. pottery; as Vardarophtsa, built on the same escarpment as Vardina, was founded at the time of the fifth settlement at Kritsana, it is likely that some of the new pottery reached Vardina before the foundation of Vardarophtsa and the abandonment of Vardina. See *PM* 35.

1 Gajtan
2 Vučedol
3 Stobî
4 Tsepicovo
5 Suvodol
6 Crnobuki
7 Bukri
8 Kravari
9 Porodin
10 Pazhok
11 Malik
12 Armenokhori
13 Arnissa
14 Vajzë
15 Vodhinë
16 Aphiona
17 Terovo
18 Kilindir
19 Vardarophtsa
20 Gona
21 Sedhes
22 Kritsana
23 Saratse
24 Gioumenitza
25 Hagios Mamas
26 Molyvopyrgo
27 Vergina

Lake Skutari

Sitnica

•Priština

•Liplian

Mora

MT. ZRNA GORA

•Scodra
1

ZADRIMË

Drin

White Drin

•Prizren

Kačanik

•Kukës

•Tetovo

Kumanovo

Skopje
2

Gostivar•

ŠAR PLANINA

Tresca

Titov Veles

Vardar 3

•Kitsevo

MT. BABUNA

Epidamnus•

IONIAN

Mati

Black Drin

•Prilep

Cer

MT. BARNOU

GULF

Elbasan•

Shkumbi

10

Devoli

Ochrid•

Lake Ochrid

Cerna

4

5 6 7

Monastir•
8
9

Cerna

MT. BARNOU

Semeni

Apollonia•

•Berat

Osum

Aous

Lake Malik

11
Koritsa•

Lake Prespa

Florina•

Lake Ostrovo
12

Edessa
13

Valona•

14

Shushicë

Aous

Drin

Kastoria•

Lake Rudnik

Naoussa•
MT. BERMION

MT. GRAMMOS

Haliacmon

•Kozani

Servia•

15

Konitsa•

Aous

Grevena•

Kalamas

MT. PINDUS

16

Arachthus

Achelous

Peneus

•Triccala

CORCYRA

Ioannina•

Dodona•

17

MAP 20. EARLY AND MIDDI

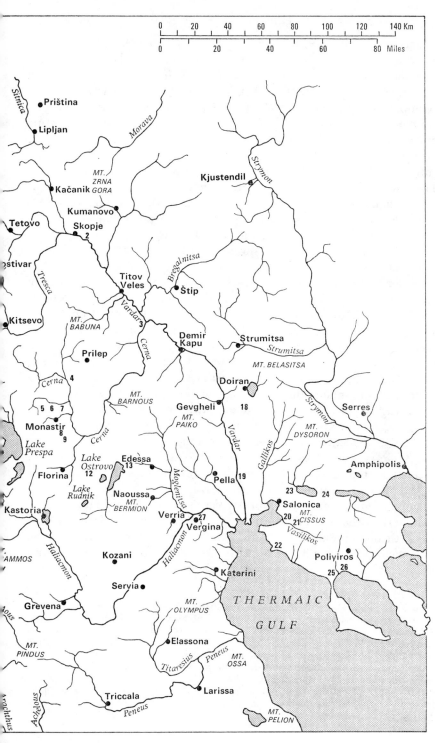

Priština
Lipljan

Sitnica
Morava

MT.
ZRNA
GORA
Kačanik

Kjustendil
Strymon

Kumanovo

Tetovo
Skopje
2

estivar
Tresca

Titov
Veles

Bregalnitsa

Štip

Kitsevo
MT.
BABUNA

Vardar
3

Cerna

Demir
Kapu

Strumitsa
Strumitsa

MT. BELASITSA

Prilep

Cerna
4

Doiran

MT.
BARNOUS

Gevgheli
18

Serres

5 6 7

MT.
PAIKO

MT.
DYSORON

Strymon

Monastir
8
9

Cerna

Lake
Prespa

Vardar

Gallikos

Lake
Ostrovo
12

Edessa
13

Moglenitsa

Amphipolis

Florina

Pella
19

Lake
Rudnik

Naoussa
MT.
BERMION

23
24

Kastoria

Verria
27
Vergina

Salonica
20
21
MT.
CISSUS

Haliacmon

Vasilikos

AMMOS

Kozani

Haliacmon

22

Poliyiros

25 26

Servia

Katerini

Grevena

MT.
OLYMPUS

THERMAIC

GULF

ous

MT.
PINDUS

Elassona

Titaresius
Peneus

MT.
OSSA

rachthus

Acheloos

Triccala
Peneus

Larissa

MT.
PELION

RONZE AGE SITES

are known at Malik and Kastoria (see pp. 229 f. above). The newcomers spread evidently into the western part of the central plain, as the Late Neolithic settlements at Nea Nikomedeia and Nea Nikomedeia East and those near Naoussa were all abandoned.[1] This intrusion was no doubt accompanied by a withdrawal, in part at least, of the earlier peoples into the higher cantons of Macedonia.[2] Meanwhile peoples of the same general origin occupied eastern Greece, especially south of Mt. Othrys; and it is probable that some at least came via southern Thrace and the central plain of Macedonia, and entered Thessaly.[3] As we shall see from the evidence at Servia, it is apparent that the invaders proceeded at first through Pieria and not through Elimea. We may assume then that Pieria also received a new layer of population, which occupied the rich coastal plain of Pieria down to the river Peneus.

In north-eastern Macedonia the Neolithic Age overlapped with the early phase of the Early Bronze Age of south-eastern Macedonia. The reason for this is that the newcomers did not penetrate to the north of Amphaxitis. But other intruders entered the upper Vardar valley, coming from the north and bringing a culture named Bubanj-Hum I after Bubanj-Hum near Niš.[4] They probably used the pass east of Mt. Zrna Gora and occupied the valley of the Vardar and its tributaries down to Demir Kapu. Their pottery, characterized by rippled or grooved ware, crusted ware, and coarse impressed ware with plastic moulding, predominated throughout this area; one of their sites was at Skopje on a high crag, a typical site for the Bubanj-Hum peoples, and they occupied Vršnik near Štip. One house of this period has been found at Demir Kapu; it is a rectangular house with a timber frame, superior to the contemporary huts of the central plain.[5] When pottery of the E.B.A. Macedonian type begins to appear in the area, it seems to have come not via Valandovo nor through the Demir Kapu pass, but via Lyncus and Pelagonia. On the other hand, one typical piece of Bubanj-Hum I ware was found in the first of the Bronze Age settlements at Kritsana.[6] To the north of the Vardar valley the Bubanj-Hum peoples overran the Predionica civilization in the Kossovo area and drove its survivors into the mountains.[7]

---

[1] See R. J. Rodden in *BS* 5 (1964) 115 f.

[2] Such a withdrawal may be seen not only in the positions of the Almopi, Crousaei, and Bottiaei of the classical period but also in the more recent situation in Epirus (see *Epirus* 27).

[3] In southern Thrace Akropotamos and Polystylo just east of the Strymon were abandoned at the end of the Neolithic period (*PAE* 1938. 103 f.), and Paradimi and Dikili Tash further inland suffered the same fate (*AS* 11 (1961) 103 f.). In Thessaly at Argissa a burnt layer and anchor-shaped hooks suggest the destruction of the site in E.H. II/III.

[4] For this culture see M. Garašanin in *39 BRGK* 53 f.   [5] Ibid. 120 f.

[6] *PM* 168 fig. 39i and Garašanin, op. cit. 63 n. 345, where he mistakenly refers the piece a pointed-base cup, to Vardarophtsa.

[7] *AI* 4 (1963) 14–15.

In Western Macedonia the last settlement of the Late Neolithic Age at Servia overlapped the beginnings of the Early Bronze Age in the southern part of Central Macedonia. In the uppermost levels Neolithic sherds and some Macedonian E.B.A. pottery were found and an anchor-shaped hook of clay. Heurtley dated this pottery to the same time as the first pottery at Vardarophtsa, corresponding to the third of the four Bronze Age settlements at Kritsana. The settlement at Servia was destroyed, probably by fire, and was abandoned.[1] It seems likely that this destruction was due to the new people of the central plain, who will have reached Servia by proceeding through Eordaea and Elimea. A settlement was founded at Armenokhori on an escarpment in the central plain of Lyncus in the Late Neolithic Age there, but probably within the Early Bronze Age of South-eastern Macedonia. Post-holes for a timber frame and a foundation wall of stones give an indication of the type of house at this time.[2] Here an anchor-shaped hook of clay was found, and the pottery shows the undoubted influence of Macedonian E.B.A. forms, especially in the two-handled tankard; moreover, as we have noticed above (p. 238), this influence spread from Armenokhori through Pelagonia into the Vardar valley. But a clear distinction was drawn by Heurtley between the pottery of Armenokhori and that of Southern Macedonia. Most of the divergent elements at Armenokhori (everted rims, plastic decoration especially of the tubular handles, and pockmarked bands and rims) are now seen to have been derived from Porodin and Crnobuki, which have been excavated since he wrote.[3] The settlement at Armenokhori came to an end probably early in the Macedonian Middle Bronze Age.[4]

In North-western Macedonia the Crnobuki culture in Pelagonia declined gradually, a result no doubt of the general turmoil to the east and to the south-east, and it came to an end when the Bubanj-Hum II peoples established themselves near Tsepicovo and at Suvodol.[5] At this stage the Armenokhori settlement was already established,[6] and it was the influences of the Macedonian Bronze Age there which predominated and even spread northwards and eastwards at the expense of the

[1] *PM* 55, 110, 203 fig. 67*f* (anchor-shaped hook).

[2] *PM* 57 and 81.

[3] *PM* 203 fig. 67*h*. *PM* 85 and 192 nos. 314 f. Compare M. Grbić, *Porodin* (1960) pl. 18, 3, 4, 5, 7, pl. 19, 1, 2, 5, 6, 8, pl. 20, 2, pl. 23, 4 and M. Garašanin in *Arheološki Vestnik* 4. 1 (1953) fig. 2*f*, fig. 6, fig. 7*a* for everted rims; *Porodin* pl. 22, 3, 7, 8, pl. 23, 1, 2, and pl. 24 and *Arheološki* figs. 14*d*, 17*b*, and 18 for various forms of plastic decoration of handles; *Porodin* pl. 15, 5, pl. 16, 3, 4, pl. 20, 2, 4, pl. 22, 7 and *Arheološki* fig. 7*b* for pockmarked bands and rims (cf. *PM* nos. 315, 321, 332, 346, 350, 355, 356, 358, 364–8, 371 for plastic decoration and pockmarking). The clay whorls with a flat base from Armenokhori (*PM* fig. 67*w–aa*) resemble *Arheološki* fig. 17*b* and *c*.

[4] *PM* 59 and 85.   [5] *AI* 4 (1963) 15.

[6] Some overlap seems to be indicated by the presence at Crnobuki of the Armenokhori type of two-handled tankard (*39 BRGK* 123).

Bubanj-Hum II culture. The new centres were at Bukri and Kravari in southern Pelagonia.[1] The peoples of northern Lyncus and Pelagonia seem to have revived and to have created there a particular form of Macedonian M.B.A. culture, which was noted by Heurtley.[2]

The general picture, then, in Western Macedonia is the progressive overthrow of the more artistic and advanced cultures of Servia and Crnobuki by two cruder cultures which impinged upon them, one coming from Central Macedonia and the other from the upper Vardar valley. The burning of the settlement at Servia suggests that the disaster was caused by descendants of the inaugurators of the Macedonian Bronze Age. Later Armenokhori was occupied by a further advance of the Macedonian Bronze Age people, perhaps in collaboration with the existing population. Soon afterwards Crnobuki came to an end through an invasion by Bubanj-Hum II peoples who made their own settlements in Pelagonia. Finally, already in the Middle Bronze Age, the Macedonian Bronze Age civilization, modified by the continuing population in Lyncus and Pelagonia, gained the ascendant and controlled the whole of Lyncus and Pelagonia. The pressure of these invasions must have tended to drive many of the earlier inhabitants from Western Macedonia westwards into central or southern Albania and from the Haliacmon valley westwards towards Epirus, areas into which they must have sent their sheep for winter pasture when Central Macedonia was hostile. There was at this time an intermingling of ideas in Western Macedonia. Weapons improved with the working of metal and with the perforation of celts and picks which were made in stone and horn as well as in metal; arrowheads were made, especially at Servia,[3] and the use of slings spread. The horse had appeared already in the Late Neolithic Age at Porodin and Tsiplevets as we see from figurines (Fig. 2f and 13j), and horse bones have been found in Central Macedonia in an E.B.A. context.[4]

The fusion of ideas produced new developments in pottery. The potter's wheel was used in the first of the E.B.A. settlements at Kritsana, and Heurtley suggested its use at Servia but with a question mark. In general pottery continued to be hand-made, but the technical knowledge of the wheel is likely to have spread.[5] The Bubanj-Hum II culture produced an unusual make and shape of pottery, which is almost indistinguishable from the ware which earned the name Minyan in Central

[1] *AI* 4 (1963) 15 and chronology on pl. 3. In the Monastir Museum I saw three very large stone perforated hammer-axes from Kravari, *c.* 7 inches long; iron ones of the same shape are used today near Demir Hissar for quarrying stone. One is shown in Fig. 13m.

[2] *PM* 85.   [3] *PM* 163 and 201, 77, 86.

[4] *PM* 88 in Early Bronze Age and 93 in Middle Bronze Age both 'in Central Macedonia'. Unnecessary doubts have been cast upon Heurtley's accuracy in this matter, e.g. by J. L. Caskey in *CAH*[3] I. i (1971) 775. The stone horse from Tsiplevets is in the Monastir museum, unpublished; the harness-lines show the horse was domesticated, as Professor Gimbutas pointed out to me.   [5] *PM* 80 n. 1 and 190.

Greece in Middle Helladic times.[1] The Bubanj-Hum pottery in the Middle Balkans was known in Pelagonia at an earlier date than in Greece. When this type of pottery became familiar to the artistically gifted peoples of Pelagonia, they produced a pottery which was a blend of the Bubanj-Hum pottery and of the Macedonian E.B.A. pottery. This blend foreshadowed even more closely the Greek type of Minyan pottery. When Heurtley wrote in 1939 that 'it is especially interesting to find that vases like Minyan in form and fabric . . . could evolve (i.e. in Pelagonia) without external influences',[2] he was thinking of the later situation in Greece. It is a point of special interest that two of the features normally associated with the coming of 'the Greeks', namely the horse and pottery of 'Minyan' type appeared in Western Macedonia some time before they made an appearance in Greece.

When we look further west, we find that the large and flourishing settlement at Malik entered a less rich period, but without any sign of an abrupt break in the continuity of its culture. This period, called IIb by the excavators, seems to have begun after the irruption of the newcomers into Central Macedonia and the severing of the trade routes with the Thermaic Gulf and later with Thessaly.[3] There is now a less wide range of painted pottery and of decoration, and there is little contact with Macedonia. An anchor-shaped hook of clay comes from Malik IIb, indicating some contact with the invaders of Central Macedonia (Fig. 4a).

The pottery is still of a very high quality, but different shapes come into fashion: wide bowls with an almost vertical collar (Fig. 4b), which occur in Macedonia only at Servia;[4] basins with thick inturning rims, sometimes ornamented with grooves (Fig. 4c),[5] which are found in Late Neolithic Macedonia but with such an ornament only once at Armenokhori; one-handled cups (Fig. 4d), occurring in Macedonia but not of the same shape;[6] and large squat jars with dwarf handles high on the shoulders and an almost vertical collar (Fig. 4e), which are unlike anything in Macedonia.[7] There is a fondness now for fluting, again unlike anything in Macedonia.[8] These wares with vertical collars and fluting (Fig. 4f) seem to imitate shapes and decoration appropriate to metal

---

[1] M. Garašanin in *39 BRGK* 63 wrote 'In Form und Machart ist in Rahmen unseres Stufe manches von den Begleiterscheinungen der mynischen Ware kaum zu trennen'. He refers to Minyan ware at Eutresis, Korakou, Asine, and Lerna.   [2] *PM* 85.

[3] Only one piece of graphite ware shows contact with the eastern part of Macedonia. It comes early in IIb; *SA* 1966. 1. 261.

[4] Ibid. 260 f. and pl. xi, 16, 18 and 21–5; *PM* 144 nos. 50, 51, 82–4. For the hook pl. iii*f*.

[5] *SA* 261 and pl. xi, 15; the shape at Gioumenitza (*PM* 155 nos. 129 and 130) is Late Neolithic Age, and the decoration on a basin is from the L.N.A. level at Armenokhori (*PM* 151 no. 104).   [6] *SA* pl. xi, 1–5.   [7] Ibid. pl. xi, 17.

[8] Ibid. pl. xi, on ten of the twenty-five vessels illustrated for this period; in the text p. 261 Prendi describes the fluting as 'cannelures'.

vessels. The closest parallels for the shapes are to be found in the silver pots and vases of the 'Kurgan' peoples who buried their chiefs in pit-graves under a tumulus (*kurgan*); there too the large squat jars with high-set dwarf handles are found.[1] These are dated in South Russia to Troy II and onwards, which accords with the Macedonian Early Bronze Age.[2] The marked change in pottery can be explained best by the arrival at Malik and further west in central Albania of a people with a new Kurgan-like culture. Another site with Malik IIb culture has been found at the Cave of Tren, on the south-west side of Little Prespa Lake; it stands 856 m high and is near the route from Malik to Macedonia.[3] On the Macedonian analogies this phase seems to end soon after the destruction of Servia.

The last stage of Malik IIb overlaps with the beginning of Malik IIIa. A new type of two-handled tankard appears (Fig. 4 *g* and *h*), different from the Macedonian E.B.A. tankard but designed probably for the same sort of drink.[4] The celts, including the flat celts, almost disappear. Instead there are hammer-axes and hammers, well polished and per-forated; at this time these weapons were widespread in the Danubian area and were used by Kurgan peoples.[5] An unusual type of barbotine decoration on thick-walled ware begins at the end of Malik IIb, is popular throughout Malik IIIa, and then disappears altogether. This decoration produces a rough surface of small lumps, as if clay had been splattered on the pot before firing. As Prendi points out, this form of decoration is typical of the coarse ware of Porodin and occurs in the Bubanj-Hum pottery, as well as further afield in northern Yugoslavia and in Bulgaria. In particular it occurs at Cnossus but only in M.M. Ia and Ib.

This fact enables us to date the beginning of Malik IIIa approximately in E.H. III, that is in terms of Macedonian chronology to the time of the last E.B.A. settlement at Kritsana.[6] The occurrence of this barbotine

---

[1] Gimbutas, *Prehistory* i pl. 10 from Maikop, pl. 11, 1 from Kuban, and pl. 18 from the catacomb-graves (later in date than the pit-graves); for the jars pl. 12, 4 and 5 from Tsarskaia. Compare too the globular handle-less pot in *SA* pl. xi, 11 with that in *Prehistory* pl. 11*i* from Staromyshastovskaia in Kuban.

[2] M. Gimbutas, *Prehistory* 91 and V. Milojčić, *Chronologie* 46.

[3] *SA* 1967. 1. 142 f.; it is near the point where the Ventrok irrigation canal draws water from the lake. Hearths with polished sides and several layers of clay slip were found.

[4] The two handles are set low: *SA* 1966. 1. 261 and pl. xi, 6–8.

[5] Ibid. 262; Childe, *Danube* 121 and fig. 76*d*; M. Gimbutas, *Prehistory*, 57 and 107 with fig. 59, 18 and 19.

[6] *SA* 1966. 1. 263–4 and pl. xii, 20; M. Grbić, *Porodin* pl. 15, 1 and 2 and pl. 35 upper middle; A. J. Evans, *The Palace of Minos*, 1. 179 f. and figs. 128 and 129*a*. Frano Prendi in *SA* 277 has noted an overlap in ornamentation between the pottery of the middle stage of Malik IIIa and the pottery of Kostolac, for which a C-14 date of 1900 B.C. ± 100 has been given. This supports the proposed dating of Malik IIIa. For the Kostolac or Cotofeni culture see M. Gimbutas, *Bronze Age Cultures in Central and Eastern Europe* (1965) 185 f.

decoration at Malik shows that some of the Porodin people of Pelagonia had moved through the corridor of the lakes and formed part of the community near and in Malik at this time; their move was a result no doubt of the impact of the Bubanj-Hum invaders (see p. 240 above). But the dominant people at Malik, when the M.H. period began, were those who had come from the north with hammer-axes, hammers, and two-handled tankards. They seem to have avoided Pelagonia by following the Tresca valley and the Saletska valley into the corridor of the lakes (see pp. 95 f. above).

Against this background of the movements of peoples in Western Macedonia we may set the two burials which Heurtley regarded as the most important find of his excavation at Servia.[1] The place of burial was well within the settlement. A circular shaft, 1·20 m in diameter, had been cut through the layer of clay and burnt debris, which had been a house-floor of the last Early Neolithic settlement, and sunk to a depth of o·60 m, and the body was laid on its right side in a contracted position, the head facing westwards, on the hard earth floor at the bottom of the shaft (Fig. 5a). The sides of the shaft had probably been lined with cobbles, and, as we shall see from analogies elsewhere, the mortuary chamber is likely to have been roofed. When the shaft was excavated, Heurtley noted that the cobbles had fallen in, that soft dark earth 'unlike the clay which otherwise covered the area' was in the shaft, and that above the body there was a layer of wood-fire ash lying on a slope in relation to the floor of the shaft. I should account for this sloping but intact layer by supposing that the roof collapsed first on one side of the shaft and that soil came in on the other side later. In the layer of ashes there were fragments of vases, 'some apparently broken before they were placed in the ashes', and in the soft dark earth of the shaft there were bones, some of them burnt; from this it is clear that a funerary sacrifice or feast with a fire took place, and that the broken pottery and the ashes were spread over the roof of the mortuary chamber.

At a later time a secondary burial was made. The body was laid just above the original burnt level, and it seems likely that it was partly above and partly beyond the edge of the original shaft, as the positions of the skull and of the bones (5 and 4 in Fig. 5a) indicate.[2] In other words the secondary burial was made when the roof of the primary mortuary chamber was intact. It follows that a mound of earth was raised above the secondary burial, in order to protect the corpse from scavengers.

[1] The description is rather scattered in *PM*, the main points being made on pp. 54 f. and p. 79; figs. 44 and 45 show the head faced westwards; fig. 50 shows the position of the corpse. One vase is shown as the frontispiece in *PM*.

[2] Heurtley remarked on p. 79 that 'of the later burial the bones and part of the skull were found but all was in confusion'; as this burial had not been robbed, the confusion may have been caused by the collapse of the roof over the original burial.

It is probable then that a tumulus of this 'soft dark earth'[1] stood originally over these two burials. We shall see similar examples in Albania.

At the bottom of the shaft under the right arm of the skeleton an obsidian blade was found, and in the crook of the arm part of an incised zoomorphic vase (Fig. 4*k*). From the sherds in the layer of wood-ash three vases were restored (one in Fig. 4*j*), and the foot of one of them contained red matter, 'perhaps ochre';[2] at the same level as the sherds were five waisted pebble-axes (as in Fig. 4*i*), a small celt, and a piece of a rectangular whetstone—objects dedicated presumably to the dead man. Associated in the same way with the secondary burial were two waisted pebble-axes, two small celts, an obsidian blade, part of a bracelet and a lid both of marble, two broken pins of bone, and a clay phallus vertically perforated (as in Fig. 3*c* 1). It is to be noted that the zoomorphic vase, the use of ochre, the waisted pebble-axe, the marble bracelet, and the phallus are, to quote Heurtley in a different context,[3] 'at home in the Danube region and appear *intrusively* in Macedonia'. The manner of burial too is of northern origin; for it appears to be that used for the chieftains of the Kurgan peoples.

A clue to the date of the secondary burial is afforded by a vase which stood beside it, Heurtley's no. 76 (Fig. 4*m*), assigned to the later phase at Servia, that is to the later part of Servia IIb.[4] If my inference is correct

---

[1] Similar black soil was used for the tumulus over Grave Circle B at Mycenae; it was found there on both sides of the wall and elsewhere, and it was unlike the red soil which was dumped there later. See my article in *BSA* 62 (1967) 86 f.

[2] *PM* 79 n. 4 in vase no. 42.

[3] *PM* 114 f., writing generally of the Macedonian Late Neolithic Age. The quotation is from p. 116. Waisted pebble-axes are found in considerable numbers at Servia (see fig. 33*m* and pp. 77, 79, 86); only one possible example is from Central Macedonia (at Molyvopyrgo, fig. 65*o* and p. 86 n. 2). Heurtley saw many specimens of this axe from Csoka in the museum at Szeged in Hungary (*PM* 120). Subsequent discoveries have shown the correctness of Heurtley's view. This type of zoomorphic vase and the phallus are characteristic of the Danilo and the Kakanj cultures of central Yugoslavia in the Middle Neolithic Age, except thàt the incisions on the vases there are not filled with white. The zoomorphic vase is typical also of the Neolithic Copper Age site at Kodjadermen in north-east Bulgaria (*Bull. de la soc. archéol. bulgare* vi (1916) pl. iv, 1 and 2), and a leg of one with white filling of the incisions was found at a Neolithic site near Salmanovo in the same part of Bulgaria (ibid. iv (1914) 152 fig. iii). In Greece the earliest examples of the zoomorphic vase with white-filled incisions come from Corinth and Elatea, where S. S. Weinberg dates them to the Middle Neolithic Age (*Hesp.* 31 (1962) 190 f., and *CAH*[3] 1. i. (1970) 598). I saw a piece of another example in the museum at Monastir in 1968; it came from Tsiplevets near the Cerna Reka in Pelagonia, and is unpublished. One from Tsangli is illustrated in *PTh* fig. 50*a*, and it is dated to the Late Neolithic Age in Thessaly (*PTh* 99 and 114). Another was found in the tumulus at Chaeronea (*AM* 30 (1905) 123 fig. 2*c* and 137 fig. 9). The earliest phallus with testicles comes from Elatea (*Hesp.* 31. 202 and pl. 68, 2); next is a phallus with red paint from Tsangli (*PTh* 123 and fig. 76*j*) of the Middle Neolithic Age; phalli with testicles and without testicles were found at Malik IIa of the Late Neolithic Age (*SA* 1966. 1. pl. x*b* = Fig. 3*c* here), both types occurring also at Servia. The zoomorphic vase and the phallus are thought to have been the female and the male aspects of a fertility rite.   [4] *PM* 73 and 147.

that the secondary burial was made not long after the first burial, the first burial was rather late in Servia IIb; and this seems to be confirmed by the fact that one of the vases in the layer of wood-ash was a four-legged table vase, Heurtley's no. 91 (Fig. 4*l*), also assigned by him to the later phase at Servia.[1] Thus the evidence inclines towards a date corresponding in Greece to E.H. I.

My conclusion is at variance with that of Heurtley, who put the first burial in the time of Servia IIa, that is in the Neolithic Age, and the secondary burial in Servia IIb, the latter with a mark of interrogation. He did so probably because the cut of the shaft was through the burnt layer of the last Early Neolithic settlement, and he inferred that the shaft 'followed the destruction' of Servia I more or less immediately.[2] But the inference is not a necessary one. If we suppose that a tumulus was raised at once over the burnt layer of Servia I, it is possible that a long time elapsed before a burial was made in it; for this is what J. L. Caskey believes to have occurred at Lerna, where the debris was shaped into a low tumulus on the destruction of the House of Tiles at E.H. II/III and the first burial was made in the Middle Bronze Age, when a shaft was sunk through the tumulus and the burnt layer and was then continued below it.[3] On the other hand, if at Servia the burial was made and the tumulus was raised with 'the soft dark earth' immediately afterwards, it is probable that the space was cleared down to the hard burnt layer just before the burial-shaft was dug.

While the analogy between Servia and Lerna is fairly close in kind, the analogy between Servia and the earliest tumulus-burials in Leucas is closer in date; for the sauce-boats and the fruit-stand found there in R 1, R 16, and R 26 C are typical of E.H. II, and may even date to E.H. I.[4] The rectangular shaft of R 1 was sunk 0·85 m below the then ground level; the mortuary chamber had walls of round stones or cobbles, and, as Dörpfeld inferred,[5] a roof of stone slabs set on wooden rafters (Fig. 5*c*). At the bottom of the shaft the primary burial was in a pithos containing some very decayed bones and a gold necklace, a silver armband, 18 obsidian blades, 2 flint scrapers, a thin copper plate with two perforations, and 4 pots; and outside the pithos were 2 obsidian blades, some flakes of flint, a spinning-weight and a pot. Above this burial there was a layer

---

[1] *PM* 73 and 150. Vase no. 15, also associated with this burial, may be of an earlier style in Servia II, but it had been much mended; it is shown as the frontispiece and is described on pp. 67 and 141.

[2] *PM* 54 and the notes to fig. 49.

[3] *Hesp.* 25 (1956) 165 and fig. 3; *CAH*[3] II. 1. 125 The second shaft-grave was outside the tumulus. Heurtley wrote of course before the excavation of Lerna.

[4] So A. J. B. Wace in *BSA* 25. 124 and J. L. Caskey in *CAH*[3] II. 1. 128 *contra* F. H. Stubbings in *Companion to Homer* 411 f. See my article in *BSA* 62 (1967) 77 f.

[5] *Alt-Ithaka* I. 223 f.

of flat slabs, sunk in the centre (perhaps the covering of a collapsed roof), and above this layer Dörpfeld thought there had been a secondary burial, robbed in ancient times. The whole had been covered with a low tumulus of soil, retained by a low dry wall of white stones forming a ring 9·20 m in diameter.[1]

While there are points of difference between the burials at Servia and the earliest burials at Leucas, such as the use of a pithos and stone slabs at Leucas, there are numerous features in common—the shaft sunk below ground level, the association with the corpse of three or four vases, weapons, tools, and jewellery, the roofed mortuary chamber, the secondary burial above the roof, and some sort of tumulus—and these features are completely distinctive. This type of burial is unknown in Central and in Eastern Macedonia, but such a burial was made at Vergina on the southern side of the Haliacmon river in Tumulus Γ, which is 1 m high and 16 m in diameter. In the centre of the tumulus Andronikos found the remains of a deep shaft. For the first 0·40 m it was 2·10 × 1·20 m with one rounded end and reached the original ground surface; for the next 0·65 m it was a circular shaft 1·20 m in diameter and at the bottom there was a layer of sand 0·05 m thick except in one sector (see Fig. 5*b*); for the next 0·45 m the shaft continued down to the virgin soil of sandy gravel. The whole of the shaft was filled with very soft, damp, clean soil. The analogy with the pit at Servia is striking: the soft, dark earth, the circular shaft 1·20 m in diameter, the depth 0·60 m at Servia and 0·65 m down to the layer of sand at Vergina. The layer of sand is immediately explained by the layer of ash, which came between the two burials at Servia. The sandless sector evidently marks an entry made into the lower burial in order to remove the remains. Thus, as at Servia, we have evidence of two burials one above the other, made in a circular shaft driven below ground level and covered with a tumulus. Nothing was found in the shaft except a sherd of unpurified clay from a large pot with a tongue-shaped lug at the north-west edge of the shaft 0·10 m down. The remains of both burials, including the pottery, had evidently been removed.[2]

It is natural to look westwards in search of a common origin for these customs at Servia and Vergina and at Leucas in E.H. I–II, especially

---

[1] Some of the objects from R 1 are illustrated in *Alt-Ithaka* 2 Beil. 64, 1–3; Beil. 60, 1 and 5; Beil. 62, 10; Beil. 61 b 7; Beil. 63, 6. The ring-wall of the tumulus varied in height from something less than 15 cm to something like 50 cm, and the individual stones were from 4 cm to 15 cm thick. In *BSA* 62 (1967) 92 f. I discuss also R 16 and R 26 C which are other early burials; for the sauce-boat in R 16 see Beil. 65, 1.

[2] *PAE* 1952. 227 and fig. 12. Andronikos did not refer to the burial at Servia but to a burial pit in Poland, which has less similarity (Childe, *Danube* 149 and fig. 93). In his final publication, *Vergina*, p. 14, he attributes the pit to the action of ancient tomb-robbers, but I cannot believe that tomb-robbers would have dug so neat a pit and introduced a layer of sand. For the Vergina cemetery see pp. 328 f. below.

as some of the objects with the primary burial at Servia recur at Malik IIa.[1] In the years since 1952 a large number of tumulus-burials have been excavated in Albania in the plain of Zadrimë, in the valley of the river Mati, in the sink between the Shkumbi and the Devoli by Pazhok, at Vajzë not far from Velcë, and at Vodhinë and other places in the valley of the Kseria river, which is a tributary of the Drin in north Epirus.[2] Although the excavators dated them at first to the end of the Bronze Age or to the Early Iron Age, I have shown in my book on Epirus that some objects associated with the earlier burials were of M.H. date.[3] Such a date was subsequently given by the excavators in 1964 for some objects found at Pazhok. It seems then that we should place the common origin of the customs seen at Servia and at Leucas in the area of northern and central Albania.

At the risk of trespassing on the Middle Bronze Age I may mention here some points in the burials at Pazhok which show kinship with those at Servia and at Leucas. Thus the body was laid on the right side, the legs bent, the head usually looking towards the west;[4] this is the position at Servia also. The primary burial in the inner (older) tumulus of one double tumulus at Pazhok was in a circular shaft, sunk somewhat less than a metre below the then ground level (Fig. 5*d*), as at Servia, and the primary burial in another was in a rectangular shaft lined with unworked stones or cobbles and probably roofed, as in R 1 at Leucas.[5] The periphery of each tumulus was marked by a ring of stones: of orthostats in the inner tumulus with the circular shaft, and of roundish white stones in the outer tumulus, as at Leucas. The diameter of the ring of the inner tumulus at Pazhok has been estimated by me to be 11 m, while that at Leucas was 9·20 m.[6] Secondary burials were found in both inner tumuli at Pazhok, as at Servia and at Leucas. An ox had been sacrificed in the inner circular shaft at Pazhok; this may be compared with the evidence of a sacrifice or a feast at Servia over the primary burial. Associated with the burials at Pazhok were weapons, tools, jewellery, and a number of pots. The excavators dated the objects from the central burials to 1800–1700 B.C. However, as the preliminary report of Pazhok is exceedingly brief, it would be rash to exclude the possibility of an E.H. date for the

[1] Thus Malik IIa has the waisted pebble-axe, the same kind of phallus, the zoomorphic vase, and the four-legged table vase or altar (*SA* 1964. 1 pl. xa 1, *b*, *c*, and *h*; also Pl. v, 27; and p. 260 especially).

[2] *SA* 1964. 1. 101 (Zadrimë); *BUSS* 1955. 1 and *SA* 101 (Mati valley where thirty-five tumuli were excavated); *SA* 101 (Pazhok where there are some twenty-five tumuli); *BUSS* 1957. 2. 76 f. (Vajzë); *BUSS* 1956. 1. 180 f. and *BUST* 1959. 2. 190 f. (Vodhinë, etc.). I have reported fully on these in *Epirus* 201 f. and in *BSA* 62 (1967) 77 f.

[3] *Epirus* 203, 228 f., 310 f. and 340 f.

[4] *SA* 1964. 1. 96 and *BSA* 62 (1967) 79.

[5] The shafts are illustrated in *SA* 1964. 1. pl. v, 2 and 4 and in *BSA* 62 pl. 18, 2, 3, and 4.

[6] *SA* pl. v, 2, and *BSA* 62 pl. 18, 2.

earliest burials. The same may be said of the tumuli excavated at Vajzë and at Vodhinë.[1]

We may conclude from the evidence at Servia, at Leucas, and at Pazhok, Vajzë, and Vodhinë that chieftains, who were buried in the Kurgan manner, were already established in E.H. I in the lowlands of central Albania. One branch of them had possession of Servia on the route of trade with Thessaly. Another branch learned seafaring, perhaps on Lake Scodra with its navigable river into the Adriatic Sea, and took possession of the Nidhri Plain, which overlooks the southern entry to the Channel between Leucas and the mainland. One distinctive ornament on the Kurgan pottery was made by pressing cord on the wet clay. This so-called 'corded ware' or 'Schnurkeramik' was found at the Nisos site on Aphiona, a peninsula of north-west Corcyra, and it was dated there to the Late Neolithic and Early Bronze Ages.[2] These Kurgan chieftains were no doubt in control of the trade route which led by sea and by land from the Mediterranean areas into the Adriatic Sea and then via the island of Hvar to central Europe. A distinctive possession of the Kurgan people was the horse, and the figurine of a horse's head at Porodin[3] in Pelagonia indicates that some Kurgan people reached this area as early as the latter part of the Late Neolithic Age. If so, they were an offshoot of the so-called 'Kurgan IV' wave of Kurgan peoples, which has been dated to *c.* 2500 B.C.[4]

These Kurgan chieftains and their followers during the E.H. period were far more gifted and enterprising than the peoples who spread from the east over Central Macedonia, and also than the carriers of the Bubanj-Hum culture who came from the north into the Vardar valley. However, by the end of the E.H. period it was the two latter peoples who seem to have advanced, the one to Armenokhori and the other to Bukri in north-western Macedonia. The pressures they exerted seem to have pushed some of the Pelagonian peoples into Albania, following the course taken earlier by some carriers of the Porodin culture. And it was perhaps from Albania and Leucas that the people came who built a low tumulus at Lerna at the transition of E.H. II to III and brought with them the perforated hammer-axe of stone.

---

[1] For instance the kite-shaped dagger shown in *BUSS* 1957. 2. Fig. 15a = *Epirus* 329 and fig. 21, D2, is of M.H. date (I saw a similar one in Vienna) ; it came from Grave 14 in tumulus A at Vajzë. Again the M.M. daggers come from the burials of stage 2 of the Vodhinë tumulus, and there is no clue to the dating of Grave 18, the earliest in stage 1 of the tumulus (see *Epirus* 203).

[2] *AM* 59 (1934) 174 fig. 7 and 188, being Kanze's dating. For corded ware and the Kurgan peoples see R. A. Crossland in *CAH*[3] I. ii (1971) 872, and M. Gimbutas, *Bronze Age* 185.   [3] M. Grbić, *Porodin* (1960) pl. 32, 6 ; see p. 224 above.

[4] Gimbutas, *Prehistory* 70 naming this earliest form 'the Pit-grave phase', that is burial in the pit or shaft under a tumulus or barrow, which is exemplified by those at Pazhok. See also Crossland, loc. cit., and my article in *RSA* 62 (1967) 77 f.

Before we leave the Early Bronze Age we must refer briefly to the excavations made in 1961–3 at Gajtan, which is in the plain some 5 km east of Scodra. The site is at the foot of a hill, which was fortified later, and in many ways it resembles the Bronze Age site at Kastritsa near the Lake of Ioannina. In a preliminary report in *SA* 1964. 1. 97 f. Selim Islami and Hasan Ceka dated the two earliest layers to the close of the Bronze Age and to the Early Iron Age, but a study of their report and of the illustrations led me to date them to the same periods as Malik II and Malik III. I gave my reasons in *BSA* 62 (1968) 103 f. Meanwhile a fuller report has been published by Bep Rebani in *StH* 1966. 1. 41 f. with the title 'Keramika ilire e cytezës se Gajtanit'; it is written in a dialect of Albanian which I find difficult to understand, but it has useful illustrations. Rebani has followed his colleagues in a late dating of the finds, but the analogies with Malik II and with Porodin show that the early dating which I suggested in *BSA* is correct.

In the earliest layer, Gajtan I, there is a deeply-incised ware with many round punctures, sometimes arranged in bands and sometimes scattered (*StH* 44 fig. 2 *b*, *c*, and *e*). Such systems of punctures are very common at Porodin (Grbić, *Porodin* pl. xiv. 3, 4, and 6), and they occur quite often at Malik IIa and at Malik IIb (*SA* 1966 1 pls. viii and ix). Incised parallel lines or parallel grooves, lines of jabs, and thin lines are common to Gajtan I and Malik IIa (*StH* 44 and *SA* pl. viii). The use of plastic mammiform knobs is common to Gajtan I, Porodin, and Malik II (*StH* 43 fig.1*a*; *Porodin* pl. xvi. 1; *SA* pls. ix and xi. 20). Only a few shapes of vessels from Gajtan are shown in *StH* pls. i and ii; they resemble those of Malik IIb in *SA* pl. xi.

However, the ledge-lug and the tongue- or teat-shaped lug of Gajtan (*StH* 43 fig. 1 *b* and *c*) are not at all typical of Malik II, and they show that Gajtan was subject to influences from the north. One of these influences is indicated by the occurrence of 'corded ware' ornament, used in combination with rows of punctures and jabs (Fig. 4*n*), and another is the use of related kinds of incision which have been called 'falsches Schnurornament' by M. Ebert in *Reallexikon der Vorgeschichte* xi 304. Their appearance at Gajtan I is of value for dating, and it also shows that the makers of a 'corded ware', probably a Kurgan people, were in control of this rich plain in the Late Neolithic Age and in the Early Bronze Age. A few pieces of corded ware have been found further south in the E.B.A. settlements at Hagios Mamas and at Kritsana in Chalcidice (*PM* 83 and 172); at Aphiona in Corcyra in a settlement of L.N.A. or E.B.A. date; and at Kastritsa near Ioannina, where it may be of E.B.A. or of early M.B.A. date (*Epirus* 309).

In Gajtan II some features of Gajtan I continue in use, such as the plastic mammiform knobs (*StH* 52 fig. 2 *b* and *c*), the punctures and the incised parallel grooves (*StH* 55 fig. 8 *h* and *k*), but there are many more geometric arrangements of incised decoration, which resemble closely those of Malik IIb (*StH* 55 fig. 8 *a* to *g, j*; *SA* pls. xi. 19, xii. 11, and xiii. 11 and 25). The use of tiny punctured or pricked decoration is common to Gajtan II and Malik IIb (*StH* 55 fig. 8*e*, and *SA* pl. xiv, second row from the foot) and so are the uses of plastic coils, both plain and finger-impressed, plastic handles shaped like an ear or like two ears back to back, and fluting on the shoulder of pots (*StH* fig. 9 and pl. V; *SA* pl. ix right-hand corner, pl. xi. 21 and 23, and pl. xiv). The plastic coils carry us into Malik IIIa. One remarkable plastic ornament in Gajtan II is an anchor-shaped hook with indications of four perforations in its shank (Fig. 4*o*); an actual hook of this kind in clay was found at Malik IIb (Fig. 4*a*). As we have seen, hooks of this shape are thought to have been introduced into Macedonia by eastern invaders at the beginning of the Early Bronze Age, and to have spread thence during the Early Bronze Age. In shapes of vessels there are similarities between Gajtan II and Malik IIb, especially in the cups (*StH* pls. iii–ix; the cups in pl. viii may be compared with those of Malik IIb in *SA* pl. xiii), but there is a wider range of experiment in the shapes of handles at Gajtan than at Malik. It would seem then that Gajtan Ia and Gajtan II were approximately contemporary with Malik IIa and Malik IIb, with the last part of Gajtan II overlapping the start of Malik IIIa. The site was abandoned early in the Middle Bronze Age.

IX

THE REMAINS OF THE MIDDLE BRONZE
AGE, AND THE CONNECTIONS WITH
THE TUMULI AND THE CIST TOMBS
IN GREECE

WHEREAS imports to Kritsana in the E.H. period were limited to one sherd and perhaps two bits of obsidian, the history of Molyvopyrgo in the M.H. period is one of imported 'Minyan' pottery from the south, so much so that the site was probably in the hands of southern settlers.[1] The pottery at Molyvopyrgo is both wheel-made and hand-made, and local Macedonian shapes such as the jug with cut-away neck and the wish-bone handle were made there in proper Minyan fabric. On the other hand, the local and rather stagnant style of the Early Bronze Age continued at other sites in Chalcidice, and even nearby Hagios Mamas was unaffected by the Molyvopyrgo 'Minyan' pottery until late in the Middle Bronze Age. Then a local variant of Minyan ware with grooved ornamentation appeared at Hagios Mamas and spread through Chalcidice.[2]

Central Macedonia stagnated. It seems to have lost touch with Chalcidice; for imported sherds of proper Minyan ware numbered only two or three, found at Vardarophtsa and Kilindir. The pottery was mainly a continuation of the E.B.A. incised and plain wares. A submergence of those Anatolian elements which had been introduced by the invaders early in the Early Bronze Age was noted by Heurtley, and the individual sites began to develop local preferences in the use of particular ornaments in the incised wares.[3] The only general change was the growing popularity of the wish-bone handle (Fig. 8 *i–l*), which became a distinguishing characteristic of Macedonian culture, and the introduction of a toothed instrument for making several incised lines, just as a multiple brush makes several parallel lines in painting. Tools were comparatively rare, metals rarer even than in the Early Helladic, and very few building remains or imported objects have been found

---

[1] *PM* 91 f. and 123. We do not know whether such settlers came from Thessaly and central Greece, as Heurtley was inclined to suggest in *PM* 123, or from further south as Mylonas thought in Πρακτικὰ τῆς Ἀκαδημίας Ἀθηνῶν 1931. 106–13. 'Minyan' pottery might have come from Troy as well, since Molyvopyrgo was near the coasting route from Greece to Troy.

[2] *PM* 91 and fig. 75.   [3] *PM* 89 f., 111, 122 f.

except at Molyvopyrgo, itself probably a foreign settlement. Animal bones include those of the horse, as in the Early Bronze Age. Overland contact with the south and with the west seems generally to have ceased.[1] Servia was no longer occupied.

The story is much the same in the Vardar valley north of Demir Kapu. The slow-moving influence of Central Macedonia seems to have penetrated this area, coming via Armenokhori, and there was some fusion of that influence with the Bubanj-Hum culture in the areas of Stobi and Skopje, where Macedonian incised wares appear.[2] In Pelagonia the influence of Central Macedonia spread likewise via Armenokhori and became strong at such sites as Bukri. It was in Pelagonia, as we have seen (p. 241 above), that the mixture of the Bubanj-Hum style and the Crnobuki style had led to the emergence of what may be called the Macedonian form of Minyan pottery. During the M.H. period a small amount of this type of pottery appeared in Central Macedonia, while the true or Greek type of Minyan ware was restricted to Molyvopyrgo until the last phase of the period.[3] Thus what is strictly speaking the West-Macedonian form of Minyan pottery is chronologically and geographically independent of the Greek Minyan pottery of Molyvopyrgo; it was an original creation in Pelagonia, whereas it was imported at Molyvopyrgo, and it began in Pelagonia either late in the Early Helladic or very early in the Middle Helladic period. Throughout the M.H. period Pelagonia seems to have remained well-populated and more inventive than the rest of Macedonia.

It has long been maintained, and it seems likely to be true, that Greek-speaking peoples of the Indo-European group entered the Greek peninsula in the course of the M.H. period; that on linguistic evidence these peoples herded sheep and cattle, had domesticated the horse and the dog, and first met the sea in the vicinity of Greece; and that in general terms they had come from the north, that is overland into the southern Balkans. As far as Central Macedonia, the vicinity of Servia, and the Vardar valley north of Demir Kapu are concerned, we can say that Macedonia was a backwater, generally stagnant and shut off from outside influences, indeed still dominated by the unenterprising peoples who had come from Anatolia and introduced the Bronze Age. On the present evidence it is obvious that the Greek-speaking invaders of the peninsula did not start from that part of Macedonia or make their passage through it. We must look rather to Pelagonia and to the areas further west. We must also bear in mind the probability that the invaders had lived for

---

[1] *PM* 123. 'Thus, apart from Chalcidice, there is really no special evidence either from the pottery or the metal objects of external relations at this time.'

[2] M. Garašanin, *39 BRGK* 120 f. with influences coming via Armenokhori (p. 123) and a summary of the Middle Bronze Age (p. 124).

[3] *PM* 85 and 91 f.

some length of time in a zone of transitional climate between central Europe and Mediterranean Greece, before they moved forward in the M.H. period and settled in the south. Such a zone includes the coastal plain of Albania, the lowlands of Epirus, the lowlands of Macedonia, and the seaward-facing base of the Chalcidic peninsula.

The first striking feature of the Middle Bronze Age in the west is the occupation of northern and central Epirus, hitherto very thinly inhabited, by 'a shepherd people, whose culture was derived from Macedonia', and the spread of peoples with a similar, though generally less crude culture into Corcyra, Leucas, Ithaca, and Aetolia.[1] Since I wrote to that effect in 1964, I have become familiar with the publication of the Porodin culture. It is obvious at a glance that there is almost identity between the unpainted potteries of Porodin and Epirus. They both have raised plastic bands impressed with round pock-marks running just below the rim or round the shoulder; rough blobs, mammiform protuberances, large and small lumps of different sizes added to the surface of the pots; jags, commas, and round holes punched in the surface with some tools; and moulded arcading below the rim.[2] Some examples are shown in Figs. 6–8. The range and the profusion of these plastic forms of decoration are peculiar to Porodin and Epirus. Individual examples occur elsewhere, for example at Velcë and at Malik, but not in such concentration. It seems likely, as we mentioned above (p. 243), that some people with the Porodin culture were driven westwards into the corridor of the lakes at the very end of the Neolithic Age and that the influence of their proximity is apparent at Malik in settlement IIIa of the latest E.H. period, when some plastic decoration of the Porodin type first became common. It is evident that at that time some Porodin peoples were moving southwestwards into Epirus, driving their sheep to new coastal pastures and returning in the summer to the high mountains of Grammos and north Pindus.

At the same time in Pelagonia itself there was probably some continuity in the population, overlapping the Porodin culture and the Crnobuki culture there, and continuing into the M.H. period with its own West-Macedonian type of Minyan ware. One interesting thing is that early in the M.H. period, *c.* 1800 B.C., we have people of the same culture and the same way of life living in an area which extended from Pelagonia through what later became Dassaretis, inland Chaonia and Molossis to

---

[1] *Epirus* 307 f.; for Aphiona in Corcyra see *Epirus* 365, and for Hermones (south of Aphiona), where there are wish-bone handles, see *AD* 20 (1965 [1967]) 2. 378 and pl. 438a. Much evidence of this culture in Corcyra has been found recently; see A. Sordinas in *Kerkyraika Chronika* 14 (1968) 80 f.

[2] *Porodin* pls. 14, 15, 16, 35; *Epirus* fig. 5, 1 and 3 (Velcë); fig. 7, 2, 3, and 4 (Kastritsa); fig. 12 (Dodona); figs. 14–16 (Koutsoulio and Terovo); *Ep. Chron.* 1935 pls. 6a, 7b, 8a and b, 9a.

Dodona and Terovo. The same pattern was apparent a thousand years later, when this large group of peoples was probably called 'the Molossian tribes', and persisted sometimes with the name 'the Epirotic tribes' for yet another thousand years.

The Middle Bronze Age at Malik was a lively period, quite unlike the stagnation in Central Macedonia. The excavators have distinguished three stages: IIIa which, as we have seen, began in E.H. III and extended into M.H.; IIIb very like IIIa but differentiated by the cessation of the particular type of barbotine decoration found at Cnossus in M.M. Ia and Ib (see p. 242 above), and by the appearance of some new forms in shape and in decoration; and IIIc marked by a considerable advance in technical skill.

From settlement IIIc come three objects which are of M.H. date. A bronze knife, *c.* 12 cm long, with no tang and with two rivet-holes set at a right angle to the back, which is mainly straight but has a slight curvature towards the tip (Fig. 10*d*); this resembles a bronze knife from Vajzë. Another bronze knife, *c.* 11 cm long, with no tang and with a rivet and a rivet-hole set at a right angle to the back, a straight back, and a worn-down blade (Fig. 10*e*); this knife is like one from Dodona but without the snout. These knives are of a type which is found at Sesklo in the M.H. period. A bronze ring-pin, *c.* 21 cm long (Fig. 10*a*), is a fine example of a class typical of the earliest Bronze Age in the Aunjetitz culture of Hungary. A bronze spear-head, 21 cm long (Fig. 10*b*), has an almost fiddle-shaped blade; a javelin-head of this unusual shape was found at Vodhinë with M.H. pottery.[1] In addition a bronze knife with a curving back and one blade, 14 cm long (Fig. 10*c*), is of a northern type, and it can be dated here by association to the Middle Helladic. These objects and other associations in the pottery show that Malik IIIc was still inside the M.H. period. Another link with the Aunjetitz culture of Hungary may be seen in a hammer-stone from Kravari in Pelagonia (Fig. 13*l*); it is waisted and grooved for a binding-thong, and it is a form typical of the Aunjetitz culture, being widely dispersed and connected with mining.[2]

Malik IIIa had a rich variety of shapes, handles, lugs, and forms of plastic decoration (Fig. 8 *m–p*); but there was a gradual decline in technique, associated with an increasing proportion of coarse ware and with a restriction in the use of paint to a tarry black.[3] A number of features

---

[1] *SA* 1966. 1. 266 and pl. xx; *Epirus* 328 and fig. 21A (Vajzë); ibid. and *Ep. Chron.* 1935. 242 no. 132 and pl. 21 b 5 (Dodona); cf. *Alt-Ithaka* 310 = N. K. Sandars in *PPS* 21 (1955) fig. 4 no. 2, a knife from Grave S 10 at Leucas. For the ring-pin see Ebert 2. 76 and pl. 30 no. 13, and 8. 402; Jacobsthal 135; this type of pin was popular in Illyria later (*WMBH* 8 pl. 2, 9–11; 8. 30 fig. 51). For the spear-head see *Epirus* 338 f.

[2] I saw this hammer-stone in the museum in Monastir, where I was told it is unpublished. It is some 6 inches long, and 3½ inches wide. See Childe, *Danube* 227 fig. 130 for a parallel, which is closer than the remarkable 'pre-ceramic' one from Sesklo (*PAE* 1966, pl. 2*a*).

[3] There are only a few illustrations of this painted style: *SA* 1966. 1. pl. xiv, last row, and

are now common at Malik and rare in Macedonia, and the fact that they occur also at two sites in Leucas indicates that their home is to be sought rather in Albania; such are the use of pricked dots within incised triangles,[1] smooth plastic coils,[2] and plastic knobs or discs (Fig. 9 *a–j* and *q–v*).[3] Examples in Macedonia belong to E.H. III and the Middle Helladic, while those in Leucas are of M.H. date and later. On the other hand, there are influences originating in Central Macedonia and spreading westwards, such as an increasing use of the wish-bone handle and a greater frequency of the anchor-shaped hook of clay.[4] At the same time the proximity of peoples who had inherited the Porodin culture is clear from the common occurrence of pock-marked plastic strips and miniature round altar-tables.[5] Signs of a Kurgan-like culture still continue in some collared jugs of metallic shape and the use of fluting,[6] but they are now diminishing. Frano Prendi derives from the north a particular type of incised decoration which is found on the surface of the pot elsewhere, e.g. at Vučedol in northern Yugoslavia, but only on the base at Malik (Fig. 9 *l–n*).[7] I suggest that this is the mark not of the potter but of the owner, for whom it was a stamp, like the stamp impressed by a pintadera; and the choice of the design shows that the owners were northerners. They are probably the people who brought the hammer-axes and the particular type of barbotine decoration to Malik (see p. 242 above). Frano Prendi marks as characteristic of Malik IIIa the rising handles on the tankards,[8] which derive from the West-Macedonian form of Minyan pottery, and it is clear that the popularity of this ware was spreading westwards.

Malik IIIb derived most of its shapes and forms of decoration from Malik IIIa, and there is an increase in the frequency of the wish-bone handle. Bowls with perforated ledge-lugs are also more common; they

pl. xvii, 23. It continued in use as long as the site was inhabited, and I have not noticed a parallel to it in Macedonia and Thessaly.

[1] *SA* 1966. 1 pl. xiv, row 7, and 1964. 1. 113 and pl. iv, 7 and 8, compared with *PM* 146 no. 62 (Servia, L.N.A.) 172 fig. 46*c* (Hagios Mamas, E.B.A.), and especially 204 fig. 68*c* and *d* (Vardarophtsa, M.B.A.), and *Alt-Ithaka* Beilage 66, 1 (E.B.A.–M.B.A.) and variants at Choirospilia in Beilage 83 b 2.

[2] *SA* 1966. 1. pl. xiv, rows 3 and 4, compared with *PM* 176 fig. 47*g* (Hagios Mamas, E.B.A.), 177 fig. 51 (Molyvopyrgo, E.B.A.), 170 fig. 42 *a*, *b*, *d*, and *e* (Kritsana, E.B.A.), and *Alt-Ithaka* Beilage 84 a at Choirospilia. In 1968 I saw a plastic coil and a stylized plastic face on an unpublished pot from Tsiplevets.

[3] *SA* 1966. 1 pl. xiv, row 5, compared with *PM* 169 fig. 39 (ii) *f*, *g*, and *i* (Kritsana, E.B.A.), 174 no. 201 and 178 fig. 47*b* (Hagios Mamas, E.B.A.), 212 fig. 82 (Molyvopyrgo, M.B.A.), and *Alt-Ithaka* Beilage 84 a 4, c 1 and 10, 85 a and b at Choirospilia.

[4] *SA* 1966. 1. 265 compared with *PM* 87 fig. 67 *f–j*.

[5] *SA* 264 f. and pl. xii, 25; pl. xiii, 21, 27; pl. xiv, row 1.

[6] *SA* pl. xiii, 9 and 3.

[7] *SA* 264; pl. xii, 11 and pl. xiv, row 6; and for Vučedol see N. Tusić, 'Curčevačka Glavica' in *Starinar* n.s. xi (1961) 147 figs. 10–11.

[8] *SA* 263 and pl. xiii, 12–15.

occur earlier in Chalcidice and probably at about this time at Choirospilia in Leucas.[1] Novelties which are characteristic of Malik IIIb are
bowls with two handles, semicircular or wish-bone, rising at an acute
angle outwards from the rim or from just below the rim (Fig. 9 *y* and *z*),[2]
and a rather heavy two-handled bowl (Fig. 9 *w* and *x*), such as occurs
at Armenokhori.[3] The latter is found also in the tumuli at Vodhinë and
in Leucas.[4] There is now a marked increase in plastic ornament of all
kinds. This is a concomitant of its dispersal over central Epirus and beyond (see p. 253 above).[5]

Malik IIIc is richer and more artistic; the pottery has a finer technique and larger repertory of shapes. What were novelties in Malik IIIb
now become characteristic. High-handled cantharoi of the Minyan style
are now common, and the wish-bone handles are elaborated (Fig.
9 *aa–ff*).[6] Other shapes move away from the contemporary styles of
Macedonia; among them are water-jugs with a short spout set at a
right angle to the line of the handle, pear-shaped vases with two long
vertical handles (Fig. 9*gg*), bowls with two high, horned handles (Fig.
9*hh*), four-handled pots, large urns with two vertical down-turned hooks
for handles, and biconical jars with two vertical handles set on the
shoulder.[7] Almost all the decoration is plastic; incision is rare. But
there is a revival of painted pottery, which foreshadows the chief development of the next settlement, Malik IIId.

The contrast between Malik on the one hand and Central Macedonia,
the Vardar valley, and Chalcidice on the other could hardly be more
striking. For Malik was affected throughout the period from E.H. III to
late in the Middle Helladic by movements of peoples and cross-currents
of ideas in pottery. These came from east, north, and probably west.
They resulted in further movements of peoples and ideas by land into
Epirus and beyond, and by sea into Corcyra and Leucas; those who
went by land seem to have been derived predominantly from the stock
of the Pelagonian peoples who had developed the Porodin culture, but
those who went by sea were at first associated with chieftains who were

[1] *SA* 265 and pl. xv, 23 and 27, compared with *PM* 169 fig. 39 (ii) *a–d* (Kritsana, E.B.A.),
171 fig. 45*i* (Hagios Mamas, E.B.A.), 177 no. 212 (Molyvopyrgo, E.B.A.), and *Alt-Ithaka*
Beilage 87, 3, 4, 5 at Choirospilia.

[2] *SA* 265 and pl. xv, 21, 22, compared with *PM* 207 no. 381 and nos. 385 f. (Molyvopyrgo,
M.B.A.).

[3] *SA* pl. xv, 20 compared with *PM* 192 no. 316 (probably M.B.A.).

[4] *Epirus* fig. 17, 1, 3, and 7 (M.B.A.), and *Alt-Ithaka* Beilage 72, 3 and 4 from Grave S
(M.B.A.).

[5] See esp. *Ep. Chron.* 1935 pl. 6, 1–7 (plastic coils) as in Malik IIIa and IIIb; ibid. pls.
6*a*, 7*b*, 8 *a* and *b*, and 9*a* for plastic forms of decoration.

[6] *SA* pl. xvi, 1–4; cf. pl. xiii, 15 of Malik IIIa; and pl. xvi, 6 and 25–7. The cantharoi
resemble very closely those from Grave F at Leucas (*Alt-Ithaka* Beilage 73, 3, 7, and 9,
M.B.A.).

[7] *SA* pl. xvi, 16, 5, 6, 12, 21, 22, in the order of the text.

buried in tumuli after the manner of the Kurgan peoples. Such tumuli are not found at Malik. Indeed it is to be noted that at Malik III a, b, and c there are no building remains, except an occasional hearth and layer of mud, indicative perhaps of some decayed mud-brick,[1] no graves of any kind, and weapons and tools only of horn, bone, or stone, until the bronze knives and ring-pin of Malik IIIc. If the main stream of the Greek-speaking peoples came through Malik and Albania, as seems wellnigh certain from the contrast between Malik and Central Macedonia, they were in need of more formidable leaders than seem to have been available at Malik.

We owe to the work of Frano Prendi and his colleagues, Selim Islami and Hasan Ceka, our knowledge of the very numerous tumulus-burials of Albania. It is clear from the weapons and the pottery found in them that some tumuli were made in the M.H. period in the plain of the Mati valley, in the sink by Pazhok between the Shkumbi and the Devoli, at Vajzë inland of the Bay of Valona, and at least one in the valley of the Kseria river at Vodhinë.[2] The chieftains buried in the Kurgan manner were well armed with bronze weapons of Mainland, Minoan, and Cycladic kinds—swords, spears, javelins, knives, daggers—while the hill-men of Malik had perforated hammer-axes and hammers of stone, bows of wood, arrow-heads of stone, slings with clay bullets, and spears of wood. The Kurgan chieftains had used the domesticated horse for many centuries, probably for hunting and fighting as well as for drawing carts. They or their kinsmen had reinforced the E.H. settlements at Leucas, where they were well placed with their ships to undertake trade or to prey on trade between the Mediterranean and the Adriatic Sea, the latter still affording the main trade route from the central Mediterranean to central Europe. As a chief source of wealth in Albania and especially in the district of Malik has always been the herding of sheep, and as transhumance is a necessary condition of the pastoral life on a large scale, the peoples in the vicinity of Malik were accustomed to moving through the high passes of Mt. Pindus and were familiar with the coastal plains of northern and central Greece, particularly with the great plain of Thessaly. It seems from the evidence of the tumuli and the settlements at Malik that they lived in round huts or rectangular bothies, made of wattle and daub, or sometimes perhaps of mud-brick, and containing a hearth.

The only durable monuments of the Kurgan chieftains in Albania in the M.H. period are the tumuli, raised originally over a central pit-grave or shaft-grave, and used subsequently for secondary burials. Cremation,

---

[1] *SA* 262.

[2] All the tumuli, except two at Pazhok, were dated by the excavators to the very end of the Bronze Age and to the Early Iron Age, but I have shown the reasons for dating some in each area to the M.H. period at the latest in *Epirus* 202 f., 228 f., and 341 f., and in *BSA* 62 (1967) 77 f.

partial cremation, and inhumation occur, the last being the most frequent; skeletons are sometimes complete, but often only part of a skeleton was found, and occasionally the grave was a cenotaph with offerings. Weapons, jewellery of gold and of less precious materials, and pottery were placed above or/and with the dead. A funerary feast or sacrifice, usually a burnt sacrifice, was held, before the tumulus was completed, or before the shaft was refilled with soil. Of the earliest graves, whether M.H. or perhaps earlier, some are in shallow pits, some in circular shafts, some in stone-lined rectangular mortuary chambers, some in slab-lined cist tombs, and some in cists of wood or trellis. Some are covered with a roof on wooden rafters, some with a cairn of stones, and some with a slab.[1] The floor is often covered with pebbles or stones.

The earliest tumuli are large, e.g. 24 m in diameter at Vajzë and 12 to 30 m in the Mati valley, and originally perhaps some 3 or 4 m in height.[2] The periphery of the tumulus is marked sometimes by a circle of orthostatic slabs and sometimes by a circle of unworked, usually white stones, single or laid in twos side by side with one now and then laid across.[3] In other cases there is no circle of stones. One tumulus at Pazhok (Fig. 5*d*) and one tumulus at Vodhinë were covered over entirely with smallish stones, forming a dome as it were.[4]

The E.H. and M.H. tumulus-burials in Leucas usually have smaller tumuli and such variations as a circular platform of stones (occurring later at Bodrishtë in the Kseria valley), burial inside a recumbent pithos, and a circle consisting of a low wall—e.g. 0·60 m high retaining the tumulus of Grave R 1 (occurring later at Kakavi in the Kseria valley). They contain weapons and pottery similar to those found in the Albanian tumuli of M.H. date; but while most of the beads in the Mati valley tumuli are of amber, there are none of amber in Leucas.

Both in Albania and in Leucas the tumuli are in groups. The earliest of all are frequently in pairs, e.g. at Pazhok and in Leucas (R 1 and R 26, the largest of the R group, being 9·30 m and 9·60 m in diameter, and the earliest; R 16 is close to R 1 in place and time).[5] The number of burials in a tumulus varies from a few to as many as twenty, and they are placed

---

[1] *BUSS* 1956. 1. 180 f. (Vodhinë for shallow pit, cremations, inhumations, cairn of stones, and slab-lined cists); cf. *Epirus* 202 f. *BUSS* 1957. 2. 76 f. (Vajzë for partial cremation, inhumations, and cairn of stones); cf. *Epirus* 229. *SA* 1964. 1. 96 (Pazhok for circular and rectangular mortuary chambers, sides and floor lined with stones, funerary sacrifice of an ox); cf. *BSA* 62 (1967) pl. 18. 3 and 4. *SA* 1964 1. 102 (Mati valley for cenotaphs and parts of skeletons).

[2] *BUSS* 1957. 2. 78, the actual height being 2. 22 m.

[3] *SA* 1964. 1 pl. v, 2 shows the orthostats, some still upright, at Pazhok; cf. *BSA* 62 (1967) pl. 18. 2. *BUSS* 1956. 1. 182 for the circle of unworked stones at Vodhinë; cf. *Epirus* fig. 1.

[4] Showing in the plates and figure mentioned in the last note, and stated in *BUSS* 1956. 1. 181 for Vodhinë. The Pazhok report is exceedingly brief, even for a preliminary report.

[5] For the dating see my article in *BSA* 62 (1967) 94; for positions in Leucas see *Alt-Ithaka* ii pl. 13.

Remains of the Middle Bronze Age 259

at different depths within the fill of the tumulus. The earliest burials in a tumulus are generally below the original ground level, and others are sometimes.

Tumulus-burials of M.H. date have been found in Greece. In some instances the tumulus has survived intact, as at Marathon, and in others the tumulus has been depleted or removed. The concentration of tumuli in Albania, and indeed far inland at Pazhok and Vodhinë, and in Leucas, quite apart from the connection of this form of burial with the Kurgan culture in the north, leaves us in no doubt that the tumulus-burials in Greece are monuments to the advance of peoples from the general region of Albania and Leucas and to their settlement as rulers in possession of newly-won realms.[1] Their presence in the M.H. period may be noted at Same in Cephallenia (perhaps);[2] at Samikon (Kleidhi) in north-western Peloponnese (perhaps);[3] at the Elean Pylos on the border of Elis and Achaea;[4] at Papoulia near the Messenian Pylos;[5] at Peristeria near the Messenian Pylos;[6] at Malthi in Messenia;[7] at

[1] I have argued this in detail in *Epirus* 341 f. and in *BSA* 62 (1967) 77 f. and 96.
[2] S. Marinatos has recently discovered burials at Roupaki which he finds similar to the Leucas ones, the latter being dated by him to the Early Helladic and the Middle Helladic; a fuller investigation is expected. The report is in *AE* 1964 [1967] 26 f.
[3] *Arch. Reports* 1955. 17; the tumulus was 5 m in diameter, its soil was retained by a wall of rough stones 0·60 m. high, and it contained ten or more burials in three layers; N. Yialouris reckoned the pottery from the tumulus to be earlier than any other Mycenaean vases found in the western Peloponnese, so that the earliest burial was probably in M.H. times.
[4] *AD* 20 (1965 [1967]) 2. 216 at Agrapidhokhorion. Three tumuli were found; the largest was 20 m in diameter, one probably had a circle of unworked river-stones, all yielded prehistoric sherds, and one yielded M.H. sherds.
[5] *Arch. Reports* 1954. 35 and fig. 7; the tumulus was 14 m in diameter and 2·50 m high; its soil was retained by a wall 2 m high, made of stone slabs, among which burials in recumbent pithoi were placed, and the pottery was dated to the Middle Helladic by S. Marinatos.
[6] *PAE* 1964. 92 f. The tumulus is 16 to 20 m in diameter, 3 to 4 m high but on a humpbacked site, its soil was retained by a circular wall of river-stones, and it contained at least two pithos-burials. There was a layer of ash, some 2 to 3 cm thick, at what was probably the original ground level, and below the layer of ash was a pithos-burial, dated by S. Marinatos to early in the M.H. period.
[7] M. N. Valmin, *The Swedish Messenian Expedition* (Lund, 1938) 188 f. and 'Das Adriatische Gebiet' in *Acta Universitatis Lundensis* 35 (1939) 1. 32 f. The tumulus is situated, like Grave Circle A at Mycenae, on the right as one enters the M.H. citadel through a main gate. Its soil was retained by a double row of orthostatic slabs, which formed a rough spiral and not a circle, as the area enclosed between a rock cutting and the road was irregular in shape. The central burial of the tumulus (Grave XXXIX) was a cist tomb, partly rock-cut and partly formed by upright slabs, which contained the skeleton of a man six feet or more tall; the bottom of the tomb was on the stereo, the corpse had been placed in a sitting position, and there were signs of a covering of cloth or the like having been placed on the floor under him (as noted in some Grave Circle B graves at Mycenae, and in some Kurgan burials, in which a fleece was used). Two collections of bones and sherds (ossuaries rather than graves) were found, one partly underneath the ring of orthostatic slabs and the other at the same depth within the ring. They seem to antedate the tumulus and be unconnected with it; they were of E.H. date. Valmin's final dating of the tumulus and the central cist tomb was at latest early in the Middle Helladic, and this seems acceptable. His supposition that the double row of orthostats was a foundation at one point for the circuit-wall is most improbable;

Lerna;[1] at Mycenae;[2] in Ceos;[3] at Aphidna and Marathon;[4] earlier at Chaeronea;[5] and at Elatea (Drakhmani) in Phocis.[6] In many cases the tumuli are close to citadels which became centres of Mycenaean power in the L.H. period, and it is likely that the burials in the tumuli were respected then as those of the founders.

I have referred elsewhere to some of the resemblances between the

for orthostats are not suited to carry great weights in dry walling. Moreover, we now have examples of orthostatic slabs in tumulus rings not only at Mycenae but also at Pazhok and in Ceos, where they are related only to the tumulus or to the decoration of the ring.

[1] Two shaft-graves were found, one sunk into the earlier stone-covered tumulus, itself 19 m in diameter with a ring of rounded stones, and one outside the tumulus (the latter perhaps within an outer tumulus, if the stone-covered one was capped by a tumulus, as at Pazhok and Vodhinë); the graves are dated to late M.H. times by J. L. Caskey in *Hesp.* 25 (1956) 165 f. with fig. 3 and in *CAH*[3] ii. i. 125.

[2] Grave Circle B had a retaining wall two stones thick (the stones were laid side by side) up to 0·85 m high; it contained black earth originally (as at Servia, p. 243 above), a number of burials at varying depths, and remains of funerary feasts. Grave Circle A, which is some 26 m in diameter in its monumental form and was surrounded by a ring of orthostatic slabs (as at Pazhok and Ceos), had originally a circular retaining wall of a construction similar to that seen in Grave Circle B, contained a number of burials at varying depths, and remains of funerary feasts. For a detailed comparison and for the suggestion that the two circles were each covered with a tumulus see *Epirus* 343 f. and *BSA* 62 (1967) 83 f.; for the original retaining wall of Grave Circle A see A. E. Mylonas in *AE* 1962 [1966]. 112.

[3] J. L. Caskey described the circle and showed slides of the ring of orthostatic slabs, when he was lecturing at the Institute for Advanced Study at Princeton in April 1968.

[4] *AM* 21 (1896) 388 f. The tumulus, 24 m in diameter (p. 400), contained thirteen graves at depths which varied within a range of 2 m; these were pit-graves and shaft-graves, both with stones set on the upper edge of the grave (as at Mycenae), pithos-graves (as in Leucas), and cists made of slabs (as at Vodhinë in stage 2) or of large stones (as at Elean Pylos), usually with a floor of pebbles. The upper part of Grave I was either a cenotaph with stones set above it (ibid., pl. xiii) or an elaborate two-storied mortuary chamber; some graves had a skull and only a few bones (e.g. Grave 7), and some had a skeleton (e.g. Grave 9). There were signs of fire, attributed by the excavator, S. Wide, to a sacrifice over the burial (p. 398). Many graves had been robbed; the surviving offerings were pots, rings of gold, silver, and bronze, crystal-like beads, spinning weights, a knife and an arrow-head, both of obsidian. The plan (pl. xiii) shows remains of a single-stone circle (as in the outer tumulus at Pazhok), to which Graves I and XIII are central; these two alone are below the ancient ground level (as at Pazhok in the central burial, or burials, of the earliest tumuli). Judging by the Albanian tumuli, we reckon Grave XIII the earliest, then Grave I, then Grave III, the two last overlying the first (p. 396). The rings of gold, silver, and bronze, the crystal-like beads, and the obsidian knife and arrow-head were in I and III. These and other objects date the tumulus to the Middle Helladic; so J. L. Caskey in *CAH*[3] ii. i. 125. I saw the Marathon tumulus in 1971.

[5] *AM* 30 (1905) 120 f.; *AE* 1908. 65 f., *PAE* 1909. 123 f. and *REG* 25 (1912) 263 f. The tumulus was 20 m in diameter and about 3·50 m high; containing two burials, it had at the bottom a layer of ash (as at Peristeria), and the remains of a funerary feast or burnt sacrifice. A. J. B. Wace in *PTh* 197 f. thought it to be the residue of a tiny settlement, but discoveries since he wrote justify Sotiriadis in his belief that it was a tumulus constructed for the burials. The pottery in the tumulus indicates a date probably earlier than the Middle Helladic. See p. 262 note 14 below.

[6] *AE* 1908. 94 f. and *AM* 31 (1906) 402 f. The tumulus, 'of small diameter' (? as compared with a habitation mound) and some 3 m high, contained one burial, over which was a cairn of stones (as at Vodhinë), and had remains of a funerary burnt sacrifice or feast. Beside the breast of the corpse a bronze snouted knife and the thigh-bone of an ox (like the ox-head in the Pazhok burial) were found. The knife is of M.H. date, and vases imported from Crete are dated to the M.M. period (*AE* 1908. 94 and Wace in *PTh* 204).

objects found in the M.H. tumuli in Albania and those found in the M.H. tumuli in Greece, particularly at Mycenae.[1] I mention here one or two points which show that the tumuli at Aphidna and Elatea in east central Greece are not separate but derive also from the north-western area. Thus the tomb in the tumulus at Elatea yielded four gold pieces. The first was a plain gold ring. Such rings in gold, silver, or bronze have come from Grave III and Grave IV of Circle A at Mycenae (both silver),[2] from Grave F 5 in Leucas (one silver and one bronze),[3] from tumulus B Grave 11 at Bodrishtë in the Kseria valley (in bronze),[4] from tumulus C Grave 7 and its soil at Vajzë (in bronze), and from tumuli in the Mati valley (metal not specified).[5] The second is a piece of gold wire forming a single coil with overlapping ends. The earliest such coil comes from the E.B.A. layer of Saratse in Macedonia,[6] and such gold wire was particularly common in Grave III of Circle A at Mycenae, where two such single coils were found, each supporting an elaborate pendant;[7] and six in gold and one in silver came from Grave III, a pithos-burial, in the tumulus at Aphidna.[8] Now it was noted at Aphidna that three of these single coils had been formed into a chain of three, and two such chains of three appear in R 24 at Leucas (in gold).[9] A single spiral coil in gold was found at Pazhok in the upper tumulus of the largest double tumulus,[10] and a chain of eighteen such coils in bronze is illustrated as coming from the Mati tumuli, apparently in linked sets of three each.[11] The third and fourth objects at Elatea are gold ear-rings, each made of a single coil which is much heavier on one side than on the other; such were found in a more elaborate form in Grave III of Circle A at Mycenae (in gold)[12] and in a simple form in bronze in Grave 6 of Tumulus A at Bodrishtë in the Kseria valley.[13]

Spirals of a more notable form were found in the tumuli of the Mati valley. Two gold-wire coils of some ten turns each were found there in the company of two Mycenaean swords.[14] Another such gold hair-coil

[1] Amber may be added; it is common at Hvar (*AI* 3 (1959) 24) and in the Mati valley tumuli (*SA* 1964. 1. 103), and 1290 amber beads were found in Shaft Grave IV at Mycenae.

[2] *AE* 1908. 94 fig. 16; G. Karo, *Die Schachtgräber von Mykenai* (Athens, 1915–16) 109 no. 502 pl. xcix.

[3] *Alt-Ithaka* 1. 216 and Beilage 73. 4.   [4] *BUST* 1959. 2. 205 fig. 18c.

[5] *SA* 1964. 1 pl. xv, 10; *Epirus* 349. Such rings have been found at Dodona (*Ep. Chron.* 1935 pl. 22b 6), which was a shrine from the Early Helladic onwards.

[6] *PM* 88 and 203 fig. 67qq. Also one in bronze at Dodona (op. cit., pl. 22b 20).

[7] Karo, op. cit. 52 no. 61 pl. xx.   [8] *AM* 21 (1896) 392, item 4.

[9] *Alt-Ithaka* 1. 289 and Beilage 61 a 5 and 61 b 2.

[10] *SA* 1964. 1. 96 f.

[11] Ibid., pl. xiv; they are shown underneath a fibula, but it is not clear whether they are a pendant to it.

[12] Karo, op. cit. 52 no. 55 pl. xx; another in Athens Nat. Mus. no. 2448.

[13] *BUST* 1959. 2. 198 fig. 9c. One such ear-ring was found in R 4 at Leucas (*Alt-Ithaka* Beilage 61 b 1) and another at Dodona (*Ep. Chron.* 1935. pl. 22b 7).

[14] *SA* 1964. 1. 102 and pl. xv, 2.

was found in the soil (not in any of the graves) in tumulus A at Vajzë.[1]
Six pieces of such hair-coils in gold have been found in and outside a cist
tomb, beside which there had been a secondary burial, at Cirrha near
Delphi in the M.H. period.[2] Heavy arm-bands made of bronze wire in
multiple rings were found in the Mati tumuli;[3] such were found in silver
in R 1, R 4, and R 15 b in Leucas,[4] and in gold with additional little
spirals in Grave III of Circle A at Mycenae.[5] The last object found in the
tomb in the tumulus at Elatea was a one-edged snouted knife of bronze.[6]
One-edged knives were in Graves III (two specimens) and IV of Circle
A at Mycenae,[7] in a shaft-grave of the M.H. period at Kephalovryson
(Grave I),[8] in S 10 of the M.H. period and R 17 a of L.H. II or III
in Leucas,[9] in Tumulus A of the M.H. period at Vajzë (four specimens),[10]
and in the Mati tumuli.[11] Snouted knives (i.e. with a small lump on the
back near the tip) come from Elatea, from Kephalovryson, perhaps from
Mycenae Grave IV,[12] from Leucas Grave S 10, perhaps from Ithaca,
and from Dodona.[13]

On the basis of our present information the earliest examples of
tumulus-burials are at Servia in Macedonia and at Chaeronea in
northern Boeotia,[14] both being in the Late Neolithic Age and probably

---

[1] *BUSS* 1957. 2. 89 figs. 14*a* and 91.

[2] L. Dor, et al., *Kirrha* (Paris, 1960) 100 and 142 from Tombs 42, 56, 57, and 58. A feature
common to Cirrha, Mycenae, and the tumulus at Elatea is the handsome urn which forms the
frontispiece to *Kirrha*; it is in *AE* 1908. 95 and additional plate iii no. 1 (Elatea), and occurs
in pottery in the Shaft-Graves at Mycenae (Karo, op. cit., pl. clxxi nos. 590–1 in Grave IV
and pl. clxxiv no. 948 in Grave VI).

[3] *SA* 1964. 1. 103 and pl. xv, 9.   [4] *Alt-Ithaka* 1. 290 and Beilage 60. 5–8.

[5] Karo, op. cit. 53 no. 66 and no. 65 pl. xxi.   [6] *AE* 1908. 94 fig. 16.

[7] Karo, op. cit., pl. cii no. 457 and pl. cxlix no. 154.

[8] *PAE* 1964. 82 f. and pl. 91 *a* and *b*.   [9] *Alt-Ithaka* Beilage 63 b 8.

[10] *BUSS* 1957. 2. 88 fig. 13; cf. *Epirus* 328 f.   [11] *SA* 1964. 1. 102 and pl. xii, 3.

[12] Perhaps no. 457 of Karo, op. cit., pl. cii.   [13] N. K. Sandars in *PPS* 21 (1955) 196.

[14] The site at Chaeronea has been the subject of some controversy. Wace in *PTh* 199 (1912)
argued that the site was a mound caused by successive settlements; and he is clearly correct,
since the mound was 120 × 120 m (*AM* 30 (1905) 120). The claim of the excavator, G.
Sotiriadis, was that at the bottom of the excavated part there was an original tumulus some
20 m in diameter and originally some 3·50 m high; and he showed this tumulus in a general
plan of the site, which is perhaps rather simplified (ibid., p. 121). Moreover, he saw a similarity
in the method of burial with the Kurgan-type burial at Helmsdorf in Germany (*AE* 1908. 76).
The nature of the tumulus is as follows. As the site is close to the river, the water table was
high and Sotiriadis did not get down to virgin ground. At the bottom of the excavated part he
found a layer of ash, extending over the area, and on this layer a tumulus, its periphery
marked originally by a palisade of wattle and daub (such a palisade was used at Malik in
settlement IIa) The skeleton of a young man lay on the layer of ash; it had been covered
with black earth (as at Servia). At a slightly higher level in the tumulus a part only of the
skeleton of an older man lay in the usual clayey soil of the tumulus, and this part of the skeleton seemed to have been lightly burnt (both practices are seen in the Albanian tumuli). Small
layers of ash mixed with animal bones were indications of funerary sacrifices or feasts, and
two hearths were noted inside the periphery of the tumulus (there was one at Servia beside the
edge of the burial-shaft). Stone tools or weapons, obsidian blades, and clay figurines were
found (*AE* 1908. 71 f.). There are a number of links in the finds with north-west Macedonia

overlapping with the start of E.H. I further south. They were associated with a flow of people from the north into Thessaly, especially at Dhimini and Sesklo, and north-east Greece towards the end of the Late Neolithic Age, a flow which may have ebbed back again with the spread of peoples from the east during E.H. I and II.

The next groups of tumulus-burials appear in central Albania and in Leucas, beginning probably in both areas in E.H. II with an extension to Lerna in the Argolid, where a tumulus was made at the transition from E.H. II to E.H. III. There is already a distinction between Albania and Leucas. Albania had larger tumuli, often 20 m in diameter, the top sometimes covered with stones, and Leucas had smaller tumuli and sometimes used pithos-burial. Representatives of both types appear in Greece in the M.H. period. The pithos-burials in the tumulus at Peristeria near Messenian Pylos, which are early in the Middle Helladic, are closer to the Leucas type; so too is the small tumulus at Samikon in north-western Peloponnese. Others belong rather to the Albanian type of large tumulus with a ring of stones or orthostats—e.g. those at Elean Pylos, Lerna, Mycenae, and Ceos. It is to be noted also that in Albania in the M.H. period there were groups of tumuli in the Mati valley, at Pazhok in central Albania, at Vajzë inland of the Gulf of Valona, and in the Kseria valley near the modern border with Greek Epirus. If the carriers of the Leucas type went by sea, the carriers of the Albanian type certainly moved by land; for the tumuli in Albania are mostly far inland, and the peoples of those parts have rarely been seafarers. We must then assume that a large-scale invasion or a long-lasting infiltration brought these tumulus-using chieftains from Albania into Greece by land. The main route was surely down the western flank of Greece north of the Corinthian Gulf, and then eastwards or/and southwards.[1] We may add to the evidence of the tumuli the graves at Cirrha with the gold hair-coils, and the occurrence of anchor-shaped hooks of clay and other

and Malik IIa and IIb: a zoomorphic vase, black with white-filled incision (such a vase lay with the primary burial at Servia = *PM* 79 and 140 fig. 9*i*, and zoomorphic vases occur at Porodin and Malik; Chaeronea = *AE* 75 fig. 7 and 86, and *AM* 123 fig. 2*c* and 137 fig. 9), three-legged and four-legged altar vessels (*AE* fig. 7 no. 3 and pp. 86–7; at Servia, Malik, and Porodin), piles of clay sling bullets (*AE* 93; especially at Porodin), plastic knobs or warts in profusion on plain ware (*AE* 85–6; especially at Porodin and Malik), two figurines of a dog (*AE* 94; one at Servia, *PM* 78 and fig. 35*o*), bowls with high upright collars (*AE* figs. 4, 5, 8 and additional plate i; at Malik IIb), in the variety of painted pottery and some designs in grey on grey (*AE* fig. 5 and Malik in *SA* 1966. 1 pl. v. 16; *AE* especially fig. 11, 4 and at Malik in *SA* 259 and pl. vi*a*, especially middle near the bottom). It seems probable that we have in the earliest layer excavated by Sotiriadis at Chaeronea a tumulus with two burials contemporary more or less with the two burials at Servia, i.e. in Macedonian terms in the Late Neolithic Age and in Greek terms very early in the Early Helladic; it has some links with the north-west. The people at Chaeronea, who certainly had many sheep (*AE* 93), probably belonged to the nomadic shepherd peoples who moved their flocks to the Pindus range for summer pasture.

[1] See *Epirus* 34 and 149.

objects of northern origin at Mega near the Schiste Hodos;[1] for both places are on the main route from the west towards Boeotia and Attica.

The pottery which was found at Mega near the Schiste Hodos[2] provides an intermediate point between the north and the Peloponnese. One sherd from Mega shows a plastic band in the form of a zigzag; this is paralleled at Malik III a–b in pottery and at Mycenae in Shaft-Grave IV in gold leaf.[3] Two sherds from Mega are incised, one with a line of punctured dots beside an incised groove and the other with jags in incised triangles; both schemes of decoration are found at Servia,[4] at Malik IIb–IIIb (as in Fig. 9s),[5] and in combination in Grave III of the tumulus at Aphidna,[6] and the punctured dots alone on incised pots at Lerna, which are mentioned just below. Two sherds from Mega are shown with what Heurtley called 'deep incised continuous lines' in the form of S-shaped spirals (Fig. 4p and pp). This unusual form of incised decoration is found at Servia on pottery,[7] at Mycenae very frequently on the stone *stelai* and on gold objects in the Shaft-Graves, and at Lerna on a flask-like pot and some others.[8]

At Lerna the flask-like pot and others of this shape are bored for suspension, being handleless. They were found in the layer immediately following the destruction of the E.H. III settlement and inaugurating Lerna V, the M.H. settlement. 'The ware, the shape and the style of decoration' wrote J. L. Caskey of these pots,[9] 'are foreign to this region of the Peloponnesos, and leave no doubt that we have here a group of imported pots. The closest parallels appear to be in the central Balkans. Dr. M. Garašanin of Belgrade, who saw much of the material in our workrooms, informed us that it resembled—indeed duplicated—certain pots that he had found in deposits of period Ia at Bubanj, near Niš.' As we have seen above (p. 238), the Bubanj-Hum I culture entered the Upper Vardar valley at a time corresponding to E.H. I–II,[10] and some of its influences affected Malik and Servia. We can therefore help to fill

---

[1] *AE* 1908. 91 and additional plate ii, 6 and 9; others were found at Orchomenus. Sotiriadis illustrates six sherds from Mega (ibid. 15–17 and 21–3), of which the first group has analogies in Malik IIIa (*SA* 1966. 1 pl. xiv) and the second group resembles pottery from Servia IIb (*PM* 146 fig. 13 (i) *a–c* and 142 fig. 11 *h–l*).

[2] Sotiriadis published only six sherds, presumably as typical, in *AE* 1908. 91 and additional plate ii, 15–17 and 21–3.

[3] *SA* 1966. 1 pl. xiv, row 4 (Malik); Karo, op. cit., pl. xxxvi no. 232, pl. lxxix nos. 284, 300, 301 (Mycenae).

[4] *PM* 145 no. 56 = fig. 11*f* and 146 no. 62, Late Neolithic Age.

[5] *AM* 21 (1896) pls. viii, ix, xiv.   [6] *AM* 21 (1896) pl. xiv, 1 and pl. xv, 3.

[7] *PM* 146 fig. 9*f* and fig. 13 (i) *a–d*, 'later incised' in the Late Neolithic Age. There is similar incision but with a less continuous line at Rakhmani in north Thessaly in *PTh* 31 fig. 9 of the Late Neolithic Age.

[8] *Hesp.* 26 (1957) 150 and pl. 40 *d* and *f*; and *Hesp.* 25 (1956) 160 and pl. 43*b*.

[9] The quotation is from *Hesp.* 26 (1957) 150; he refers to the pots also in *CAH*[3] ii. i. 125.

[10] At that time M. Garašanin dated Bubanj-Hum I to Early Helladic III and Bubanj-Hum II to Middle Helladic (*AI* i (1954) 19).

the gap between Niš and Lerna by adding examples of the same shape at Porodin (Fig. 4*s*), at Malik IIa and onwards (Fig. 4 *q* and *r*),[1] at Dodona, at Tsani in west Thessaly from the Late Neolithic Age onwards, at Cirrha dated within M.H. Ib,[2] at Asea in Arcadia, and from tomb III at Kephalovryson near Pylos,[3] where the two one-edged snouted knives were found. It would seem likely that these flask-like pots were brought by invaders early in the M.H. period. Frano Prendi thought they were milk-containers at Malik. Bones of horses were found at Lerna at the same level,[4] and horses too are usually attributed to the invaders.

Evidence of intruders with possessions like those of the tumulus-using people of Albania is also to be seen at Sesklo in the M.H. period, where some M.H. cist tombs, made of slabs, contain objects distinctive of the tumulus-burials, even as those at Cirrha do. Sesklo Grave 25 with three burials is a good example: it contained a dagger, a one-edged knife of a north-western kind, a plain bronze ring and three gold hair-rings.[5] The last were found in silver in other graves, three by the head in Grave 41, and four together with a bronze ring in Grave 28.[6] A very small silver ring was found in Grave 40 together with bronze tweezers. Such tweezers have been found in the central M.H. burials in two large tumuli at Pazhok, in the Mati tumuli, and in Shaft-Graves V and VI at Mycenae in silver and in bronze.[7] Grave 22 had a bronze dagger and bronze tweezers.[8] Grave 50 had a bronze one-edged knife of the north-western kind.[9] Grave 55 had a bronze shoed spear-head, of which there are two examples from Tumulus A at Vajzë, one from Leucas F 7, and one from

[1] M. Grbić, *Porodin* pl. xiii, 4 with four small pierced lugs; *SA* 1964. 1. pl. ii, 8 and 1966. 1. pl. iv, 11 with borings; *SA* 1964. 1. pl. ii, 6 and 1966. 1. pl. iv, 13 and 14 with dwarf handles; *SA* 1966. 1. pl. v, 11 with one pierced lug set very low down. In the museum at Titov Veles in 1968 I saw an unpublished specimen with two dwarf handles and one mammiform lump visible.

[2] *Ep. Chron.* 1935. 196 and pl. 2*a* 2; *PTh* 144 and fig. 86*e*: five examples are mentioned and the one illustrated has bore-holes for suspension. L. Dor, et al., *Kirrha* pl. xliv no. 34 and pp. 87, 130, and 148.

[3] E. J. Holmberg, *The Swedish Excavations at Asea in Arcadia* (Lund, 1944) 88 fig. 89*a*, with unusual vertical lugs, vertically pierced; it was found in the burnt layer between the Early Helladic and the Middle Helladic, had been incised with lines and crosses and then been painted, and was certainly not of local manufacture. *PAE* 1964 pl. 94*b*.

[4] *CAH*[3] II. i. 125.

[5] Tsountas, *Dimini and Sesklo* 136 with the dagger in pl. 5, 16, the knife in pl. 4, 13 = Sandars in *PPS* 21 (1955) 182 fig. 4 no. 5, and the hair-rings in pl. 5, 1.

[6] Ibid. 139 and 143.

[7] Ibid. 143; *SA* 1964. 1. 96 and 103 and pl. xiv, 11–12. Tweezers are found later in a grave at Kalbaki in Epirus (*PAE* 1956. 116 fig. 2, 5–6 and 126 f., two in bronze) and at Kakavi in the Kseria valley in Grave 4 of the tumulus (*BUST* 1959. 2. 194 and fig. 6*d*, in iron); Evangelides found 5 bronze tweezers at Dodona (*Ep. Chron.* 1935. 241 and fig. 18), and Carapanos published some (*Dodona* pl. 50, 20–1). For Mycenae see Karo, op. cit. 37 and 45.

[8] Tsountas, op. cit. 136; the dagger is in pl. 4, 9.

[9] Ibid. 144 and pl. 4, 14.

Shaft-Grave IV of Circle A at Mycenae.[1] Of the fifty or so graves listed at Sesklo those I have mentioned are the only ones which contain weapons. The similarities of the contents of the graves to those of the tumulus-burials are therefore very significant. Another point of interest is the anchor-shaped hook of clay. Such hooks have not appeared in any of the tumulus-burials, but we have seen the spreading of them from East Macedonia to Malik. Five such hooks were found on the top layer, that is the M.H. layer, at Sesklo.[2] Two were found at Mega near the Schiste Hodos.[3] Others occurred at Lerna IV in E.H. III, that is after the construction of the tumulus there.[4] The connection between Sesklo and the tumulus-using group in Albania is explicable only if chieftains of the same culture were in occupation of Sesklo.

In the cemetery at Vergina on the south side of the lowest reaches of the Haliacmon there is some evidence of M.H. burials. In Tumulus Z, some 2 m high and 15 m in diameter with remains of a circular peribolos of single unworked stones, a two-handled *cantharos* of the Middle Helladic, not to say Minyan, type was found in fragments just inside a piece of the peribolos. The centre of this tumulus had been excavated in the Hellenistic period to accommodate a very large built tomb, and the natural explanation of the M.H. *cantharos* is that it is a survivor of an original M.H. burial in the centre of the tumulus. In some other tumuli Andronikos noted that the earliest burials were in shaft-graves sunk below the original ground level; that some of them were filled with pure, dark earth; that their sides had been supported with stones; and that some had had a roof of timber or branches. One tumulus with such burials, Tumulus A, was 20 m in diameter. The indications are that we have at Vergina examples of the burial customs which were practised in the M.H. period in central Albania.[5]

When the level of the water in Lake Ostrovo fell, Ph. Petsas reported that a grave circle of orthostats was revealed at Arnissa.[6] The diameter of the circle was 11·50 m, and some ten cist-graves were noted inside the circle. Other graves could be distinguished outside the circle. In all probability this is a double tumulus, similar to that at Pazhok, where the inner tumulus was defined by a circle of orthostats, and to that at Vodhinë. In both cases the inner tumulus was of M.H. date at the latest. Nothing more has been heard of the circle at Arnissa since the report by

---

[1] Tsountas, op. cit. 146 and pl. 4, 10; *BUSS* 1957. 2 fig. 11 *a* and *c* = *Epirus* 337 and fig. 23 *b* and *c* (Vajzë); *Alt-Ithaka* Beilage 73. 16; and Karo, op. cit., no. 413 pl. 73. A mould for making such spear-heads was found at Sesklo.   [2] Tsountas, p. 346 figs. 280–2.

[3] *AE* 1908. 91 and additional plate 11, 6 and 9.

[4] *Hesp.* 25 (1956) 162 and pl. 47 *l–p*.

[5] *PAE* 1953. 146 and fig. 1, and *Vergina* pl. 40 z 35; *PAE* 1952. 219 f.

[6] *Arch. Reports* 1953. 159. When I was at Arnissa, I was unfortunately not aware of this circle.

Ph. Petsas. We may, however, assume for the time being that it is a link in the chain between Vergina and the Albanian M.H. tumuli.

Links with the north-west appear frequently in the Neolithic and Bronze Ages at Tsangli, which is situated in the valley linking the western Thessalian plain to Sesklo, itself near the Gulf of Pagasae.[1] An unusual form of dipper, occurring at Vodhinë in two cremation sets of pottery in tumulus-burials of the M.H. period, was found at Tsangli.[2] Fragments of zoomorphic vases and of three-legged and four-legged altar-tables, which we have noted at Servia, Porodin (Fig. 1 *b* and *f*), and Malik (Fig. 3*e*), were also found there.[3] Other points in common are clay phalli (at Servia and Malik, Fig. 3*c*);[4] figurines with detachable heads, cruciform figurines, and figurines of animals at Porodin (Fig. 2) and Malik (Fig. 3 *d* and *f*);[5] and clay sling bullets (Porodin especially).[6] There are striking similarities with Malik: two bases of pots have incised stamps of the same design as at Malik IIIa (Fig. 9 *l–n*),[7] 'the most interesting' complete figurine is exactly like one at Malik (Fig. 3*d*),[8] and a small lamp of 'exceptional shape' is like one from Malik IIIc.[9]

The horse made its appearance at Porodin and Tsiplevets in the Late Neolithic Age, in Central Macedonia in the Early Bronze Age and, for the first time yet known in Greece, early in the M.H. period at Lerna V, where the two shaft-graves were made later on, one of them being sunk in the earlier tumulus,[10] and on the *stelai* of the shaft-graves at Mycenae late in the Middle Helladic. Already at Mycenae the horse was used to draw the chariot with two-spoked wheels and the wagon with four-spoked wheels, both in war and in hunting. The spoking, thick and in the form of a cross, is simply shown on the *stelai*; a spoked wheel of exactly this form is shown at Malik IIIa as a plastic ornament on a pot (Fig. 9*k*).[11] The hunting scenes at Mycenae[12] portray the lion and the wild ox or aurochs; these were certainly familiar to the inhabitants of Macedonia and northern Pindus, but it is improbable that they were to be found in the Argolid.

[1] *PTh* 241 and map facing p. 1.

[2] *PTh* 89–90 and fig. 40*d* and *Epirus* 310 f. with fig. 17.

[3] *PTh* 99 and fig. 50*a*; figs. 42*d*, 57*g*, 58*b*.

[4] *PTh* fig. 76 *j* and *k*, and Malik in *SA* 1966. 1 pl. x*b*.

[5] *PTh* 122 f. and fig. 74*a* and *b* and fig. 77*b*, compared with *SA* 1966. 1. pl. x*a* and *c*.

[6] *PTh* 125.   [7] *PTh* 90 and fig. 43, and *SA* 1966. 1 pl. xii, 11 and pl. xiv, row 6.

[8] *PTh* 124, figs. 71*b* and 76*l*, and *SA* 1966. 1 pl. x*a*, bottom row left = here Fig. 3*d*, on left.

[9] *PTh* 113 fig. 61*c*, and *SA* 1966. 1 pl. xvi, 16. I saw another from Mesemeri near Kritsana in the Salonica Museum, unpublished.

[10] *CAH*[3] ii. i. 125; or even in E.H. III if Caskey's 'equine animal' (ibid., p. 136) counts as a horse.

[11] *SA* 1966. 1 pl. xiv, row 5 right. A clay model of such a wheel from Slovakia is shown in M. Gimbutas, *Bronze Age*, pl. ii, 1. The more developed wheel with six spokes appears at Choirospilia in Leucas in a miniature bronze of later date (*Alt-Ithaka* Beilage 83 a).

[12] For a brief account see E. Vermeule, *Greece in the Bronze Age* (Chicago, 1964) 90 f. For the aurochs see p. 201 n. 2, above.

The new rulers must have come from a people which had been familiar with the domesticated horse for many generations, and had trained it and evolved suitable vehicles for transport, hunting and war. It has often been remarked that chariot warfare was invented where there were wide, stoneless plains, and such plains are typical of central Albania, Western and Central Macedonia, and southern Yugoslavia. Even today wedding processions are mounted on a string of decorated horse-drawn wagons in the plains north of Kačanik. There are thus many reasons for supposing that the people to which the rulers of Mycenae belonged had been in, or in the vicinity of, Porodin in Pelagonia since the Late Neolithic Age.

X

SOME ETHNOLOGICAL INFERENCES ABOUT THE GREEK-SPEAKING PEOPLES IN THE EARLY AND MIDDLE PERIODS OF THE BRONZE AGE

EVEN our earliest use of the term 'The Greeks' must be taken to have a connotation of language and not of race. If this definition is accepted, no one will disagree with the view that the invaders who came from the north in the M.H. period were in a general sense 'The first Greeks'; for they introduced into the southern peninsula the Greek language which has persisted ever since that time. The decipherment of Linear B (Mycenaean) script, which was devised as a vehicle to express the Greek language for the purpose of the governing class, has confirmed the view that the rulers who established themselves, for instance, at Mycenae spoke Greek at the time of their arrival. These rulers practised a form of burial of which a large low tumulus was the outer mark. Its continuous use, whether it covered pit-graves, shaft-graves, or a tholos tomb,[1] shows that families of the same stock were in power until c. 1300 B.C., when the monumental reconstruction of the top of Grave Circle A of c. 1650–1500 B.C. was undertaken as a memorial. Within the period to c. 1300 B.C. the earliest Linear B tablets certainly fall.

At the same time we must notice that from the invasion onwards there was a clear distinction between the ruling or governing group on the one hand and their followers on the other hand. Only the former have tumuli; it is they who appear driving chariots and wagons in scenes of hunting and of war on the *stelai* of the tumuli, and they who have the distinctive death-masks, the jewellery, and the weapons. Their followers in the invasions are dimly discernible, but mainly in new types of pottery or figurines or amulets, such as anchor-shaped hooks of clay, or in humbler weapons, such as the sling and the bow.

In the same way we know more of the earlier history of the ruling group

---

[1] The tholos tomb evolved, one imagines, from the mortuary chamber in the Shaft-Grave, whether circular or rectangular, and the earliest known tholos tomb, dating to the end of the Middle Helladic, was built near Pylos, where it had been preceded by tumulus-burials; for the tumuli with circular retaining walls over the tholoi see references in my article in *BSA* 62 (1967) 88 and N. Valmin 'Tholos Tomb and Tumuli' in *Skrifter utgivna av Svenska Institutet i Rom* 2. 216 f. See now the sequence of tumuli and tholoi at Marathon.

than of that of their followers. For the ruling group belonged to the so-called Kurgan culture of which the features are well known and have been summarized as follows.

Burial of the dead in particular contracted positions, often painted with red ochre, individually or in pairs or in small groups in pits, usually under a small barrow (*kurgan* in Russian); remains of domesticated horses; 'battle-axes' i.e. shaft-hole axes of particular types in stone but imitating metal prototypes; also, according to some interpretations, pottery of types classed as 'Corded Ware' . . . or supposed prototypes of them.'

The general view is that the Kurgan peoples were migrating into the areas north and west of the Black Sea during the period between 3000 and 2500 B.C. and that from there some groups, already driving horse-drawn vehicles and possessing such weapons as the battle-axe, migrated into and beyond the Danubian region, imposing themselves as rulers upon the earlier populations. The new evidence provided by the tumuli in Albania and by a consequential reassessment of the burials at Servia and in the tumuli in Leucas is in accord with this general view. There the earliest traces of Kurgan peoples fall within the bracket of the Late Neolithic Age to E.H. I/II which we may reckon *c.* 3000 to 2400 B.C., and in what follows I propose for convenience to place the first burial at Servia *c.* 2600 B.C.[1]

It is usually maintained that the Kurgan peoples were the main reservoir of the Indo-European languages; and that they were so far differentiated one from another, before the first migration into central Europe started, that individual sections of them spoke separable languages,[2] such as Greek and Illyrian, in however primitive a form. This hypothesis is borne out by the more recent evidence. In Yugoslavia, there are tumuli with central cist graves and pyres, offerings over the place of burial, irregular stone circles, and stone markers, which range from c. 2000 B.C. at Belotić down to late Hallstatt times; and from c. 1600 B.C. in the Dobrača area the largest tumuli are 20 m in diameter, they often contain two cist-graves with urn-burial, vases for food and drink, and sometimes the double cup. Thus the tumuli begin with the second millennium and recur again in Hallstatt C and D. The group of Kurgan peoples in central and western Yugoslavia must have spoken Illyrian, not Greek, if they brought to this area its first and lasting Indo-European language.[3] On the other hand, our group of Kurgan peoples who came into central Albania and then entered the Greek peninsula

---

[1] The quotation is from R. A. Crossland in *CAH*[3] I. ii (1971) 870. S. Piggott, *Ancient Europe* (Edinburgh, 1965) 85, gives *c.* 2500 B.C. as a C-14 date for Kurgan peoples reaching the Rhine. My date for Servia II rests on *PM* 127 and my table in *HG*[2] 21.

[2] Ibid. 50, referring to a period in the Volga region, when there was time for 'the incipient differentiation of their language into dialects, which the historical pattern of isoglosses suggests, before extensive emigration began'.

[3] I take the view—which is often contested—that Albanian is descended from Illyrian.

in the M.H. period evidently spoke Greek, not Illyrian.[1] There is in fact an interesting overlap later in central Albania; for on my interpretation the Mati valley contains tumuli of both groups, M.H. tumuli of Greek-speaking Kurgan peoples and EarlyIron Age tumuli of Illyrian-speaking Kurgan peoples, who had spread southwards from West Yugoslavia (see pp. 375 ff. below).

The existing populations into which the Kurgan peoples forced their way were already old in the sense, for instance, that a place like Nea Nikomedeia had been occupied late in the seventh millennium, and mixed in the sense that different cultures and probably different peoples had impinged at different times, for example, upon the upper Vardar valley. We shall not be far wrong if we visualize the Kurgan invaders moving south or west with their weapons, loot, wagons, and families much as the Goths of Theodoric did in A.D. 475 (see p. 34 above).

On their arrival the first group of Greek-speaking Kurgan peoples took control of Servia and probably Vergina in the Haliacmon valley and of adjacent areas, and gradually converted the existing populations to the use of the Greek language. For the latter process a period of some seven hundred years ensued, before the transplantation of the Greek language into the southern part of the peninsula got under way. During this period of some seven hundred years the Greek language became differentiated into strong dialects, which themselves proved to be long-lasting and survived transplantation at different dates not only between 1900 B.C. and 1100 B.C., but also between 1100 B.C. and 550 B.C. The geographical nature of Western Macedonia and Albania is such that strongly differentiated tribal groups and strongly differentiated dialects have evolved and persisted in all historical periods down to very recent times. Thus even in the last century the Gegs, the Tosks, the Liaps, and the Tsams were tribally and dialectically distinct groups of the Albanian-speaking people.[2] In the same way we may assume that tribally and dialectically distinct groups of the Greek-speaking people grew up in the course of the long period from *c.* 2600 to 1900 B.C.

The earliest Greek tradition about the origins of the Greeks is preserved by Hesiod (fr. 9) in the form of a genealogy. It is located in the first part of Greece proper into which the Kurgan peoples penetrated, that is in Thessaly near the end of the Late Neolithic Age. There 'the war-loving

[1] The alternative possibility is that this group of Kurgan peoples arrived speaking an Indo-European language other than Greek and adopted the Greek language from the population, say, of Pelagonia; and that after its adoption there was time for different dialects to evolve in West Macedonia and Albania before the southwards migration began. This runs counter to the current idea of a single and central area of diffusion for the Indo-European languages.

[2] See *Epirus* 31, and map in *SA* 1966. 2. 50. The complete adoption of the Greek language seems to take several centuries, if we judge by the Albanian immigrants of the fifteenth and following centuries whose descendants in Attica and at Perachora were still bilingual in many cases in the 1930s.

king Hellen [son of Deucalion] begat Dorus, Xouthus (father of Ion), and Aeolus who fought from a chariot'. These names indicate the common origin in Thessaly of three tribally and dialectically distinct groups of the Greek-speaking people, the so-called Dorieis, Iones, and Aeoleis. To these three groups we may add a fourth called by dialectologists 'the North-West Greeks', who were more closely akin to the Dorieis than to the Iones and the Aeoleis. The dialects developed between 2600 and 1900 B.C. not only among the Kurgan peoples themselves but also among the peoples who came to adopt Greek speech. Thus we may be able to suggest the particular regions in which the particular dialects developed within the general area under the control of Kurgan peoples, that is within the area extending from the Haliacmon valley to Albania and then Leucas.

One of the existing populations which was converted to the use of the Greek language was the Porodin group in Pelagonia; for we find a part of this group moving westwards into central Albania and then southwards into central Epirus in the company of tumulus-using chieftains, as far at least as the Kseria valley. As we have seen, the peoples of the Porodin culture had been for many centuries, and indeed continued to be, conservative in their way of life; and the remarkable number of habitation mounds in Pelagonia and northern Lyncus suggests that from very early times they were split into small tribal or familial units. During the M.H. period peoples of this culture settled in central Epirus, while others of their kindred in Pelagonia and Lyncus stayed where they were. Thus a group of Greek-speaking peoples with a distinctive culture and no doubt a distinctive dialect came into existence as early at least as the M.H. period. It straddled the Pindus range from north-west Macedonia to the upper basin of the river Kalamas at least, and it continued in existence until its partial disruption by the Romans under Aemilius Paulus and until its final disruption at the break-up of the Roman Empire. This group of peoples was called at one time 'the Molossian tribes', at another 'the Epirotic tribes', and at another a separable but constituent part of 'Macedonia',[1] terms which were primarily of a political colour. If we prefer the colourless language of the dialectologists, we may call them a separable but constituent part of the North-West Greeks.[2]

Another distinguishable group of our early Greek-speaking peoples seems to have lain in the southern part of Macedonia, particularly in the Haliacmon valley. The earliest traces, indeed, of Kurgan people were at Servia in that valley, and it was from Servia that they entered Thessaly late in the Late Neolithic Age. There was probably some retraction from

---

[1] Strabo C 326 fin.

[2] In *Epirus* 422 f. I give some of the arguments based on evidence of the classical period for maintaining that this group was from early times Greek-speaking and belonged to the north-west family. Acarnania was another member probably.

Thessaly in E.H. I–II, but we find Tsangli (in northern Phthiotis) and Sesklo (but not Dhimini), in what Herodotus called Histiaeotis, occupied by people with Kurgan characteristics in the M.H. period. Here again an ebb may have set in during the L.H. period. Herodotus preserves the ancient tradition that this group was 'the Dorian–Macednan group'. It held at first the region of Thessaly called Phthiotis and then the country under Mt. Ossa and Mt. Olympus. From there it was driven into the Pindus range (north-westwards) by the Cadmeans (who entered Greece *c.* 1350 B.C.).[1] We may well accept the sobriquet used by Herodotus Δωρικόν τε καὶ Μακεδνὸν ἔθνος (8. 43) as the name for this tribal and dialectical group; and we may see signs of the group's movements in the ebb and flow which is apparent in the archaeological evidence at Sesklo and Tsangli in particular.

We are left with the tumulus-using chieftains and the peoples of Leucas and Albania. It is these, as we have seen, who occupied places in east central Greece and in the Peloponnese, as well as in Ceos, in the M.H. period. Here a very broad distinction may be drawn: on the one hand we have the sea-going chieftains and people of Leucas and whoever from further north were associated with them; and on the other hand the inland chieftains and peoples of Albania, who are likely to have moved overland. This distinction may be related to the fact that some settlements in Greece were made fairly early in the M.H. period and some settlements very late in the M.H. period. It seems likely that it was the group with the sea-going leaders which made the first settlements in central and southern Greece; for these settlements were reached easily by sea—at Leucas in E.H. II, perhaps at Roupaki in Cephallenia where the graves resembled the R Graves in Leucas,[2] at Lerna in the transition from E.H. II to E.H. III, at Peristeria near Pylos early in the Middle Helladic and at Samikon in Elis perhaps early in the Middle Helladic. It seems most probable that these places were captured by sea-borne expeditions.

There are tumuli in east central Greece which seem also to be early. That at Elatea in Phocis is dated to the earliest phase of the Middle Helladic by imported vases from Crete.[3] That at Aphidna in Attica has some early features and also particular links with the west. It has three types of burial, namely pithos-graves, cist-graves of slabs, and graves in earth pits, and this is a combination found at Leucas in the

[1] For the date see *HG*² 654.

[2] S. Marinatos in *AE* 1964 [1967] 26 f.

[3] Wace in *PTh* 204, though sceptical on p. 239 of Sotiriadis's dating elsewhere, sees the vase illustrated in *AE* 1908. 87 fig. 13 = *PTh* fig. 140*d* as typical of M.M. I. The pot shown in *AE* 1908. 91 fig. 15 from Elatea tumulus is exactly like one in *Hesperia* 26 (1956) pl. 42*d* from Lerna late in the Early Helladic. An unusual kind of light incision of parallel and hatched lines at Elatea (*AE* 1908. 74 fig. 6 top) occurs at the Ayios Sotiros site in Leucas (*Alt-Ithaka* 281 and Beilage 56 b and 57 b).

R Graves but not in the Albanian tumuli.[1] The earliest pithos-burial, Grave III, at Aphidna resembles pithos-burials in the R Graves in having much ash lying outside the pithos at either end, partly burnt bones in the ash, a large stone blocking the mouth of the recumbent pithos, and a bed of stones under it (at Leucas the stones are usually described as being all round it). The pottery in Grave III included an urn and sherds with incised decoration of kinds found at Mega, at Lerna very early in the Middle Helladic, at Servia, and at Malik, and two unique vessels, reconstructed from sherds and shown only in a drawing, which Dörpfeld noted as examples of the twin-vessel ('Zwillingsgefäss'), although of a more elaborate kind.[2] Twin-vessels of this period are found in tumuli: two in R Graves at Leucas, one in the M.H. shaft-grave at Kephalovryson which contained the one-edged snouted knives, and one in Tumulus A Grave 3 at Vajzë in Albania.[3] More interesting still is the report that the tumulus-burials of the Dobrača area sometimes had a double-cup.[4] It seems likely then that the burials in the tumulus at Elatea and the earliest burials in the tumulus at Aphidna should be classed with the early group.

Of the two remaining groups of Greek-speaking peoples, the Iones and the Aeoleis, it is the Iones whose gifts lay in seafaring. In the ancient tradition they were the first Greek-speaking settlers of Attica and probably of other places too in Greece. Thus Herodotus reports that the Iones of Attica were 'the first of the Greeks' to have encountered 'the Pelasgians' (Hdt. 2. 51), a term which means *inter alia* non-Greek-speakers, and Thucydides thinks of them as holding Attica for many generations before the time of Theseus (1. 2. 3 f. and 2. 15. 1), and as not being displaced by the migrations which ended the Late Bronze Age. They figure as the Iaones in *Iliad* 13. 685. Being the first of the Greek-speakers to arrive in Attica, the Iones claimed to be autochthonous.[5] So did the Iones of Cynouria, who were there when the Dorians came at the end of the Bronze Age (Hdt. 8. 73. 3). Iones held Achaea also before the Dorians and their associates came to expel them (Hdt. 1. 145). Traces of Ionic dialect in Troezen indicate that Troezen was Ionic in the Late Bronze

---

[1] *AM* 21 (1896) 389; *Alt-Ithaka* 249.

[2] *AM* 21. 391 f. and pls. xiv and xv.

[3] *Alt-Ithaka* 302 and Beilage 64. 7 and 66. 2a and 3; *Arch. Reports* 1965. 13 fig. 14*b*; *BUSS* 1957. 2. 81 fig. 5*b*. Those from Leucas and Vajzë have several pierced lugs; see also *Epirus* 311 and fig. 17, 11 and 13, where I dated the double-vessel at Vajzë later; I think now, mistakenly. Two other pots from Aphidna Grave III are similar in shape, though with higher handles, to a cup from the E.H. III layer at Lerna (*AM* 21 (1896) pl. xv, 6 and 7, and *Hesp.* 25 (1956) pl. 43*d*). I saw in 1968 an unpublished double-cup from the Voïon area (Grevena–Kastoria) in the museum at Kozani; a similar one of M.H. date comes from Tsangli (*PTh* 109 fig. 59*c* and 113).

[4] *AI* 2 (1956) 12 with illustrations. Also at Komarevo in the Vrattsa region of Bulgaria; see Археология, 4. 4 (1962) 68 fig. 7.

[5] Solon called Attica the oldest land of 'Iaonia' (fr. 4).

Age. These districts, Cynouria, Achaea, and Troezen, look like places of refuge, and it may be that in even earlier times the Iones held richer parts of the Peloponnese such as Lerna or Elis, and the unique expression in *Odyssey* 18. 246 ἀν᾽ Ἴασον Ἄργος for the Peloponnese may stem from an early Ionian memory.[1] Hdt. 5. 58. 2 f. preserves the tradition that when the Cadmeans came to Boeotia, that is *c.* 1350 B.C.,[2] the areas round Boeotia (which include Attica) were held by Iones. It looks then as if the earliest tumuli—those at Elatea and Aphidna, at Lerna, and in the western Peloponnese—may be evidence of Ionian settlement early in the M.H. period, in the sense that the leaders and the bulk at least of their followers spoke the (earlier form of the classical) Ionic dialect of Greek. They had come, on my interpretation, from the 'Ionian Gulf', which was named after them, and from its hinterland.

The late wave of settlement which took place towards the end of the M.H. period was the most powerful in its effects; for it led directly to the growth and the spread of what we call Mycenaean civilization. The key site is Mycenae. Here the earliest graves—namely those in the defective circle preceding Grave Circle B, the earlier ones in Grave Circle B, and the earlier ones in Grave Circle A[3]—are clearly to be derived from the earlier M.H. burials in the tumuli of central and southern Albania and not from those in the tumuli of Leucas. There are close analogies in the details of the burial customs, the structure of the mortuary chambers, and the contents of the graves. The same taste is apparent in Albania and at Mycenae; and as the wealth of Mycenae increased at the end of M.H., it took the form of a barbaric splendour, which marked the later graves. The scenes on the *stelai* and the armaments of the chieftains are typical of a hunting and military élite, who fought from chariots and wagons. They are landsmen, not seamen; forerunners not of the Milesians but of the Macedonians; and their delight is not in ships but in horses. These are the people of 'Aeolus who fought from the chariot' and of the Aeolidae, namely Cretheus (founder of Iolcus), Deïon (king of Phocis), Athamas (king of Minyan Orchomenus), Sisyphus (builder of Ephyra, viz. the later Corinth), Salmoneus (on emigrating from Thessaly founder of Salmone in Elis), and Perieres (king of Messenia).[4] They held most of the areas which in

---

[1] I do not agree with those who place no reliance at all on the ancient literary evidence and maintain that Ionic developed after the migrations to the east (see J. Chadwick in *CAH*[2] 2. 39. 16). The name Iasos occurs in *Iliad* 15. 332 as that of the leader of the Athenians. The early names, under which the Greek speakers in Attica went, are reflected in Hdt. 8. 44. 2 (cf. 7. 94), but they are never ascribed to any other group than the Ionic one. For Ionians as a considerable element in the Peloponnese in L.H. III see Hdt. 7. 94 and 9. 26. 3 and Paus. 2. 37. 3.

[2] For the value and the date of this tradition see *HG*[2] 654.

[3] See my article in *BSA* 62 (1967) 90 f.

[4] Hes. fr. 10, omitting Deïon who figures in other lists.

the Late Bronze Age spoke the Aeolic dialect, namely Thessaly, Phocis, and Boeotia in the east and Aetolia in the west, Corinthia and the Argolid, and probably other parts of the Peloponnese such as parts of Elis and Messenia.[1] Signs of their arrival may perhaps be seen not only in the Grave Circles of Mycenae but also in the tumuli at Malthi in Messenia and at Pylos in Elis, in the shaft-graves sunk into the (earlier) tumulus at Lerna in the Argolid, and in the tumulus in Ceos.

Although the archaeological evidence is patchy and broad distinctions have been drawn between tumulus-users in Leucas and tumulus-users in Albania and between early and late settlements in Greece, whereas in practice there may have been more overlap, yet enough emerges to justify the ancient division into Ionians, Aeoleis, Dorieis, and what were called probably by Hecataeus 'Molossika ethne'. We are left with another part of the earliest genealogy we have of the Greek race, namely that which is concerned with the descendants not of Deucalion's son Hellen but of Deucalion's daughter Thyia, who bore to Zeus two sons 'Magnes and Macedon who fights from the chariot, and they had their dwelling around Pieria and Olympus' (Hesiod, *Eoeae* fr. 7). This tradition relates to a time before Magnes moved into the north-eastern part of Thessaly, which received the name Magnesia (Hesiod, *The Great Eoeae* fr. 256) and before the Trojan War when the Magnetes lived round the Peneus and Mt. Pelion (*Il.* 2. 757).[2] Now the name which Hdt. 7. 131 gives to the mountain north of Olympus is 'the Makedonikon oros', which is in Pieria; and this name is evidently related by Herodotus at 1. 56. 3 to the 'Makednan' name adopted by the Dorian group when it moved from Olympus to Pindus at some time after *c.* 1350 B.C. If our interpretation of the earliest genealogy is correct, the Macedones being, like the Molossian group, a collateral branch of the Greek-speaking peoples were in the northern mountainous part of Pieria in the centuries *c.* 1900–1600 B.C. which we know as the M.H. period.

[1] Hdt. 7. 176 (Thessaly); Aeolic influence survived in the dialect of the classical period in Phocis, which was mainly North-West-Greek; Thuc. 7. 57. 5 (Boeotia); Thuc. 3. 102. 5 (Aetolia); Thuc. 4. 42. 2 (Corinthia); the decipherment of the Linear B Script suggests that the kings of Mycenae spoke an Aeolic form of Greek; Aeolic influence survived in the dialect of the classical period in Elis, which was mainly North-West-Greek; and the link between Messenia and Aeolic Thessaly recurs again with the tradition of Neleus coming from Thessaly to Messenian Pylus.

[2] My reasons for believing that the Homeric Catalogue of Ships describes conditions of *c.* 1200 B.C. are given in *HG²* 64 f.

XI

THE LATE BRONZE AGE

1. *The Local Potteries of Macedonia and their Distribution*

THE transition from the Middle Bronze Age to the Late Bronze Age in Central Macedonia and in Chalcidice was marked for Heurtley by the beginnings of a matt-painted pottery, and it was on this criterion that he dated the transition to *c.* 1500 B.C. in Central Macedonia and to a little later in Chalcidice (*PM* 126), the difference in time being due to his belief that the matt-painted pottery originated in Central Macedonia and spread thence into Chalcidice. From 1500 to 1150 B.C. these two districts were very closely associated with one another, especially in their pottery (*PM* 112). When Mycenaean objects began to appear *c.* 1350 B.C., they came 'almost simultaneously' to both areas and did not affect their close interrelationship. So far then as external relations were concerned, it appears that in the period 1500–1150 B.C. Central Macedonia and Chalcidice looked eastwards and southwards. This appearance is supported by the fact that almost all the sites in Central Macedonia were on the east side of the Axius river. By way of contrast 'Western Macedonia remained isolated' from Central Macedonia and Chalcidice (*PM* 112).

In fact two new wares marked the transition to the Late Bronze Age in Central Macedonia and Chalcidice: the matt-painted ware and an incised ware. Heurtley held that they were both descended on parallel lines from the earlier incised pottery of Central Macedonia (*PM* 94 f.). Soon after the establishment of these two wares there appeared at Vardarophtsa, Vardina, Saratse, and Sedhes an incised ware of a distinct and simpler kind; this ware too was thought by Heurtley to have been an internal growth from an earlier tradition. The shapes too of the vessels are marked by a very conservative trend. Heurtley noted only two possible influences entering Central Macedonia before 1350 B.C.: one from Bosnia in respect of the 'thumb-grip' handle (Fig. 14*a*), in which the vertical member of a triangular handle was prolonged above the horizontal member and provided a rest for the thumb (*PM* 124 with n. 1), and the other from Vučedol in northern Yugoslavia, where some incised decorations resembled those of the later incised ware at Vardarophtsa, etc. (*PM* 96 n. 1). Within Central Macedonia there was an enlargement of some sites which had been occupied in the Middle Bronze Age;

1 Gajtan
2 Visoï
3 Pazhok
4 Bulçar
5 Tren Cave
6 Kravari
7 Saraj
8 Malik
9 Symize
10 Ventrok
11 Benje
12 Vodhinë
13 Bodrishtë
14 Boubousti
15 Tsotyli
16 Omali
17 Palaiogratsiano
18 Vergina
19 Kilindir
20 Chauchitsa
21 Vardina
22 Vardarophtsa
23 Sedhes
24 Saratse
25 Petralona
26 Hagios Mamas
27 Kastritsa
28 Koutsoulio
29 Volustana Pass
30 Portes Sarandaporou

Priština
Lipljan
MT. ZRNA GORA
Kačanik
Kumanovo
Skopje
Sitnica
Morava

Lake Skutari
Drin
White Drin
Prizren
Kukës
Tetovo
Gostivar
Titov Veles
Vardar
Treska

Scodra
1
ZADRIMË
ŠAR PLANINA

Matt
Kitsevo
MT. BABUNA

Epidamnus
IONIAN
Black Drin
Prilep
2
MT. BARNO

GULF
Elbasan
Shkumbi
3
Ochrid
Lake Ochrid
Monastir
6
7
Cevna
MT. BARNO

Devoli
Lake Prespa
Edess

Semeni
4
Berat
Lake Malik
8
9
5
10
Florina
Lake Ostrovo

Apollonia
Aous
Osum
Koritsa
Kastoria
Lake Rudnik
Naouss
MT. BERMIO

Valona
Shushicë
Aous
11
MT. GRAMMOS
14
Haliacmon
Kozani

Drin
12
13
Konitsa
Aous
Grevena
15
16
Servia

Kalamas
MT. PINDUS
Arachthus
Acheloüs
Triccala
Peneu

CORCYRA
Ioannina
28 27
Dodona

MAP 2I. LAT

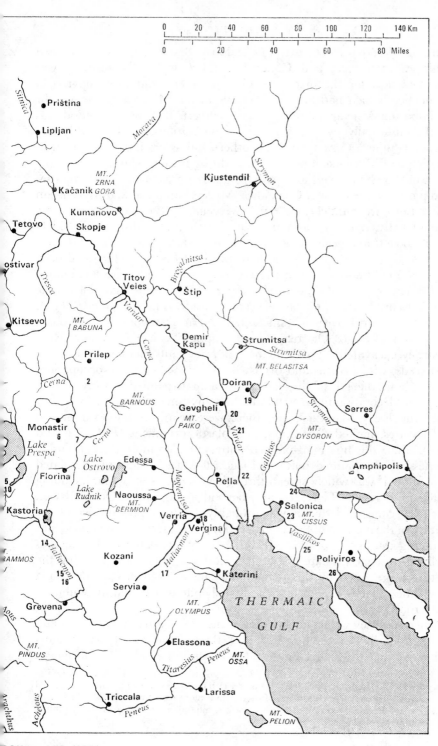

RONZE AGE SITES.

Vardina, deserted since early in the Early Bronze Age, was occupied again *c.* 1350 B.C.; and Chauchitsa (Heurtley's 'Tsaoutsitza') was occupied now for the first time. On the other hand Molyvopyrgo in Chalcidice, which had been remarkable in the Middle Bronze Age for its imported Minyan pottery, now lay deserted. Thus the period was marked internally by slowly improving conditions and by hardly any outside contacts. *Circa* 1350 B.C. southern influences began to return in the shape of Mycenaean pottery, brought by traders who sailed into the delta of the Axius river, and perhaps upstream as far as Vardarophtsa, and put in on the coast of Chalcidice. Mycenaean forms and Mycenaean decorations were quickly adopted. Mycenaean types of pottery were made locally, especially at Vardarophtsa; they were distributed widely after 1300 B.C. and began to penetrate into Western Macedonia (*PM* 124).

In north-western Macedonia the towns of Pelagonia, which had been inhabited continuously since the Late Neolithic Age, were abandoned at the end of the Middle Bronze Age, and it seems that the people moved to hill-sites and may have become pastoral and nomadic (*PM* 93). An interesting discovery was made in Western Macedonia at Boubousti, south-west of Argos Orestikon, in the upper Haliacmon valley. Here Heurtley excavated a tiny settlement of a few huts, made of mud-brick and reeds, with hearths and ovens; he noted two stages of occupation. Throughout the life of this settlement a matt-painted pottery was in use with 'decoration more elaborate than anything known in Macedonia since the Early Neolithic', and there were relatively few examples of plain wares, incised decoration, and plastic ornament (*PM* 40 f. and 99 f.). Since this fine matt-painted pottery has no more than 'a family likeness' to the painted pottery of Central Macedonia, and as isolated finds show it was widely spread through Western Macedonia, including Pateli in Eordaea (Fig. 14*e*), and beyond as far as the Ochrid basin, Heurtley concluded that it was probably a later representative of the culture of the mounds of Pelagonia (*PM* 99–100). Heurtley had no means of dating the first appearance of this pottery at Boubousti, but he was inclined to suggest a date *c.* 1300 B.C. In doing so he remarked that the culture represented by this pottery may have 'been in existence for a long time', that is long before the first shepherds camped at Boubousti (*PM* 100).

Since Heurtley wrote, further discoveries have been made. In the plain of Ioannina in Central Epirus S. I. Dakaris found two types of matt-painted pottery, which I have called K 4a and K 4b.[1] The former is

[1] See *Epirus* 292, with references. S. I. Dakaris published both painted wares at first as Category IV in *PAE* 1951. 180 f. but as IVa and IVb in *PAE* 1952. 373 f., where he stressed the essential difference between them. However, in a more recent work in *PAE* 1966. 401, he writes as if they were one and the same, as he attributes them to invaders whom he thinks to have been the Molossians.

identical with that of Boubousti, except that a high-footed Mycenaean type of goblet with a geometric design has no parallel at Boubousti. The latter, K 4b, may have derived from a painted pottery found at Vardarophtsa in Central Macedonia, where it was in use from early in L.H. III, i.e. from *c.* 1350 B.C. I have suggested elsewhere[1] that the bearers of these two painted potteries were nomadic shepherds who stayed a relatively short time in central Epirus; that those whose contacts were with Vardarophtsa were perhaps the earlier of the two; and that the influences of Macedonian painted pottery and its forms which Heurtley noted at Choirospilia in Leucas, at Thermum in Aetolia, and at Pelikata in Ithaca[2] may have come from Macedonia through Epirus. More important still, Frano Prendi has found at Malik in the last settlement, known as IIId, a matt-painted pottery superior in quality to any of the earlier potteries there and having very close affinities with the Boubousti pottery.[3] He and his colleagues have found similar pottery on a nearby hill-site called Symize, to which the people of Malik probably moved; at Tren on the Albanian side of Lake Little Prespa; at Bulçar in Gramsh on the middle Devoli; at Pazhok in a tumulus; at Benje near Permet on the middle Aous; and at Vodhinë in a tumulus.[4] These discoveries have made it clear that Boubousti lay not at the centre but on the periphery of a zone of culture characterized by this excellent matt-painted pottery, which in Frano Prendi's phrase 'bears the veritable stamp of art'.[5]

When we try to date the beginnings of this pottery, the important site is Malik. The first examples of it appeared in Malik IIIc, which we have dated within the Middle Helladic period (see p. 256 above), and then without any break[6] in the settlement this pottery became dominant in IIId. At the same time there was a marked continuity between IIIc and IIId in the shapes of the vessels. Some features in IIId pottery are imitative of metalwork: plastic rivet-heads and rivet-holes grouped at the places where the handle joins the wall of the vessel, the 'split handle', and the triangular handle (Fig. 12, *c*, *i*, *j*, *m*, *t*, *v*, and *ee*).[7] These features are close to the Minyan style of the Middle Helladic period.

[1] *Epirus* 313.
[2] *PM* 131.
[3] *SA* 1966. 1. 267 f.: 'Les plus grandes similitudes de la poterie peinte de cette phase de Maliq . . . sont avec la poterie peinte en mat du bronze récent de Bubušt.'
[4] *SA* 1966. 1. 227 f. where *IId* is a slip for *IIId*. For Pazhok see *SA* 1964. 1. 119 pl. vii, 2, and for Vodhinë see *Epirus* 310 with references.
[5] *SA* 1966. 1. 267: 'la variété de composition de ces motifs géométriques, en concordance avec les formes d'une belle venue des récipients aux lignes élégantes et lestes, donnent au groupe de poterie peinte le véritable sceau de l'art'.
[6] *SA* 1966. 1. 275.
[7] Ibid., pl. xvii, 9, 10, 13, 14, 26 (rivet-heads and holes), comparable with *PM* 92 and 210 fig. 76 *c* and *d* in the Middle Bronze Age at Molyvopyrgo; pl. xvii, 13 and 20 (split handles); pl. xvii, 31 (triangular handle).

Thus the evidence at Malik suggests that Malik IIId began late in the Middle Helladic rather than early in L.H. I. Such a date fits well with the appearance of a similar matt-painted pottery at Lianokladhi III in the Spercheus valley, there associated with imported Minyan ware and attributed by Wace and Thompson and others to the M.H. period.[1] I conclude, then, that this particularly fine matt-painted pottery with geometric linear ornaments was developed late in the M.H. period in the district of Malik and that it spread from there throughout Albania, down the Haliacmon valley to Boubousti, into Epirus, and as far as Liano- kladhi. In the light of the new evidence it is advisable to look again at variations within the group and to bear in mind the need perhaps to revise the datings made by Heurtley and others.

Within the group there are regional differences. The matt-painted pottery at Malik is described by Frano Prendi as follows.[2] The paint of which the colours are chestnut, dark chestnut, and red was applied direct to the natural surface of the pot, which varied in tone from grey to ochre and red. The painted linear geometric designs were used in a variety of combinations to enhance the graceful shapes of the vessels. Typical designs, which are shown on two plates in Prendi's report[3] (he does not show actual vases), are reproduced here as Fig. 11. The designs include triangles either solid with paint or filled with parallel lines or filled with criss-crossed lines, triangles apex to apex forming various shapes, chess-board patterns, straight bands either solid with paint or filled with criss-crossed parallel lines, dentated lines, herring-bones, ladders, zigzags, and so on. Curves do not appear, except that the tips of some slender triangles are curving. The designs were evidently grouped round the neck, the handles, and the shoulder of the vessels, as we see from a pot found in an upper tumulus at Pazhok.[4]

Some shapes in this ware were identical with those of Malik IIIc; others were variations of them, having more developed handles and more decoration. In his outline drawings Prendi shows the following shapes of IIId pottery.[5] (1) The two-handled tankard or *cantharos* (Fig. 12, *a*, *d*, *g*, and *h*). (2) The two-handled bowl, sometimes with handles rising high from the rim, sometimes with elongated tips to the handles, and some- times with wish-bone handles rising from the shoulder (Fig. 12, *c*, *f*, *i*, *j*, *m*, *n*, and *p*). (3) The bowl with two lug-like handles set below the rim, or with two heavy and almost triangular handles set below the rim, or with two heavy horizontal loop-handles (Fig. 12, *k*, *o*, and *q*). (4) The handleless small bowl (Fig. 12, *b* and *e*). (5) The handleless large bowl with a rippled rim (Fig. 12*r*). (6) The water-pot with the

[1] *PTh* 180 f. and 236 f. J. L. Caskey in *CAH*[3] II i. 122, places Lianokladhi III in the Middle Helladic.   [2] *SA* 1966. 1. 267 f.   [3] Ibid., pls. xviii and xix.
[4] *SA* 1964. 1. 96 and 119 pl. vii, 2.   [5] *SA* 1966. 1 pl. xvii.

tops of the handles and the rim forming a straight line (Fig. 12*l*). Handles include wish-bone handles with and without elongated tips, ledge-lugs pierced and unpierced, high loop-handles, split handles, and triangular handles. Some handles are decorated with plastic rivet-heads or rivet-holes at the places where they join the wall of the pot. Some lugs have extensions, which fit through the wall of the pot (Fig. 12*cc*).[1]

A plain ware at Malik IIId has the same shapes. Some vessels of plain ware are shown from an upper tumulus at Pazhok.[2] There are three two-handled tankards, one with elongated tips to the handles. There is also from there a tall water-jar with a cylindrical neck. An incised ware at Malik IIId often has the same designs as the matt-painted ware. Prendi does not illustrate any of the incised ware of Malik IIId, but he sees an analogy in the decorations of the incised ware at Gajtan near Scodra.[3] The incised designs which are illustrated in the publication of Gajtan show that the designs of Gajtan II pottery are cruder than those of the matt-painted ware. On my dating of the layer, the Gajtan pottery is probably earlier.[4]

On the matt-painted pottery at Boubousti, as described by Heurtley,[5] the paint is purple when the pot's surface is buff or grey, and black when it is red. The decorative systems are rectangular, and they are usually concentrated on the neck and upper parts of the jar. 'Slender triangles hatched, latticed, or closed, of which the apexes are prolonged almost to the base of the vase' are very frequent. The illustrations in *Prehistoric Macedonia* show examples of almost all the designs which are found at Malik IIId, and the only curving lines on the Boubousti pottery appear in the apexes of slender triangles as at Malik.[6] The shapes at Boubousti are as follows. (1) The jug with sloping, sometimes cut-away neck (Fig. 14*b*). (2) The globular bowl with broad everted rim; it has sometimes horizontal lugs (Fig. 14*c*), sometimes wish-bone handles, and sometimes rims extended to form a triangular grip. (3) The tankard with two ribbon-handles rising from the rim (Fig. 14*d*). (4) The jar with conical neck and vertical lugs, and the jar with cylindrical neck and horizontal lugs (as in Fig. 14*e*). (5) The bowl with a broad flat rim. Among the handles at Boubousti there are split handles and also loop-handles with extensions to go through the wall of the pot, as at Malik.[7] An unusual type of handle is derived probably from acquaintance with Mycenaean pottery.[8] A plain ware at Boubousti had shapes 2 and 4 of the painted ware. An incised ware at Boubousti was represented by one

[1] *SA* 1966. 1 pl. xvii.
[2] *SA* 1964. 1. 119, 3–5; reproduced in *BSA* 62 (1967) pl. 20.
[3] *SA* 1966. 1. 278.   [4] *StH* 1966. 1. 55 figs. 8 *a–d*, *g*, and *l*.
[5] *PM* 99 and 227 f. and *BSA* 28 (1926–7) 167 f.   [6] *PM* 227 no. 460.
[7] *PM* 229 fig. 101 *l*, *m*, and *n*; *SA* 1966. 1 pl. xvii, 13, 20, and 29.
[8] *PM* 100 and *BSA* 28. 173, figs. 21. 8 and 28. 4.

sherd only; it had a row of plain and hatched triangles, a design which appeared also on matt-painted wares there.

When we compare the matt-painted wares of Malik IIId and Bou-busti, we see an immediate similarity and sometimes an identity, as Prendi remarks,[1] in the linear geometric designs, the repertory of motifs, the concentration on the structural parts of the vessel, and the avoidance of any curvilinear devices such as the wavy line, the spiral, and the pot-hook. As regards the shapes Malik IIId and Boubousti have in common the two-handled tankard (Malik 1 and Boubousti 3), a shape which was typical of Armenokhori in Lyncus late in the Early Bronze Age, and the bowl with two lug-like handles set below the rim (Malik 3 and Bou-busti 2).[2] On the other hand, Malik alone has the handleless bowls, the two-handled bowls with various kinds of handles, and the water-jar with the straight top, and Boubousti alone has the jug with sloping or cut-away neck, the jars with conical and cylindrical necks, and the bowl with a broad, flat rim. It is clear that Malik and Boubousti each derived these shapes from their own local tradition: Malik from its own earlier phases and Boubousti from Central Macedonia, where both kinds of jug had a history in the Middle Bronze Age. Malik and Boubousti have in common the split handles and other kinds of handles, and the same device of extensions which fitted through the wall of the pot. They both have plain and incised wares, and in both places these wares bear the same relationship to the matt-painted ware.

In short, Malik appears to be the leader in this school of matt-painted pottery; for the quality of its pottery is finer, the designs are more varied, and the forms of some pots are more primitive. Boubousti is an offshoot of the school; but it has some shapes deriving from Central Macedonia and some knowledge of Mycenaean shapes, gained probably after 1300 B.C.

At Tren, on the south-west shore of Little Prespa Lake, where a part only of the cave has been excavated, the excavators (Muzafa Korkuti, Frano Prendi, and Zhaneta Andrea) have found a culture which is sub-sequent to Malik IIId but is clearly a close descendant of it. There was a gap in the habitation of the cave between the layer typical of Malik IIb culture (see p. 242 above) and the layers under consideration. In these layers 'a pot of Late Helladic date, imported from the Aegean world' gave a date within L.H. III for a part at least of this culture. If my dating of Malik IIId is correct (see p. 282 above), the start of the culture found at Tren was in L.H. III. The two principal shapes of the pottery at Tren

[1] *SA* 1966. 1. 267 and 275.

[2] *SA* 1964. 1. 94 and 109 pl. ii, 15; *SA* 1966. 1 pl. xvii, 1, 3, 4, 6, 7, 8; and *PM* 99 and 227 nos. 461 and 462 for the tankards. *SA* 1966. 1 pl. xvii, 11 and *PM* 227 nos. 459, 460, 466, and 467 for the bowls.

are the tankard with high vertical ribbon handles from shoulder to rim, that is the Boubousti shape no. 3, and the open bowl with two horizontal handles and everted rim, on the inner side of which small squares and similar designs are painted, that is the Boubousti shape no. 2, which has similar designs on the rims (Fig. 14c).[1] There are only two sherds which belong to jugs with sloping necks, that is of the Boubousti shape no. 1;[2] this suggests that Tren is on the last fringe of influence from Central Macedonia where this type of jug was typical. There are other shapes of vessels and also a number of handles at Tren, such as the horned handle, large lug, and perforated small lug, which appear rarely or not at all at Boubousti but are in the Malik tradition.[3]

The colour of the clay, reddish or grey, the polished surface, and the matt paint of bright or dark chestnut, applied direct to the surface, are very much as at Boubousti.[4] The range of painted motives includes those found at Boubousti and others as well.[5] Particularly typical of Tren are the square, filled with parallel lines or crossed lines; the groups of parallel lines; the bands filled with zigzag lines; and the bands of small rhombi (Fig. 14 *f* and *j*). Tankards with pendent slender triangles from the shoulder were not found. Both at Tren and at Boubousti the handles are decorated with painted lines which seem to imitate strings (Fig. 11, the last two).[6] This finely painted pottery is the commonest pottery at Tren. Next comes pottery with plastic decoration, such as raised bands with impressed pock-marks. There were only two sherds with incised decoration. A very small amount, less than 5 per cent, of the pottery was made on the wheel. In Macedonia in the Late Bronze Age only one wheel-made pot was known to Heurtley and that was at Boubousti with a question mark.[7] The excavators have dated the end of this culture at Tren to the end of the Bronze Age, although noting that some of its features are found elsewhere in Albania in the Early Iron Age. Other finds were two flat celts of the shape common earlier at Malik, a worn flint instrument, a biconical bronze bead, and many fishing-weights. The terrace outside the cave was also occupied at this time.

Only a few examples of matt-painted ware from other parts of Albania have been described or illustrated. The jug from an upper tumulus at Pazhok has typical patterns of linear geometric design, and its shape seems to imitate a metal original.[8] Of the plain ware there the

---

[1] *SA* 1967. 1. 143 (Tren) and *PM* 227 no. 461 (Boubousti) for the tankard. For the bowls and the designs on the rims *SA* 1967. 1. 143 and fig. 4, 18 and 19, (Tren), *PM* 227 nos. 459 and 460, 229 nos. 466 and 467, and *BSA* 28 (1926–7) 171 and figs. 13, 23a and 28, 5 (Boubousti). [2] *SA* 1967. 1 fig. 3 nos. 17 and 19.
[3] Ibid. 143 and fig. 3. [4] Ibid. and *BSA* 28. 167 and 169.
[5] Compare *SA* 1967. 1 figs. 3 and 4 with *BSA* 28. 176 fig. 24.
[6] *SA* 1967. 1. fig. 4, especially 18 and 19, and *BSA* 28. 173 fig. 21, 9 and 11, and 175 fig. 23A.
[7] *SA* 1967. 1. 143 and 144; *PM* 228. [8] *SA* 1964. 1. 96 and pl. vii, 2.

two-handled tankards are of the kind found at Malik and Boubousti, and the water-jug with the cylindrical neck, globular body, and vertical handles on the shoulder resembles one from Armenokhori, dated late in the Early Bronze Age, and several of a more primitive kind from Gajtan.[1] A two-handled tankard from Grave 12 in the tumulus at Vodhinë in the Kseria valley is decorated in matt paint of café-brown colour on a light ground: two fine wavy lines run round the top and the bottom of the neck, there are between them six diamonds filled with geometric designs in paint, and below the lower wavy line the body of the pot is decorated with pendent slender triangles of which the apexes hang downwards (Fig. 14*l*).[2] Prendi reported just such another pot from Ventrok near Koritsa.[3] This shape in a plain ware is not uncommon in the tumulus-burials of Albania. There are three examples of the water-jar with the straight top from the tumulus-burials at Bodrishtë in the Kseria valley; they are like shape 6 of Malik IIId (Fig. 12*l*). It seems, then, that the Albanian varieties of matt-painted wares and their counterparts in plain ware go mainly with Malik IIId.[4] Pottery typical of Tren, which came after the end of Malik IIId, has been found at Bulçar in Gramsh and in a cave at Benje near Permet on the Aous.[5]

Across the Greek border S. I. Dakaris saw 'undoubtedly a direct relationship' between the matt-painted K 4a ware (found at Kastritsa and at Koutsoulio in the plain south of Ioannina) and the Boubousti matt-painted ware. The full range of linear geometric designs is represented there, and in addition the odd pot-hook spiral occurs. The technique is the same as at Boubousti and Malik. An incised sherd at Kastritsa has a design which appears also in paint.[6] Here the relationship is closer with Boubousti than with Malik; for Kastritsa has jugs with cut-away necks (Boubousti shape 1, found in Albania only at Tren) and jugs or jars with high narrow necks.[7] There is a connection not with Boubousti but with Central Macedonia in the pot-hook spiral on the matt-painted K 4a ware at Kastritsa.[8] At the same time Malik's shapes 2-6 seem to be lacking at Kastritsa. But once again we find the common denominator between all these sites not only in the technique and designs of the matt-painted ware but also in a two-handled tankard at Kastritsa decorated with two paint-filled wavy-edged lines at the top and the

[1] *SA* 1964. 1 pl. vii, 6 (Pazhok); *PM* 195 no. 352 (Armenokhori); *StH* 1966. 1. 54 and pl. xii, 6, 8, 9, and 10 (Gajtan; of these no. 9 from Gajtan II is inscribed with groups of crisscrossed lines in the form of design used on the matt-painted ware of Malik IIId).

[2] *BUSS* 1956. 1. 184 and fig. ii, 3 = *Epirus* 310 and fig. 10*m*.

[3] *BUSS* 1956. 1. 184.

[4] *SA* 1966. 1 pl. xvii, 12 (Malik); *BUSS* 1959. 2. 198 fig. 9*a* and 204 fig. 16 *a* and *b*.

[5] *SA* 1967. 1. 143 and 145.

[6] Dakaris in *PAE* 1951. 180 f. and 1952. 373 f.; see also *Epirus* 295 f.

[7] *PAE* 1951. 182 with fig. 6, 2 and 3 = *Epirus* fig. 8; *PM* 227 nos. 463 to 465 and fig. 98 *d* and *i*. [8] *PAE* 1951. 180 f. and fig. 6, 2; *PM* 219 figs. 89 and 90.

bottom of the neck and a line of slender triangles pendent from the shoulder with the apexes pointing downwards (Fig. 14g).[1] At Kastritsa, as at Boubousti, a separate and later shape appears as the result of some contact with Mycenaean pottery: for high-footed goblets were found, mostly in a plain ware but in one case with a geometric design in matt paint, and these goblets are unlike anything from Albania or from Boubousti.[2] This part, then, of central Epirus in contrast to the Kseria valley sites, just north of the frontier, seems to have its contacts with Boubousti and Central Macedonia rather than with Malik.

The pottery of Lianokladhi III in the Spercheus valley which is known as Δ1β appeared suddenly there and seemed, in Wace's words, 'peculiar to Lianokladhi'.[3] The technique is that of the other matt-painted wares which we have so far described; for the paint, which is black, is applied directly to the surface of the reddish clay, and the pottery is hand-made. The pots have no bases but merely flattened bottoms, as is the case at Malik, Boubousti, Pazhok, Vodhinë, and Kastritsa (except for the Mycenaeanizing goblets). The designs are of the familiar linear geometric types; the repertoire is very like that found at Boubousti, and it is paralleled and even exceeded by the repertoire at Malik.[4] The designs are applied to the same parts of the vessels. There are some particular features: spirals and pot-hook spirals are common as in Central Macedonia[5] (occurring also at Kastritsa), the slender triangles pendent from the shoulder are lacking, and many vessels have a crossed circle on the bottom, a decorative practice noted at Malik II and Malik IIIa.[6] The shapes at Lianokladhi are as follows. (1) The water-jug with a cylindrical neck and a globular body, as at Boubousti, Pazhok, and Gajtan, but less tall at Lianokladhi.[7] (2) The two-handled tankard,[8] similar in shape to those of Malik, Boubousti, etc. (Fig. 14l). (3) The shallow, open bowl with loop handles on the rim. (4) Amphorae usually without handles. (5) Handleless round jars with a tall narrow neck, sometimes with two small lugs on each side.[9] Wace's Δ1γ ware is also matt-painted; it has shallow bowls with a flattened bottom and raking handles, which are of a shape known in Macedonia and which occur in this matt-painted

---

[1] *PAE* 1952. 374 fig. 11 = *Epirus* fig. 10k. The extension of the handle to fit through the wall of the pot occurs also in Epirus; see *PAE* 1952. 375 fig. 13, 3 and *Epirus* fig. 11 b 6 = fig. 13 b 6 (from Terovo).

[2] *PAE* 1951. 182 fig. 7 and 1952. 365 fig. 3, 1–3.   [3] *PTh* 180 f.

[4] Compare *PTh* figs. 125–33 with *PM* 227–9 and *SA* 1966. 1 pls. xviii and xix.

[5] Spirals and pot-hook spirals appear in the Late Neolithic Age at Malik IIa (*SA* 1964. 1. 93 and *SA* 1966. 1 pls. vi–viii), at Servia (*PM* 74 with fig. 9f and fig. 13 (i) c), and at Kritsana and Olynthus (*PM* 75 f. with fig. 29b, fig. 32g and no. 148). They appear next in the Middle Bronze Age at Kilindir, Saratse, and Vardarophtsa (*PM* 90 f. and 205 f.), and again in the Late Bronze Age in Central Macedonia (*PM* 94 f. and 218 f.).

[6] *SA* 1966. 1. 264.

[7] *PTh* 181 fig. 125; *BSA* 28. 170 fig. 18 (Boubousti); *SA* 1964. 1. 119 pl. vii, 6 (Pazhok); *StH* 1966 1 pl. xii.   [8] *PTh* 182 fig. 126 c and d.   [9] *PTh* 184 and fig. 133.

style at Malik IIId. This shape is found also in a plain, unpainted form. These wares, then, are closely related to the matt-painted group, but they have some characteristics which seem to be earlier and to derive from Malik II or IIIa, notably the decorating of the bottom of vessels and the use of small lugs. There are signs of Macedonian influence too, as Wace and Heurtley remarked,[1] but some of them may have been transmitted via Malik.

Lastly, one may note that very similar designs occurred on matt-painted bowls in the tumulus at Aphidna in Attica (Fig. 14*m*).[2] In one case the paint is on the natural surface, and in four cases the paint is applied to a yellowish slip. Four are hand-made, and one is wheel-made; the other pottery is generally wheel-made. The tumulus contained shaft-graves, cist-graves, and pithos-burials. The bowls were found only in the pithos-burials (III, IV, VI, VII, and IX), one to each pithos, except in pithos-burial VIII, which had been plundered and contained remains of the pithos only. In four cases the bowl was near the mouth of the pithos, and S. Wide conjectured that it had covered the aperture of the pithos. His conjecture is confirmed by a pithos-burial at Gajtan III, in which a similar bowl was found upside down over the mouth of the up-right pithos.[3] The fine bowls at Aphidna are all of the same shape—large, with a slightly incurving top, some decoration on the rim, main decora-tion on the exterior of the incurving part, and two small horizontal handles more suggestive of perforated lugs than actual handles (Fig. 14*m*). The bowls are from 34 to 42 cm wide but have a relatively small flattened bottom. They are evidently ritual vessels, used in this form of pithos-burial. The one at Gajtan III is not dissimilar in shape but has different handles.

We have already shown the connections of the tumulus at Aphidna and some of its contents with the north-western region (see p. 273 above). It is therefore interesting to find this shape of bowl without handles at Malik IIIa (Fig 4*c*) (E.H. III–M.H. I), Servia (L.N.A.) (Fig. 4*m*), Armenokhori (L.N.A., with lugs), and Vardina, Gioumenitsa, and Kritsana (all L.N.A.); and with handles of various kinds in the Macedonian Early Bronze Age at Servia, at Central Macedonian sites, and in Chalcidice.[4] It does not appear at Malik after M.H. I. or in Macedonia after the Early Bronze Age. The closest parallel to the handles on bowls of this shape occurs at Kritsana and at Servia, both in the Early

---

[1] *PTh* 185 and *PM* 130 'Macedonians turn up at Lianokladhi in the full Middle Bronze Age'.   [2] *AM* 21 (1896) 391 f. and pl. xv, 4–6.

[3] *StH* 1966. 1. 58 fig. 10.

[4] *SA* 1966. 1 pl. xii, 16 (Malik), *PM* 147 f. nos. 75 and 76 (Servia), 151 no. 108 (Armeno-khori), 153 no. 116 (Vardina), 155 no. 129 (Gioumenitsa), and 158 nos. 134 and 137 (Kritsana); then in the Early Bronze Age *PM* 190 no. 307 (Servia), and *PM* vessels nos. 162–5, 178–80, 209, 216, 241–2, and 249–52.

Bronze Age; such handles are found on vessels of different shape at Malik IIId and at Boubousti.[1] The indications are thus strong on the evidence of these bowls that the tumulus at Aphidna falls at the latest early in the M.H. period and that its makers came from the north-western area, probably from Albania.

In publishing pottery found in the tumulus at Elatea G. Soteriades remarked that a design of pendent triangles in matt paint resembled the design on one of the bowls from the tumulus at Aphidna.[2] The linear geometric designs in matt paint (and contemporaneously in bright paint) and the shapes of some handles which resemble perforated lugs set horizontally at Elatea are indeed very similar to those found at Aphidna and in the north-western region.[3] It is likely that this tumulus had connections with that region in the M.H. period (see p. 261 above).

Turning now to the dating of all these examples, we should place early in the M.H. period the pottery from the tumuli at Aphidna and Elatea, and within the M.H. period all the pottery of Lianokladhi III (found with Minyan pottery from the south)[4] and the beginnings of the pottery of Malik late IIIc and early IIId (having some Minyan features). It may be noted that the two-handled tankards decorated with slender triangles, of which the apexes hang downward towards the foot, do not occur at any of the M.H. sites. They appear first at Malik IIId, where we may attribute them to the L.H. phase of Malik IIId. Prendi noted that Malik IIId lasted for a relatively short time, since the depth of the IIId deposit is only 50 to 70 cm. The Malik IIIc deposit has a maximum depth of 130 cm. We may guess, then, that Malik IIId was less thickly populated in L.H. I and II, and that it was probably abandoned very early in L.H. III. Such a date accords with the absence of Mycenaeanizing influences and with the differentiations between Malik IIId and Boubousti and between Malik IIId and Tren. One of the upper tumuli at Pazhok is dated by various objects to a period from late M.H. to L.H. III B/C, and the pot of metallic shape with the design in matt paint from an upper tumulus there is probably of M.H. III/L.H. I.

It is possible that the abandonment of the large site at Malik very early in L.H. III coincided with a resumption of pastoral life on a large scale, and we may see an example of such a way of life in the occupation of Symize and Tren and the founding of the small settlement at Boubousti, perhaps in L.H. III A, a date appropriate to the overlap in tradition with

---

[1] *PM* 167 no. 165; 190 no. 307; *SA* 1966. 1 pl. xvii, 11 (Malik); *BSA* 28. 175 fig. 20. 3 and fig. 23A (Boubousti, handle only) and *PM* 227 nos. 459, 460, 466, and 467 (Boubousti, handle only).

[2] *AE* 1908. 95.   [3] *AE* 1908 pl. 5, 1; and for the handles pl. 5, 3.

[4] *PTh* 186. So dated by J. L. Caskey in *CAH*[3] ii. i. 122; he suggests tentatively a reflection of a Peloponnesian E.H. III style in the matt-painted pottery, but the geographical situation of Lianokladhi makes this most unlikely.

Malik IIId and to the contacts with Central Macedonia. As the matt-painted ware of this kind at Kastritsa and Koutsoulio, called K 4a, has connections not with Malik but with Boubousti and Central Macedonia, its beginning there may be dated to L.H. III, either to L.H. III A or to L.H. III B. The other examples of this style in Albania—in Pazhok, Bulçar in Gramsh, Benje near Permet, and Vodhinë in the Kseria valley—are likely to fall within the Late Helladic, though some may belong to the Middle Helladic. On the present evidence this type of pottery remained in use to the end of the Bronze Age, and even beyond it at Vodhinë in tumulus-burials, at Kastritsa and at Boubousti; and Prendi suggests that this was so also in the tumulus-burials of the Mati valley and of Vajzë.

If our datings are even approximately correct, we are faced by a remarkable phenomenon: the reappearance repeatedly of the same basic love of geometric design used to stress the structure of certain shapes of vessel over a period of some 800 years, if we start Middle Helladic at 1900 and place the end of L.H. III *c.* 1125 B.C. The centre which repeatedly gave off this style of design seems to have been Albania. As we have concluded on other grounds that this area was a reservoir of Greek-speaking peoples from an even earlier period, it is difficult to deny the likelihood that the peoples who were so given to the geometric type of decoration were Greek-speaking peoples. It would appear then that groups of such peoples were in occupation of the upper Haliacmon valley (for Boubousti is a symptom of widespread settlement there), the Malik area, and much of Albania; and from early in L.H. III central Epirus. On the other hand, Central Macedonia was still held by a relatively unenter-prising and culturally less developed people, which had spread outwards into coastal Pieria, Eordaea, Lyncus, and finally Pelagonia. Meanwhile the uppermost Vardar valley was still held by the Bubanj-Hum people, who had spread into parts of Pelagonia. The abandonment of sites in the plain in Pelagonia and in Lyncus in L.H. I and again at Malik very early in L.H. III seems to indicate that these sites lay in the area of con-flict between these peoples and the Greek-speaking group which was in possession of the upper Haliacmon valley, Albania, and central Epirus.

2. *The first period of Mycenaean contact, c. 1350–1200 B.C., and the geography of Macedonia in the* Iliad

The first appearance of Mycenaean pottery in Central Macedonia was dated by Heurtley to *c.* 1350 B.C., and subsequent evidence supports that date.[1] The pattern of sites shows that Mycenaean traders came to the

[1] *PM* 126; Petsas in *AE* 1953–4. 2. 113 and 119, reporting a Mycenaean sherd of pre-1300 B.C. date from Toumba Paionias, on the right bank of the lower Vardar. V. R. d'A. Des-borough, *TLM* 139 f., reviews Heurtley's conclusions and agrees with a date in L.H. III B for the earliest imports.

coast of eastern Central Macedonia. There they dealt directly with ports near Sedhes and with sites on the river Vardar; for in Chalcidice Mycenaean pottery has been found at only one site, Hagios Mamas.[1] The chief depots were Vardarophtsa and Vardina. Here pottery of Mycenaean type was made locally; it was the main pottery in use from *c.* 1350 B.C. to *c.* 1125 B.C., that is until the end of L.H. III C.[2] Heurtley noticed that this pottery was 'strictly true to type', a phenomenon to be explained only if these depots remained closely in touch with Mycenaean trade for some two centuries. On the other hand, very little Mycenaean ware was imported, and we may infer from this that southern Greeks from Mycenaean centres did not come to settle in places such as Vardarophtsa and Vardina. What brought Mycenaean traders to this coast was probably timber for the building of ships; for the forests of Mt. Cissus above Sedhes were always famous, and the floating of logs down the Vardar has been common at all times. Copper and gold may also have been attractions.[3] We do not know what the inhabitants of Macedonia were given in exchange, except that it was not anything packed in Mycenaean pottery. The taste for the local type of Mycenaean pottery spread inland in Central Macedonia but, as far as we know, only east of the Vardar; Saratse by Lake Koronia in Mygdonia became a secondary centre of distribution, and a small quantity has been found at Kilindir, situated on the south side of the pass leading to Lake Doiran.

The other area in which Mycenaean pottery has been found is southwestern Macedonia. The chief site is Kozani, where Petsas maintains that the proportion of Mycenaean ware was considerable.[4] Of thirty sherds from there he ascribed six to L.H. III B and the rest to L.H. III C; and as he observed that the sherds differed individually in the clay, the technique, the ornament, and so on, it is apparent that we are dealing not with pottery made locally at Kozani but with pottery brought to Kozani. One of the shapes at Kozani is the high-footed goblet. Such a goblet with two small handles and an aryballos of 'closed angular-cylindrical shape' (as in Fig. 14n) of L.H. III B type were found at Portes Sarandaporou in Perrhaebia.[5] The base of a high-footed goblet came

[1] *PM* xxii–iii: Hagios Mamas, Vardarophtsa (Axiokhorion), Vardina (Limnotopos), Kilindir (Kalindoia), Chauchitsa, Giatzilar (Xylokeratia), Saratse, Gona, Sedhes, Tsair; and Toumba Paionias (see last note) and Kalamaria (*BSA* 23. 26).

[2] I am following the chronology given in *HG*[2] 21 for the end of L.H. III C, rather than that of Desborough, *TLM*. See p. 312 below.

[3] For copper, perhaps from near Gevgheli, see O. Davies in *PM* 254 f.; and for 'what is probably gold slag' at Vardarophtsa at the end of the Late Helladic see *PM* 102.

[4] *AE* 1953–4. 2. 113 f.; and Kallipolitis in *Ergon* 1958. 88 and fig. 94.

[5] Seen by me in the collection at Kozani in 1968, and said to have been found in 1961. The goblet is like that from Vardina in *PM* 217 no. 414; the aryballos is described in the terminology of Furumark, *The Mycenaean Pottery* (Stockholm, 1941), 43 and resembles his type 94 of L.H. III B. For such aryballoi see *PAE* 1953. 131 fig. 11 (from Pharsalus).

from Tsotyli, a sherd from Omali, and two from Boubousti—one from Heurtley's site, the other from the hill called Prophet Elias.[1] The distribution of the sites and the contrast between locally made Mycenaean-type pottery in east Central Macedonia and imported Mycenaean pottery at Kozani make it most likely that this pottery came from Thessaly into the middle Haliacmon valley over the pass of Volustana, that is through Perrhaebia.[2] There are slight signs of Mycenaean influence also in the cemetery of tumuli at Vergina on the south side of the lower Haliacmon valley: one pot of Mycenaean shape locally made, and two aryballoi of 'closed angular-cylindrical shape' of L.H. III B, of which one at least was locally made[3] (Fig. 14*n*).

Objects other than pottery which may have a Mycenaean connection are very rare in Central Macedonia: a figurine of a horse at Hagios Mamas, and a bronze socketed javelin-head with two rivets at Vardina (Fig. 13*k*).[4] They are less rare in south-western Macedonia. Thus the Voïon area, which lies on the west of the upper Haliacmon valley from Grevena to the mass of Mt. Grammos, has produced two small bronze spear-heads, one being broad-bladed with a medial ridge and the other having a split socket and two rivet holes.[5] The district of Grevena has yielded two bronze swords of Mycenaean types, one of the horned type and the other of the cruciform type (Fig. 10 *g* and *h*); both may be attributed to 1400–1350 B.C. approximately.[6] Another sword of that period came from Tetovo, north of Pelagonia.[7] At Boubousti Heurtley found a bone pommel from a sword, which he dated to L.H. III B.[8] And at Vergina, which is on the lower Haliacmon and far removed from the Voïon district, the tumulus-burial C*Δ* contained a bronze sword of Catling's Type II Group I, which may be dated to L.H. III C (Fig. 10*l* and Fig. 13*a*).[9]

The distinctions which we have drawn between east Central Macedonia and the Haliacmon valley of south-western Macedonia are supported by the distinction in local pottery, that is between the incised and

---

[1] *PAE* 1953. 48 f.; *PAE* 1937. 70; *BSA* 28 (1926–7) 177 and fig. 29. 3, where Heurtley gives 'a late Mycenaean (L.H. III B) date'; and *PAE* 1938. 54.

[2] For L.M. II vases from Maghula near Elassona see *PTh* 207.

[3] *BS* 2 (1961) 96 and *PAE* 1952. 234 and 258, where it is described as an alabastron.

[4] *PM* 101 and fig. 104*y*, and 101 and fig. 104*cc*.

[5] In the collection at Kozani, where I saw them in 1968; they were said to have been chance finds. It is possible that they are javelin-heads. That with the split socket should be early, perhaps of L.H. I–II; for M. N. Valmin, in *The Swedish Messenian Expedition* (Lund, 1938) pl. xxx, 2, dates such a spear-head to late in the Middle Helladic, and S. I. Dakaris in *AD* 20 (1965) *Chron.* 350 fig. 3*b* dates one from Dodona to L.H. III A or B, which is perhaps too late.

[6] *Epirus* 322 f. with references, to which add now Ph. Petsas in *AE* 1953–4. 2. 120 n. 1.

[7] *AJA* 67 (1963) 120 and 145.   [8] *BSA* 28. 177 and fig. 29, 2.

[9] *AD* 17 (1961–2) 1. 242; see p. 316 below. I follow Catling's classification in *Antiquity* 35 (1961) 116 f.

matt-painted wares of Central Macedonia and the so-called Boubousti ware of the Haliacmon valley. When we consider wider contacts, it is clear that, as in Boubousti ware, so too in other respects the Haliacmon valley goes with central Albania and central Epirus, rather than with Central Macedonia. The cave at Tren by Little Prespa Lake has yielded a Mycenaean pot of L.H. III date, and tumulus-burials at Pazhok a two-zoned cylindrical cup of L.H. I–II A and other L.H. pottery; high-footed goblets come from Kastritsa near the Lake of Ioannina, from Dodona, and from Xylokastro by the Nekyomanteion on the river Acheron.[1]

Bronze swords and bronze spear-heads of types such as we have been describing are surprisingly numerous in central Albania and central Epirus.[2] As I have argued elsewhere, the main route for the traffic in such weapons was through central Epirus and along the east coast of the Adriatic Sea to central Europe.[3] There is no sign at all of any trade in bronze weapons through the ports of Central Macedonia. There may well have been a subsidiary land route through Pelagonia and the Kačanik pass; but it was probably an offshoot from central Albania. Thus there is a Type II Group II sword from the area of Monastir;[4] a sword of an earlier type (Fig. 10*i*), a spear-head and a javelin-head (Fig. 13*h*) from Prilep;[5] and a sword of Type II Group II 'developed' (Fig. 10*j*) and four spear-heads from a tumulus at Visoï near Prilep.[6]

---

[1] *SA* 1967. 1. 143 (Tren); *SA* 1964. 1 pl. vii, 1, and *BSA* 62 (1967) 81 and pl. 20, 1 (Pazhok); *PAE* 1951. 182 fig. 7; 1952 fig. 3, 1–3; a stirrup-jar in *PPS* 33 (1967) 31, of L.H. III B–C date (Kastritsa); ibid. a sherd of L.H. III B–C date from Dodona; and *Epirus* 313 with references (Nekyomanteion).

[2] *Epirus* 318 f. (swords from Dodona, Tseravina, Mesoyefira, Nekyomanteion, Vajzë, Kakavi, and the Mati valley) and *Epirus* 337 (spear-heads of this period from Kiperi, Kalbaki, Lakhanokastro, Gribiani, Koukousos, Vajzë, and Vodhinë). Add *BSA* 62 (1967) 79 (swords and spear-heads from Pazhok); *PPS* 33 (1967) 32 (sword from Kastritsa, sword and spear-head from Paramythia); *AD* 20 (1965) *Chron.* 350 fig. 3*b* (javelin-head from Dodona). [See H. W. Catling in *BSA* 63 (1968) 98 ff. and my article in *BSA* 66 (1971) on these swords.]

[3] *Epirus* 327 f.

[4] *Antiquity* 35 (1961) 118 no. 33. As it is attributed to Russian excavations in 1899, it may have come from Pateli.

[5] The sword and the javelin-head are illustrated by M. Garašanin in *39 BRGK* 125 fig. 26 = Ć. Truhelka, *Glasnik Skopskog* Naucnog Društva 5 (1929) fig. 3 *a–c*. Garašanin dated the sword *c*. 1200 B.C., but its length (0·76 m) and long, narrow blade suggest a date perhaps in the fourteenth century (see Nestor, *Sargetia* 1 (1937) 155 f.). The socketed javelin-head, some 12 cm long, with a very small part of the socket below the blade, resembles closely two javelin-heads from central Albania (see *Epirus* fig. 24, 5 and 6). The spear-head is published in *Arheološko Društvo Jugoslavije Praistorijska Sekcija* i (Ochrid, 1960) pl. i no. 8; see *Epirus* 340 n. 1, where it is compared to a spear-head from Koukousos, which is of Hallstatt A type.

[6] Unpublished; so labelled in the museum at Monastir in 1968. The sword, in two pieces and at a guess some 0·65 m long, resembles in its flanged hilt and shoulders the sword from Vajzë (*BUSS* 1957. 2 fig. 19), and is similar to Catling's Type II Group II 'developed'. The shoulders of the sword and the shape of the blade resemble those of a shorter sword from Joševa, illustrated in *39 BRGK* 100 fig. 22. [The sword may come from Raštani in Pelagonia, not Visoï; for a similar sword is shown as coming from Raštani in I. Mikulčić, *Pelagonia* (Skopje, 1966), a work which I saw in Sofia when this book was in proof.]

Another token of the affinity between these areas is the occurrence of tumulus-burials at Vergina on the lower Haliacmon, at Visoï near Prilep in Pelagonia, in the Mati valley from which comes the bronze sword in Fig. 10*k*, in the Zadrimë plain and Pazhok in central Albania, and at Vajzë and Vodhinë in central Epirus. Bronze swords of Type II were found at the last three places. A sword in the Museum of Skopje, from an unknown site, is said to be of early Mycenaean type;[1] such swords have been found at Vajzë and Pazhok and in the Mati valley.

We have already referred on p. 276 above to the literary evidence which shows that, while the Magnetes were driven southwards, the Macedones stayed in the hill-country of north Olympus, and that at some time after *c.* 1350 B.C. the people later to be called 'Dorians' moved from north-east Thessaly on to the slopes of Pindus and took the 'Makednan' name (Hdt. 1. 56 οἴκεε ἐν Πίνδῳ Μακεδνὸν καλεόμενον).[2] Their main route was evidently through the Volustana pass, up the middle Haliacmon valley, and into the district of Voïon. Here they were on the slopes of Pindus. The word Μακεδνός meaning 'tall' may have been that of the high country[3] now known as Voïon, and the incomers who settled there took its name. A related form was used of the 'Makedonikon oros', that is the range north of Olympus. It looks likely, then, that the Makedones held northern Pieria and the middle Haliacmon valley, and that the 'Dorians-to-be' settled among them in Voïon. Thus the introduction of Mycenaean pottery and weapons into this area before and after 1300 B.C. was probably due to the movement which Herodotus described. It is possible that these people were responsible for the destruction of Malik IIId, which fell before Mycenaean influences showed themselves in the pottery.[4] On the other hand, we have no literary evidence for Central Macedonia at this early period, and the inference is a probable one that it was occupied by non-Greek-speaking peoples.

An interesting light is shed upon the scene by the two Catalogues in the *Iliad*. In my opinion they contain an accurate record of the situation as it was *c.* 1200 B.C. The Achaean Catalogue of Ships ends with two

[1] *39 BRGK* 124; it has been compared to the swords illustrated by F. Matz in *Handb. d. Arch.* 2 Textband (1950–4) 266 n. 1 pl. 34, 2–3, which are from Shaft-Grave V at Mycenae; and mentioned by Petsas in *AE* 1953–4. 120 n. 1.

[2] I have discussed the value of the tradition on which Herodotus was drawing in *BSA* 32. 172 f., *CAH* 2². 36. 25 f. and *Epirus* 374 f. The movement out of north-east Thessaly was due to pressure from the Cadmeans, who came to Thebes *c.* 1350 B.C. (see *HG*² 654). How and Wells in their *Commentary on Herodotus* 1. 78 and 2. 28 put Hdt. i. 56 and Hdt. 5. 61. 2 together and conclude that the Cadmeans were in flight from Thebes, when they pushed the 'Dorians-to-be' out of north-east Thessaly. This is not what Herodotus says; nor is it likely that the defeated Cadmeans would have had sufficient strength. We need a time when the Cadmeans were at the peak of their power.

[3] The land would be called Μακεδνή; we may compare Πελαγονία, Ὀρεστίς, and Ἠμαθία, which are all Greek words descriptive of terrain.

[4] *SA* 1966. 1. 267 and 275.

contingents from the outlying (later Perioecic) parts of Thessaly, which were inhabited by Aenianes, Perrhaebi, and Magnetes. The last, as we have seen, had been ejected recently from Pieria, and their leader Prothoos has no pedigree. The other two have a leader without a pedigree, but their habitats are described with more detail:

> τῷ δ' Ἐνιῆνες ἕποντο μενεπτόλεμοί τε Περαιβοί,
> οἳ περὶ Δωδώνην δυσχείμερον οἰκί' ἔθεντο,
> οἵ τ' ἀμφ' ἱμερτὸν Τιταρησσὸν ἔργ' ἐνέμοντο,
> ὅς ῥ' ἐς Πηνειὸν προΐει καλλίρροον ὕδωρ,
> οὐδ' ὅ γε Πηνειῷ συμμίσγεται ἀργυροδίνῃ,
> ἀλλά τέ μιν καθύπερθεν ἐπιρρέει ἠΰτ' ἔλαιον·
> ὅρκου γὰρ δεινοῦ Στυγὸς ὕδατός ἐστιν ἀπορρώξ.   (2. 749 ff.)

The Enienes, later called Aenianes, had been driven out of the Dotian plain of Thessaly and had settled near the Aethices, who were in northwest Thessaly; at the time of the Trojan War the Enienes held both sides of the Zygos pass which leads from Thessaly to Dodona.[1] As the name Peraebi probably means 'beyond the Aias', that is the later Aous river, these people too had probably moved fairly recently into what was henceforth called Perrhaebia.[2] The river Titaressus, by which their position is defined, rises from Mt. Titarium, north-west of Mt. Olympus (see p. 117 above), and flows into the Peneus;[3] and its reputation as a part of the Styx was probably due to its closeness to the home of the gods on Mt. Olympus. The Peraebi held the important pass of Volustana leading from Thessaly into Macedonia. The Enienes and the Peraebi were not in fact contiguous; but they held the important passes, lived in the hill-country above the plain, and were grouped together under Gouneus. The movements of these and other peoples remind us that north Greece was a troubled area towards the close of the Late Bronze Age.[4]

In Homer's geography there is a gap between the gods and Muses of Olympus–Pieria and the allies of Troy by the river Axius. A goddess passes once through this no-man's-land. On leaving Olympus Hera set foot on Pieria and then on Emathia, as she rushed towards Thrace (*Il.* 14. 226). Emathia 'the sandy place' suits the plain of Lower Macedonia. But a tradition preserved by Strabo (see p. 153 above) fills the gap between Pieria and Emathia by calling an intermediate part of the plain

---

[1] See *Epirus* 375.   [2] Ibid. 373.

[3] T. W. Allen, *The Homeric Catalogue of Ships* (Oxford, 1921) places both the Enienes and the Peraebi by Dodona, and therefore removes the river Titaressus from the position which Strabo 7 fr. 15 gives (see p. 122 n. 1 above). The phenomenon at the juncture of the Titaressus and the Peneus which Homer described has been seen by M. Georgiades, *Thessalia²* (1894) 23, where the river of Elassona falls into the Peneus. The ancient Titaressus is the modern Sarandaporos and its continuation down to the Peneus.

[4] Similar movements were occurring in Pelagonia and near Malik, where men moved to new hill-sites.

'Bottiaeis', attributing the name to a Cretan follower of Minos, named Botton, and connecting the settlement in time with that of Taras. If the tradition is sound,[1] it refers to the fourteenth century B.C., but there is no archaeological evidence of that period in its support. In the Trojan Catalogue the Paeones come from the Axius:

$$\text{αὐτὰρ Πυραίχμης ἄγε Παίονας ἀγκυλοτόξους,}$$
$$\text{τηλόθεν ἐξ Ἀμυδῶνος, ἀπ' Ἀξιοῦ εὐρὺ ῥέοντος,}$$
$$\text{Ἀξιοῦ, οὗ κάλλιστον ὕδωρ ἐπικίδναται αἶαν.}\qquad\text{(2. 848 ff.)}$$

Amydon and the Axius are 'far off' to the Trojan, as Dodona is to Achilles (16. 233), and the same expression is used of Paeonia at 21. 154:

$$\text{εἴμ' ἐκ Παιονίης ἐριβώλου, τηλόθ' ἐούσης.}$$

Thus Amydon, the Axius, and Paeonia are the western frontier-province of the Trojan Alliance, hostile to Mycenaean Greece. The geographical details are most apt here and elsewhere in the poem: the wide-flowing Axius (2. 849; 16. 288; 21. 141, 157, 186), the inundation of the deltaic plain (2. 850; 21. 158) and the very rich soil (17. 350; 21. 154).

As the archaeological evidence shows, the delta of the river and the coast by Sedhes were well known to Mycenaean traders from c. 1350 B.C. onwards, and we may hazard the guess that Vardarophtsa, the chief entrepôt on the Axius, was the Amydon of Homer. Now it is most probable that the Axius formed the defensible frontier, and the archaeological evidence makes us regard the territory east of the Axius as a cultural unity. Thus east Central Macedonia was called Paeonia c. 1200 B.C., and its inhabitants were the Paeones. Their weapons were the bow (2. 848) and the long spear (21. 155). Asteropaeus, one of their champions, threw two spears at Achilles and then apparently had no weapon; Achilles dispatched him with a sword (21. 162–82). It may be that the Paeones did not have the sword, as indeed the archaeological evidence suggests. On the other hand, they are the only people who are called ἱπποκορυσταί 'fighters from chariots' (16. 287; 21. 205), and such fighters do not need the sword. The use of chariots in war develops among people who are familiar with horses and live in wide stoneless plains. In Macedonia the horse was an early arrival, and the plains of Upper Macedonia and Lower Macedonia are most suitable for chariots. It may be noted too that Hesiod used an epithet of the same meaning, ἱππιοχάρμης when he named the heroes 'Makedon' and 'Aiolos' (frs. 7 and 9 Merk.– West), whose realms were in Pieria and in Thessaly.[2]

[1] The tradition concerning Sicily and Taras was true, and one can imagine a dispersal of Minoan Cretans after the sack or destruction of Cnossos c. 1400 B.C.; for the date see *HG²* 47.

[2] These epithets come from an earlier stage in the epic tradition, when wars in northern Greece may have provided material for the bards; it has been suggested above (p. 268) that the chariot was in use late in the M.H. period in Albania and Macedonia.

The first leader of the Paeones, Pyraechmes, was killed by Patroclus (16. 287); the second, Asteropaeus, by Achilles (21. 179). The killing of the latter is a substantial episode, and the genealogy of the hero is given. Axius (the god of the river) and Periboea, daughter of Acessamenus, were the parents of Πηλεγών, the father of Asteropaeus (21. 141 ff.). Pelegon himself was born of the intermingling of Periboea with the waters of Axius (21. 143), and there is little doubt that Periboea is the nymph of the main tributary of the Axius, the Cerna Reka, the later Erigon. In the insulting rhetoric of Achilles his birthplace is brought down to 'briny rivers', referring to the delta of the river in the Thermaic Gulf.[1] Now Pelegon has the appearance of a tribal patronymic; and if Periboea is the nymph of the Cerna Reka, then the Pelegones lived *c.* 1200 B.C. by the Cerna Reka, just where the Pelagones lived in classical times. As a son of Pelegon led the Paeones, the Pelegones and the Paeones must have been closely associated geographically, and it is thus probable that the Paeones held the Demir Kapu and the eastern side of the middle Vardar valley by Stobi.

The extension of Troy's influence in Europe as far as the Axius and Pelagonia is not surprising if we recall the analogies of Persia and Turkey, for instance, in historical times. According to the tradition preserved by Hdt. 7. 20. 2 this influence had been established by force of arms 'before the Trojan War', an expression which refers probably to the latter part of the thirteenth century B.C. The Mysi and the Teucri (his term for Trojans) crossed then into Europe, conquered all the Thracians, descended to the Ionian Sea, and drove southwards to the river Peneus. Such an expedition would cross the Balkan chain either at the Tsangon pass or north of Lake Ochrid on the later Via Egnatia route. At the time of the Trojan War, the power of Troy operated still in Pelagonia, a district which dominated the eastern side of the Via Egnatia route. Other important places on the route between the Ionian Sea (the southern part of our Adriatic Sea) and Asia Minor are the crossings of the Axius and the Strymon. The first of these was held by Troy's allies, the Paeones of Amydon. The second was held evidently by a military colony planted by the Teucri. Herodotus refers to this twice: at 7. 75. 2 the Teucri and the Mysi expelled the Thracian people called Strymonii from their habitat, and at 5. 13. 2 the Teucri of Troy planted settlers in the Strymon valley who took the name of Paeonians.[2] These remarks made

[1] It is possible that Homer is adapting to the Scamander an episode which was at home on the Axius or the Cerna Reka. The reference to the briny waters suggests that Homer had no idea where Periboea and the Pelegones were situated and brought the birthplace to the mouth of the Axius, which was known better than the interior.

[2] As the Athenian settlers at Chalcis are called Chalcidians by Herodotus (6. 100 and 8. 1) How and Wells's suggestion that the Paeonians regarded Teucrians from Troy as their ancestors is based on an unwarranted inference from the passage.

by Herodotus *en passant* are based evidently on a well-known and accepted tradition. We gain from it some insight into the power of the Teucri and of their chief city Troy, and the use to which they put their control of the Hellespont. The Mysi controlled the Bosporus (Str. 566). The advance of these powerful peoples to the Tempe pass on the river Peneus may have been a factor in the displacement of the Magnetes from the coastal district of Pieria (Hes. fr. 7) to the historical Magnesia, where they were at the time of the Trojan War (*Il.* 2. 757). The Mycenaeans responded to this advance as the Greeks responded later to the advance of Persia. They made a combined effort to capture 'the narrows' between Europe and Asia.[1]

We can thus see the position in Macedonia at the time of the Trojan War, i.e. late in L.H. III B. *c.* 1200 B.C. I shall discuss later who was in possession of coastal Pieria.[2] The history of the other peoples may be summarized briefly as follows. The Paeones are evidently the unenterprising and culturally conservative people who occupied east Central Macedonia at the beginning of the Bronze Age; thereafter their power spread slowly beyond the Vardar through the plain to the Ludias river, then into Eordaea, Lyncus, and finally Pelagonia, as well as up the Vardar to Stobi or beyond. Further north in the upper Vardar valley lay the carriers of the Bubanj-Hum culture; these too had pressed down from the north upon Pelagonia. The Paeones were a warlike people; they brought the perforated battle-axe with them, they had the spear and the bow, and they fought from chariots. It is possible that Minoan Cretans established themselves west of the Vardar in the fourteenth century and confined the Paeones of the plain to the east of the river. Inland Pieria and northern Olympus were held by Greek-speaking Macedones, and the middle Haliacmon valley by a mixture of Macedones and 'Dorians-to-be' who had emigrated from north-east Thessaly. By 1200 B.C. the Peraebi held the pass between them and Thessaly. Other Greek-speaking peoples held Lyncus and Pelagonia, central Albania, and central Epirus.

---

[1] The passage in Herodotus has received little attention since scholars, Hellenistic and modern, got embroiled in arguments about the Mysi. The Teucri, however, are not in dispute, and the tradition itself is clear about them. As regards the Mysi it is probable enough that the Mysi on the Asiatic side of the Bosporus (*Il.* 2. 858 f.) were an offshoot of a nomadic European tribe of the same name (*Il.* 13. 5); for there are many analogous cases in later centuries of European tribes entering Asia Minor. In commenting on Hdt. 7. 75. 2 How and Wells assume that the Thracians who were expelled from the Strymon valley then invaded Bithynia; this assumption is not justified in the context, and the time sequence was not immediate. R. W. Macan ad loc. makes the same assumption and then exclaims that the result is 'almost an absurdity'. Indeed How, Wells, and Macan apparently felt free to choose one or other of the two movements—one by the Teucri and the Mysi before the Trojan War, and the other by the Phrygians and ? the Mysians some centuries later—and reject the other, much as if a historian of the future may feel free to choose one World War and reject the other. Thus Macan writes happily on Hdt. 7. 73 'for the Myso-Teukrian invasion of Europe . . . must be substituted a Phrygo-Mysian invasion of Asia Minor and the Troad'.

[2] See p. 416 below.

Their way of life was mainly pastoral. They were well armed with bronze weapons, and they were well led.

One type of weapon which belonged probably to this period was a powerful axe of bronze. Recently a hoard of bronze flat celts (Fig. 13*e*) and bronze axes of this kind was found at Petralona in the interior of Crousis.[1] The family to which these axes belong had its origin in the region of Laibach, near the head of the Adriatic in the upper valley of the Drave. Thence it spread into Hungary, where it was adopted by the Urnfield culture. Later it passed south-eastwards into Bulgaria and went as far as Troy VII, and southwards into Serbia, Albania, and Epirus.[2] The axes from Petralona are not yet published. Some of them were on view in the museum at Thessalonica in 1968 (see my sketch of three in Fig. 13 *b–d*),[3] and one with a collar, on which there were raised ribs of ornament (Fig. 13*c*), was of the type found at Scodra in north Albania. The hoard at Petralona may be indicative of trade with the north or north-west, or it may reflect the pressure of Hungarian peoples from the north on north-eastern Macedonia. One other example is reported (but unpublished) from Central Macedonia.[4] It is probable that the hoard at Petralona was deposited in the period *c*. 1250–1200 B.C. When I visited the museum at Monastir in 1968 a show-case contained a bronze axe very similar to that shown in Fig. 13*b*, but a little shorter in the neck, and in addition a mould for making these axes. The axe and the mould came from Kravari in southern Pelagonia. They are unpublished. There was also on show from Kravari a fine bronze double-bladed axe, perforated and having a collar on the top only (Fig. 13*f*). The blades are not swallow-tailed. It is of the same family as an axe from Dodona.[5] This axe from Kravari and a collared bronze axe of the same family

[1] *Mak.* 7 (1966–7) 292 and *Chron.* pl. 4.

[2] Ebert 2, pls. 100–1 (Bulgaria); W. Dörpfeld, *Troja und Ilion* (Athens, 1902) 405 fig. 404 (Troy VII); *Epirus* 331 f. for the numerous axes and for the literature on the subject (Serbia, Albania, and Epirus).

[3] The museum's numbers are *Π* 732 f. There were in the show-case 18 celts, 3 axes, and an unusual bronze 'cold chisel', *Π* 730. Two of the axes were broken, and this shows that they were not in use as a form of currency.

[4] Casson, *Macedonia* 141 n. 2; the axe is in the Liverpool Museum. I give my arguments for the dating of this class of axe in Serbia, Albania, and Epirus in *Epirus* 333. It seems probable that the additional examples at Kravari in Pelagonia and at Petralona should be associated with their fellows in the Balkans and not with the similar axes of Poliokhni in Lesbos, which stem from Asia Minor (see Bernabò Brea, *Poliochni* (1964) i. 661 for discussion and ii pl. clxxiii). However, it should be noted that C. Renfrew has dated the Petralona axes by those of Poliochni to the E.B.A. period 2; if he applied the same date to the mould and the axe at Kravari, it would place the evidence of metallurgy in bronze in the Balkans unexpectedly early (see p. 313 below). For axes like those at Petralona which are of L.B.A. date in Bulgaria see for instance one from Varbica in the Pleven region in a hoard which included a Naue Type II bronze sword (Археология 9. 2 (1967) 55 figs. 5 and 6); for such in Albania see *BUST* 1958. i. 207 with specimens from Malessia Madhe in the Scodra district, from Mirditë, and from Shelcan in the Elbasan district.

[5] See *Epirus* 333, item C.1.

from Kilindir (Fig. 13*g*) should be dated to the period 1250–1150 B.C.[1] All these axes were battle-axes of a formidable kind, not in use in the contemporary Mycenaean world.[2] A bronze 'sickle' from Kilindir (Fig. 10*f*) may have been a weapon too.

3. The second period of Mycenaean contact, c. 1200–1125 B.C., the Nostoi, and the coming of the Phrygians to Macedonia

The sack of Troy was followed by a period of unrest not only on the Greek mainland but also further north. There were raids by land and by sea, seizures of sites, and movements of peoples, as well as internal dissensions. Traditions of the period have survived in the *Odyssey* and the Epic Cycle.[3] It is most probable that these traditions 'came down in the body of epic saga which derived from the twelfth century and was originally composed in that century'.[4] Several of them are concerned with Thrace, Macedonia, and Epirus and with the overland routes through the Balkan chain, which the expedition of the Mysi and Teucri had used. Adventurers were exploiting the collapse of Trojan power or seeking new kingdoms. These traditions give us an insight into the period of unrest.

Neoptolemus, son of Achilles, was an important figure in the *Ilias Parva*, composed probably in the seventh century, and in various *Nostoi*. In the *Nostoi* of Hagias of Troezen Neoptolemus was advised by Thetis to make his journey home by land ($\pi\epsilon\zeta\hat{\eta}$). On his way he met Odysseus at Maronea in Thrace and later he came to the Molossians; as we are told by other sources,[5] he founded the royal house of the Molossians and planted the city Byllis. As Byllis lay in the latitude of the Gulf of Oricum,[6] we may put the Molossians in the lower valley of the Aous at that time, i.e. c. 1180 B.C. The route overland which Neoptolemus is likely to have taken followed the middle and upper Haliacmon valley, crossed the main range by the Tsangon pass, and descended via Leskoviq into the Aous valley. This route had been taken already by the 'Dorians-to-be', who were by this time in central and southern Epirus.[7] If he came to the

[1] Casson, *Antiq. J.* 6 (1926) no. 1 pp. 67 f. and pl. xvii no. 2; *Macedonia* fig. 45, facing p. 136.

[2] I suggested in *Epirus* 333 n. 3 that the axes of these two kinds and the northern swords of Type II came, at least in part, via the Vardar route from the Danube area to Epirus. The axes at Kravari and at Petralona give added support to this suggestion.

[3] Thuc. I. 12. 1–2 summarized the situation from his knowledge and understanding of epic material mostly lost to us. For examples of traditions of this period which have been proved dependable through archaeological evidence see Hammond *CAH*[2] 2. 36 (1962) 22 f.

[4] *Epirus* 389, with reference to the significance of epic saga in north-western Greece, where the epic tradition is stronger and more detailed.

[5] O.C.T. Homer, vol. 5 p. 108; see *Epirus* 383 f. for the other sources.

[6] Probably at Plaka, where I found Mycenaean sherds; see *Epirus* 472.

[7] See *Epirus* 390 f.

Molossi before he went to Thessaly,[1] he may have crossed Central Macedonia and gone via Beroea or the Edessa of classical times into Eordaea and Elimea. Another legend brought Locrians of Thronium and Abantes of Euboea to the Gulf of Oricum by sea, their ships having been scattered on the way home from Troy, and these peoples founded Thronium, Abantis, and Oricum. Strabo 10. 1. 15, C 449, preserves the next stage of the journey of those who had come from Euboea. 'Of the Euboeans coming back from Troy some landed in Illyria and setting off homewards through Macedonia stayed in the vicinity of Edessa, as they were helping their hosts there in a war, and they founded a city Euboea.'[2] These Euboeans probably used the later Via Egnatia route from Illyria, intending to proceed from Edessa to the western side of the Thermaic Gulf rather than to the eastern side, where the Paeones were hostile.

These routes had been familiar to the Trojans since the time of the Teucro-Mysian expedition. One of them was used by the Trojans associated with Neoptolemus. These were Andromache, Aeneas, and Helenus. Andromache went with her captor to the Molossi. There are variant accounts of Aeneas. In the *Ilias Parva* Andromache and Aeneas were carried off by Neoptolemus to his home in Thessaly;[3] they went probably to the Molossi before they reached Thessaly, but the fragments do not mention this stage. According to Hellanicus (*FGrH* 4 F 31 and F 84) Aeneas escaped defeat, withdrew from the Troad, came by sea to Pallene in Chalcidice and later went 'from the Molossians to Italy'; in this legend it seems that Aeneas too crossed the Balkan range, presumably by the same route. Helenus was associated with the foundation of an 'Ilion in Macedonia' by Stephanus Byzantius,[4] and was active in the west among the Chaones of northern Epirus; he too may have used the same route.

The tradition of an independent Aeneas may have arisen from the movements of peoples westwards from north-western Asia Minor. His independence was explained either on the lines of Hellanicus' fragment, or on the grounds that he was set free by the Greeks, at the time of the sack of Troy or after the death of Neoptolemus. The latter was the version of the *Ilias Parva*.[5] In it Aeneas settled 'first' on the east side of the

[1] This is implied in the summary, where after coming to the Molossians he was recognized by Peleus (as Odysseus was recognized by Laertes).

[2] The ultimate source is no doubt an epic *nostos*. See also Callimachus fr. 259 Schn. = Aetia fr. 12 Tryp.; St. Byz. s. vv. *Abantis, Amantia,* and *Euboia*; *Et. Gen.* (A.B.) s. v. *Amantes*; Lyc. 1042 f. and Tzetz. ad loc.; Schol. to Ap. Rhod. 4. 1175.

[3] O.C.T. Homer, vol. 5 pp. 134–5.

[4] St. Byz. s.v. *Ilion*. In *Epirus* 697 n. 2 I suggested that this Ilion might be the Ilion in Epirus, but it is perhaps better to attribute the citation in St. Byz. to a Greek source rather than to a Roman source. A Greek source would not have included Epirus in Macedonia.

[5] O.C.T. Homer, vol. 5 p. 135 no. xxi.

302 *The Late Bronze Age*

Thermaic Gulf, where he founded 'the Macedonian cities in the district of Rhaecalum and Almonia, the cities being situated near the Cissian mountain, and Rhaecalum was called Aenus after him'. This area, being near Sedhes, was known to Mycenaean traders. It is the area and not a town which was called Aenus after Aeneas, and in fact the earlier name of the area, 'Rhaecalum', prevailed; but Aenus survived in the name of its cape, 'Aeneia', and in the name of its (later) town 'Aeneia', which put the head of Aeneas upon its coins in the sixth century B.C. (see Head *HN* 214). The next place where Aeneas settled was presumably among the Molossi;[1] if so, he may have crossed the Balkan range via the Tsangon pass.

Another group of migrants who may have made a similar crossing were the Tyrreni. Their king, Elymus or Elymas, was reputed to be the founder of Aeane and Elimia; and if Elimia is identified with Palaio-gratsiano, which has Early Iron Age remains, it is probable that the Tyrreni came to Palaiogratsiano from the mouth of the Haliacmon river via Vergina along the southern side of the great Haliacmon gorge.[2] The tradition that Tyrreni, as well as followers of Aeneas, were in Mace-donia cannot be lightly dismissed; for both Herodotus (1. 57. 1) and Thucydides (4. 109. 4) believed that in their own time 'Tyrseni' were living in the Athos peninsula or in its hinterland in Chalcidice. Herodotus further held that a group of the Tyrseni, presumably that group which left traces in Chalcidice, reached Umbria in Italy (1. 94. 6), and the most probable route is that indicated by the tradition of King Elymus founding Aeane and Elimia, that is overland via the Haliacmon valley and the Tsangon pass to the Adriatic coast.

On the chronology which I am using the fall of Troy was about 1200 B.C., and the movements of Neoptolemus with his Myrmidons, of the Abantes from Euboea, and of the Trojans associated with Neoptolemus were in the decade 1200–1190 B.C.[3] The further movements of Trojans, if separate from those of Neoptolemus, and of Tyrreni may have been either then or later, e.g. after *c.* 1100 B.C. when Troy VII B 2 was deserted. There is another important movement of peoples which is attached to a time after the return of Odysseus to Ithaca, that is after *c.* 1190 B.C. As we learn from a summary of Eugammon's *Telegony*, written *c.* 565 B.C., Odysseus went to Thesprotia and led the Thes-protians in a war against the Brygi, who were at first victorious.[4] In the foundation legend of Epidamnus, later called Dyrrachium, which is preserved in Appian *BC* 2. 39, some activities of Heracles in the region are followed by the arrival at a later time of Briges 'coming back from (the) Phrygians'. These Briges seized the city and its territory; they

[1] See *Epirus* 384 f. [2] See p. 117 above. [3] *HG²* 654.
[4] O.C.T. Homer, vol. 5 p. 109; cf. *Epirus* 385 f.

were displaced by the Taulantii, 'an Illyrian tribe', who were in turn succeeded by another Illyrian tribe, the Liburni, and only on the expulsion of the last did the Greeks found a colony there. The expression 'coming back from (the) Phrygians' suggests that the legend drew on a *nostos*,[1] and that 'the Phrygians' are those of the *Iliad* who lived by Lake Ascania on the south shore of the Propontis.[2] Whatever we may make of this connection with the *Iliad*, there can be little doubt that the Brygi who defeated Odysseus and the Briges in the foundation legend are the same people. It seems then that they pressed down from central Albania upon Epirus, which was held by the Thesproti;[3] that they had come from the east side of the main Balkan range; and that they were not 'an Illyrian tribe' but were earlier than the Illyrians.

If we had these two legends alone, the rationalist might try to explain them away as later inventions. But there are other pointers. In classical times there were still some Brygi inland of Epidamnus; moreover, there were Briges on the east side of the Balkan range in a remote pocket north of Pelagonia, these Briges being distinct from the Illyrian Penestae to the west, the Paeonians to the east, and the Pelagones to the south;[4] and there were 'Brygi Thracians' somewhere north of Chalcidice who attacked the Persians in 492 B.C. (Hdt. 6. 45). One of the leaders of Homer's Phryges in *Iliad* 3. 186 is Mygdon, and we find later a Mygdon as the eponymous hero of Mygdonia, that is of the plain east of the Axius mouth and north of Chalcidice (see p. 182 above).[5]

Philologists tell us that the name Edessa is derived from the Phrygian word for water. Now this was the earlier name of the place which the Argeadae renamed Aegeae, and it was also the name of a classical city. Both places were on the western side of the Central Macedonian plain. It may be doubted whether Herodotus possessed this piece of philological knowledge; yet he placed the so-called gardens of Midas, son of Gordius, the founder of the post-Homeric Phrygian dynasty in Asia Minor, 'under Mt. Bermium' i.e. in the vicinity of the classical Edessa. Strabo 7 fr. 25 gives the 'Briges, a tribe of Thracians', as the 'earlier' inhabitants of Mt. Bermium. Here Herodotus and Strabo may be drawing on a common source, probably Hecataeus.[6] When we take

---

[1] App. *BC* 2. 39 ἐπανελθόντας; compare Str. 10. 1. 15, C 449, τῶν δὲ ἐκ Τροίας ἐπανιόντων Εὐβοέων. [2] See T. W. Allen, *The Homeric Catalogue of Ships* 154 for their habitat.

[3] See *Epirus* 480.

[4] Str. 7. 7. 8, C 326, derived probably from Hecataeus (see *Epirus* 466 f.); in Strabo's abbreviated version the Brygi are lumped together with the adjacent tribes as Illyrians. But at 7, fr. 25, the Briges become a Thracian tribe. These tribal terms in Strabo are less likely to be correct than those in the foundation legend of Epidamnus.

[5] The name of the plain 'Mygdone' persisted on the south shore of the Propontis (Hecataeus, *FGrH* 1 F 217).

[6] The fragment of Strabo is brief: ὅτι αὐτοῦ που καὶ τὸ Βέρμιον ὄρος, ὃ πρότερον κατεῖχον Βρίγες Θρᾳκῶν ἔθνος, ὧν τινες διαβάντες εἰς τὴν Ἀσίαν Φρύγες μετωνομάσθησαν. Herodotus

all these bits of evidence together, there is a very strong case for believing that the Briges were a very powerful people who held part of Pelagonia, occupied the western part at least of the plain of Central Macedonia, and also occupied central Albania and threatened Epirus; that the first invasion of north Epirus by these people happened in the decades immediately after 1190 B.C.; and that they were in some sense related to 'Phrygians' as they bore a very similar name, Brygi or Briges.

It is now necessary to investigate the traditions about the Phrygians in Asia. These traditions are sometimes lumped together, but they refer in fact to three entirely different periods:[1]

1. Before and during the Trojan War the 'Phryges' occupied a territory called Phrygia on the southern side of the Propontis; in Priam's younger days they had fought against the Amazons at the Sangarius river, and they were allies of Troy in the Trojan War (*Il.* 3. 184 f. and 2. 862 f.).[2] In the *Iliad* they alone have the epithet αἰολόπωλοι, 'with gleaming horses' (also in the *Hymn to Aphrodite* 137). Homeric epic knew also of Tantalus and Pelops; they were 'Phryges' and not 'Lydi', a people unknown to epic saga. The land allotted to the Phryges in the Trojan Catalogue was a district which, according to R. D. Barnett, 'may very well mark the earliest area of Phrygian settlement'.[3] We may for convenience call it Hellespontine Phrygia. It was held by Phryges from *c.* 1260 B.C. at the latest.

2. 'After the Trojan War the Phryges came from Europe and the region left of the Pontus', wrote Xanthus the historian *c.* 460 B.C.[4] The opening phrase refers, as usual, to the period of the *Nostoi*, and the record here is of Phryges crossing from Europe into Asia and in particular from the Ukraine into inland Phrygia[5] at some time after 1200 B.C. Archaeologists have seen traces of invaders, who, they thought, might have been Phrygians, in Troy VIIb; and the archaeological date is *c.* 1150 B.C.[6]

3. There is no reference to the Trojan War or to its aftermath in the traditions of Gordius and his son Midas and of their Briges leaving Macedonia and founding the famous dynasty in inland Phrygia. That movement was much later. We discuss it below (p. 412).

Returning now to the Brygi in the *Telegony* we can see that, as far as the epics are concerned, the Brygi who threatened the Thesproti were

mentioned ὄρος Βέρμιον οὔνομα at 8. 138. 3 and wrote at 7. 73 οἱ δὲ Φρύγες, ὡς Μακεδόνες λέγουσι, ἐκαλέοντο Βρίγες χρόνον ὅσον Εὐρωπήιοι ἐόντες σύνοικοι ἦσαν Μακεδόσι, μεταβάντες δὲ ἐς τὴν Ἀσίην ἅμα τῇ χώρῃ καὶ τὸ οὔνομα μετέβαλον. Both authors make the same points and use the same form of the name, Βρίγες. For Hecataeus as a common source see p. 153 above.

[1] See Eitrem in *RE* 15 (1932) 1526 and E. A. Fredericksmeyer, 'Alexander, Midas and the Oracle at Gordium', in *CP* 56 (1961) 160 f.

[2] See T. W. Allen op. cit. 162 f.

[3] In *CAH²* 2. 30 (1967) 4.   [4] *FGrH* 765 Xanthus F 14.

[5] Xanthus came from Lydia, and he was probably describing the origins of the Phrygian kingdom of the historical period.   [6] *CAH²* 2. 30. 4 with references.

entirely separate from the Phryges in Hellespontine Phrygia and from the Phryges mentioned by Xanthus. It is clear that the epic saga kept them distinct; and that the Brygi north of Thesprotia were the epic predecessors of the Brygi who lived not only near Epidamnus but also north of Pelagonia, below Mt. Bermium and north of Chalcidice. There is only one passage which confuses the Brygi and the Phryges of epic saga, namely Appian *BC* 2. 39, recording the foundation legend of Epidamnus; and we may surely dismiss the confusion as an attempt by the Greek founders of the colony to link the Brygi in that area with the Phryges of the *Iliad*.[1] We are still left with the similarity of the names, Brygi being a dialectal form of Phryges, and with the place-name Edessa, which indicates that the Brygi spoke Phrygian. The easiest explanation is that the Briges–Brygi and the Phryges of Xanthus came from a common stock in central Europe and invaded respectively the southern Balkans and north-west Asia Minor in the troubled period after 1190 B.C.

If we take the mentions of the Briges–Brygi as pointers, it seems most likely that they came via the upper Vardar into Pelagonia and Lyncus. From there one group turned westwards into central Albania, and later threatened the Thesproti in what became Epirus. Another group proceeded along the route used later by the Via Egnatia, entered the Central Macedonian plain below Edessa and occupied the part west of the Axius, subduing the Bottiaei of Minoan origin. They anticipated the successes of two groups of Goths, those under Theodoric and Theodimund and those under Theodoric and Thiudimer; but they were more powerful than the Goths, because they threatened Epirus and they kept the conquered territories. In their defeat of the Thesproti they may be compared with the Dardanians of Bardylis who defeated the Molossians in the fourth century B.C.

It is natural to expect that the Briges–Brygi left their mark in the archaeological evidence. On the basis of present knowledge, they were in all probability the carriers of the so-called Lausitz culture. Heurtley noted this intrusive culture mainly at two sites, close to one another on the east bank of the river Axius: Vardarophtsa and Vardina. He identified 'a burnt layer', 1·50 m deep, from 'two settlements at least', which contained intrusive Lausitz pottery at Vardarophtsa; and he saw in this 'a clear record of an invasion, though not necessarily a hostile one, of makers of Lausitz pottery at the end of the Mycenaean Age'.[2] The very top of the burnt layer marked the end of the settlement which had

---

[1] The suggestion that Phryges 'returning' from Hellespontine Phrygia came to Epidamnus makes no sense in itself; and if any Phryges fled from Hellespontine Phrygia after the fall of Troy, they would not have been strong enough to acquire Epidamnus and defeat the Thesproti under Odysseus.

[2] *PM* 39. The early Lausitz culture, 'Lausitz A', is still dated to this century, 1200–1100 B.C. (see Gimbutas, *Bronze Age* 131).

intrusive Lausitz pottery, and the very top had some sherds of the Granary style of Mycenae; indeed there were some sherds of this style just above the burnt layer and they belonged to the next settlement. Now the Granary style was in vogue at Mycenae when the Granary there was burnt *c.* 1120 B.C., a date based on the chronological date of Thuc. 1. 12. 3 but acceptable also to those who disregard the literary evidence. However, the Granary style may have lasted at Mycenae and elsewhere for some time after *c.* 1120 B.C., and at Vardarophtsa it was in vogue until 'the first compass-drawn concentric circles' appeared in 'the occupation layer which rests partly on the debris of the Lausitz'.[1] If we date the first compass-drawn concentric circles to *c.* 1050 B.C. as Heurtley and others do, the stratum with intrusive Lausitz pottery ended some time before the last appearance of Granary style sherds, say *c.* 1080 B.C. The total period of Mycenaeanizing pottery *c.* 1350 B.C. to *c.* 1080 B.C. covered some 270 years, and the stratum with intrusive Lausitz pottery occupied three-thirteenths of the whole, i.e. some sixty years if the rate of deposition was fairly constant. The stratum began then *c.* 1140 B.C. The date 1150 B.C. was given by Heurtley on other grounds.[2]

The evidence at Vardina is similar. The Mycenaeanizing phase was represented by three settlements, of which the last had intrusive Lausitz pottery. Immediately below this last stratum and thus antedating it there was found a violin-bow fibula with a flattened bow; and Heurtley saw parallels to this fibula at Mycenae in the period immediately before the destruction of Mycenae, i.e. before *c.* 1120 B.C.[3] We may thus put the start of this last stratum at Vardina *c.* 1140 B.C. at the earliest.

It is probable that the destruction of Vardarophtsa *c.* 1140 B.C. should be related to the destruction of the settlement at Kilindir, a destruction caused also by fire. Kilindir was not reoccupied for many centuries. In the burnt soil at Kilindir Casson found a Mycenaean stirrup-jar, 'itself blackened by fire', and he therefore dated the destruction *c.* 1150 B.C. At the nearby site of Chauchitsa a burnt layer marked the destruction of the settlement, and Casson put this just before the end of the Bronze Age. Here too a date around 1150 B.C. is appropriate. At Chauchitsa habitation of the site continued after the fire.[4]

It was a strange feature of Casson's and Heurtley's excavations that at Vardarophtsa and Vardina alone was Lausitz pottery found together with Mycenaeanizing pottery. At other sites east of the Axius, where

---

[1] *PM* 96 n. 5.

[2] *PM* 125, on an inference from the Trojan War situation.

[3] *AAA* 12 (1925) 34 and pl. xix, 12*b* = *PM* fig. 104*aa*. I disagree with Desborough *TLM* 142, who says 'the excavators could even be right' to date the invasion as late as 1050 B.C.; Heurtley, *PM* 125, said 1150 B.C.

[4] *Antiquaries J.* 6 (1926) 62 and 71 (Kilindir); Casson, *Macedonia* 128 f. and *Archaeologia* 74 (1923–4) 78 (Chauchitsa).

Mycenaeanizing pottery was found, there was only the local pottery with it. This shows that the Lausitz people had only a very limited foot-hold geographically to the east of the Axius, and that their main zone of occupation was west of the Axius. Nor can the dates at these two sites be taken to mark the upper and the lower dates for the presence of the Lausitz culture in Macedonia. It is indeed likely that Vardarophtsa and Vardina were the last places won and the first places lost by the Lausitz people. We may indeed conclude from the archaeological evidence that they had come from west of the Axius.

Heurtley deduced from the pottery at Vardarophtsa and Vardina—particularly from the fluted or grooved bowls and jugs, perhaps the plain grey cup with a high handle and pedestal foot, and the twisted handles which derived (he thought) from the fluted handle—that the intruders were members of 'the Lausitz people who about this time were spreading from their focus in Bohemia through the Balkan penin-sula, presumably in search of minerals'. As he found the pottery at these two sites only, he made the observation that 'they do not seem to have stayed long in Macedonia'.[1] My own deduction from the geographical position of these two sites is different; and my view is due in part to the fact that further traces of Lausitz people have been found since Heurtley wrote in 1939. In the cemetery of tumulus-burials at Vergina a con-siderable amount of the fluted ware which is typical of the Lausitz culture has been found, and the twisted handle is very common.[2] Some pottery of Lausitz type occurs together with pottery of Mycenaean shape, as at Vardarophtsa and Vardina, and should be dated *c.* 1150–1075 B.C. Other pottery of Lausitz type is associated with an iron sword of northern type, and with a wide variety of objects. At the lower end of the scale Andronikos reckoned that some of the Lausitz pots should be dated within the ninth century B.C.[3] We may take the period *c.* 1150–800 B.C. as a rough-and-ready estimate of the time during which some Lausitz people were continuously in the vicinity of Vergina.[4]

The site of Gajtan, just south of Scodra, has produced pottery with

[1] *PM* 124, citing Childe, *Danube* 326 and 411. Heurtley illustrates the Lausitz pottery on pp. 216–18 and 233.

[2] *Ergon* 1960. 88 in AF XI and in LXV *Ξ*; *PAE* 1952. 234 in *Δ* 5 and *Δ* 24; 241 in A10 and B4; 258; *BS* 2 (1961) 95 f. (jugs with cut-away necks having the twisted handle) and pl. viii, 19; *Studies in Med. Arch.* 13 (1964) 5.

[3] See last note, especially *Δ* 5, AF XI, and LXV *Ξ*, regarded by Andronikos as one of the oldest burials. The date 900 B.C. in *PAE* 1952. 258 is revised to become the ninth century in *Vergina* 188 ff.

[4] I am opposed to the tentative suggestion which Andronikos has made in *Vergina* 190, that the Mycenaean sherds and the Lausitz pottery at Vardarophtsa and *a fortiori* the Lausitz pottery at Vergina should be down-dated to some time after 1000 B.C. Andronikos was developing a view put forward by H. Müller-Karpe, *Chronologie* 123 f. The traditional dating of the Granary Class of Mycenaean sherds should be retained in Macedonia as else-where.

fluting not only on the body of the bowl but also on the rim (Fig. 14*k*) and on the handle, such distribution of the ornamentation being typical of the Lausitz ware. One handleless biconical collared bowl which is illustrated is of a characteristic Lausitz shape (Fig. 14*h*).[1] This fluted pottery occurs first in Layer 3 at Gajtan, which, I have argued else-where,[2] belongs to the Late Bronze Age and Early Iron Age. There are other styles of pottery, which are not of the Lausitz type. We may see a strong Lausitz influence rather than a Lausitz settlement at Gajtan. The cemetery of tumulus-burials in the Mati valley has yielded a large amount of fluted pottery. As Selim Islami and Hasan Ceka put it, 'on emploie largement aussi l'ornement à cannelures, qui souvent recouvre non seulement le corps mais également les anses, en leur donnant parfois l'aspect de l'échelonnement d'une corne de chèvre'. Four pots with this fluting are illustrated. Islami and Ceka consider the shapes generally to be those of the end of the Bronze Age; to judge by the illustrations some are likely to be of the Early Iron Age.[3] Here perhaps we may see a Lausitz people settled for a long time in the Mati valley which lies north-east of Epidamnus. There are a few signs of Lausitz influence in central Epirus,[4] and some in northern Thessaly.

Thus the archaeological evidence fits very well with the literary evidence of the places where the Briges or Brygi settled—namely in Albania in the vicinity of Epidamnus, and in Macedonia 'below Mt. Bermium', that is in that part of the plain of Central Macedonia which lies between Vergina, south of the Haliacmon, and Vardarophtsa–Vardina, just east of the Axius. We may give the name Briges to the Lausitz invaders. Moreover, we can see some of the effects of their invasion. They entered central Albania first and pressed hard upon the Thesproti in Epirus at a time when Odysseus had come home and was still alive, i.e. between 1180 and 1160 B.C. At that time or earlier other invaders, who came, like the Lausitz people, from Hungary and were armed with battle-axes, had entered central Albania and pressed down upon Epirus.[5] The pressure of these invasions set in motion the so-called Dorian invasion which

[1] *StH* 1966. 1. 60 and pl. xi, 5, 6, and 9 (in a difficult dialect of Albanian; but using 'kanelyra' for the French 'cannelures'); see the much briefer report in *SA* 1964. 1. 100 where fluting is mentioned but attributed to layer 2. Pl. xi, 6 is the characteristic shape; see Schránil 149 and pls. xxvii, 13, 25, 29, 34 and xxix, 11 (the Knovizer culture being Lausitz B), and compare the Lausitz pot at Vardarophtsa in *PM* 217 no. 410. *StH.* pl. xi, 5 with fluted rim resembles *PM* 217 f. nos. 415–418.
[2] *BSA* 62 (1967) 103; the excavator, Bep Rebani, puts Layer I at the end of the Bronze Age.
[3] *SA* 1964. 1. 103 and pl. xvi, 8–11. The pots have two unusually high handles which are not unlike the single high handle on the grey cups in *PM* nos. 471 and 484 of the Early Iron Age.
[4] *Epirus* 293, citing Dakaris in *PAE* 1952. 378 with fig. 12, 2 for fluted and ringed handles at Kastritsa and Terovo.
[5] See *Epirus* 353 and 392.

started with the Thessali leaving Thesprotia to invade north-eastern Greece *c.* 1140 B.C. and with the Dorians entering the Peloponnese *c.* 1120 B.C.[1] Meanwhile Central Macedonia was itself invaded from the north-west by another branch of the Lausitz people, and this invasion ended with the Lausitz occupation of the western part of the central plain. The Macedonians held firm in mountainous Pieria and in the middle Haliacmon valley, and the pass between that valley and Thessaly remained in the hands of the Peraebi.

We have still some traditions to consider. We have already noted that ἡ Μακεδονὶς γῆ and τὸ Μακεδονικὸν ὄρος were the areas north of Mt. Olympus extending up to the Haliacmon at the time of the Persian War, and that when the Dorians-to-be were living on Pindus they were called 'Makednon' (sc. *ethnos*) *c.* 1300 B.C. From these and other passages we have concluded that at the end of the Bronze Age the habitat of the Makedones included the southern side at least of the middle Haliacmon valley. The term Makednon, meaning 'tall' or 'high', seems likely to refer to the 'highlands' (of this part of Pindus), and suggest that Μακεδνὴ γῆ or ἡ Μακεδνία was the early name of this area. And in their turn the classical words 'Makedon' and 'Makedonia' grew out of the Bronze-Age Makednos and Makednia. There was, however, in classical times a variant both for the ethnic and for the area: Μακέτης with a feminine Μακέτας or Μάκεσσα, and Μακετία. These were explained by the lexicographers as deriving from Μάκετα, the name of a part of Macedonia and in particular the name of Orestis: καὶ τὴν Ὀρεστείαν δὲ Μάκεταν λέγουσιν ἀπὸ τοῦ Μακεδόνος (*FGrH* 135/6 Marsyas F 10).[2] Here Marsyas derives Μάκετα from the eponym of Macedonia, Μακεδών; but a political motive may be detected, since the Orestae were Molossian and not Macedonian, and the derivation is linguistically improbable. I suggest another explanation. The name Μάκετα was evidently the earlier name of the district later called Orestis. One citation in Stephanus Byzantius[3] places Orestis next to ἡ Μακεδονικὴ γῆ, which is probably a term for the Macedonian homeland: Ὀρεστία, πόλις ἐν Ὀρέσταις, ἐν ὄρει ὑπερκειμένῳ τῆς Μακεδονικῆς γῆς. It is thus likely that before the Orestae arrived, the upper Haliacmon valley was called Μάκετα, and the

[1] Thuc. 1. 12. 3; see my remarks in *CAH*[2] 2. 36 (1962) 31 f.

[2] The fragment of Marsyas occurs in St. Byz. s.v. *Makedonia*. The earliest mention is *FGrH* 323 Cleidemus F 3 in his *Atthis*, which is cited by St. Byz. s.v. *Makedonia*. The information is given also by Const. Porphyr. *De them.* 2. 2 (reading Ὀρεστίαν for Ἡρεστίαν) and p. 48, 9 ed. Bonn; Eustath. ad Dion. Perieg. 427; and Hsch. s.v. *Maketia*. Dindorf and others emended Μάκετα to Μακετία, but the manuscript tradition is clear that the former is the name of the district and the latter is the name of the greater Macedonian realm. With Mak-etai we may compare Dassar-etai.

[3] St. Byz. s.v. *Orestia*. In this passage Eordaea and Elimea have no place; it is probable that the passage comes from a discussion of an earlier situation in Macedonia. See p. 311 n. 1 below.

middle Haliacmon valley was called Μακεδνία—each with the adjacent highlands. If the Makedones proper came from Μάκετα and Μακεδνία originally, they could have taken their name from both districts and so have been called both Μακέται and Μακεδνοί, and the area they finally controlled could have been called both Μακετία and Μακεδνία or Μακεδονία.

The word Orestae, like the word Μακεδνοί 'highlanders', means 'mountaineers'. According to Hecataeus (*FGrH* 1 F 107) the Orestae were not Macedonian but Molossian. In other words they belonged to the Molossian group. They revived the association when they appeared as Ὀρεστοὶ Μολοσοί in an inscription of 164 B.C. at Dodona.[1] The bulk of the Molossian group lay west of the Balkan range, and we have noted (above, p. 300) that at the time of the *Nostoi* the Molossoi were in the district of the lower Aous valley.[2] It seems likely, then, that the Orestae lay at one time on the western part of the highlands and subsequently moved eastwards into the upper Haliacmon valley, as a result perhaps of the general movement southwards from Albania through central Epirus which stimulated the so-called Dorian invasion.

The evidence which we have considered for Macedonia makes it certain that the so-called Dorian invasion was not launched from Central Macedonia, nor did the Dorian invaders pass from Central Maceonia into Thessaly. On negative evidence, as well as on positive evidence, the Dorian invaders passed through central Epirus and thence eastwards and southwards.[3] One wing of the movement occupied south-west Thessaly and gave that country its classical name. The newcomers spread late and gradually into north-east Thessaly. The so-called Aeolian migration which drew emigrants from Thessaly, Phocis, Locris, and Boeotia was of long duration and lasted from *c.* 1130 to *c.* 1000 B.C. or later.[4] During much of this period north-east Thessaly continued to be Aeolian in speech, and the emigrants were using the north-eastern route overseas along the coast of the Thermaic Gulf and Chalcidice. Thus there was a relatively undisturbed area, which lay between the irruption of the Briges into western Central Macedonia and the irruption of the Thessali into south-western Thessaly, and it was in this relatively undisturbed area that for some time a continuous tradition ran on in the evolution of pottery and in the transmission of epic. But here too conditions were to worsen later on.

The first group of Aeolian migrants was led to the coast of Thrace by Penthilus, son of Orestes. With this tradition we pass out of the *Nostoi*

---

[1] See *Epirus* 462 f. and 811.

[2] As the people of the middle Aous valley, the Parauaei, belonged to the Thesprotian group (see *Epirus* 703), we have to put the Molossi of that period further to the north or west.

[3] *CAH*[2] 2. 36 (1962) 31 f.　　　　　　　　　　　　　[4] See *HG*[2] 82.

cycle of epic; for Orestes is not one of the company who fought at Troy. Orestes figures in some traditions which concern the Orestae. According to Str. 7. 7. 8, C 326, Orestes gave this name to the country and founded Argos Oresticum; according to Theagenes (*FGrH* 774 F 10) Orestes came to the country and had a son Orestes, during whose rule the people were called Orestae.[1] The version of Strabo occurs in Eustathius ad Dionys. Perieg. 680 (*FHG* ii. 339) Ὀρέσται ἔθνος εἰσιν Εὐρωπαῖον, Μολοσσικόν, ἀπὸ Ἀγαμεμνονίδου Ὀρέστου καλούμενοι. As the attribution of the Orestae to the Molossian group of tribes comes from Hecataeus,[2] it is possible that this link between Orestes and the Orestae was reported by Hecataeus. But the link remains highly improbable. The aetiologizing motive is patently obvious, the more so as the word Orestae has an obvious derivation from ὄρος and the west-Greek ethnic termination -estae.[3] It is therefore prudent to reject the idea of any connection between Orestes and the Orestae.

[1] Theagenes concerned himself with the Macedonian traditions, and the named fragments are all preserved by Stephanus Byzantius. It is possible that some other entries in St. Byz. and especially the entry s.v. *Orestia* may come from Theagenes. The fragment of Theagenes is sometimes made to include the next sentence, in which Orestes is said to have died of a snakebite; but this sentence evidently came from Asclepiades Tragilensis (*FHG* 3. 304 no. 15), or from a source common to Asclepiades and St. Byz. Theagenes alone introduces Orestes, son of Orestes; perhaps this was for reasons of chronology, if for instance he put the arrival of the Orestae in 'Maketa' in the generation of Penthilus, i.e. *c.* 1130 B.C.

[2] See *Epirus* 462.

[3] Orestai and Orestoi may be compared with the Enchestoi, Hyncestoi, Kyestoi, Peukestoi, and Ethnestai of Epirus and the Lynkestai of Lyncus.

XII

THE TRANSITIONAL PHASE
LEADING TO THE EARLY IRON AGE

c. 1125 TO 1050 B.C.

IN most parts of the Aegean area it is very difficult to put a date to the transition from the Bronze Age to the Iron Age. One reason is that scholars follow different conventions. Some close the Bronze Age, as I do here, at *c.* 1125 B.C.; they include in the Early Iron Age a sub-Mycenaean phase, which occurs in some areas (e.g. in Central Macedonia) and precedes the first appearance of Proto-Geometric pottery at Athens and at Corinth *c.* 1075 B.C.[1] Others close the Bronze Age at *c.* 1050 B.C., when there is a larger spread of Proto-Geometric pottery; they either keep the sub-Mycenaean period as the last phase of the Bronze Age or abolish the term and extend L.H. III C to *c.* 1050 B.C.[2] When these conventions are not understood, an extraordinary confusion in the dating of particular objects may result. I am retaining the term 'sub-Mycenaean period', which arose originally from distinctive finds in some areas, and I am describing it as the first, or transitional, phase of the Early Iron Age.

Whatever nomenclature is used, the basic distinction between the Bronze Age and the Iron Age is the introduction of iron for the making first of knives, later of swords, and finally of other weapons and tools. Now Macedonia has always been very well off for minerals. The Romans made arrangements to control the mining there of gold, silver, copper, and iron. In modern times the same metals are exploited, and iron is mined particularly in Chalcidice.[3] The working of metal was practised in Macedonia during the Bronze Age. Gold slag has been found at Vardarophtsa in contexts dating to the Early Bronze Age, the end of the Late Bronze Age, and the first E.I.A. settlement which began *c.* 1075 B.C.,[4]

---

[1] These are the dates which I gave in *HG²* 21 and 84.

[2] For instance, Desborough, *TLM* 241. There has also been a tendency to keep the Proto-Geometric dating close to the Geometric. Thus Desborough used to date the beginning of Proto-Geometric pottery at Athens to 1025 B.C., and he has recently put back the date to 1050 B.C. (ibid. 258).

[3] Livy 45. 29; Casson, *Macedonia* 57 f. and O. Davies in *PM* 253 give brief accounts of mineral resources and mining. See pp. 12 f. above and Map 1.

[4] The slags are listed in *BSA* 28 (1926–7) 197; the two later ones come from settlement 16 and settlement 18, which are defined in *BSA* 27 (1925–6) 10 and 63, where Heurtley dates the end of the burnt layer and so of his Period C *c.* 1050 B.C. For my date see p. 306 above.

and also at Saratse in an E.B.A. context. This suggests that the Paeonians and probably the Lausitz people at Vardarophtsa were skilled in working metal. The mould for making bronze axes at Kravari in Pelagonia shows a similar skill there *c.* 1250–1150 B.C. It is probable that the bronze was made from local copper.[1] For copper objects in Macedonia contain an unusual amount of lead, and O. Davies has suggested that a copper which has this amount of lead was mined at Tsatzile (south-east of Kilkis) or at Gevgheli in the Bronze Age and later.[2] A lump of lead was found at Vardina in a L.B.A. layer; lead rivets were used in mending pottery there throughout L.H. III and at Vergina in the Early Iron Age; and a lead ring and two lead beads were found in burials of the Early Iron Age at Vergina.[3] Lead is still obtained in Macedonia (see Map 1).

When such knowledge of metal-working was present, it is not surprising that iron too was worked early. A large boulder of magnetite, an iron ore, which was found at Kilindir in a M.B.A. level, may have been intended for smelting.[4] A lump of slag 'apparently derived from cast iron' was found at Vardarophtsa in a pre-Mycenaean level, i.e. before *c.* 1350 B.C.[5] Iron extracted in this casting method was too brittle to be used for weapons. Another iron slag, found at Vardarophtsa in the twentieth settlement, was the result of a different method which produced a mild steel; and it was from this mild steel that the knives and other weapons of the Iron Age were made. The twentieth settlement, however, is the third of four settlements within Heurtley's Period D, which runs from *c.* 1050 to 350 B.C., and it is itself dated after the late seventh century B.C.[6]

As iron pyrites, molybdenum (used nowadays for alloying steel), and metallurgical skill were present in Central Macedonia on either side of the conventional dates for the transition from the Bronze Age to the Iron Age, it is reasonable to suggest that mild steel for making weapons of iron may have been produced relatively early in Macedonia. When I studied the bronze and iron weapons of this period in Epirus, the incidence of iron knives, in one case with bronze rivets, and of iron weapons which were replicas of weapons in bronze pointed 'to the conclusion that iron was used for weapons in Epirus at an earlier date than

[1] For the mould see p. 299 above. Davies noted in *BSA* 28 (1926–7) 196 that the analysis of some bronze objects found at Vardarophtsa showed them all to have been made from a copper with a high nickel content, which had been taken apparently from one and the same mine. For copper see Map 1.   [2] *PM* 255.

[3] *PM* 102; *AD* 17 (1961–2) 1. 274 in LXV burial *O*, and 281 in LXV *AK*; *PAE* 1952. 239 in Tumulus E; *Vergina* 260.   [4] Casson in *Antiquaries J.* 6 (1926) 64 n. 1; and *PM* 255.

[5] *BSA* 28. 197 and 199 'in association with the earliest Mycenaean sherds', and *PM* 101–2 immediately below the Mycenaean level and 255 'in the pre-Mycenaean level'. A. M. Snodgrass in *PPS* 31 (1965) 239 is mistaken in putting this slag in 'the period contemporary with the latest Mycenaeans'.

[6] *BSA* 28. 197 f. and *BSA* 27. 10 and 61. Snodgrass loc. cit. is mistaken in putting this slag 'in the immediately succeeding period' after his 'latest Mycenaeans', and his argument that it antedates the earliest tombs at Vergina is very wide of the mark.

in Attica and Cyprus, indeed at a date which preceded the so-called Dorian invasion'.[1]

Since the time of that study excavations at Vergina have produced further evidence for the working of iron in Macedonia. Andronikos has pointed out that the bronze and iron objects at Vergina were made locally not by casting in a mould but by hammering; in iron spear-heads, for example, the socket is often not closed. Sometimes iron and bronze were used in the same object. In Tumulus LXV burial *AP*, which I date to the eleventh century (see pp. 331 f. below), an arched fibula of bronze with two buttons had an iron pin, apparently a repair.[2] LXVIII *Z* contained a sword with an iron blade, a bronze hilt, and a wooden scabbard with a bronze covering at its tip;[3] Tumulus XVI had iron nails with bronze heads;[4] and LXVIII *E* had a long bronze coil (for the hair) with an iron termination.[5] Working with two metals was not restricted to Vergina; for at Chauchitsa a sword with an iron blade and a bronze hilt was found, and a shield-boss was strengthened with six rivets of iron. There are also rare specimens in iron of objects which were commonly made in bronze, and these are best explained as experiments by local smiths. In LXV *AP*, which I date to the eleventh century, both iron and bronze rings were associated with the long bronze coils.[6] In the fill of Tumulus E there was an arched fibula of iron with two buttons (a piece of inferior workmanship) and another in *AΓ* III; this type is of the eleventh century.[7] In *AZ* VII, dating to *c.* 900–850 B.C., one phalaron or belt-boss was made of iron,[8] and in LXV *Γ* of the ninth century there was a pair of tweezers of iron.[9] The very numerous iron weapons are difficult to date. The swords, all of the northern Naue II type, are considerably longer and broader than their counterparts further south— corresponding no doubt to differences in physique—and some of them are assigned by Andronikos to the tenth century, and others to the eighth century.[10] Knives and spear-heads, some very large, cannot be dated with any precision.

It is clear from this evidence that the working of iron was practised in Epirus and Macedonia long before it was practised in central Europe, where the commencement of the Iron Age is put usually *c.* 750 B.C. As

[1] *Epirus* 358 f.

[2] *AD* 17 (1961–2) 1. 285; for casting and hammering see Andronikos in *Vergina* 224.

[3] *AD* 18 (1963) 2. 222; remains of a wooden scabbard bound with strips of bronze, together with an iron sword, were found in Tumulus Z (*PAE* 1953. 145).

[4] *AD* 17. 1. 237; the tumulus contained prehistoric objects and a Hellenistic burial, so that the nails could be of either period. I have not included in my list the bronze-headed iron pins of Tumulus LXVII *Γ*, which are of the orientalizing period (*AD* 18. B 2. 219).

[5] *AD* 18. B 2. 222. [6] *AD* 17. 1. 285.

[7] *PAE* 1952. 240 and 256–7 = *Vergina* E on p. 22, and A III on pp. 63 and 135.

[8] *Ergon* 1961. 102. [9] *AD* 17. 1. 270; I noted six tweezers in bronze.

[10] *BS* 2 (1961) 95, and *Vergina* 265.

between Epirus and Macedonia it is probable that Epirus has some priority; but being itself devoid of minerals Epirus must have drawn the ore and the skill from a near-by source, namely Northern Macedonia or the vicinity of Florina. For it seems most unlikely that the inhabitants of Epirus and Macedonia derived any such ore or the knowledge how to use it from Greece itself, where iron was not worked until the Proto-Geometric period, commencing about 1050 B.C. From what quarter, then, and from what people did the knowledge of iron-working come into Macedonia and Epirus so early?

There is one tumulus at Vergina which is of special interest for the transition from bronze to iron. Tumulus C had been disturbed in post-Byzantine times and again in recent times, but the excavators found some pieces of a circular peribolos, consisting of a double line of unworked stones. The diameter was estimated at some 14 m, and this makes burial Γ the central burial.[1] The tumulus contained the following burials. Burial A, without any surround, had two bronze 'arched' fibulae of a simple kind (Fig. 17*q*) and a jug with cut-away neck; B, with a surround of massive stones, had bits of an iron sword, four bronze finger-rings, and a pot with three mammiform projections on the shoulder, inspired probably by Lausitz pottery;[2] Γ, a trench with bones collected at each end and at one end 'by the skull',[3] had no offerings; $\varDelta$, with a surround of massive stones, had among the stones a two-handled cantharos with short vertical parallel lines incised on the shoulder exactly like one of the early Lausitz culture, a bronze finger-ring, and a bronze sword 72 cm long in excellent condition, similar to Type II Group I (Fig. 10*l* and Fig. 13*a*);[4] Z, without any surround, had two jugs with cut-away neck, a bowl with extended rim perforated to provide two handles, and a drinking-bowl with thumb-rests;[5] $\varTheta$, inside a pithos, had a jug with cut-away neck and a drinking-bowl with thumb-rests;[6] and there were two burials of Christian times.

Of the prehistoric burials the deepest, Γ, is probably the earliest; the next deepest, B and $\varDelta$, being constructed in the same way and being on the same level as one another, are also early; A, being higher up and

---

[1] *AD* 17. 1. 241 and fig. 28. The central position of Γ is shown also by the fact that burials $\varDelta$ and $\varTheta$ near the periphery are about equidistant from Γ in fig. 28. Views of the tumulus in pl. 114 and pl. 115.

[2] For the fibulae pl. 114*y* and pl. 145*a*, objects CA2 and CA3, and for the jug pl. 114*y* and pl. 115*a* 1; for burial B pl. 145*a*, objects CB 7–10, and pl. 115*a* 2, to which Schránil pl. xxvii, 5, 13, and 15 may be compared for mammiform projections (early Lausitz). The four rings in B may be hair-rings; but I translate Petsas's δακτύλιοι as finger-rings.

[3] The collection of bones in this way is very rare at Vergina and may imply a special reverence.

[4] Pl. 115*e* and Schránil 141 and pl. xxvii, 6 for an almost identical cantharos with this incised ornament (early Lausitz); pl. 115*d* and *Mak.* 7 (1966–7) pl. 42*b*.

[5] Pl. 119*d*.

[6] Pl. 119*e*3.

probably directly above a part of *Γ*, is later than *Γ*, *B*, and *Δ*; *Z*, with no surround (like *A*), is also later; and *Θ* latest, if the pithos-burial is a later form generally. Bronze swords of Type II Group I are dated to the decades on either side of 1200 B.C.; and the sword of burial *Δ*, being in prime condition, was interred presumably in L.H. III C before the end of the Bronze Age.[1] If we place the Lausitz type cantharos near the time of the Lausitz invasion of Central Macedonia, one may date grave *Δ* to *c.* 1140–1120 B.C. A tumulus at Vodhinë in northern Epirus provides an analogy. It is a double tumulus, the inner tumulus being sealed off by a layer of shingle. The earliest burial, that in the centre, had no offerings; a subsequent burial had a bronze sword of Type II Group I; and in the upper tumulus a long bronze pin and a bronze spectacle-fibula provided a date before which the lower tumulus with the bronze sword was constructed. At Vergina, as *B* and *Δ* were at the same level, were both surrounded by massive stones, and both had bronze finger-rings and pottery influenced by the early Lausitz culture, it is probable that they were fairly close in time. One might suggest that *B* and its iron sword are to be dated to the very beginning of the Early Iron Age, *c.* 1120–1100 B.C.[2] The arched fibulae of burial *A* may be of the eleventh or tenth century B.C. (see p. 386 below); and this burial is certainly subsequent to burial *Δ* and burial *B*.[3]

There is an interesting parallel to Tumulus C in a tumulus at Visoï near Prilep in Pelagonia. The results of the excavation there have not been published, but I saw a model of the excavated tumulus, in which there were relatively massive stones as in Tumulus C.[4] Among the finds on display were two swords: a bronze sword in two pieces (Fig. 10*j*),

---

[1] Dated originally by Petsas in *AD* 17. 1. 242 and Daux in *BCH* 85 (1961) 794 to 'the end of the Bronze Age'. Catling in *Antiquity* 35 (1961) 119 puts three swords of this category in the period 1225–1175 B.C. and one in 1200–1125 B.C. H. L. Lorimer, *Homer and the Monuments* (London, 1950) 367, pointed out that 'the iron sword follows the bronze in Greece at a very brief interval . . . after them [the bronze pair from Tiryns at the very end of L.H. III] the bronze sword is no more seen on the mainland'. Bronze swords of Type II in tumuli of northern and central Epirus fall within Catling's dates, 1225–1125 B.C. (see *Epirus* 320 f., 351, 355). In *PPS* 31 (1965) 239 A. M. Snodgrass disagreed with Petsas's dating of the bronze sword at Vergina, because he thought that burial B containing an iron sword was 'the central (and presumably primary) burial' in the tumulus. This is not demonstrably so, because the tumulus and the stones were disturbed and displaced in later times. The depth of the burials is a better guide. He writes of stray finds of such swords in Greece in Geometric contexts; but that is irrelevant, since this sword was no stray but was placed, while in excellent condition, in the grave of a warrior.

[2] *Epirus* 202 f. (Vodhinë). The fill of Tumulus C yielded a unique piece at Vergina, namely a small bronze piece of horseshoe shape, shown in pl. 145 as C11. If it is part of what had been a pendant, then it is of the later Lausitz type (Knovizer culture) shown in Schránil pl. xxx no. 32.

[3] A similar plain arched fibula in Grave C at Theotokou in south-east Magnesia (*PTh* 212 fig. 147*b*) is dated *c.* 1050 B.C. by Desborough, *PGP* 148 f.

[4] In the museum at Monastir in September 1968. There was only a very small show of the finds. [See addition to p. 293 n. 6, above, for the bronze sword.]

belonging to Catling's Type II Group II 'developed', and an iron sword, long-bladed and with a fish-tail haft of the Type II Group I kind. These two swords may be dated similarly to just before and just after 1120 B.C. As we shall see below (p. 337), other objects from the tumulus at Visoï are closely related to objects characteristic of the Vergina tumuli. A tumulus at Pateli may be of this period (p. 341 below).

The probable conclusion, then, is that in Pelagonia and Central Macedonia, as well as in Epirus and Albania, the Iron Age commenced *c.* 1120 B.C. with swords (and no doubt knives)[1] made of iron. The first appearance of these swords seems to be associated with the arrival of the Lausitz invaders, whom we have identified as the Briges, related in some way to the Phryges of north-western Asia Minor. It may be more than coincidence that Greek tradition attributed to the Phrygian Dactyli, named Celmis ('smelter'), Damnameneus ('hammerer'), and Acmon ('anvil'), the discovery of the working of iron—a working, which, to judge from the names, involved not cast iron but the mild steel of which we have written. It is most likely that the Briges of the Balkans shared a knowledge of this discovery with the Phryges of Asia Minor or derived it from them, and were early workers of iron. The famous mine near the territory of the Briges of Pelagonia took its name 'Damastion' from the same verb as the Dactyl Damnameneus, and it probably refers to the working of wrought rather than cast metals.[2] Greek tradition, as preserved by Str. C. 680, attributed the wealth of Midas to 'the mines by Mt. Bermium'. Perhaps the mines by Mt. Bermium yielded the iron from which the very numerous iron weapons in the Vergina cemetery were made. Thus the literary evidence and the archaeological evidence coincide in indicating that the use of mild steel in the southern Balkans originated with the Briges in the lands immediately north of Greece, probably *c.* 1120 to 1100 B.C.

If there is substance in our arguments that the Briges were related in some way to the Phryges, bore marks of Lausitz culture and were early workers of iron, we should expect to find something in common between the two peoples in the areas where they settled. Did they, for instance, arrive about the same time? We have dated the irruption of the Briges into central Albania to *c.* 1160 B.C. and into Central Macedonia to *c.* 1140 B.C., and in the latter area their occupation of Vardarophtsa and Vardina was within the period of the Granary class of Mycenaean pottery,

---

[1] An iron knife with a bronze rivet was found together with a bronze sword of Type II Group I at Kakavi in Epirus (see *Epirus* 358); it should be dated towards the end of L.H. III. The knives from Petsas's excavations at Vergina have not yet been illustrated.

[2] This seems to be the obvious etymology of the name. See L–S–J[9] for the epic and later forms s.v. δαμάζω. The name Damnameneus is in the Aeolic dialect, and it is probable that the traditions of the Phrygian occupation of the Troad entered the Aeolian epic during the time of the Aeolian migration.

and was indeed succeeded by further examples of Granary pottery, so that we dated the occupation of these two sites *c.* 1140–1080 B.C. The evidence for dating the irruption of the Briges into central Albania came initially from the Epic Cycle. So does that for dating the irruption of the iron-working Phryges into north-western Asia Minor. Strabo C 473 says that 'when Troy had been sacked', τῆς Τροίας ἐκπεπορθημένης, Phrygians gained control of the Troad, and that the Phrygian Dactyls were the first to discover and work iron on Mt. Ida; he cites Sophocles for the latter part, and it is clear that he derived the names of the three Dactyls from the Cyclic Epic *Phoronis*,[1] which was composed *c.* 600 B.C. but used traditional saga of earlier times. If we put the sack *c.* 1200 B.C. and allow a generation for the legends of some Trojan heroes remaining at or near Troy, we may date the coming of the Phrygians into the Troad to *c.* 1160–1130 B.C.

What then of the archaeological evidence? Within the area of the Troad Troy VII b 1 was an impoverished version of the great Troy, and the first 'notable decorative innovations' appeared in Troy VII b 2. Both settlements were of short duration, and both were marked by the Granary class of Mycenaean pottery. The archaeological evidence puts the life of Troy VII b 2 on either side of 1120 B.C., say *c.* 1150–1070 B.C. Blegen and his colleagues, following a higher chronology which puts the sack of Troy *c.* 1250 B.C., held that Troy VII b 2 lasted on 'well into the twelfth century while the pottery style of Mycenaean IIIc prevailed',[2] and this means on my chronology into the early eleventh century at the latest. Blegen and his colleagues attributed the innovations of Troy VII b 2 to invaders, and indeed to the first invaders who came after Troy had been sacked. The literary and the archaeological evidence lead us to the same date approximately for this invasion. Moreover, the literary evidence supplies the name of the invaders, the Phryges. Thus the Briges occupied areas in Albania, Pelagonia, and Macedonia, and the Phryges occupied the Troad at approximately the same time, *c.* 1150–1080 B.C. The Briges had or acquired the art of making mild steel; and if we accept the literary evidence, despite the absence of iron objects in Troy VII b 2, the Phryges also had or acquired this art in the Troad. They inaugurated the Iron Age in these two regions somewhere around 1120 B.C.

One last test remains. Were the Phryges bearers of a Lausitz culture? Were the innovations of Troy VII b 2 'Lausitz' in kind, and if so do they resemble the Lausitz phenomena in Macedonia and Albania? Blegen and his colleagues have confirmed the view of their predecessors, that there was an 'unmistakable general family similarity'[3] between the new

[1] Str. 10, C 473 and Schol. Ap. Rhod. 1. 1129 = *FEpG* fr. 2.
[2] Blegen in *CAH*² 2. 21 (1964) 15.　　　[3] *Troy* iv. 1. 144.

ware of Troy VII b 2—the so-called Buckelkeramik or Knobbed Ware—
and the pottery of 'Hungary', but they did not make particular comparisons either with individual cultures in Hungary or with the pottery of
Macedonia. This we must now do.

The Knobbed Ware of Troy VII b 2 was named after the protuberances
which vary from regular horns to small mammiform protuberances,
sometimes ringed concentrically with grooves.[1] In the older Lausitz phase
in Hungary 'das Grundelement des plastischen Dekors ist der Buckel',
and a similar variety of protuberances, some with the concentric grooves,
are shown by Schránil.[2] In the Albania–Macedonia region horn-like
protuberances occur at Gajtan, pointed knobs on the shoulders of pots
at Pateli, and knobs usually of a less emphatic form at Vergina;[3] and one
peculiar case of a knob on top of a handle at Troy VII b 2 is paralleled by
such a case at Saraj near Brod in Pelagonia.[4] The rippling, as Blegen
calls it at Troy VII b 2, is precisely like the 'flache Kanelierung' of the
older Lausitz phase in Hungary, the 'fluting' or 'grooving' of Heurtley's
Lausitz pottery in east Central Macedonia, the ῥαβδώσεις of Andronikos'
Lausitz-type pottery at Vergina, and the 'kanelyra' illustrated in the
reports of Gajtan and the Mati valley sites in Albania.[5] This fluting is
particularly striking on the handles; it occurs there in all the areas I
have mentioned.[6]

At Troy VII b 2 this pottery was always hand-made, though other
pottery was wheel-made; it was always hand-made both in Macedonia,
where the wheel was in use, and in Albania, where its use is uncertain.
In all cases the pottery is of a 'dark monochrome colour but burnished'.[7]
At Troy, in the Lausitz homeland, and in the Mati valley a strong ad-
mixture of sand in the clay has been noted. In Troy VII b 2 the Knobbed
Ware was remarkable for a number of small vessels; so was the older
Lausitz culture in Hungary. Troy VII b 2 had cups and drinking-bowls

---

[1] *Troy* iv. 1. 179, and iv. 2 figs. 259, centre; 260. 2; 264. 3; 265. 4 and 5; 271. 4, 15, and 19; 280; and 282.   [2] Schránil 142 and pl. xxvii, 5, 13, 14, and 15.

[3] *StH* 1966. 1. 48 'vegje në formë mjekrre të rrafshtë ose me maje të kthyeme nalt' and pl. iv, 7 (Gajtan, perhaps of an earlier date). *PM* 105 and pl. xxiii *a, f, j, l, w* (Pateli, being a common form there). *AD* 17. 1 pl. 103*a*, pls. 115*a* 2, 149*b*, and 151*η*; *AD* 18 (1963) 2, pl. 261*a* 2 (Vergina). *Vergina* pl. 30, 13; pl. 31, 16, 18, 22, and 24; pl. 33, 10; pl. 36, 4, 9, etc.

[4] *Troy* iv. 2 fig. 265 no. 36. 1097. At Saraj the knob is on a vertical rounded handle, which is an extension of the rim of an open bowl. I saw it in the museum at Monastir in 1968; it is unpublished.

[5] *Troy* iv. 1. 179, and iv. 2 fig. 281; Schránil 142; *PM* 98; *BS* 2 (1961) 96; *StH* 1966. 1 pl. xi, 5, 6, 9; *SA* 1964. 1. 103 'on emploie largement aussi l'ornement à cannelures' and pl. xvi, 8 and 9; *Vergina* pl. 32, 4; pl. 35, 24; pl. 57, 24; pl. 61, 10; pl. 64, 25; pl. 70, 33.

[6] *Troy* iv. 2 fig. 272, 19–21; Schránil pl. xxix, 7; *PM* 98 and fig. 87; *SA* 1964. 1. 103, where the fluted handle of the Mati tumuli is compared to a goat's horn, and pl. xvi, 9 and 10; *Vergina* pl. 73, 28.

[7] Troy iv. 1. 180; Schránil 142, 'eine dünkelgefarbte und geglättete Keramik'; *PM* 98 'fine dark polished surface'; *BS* 2 (1961) 96, very dark in colour from grey to black; *SA* 1964. 1. 103 'de couleur gris'.

with disproportionately long, rather high-standing handles. Such handles
are a feature of the Mati valley pottery. Both the handles and the shapes
of cups and drinking-bowls at Troy are very similar to the pottery of the
later Lausitz phase in Hungary.[1] A ceramic curiosity in the Lausitz
homeland is a group of such two-handled, rippled drinking-bowls which
stand upon two little feet, formed like human feet (Fig. 15*aa*). Blegen
and his colleagues found in Troy VII b 2 one such human foot and
published it as 'from the foot of a vessel', correctly but without knowledge
of the Lausitz analogy.[2]

The 'general family similarity' can thus be defined more closely as
a direct relationship of the Knobbed Ware of Troy VII b 2 to the older
Lausitz culture of Hungary, and at the same time as a collateral relationship to the cultures of Macedonia, probably Pelagonia, and Gajtan and
the Mati valley in Albania—this collateral relationship being due to
common descent from the Lausitz culture of Hungary. From the limited
material which has been published[3] it appears that the collateral relationship of Troy was strongest with Macedonia, probably because there was
some traffic along the coast between the Thermaic Gulf and Troy
VII b 2 throughout the second half of the twelfth century B.C.

In 1925, when Heurtley was reporting on his excavation of the mound
at Vardina in Central Macedonia, he noted several points of similarity
between the Vardina pottery and that of Troy VII b: a form of incision
'mechanically made, apparently by laying a stick on the wet clay', incised circles made with a stamp, ribbed handles, and incised tangential
circles.[4] He was concerned not with a relationship but with a cross-dating,
because 'various analogies to the pottery from the second seventh city at
Hissarlik' confirmed the date *c.* 1100 B.C. which he and Casson proposed
for the immediately post-Mycenaean phase and the inauguration of the
Iron Age at Vardina and Chauchitsa.[5] Now that we have the work of

[1] For small vessels see pl. xxvii in Schránil. For cups and bowls see *Troy* iv. 2 figs. 260 and
261; *SA* 1964. 1. 137 pl. xvi, 8 and 9; and Schránil 151 and pl. xxvii, 32 and 33, illustrated
as being of the earlier Lausitz culture and described in the text relating to the later Lausitz
culture = older Knovizer culture.

[2] Schránil 151 'die auf zwei in der Form von Menschenfüssen modellierten Füsschen stehen'
and pl. xxvii, 33; *Troy* iv. 1. 177, and iv. 2 fig. 275 no. 8 (*a*) and (*b*). These bowls were unique
not only in having these feet but also in having two little horns on each handle (the so-called
'ansa lunata'). They were probably cult vessels; the human feet with the toes marked (see
the examples at Troy) should then have some local religious significance. Do they explain
the name of the Phrygian 'Dactyls' (toes) in a more acceptable manner than Strabo's derivation of it from the foothills of Mt. Ida (C 473)?

[3] Very little pottery from the earlier excavations at Vergina, very little indeed from the
Mati valley, some from Gajtan, and none from the tumuli near Prilep in Pelagonia. We rely
mainly on Heurtley's material, the publication by Petsas of some pottery from Vergina,
and now Andronikos, *Vergina*.

[4] *AAA* 12 (1925) 27 n. 1; 28 n. 2; 35 with n. 1. He was making comparisons with objects
nos. 3318, 3321, 3491, and 3554 in H. Schmidt, *Heinrich Schliemann's Sammlung trojanischer
Altertümer* (Berlin, 1902).   [5] *AAA* 12. 35.

Blegen and his colleagues, we can see the extent of the relationship between Troy VII b 2 and east Central Macedonia. Blegen was able to associate with his Knobbed Ware a considerable range of impressed, stamped, and incised decorations of a distinctive kind, sometimes filled with white and sometimes not. Almost the same range of decorations, both filled and unfilled, occurs at Vardina and Vardarophtsa.[1] I show in Fig. 15 a selection of these decorations on sherds from Troy and Macedonia. Their similarity, coupled with the similarities in the Knobbed Ware, seems to put beyond reasonable doubt the lines of development from the older Lausitz culture of Hungary to Albania–Macedonia on the one hand and to Troy VII b 2 on the other hand, and in consequence the identification of the Lausitz-culture bearers of this period in Albania–Macedonia and in Troy VII b 2 with the Phrygian group of peoples, called Briges in Europe and Phryges in Asia.

As regards the Briges in Europe, we may attribute to them some tombs which have been excavated in Pelagonia. Two cist-tombs, lined with slabs, were opened near Prilep. One had been rifled, the other was intact. In addition to the skeleton there were in it two arched fibulae with linear engraving on the arches, like the two fibulae in Mouliana Grave A in Crete; two bronze armlets of five spirals each, rectangular in section; five heavy bronze armlets and a piece of a sixth, which are open-ended (Fig. 20x) and of a shape typical of the early Lausitz culture; a finger-ring of bronze band, the ends meeting at an oblique angle (Fig. 20w), and a small piece of spiralling bronze wire, which evidently belonged to the ring, the whole ring being in the early Lausitz manner; two amber beads; and one bead of glass paste.[2] The two fibulae were dated by the excavator to Hallstatt A, 1200–1000 B.C., and Mouliana Grave A has been dated to early L.M. III C, 'after rather than before 1200'.[3] The excavator compared the heavy armlets to some found together with fibulae of the Peschiera type at Glasinac, which were dated there to L.H. III C before the fall of Mycenae. A cross-check for the two fibulae is provided by precisely similar fibulae in Phase I cist-tombs of the Liburnians on the

---

[1] *Troy* iv. 1. 179, and iv. 2 figs. 259, 260, 263 no. 1, 265 no. 2, 271 nos. 17, 18, 21, and 23, 280, 282, and 288; *AAA* 12 pl. xiii, 20, 23, 24, pl. xiv, pl. xviii (Vardina); *PM* 95 f., 221 fig. 92, 222 fig. 93, 232 fig. 105, and 235 fig. 109. My Fig. 15 shows in Blegen's terminology the dotted circles connected by tangents (*a, b,* and *h*); paired concentric circles (*i* and *k*); spirals connected by tangents (*c* and *d*); incised chevrons of several kinds (*e, f, g,* and *n*); punctuated round impressions (*g, j,* and *n*); and two parallel lines with a filling of transverse dashes (*l* and *m*).

[2] *Starinar* 11 (1960) 209 f. The two fibulae, shown there in figs. 2, 3, and 4, are Blinkenberg's Type II 11a fig. 44, a reproduction of a Mouliana fibula. The heavy armlets, shown there in figs. 7–12, are as in Schránil pl. xxviii, 43 but undecorated. The finger-ring ends and the small spiral, shown there in figs. 13 and 15, may be compared with Schránil pl. xxviii, 16, 32, 35, and 45.

[3] N. K. Sandars in *AJA* 67 (1963) 134 f.; see *Epirus* 356 f. for probable connections between Mouliana Grave A and Epirus.

Adriatic coast, where they have been dated to Hallstatt A2 and B1, i.e. 1100–900 B.C.[1] Lastly, the early Lausitz culture is dated by M. Gimbutas to the period 1200–1125 B.C.[2] We may date this cist-tomb within the period 1200–1100 B.C.

There is a very brief report of objects from other cist-graves, lined with slabs, at Prilep. These are a one-handled mug in a good black ware, a bronze spear-head, and a long bronze sword of the Naue Type II (Fig. 10i), which J. Korošec dated around 1200 B.C. 'at the end of the Bronze Age'. Other pottery, decorated with geometric designs in black paint on a bright red ground, was of the Boubousti type.[3] One at least of these cist-graves is to be dated within the period 1200–1100 B.C.

In southern Pelagonia at Saraj near Brod a cemetery of twenty cist-tombs beside the Cerna Reka was excavated, and it was found that one tomb, no. XI, was separate from the others in its position. It was certainly earlier than the others, which are described on p. 339 below. It contained a fibula of the Peschiera type; a number of round bronze buttons with a tiny loop on the back; one bronze button with two points, diametrically opposite one another, which projected from the circumference; a solid bronze arm-band, ribbed and engraved with three lines so as to simulate four coils, and open-ended (Fig. 19m); and a one-handled cup.[4] The Peschiera fibula gives us a date towards the end of the Late Bronze Age; the bronze buttons and the arm-band are typical of the early Lausitz culture of 1200–1125 B.C.[5] Thus this tomb also may be dated within the period 1200–1125 B.C. It was presumably that of a chieftain, who was regarded as a hero by those who were buried later in a group near him.

At the northern end of the great Vardar defile by Demir Kapu, on the road thence to Budur Čiflik, a child's tomb was found to contain an arched fibula with a fairly large spring, a tiny catchplate, two buttons, and a slight swelling of the arch (as in Fig. 17r), and two bronze armlets with overlapping ends. The fibula is of a sub-Mycenaean kind, and the grave may be dated c. 1125–1050 B.C.[6] A pair of such fibulae with a larger swelling of the arch are mentioned below (p. 333).

A sign of overseas contact in the transitional period is the presence of sub-Mycenaean pottery. It has been found at Mikro Karaburnu,

---

[1] *AI* 6 (1965) 57 with figs. 7 and 8 in the article by Š. Batović, 'Die Eisenzeit auf dem Gebiet des illyrischen Stammes der Liburnen'.

[2] M. Gimbutas, *Bronze Age* 131 and 310.

[3] *Zbornik Arheološkog Muzeja* i (1956) 125 with fig. 26, 1–3.

[4] *Starinar* 11 (1960) 199 f. with figs. 20–3.

[5] Schránil 144 'es beginnen auch gegossene Knöpfe mit flachem Kopf und halbkreisförmiger Öse an der Unterfläche aufzutauchen' in the early Lausitz culture, and pl. xxviii, 36 and 42; and for the arm-band Schránil 126 with pl. xxv, 8 and 143, for the south -and west-Bohemian culture and its heir, the early Lausitz culture.

[6] *Starinar* 12 (1961) 243; the fibula is of Type II 10a in Blinkenberg's classification.

evidently a main port of entry;[1] at Saratse in the Langadha basin, which is reached by a direct route from Mikro Karaburnu; at Vardarophtsa and Vardina on the east bank of the Vardar river, the former being probably a port on the navigable stretch of the river; and at Vergina, south of the Haliacmon river.[2] As in the preceding period, the distribution suggests that sub-Mycenaean pottery was associated with ports of entry and trade inland. Contact was probably with north-eastern Thessaly, where, apart from the destruction of the palace at Iolcus in early L.H. III C, there was unbroken continuity of Mycenaeanizing pottery until the first appearance of Proto-Geometric pottery.[3] At this time too the Aeolian regions of Thessaly were kept in touch with north-west Asia Minor by the Aeolian migration, and this involved a use of the ports of the Thermaic Gulf and of Chalcidice on the coasting route.

[1] *Mak.* 7. 303 no. 84, citing *BCH* 79 (1955) 274 and *Arch. Reports* 1954. 39.
[2] *PM* 29 and 105; *AAA* 12. 35 f.; and for Vergina, e.g. *PAE* 1952. 258, *Ergon* 1958. 82 and 84.
[3] *Ergon* 1961. 54 f.

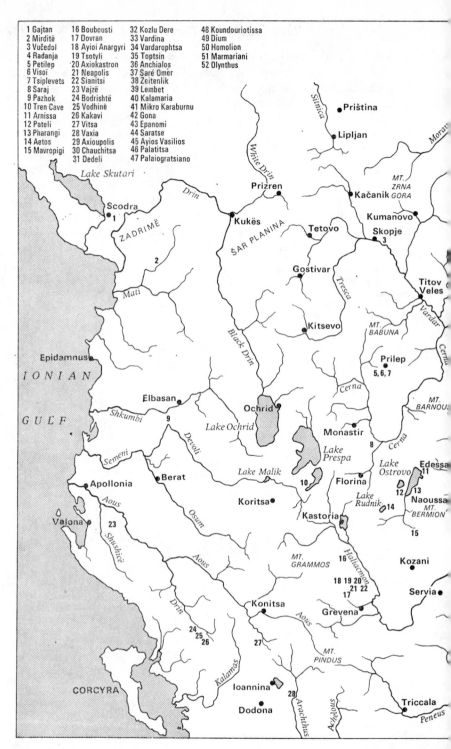

1 Gajtan
2 Mirditë
3 Vučedol
4 Radanja
5 Petilep
6 Visoi
7 Tsiplevets
8 Saraj
9 Pazhok
10 Tren Cave
11 Arnissa
12 Pateli
13 Pharangi
14 Aetos
15 Mavropigi

16 Boubousti
17 Dovran
18 Ayioi Anargyri
19 Tsotyli
20 Axiokastron
21 Neapolis
22 Sianitsi
23 Vajzë
24 Bodrishtë
25 Vodhinë
26 Kakavi
27 Vitsa
28 Vaxia
29 Axioupolis
30 Chauchitsa
31 Dedeli

32 Kozlu Dere
33 Vardina
34 Vardarophtsa
35 Toptsin
36 Anchialos
37 Saré Omer
38 Zeitenlik
39 Lembet
40 Kalamaria
41 Mikro Karaburnu
42 Gona
43 Epanomi
44 Saratse
45 Ayios Vasilios
46 Palatitsa
47 Palaiogratsiano

48 Koundouriotissa
49 Dium
50 Homolion
51 Marmariani
52 Olynthus

MAP 22. EARLY

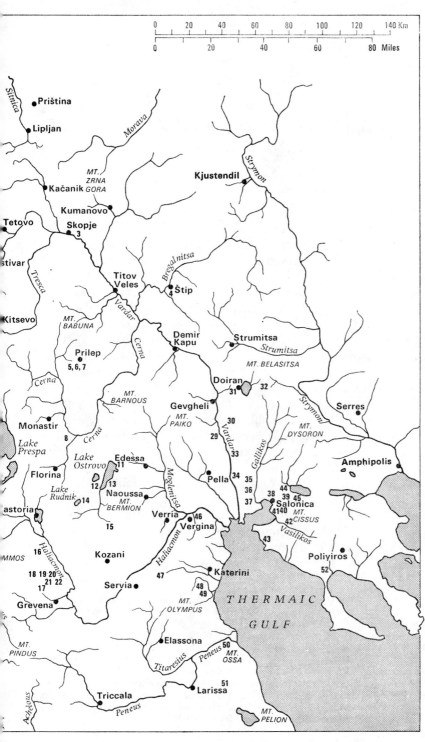

XIII

THE REMAINS OF THE EARLY IRON AGE,
c. 1050 TO *c.* 550 B.C.

1. *In East Central Macedonia*

THE period began in Central Macedonia, east of the Vardar, when the
Lausitz phase at Vardarophtsa and at Vardina had come to an end
c. 1080 B.C. The evidence for this area was assembled by Heurtley.
Of the wheel-made pottery the Mycenaean Granary style, which re-
appeared briefly after the Lausitz phase at Vardarophtsa, was followed
by the first appearance of compass-drawn concentric circles. This form
of decoration may be taken to mark the beginning of the Proto-Geometric
style. As it appeared first in the 25 cm overlying the burnt layer at Vardarophtsa,[1] it may be dated to *c.* 1050 B.C. (see p. 306 above). Its appearance at Vardina and elsewhere in Macedonia is not associated with
any sign of intruders. As Heurtley pointed out,[2] it is too late to be a
direct result of the Lausitz invasion; and he attributed it to contact with
'the South'. One need not perhaps look further south than north-east
Thessaly, where Mycenaeanizing pottery led on into a local Proto-
Geometric style at a relatively very early date.[3] Mycenaean and Proto-
Geometric forms of ornamentation were used also on pottery of local
types, and the Mycenaeanizing class in particular was very similar to
that of Chalcidice. The Proto-Geometric class was not followed in general
by Geometric ware, but it went on until the first Corinthian pottery
arrived *c.* 600 B.C.[4] The explanation of these phenomena is that Central
Macedonia and Chalcidice continued to be in contact with traders from
the Greek mainland until some date within the Proto-Geometric period.[5]
We have suggested that this contact was due mainly to the so-called
Aeolian migration of *c.* 1130 B.C. to *c.* 1000 B.C. This suggestion receives

---

[1] *PM* 105 n. 6. Proto-Geometric pottery in east Central Macedonia has been found at
Kalamaria, Mikro Karaburnu, Lembet, Gona, Sare Omer, Toptsin, Vardarophtsa, Vardina,
and Saratse (*PM* 232 f. and Rey figs. 48, 50, 52, pls. 50, 51).

[2] *PM* 125 n. 1, opposing a view advanced by T. C. Skeat.

[3] *Ergon* 1960. 60; 1961. 54 and 59. Theokharis dated the start of Proto-Geometric to *c.*
1100 B.C.   [4] *PM* 106 and 125.

[5] The theory advanced by J. L. Myres, *Who Were the Greeks?* (California, 1930), 453 f.
and discussed by T. C. Skeat, *The Dorians in Archaeology* (London, 1934), 4 f., that the
concentric circle originated with the Lausitz people, was rejected by Heurtley *PM* 125 n. 1,
and the lack of this device on the pottery of Lausitz type found since then at Vergina, Gajtan,
and in the Mati valley seems to support Heurtley decisively.

some support from the occurrence in Central Macedonia of a wheel-made grey cup of a particular shape (Fig. 16a) which 'has points of contact with the grey bucchero which was distributed over Lesbos and western Asia Minor at the end of the Mycenaean Age and the beginning of the Iron Age'.[1] A general poverty marked the sites of east Central Macedonia in this period. Metal was very rare and tools were made mainly of stone and bone. The people of this region, that is the Paeones, were evidently unenterprising and conservative; they did not initiate any traffic with the south; and in the Geometric period, when the Aeolian migration had ended, they made hardly any contact with the Greek mainland.

The Local Ware of Central Macedonia east of the Vardar was mostly hand-made and had a very limited repertoire of shapes: (1) bowls with extended flat rims, perforated to provide handles, some of which were horizontal wish-bone handles (Fig. 16b), (2) jugs with cut-away neck (Fig. 16c), and (3) trigger-handled cups (Fig. 16d). The distribution of these shapes outside east Central Macedonia is interesting. The bowls are very common at Vergina and in south-west Macedonia; but only one has been found in Chalcidice. The jugs are very common throughout Macedonia and Chalcidice, and they occur also in Thessaly. On the other hand, small jugs which are found in Chalcidice do not occur in east Central Macedonia. Thus Chalcidice and east Central Macedonia were both open to contacts with the south, but they did not share all the contacts within Macedonia. Each district tended to go its own way, and there was a lack of co-operation between them.

The sites of east Central Macedonia where Heurtley found Early Iron Age pottery were (1) close to the Vardar, namely Chauchitsa, Vardina, Vardarophtsa, and Toptsin; (2) Saré Omer on the Gallikos and near the coast; (3) Saratse near Lake Koronia; (4) three sites on the eastern side of Thessalonica, namely Kalamaria, Lembet, and Mikro Karaburnu; and (5) Gona in the Vasilikos valley below Mt. Cissus. All these sites, except Chauchitsa which lies on the route inland up the Vardar valley and Saratse which was, as in the Mycenaean period, a secondary centre of distribution, are close to the waterways of the Thermaic Gulf. The main additions to Heurtley's reports concern Mikro Karaburnu, where Petsas collected Proto-Geometric pottery and then 'pre-Persian' pottery from the remains of houses, storehouses, storage-pits, and tombs;[2] and Anchialos (Inglis) where pottery of the Local Ware was found belonging to categories (1) and (2) above.[3] It is clear that Mikro Karaburnu was

---

[1] *PM* 107. Heurtley and others disregarded the Aeolian migration in this connection.

[2] *Mak.* 7. 303 no. 84; see *BCH* 79 (1955) 274, and *Arch. Reports* 1954. 39.

[3] *Mak.* 7. 305 no. 98, pl. 16 a–e. The pot with two high handles and linear ornament, shown as *b*, is like one from Chauchitsa (*PM* 235 no. 482); it has closer parallels at Vergina.

a considerable site, perhaps being the city which had the main port on this side of the Gulf. Here, as elsewhere, Geometric ware was absent. The road inland from it branches at Anchialos into two roads leading into the areas of Kilkis and the Vardar valley respectively.

Stone, bone, and clay were used for tools and ornaments in the sites of east Central Macedonia, and pieces of metal were very rare: fragments of bronze tweezers and of a bronze pin; and a socketed javelin-head at Vardina (Fig. 13*k*). A mould for making bronze plaques, found at Saratse, was attributed by Heurtley (*PM* 108 and fig. 112*b*) 'probably to this period'. Two collections of bronzes, which the dealers said came in part from Crousis and from Chalcidice, will be described later (pp. 355 ff. below).

2. *In Southern and Western Macedonia*

The most exciting discoveries since Heurtley wrote have come from the cemetery of tumulus-burials at Vergina, just south of the lower Haliacmon river. A miniature bronze jug and some bronze armlets had been reported as coming from the vicinity of Verria, and then early in the last war the makers of a new road from Verria to Palatitsa opened two graves. They contained three large and one small arched fibulae of bronze, two 'eight-shaped fibulae with double-spirals' of bronze, three armlets of thick bronze and one of thin bronze, two bronze armlets of several coils each, a small bronze double-axe with a hole in the middle, three bronze 'shield-bosses' (probably belt-bosses), and an iron ring.[1] Part of this cemetery was excavated by M. Andronikos in 1951 and later years, and another part was excavated in 1960 and 1961 as a matter of urgency by him, X. Zerzelides, and Ph. Petsas. The preliminary reports were brief but admirably clear and well illustrated, and we now have the wholly excellent book by Andronikos on his own excavations.[2]

The excavators have not made any comparison with the cemeteries of tumulus-burials in northern Epirus, or in Central Albania, or in the area of Prilep.[3] At an early stage M. Andronikos expressed the opinion that all the burials in these tumuli were subsequent to 1000 B.C. (on

[1] Casson, *Macedonia* 171 and *Arch. Anz.* 1942. 187.
[2] The reports are in *PAE* 1952, 1953, 1957–61; *Ergon* 1957–61; *BCH* 1952–4 and 1957–62 Chronique; *BS* 2 (1961) 85 f.; *VIth International Congress of Prehistoric and Protohistoric Sciences in Rome*, 1962; *Studies in Med. Arch.* 13 (1964); *AD* 17 (1961/2 [1963]) 1. 218 f.; 17. 2. 230 f.; *AD* 18 (1963) B 2. 217 f.; *Mak.* 7 (1967) 324 f. Add now *Vergina* (1969).
[3] The reports on the Albanian tumuli were published in *BUSS* 1955. 1; 1956. 1; 1957. 2; 1959. 2; *SA* 1964. 1; 1966. 1. I have described the tumuli in *Epirus* 201 f. and 228 f. and in *BSA* 62 (1967 [1968]) 77 f. The reports of these tumuli had been overlooked (in non-Communist countries at any rate) until I mentioned them in *Epirus* (1967). The tumuli near Prilep are in the main unpublished; I learnt of them in 1968 when I visited the museum at Monastir.

occasion he suggested 1050 B.C.), and he has been supported by the other excavators.[1] The same thing happened when the Albanian tumuli were excavated. There all the burials were dated by the excavators at first to the very end of the Bronze Age or to the beginning of the Iron Age. In my book on Epirus I showed that some of the burials in these Albanian tumuli were of M.H. date, indeed perhaps of an earlier date. Recently further discoveries have been made in tumuli at Pazhok in central Albania, and these have led the Albanian excavators to recognize that some burials there were of M.H. date.[2] A similar error seems to have arisen at Vergina. Some burials in some tumuli in the cemetery at Vergina were of M.H. date and others were of L.H. date, as I have argued above (pp. 266 and 316).[3] The re-use of tumuli after considerable intervals of time was not uncommon in central Europe. It may well be expected to have occurred in this part of the Balkans.

As the great bulk of the burials are of the Early Iron Age, I have postponed a general description of the site until this point. Standing on higher ground, one is amazed at the great size of the Vergina cemetery which covers a square kilometre. The tumuli are close-packed. They lie beside a stream which runs on through the plain into the Haliacmon river.[4] There are more than three hundred tumuli. The cemetery must have been known to very many generations; for the direct road from below Beroea to Pieria, which skirts the edge of the plain, passes along the side of the cemetery.[5] The addition of Hellenistic burials and of Christian burials to the tumuli shows that in those periods too the cemetery was a matter of common knowledge. The site occupied by the users of the cemetery in the Early Iron Age has been identified. It lies on higher ground to the north of the so-called Hellenistic 'Palace' of Palatitsa.[6]

The choice of a cemetery beside a main route and beside a stream bed on flat ground is typical of the 'kurgan' people. The cemeteries of tumuli in the Zadrimë plain, the Mati valley, the Pazhok area, the Vajzë plateau, and the Kseria valley (at Vodhinë, Bodrishtë, and Kakavi) hold positions of the same kind. The tumuli within the Vergina cemetery are in groups of 4 or 5 and up to 8 or 9; those of the Mati valley are in groups of 'de 3–5 à 15 tertres', and those of the Kseria valley by Vodhinë are

---

[1] *PAE* 1952. 3; *BS* 2 (1961) 88; *Ergon* 1960 [1961]. 92; *Studies in Med. Arch.* 13 (1964) 3; *Mak.* 7 (1967) 328.

[2] *Epirus* 201 f. and 228 f.; *BSA* 62 (1967) 77 f.; *SA* 1964. 1. 96.

[3] I referred to the Vergina tumuli in *Epirus* 355 ff. and 401 ff., and noted that Tumulus C was to be dated 'probably before the end of the Bronze Age'. The reason for the error is that the more obviously datable objects are often the later ones, and that excavators tended to regard a prehistoric tumulus as containing burials of a restricted period.

[4] For views of the site see *AD* 17 (1961/2) 1. pls. 92, 95, and 97.

[5] A modern road was built in 1960 to link the crossing by the Haliacmon dam to the main road to Athens; it cut through the cemetery (see *AD* 17. 1. 218).

[6] It was noticed by Bakalakis (*Ergon* 1959. 56).

in separate groups.[1] In each case the excavator noticed this independently and suggested independently that the groups belonged to clans or families. There is no doubt that some tumuli were used for burying members of royal families; for diadems have been found at Vergina and in the Mati valley.

At Vergina it was noted that, when a Hellenistic burial was made within a tumulus, as in Tumulus LXV, the shaft was dug unusually deep and might obliterate an earlier burial, but the adjacent earlier burials were not pilfered. This respect was shown probably because people in the Hellenistic period supposed themselves to be of the same family or stock as the dead within a particular tumulus. It was noted also that some tumuli contained only Hellenistic graves and had apparently been constructed in the Hellenistic period. There was during that period a revival of tumulus-burial at Vergina. However, when burials were made in a tumulus in the Byzantine period and thereafter, the adjacent tombs were pilfered, and the objects which survived, for instance in Tumulus C, lay under heavy stones and so escaped detection. Despite this and other pilfering, a vast amount of pottery and great quantities of bronze and iron objects have been found by the excavators.

Within a work of this scope it seems best to describe a single tumulus of the Early Iron Age period. I have chosen Tumulus LXV, which, among those excavated in 1960 and 1961, was the highest, being 2·10 m high, and the largest, being some 23 m in diameter. There was no peribolos of stone, but the burials covered a roughly circular area. The tumulus over this area was made of soil, a few stones, and sherds in the northern part, and of stones, a little soil, and very many sherds in the southern part. As the fill of the tumulus contained prehistoric objects which were not in individual graves, we may infer that the fill had been repeatedly disturbed during the addition of burials and that it was evidently the original fill. There were at least fifty burials, all of prehistoric date, because only one Hellenistic sherd was found in the fill. Burial Γ was more or less in the centre, and it was partly overlaid by burial Σ.[2] The burials were at different depths within the fill, and some were in virgin ground beneath the fill.[3]

Four forms of burial were employed in this tumulus. (1) Within a roughly rectangular peribolos of field stones, sometimes several courses high[4] and designed presumably to carry a roof of boughs or planks; in some cases there were stones on the two long sides only, or on these two and one other only. All are technically cist-tombs. (2) Within a cairn of

[1] *Studies in Med. Arch.* 13. 4; *SA* 1964. 1. 101; *Epirus* 201.

[2] *AD* 17 (1961/2) 1. 269 and 276. Burial $B\Theta$ was also early, being overlaid by AE; $B\Theta$ lay near the top of the tumulus.

[3] For example, burial Θ (p. 271).

[4] In Y the courses were 0·40 m high (p. 276).

stones—one example only. (3) Within a large pithos, of which the mouth was closed by a pot or a flat stone; there were sixteen examples.[1] (4) Without any surviving surround or covering.[2] Of these forms of burial the first may be the earliest, because it was used in *Γ*, *AP*, and *BΘ*, which were overlaid by later burials. All burials were inhumations, even where no bones were found, and there were no signs of cremation.[3] The body had usually been laid on its back in an extended position either on the ground or in a pithos.

The offerings which were placed with the dead are known from un-disturbed burials, disturbed burials, and objects in the fill of this tumulus. They are remarkably uniform. As an example we may take the undis-turbed burial *Γ*.[4] A jug and a drinking-vessel were laid one on either side of the head, and a bowl or a jar for a solid food was placed beyond the feet. Where the head lay, there were long bronze coils, shaped like very tight hair-curlers, and these coils were suspended from bronze buttons, shaped like the top half of a bicycle bell (Fig. 17*a*). The bronze buttons had evidently been attached to the head by something perishable such as a cloth band, and the coils may have formed the centres of bunched strands or plaits of long hair. In this burial three coils lay on the left and four coils lay on the right of where the head had been. In addition there were three coils of gold wire, wider in diameter than the bronze coils but shorter, being of several turns only, and there was a bronze ring; these served evidently to hold the hair. There was also a pair of iron tweezers. Below the lower ends of the bronze coils thirteen necklace-beads of carnelian were found. The material of these beads, as of those found in other tombs, was reported at first as amber. Below the position of the necklace, that is at the level of the shoulders, there were two spectacle-fibulae, made of bronze wire (Fig. 17*b*), one on either side, which had fastened the clothing of the corpse. Towards the position of the loins a bronze ring lay in the centre and on each side a bronze 'phalaron' or belt ornament (Fig. 17*c*). These pieces had probably been the attachments of a belt of perishable material. The corpse had dis-integrated into dust.

As an example of a child's burial we may take grave *Π* which had no surviving covering or surround.[5] It contained the usual three pots (as in *Γ*) and an additional jug, two long bronze coils attached to a button, a bronze hair-coil, two necklaces of twisted bronze wire of which the

---

[1] A pile of stones lay on top of one pithos, K (p. 272).

[2] For instance, *Ξ* (p. 274). The conditions at Vergina were such that most skeletons rotted into dust, and we may suspect that the corpses were covered with trellis or boards which have left no trace.

[3] In one case, *AΞ* (p. 284), Petsas writes of the pithos as a cinerary urn in his summary on p. 297.   [4] See the illustrations pl. 132 *γ* and *δ*, and pl. 133 *γ*.

[5] Pls. 134 *ε* and 135 *α* and fig. 10 object LXV *π* 66.

ends turn slightly outwards (Fig. 18*d*), a small spectacle-fibula of bronze, a relatively heavy bronze ring, several bronze ornaments (also in *Ξ*) which consisted of two concentric spirals with an upstanding extension between them (Fig. 17*i*), some bronze buttons, and a gold ring. As an example of a pithos-burial we may take burial *E*, in which the mouth of the pithos was covered by a pot.[1] Here there were two bronze rings (for the hair), six long bronze coils, and five bronze buttons. The only example of a burial inside a cairn of stones in this tumulus is burial *P*, where remains of bones, an iron knife, two biconical bronze beads and a jug were found.[2] Another type of ornament, which did not appear in the burials we have described, but was common in others, was an armlet consisting of a single coil of bronze wire with overlapping ends (Fig. 17*f*); sometimes the ends were strengthened.[3]

When we consider all the finds in this tumulus, a number of other objects remain to be described. Two other types of ornament made of spiralling bronze wire occur: one resembles a spectacle-fibula, save that the two round pieces are joined by a bridge of wire (Fig. 17*h*),[4] and the other has a ring of wire set at right angles to the two round pieces (Fig. 17*j*).[5] The excavators mention also '8-shaped' ornaments, which may be simpler versions of these two types. Bronze strips about 0·15 m wide, found in some burials and also in the fill, belonged to diadems worn on the forehead of the corpse; one such diadem was decorated with a triple row of impressed dots (Fig. 17*g*).[6] Beads of carnelian (reported as amber) were very common; biconical beads of bronze and of clay were also common; bone beads were rare; beads of glass-paste were found only in the fill. Tweezers were made generally of bronze; only one pair was of iron. All the weapons were of iron: sixteen knives, five spearheads, five javelin-heads (or arrow-heads), and one sword. Objects of stone were rare: two hones perforated towards one end, and a perforated red stone.

Only one example of the following objects occurred in this tumulus. In burial *Ξ*, which had no covering or surround that survived, there was an unusual pendant of bronze (Fig. 17*k*, from *Φ* III).[7] It consists of a long flattened rod, carrying three flat double-axes, one above the other; the rod protrudes further at one end than at the other end, the longer end being pierced for suspension and the shorter end culminating in two small spiral coils, one on either side. In burial *Φ* there was a bronze ring with a loop for attachment as a pendant (Fig. 17*l*).[8] In burial *AΓ* there

---

[1] Pl. 133 β.   [2] Pl. 135 β.   [3] Pls. 139 γ and 145 γ.
[4] See object no. LXV *AΘ* 198 on fig. 10, and pp. 267 and 274 for examples in LXV *Ξ*.
[5] See p. 227, fig. 10 object no. LXV *Ξ* 48*a*.
[6] Found in the fill and in burials *T*, *AB*, and *AΘ*.   [7] Pl. 134 δ.
[8] LXV *Φ* 104 on fig. 10; a pendant of the same shape but with an addition in *AZ* VII (*Ergon* 1961. 101).

was a biconical bronze amulet with engraved sets of dot-centred concentric circles (Fig. 17*m*).[1] In *AA* a bronze cup with a long stem had a detachable lid with two upstanding ends, which were shaped at the top like a bird's head (as in Fig. 17*o*); it was described as a pendant by the excavators. It seems likely that it contained herbs (as village ossuaries in Voïon do today), and I shall call it a herb-cup pendant. Another, 7 cm high, was found in a pithos; it was a chance find in a field at Vergina.[2] In *AA* there was also a mysterious bronze piece with a socket for a wooden shaft; the blade is shaped like that of a turf-cutter (like Fig. 17*p*, from Chauchitsa).[3]

The pottery in the tumulus has a limited number of shapes. Some are paralleled in east Central Macedonia: the jug with cut-away neck (Fig. 16*c*; category 2, above on p. 327), the jug with a straight rim (Fig. 16*e*), the bowl with the extended flat rim, perforated to provide two handles (Fig. 16*b*; category 1 above) and the two-handled cantharus.[4] Others are not so paralleled. The most striking of these are a shallow, usually two-handled drinking-bowl, often with a rounded bottom, which has above the rim or above the handle-tops two projections, flat-topped and tapering downwards, to serve as thumb-rests (Fig. 16*f*);[5] and a very shallow, basket-like bowl, often with a rounded bottom and usually with two loop-handles on the rim and two pinched-out extensions of the rim (Fig. 16*g*).[6] Both of these appear to be ritual vessels, as they are so unusual in shape and are so common in the burials of this and other tumuli. There are also a few examples of a pot with a collared or cylindrical neck and with two handles rising at a steep, almost vertical angle from the shoulder; this pot, too, often has a rounded bottom (Fig. 16*h*).[7] It is very unusual in east Central Macedonia.[8]

Now that we have described Tumulus LXV, we may note that it is a fairly typical example of the Iron Age tumuli. There are a few additions to be made, if we are to have a full picture of the Early Iron Age at Vergina. In Tumulus E there were some 'arched' fibulae (Fig. 17*r*), four of bronze and one of iron, and in Tumulus LXV burial *AP* there were two arched fibulae of bronze, of which one had been apparently repaired with a pin of iron.[9] As this type of fibula is dated usually from the late

[1] LXV *AΓ* 156 on fig. 10.
[2] Pl. 137 δ, and p. 277; *BCH* 79. 279, found together with a spectacle-fibula.
[3] LXV *AA* 169 on fig. 10.   [4] Pl. 149 *a* and pl. 151 *a* 2 and δ 1.
[5] Pl. 150 ζ 1 and pl. 151 β 1 and ε 1. The knobs or discs on handle extensions at Saratse (*PM* 236 nos. 486–7) and at Olynthus (*PM* 239 nos. 499–500) are differently shaped and on different vessels.
[6] Pl. 149 δ 1 and 3, pl. 150 γ 2, pl. 151 δ 2 and ε 2, pl. 152 β 2, pl. 153 β 1, γ 1, δ 1, and ε 3.
[7] Pl. 149 β and γ, pl. 150 β, pl. 151 η 2.
[8] *PM* 237 no. 494 from Saratse (E.I.A.), but with a ring foot.
[9] *PAE* 1952. 240 in burials E o, E φ, E ψ, E ψ 1, and E ω 3, and *BS* 2 (1961) 97; and *AD* 17. 1. 280 and fig. 58.

twelfth century into the Early Iron Age, it is interesting to note that Tumulus E, some 17 m in diameter, contained a cairn of stones, within which there had been a burial, and round which there was burnt ground —the result either of the cremation of a corpse or of a burnt sacrifice; there are analogies in Albanian tumuli. In this tumulus in burial *Eω* there was found, together with the arched fibula of iron, a bronze mini-ature four-spoked wheel (like Fig. 18*t*, being E VIa, and another such one in Tumulus A burial *Z*).[1] We have noted an example of this wheel on pottery at Malik in a much earlier context (p. 267 above). The closest analogy in time is found in the Milavečer stage of the Lausitz cul-ture, which employed cremation, covered a burial with a pile of stones, and then raised a tumulus of soil or of a mixture of soil and stones. Associated objects in the Milavečer burials include the miniature four-spoked wheel of bronze and also a pendant bronze ring with a small ring for suspension, such as we noted in LXV burial *Φ* and occurs in *AA* VII (Fig. 17*l*).[2] In Tumulus LXV burial *AP* there were found to-gether with the two arched fibulae the usual long bronze coils and rings for the hair, but the rings were some of bronze and others (unusually) of iron; and two finger-rings of bronze with an (unusual) covering of gold leaf.[3] As we have noted above (p. 331), burial *AP* belonged to the category of the earliest burials in Tumulus LXV. The mixture of metals in these and other burials has been noted above (p. 314).

Tumulus LXV burial *AΓ*, which belongs to the category of the earliest burials, contained the unusual amulet of bronze, biconical in shape, which has been mentioned; it is decorated with two sets of three engraved dot-centred concentric circles, one set on each shoulder, and pierced vertically through the centre (Fig. 17*m*).[4] Very similar bronze amulets were found in a burial at Gajtan and in a tumulus burial in the Mati valley (Fig. 17*s*).[5] In Tumulus LXV burial *Ξ* there were six examples of a ring set at right angles to two spiralling terminals (Fig. 17*j*); they are a type of finger-ring found in the Lausitz culture especially in the later (Knovitzer) stage. Armlets of the same Lausitz type have been found at Dodona.[6] The looped spiral ornaments (Fig. 17*i*) may be due to Lausitz influence. One of several found in LXV *Π* resembles an early Lausitz type, but that type may be rather early for burial *Π*, which, having no

---

[1] *PAE* 1952. 246 and 256; *Ergon* 1961. 102; *V* 255 fig. 90.

[2] Schránil 157 f., fig. 15 and pl. xxxiii nos. 28 and 32. The pendant in *AZ* VII shows in fig. 97 of *Ergon* 1961. 101 = *V* pl. 125 ε.

[3] *AD* 17. 1. 285. The pottery does not help in any closer dating.

[4] *AD* 17. 1. 280 and fig. 10 object LXV *AΓ* 156.

[5] *StH.* 1967. 3. 167 with references to *BUSS* 1955. 3. pl. vii, 4 and 1958. 2. 127.

[6] *AD* 17. 1. 275 and fig. 10 object LXV *Ξ* 48*a*; Schránil, 144 and pl. xxviii, 32 of earlier Lausitz culture; Childe, *Danube* 377 and pl. xiv, 2; Schránil, 166 and pl. xxx, 45; *Ep. Chron.* 1935. 242 and pl. 22 *β* 2 and 3 (armlet, as in the Knovizer stage = Schránil 165 and pl. xxx, 37 and 44.

peribolos of stone, does not belong to the category of early burials in Tumulus LXV.[1]

The pendant in the form of a rod with three flat double-axes of bronze, all cast in one piece, which was found in LXV *Ξ*, is matched by four others, found in *Φ* III (Fig. 17*k*), *ΑΔ* I, *AE* V, and *AH* II.[2] Each was in a woman's grave with ornaments of exceptional richness. The graves had no surviving covering or surround (as far as one can judge from the photographs). The pendants vary only in detail (one has two double-axes of the normal size and a smaller third one). The rods all have a hole at one end, presumably for suspension. The hole was at the end nearest the head of the corpse in *Φ* III, *AH* II, and LXV *Ξ*, but not in *ΑΔ* I and *AE* V. The position of the two armlets in *ΑΔ* I shows that the pendant was not held in one of the woman's hands, and the probability is that it was attached to a head-dress. In three cases (*ΑΔ* I, *AE* V, and LXV *Ξ*) a number of small bronze studs were found by the cheeks and forehead which had been on a head-dress, probably of leather;[3] in the other two cases there may have been a head-dress with no metal studs. Four of the women had gold hair-rings, at least three had belts decorated with many bronze studs, and one had bronze bosses for her belt in addition. They had different kinds of necklaces; two had a central glass-paste bead in a necklace of carnelian beads (reported initially as amber beads). One of them had a second and smaller pendant (Fig. 17*t*), found at the position of the throat.[4] In three cases the woman's grave was alongside that of a man: *ΑΔ* I beside *ΑΔ* II with an iron sword in a wooden scabbard, three spear-heads, and a small knife (unusually rich for a man's grave); *AE* V beside *AE* VI with two small iron knives and a small spear-head (? javelin-head); and LXV *Ξ* beside LX *Y* with an iron knife. There is no report of the burials in Tumulus *Φ*. There was 'almost nothing worthy of mention' in the other six graves of Tumulus AH. One imagines that the wearer of this special pendant was a queen or/and a priestess, whether married or single. Her office was not confined to membership of one family or clan, if we are right in attributing tumuli to families and groups of tumuli to clans.

The double-axe of thin bronze is familiar in Minoan worship, where it has been remarked that 'it is often shown in art carried by women,

[1] *AD* 17. 1. 275, pl. 135 *a* below the jug, and fig. 10 object LXV *π* 66; Schránil 144 and pl. xxviii, 14 (cf. Childe, *Danube* 373 fig. 209); Petsas in *AD* 17. 1. 275 n. 17*a* refers to Evzen Plesl, *Luziská Kultur* (Prague, 1961) pl. lii, which I have not seen.

[2] *Ergon* 1959. 56 and fig. 55; 1960. 88 and fig. 102; 1960. 91 fig. 105; 1961. 103 figs. 98 and 99; also in *BS* 2 (1961) 94 pl. v, 10 and 11. For LXV *Ξ* see *AD* 17. 1. 275 and pl. 134 δ; see also *Mak.* 7, pl. 40b.

[3] For LXV *Ξ* see n. 16 on p. 275 of *AD* 17. 1. This head-dress was not peculiar to wearers of this pendant. See *Ergon* 1961. 101 fig. 97, where the head-dress appears to have had a strap round the lower jaw. Perhaps the pendant was attached to the chin-strap, as it lay over the breast in LXV *Ξ* pl. 134 δ. [4] *Ergon* 1960. 89 fig. 102.

probably priestesses or worshippers'.[1] It was adopted on the Greek mainland in Mycenaean times, but we can hardly attribute its importance at
Vergina to Mycenaean influence, which was, as we have seen, minimal
in this part of Macedonia. There is also the further phenomenon that
the cult of the double-axe is widespread in the Balkans at this time and
occurs even in south Russia. As C. F. C. Hawkes remarked in his study
of the double-axe, 'there are double-axes with their own Aegean origin
apparently not earlier than Late Minoan times'.[2] An overland route
of dispersal has therefore been postulated but not identified. Now the
tradition that the Bottiaei of Lower Macedonia were Minoan Cretans
who had settled there in what we should call the fourteenth century B.C.,
within the Late Minoan period, certainly supplies a particularly appropriate source for the dispersal of this cult into the Balkans. Moreover, it
accounts for the cult at Vergina, a site which looks out over Bottiaea.
We conclude then that the cult of the double-axe was brought to Macedonia by the Bottiaeans in the fourteenth century B.C., whence it spread
inland through the Balkans. It was adopted by the people who occupied
Vergina at some time in the Early Iron Age.

When the reports of the Vergina tumuli became available, I studied
them in connection with my work in Epirus, and I wrote in 1964 as
follows (*Epirus* 404): 'So far as the evidence goes, it looks as if the people
at Vergina came from the north-west into the Haliacmon valley. There
they met other influences which quickly affected them; these influences
came from the Lausitz invaders and from South Greece.' I turn therefore
to north-west Macedonia. In 1968 I visited the museum in Monastir,
and I was surprised and delighted to find material, unpublished, I was
told, from some tumuli situated between Monastir and Prilep. There
was a model of a tumulus which had been excavated at Visoï, a place
beside the main road from Monastir to Prilep and some 10 km short of
Prilep. In the centre of the tumulus-area, which was circular in shape,
there were two cist-tombs, lined with rough slabs; these two tombs lay
within a circular peribolos, which was only one stone thick, and which
consisted of whitish crystalline stones. In the area between this peribolos
and the outer peribolos, which was two or three stones thick, and which
consisted of large, dark stones, there were nearly forty cist-tombs, lined
with rough slabs; these burials were set among many large stones. The
central burial of the tumulus viewed as a whole was one of the two burials
in the smaller peribolos. In size, then, this tumulus at Visoï was like
Tumulus LXV at Vergina, which contained some fifty burials. It is

---

[1] See H. J. Rose in *A Companion to Homer* 476 n. 11; for a woman holding a double-axe
in each hand see *AE* 1900 pl. 4a and 1953–4. 2. 215 f., with fig. 1.

[2] *BSA* 37 (1936–7) 158. There was a much earlier dispersal of this cult into western
Europe during the third millennium. That of the Late Minoan period is a separate one which
affected a different area. See also Childe, *Dawn of European Civilisation* (London, 1925) 106–7.

possible that it was a double tumulus, the inner marked by the peribolos of whitish stones and the outer by the peribolos of darkish stones; if so, it resembled the double tumuli of Pazhok and Vodhinë. On the whole it seems more likely that it was not a double but a single tumulus with an original burial or perhaps two original burials marked off by their own special peribolos. Some objects from this tumulus were on show: a bronze sword of Type II Group II 'developed' in two pieces (Fig. 10*j*); an iron sword, long-bladed and with a fish-tail haft of Type II Group I shape; a heavy iron cutlass of the 'makhaira' type; four bronze spear-heads with medial ridge, long socket, two nail-holes near the base, and worn blades; one large bronze spectacle-fibula and two small bronze spectacle-fibulae; three open-ended bronze bracelets for the arm, two very heavy bronze bracelets with thickened ends (as in Fig. 17*z*); a bronze armlet of nine coils (as in Fig. 17*e*), diminishing in diameter; a bronze finger-ring; a piece of long bronze coil (as in Fig. 17*a*); a bronze herb-cup with a long stem and a detachable lid with two upstanding ends, which were shaped at the top like a bird's head (as in Fig. 17*o*); three double-axes of thin bronze sheet, each with a substantial waist, which was perforated (Fig. 17*u*); a long hollow rectangular bronze tube, of which the sides were fretted with small triangular apertures for three-quarters of their length; and a very small bronze statuette of a horse with an arched neck.

Most of these objects are familiar at Vergina. The herb-cup is the same as the one at Vergina. The three double-axes puzzled me at the time (for I thought they were votive axes but saw no point in the strong perforated waist); later I remembered the pendants with three flat double-axes at Vergina (Fig. 17*k*). Evidently a similar pendant (or sceptre) was made with a detachable rod at Visoï. A small bronze double-axe with a hole in the middle was reported from the vicinity of Vergina (p. 328 above), and two more were found by Andronikos in his excavations; they were of the same kind as that at Visoï. Hollow rectangular tubes with similar fretwork have been found at Axioupolis on the Vardar valley (see Fig. 19*b* and below). A small horse set on a bronze stand was in Tumulus LXVI burial *A* at Vergina.[1] There were three objects in an unlabelled show-case which, I gathered, came from the Visoï tumulus (if not, they came from a near-by tumulus). These were a violin-bow fibula with a broad flattened bow, similar to one from Vardina (p. 306 above), which may be dated around 1150 B.C.; a pendant of bronze plate in the shape of a double-axe with two holes at its centre (Fig. 17*v*),

---

[1] *Vergina* 25 in Z pithos burial 1 and 119 in I γ (double-axes). *AD* 18 (1963) B2. 218 and pl. 259*b*. There is a mention of 'les pendentifs en forme de hache double-labrys' in *AI* 5 (1964) 74, where it was said that the material was unpublished but references were given to I. P. Mačkić, D. Simoska, 'Terenski radovi Bitoljskog muzeja u 1954 godini', *Muzeji* 9 (1954) 208–10, and 'Naod na lokalitetot Visoï key Bitola', *Vesnik na mue muzejoskoi konservatorsko društvo na NR Makedonija* iii 3–4, 75–8. I have not had access to either article.

which is paralleled in shape and in material by a piece from the later Lausitz culture (older Knovizer culture);[1] and a long bronze pin with an angular knob at the top end.

No pottery was on show from Visoï. But there were a few pieces of pottery from a tumulus at Saraj near Brod on the Cerna Reka and from a place called Petilep near Visoï (perhaps also a tumulus). From Saraj came a magnificent example of the drinking-bowl with a rounded bottom and the flat-topped conical thumb-rests, typical of so many burials at Vergina (Fig. 16*f*); it was very large, red, and polished, and it had a line of small dog-teeth incised on the shoulder. There were also two high two-handled cantharoi with painted decoration of the Boubousti type; both had painted triangles, pendent in one case from the shoulder to the base (Fig. 16*j*), and in the other from below the shoulder to the base. The handles of the former had the angular outline, due to a twisting of the handle, which occurs rather often at Vergina (e.g. in LXV *Γ*, *AD* 17. 1 pl. 149*a*) and more often at Chauchitsa (Fig. 16*i*). Another was an open bowl with an extended flat rim and two horizontal rounded handles—a very common shape at Vergina; the end of each handle turned up very slightly, and had a little knob on it. There was a jug with a straight rim continuing into the handle and a ring foot, as at Vergina in Tumulus XXXIII *Γ* 16 (*AD* 17. 1 pl. 148*b*1); the handle is split double as in Tumulus LV *Δ* (*AD* 17. 1 pl. 147*a*). Lastly a graceful amphora is like one from Vergina in Tumulus LXV *N*, but has a pedestal foot.

From Petilep come the following: a very shallow bowl with two loop-handles on the rim and two pinched-out extensions of the rim—a very common shape at Vergina (Fig. 16*g*); two little jugs with a high handle (one having round the neck an incised band which contained upturned acute triangles and below the band incised pendent triangles with parallel lines inside each); an unusual two-handled cup with a collar and with incised lines on one side which suggest a human face; three two-handled cantharoi of varying sizes, the handles rising above the rim; and a pot with a globular body, from the middle of which rise two small semicircular handles at an angle of 50°, and with a tall cylindrical neck, on which a vertical handle is set below the everted rim (Fig. 16*u*). This pot has a close parallel in Tumulus *AΓ* at Vergina, and there are similar vessels in Tumulus E and Tumulus N (*Vergina* pl. 37, 24 and Pl. 43, 8 and 16). Another pot of this kind was on show from Progon, a place near Visoï.

There is thus no doubt that the plain below Prilep contains a cemetery of tumuli which have the same construction, and some of the same weapons, ornaments, and pottery as the cemetery of tumuli at Vergina. The tumulus at Visoï had one or more burials of the period *c*. 1200–

[1] Schránil pl. 30, 33, described as a razor in the text, p. 156.

1120 B.C., as is shown by the bronze sword and the violin-bow fibula.[1] Otherwise all the objects on show in the museum indicate that the burials were made mainly in the same period as the bulk of the burials at Vergina, that is from 1050 B.C. onwards. That the flow of influence was from Prilep to Vergina rather than vice versa may be inferred from the fact that there were no Proto-Geometric vases on display from Prilep and that the most typical of Central Macedonian vessels at this time—the jug with cut-away neck—was absent. What we can see at Prilep is rather the source, or a place between the source and the recipient, of the influences which came from the north-west into Central Macedonia and produced the phenomena typical of the Vergina tumuli.

Since my visit to the museum at Monastir I have found a short account of the cemetery at Saraj. It contained twenty cist-tombs lined with stone, and the bodies were aligned to the flow of the adjacent river, being roughly north to south; they were compared by Maja Parović-Pešikan to the burials of the Visoï tumulus. One tomb, no. XI, which lay rather apart from the rest, has been dated to the twelfth century B.C. (see p. 322 above). From the main group of burials comes an ornament made of two spirals and a connecting spiralling spring, a variant of Fig. 17*h*, and it is this variant which is typical of the early Lausitz culture. There are also open-ended single-coil armlets, iron spear-heads, a crater of a Late Geometric type, a *cothon* not earlier than the sixth century B.C., and a plain pyramid-shaped ear-ring not earlier than the late sixth century B.C. The local pottery which is illustrated in the report has pots of the kind I described from my visit to the Monastir Museum, including one as in Fig. 16*u*. We have then a familiar kind of tumulus with at least one burial of the twelfth century B.C. and with burials of several periods from then until the sixth or fifth century B.C. We should resist the dating of all the burials except no. XI to the eighth century B.C. as V. Trbuhović suggested.

There are intermediate stations in the districts near Vergina and between Vergina and Prilep, to which we must now turn. At Koundouriotissa in Pieria by the source of the river Baphyras which flows to Dium, spectacle-fibulae of bronze, two examples of the drinking-bowl with the thumb-rests so distinctive of Vergina (Fig. 16*f*), and a skyphos with painted concentric semicircles, have been found. These pieces came probably from the excavation of twelve slab-lined cist-tombs, some 50 cm below ground-level, between Koundouriotissa and Kalyvia; the joints between the slabs and also the corpses themselves had been smeared with clay ('Tonerde'), and a tumulus 0·50 to 0·80 m high stood over each grave.[2] I saw a skyphos with concentric semicircles at Dium in the

---

[1] But see p. 213 n. 6 fin.
[2] I saw these in the museum at Salonica in 1968. The report is very brief in *Arch. Anz.* 55 (1940) 273.

museum in 1968. At Beroea, on the route from Vergina to Lake Ostrovo, a pithos-burial contained two of the same drinking-bowls and a shallow bowl of a type also found at Vergina; another pithos-burial contained two spectacle-fibulae, and a broken 'prehistoric vase'; as a cist-tomb had been found on this spot, it seems that Beroea's cemetery was at this place at this time.[1] Bronze objects from tombs of the period are also reported from Beroea.[2]

In Eordaea there are a number of Early Iron Age sites. We have already referred (p. 266 above) to what was probably a double tumulus at Arnissa at the north end of Lake Ostrovo; on the analogy of the double tumuli in Albania at Pazhok and Vodhinë, some of the outer burials are likely to be of this period. The most remarkable site is at Pateli (Ayios Pandele-ëmon) on the south-west side of the lake. Its size was not appreciated by Casson, Rey, and Heurtley, when they wrote of Pateli.[3] A fuller description was given first by Th. Makridis in *AE* 1937. 2. 512 f. I begin with his description. The railway line was driven straight through a cemetery, from which the finds were taken to the Russian Archaeological Institute in Constantinople, and the Russians excavated 154 graves in 1898 and 222 more in 1899. Some of the finds went to the museum at Constantinople. The reports in Russian were very brief. Makridis gives a summary from one such report.

According to this report all burials were in cist-tombs, of which the sides were formed by 'a series of quandrangular stones', while the bottom was paved with similar stones and was usually covered with pebbles or sand. The dead had been laid on their backs, except in two instances; there was no concern for the orientation of the corpse; and some tombs had two or more corpses, laid parallel or in opposite directions. In very many tombs there were piles of bones from earlier burials. These piles were organized in one of two ways: either the bones of each skeleton were piled together with its skull on top, or the skulls alone were arranged as a frame round the complete skeletons and the other bones were stored in stone boxes or amphorae. The cemetery was evidently in use for a long period of time. During the second year of excavation, in 1899, a space surrounded by a thick circular wall was found to contain fourteen tombs, which, the excavator thought, belonged to the rulers or leaders of the place. These fourteen tombs produced arched[4] and spectacle[5] fibulae of bronze, a large hemispherical bronze cup, a small bronze statuette of a horse,[6] amulets in the shape of a bird,[7] a bronze sword, a bronze breastplate,

---

[1] *AD* 21 (1966 [1968]) B2. 355 f. and pl. 380.   [2] *PTh* 216 n. 11.

[3] *BSA* 23. 30; Casson, *Macedonia* 144, 150, and figs. 63 and 66; L. Rey in *Albania* 4 (1932) 44 f. and figs. 10 and 11; Heurtley *BSA* 28. 183 fig. 30 and 191, and *PM* 100, 104 f., fig. 112 and pl. 33.   [4] Rey, loc. cit. fig. 10; *PM* fig. 112*k*; Makridis in *AE* 1937. 2. 514.

[5] Rey fig. 10; *PM* fig. 1120.

[6] Possibly the horse in Rey fig. 10; *PM* fig. 112*m*; Casson fig. 66.   [7] Rey fig. 11.

miniature bronze vases,[1] a stone object (apparently an idol), bronze diadems of which one had decorations, four gold ornaments, bronze
tweezers, a carved wooden handle, and 'pottery related to primeval
Mediterranean ceramics'.

The total finds from the 376 tombs were 74 spectacle-fibulae, 106
fibulae of various shapes,[2] 255 necklaces and amulets, 75 rings, 46 bracelets,[3] 185 buttons of different sizes,[4] 27 nails, 8 ear-rings, 20 miniature
vases, and 68 other different objects and fragments[5]—all the above being
of bronze; 2 gold ear-rings, 4 gold ornaments; and of iron 9 bracelets,
25 nails, 25 tweezers, 9 swords, 25 spear-heads, 4 arrow-heads, 72 knives,
and 38 fragments. Also 7 necklaces of clay beads, 11 necklaces of amber
and stone beads, 11 small objects of stone and bone, 8 objects of wood, 59
objects of stone and clay, and 614 pots of various shapes 'with painted
geometric designs'. Makridis mentions also a votive double-axe,[6] and
a statuette of a horse with pricked ears, made of doubled bronze sheet.

The pottery has been described best by Heurtley, who saw eighty-five
pots in the museum at Constantinople.[7] Only five were wheel-made, the
rest were hand-made. He judged the latter 'very close in character', but
inferior in execution of design, to the pottery of Boubousti (e.g. Fig. 14e).
Incised ornament and pointed knobs of the Lausitz type occurred, as
well as the painted geometric designs. The shapes in descending order of
frequency were jugs with cut-away or sloping necks, jugs with straight
rims and often with knobs, loop-handled cups, two-handled cantharoi,
and four-handled pots with spherical body, cylindrical neck, and everted
rim. There were also two twin-vases, two bowls with upstanding handles
on the rim, and a round-bellied pot with short cylindrical neck, everted
rim, and two handles rising at 50° from the shoulder (Fig. 14e). Two
wheel-made jugs had grooved handles of the Lausitz kind. Casson reported eighty-nine or eighty-seven pots from Pateli in the museum at
Constantinople. One was a degenerate goblet of the Mycenaean kind.
What happened to the other 500 pots found by the Russians?

Before we move on to the other evidence it will be wise to note that in
the fourteen graves within the thick circular peribolos there were apparently no iron objects, whereas iron was common for tweezers and for
weapons in the cemetery as a whole, and that the one and only bronze
sword was found there. Our knowledge of tumuli makes it clear that the
thick circular peribolos was the retaining wall of a tumulus, as at Mycenae
and elsewhere;[8] that its construction may be put in the Late Bronze Age,

---

[1] Rey fig. 11. [2] Rey fig. 10; *PM* fig. 112n; Makridis pl. vi γ.
[3] Rey fig. 11. [4] Rey fig. 10. [5] Makridis pl. vi. [6] Rey fig. 11.
[7] *PM* 105 and pl. 33; *BSA* 28 fig. 30; Casson fig. 63; Rey 45; Rey criticizes Casson for
inaccuracy, correctly.
[8] See my article in *BSA* 62 (1967) 77 f.; in 1898–9 the excavators may well not have
noticed or not have reported the existence of a mound.

perhaps in the twelfth century; that some burials in it were of that time; and that others were well within the Iron Age, even though we must remember that the list of contents is not complete. In the Late Bronze Age the links of this Royal Tumulus, if we may so call it, are with Tumulus C at Vergina, with the Tumulus at Visoï—each having one bronze sword—and with the tumuli in central Albania and in north Epirus, which have yielded bronze swords. It is not clear what the Russians meant when they described the pottery from these fourteen graves as 'primeval'; at any rate the pottery there was clearly different from the general run of pottery 'with painted geometric designs'. With regard to the summary of the total finds the three chief differences between Pateli and Vergina are that Pateli has neither of Vergina's two distinctive vessels, the bowl with thumb-rests and the shallow bowl with two horizontal handles and two pinched-out extensions of the rim; that in proportion Pateli has fewer spectacle-fibulae than Vergina; and that Pateli used iron more for certain objects, e.g. tweezers. Moreover the arrangement of the skulls and other details at Pateli do not occur at Vergina.

The other evidence comes principally from Rey. Whereas Makridis drew on a Russian report in *Bulletin de l'Institut Archéologique Russe de Constantinople* 4 (1899) 149 and 6. 2–3 (1909) 472, Rey based his account on a short report read by M. P. Milioukov to the Archaeological Congress at Kiev on 9 August 1899. Now in August the current year's findings could not have been known. Milioukov's report must have referred to the excavations of the previous year, 1898. Moreover, as Rey says that Milioukov and Farmakovsky explored fifty-four tombs, Milioukov must have talked only of that group and not of all the 154 tombs which had been opened in 1898.[1] No one seems to have realized that point. Rey's account of the fifty-four tombs is that they were inhumations 'en pierres comme à Bohemica' (that is in stone-lined cist-graves) and in pithoi containing bones. The tombs, he said, were in several groups, marked off one from another by lines of rough stones, and the groups radiated from a centre, and the dead had been laid with their heads towards this centre. The centre itself was an empty space. Some tombs contained several skeletons. He drew parallels with Hallstatt in Austria and with Glasinac in Yugoslavia for the disposition of the groups and the dead particularly. Rey then described the material in the museum at Constantinople. This material came in fact not just from fifty-four graves, as he thought, but from the 376 graves. It was perhaps a small cross-section of the list given by Makridis, and it contained a few but not all of the objects Makridis

---

[1] Rey himself writes as if the fifty-four tombs were all that were ever found at Pateli; he was completely unaware of the report translated by Makridis. Everyone seems to have accepted Rey's view.

mentioned as coming from the fourteen graves of the 'rulers or leaders of the place'.[1]

Rey, Casson, and Heurtley add some more points about those bronzes which were placed in the museum at Constantinople. Some of the arched fibulae had a very developed catch-plate (Fig. 17*x*); the spectacle-fibulae were of bronze wire; there was at least one example of the double spiral ornament linked by a bridge,[2] as in the older Lausitz culture (Fig. 17*h*); armlets were of the heavy kind with overlapping ends (Fig. 17*z*); there were bracelets with up to ten coils (as in Fig. 17*e*); one pendant was a bronze herb-cup with upstanding ends shaped like a bird's head (as in Fig. 17*o*);[3] another a distaff-shaped pendant with a bird's head at the top (Fig. 17*y*); another with a pierced triangular top and an end shaped like a door-knob (Fig. 17*aa*); another with a miniature jug at the top of a knobbly stick with a bulb at the bottom (Fig. 17*cc*); another spoon-shaped with a short spout (Fig. 17*bb*); a four-spoked wheel with an extended rim, some 15 cm in diameter, all decorated with incised concentric circles (Fig. 18*a*); a two-pinned triangular fibula incised with concentric circles, circles, and zigzags (shape as in Fig. 18*c*); a long pin with three swellings and a mushroom-shaped top (Fig. 20*q*);[4] a flower-shaped bronze button with eight petals (Fig. 17*dd*); a double-pin (as in Fig. 20*b*); and a miniature jug of which there were twenty examples (Fig. 17*n*).[5] Rey noted that iron was used for weapons only. He mentioned bronze harness ('harnachement'), but he did not describe any. Casson shows a horse with ears like those of a dog; it stands on a flat plate, like one from Vergina Tumulus LXVI *A*.[6]

As the Russians said, the cemetery was in use for a long period of time. In this respect it resembles the cemeteries in the Mati valley and elsewhere in Albania. Its long life is reflected in the different methods of burial: stone-lined cists with pebbles or sand on the floor, extended corpses lying on the back, fourteen burials within a thick circular peribolos, as at Mycenae—Late Bronze Age, or even Middle Bronze Age, as far as burial practices go; the alignment of the dead towards a centre, as in a tumulus

[1] Rey thought the material in the museum was all the material and others have followed his view; but Makridis shows that the great bulk of the material disappeared, doubtless into Russia. In his account, *AE* 1937. 2. 514, he noted which objects were and which objects were not in the museum at Constantinople. For example, the bronze breastplate, the gold ornaments, the large bronze cup, etc., were not there. In the museum at Salonica I saw a pot with incised decoration as on fig. 15*e* from Pateli.

[2] Rey 45 and fig. 10; *PM* fig. 112*n*; *PM* 108 n. 3.

[3] Rey 45 and fig. 11; Makridis pl. vi.

[4] Makridis pl. vi; Rey fig. 11. Makridis p. 516. This very long pin, some 50 cm, is probably related to the one from Corinth, no. 33*a* in Jacobsthal, of *c.* 750 B.C. (see p. 355 below). The top may be local; see no. 558 and p. 172 where Jacobsthal means the pin from Pateli.

[5] Rey figs. 10 and 11.

[6] Casson fig. 66 = Rey fig. 10 = *PM* fig. 112*m*; for Vergina *AD* 18 (1963) B2. 218 and pl. 259*b*.

at Papoulia near Pylos of M.H. date;[1] the arrangement of skulls as a frame round the latest dead, unknown in Greece, I think; the burials in pithoi, usually later than those in cists elsewhere (e.g. at Vergina); and the alignment of groups of burials towards an empty centre, which has analogies at Glasinac. If the earliest burials are of the Late Bronze Age, the latest may well be of the sixth century B.C., as Heurtley observed.[2]

Other sites with a culture similar to that of Pateli appeared, when the waters of the lake receded. One is at Pharangi on the south-east side of the lake, where classical and Hellenistic objects were also found, and two are at the south end.[3] As I have argued above (p. 54), the level of the lake was very much lower then than it is today, and these sites were on the edge of a most fertile basin, through which ran the main route from southern Central Macedonia to the cantons of the north-west. Further west in Eordaea, at Aetos, WSW. of Amyndaeon, on the edge of another but smaller basin, cist-tombs of slabs have been reported, and finds are said to be of the Early Iron Age. One of them is illustrated, a high two-handled cantharos. In southern Eordaea at Mavropigi an Early Iron Age grave 'like those in Pieria', with the corpse extended on its back, was opened by Kotzias and contained a diadem of bronze plaque and a spectacle-fibula. The tomb was on the lower slope of an acropolis site.[4]

As we leave Eordaea and enter Elimea, our first site is Kozani, which lies above the middle Haliacmon valley. An important centre in the L.H. period, it continued to be so in the Early Iron Age. There are one-handled cups and a small jug with cut-away neck from Ayios Athanasios, a ward of Kozani, in the museum; they are of this period.[5] When a road was being cut, burials appeared 'at many points simultaneously along its length', and objects collected at the time were published by B. G. Kallipolitis in 1951. He ascertained that twenty-eight objects, which he listed, came from a group of six graves, numbered I–VI, and he found them to

[1] *Arch. Reports* 1955. 11, fig. 7; see my article in *BSA* 62. 90.

[2] Heurtley, *PM* 100 and 105, noted that the pottery with the designs typical of Boubousti was inferior and therefore, he supposed, later than the earlier phase of Boubousti. As this phase started c. 1300 B.C., the earliest burials with this pottery at Pateli could be of the twelfth century. But Heurtley was unaware of the 'primaeval' type of pottery at Pateli, which was evidently of pre-Boubousti date. In *BSA* 28. 191 Heurtley thought that the cemetery was used for a limited period only 'well within the Iron Age' (*PM* 100), and Rey 50, writing of newcomers at Pateli being absorbed or departing 'quickly', concluded (59 f.) that invaders entered Macedonia between 900 B.C. and 500 B.C. and at a date nearer 500 B.C. They did not know of the evidence produced by Makridis. Desborough, *TLM* 142, referring to Pateli erroneously as 'in the valley of the Tserna river', did not make use of Makridis's report.

[3] *AD* 17 (1961–2) 2. 216; *BCH* 85. 773; *BCH* 84. 767.

[4] *AD* 17. 2. 216 and pl. 253 ζ (Aetos) and *Mak.* i. 491 (Mavropigi, north-west of the village).

[5] Seen by me in 1968.

be of the classical period.[1] He wrote as if the objects from the other burials were also of that period, but there were Early Iron Age pieces among them and these pieces were neither found nor paralleled in tombs I–VI. They were as follows: a bronze distaff-shaped pendant with triangular openings; a second such with a disc at the bottom end (as in Fig. 17*y* but without the bird's head); a bobbin-shaped pendant of bronze (Fig. 19*d*); a double-pin of bronze (as in Fig. 20*b*); two heavy bronze armlets with overlapping ends (as in Fig. 17*z*); two light armlets of bronze wire with overlapping ends (as in Fig. 17*f*); three finger-rings of bronze wire; and five spectacle-fibulae of bronze wire.

Since then some graves at a distance from tombs I–VI have been excavated by Ph. M. Petsas.[2] One of them, a cist-tomb made of slabs, which he numbered XXIII, contained the skeletons of two children. A one-handled cup, a jug with cut-away neck, and a feeding-jug of the same shape lay just outside the tomb, where they had presumably been deposited, when space was made for the second interment; and inside the tomb were a similar cup, a similar jug but with a higher handle, a shallow bowl, bits of long bronze coils (as in Fig. 17*a* at Vergina), biconical bronze beads, a pendant of bone incised with geometric designs, and a clay necklace-bead dappled with little round holes. The pots are hand-made and of shapes common at Vergina. We cannot date the tomb more precisely than within the Early Iron Age.

Particular importance has been attached to tomb XXIII by V. R. d'A. Desborough, who thought it could go back into the eleventh century.[3] The lack of iron objects, to which he draws attention, is normal in children's graves, and the fact that the bases are hand-made is nothing unusual at an inland site, since only three of eighty-five pots at Pateli were wheel-made. On the evidence of the finds it could be dated anywhere within the bracket 1100 to 600 B.C. What interested Desborough about this burial was that it was made in a cist-tomb, and he associated cist-tombs with invaders. There are, however, many cist-tombs at Pateli and at Visoï, which may be dated to the eleventh century on better grounds than tomb XXIII at Kozani.

There are many Early Iron Age sites along the Haliacmon valley. At Palaiogratsiano, near the Volustana pass to Thessaly, wheel-made grey

---

[1] *AE* 1948/9 [1951] 85 f. and figs. 16, 17 (pin no. 21 only), and 18. Some years later Kallipolitis found a number of Mycenaean sherds and a piece of semicircular wall which he thought to be pre-Mycenaean (*Ergon* 1958. 88), so that it became clear that the cemetery area contained more than classical burials. For the site see also *BCH* 73 (1949) 532; 74 (1950) 306; *JHS* 70 (1950) 26; *Mak.* 2. 638 f.; *BCH* 79. 274, a tomb with an Early Iron Age pot.

[2] *Ergon* 1960. 99 f.; *BCH* 85. 777 with figs. 3–7; *AD* 17. 2. 216 fig. 6 and pls. 254 and 255; *BCH* 84. 767.

[3] *TLM* 38, 139 n. 5, and 259. The biconical bronze beads make so early a date most unlikely.

cups, hand-made grey jugs, bowls with high handles and also twisted handles have been found on the surface.[1] In a collection of objects found near Aeane there are a fine spectacle-fibula of bronze wire and some open bracelets of bronze with pointed ends.[2] Finds of spectacle-fibulae, bracelets, and other ornaments at a site which was apparently a cemetery have been reported at Dovran, two hours north of Grevena (Casson, *Macedonia* 172). In the district called Voïon, west of the Haliacmon river, chance finds have been made at several villages near Tsotyli. A fine distaff-shaped pendant of bronze with a seated male figure on the top and a disc at the foot came from Ayioi Anargyri, attributable to the eighth century.[3] A collection made at Axiokastron (Sourdhani) included a large spectacle-fibula of bronze wire; five bronze armlets with overlapping ends, as in Fig. 17*f*; pieces of spectacle-fibulae or of smaller spiralling ornaments; a bronze torque (Fig. 18*d*), and a piece of another; five bronze beads of various sizes, decorated with incised concentric circles and biconical in shape, as in Fig. 17*m* and *s*; two examples of the two-pinned triangular fibula with incised ornament of concentric circles (one in Fig. 18*c*); long bronze pins (one in Fig. 20*s*); three bronze finger-rings, decorated with the incised circle and dotted centre motive; bronze ear-rings; a twin vase (Fig. 16*k*); and a jug with cut-away neck.[4]

From Tsotyli come a fine spectacle-fibula, a pair of armlets with over-lapping ends, pieces of open bracelets, pieces of an incised broader armlet —all being of bronze—and an iron spear-head which is probably of this period.[5] By Neapolis (Liapsisti), near Tsotyli, Keramopoullos reported a number of finds from burials. The bronze objects were a spectacle-fibula, bronze coils, finger-rings with spirals (evidently as in Fig. 17*j*), an armlet, pierced beads, and a pair of tweezers. A spear-head and a knife were of iron; an arrow with two barbs was of bone; and there were boars' tusks, a piece of sawn ivory, perforated clay beads, one of which was dappled with little round holes (as in tomb XXIII at Kozani and tomb AH IX at Vergina), and a stone polisher, pierced for suspension (as in some burials at Vergina e.g. LXV *ΑΓ*). Apart from the base of a high-footed Mycenaean goblet, he noted a jug with cut-away neck, a broken bowl with four wish-bone handles set horizontally (a variant of the Vergina type of shallow bowl in Fig. 16*g*), and an imported, apparently Geometric, sherd.[6] These burials lay under the remains of some huts. At Sianitsi

---

[1] In the collection of the British School at Athens (*BSA* 31. 44); *PM* 100 n. 6 and 239.

[2] *AD* 17. 2. 216 and pl. 258*a*; *BCH* 85. 782 and fig. 19.

[3] *AD* 17. 2. 216 with n. 3 and pl. 256*a*; *BCH* 85 figs. 8 and 9. The central part is spherical and has vertical gashes.

[4] *AD* 17. 2. 214 with figs. 1–5, pls. 252*e* and 253*a*; *BCH* 85. 773 and figs. 5–6.

[5] *AD* 17. 2. 214 with pl. 252 *b* and *d*; *BCH* 85. 773 and figs. 3–4. In both places reference is made to prehistoric bronze ornaments at Siatista, which may be of this period.

[6] *PAE* 1935. 47 f. He compares the Geometric sherd to four pieces at Boubousti; these, as shown by Heurtley in *BSA* 28 fig. 29, 5–8, are Proto-Geometric and Geometric.

a tomb was excavated which contained offerings of our period.[1] It was an inhumation with the head to the west. Beside the head was a three-handled pot, a jug with a cut-away neck, and a two-handled pot; below it a bronze anchor-shaped pendant (? as in Fig. 17*p*) with a hole for suspension; a two-pinned triangular fibula with ornamental circles (evidently as in Fig. 18*c*) 'for pinning the clothing over the breast', a bit of iron plaque perhaps belonging to it, and two long bronze pins, one on each side of the breast; a bronze bead, a spiralling ring, and a long pierced bead of bronze round the waist. There were also pieces of broken pottery.

When we consider the finds at and near Pateli and those on both sides of the middle Haliacmon valley, there is a closer connection between Vergina and the Haliacmon valley than between Vergina and Pateli. It may be that the Haliacmon valley depended more upon Vergina as its outlet near the coast, and we have seen from the literary evidence and from the archaeological evidence of an earlier period that the Makedni or Macedonians proper then held northern Pieria and at least the western side of the Middle Haliacmon valley. The sites round the Ostrovo basin in Eordaea seem to be distinct in many ways both from Vergina and the Haliacmon valley sites, and the great cemetery at Pateli probably contains the burials of its royal house. The upper valley of the Haliacmon may not go with either the kingdom of Vergina or the kingdom of Pateli. For the excavated site at Boubousti, now Platania, which lasted down to *c.* 900 B.C., produced a bronze pin of a sub-Mycenaean kind, a Proto-Geometric sherd and a Geometric sherd, and much of its own typical painted ware with geometric designs, but there is no sign of the forms of pottery and of the bronzes which are associated with Vergina or with Pateli. The associations of Boubousti were rather with Tren near Lake Prespa and with central Epirus at this period. On the other hand, Pelagonia was very closely related to Vergina; for the tumuli below Prilep have yielded the same type of pottery and of objects as most of the tumuli of Vergina. This relationship is perhaps explained best by supposing that one was the offshoot of the other, and that the kingdom in Eordaea, as represented by the great cemetery of Pateli, arose as an independent power on the most direct route between them.

3. *In the hinterland of the eastern central plain*

Some interesting graves were discovered in 1916 at a place 1¼ miles south-east of Ayios Vasilios, a village on the south shore of Lake Koronia in Mygdonia. Of four cist-tombs, made of slabs of local shaly stone, two were undisturbed. One, which held the skeletons of a man and a small

[1] *PAE* 1937. 71. The tomb is there numbered Tomb 13.

child, contained an iron knife, an iron spear-head and two iron spear-butts, and two small flat bands of gold, which were associated with the child. The other contained a *cothon* or round dish with a half-loop handle, which is of importance for dating; a lozenge-shaped piece of thin gold sheet with a tooled design, measuring 8 cm by 4·25 cm, which was found near the neck; a gold bead, biconical in shape, perforated, and decorated with incised patterns; an amulet of amber; pieces of bronze fibulae of the type shown in Fig. 18*j*, found near the right shoulder and in the centre of the chest; two bronze armlets with overlapping ends; and two bronze finger-rings, one on each hand, of the type with two spirals shown in Fig. 17*j*. From the disturbed tombs a gold hairpin and a blue glass bead of an Egyptian type, dating from the 18th Dynasty onwards, were found. The *cothon* resembles in shape and in its degenerate decoration one attributed to Class *A* II of this ware and may be dated *c.* 550 B.C.[1]

Chauchitsa occupies a strategic position on the northern edge of the upper part of the plain and to the east of the first gorge of the Vardar. The route which leads from Salonica, some 60 km away, and goes up the Vardar valley via Gevgheli, has to keep east of the gorge and passes not far from the hill of Chauchitsa. Here only one cist-tomb, made of slabs, was dug by Casson during his excavations.[2] It contained a wheel-made jug with a straight rim except for a dip above the handle; two spectacle-fibulae; ten fragments of long bronze coils (as at Vergina); 101 necklace beads of bronze; a bronze pin with a flower-shaped head, shaped as in Fig. 17*dd*; one large and two small beads of the biconical shape; a heavy bronze armlet with overlapping ends (as in Fig. 17*z*); a bronze finger-ring; and two iron pins with ivory or bone adhering to them. In 1917–18 objects from graves at Chauchitsa were found during military operations, and Casson reported them twice without indicating exactly where the burials were in relation to his own excavations. The 'Bronze Age' objects of bronze were given by him as five spectacle-fibulae of the early type, as in Fig. 18*e*; bronze armlets with overlapping ends; finger-rings; a large biconical bead; a pendant with a slashed sphere (Fig. 18*f*); and a pendant of a bird perched on a bulb.[3] The two last appear to have come from a cist-tomb, made of slabs, which had also a miniature bronze amphora 4 cm high.[4] Some of these were reported by Casson as of 'classical date'.[5]

Later Casson described objects from three graves found in the same way. In Grave A, where the body lay extended on its back under a cairn

---

[1] *BSA* 23 (1918–19) 17 f., with figs. esp. 9–16 and pl. v, 2 the *cothon*, for which see *JHS* 31 (1911) 75 fig. 3; Payne, *Necrocorinthia* 335, and *Albania* 2. 56 fig. 14. An Early Iron Age site is reported at Sochos in this basin (*Arch. Anz.* 55 (1940) 272).

[2] *BSA* 24 (1919–21) 8 f., 12 fig. 9 and pl. i = Casson, *Macedonia* fig. 58.

[3] *BSA* 23. 32 f. with pl. vii*b*; for this early type see Ebert 2. 86 pl. 35, 3.   [4] *BSA* 23. 37.

[5] *BSA* 23. 36 f., listed under Grave D with references to pl. viiB, 7, 9, 10.

of stones, the pendants round the neck were a miniature bronze jug (Fig. 18*g*) and a prick-eared horse, originally on a stand (Fig. 18*h*); a large biconical bead; two heavy armlets with overlapping ends; two bracelets with sharp ends; a string of bronze beads; and two finger-rings of twisted gold. In Grave B, with no cairn, a lozenge-shaped piece of gold plaque (Fig. 18*i*) of the same size as that at Ayios Vasilios, a necklace of bronze beads with a central clay bead, a small bird-pendant of bronze, a spectacle-fibula of bronze, and two heavy bronze armlets with overlapping ends. In Grave C, with no cairn, a long bronze coil, a cup-and-lid pendant (Fig. 17*o*), a turf-cutter pendant (Fig. 17*p*), a bronze bar some 20 cm long with a hole in the centre, which was on the chest, a light bronze armlet with pointed ends, a spiral of gold, and a piece of gold leaf of the same size as that in Grave B, shown in Fig. 18*i*. The bronze horse in Grave A was dated *c.* 700 B.C. by Miss S. Benton in *JHS* 72 (1952) 119 with her fig. 1. Among objects not associated with a specific grave were a bronze pendant similar in shape to that in Fig. 17*aa* but less ornate; an iron-bladed antenna sword with a bronze hilt,[1] two bronze shield-bosses, 20 cm and 13 cm in diameter respectively, and two large bronze pins, 25 cm and 22 cm long. The larger shield-boss is of the same design as that in Fig. 18*b*; and the smaller has the same six triangular apertures.[2] Other graves were of the classical and the Roman periods.

In 1921 and 1922 Casson conducted his excavations at two mounds. The western mound was trenched but yielded only stray finds, similar to others on the site.[3] The eastern mound was formed by an outcrop of rock, some 20 feet high above the adjacent ground, and measuring on its flattish top some 25 by 45 m. There was little or no soil above the rock in some of the higher parts, and not much more than a metre of soil at many places on the sloping sides.[4] He opened thirty-six graves. The bulk of these were in the soil on the top, and only a few were on the lower slopes. Casson wrote of this as follows.[5] 'The nature of the Iron Age cemetery is peculiar. The bodies seem to have been laid either on the rock itself or in shallow depressions in still shallower earth. They were then covered with heavy stones, presumably to keep off the wolves with which this country still abounds. In the course of time a thin stratum of earth formed over both grave and cairn.' Here Casson reverses the processes of nature on a rock outcrop in the Macedonian climate. When rock surfaces and cairns exist, erosion follows and causes denudation and not accumulation of soil; this was indeed demonstrated when Casson found collapsed

---

[1] *Antiq. J.* 1 (1921) 209 f. pls. 6 and 7, and fig. 3; Casson, *Macedonia* fig. 50.
[2] *BSA* 23. 37 f. and pl. viiA.   [3] *BSA* 26. 3 and 16 (*f*)–(*j*).
[4] *BSA* 24. 6 f. and fig. 6; 26. 1 f. and fig. 2. The mound is beside a stream, as are the tumuli at Vergina, Vodhinë, and Pazhok.
[5] *BSA* 26. 9.

cairns on what is now the edge of the mound. The truth is rather that the dead were buried in a mound of soil which after the initial burial covered the rock, the graves, and the cairns set up by the relatives; in other words it is most probable that we have here the remains of a large tumulus of soil, made on a natural outcrop, and analogous not only to the tumulus with a cairn-burial at Vergina (p. 330 above) but also to the tumuli with cairn-burials at Vajzë in southern Albania.

At Chauchitsa the burials were at varying depths from the surface, and in three instances one burial partly overlaid another;[1] both features are characteristic of tumulus-burials. If we are correct, the central burial of the tumulus is likely to have been the original burial, over which the tumulus was raised. This burial is Grave (19). It was unique in that 'it was bedded upon ten or twelve large rocks, which had been built up to support it';[2] or, as I should prefer to put it, the burial was inside a large cairn. A large shield-boss, 31·5 cm in diameter, with six triangular apertures and a short spike, resembling the shield-boss in Fig. 18*b*, was found where the chest of the corpse had been. It was of bronze but riveted with six iron rivets; its spike passed through a hole, then through a small holding plate, and ended in a loop, to which the shield itself was attached. Similar shield-bosses, 18·6 and 23 cm in diameter, were found in the same position on the corpse, in Graves (18) and (20) (the former in Fig. 18*b*), and we have mentioned the two stray finds already. It is thus highly probable that the bronze bar, 20 cm long with a central hole, found on the chest in Grave C, was from a shield of different construction.[3] To return to Grave (19) and its other contents: namely, two heavy bronze armlets with overlapping ends, 7 cm in internal diameter, worn by men (as in Fig. 17*z*); a wheel-made straight-rimmed jug; and a clay whorl (? bead) of barrel shape.

The other thirty-five burials on the mound were in soil and were crushed by cairns of rough stones. My suggestion is that the corpses had been laid in a wood-lined or trellis-lined trench or coffin together with

---

[1] *BSA* 24. 7 and 26. 28. As erosion proceeded and cairns were exposed, the stones were no doubt taken, as they are scarce in the plain.

[2] *BSA* 26. 12. Casson distinguished between his two excavations by calling e.g. 'Grave 1' that of his first excavation and 'Grave (1)' that of his second excavation.

[3] This explanation of the bar is my own. It is supported by the discovery of a bronze bar, 17 cm long, pierced in the middle (a bit more than half was found), lying on the mouth in Grave (1). Casson said it had been placed there 'over the mouth of the body or in it'; but the average mouth is only 4 cm wide. Casson did not comment on the complete bar (shown in *Antiq. J.* 1. 211 pl. vii, fig. 1). For the position of the shield-boss in Grave (19) see *BSA* 26 fig. 5; the spike ibid. fig. 4; the shield-bosses in pl. 1, *BSA* 23. 37 foot and pl. viiA, and Casson, *Macedonia* figs. 59–62. I referred in *Epirus* 404 to these shield-bosses, and compared them in *Epirus* 357 to those in Leucas, Dodona, and Kaloriziki, where I was misled by a sentence in Casson, *Macedonia* 149: 'Three of the bosses were found *in situ* on the breast of a skeleton.' In fact three bosses and three skeletons were what he meant. I am grateful to A. M. Snodgrass for pointing this out to me.

their ornaments, etc.; that a cairn had been placed above the coffin, as was the case at Pazhok in central Albania;[1] and that, when the coffin rotted, the cairn fell and crushed the bones and the ornaments and offerings. All corpses lay on their backs in an extended position. The contents of the thirty-five graves may be summarized as follows. Of bronze: long coils (as at Vergina in Fig. 17*a*) of considerable length in 6 graves and bits in others; hair-rings 8; pins 6; spectacle-fibulae 9; fibulae (as in Fig. 18*j*) 3; small beads 55; large beads 15, at least one of which had incised concentric circles as in Fig. 17*m*; tweezers 4; finger-rings 12; spiral finger-rings with five convolutions 2; heavy armlets with overlapping ends (as in Fig. 17*z*) 14; armlets with several convolutions (as in Fig. 17*e*) 5; small armlets 6; thick rings 2; ringlets (in one grave only); cup-pendants (as in Fig. 17*o*) 5; jug-pendant 1; anchor-pendant (as in Fig. 17*p*) 1; bean-pendants 2; bird-pendants 4; jug-on-bird pendants (see Fig. 18*k*) 2; and animal-pendant 1. Of iron: knives 14; swords 5 (but 2 may be long knives); pins 4; rings 2. Of gold: plaques with impressed ornaments in repoussé style 5. Of amber: beads 2. Of paste: beads 6.[2]

There is clearly a marked relationship in hair-ornaments, pins, fibulae, armlets, finger-rings, beads, necklaces, and some pendants between the burials of this tumulus and those of many tumuli at Vergina. But there are marked differences: cairns at Chauchitsa, stone-surrounds to graves and tumulus-periboloi at Vergina; no double-axe pendants at Chauchitsa, only one bird-headed pendant and no bean-pendants at Vergina; no lozenge-shaped gold plaques at Vergina, no gold rings at Chauchitsa tumulus, unless Graves A and C above belong to the tumulus. Again in weapons iron knives and swords are in common; but Vergina has many spear-heads in iron, Chauchitsa has no spear-heads; belt-bosses are common and shield-bosses lacking at Vergina, and the opposite is the case at Chauchitsa. This list is far from exhaustive; but it is enough to bring out the nature of the relationship.[3]

The story is much the same in regard to the pottery. In Grave (19), the oldest on my interpretation, there was a wheel-made straight-rimmed jug with one handle of red ware. In general Casson classified the pottery in three classes: A, small vessels, hand-made, of reddish-brown clay, with twisted handles (as in Fig. 16*i*); the shapes are straight-rimmed jugs and cut-away-necked jugs, both one-handled, cups with lobe-shaped or

---

[1] See my article in *BSA* 62 (1967) 81 and pl. 19, 3.

[2] The objects are listed by graves and many are illustrated in *BSA* 24 and 26.

[3] Some small points at Chauchitsa may be understood from the excavations at Vergina, e.g. the bronze bands on an iron sword's wooden scabbard at Vergina (*PAE* 1953. 147 and *AD* 18. B2. 222), explaining the purpose of one at Chauchitsa (*BSA* 26. 12 Grave 17). The metal of a spear-head in Tumulus III burial *E* is not defined by Petsas in *AD* 17. 1. 224 and pl. 99*b*; I have assumed that, like all other spear-heads at Vergina, it is of iron.

thumb-grip handles (Fig. 16 *n* and *o*), and small saucers. To this class the pot in Grave (19) belongs, save that it is wheel-made. Some pieces have incised triangles or dots, and small stamped circles—the former found also at Saratse, and the latter at Vardarophtsa and at Saratse in the Early Iron Age.[1] B, large vessels, wheel-made, thin and fine, mostly painted with glaze paint; the shapes are two-handled cantharoi (as in Fig. 16*m*), and jugs with a cut-away neck but a high handle. One-handled *cothon*-shaped dishes in this ware were fairly common (Fig. 16*l*); the rim is not inturning as it is in the *cothon*. C, grey ware, wheel-made, ringed with wheel-made incisions; the shape being the pedestalled, one-handled cup common in Macedonia (Fig. 16*a*). There were also two examples of skyphoi, one with pendent concentric circles (Fig. 16*p*), and one without.[2] All the pottery was made of local clays, and it was therefore not imported.

When we compare Chauchitsa with Vergina, we see that they share the various kinds of jug and the two-handled fine cantharoi. Both have skyphoi with concentric circles. On the other hand, Chauchitsa has none of the characteristic Vergina pots with thumb-rests and shallow bowls with two handles extending from the rim and two pinched-out pieces of the rim; Vergina has no *cothon*-shaped dishes. Both have examples of the so-called *ansa lunata* (Fig. 16*q*).[3]

The pieces of gold plaque in the shape of a lozenge or an oblong with rounded ends are not found at Vergina. The one at Ayios Vasilios (8 cm by 4·25 cm) was found near the neck, and the breaks at the ends of its length suggest that it had been tied on. The holes for the purpose are visible in Casson's illustration of a complete one found in Grave B at Chauchitsa in 1918. An example of the oblong type was in Grave C at Chauchitsa (Fig. 18*i*). Casson's excavations at Chauchitsa produced five more, from 5 to 7 cm long and with holes or signs of holes at each end. Four similar pieces of gold plaque in the Louvre came from Zeitenlik, some 5 km north of Thessalonica, but they are larger, being up to 15·2 cm. As Casson suggested, they were probably laid on the lips of the dead, and the strings were tied behind the head. At least it is clear from the burials of warriors wearing the 'Illyrian' type of helmet at Zeitenlik that they were not diadems. At Ayios Vasilios and in Grave (22) of the tumulus at Chauchitsa they were found in each case together with a *cothon* and with a fibula of the types shown in Fig. 18*j*. Thus this form

---

[1] *PM* 232 fig. 105, 236 fig. 110 f., and 237 no. 495.

[2] *BSA* 26. 6 Graves (2) and (3), fig. 3, *c*, *d* and fig. 6 *d*; *PM* 235 nos. 480 and 481.

[3] At least there are no *cothons* in the publications and descriptions, but a great deal of pottery has yet to be published from Petsas's excavations at Vergina. The *ansa lunata* on the lid in *BSA* 26 fig. 3*f* is from Grave (14) at Chauchitsa; another example from the western mound is shown in fig. 6*b*, the shallow vessel being rather like the shallow bowls at Vergina which have such handles (*AD* 17. 1 pl. 103 *c* 1, pl. 149*d* and perhaps pl. 94*c* and pl. 153*d*).

of gold 'mouth-piece' was in use *c.* 550 B.C. in these three places. They have been found also at Kalamaria.[1]

On the other side of the Vardar from Chauchitsa more than twenty burials were found in 1918 near Axioupolis, then called Bohemitsa, which is on the southern side of the Vardar gorge.[2] The burials were inhumations, some in pithoi but most in slab-lined cist-tombs, situated on a plateau above the river. Bones, pottery, and iron objects had almost all rotted away. In a group of eighteen burials no precise arrangement was observed, except a general east–west orientation. More objects survived in Grave 2, lined with ten stone slabs, than in any other. By the head were beads of amber, two small clay beads, and 'spires en bronze'— regarded as components of necklaces, but the last are clearly the long bronze coils for the hair,[3] as at Vergina in Fig. 17*a*; bits of one or two rings of bronze; and a pair of light armlets of bronze, one with seven turns. At the centre were a circular phalaron of bronze shown in Fig. 19*e*, with a rim containing a rivet-hole and with a hemispherical centre, the diameter of the whole being 8·9 cm, and adjacent to it traces of iron; six pendants, shown in Fig. 19*a*, one being 12 cm long, the others about 10 cm; and two bronze pendants with fretted openwork, as in a similar object at Visoï, but with a stylized man, arms on knees, at one end and a mushroom top at the other end, and a total height of 8·5 cm, shown in Fig. 19*b*. At the feet pieces of pots. In other graves of this group there were the following bronze objects: heavy armlets with overlapping ends (as in Fig. 17*z*); a bit of a fibula; a finger-ring; two pendants as in Fig. 19*c*; one pendant as in Fig. 19*d*; an 'eight-petalled' button, as in Fig. 17*dd*; two pendants 'à boule' as in Fig. 18*f*;[4] and two small bronze handles. There were beads of amber, bronze, and clay.

At some distance from this group, in the embankment of the road from Axioupolis to Izvor more tombs were found with heavy bronze armlets, one being decorated on the outside with incised circles and an incised cross of St. Andrew;[5] a bronze ring with eight pendants shown in Fig. 19*dd* (three having been lost); a bronze torque as in Fig. 18*d*; a small 'cupule' in bronze; a trilobate bead in bronze; two large monolobate beads in bronze; and a bracelet of bronze 'eggs'. There was one ring of iron. A number of stray objects were recorded. These included bits of a bronze

---

[1] *BSA* 26. 23; A. de Ridder, *Catalogue sommaire des bijoux antiques* (Paris, 1924) pl. ii. 101, 103; *Albania* 2 (1927) 32 f. with fig. 11 for Zeitenlik, where the pieces of gold plaque were found by the neck, and 52 with fig. 6 for Mikro Karaburnu, where found in the position of the mouth; *BSA* 24. 21 and *JHS* 41. 274 in graves at Kalamaria. Such gold mouth-pieces are found especially in Bulgaria; see Ebert 2 pl. 109, 1–2.

[2] *Albania* 4 (1932) 40, reported by L. Rey. The finds are in the Louvre. Rey gives a map of the site on p. 43 and excellent illustrations.

[3] Rey shows them apparently in his fig. 9 (inside the torque).

[4] Rey used the term 'boule' to describe the pendants in my Fig. 19*d* (his fig. 7. 3).

[5] As in Ebert 2. 90 pl. 39 central arm-band.

spectacle-fibula; an open-ended bracelet of bronze, decorated on the outside with two rows of incised circles; 'a handle or hilt ending in a thin blade, twisted and frayed, of bronze'; and an iron spear-head planted in the soil with the point upright at 4 m distance from Grave 18 in the first group.

In several ways the finds at Axioupolis are very different from those at Chauchitsa. Amber is common at Axioupolis; one necklace had some fifty-five amber beads of different shapes. The pendants dangling from pendants occur only at Axioupolis, and the love of incised circles is stronger at Axioupolis than elsewhere. The spear-head planted upright is interesting in view of two passages. Homer describes the followers of Diomede sleeping with their spears fixed upright on the butt-end's spike (*Il.* 10. 151–3):

$$\text{ἀμφὶ δ' ἑταῖροι}$$
$$\text{εὗδον, ὑπὸ κρασὶν δ' ἔχον ἀσπίδας· ἔγχεα δέ σφιν}$$
$$\text{ὄρθ' ἐπὶ σαυρωτῆρος ἐλήλατο.}$$

The warrior in Grave 18 was sleeping the sleep of death, his spear-head upright beside him. Aristotle, *Poetics* 1461[a]3, commenting on this passage in the *Iliad*, remarked that it was in his day a custom of the Illyrii.

When we look to Illyria, we find in the tumuli of the Mati valley that of the beads there 'la plupart sont en ambre',[1] and that there are remarkable examples of pendants dangling from pendants, of which I show an example (Fig. 19*f*). Another from the Mati valley tumuli consists of forty pieces dangling in four chains from the top-piece shown in Fig. 20*f*.

The phalaron from Axioupolis (Fig. 19*e*), 8·9 cm in diameter, was in a woman's grave, as we see from the pair of light armlets, which are only 5·5 cm in internal diameter. It was attached therefore to a belt or apron. In shape it differs from the phalara at Vergina. However, it is precisely paralleled, on the one hand, in shape and even down to the rivet-hole in the tumulus burials of Černá Mýt in the south- and west-Bohemian culture of Hungary, and, on the other hand, by the side-bosses on the shield at Kaloriziki in Cyprus of the late twelfth century B.C. The illustration showing the phalara from a woman's apron at Černá Mýt contains pieces of the long bronze coils (as in Fig. 17*a*) and examples of the many small discs, called 'tutuli', which are very common in the richest women's graves in the tumuli of Vergina.[2]

Graves near Gevgheli were opened during the First World War. Among the bronzes were two miniature bronze jugs as in Fig. 18*g*,

---

[1] *SA* 1964. 1. 103.

[2] For the Kaloriziki bosses see *AJA* 58 (1954) pl. 25; Snodgrass, *EGA* 39 f. and pl. 19; Hammond, *Epirus* 357; Schránil 129 fig. 13. He explains the bits of long bronze coil as being used to hold tassels on a belt in this case. See also Ebert 2. 90 pl. 39, lower right.

a primitive form of the fibula shown in Fig. 18*j*, a pendant ending in a ball as in Fig. 17*aa*, a stylized bird-pendant, a belt-ornament consisting of three tutuli fused together in tandem, a large biconical bronze bead, and two specimens of a fusion of two such beads to form a cross-shaped junction as in Fig. 18*m*.[1]

On the east side of the Vardar valley at Dedeli, which is near the north-west side of Lake Doiran, some graves were opened during the First World War and Casson described the contents as 'of the Hallstatt type as at Chauchitsa, though perhaps later in date'.[2] To the east of the lake near the road under Mt. Belasitsa which leads to the Strymon valley, near the village Kozlu Dere, a tomb was found to contain small biconical bronze beads, glass-paste beads, a bronze button of unusual shape, decorated with concentric circles (Fig. 20*h*), and a stone pot with a long loop-handle, which resembles one from Glasinac.[3] At a village called Houma below Mt. Kojouch a very heavy armlet of bronze with over-lapping ends and engraved with a geometric design of crosses, dots, and rings was found; in its size (9 cm in diameter) and shape it resembles that in Fig. 17*z*, but has more overlap.[4]

Further up the Vardar valley a number of bronzes were found during the making of a road from Titov Veles to Skopje. The bronzes from near Titov Veles were sold to the Benaki Museum in Athens together with bronzes from two villages near Epanomi in Crousis, namely Mesokhori and Trilophos. The dealer reported these as the places of origin, but the names were firmly attached to only a few objects by Th. Makridis, who published the collection in *AE* 1937. 2. 512 f. Those definitely from Titov Veles are a most unusual rhyton, 26 cm long, shaped like an ear-trumpet, with a pierced extension of the lip for suspension; a herb-cup resembling that in Fig. 17*o* but of a variety exactly paralleled at Chauchitsa, and decorated with incised parallel lines in bands; the curving side-piece of a horse's bit, 19 cm long, similarly decorated, and having on the convex side a stylized horse, rings, and a bird-ended disc, and at one end a large disc; another side-piece, 14·5 cm long, similarly decorated, and having a ring and a knob on the convex side and a cone-shaped disc at one end; an arched fibula, 7 cm long, similarly decorated, as in Fig. 17*q*; and a pin, 51 cm long, rectangular in section at first and cylindrical lower down with a disc and two spherical swellings (Fig. 20*r*).[5] This pin is

[1] Ebert 2. 207 and pls. 105 and 106; mentioned in *Albania* 4. 48 and Casson, *Macedonia* 171. Finds in the museum of Sofia.
[2] Material in the Berlin Museum für Völkerkunde; Casson, *Macedonia* 172.
[3] R. Popov in *Godishnik Narodnja Muzei (Annuaire du Musée National de Sofia)* 1921 figs. 141–3. The material is in the Sofia Museum; mentioned cursorily by Casson, *Macedonia* 173. Popov made the comparison with Glasinac.
[4] R. Popov, ibid., figs. 139 and 140; Casson, ibid.
[5] These objects are illustrated in *AE* 1937. 2. 520 f. as pl. i *a*, *b*, *c*, pl. ii *a*, *b*, pl. iv*h*, and pl. v*e*.

to be dated *c.* 750 B.C.; its origin is Corinth.[1] On the east side of the Vardar valley a site called Radanja near Štip has yielded the following bronze objects: bird-pendants, vessel-pendants, a herb-cup top, biconical beads, 'bipyramidal tassels as at Kumanovo', and circular bronze buttons with a semicircular loop in the back.[2] At Vučedol near Skopje there are heavy bronze armlets with overlapping ends (as in Fig. 17*z*) and bronze arched fibulae with a strengthened arch and a large catch-plate.

In *Spomenik* 77 (1941–8) 271 a number of bronzes from the vicinity of Kumanovo are published. There are six miniature jugs as in Fig. 18*g*; a biconical bead as in Fig. 17*d*; a pendant as in Fig. 18*f*; a bird-pendant; a triangular-topped pendant as in Fig. 17*aa*, but with a slashed spherical bulb as the lower part; a heavy armlet with overlapping ends; a lighter armlet of two turns; a lid with bird-shaped lugs and a central handle, as for the herb-cup in Fig. 17*o*; a pendant with a large spherical centre, as at Dodona Fig. 18*u*; a bronze bead as in Fig. 17*m*; a larger bead with rounded outline as in Fig. 17*s*; a cross-shaped junction piece as in Fig. 18*m*, but with wider collars at the ends; two smaller beads; and six large buttons with semicircular loops on the back, buttons such as those to which the long coils are attached in Fig. 17*a*.[3]

The only object named as coming from one of the villages near Epanomi is a miniature jug as in Fig. 18*g*, with incised parallel lines running horizontally round the neck and just below the shoulder.[4] The other forty-four pieces in the Benaki Museum collection are unallocated as between Titov Veles and the Epanomi villages, and we can list them only as coming from one or the other region east of the Vardar. They are as follows. A double jug (Fig. 18*r*); four pendants with fretted openwork, the only complete one having a loop at the end for suspension (as in Fig. 19*b*, without the man); two cross-shaped junction pieces,[5] of which the larger is shown in Fig. 18*m* and the smaller has the same incised parallel lines in bands as those on objects known to have come from near Veles; rings with three or four knobs, shown in Fig. 18*n*; a trilobate bead,

[1] Compare Jacobsthal 11 and no. 33*a*, which is 52 cm long, from Corinth.
[2] *WMBH* 1. 101 f., figs. 182 and 187.
[3] These are all on one illustration, and the buttons are not all easy to make out. This publication by Vulic is perfunctory. M. Garašanin made further comments in *Starinar* 5–6 (1954–5) 40 f. He suggested that the objects came from a hoard. This is most improbable, since all the objects are typical of burials of the period. They are likely to be the result of tomb-robbing. [4] *AE* 1937. 2. 516 no. 3 and pl. *id.*
[5] These and others elsewhere have a hole behind the cross, which Makridis believed was to take four reins which issued separately from the four ends. The difficulty is that one is 6 cm long and the other 3·2 cm long, so that the reins would have to be excessively thin. Carapanos thought of two such objects at Dodona (4 cm and 2 cm) as axle boxes, and this is possible if the spokes and the axle were light metal pins (Carapanos i 98 no. 4 and ii pl. 52, 20). At Donja Dolina they were explained as belt-fittings (*WMBH* ix. 150 'Gurtel-bestandtheil').

shown in Fig. 18*o*; a triangular bead with discs at the points, shown in Fig. 18*p*; biconical beads as in Fig. 19 *i–l*, with and without intermediate discs, and an outsize one with knobs on the central part; necklace beads; three ball-ended pendants with and without a disc, as in Fig. 17*aa*; four pendants of the distaff type, one having a stylized jug at the top, one a crude bird-head, one a stylized bird, and one a fishtail handle; a pendant with a triangular disc-ended top, as in Fig. 17*aa*, but with a solid biconical body; four heavy armlets, and two lighter armlets with several turns, often decorated with incised parallel lines and concentric circles; a finger-ring of bronze strip with three coils; an arched fibula with a catch-plate (Fig. 20*a*); two spectacle-fibulae; a finger-ring with two spirals attached as in Fig. 17*j*; a fibula of four spirals; a broken spoon-shaped pendant, as in Fig. 17*bb*; a double-shanked pin; a bronze button with petals as in Fig. 17*dd*; two bronze buttons, Fig. 18 *l* and *s*; and two four-spoked wheels with wide rims as in Fig. 18*a*, 7 cm and 6·5 cm in diameter respectively, one having its short spike protruding on both sides.[1]

Two lots of bronzes were published separately by Forsdyke in 1932 and 1934.[2] Lot A was acquired for the British Museum from a dealer, who said the objects came from Potidaea. They are a bronze spear-head, 21 fretted-cylinder pendants 'with rectilinear engravings on the solid part of the back' (shaped as in Fig. 19*b* but without the figure on the top), 1 ball-ended pendant (as in Fig. 17*aa* but with one ring and a suspension ring), 1 slashed-sphere pendant (as in Fig. 18*f*), 1 bird-topped slashed-sphere pendant, 1 bell-and-clappers pendant, (as in Fig. 19*a*), 1 bobbin-shaped pendant (as in Fig. 19*d*), 1 jug-with-cutaway-neck pendant (as in Fig. 18*g*), 1 jug-with-incised-decoration pendant, 2 ringed biconical beads, 1 tubular three-ringed bead, 1 spectacle-fibula, and 1 fibula with a catch-plate of eighth-century date. Lot B was described by Forsdyke as an addition to Lot A and as having resulted from irregular excavations, and nothing was said of its provenience. It contained beads of amber, bone, carnelian, and glass; a pair of linked rings of bronze with knobs representing animal heads; an eight-petalled bronze button (as in Fig. 17*dd*), decorated with finely engraved circles, a bronze hook and a bit of an iron pin; armlets with several turns; and armlets with over-lapping heavy ends, on which there is simple linear engraving (as in Fig. 17*z*).

The dealer's word that Lot A came from Potidaea has been accepted. Indeed it has been extended to include Lot B, and there has been a

---

[1] I have listed these in the order of Makridis's text and excellent illustrations in *AE* 1937. 2. The fibula of four spirals belongs apparently to the class iv b of J. Alexander in *AJA* 69 (1965) 16, dated to 850–550 B.C.

[2] *British Museum Quarterly* 6 (1932) 82 f. and 8 (1934) 108.

tendency to date all objects in both Lots by the eighth-century fibula.[1] This is almost certainly wrong. Lot A has the air of a job lot; for the twenty-one fretted-cylinder pendants are so disproportionate a part of the whole that the collection cannot have come from one group of even twenty-one graves. Lot B has no connection with Lot A, as it should have if it too had come from Potidaea. There are further arguments against Potidaea as a possible site. No object resembling anything in either lot has turned up at Potidaea among the chance surface finds, in the digging of the canal, and in Pelekides's preliminary excavations.[2] There is neither evidence nor probability that Potidaea was occupied until Corinth planted its colony on this exposed site *c.* 600 B.C.; for it needed a fleet and walls for its defence by sea and by land.[3] Moreover Lots A and B have little in common with objects of this period at near-by Olynthus. With the twenty-one fretted-cylinder pendants we may compare only two which were found together at Olynthus, one broken and the other having a jug on top.[4] The rectilinear engravings are found not at Olynthus but on pendants of this kind at Axioupolis (Bohemitsa) and in the Benaki Museum collection; further, Axioupolis had six examples of the rare bell-and-clapper pendant.[5] Lot B's beads of amber, carnelian, and bone are not found at Olynthus, but amber beads occur at Axioupolis and at Chauchitsa. On the present evidence the wisest conclusion is that these two lots did not come from Potidaea, a plausible site in a dealer's mind as that of an ancient city, but very probably in the case of Lot A from Axioupolis, where trenches dug in the First World War had exposed part of a cemetery.

Olynthus holds an important place in the evidence not only because it has been thoroughly excavated and described, but also because we know something of its early history. The place was occupied by the Bottiaei, when they were expelled from their homeland in the western part of the central plain by the Argead Macedonians. This event occurred approximately in the eighth generation before the reign of Archelaus, which began in 413 B.C.[6] If we reckon a generation at thirty-three years for the upper figure and thirty years for the lower figure, we can put the

---

[1] So *Olynthus* x (1941), see Index; J. A. Alexander, *Potidaea* (Athens, 1963) 11 ff.; Th. Makridis in *AE* 1937. 517.

[2] Alexander, op. cit. 6 ff. gives an account of them.

[3] It was founded later than Olynthus, and it held a threatening position *vis-à-vis* Olynthus and its communications; it is unlikely that a native city was built there so close to Olynthus before 600 B.C.

[4] *Olynthus* x. 2624 and 2625. The numbers guide the reader to the text and to the illustrations.

[5] *Albania* 4 (1932) figs. 5 and 6, and *AE* 1937. 2. 520 pl. ii. Robinson and Alexander do not refer to the latter. For rectilinear engraving see figs. 5 and 6 in the former, and pl. i *a* and *d*, pl. ii *a* and *b*, p. 517 on objects 7–10, and p. 519 on objects 31–3 and 38 in the latter.

[6] Thuc. 2. 99. 3; 2. 100. 2; Hdt. 8. 139. See p. 433 below.

eighth generation somewhere between 675 and 625 B.C.[1] Robinson has
dated the earliest pottery and other objects of the Iron Age at Olynthus
to the seventh century and generally to not before 650 B.C.[2] As the
Bottiaei had come from their homeland close to or even including Vergina,
we should expect to find among the objects of archaic Olynthus some
signs of their origin and in particular of the cult of the double-axe (see
p. 335 above). In fact Robinson published seven 'miniature double-axes,
generally thick in the center (and perforated) with flattened sharply
curving wings' as bronze pendants. The shape of these axes (Fig. 19*h*)
is more Minoan than that of the axes from Vergina, Pateli, and Visoï
(Fig. 17 *k* and *u*), and the absence of a suspension ring shows that the
perforation on each was for a rod. A miniature double-axe of bone was
also found; it resembles in shape the triple double-axes of Vergina and
the pendant double-axe from Visoï (Fig. 17*v*).[3] The similarity in cult and
yet the difference in shape of the bronze pieces suggest that the Bottiaeans
had been the neighbours and not the users of the tumuli at Vergina.
This suggestion is confirmed by the pottery at Olynthus as compared with
that at Vergina. At Olynthus there are no shallow bowls with two
handles and two pinched-out rim-pieces (as in Fig. 16*g*), relatively few
jugs with cut-away necks, and a good many drinking-bowls with thumb-
rests; but the thumb-rests are of a different shape. At Olynthus 'the top
is pointed or rounded or flat with sharp projecting edges'[4] (see Fig. 16*t*
for the rounded or mushroom top), but at Vergina the top is flat and the
sides are conical (Fig. 16*f*.)

The archaic objects at Olynthus not only show us what the Bottiaeans
used at Olynthus in the period *c.* 650–550 B.C., with which we are at
present concerned, but also indicate what they had previously used in
Bottiaeis. The most remarkable thing at Olynthus is the great number
of the bronze beads, 134. The commonest types are the biconical collared
bead and the longer form with two additional rings, as in Fig. 19 *i–l*.
There are very few of these at Vergina and many at the Vardar valley
sites. Of those published so far, the closest analogies to the Olynthian
ones come from Titov Veles and the Epanomi area, that is from the
Benaki Museum collection; in particular an outsize one with knobs on
the central part is exactly like one in that collection.[5] There are a number

---

[1] See my remarks on genealogical reckoning in *HG*[2] 653.
[2] In *Olynthus* v, p. 4, he puts his Group I only into the 'eighth to seventh' century, but this
group of Local Macedonian Ware cannot be dated to the eighth rather than the seventh
century on its own development; it has to be dated by its context, which here is seventh
century. [3] *Olynthus* X, 438–44.
[4] *Olynthus* v, 4 and pls. xxiii and xxiv; see also xiii pl. xi.
[5] *Olynthus* x pls. viii–xi and pp. 65 f., where Robinson concludes that 'the abundant use
of such beads was more customary in the archaic town of the Bottiaeans'. In his comparisons
he did not know of Makridis's article on the Benaki Museum collection, which probably
came out after *Olynthus* x went to press. The outsize bead is in *Olynthus* x. 159 and in *AE*

of objects which are relatively rare at Olynthus and are also found at various sites in, or west of, the Vardar valley. These are truncated biconical beads, as in Fig. 17*m* but without the concentric circles decoration; bronze buttons, as in Fig. 17*dd* and Fig. 18*l* and *s*; long hair-coils, as in Fig. 17*a*; spectacle-fibulae; arched fibulae of a later kind than at other sites; bird-pendants; slashed-sphere pendants (as in Fig. 18*f*); a bell-and-clapper pendant (as in Fig. 19*a*); bobbin-shaped pendants (as in Fig. 19*d*); ball-ended pendants (as in Fig. 17*aa*); bronze tweezers; bronze rings with knobs (as in Fig. 18*n*); the same with knobs in the shape of animal heads; various plain rings; miniature four-spoked wheels (as in Fig. 18*b*); miniature jugs (as in Fig. 18*g*); disc-headed pins; a side-piece of a horse-bit, as at Titov Veles; and cold chisels, as at Petralona in Fig. 13*i*.[1] Almost all the weapons are of iron: swords, knives—some with curving back—spear-heads and spear-butts. It is clear that the Bottiaeans came to Olynthus with many characteristics of a culture which had had close contact with the peoples of Vergina and of the Vardar valley sites, and that they maintained this culture generally in 650–550 B.C.

There was no importation of Greek pottery from the Greek states in Chalcidice, with which they were probably on hostile terms. The first Greek influences came from Thessaly, probably at a time before Potidaea was founded or at least before she was strong enough to cut the maritime contacts of Olynthus. The adoption of the *cothon* at Olynthus, as at some other sites in Macedonia, is the first sign of a Greek import, and that is in the sixth century B.C. It was only after 550 B.C. that Thracian influences from the north-east affected Olynthus, especially the Thracian type of fibula.[2]

4. *The inter-relationships of the Early Iron Age remains within Macedonia*

The description which we have given is based at Vergina on the book of Andronikos and a preliminary report by Petsas, at Chauchitsa on a relatively full report, at Visoï on what was on show in a museum, at Pateli on second-hand reports of an incomplete preliminary report, and so on. Nevertheless, the total body of material is very considerable. Even when we bear in mind the partial nature of most of the reports, it seems

1937. 2. 520 pl. iiia. At Olynthus it was in Grave 516 of the Riverside Cemetery together with a ring, a bracelet, and fifteen other bronze beads of the collared kinds.
    [1] I give the numbers in *Olynthus* x in the same order and with the same punctuation: 45–8, 61; 247–52; 2621–3; 326–31; 343–4; 400–4; 405–6; 420; 414 and 418; 410–12; 1713–19; 2586–7; 2585; 833–946; 584; 2589–90; 1737–9; 433 and *AE* 1937. 2. 516 with pl. ii*b*, the sizes being almost the same; and 1647–9. I mentioned earlier the two fretted-cylinder pendants, i.e. 2624–5.   [2] Ibid. 349–61.

to provide a sufficient basis for making comparisons and reaching tentative conclusions. To this end I have drawn up the following table of objects and proveniences, including under 'Bottiaeans' objects from Olynthus and omitting objects of unknown or doubtful provenience in the Benaki Museum and the British Museum collections.

Burial customs are of particular interest. Cist-tombs in my sense of the term occur everywhere. They were lined with slabs or with rough walls of field stones, in accordance with what was available; and where the lining has disappeared, it is probable that it had consisted of sawn wood or branches.[1] Large tumuli are exceptionally numerous at Vergina; there are at least several at Visoï and near Visoï; if my arguments are accepted, there is one at Pateli, and one at Chauchitsa. It would appear then that this type of tumulus within Macedonia has a strong bias towards western and north-western Macedonia; and it is indeed in that direction that we find large cemeteries of tumuli in central Albania and in southern Yugoslavia in the Early Iron Age. The raising of a separate tumulus over each burial is found at Koundouriotissa only. This custom, we learn from Hdt. 5. 8, was practised by the Thracians when they buried a man of consequence, and it is here in southern Pieria that tradition placed Thracian settlers in the Early Iron Age (e.g. Str. C 410). The burial of a body within a cairn or the raising of a cairn over a burial occurred very rarely at Vergina, but these practices were the rule in the tumulus on the eastern mound at Chauchitsa. One may then conclude that the rulers at Vergina and the rulers at Chauchitsa came from a tumulus-using area but probably from different parts of it. The placing of skulls as a frame round the latest interment is peculiar to Pateli and in addition peculiar to one group among the burials at Pateli; the collecting of bones in a heap and the placing of the skull on top occurred often as an alternative practice in this same group at Pateli, but elsewhere it has been noted perhaps only once at Vergina,[2] where a Patelite of this persuasion may have died.

Again, we must note the absence of any of these practices in the middle Haliacmon valley, where quite a number of cist-graves have been opened. This phenomenon suggests that the people of the middle Haliacmon valley were not related, at least not closely related, to the powerful families of Vergina, Pateli, Visoï, and Chauchitsa. Of east Central

---

[1] There is a tendency among archaeologists to overplay the significance of the slab-lined cist-tomb as a racial or cultural criterion. Where schist-limestone or schist-slate is abundant and wood is rare, one uses slabs; if the opposite is the case, one uses wood; and if neither is available, one may use field-stones or just branches. Even within a single tumulus one may find slab-lined, wood-lined, and field-stone-lined burials, or any two of the three types (e.g. *Epirus* 203, 230 at Vajzë and Vodhinë; *SA* 1964. 1. 96 at Pazhok; and Tumulus LXV above, p. 330). One can hardly infer any racial change from their juxtaposition, even if one argues that the use of one is earlier than that of another.

[2] *AD* 17 (1961–2) i. 285 in burial *AT*.

TABLE OF OBJECTS AND PROVENIENCES

'Bottiaeans' = objects found at Olynthus which may belong to the period c. 650–550 B.C.
The Benaki Museum collection is not included unless the provenience was named.
?'Veles' = perhaps Titov Veles, being an object in the above collection connected by type with Veles.
The British Museum Lots A and B, allegedly from Potidaea, are not included.

Object	Vergina	Visoi	Bottiaeans	Pateli	Kozani	Voion	A. Vasilios	Chauchitsa	Axioupolis	Kumanovo
Amber	..	..	..	..	..	..	..	..	Axioupolis	..
Armlets: heavy (Fig. 17z)	Vergina	Visoi	..	Pateli	Kozani	Voion	A. Vasilios	Chauchitsa	Axioupolis	Kumanovo
light	Vergina	Visoi	..	Pateli	Kozani +Aeane	Voion	..	Chauchitsa	..	Kumanovo
spiralling of iron	Vergina	Visoi	..	Pateli	..	..	..	Chauchitsa	Axioupolis	..
Beads: carnelian	Vergina	..	..	..	..	..	A. Vasilios	..	..	..
gold	..	..	..	..	..	..	..	Chauchitsa	..	..
bronze, collared (Fig. 19j)	Vergina	..	Bottiaeans	..	Kozani	Voion	..	Chauchitsa	Axioupolis +Gevgheli	Kumanovo
bronze, biconical (Fig. 17m)	Vergina	..	Bottiaeans	..	..	..	..	..	..	..
glass-paste	Vergina	..	..	..	..	Voion	..	Chauchitsa	Axioupolis	..
trilobate (Fig. 18o)	..	..	..	..	..	..	..	..	Axioupolis	..
Birds: pendants	Vergina (once, in LXVI B)	..	Bottiaeans	Pateli	..	..	..	Chauchitsa	Gevgheli	Kumanovo
on pendants	..	..	..	Pateli	..	..	..	Chauchitsa	..	..
Bones: by the skull	Vergina (once)	..	..	Pateli (often)	..	..	..	..	..	..
Bosses: belt	Vergina	..	..	Pateli	..	..	..	Chauchitsa	Axioupolis (?)	..
shield	..	..	..	Pateli (1)	..	..	..	Chauchitsa	..	..
Burials: large tumulus	Vergina	Visoi	..	..	..	..	..	..	..	..
individual tumulus	Vergina (rare)	..	Koundouriotissa	..	..	..	..	..	..	..
cairns	Vergina +Verria	Visoi	Koundouriotissa	..	..	..	..	Chauchitsa	..	..
cists	Vergina (rare)	..	..	Pateli +Aetos	Kozani	..	A. Vasilios	Chauchitsa	Axioupolis	..
cremation	Vergina +Verria	..	..	Pateli	..	..	..	..	..	..
pithos	Vergina	..	..	Pateli	..	..	..	..	Axioupolis	..
trench (coffin or trellis)	..	..	..	..	..	Voion	..	..	..	..

Buttons:

	Vergina		Visoi	Bottiaeans	Pateli	Kozani	Voïon	A. Vasilios	Chauchitsa	Axioupolis	Veles/Kumanovo
Buttons:											
petalled (Fig. 17dd)	Vergina	..	..	Bottiaeans	Pateli	..	..	..	Chauchitsa	Axioupolis	..
pierced (Fig. 18 s, l)	..	..	..	Bottiaeans	Pateli	..	..	..	Chauchitsa	Axioupolis	..
Coils:											
gold, for the hair	Vergina	..	..	..	..	Kozani	Voïon	..	Chauchitsa	..	..
long bronze	Vergina	..	Visoi	..	..	..	Voïon	..	Chauchitsa	Axioupolis	..
Decoration in concentric circles on bronze	Vergina	..	..	..	Pateli	..	Voïon	..	Chauchitsa	Axioupolis	..
Diadems	Vergina	..	..	..	Pateli	..	..	..	..	Axioupolis	..
Fibulae:											
violin-bow	Vergina	..	Visoi	Vardina	..	..	..	..	..	Demir Kapu	Veles
arched, plain,	Vergina	..	..	..	Pateli	..	..	..	..	..	..
arched and catchplate	Vergina	..	..	..	Pateli	..	..	..	Chauchitsa	..	..
spectacle (Fig. 18e)	Vergina	..	Visoi	Koundouriotissa +Bottiaeans	Pateli	Kozani +Aeane	Voïon	..	Chauchitsa	Axioupolis	..
spectacle (Fig. 17b)	Vergina +Verria	..	..	..	..	..	..	A. Vasilios	Chauchitsa	Gevgheli	..
arched (Fig. 18j)	..	..	..	Zeitenlik	Pateli (1)	..	Voïon (3)	..	Chauchitsa	..	..
triangular (Fig. 18c)	..	..	..	..	..	..	..	A. Vasilios	Chauchitsa	..	..
Gold mouth-pieces	Vergina	..	..	..	..	..	..	..	Chauchitsa	..	..
Hones	Vergina	..	Visoi	..	Pateli	..	..	..	Chauchitsa	..	..
Horses	Vergina	..	..	..	..	..	..	..	Chauchitsa	Gevgheli	..
Hub-junction	..	..	..	..	..	..	Voïon	..	Chauchitsa(?)	Gevgheli	?Veles +Kumanovo
Ivory	Vergina	..	..	..	Pateli	..	..	..	..	..	..
Ornaments (Fig. 17h)	Vergina	..	Visoi	..	..	..	..	..	Chauchitsa	..	..
(Fig. 17i)	..	..	Visoi	..	Pateli (1)	..	..	..	..	..	..
Pendants:											
animal	..	..	Visoi	Bottiaeans	..	..	..	..	Chauchitsa	..	..
axe, double	Vergina	..	..	..	..	..	..	..	Chauchitsa	..	..
axe (on rod)	..	..	..	..	..	..	..	..	..	Axioupolis	..
bead see Beads	..	..	..	..	..	..	..	..	..	..	..
bean	..	..	..	Bottiaeans	Pateli	..	..	..	Chauchitsa	Gevgheli	..
bell+clappers	..	..	..	Bottiaeans	..	Kozani	..	..	..	..	..
ball	..	..	..	Bottiaeans	..	..	..	..	Chauchitsa	..	..
bobbin	..	..	..	..	Pateli	..	..	..	Chauchitsa	..	..
jug on bird	..	..	..	Bottiaeans	..	..	..	..	..	..	..
jug on stick	..	..	..	Bottiaeans	Pateli	Kozani	..	..	..	Axioupolis	..
jug on fretted cylinder	Vergina	..	..	..	..	..	..	..	..	..	..
distaff	..	..	Visoi	Bottiaeans	Pateli	Kozani	Voïon	..	..	Axioupolis	..
fretted cylinder	..	..	..	Bottiaeans	..	..	..	..	..	..	..

TABLE OF OBJECTS AND PROVENIENCES (cont.)

	Vergina	Visoi	Bottiaeans	Pateli	Kozani	Voïon	E. Central Macedonia	Chauchitsa	Axioupolis	Veles / Kumanovo
Pendants (cont.)										
herb-cup	Vergina (2)	Visoi		Pateli				Chauchitsa (6)	Axioupolis	Veles +Kumanovo
jug	Vergina		Bottiaeans	Pateli (20)				Chauchitsa	Gevgheli	Kumanovo
double jug			Bottiaeans					Chauchitsa	Axioupolis	?Veles
sphere, slashed			Bottiaeans					Chauchitsa	Axioupolis	Kumanovo
sphere, solid										Kumanovo
spoon				Pateli						
turf-cutter	Vergina (1)					Voïon		Chauchitsa (2)	Axioupolis	
triangle with pendants (Fig. 19c)	Vergina									
ring	Vergina								Axioupolis	
ring with pendants caduceus (Fig. 17c)	Vergina									
Pins:										
long bronze	Vergina	Visoi		Pateli		Voïon		Chauchitsa		Veles
iron				Pateli	Kozani			Chauchitsa		
double bronze	Vergina	··								
Pottery:										
drinking-bowl with distinctive thumb-rests	Vergina +Verria	Sarai (nr. Visoi)	Koundouriotissa							
shallow bowl with 2 handles and 2 extensions	Vergina +Verria	Sarai (nr. Visoi)				Voïon				
globular with cylindrical neck (Fig. 16h)	Vergina	Petilep (nr. Visoi)		Pateli						
double-vessel									•·	
ansa lunata	Vergina			Pateli		Voïon		Chauchitsa		
handle (Fig. 16i, j)	Vergina (rare)							Chauchitsa (often)		
thumb-grip handle (Fig. 16d)								Chauchitsa		
(Fig. 16o)								Chauchitsa		
Proto-Geometric conc. circles	Vergina		Koundouriotissa +Dium				many sites in E. Central Macedonia	Chauchitsa		
Rings:										
gold, ear-	Vergina			Pateli				Chauchitsa		
gold leaf on bronze	Vergina									
bronze-spiralling, finger-						Voïon		Chauchitsa		
bronze, finger-	Vergina	Visoi	Bottiaeans		Kozani	Voïon		Chauchitsa	Axioupolis	
bronze, hair-	Vergina							Chauchitsa		
bronze, ear-				Pateli		Voïon				
lead	Vergina							Chauchitsa	Axioupolis	
iron	Vergina							Chauchitea	Axioupolis	
with spirals (Fig. 17j)	Vergina					Voïon	A. Vasilios			

	Vergina	Visoi	Bottiaeans	Pateli	Voion	A. Vasilios	Chauchitsa	Axioupolis	Gevgheli
Torques, bronze	Vergina	..	..	..	..	..	..	Axioupolis	..
Tutuli	Vergina	..	..	..	..	..	..	..	Gevgheli
Tweezers: bronze	Vergina	..	Bottiaeans	Pateli	Voion	..	Chauchitsa	..	..
iron	Vergina	..	..	Pateli (25)	..	..	..	..	..
Wheel, 4-spoked amulet	Vergina (2)	..	Bottiaeans (2)	..	..	..	..	..	..
Weapons:									
breastplate, bronze	..	..	..	Pateli	..	..	..	..	..
cutlass, iron	Vergina	Visoi	Bottiaeans	Pateli (72)	Voion	A. Vasilios	Chauchitsa (14)	..	..
knives, iron	Vergina	Visoi	Prilep	Pateli (25)	Voion	A. Vasilios	..	..	..
spear-heads, bronze	Vergina	..	Bottiaeans	..	Voion	..	..	Axioupolis	..
spear-heads, iron	..	Vardina	Prilep	Pateli (4)	..	..	..	..	..
javelins or arrows, bronze	..	..	Prilep (1)	Pateli (1)	..	..	..	..	..
„ , „ iron	Vergina	..	..	..	..	..	..	..	..
swords, bronze	Vergina (1)	Visoi (1)	Bottiaeans	Pateli (9)	Voion	..	Chauchitsa	Axioupolis (1)	..
swords, iron	Vergina	..	..	..	..	..	Chauchitsa (1)	..	..
swords, mixed	Vergina	..	..	..	..	..	..	..	..

Macedonia we may make the same generalization. We may note too that the practice of tying a gag of gold plaque over the mouth of the corpse is peculiar to this area, if we include the border-site Chauchitsa within it, but that this practice may be later than most of the burials at Vergina, Pateli, and Visoï.

When we consider objects placed in the burials, we find ornaments with the women and weapons with the men in all areas. Moreover, some objects are common to all or nearly all areas: bronze armlets of all kinds (except among the Bottiaeans), bronze beads, long bronze coils (except perhaps at Pateli), long bronze pins, bronze spectacle-fibulae, and bronze finger-rings. One may therefore say that the ruling classes in most parts of Macedonia had certain features in common. These features are partly due to a common origin in the Danubian area and may be partly due to intercommunication within Macedonia. But we must not exaggerate the influence of the latter, since we are faced there with many local variations, which align themselves to some extent with the variations in burial customs.

The most marked differences are in the pottery. At Vergina two categories of ritual vessels were found in most of the burials, the drinking-bowl with the flat-topped conical thumb-rests (Fig. 16*f*) and the shallow bowl with two handles and two extensions of the rim (Fig. 16*g*). The former was found outside Vergina at near-by Verria, at Koundouriotissa in Pieria, and at far-away Saraj near Visoï; and the latter only at Verria, in Voïon, and near Visoï at Saraj and Petilep. We have enough evidence from Kozani, Chauchitsa, and east Central Macedonia and perhaps from Voïon and the Bottiaeans, to say that these two categories of ritual vessel were not in vogue there. Of Pateli in Eordaea we cannot speak with any certainty. A third category at Vergina is the hand-made, often clumsy globular pot with cylindrical neck, everted rim, slanting handles, and curving bottom (Fig. 16*h*). Elsewhere this was found at Petilep by Visoï and at Pateli, but not to the east of this line. The distribution of these three categories shows a strong bias towards the north-west, and a par-ticularly close affinity between Vergina and Visoï. But Pateli, standing on a direct route between them, seems to have been a separate centre. These conclusions are the same as those which arose from the study of the burial customs.

On the other hand, the double-vessel in pottery occurs only once at Vergina (AZ 8) and not at Visoï, as far as we know, but at Pateli and in Voïon. It has a long history on the western side of the peninsula: at Leucas from Grave R 10 c and at Malthi in Messenia in the M.H. period, and at Vajzë Tumulus A Grave 3 in the transitional phase from the Bronze Age to the Iron Age. Double-vessels have been found in cist-tombs inside a tumulus 20 m in diameter at Dobrača in western Yugoslavia.[1] It looks as if the connections of Voïon and Pateli in this respect were with the north-west. The bronze pendant in the form of a double-vessel (Fig. 18r), which came either from Titov Veles in the middle Vardar valley or from the area of Epanomi, is also likely to have derived from that direction.

The distribution of Proto-Geometric pottery, a style which remained in vogue until the end of the Geometric period, is entirely different. As we have seen, it probably developed early through contact with north-east Thessaly. This contact was no doubt maintained through the coastal route by sea and perhaps by land, as there are some examples at Dium and Koundouriotissa and many examples at Vergina. But the real home of the Proto-Geometric style in Macedonia is in east Central Macedonia, where it has been found at many sites and particularly at Kalamaria and Mikro Karaburnu. It is clearly a pottery associated with trade overseas, of which the chief outlets at this time were on the east side of the inner Thermaic Gulf, as they had been in the Mycenaean period. Proto-Geometric pottery is found as far inland as Chauchitsa, where the main route from east Central Macedonia turns northwards up the Vardar valley. On the other hand, it is not found at Pateli, in Voïon, at Visoï, or in the middle Vardar valley. The survival of the Proto-Geometric style until *c.* 600 B.C. indicates that overseas contacts with southern Greece were suspended during the Geometric period, and that east Central Macedonia continued to be an area apart in this respect from northern and western Macedonia.

The distribution of pendants is indicative also of local divisions. Voïon has hardly any. The Vardar valley sites have most. Thus we have bird-pendants from Chauchitsa, Gevgheli, and Kumanovo, and also from the Bottiaeans and from Pateli. The herb-cup is most frequent, both absolutely and in relation to the number of burials, at Chauchitsa, and there are further examples from other sites in the Vardar valley, Axioupolis, Titov Veles, and Kumanovo. It is found also at Vergina, Pateli, and Visoï. The pendant ending in a ball is found at Chauchitsa, Gevgheli, among the Bottiaeans, and at Pateli; that with a slashed sphere at Chauchitsa, Axioupolis, among the Bottiaeans, and at Kumanovo. Some types of pendant are found only at Axioupolis. Thus the bulk of the evidence suggests that the fashion for pendants came down the Vardar valley, either from south Yugoslavia or from Bulgaria via Kumanovo. But there is one pendant which goes against this stream: the triple double-axe form of pendant, which we have suggested was due to a

---

[1] For Leucas and Vajzë see *Epirus* 311 f.; for Malthi see M. N. Valmin, *The Swedish Messenian Expedition* 300 and 304 fig. 68, no. 49 (cf. idem, *Das Adriatische Gebiet* (Lund, 1939) 200 fig. 45); for Dobrača by Kragujevac in the Morava valley see *AI* 2 (1956) 'neue Hügelgraberforschung in Westserbien', pot no. 8.

worship of Cretan origin in Bottiaeis, is found principally at Vergina and among the Bottiaeans but also at Pateli and Visoï. Its distribution falls within the north-westerly orbit of influence.

Other objects are less well represented. Amber raises something of a problem. In the reports on Vergina a large amount of amber was included, but it has been stated subsequently that the amber was in fact carnelian. One wonders whether a similar confusion may have arisen at other sites. Both materials were in use, as Forsdyke stated in describing Lot B in the British Museum. If we accept the statements at their face value, amber came mainly to the Vardar valley sites; for it is found at Chauchitsa and Axioupolis, and on either flank at Pateli and Ayios Vasilios. As regards weapons, javelins and arrows come from Vergina and Pateli; shield-centres from Chauchitsa, probably Axioupolis, and Pateli; and knives, spear-heads, and swords from almost all sites, with the striking exception that Chauchitsa produced no spear-heads. Thus there seems to be a difference in armament between the Vardar valley group and western Macedonia. If bronze hub-junctions (Fig. 18*m*) come from or refer to chariots, their use belongs to the Vardar valley group. Horse-pendants or horse-statuettes come from all parts of Macedonia except Olynthus. Some forms of fibula are local: the triangular fibula (Fig. 18*c*) to Voïon and Pateli; the arched fibula with a catch-plate to Vergina and Pateli (Fig. 17*x*); and the arched fibula with the small pendent catch-plate (Fig. 18*j*) to Chauchitsa, Gevgheli, and Ayios Vasilios. Because the total number of objects reported from Vergina exceeds by far that from any other site, it is natural that it has many objects not paralleled elsewhere. Of these I note the numerous tutuli, the hook-tailed nails, the belt-bosses, the spiral ornaments (Fig. 17*i*), two unusual pendants (Fig. 17 *l* and *t*), and the gold leaf on a bronze ring.

When we put together all our inferences and conclusions from the study of burial practices and objects, we can draw the following picture with fairly firm strokes. In the south the rulers of the Katerini plain at Koundouriotissa used a Thracian form of burial. As they were on the coastal route by land and by sea from north-east Thessaly to Vergina, they were in contact with both these areas; this contact is reflected in the pottery from the burials. The rulers who lived at Vergina on the south-western edge of the central plain, practised a form of burial in large tumuli which had come from the north-west, whether from Pelagonia or from beyond Pelagonia. Their settlement was evidently the chief centre of exchange in Southern Macedonia. They had overseas contacts during part of this period. As Verria was in their sphere of influence they controlled the pass towards Kozani. They had some relationship—probably one of trade—with Pateli and Voïon, and their cultural affinity was with Visoï in Pelagonia.

The middle Haliacmon valley, and in particular the district called Voïon, did not practise tumulus-burial at all; it had less taste for pendants than most of Macedonia, it had its own type of fibula, and it had some contacts with the west. This last point is very understandable, because the upper Haliacmon valley, beginning from Boubousti, shared in the culture not of Macedonia but of central Epirus and south-west Albania (e.g. at Tren). In Eordaea the rulers of the rich basin of Ostrovo, who buried their dead at Pateli, were quite distinct from their neighbours in some of their burial customs. Their contacts seem to be almost closer with the Vardar valley sites of Axioupolis and Chauchitsa than with Voïon and Vergina, and this indicates probably that they used or controlled the entry via Edessa into the upper part of the central plain. They must have been powerful, because they were at the centre of a web of overland communications. The rulers of Pelagonia, who buried their dead in large tumuli at and near Visoï, had a cultural affinity with the rulers of Vergina, the more remarkable since the powerful dynasty of the Ostrovo basin separated them from one another.

We know least about the Bottiaeans who held the northern part of the central plain west of the Vardar river. If we may judge from the objects found in early Olynthus, the Bottiaeans had their own cult of the double-axe, no liking for bronze armlets, beads of amber and carnelian, and concentric-circles decoration, but a liking for many bronze pendants. Their central position on the route which follows the northern side of the central plain exposed them to influences from their neighbours, but they seem to have retained their identity even after their expulsion *c.* 650 B.C. and their settlement in the hinterland of the Chalcidic peninsula. The Vardar valley sites from Kumanovo in the north to the cluster at the lowest gorge of the river may have brought to Macedonia the love of pendants and the metal-centred shield. The sites at Chauchitsa, Axioupolis, and Gevgheli had a stranglehold on the route from the central plain towards the north, and the impression created by the cemetery at Chauchitsa is that its rulers were warlike and well armed with sword, knives, and shield.

Lastly, the people of east Central Macedonia form the richest of all the groups in terms of gold and trade, which attracted travellers to the ports of the east coast of the inner Thermaic Gulf during the Proto-Geometric period. This people seems to have held most of its territory against the Lausitz invaders, when the latter occupied Vardarophtsa and Vardina, and against the newcomers who took control of Chauchitsa, Axioupolis, and Gevgheli. When Heurtley remarked[1] that 'the relationship between Central Macedonian sites is very close', he was writing of the sites in *east* Central Macedonia during the Early Iron Age. These

---

[1] *PM* 112.

B b

sites were affected to a lesser degree by the movements which brought great innovations to other parts of Macedonia, and this is likely to have been because they managed to maintain their political independence at least during most of the period.

I have described the graves as those of the ruling class in each area. This is because iron weapons were the possessions of only a few, and those few were the rulers. The song of Hybrias the Cretan could have been sung at this time in Macedonia. 'My wealth is spear and sword, and the stout shield which protects my flesh; with this I plough, with this I reap, with this I tread the sweet wine from the grape, with this I am entitled master of the serfs'. The peasant population of Macedonia was descended from many races which had entered its confines from different directions during many centuries, indeed during some millennia, long before the beginning of the Iron Age. If our earlier arguments are sound, at least five languages were spoken in Macedonia at the beginning of the Proto-Geometric period: Thracian in coastal Pieria, Minoan-Cretan in Bottiaeis, Phrygian in the vicinity of Mt. Bermium and in northernmost Pelagonia, Paeonian in east Central Macedonia, and Greek of two dialects—'Macednian' in northern Pieria and the middle Haliacmon valley, and 'Epirote' in the upper Haliacmon valley, Lyncus, and Pelagonia. But power did not lie with the peasant population. It lay with the owners of iron weapons and fine horses, who imposed their rule and buried their dead with honours. In many cases they were not descendants of the Bronze Age populations of Macedonia. Whence, then, had they come during the opening centuries of the Iron Age?

XIV

MACEDONIA AND HER WESTERN, NORTHERN, AND EASTERN NEIGHBOURS IN THE EARLY IRON AGE

NORTHERN Epirus provides a precedent for the tumuli of Vergina and Visoï and for some of their contents. At Vajzë[1] Tumulus A was used in the Middle ·Bronze Age and down to the end of the Late Bronze Age; Tumulus B in L.H. III B and C and in the Early Iron Age; Tumulus C and Tumulus D in L.H. III C and in the Early Iron Age. At Vajzë an occasional cremation was found, but the bulk were inhumations, mostly in slab-lined cist-tombs and sometimes just in the soil (a wooden surround having probably rotted away). A cairn covered a central burial in Tumulus A. The weapons are mainly of bronze; the iron sword and the iron knives appear in an earlier context than in Macedonia, and the long bronze pins are like those of Vergina. Among the contents of the tumuli are 'pierced beads of bronze, biconical in shape but with the ends of the cones truncated; a pierced reel of bronze, biconical and with ringed ends, which carries on its surface sets of incised concentric circles with a drop at the centre of each set' (as in Fig. 17s); thirty-seven mushroom-shaped belt studs—such as are called tutuli at Vergina—but attached by a method which is probably earlier than that employed at Vergina; a round piece of gold leaf with the design of concentric circles in repoussé style which occurs at Chauchitsa; long iron pins; bronze finger-rings; bronze arrow-heads; biconical clay beads; and beads of glass-paste. All these objects are found also in Macedonia.

The tumuli of the Kseria valley at Kakavi, Bodrishtë, and Vodhinë[2] have many of the features and the contents of the Vajzë tumuli, but in addition some further objects which are found also in Macedonian tumuli. These are small hook-tailed nails of bronze, bronze buttons, some having loops for attachment as at Saraj, only one bronze spectacle-fibula, lines of impressed dots in repoussé style on bronze plaque (as on diadems at Vergina in Fig. 17g), and painted pottery of the Boubousti type. As almost all the burials in these tumuli are earlier in date than the great bulk of the Macedonian tumulus-burials, it is clear that we have

---

[1] *Epirus* 228 f., 311 f., 340 f., and 346 f. with reference to the original publications. The quotation is from p. 346.   [2] Ibid. 201 f., 310 f., 324 f., 349 f.

a precedent and not an immediate source. We may therefore conclude
that both lots came at different times from a common origin, which is to
be located north of north Epirus and north or north-west of Visoï and
Vergina.[1]

Some of the objects which we have seen in the Early Iron Age burials
of Macedonia are found as dedications at Dodona. I note a shield-boss,
an iron sword, iron spear-heads, iron knives including those with curving
back, a bronze hub-junction (as in Fig. 18*m*), a bronze ring with two
knobs (as in Fig. 18*n*), a bronze pendant with large spherical centre
(Fig. 18*u*), armlets of all three types, armlets with spirals attached,
spiral-ended pins, bronze hair-coils, bronze finger-rings, and bronze
plaque decorated in the repoussé technique sometimes with the concentric
circles motive.[2] Among some unpublished objects which were found in
1938 at Vaxia, in the upper valley of the Arachthus river in central
Epirus, there were pieces of thin bronze plaque decorated in repoussé
style with concentric circles pierced at the centre for nails and with
circular bosses, and some bronze pendants like those found at Axioupolis
(Fig. 19*a*).

An important site is still being excavated at Vitsa near Monodendri.
Situated 1,000 m high, it is near the Voïdhomati river, a tributary of the
Aous. The first report by Miss Kouleimane was of a cemetery with
burials in three layers; the corpses were laid on their backs in an extended
position (as in Macedonia) with one exception, and there was no general
orientation.[3] The cemetery was used throughout the Geometric period
and on into the fifth century B.C., as is shown by imported bronze vessels
and imported pottery from Corinth, and later from Athens. Burials
were made in simple trenches; in cist-tombs, lined on the sides with
upright slabs and roofed with branches, over which stones were placed;
and under a cairn of stones. Only in the fifth century were the cists
roofed as well as lined with slabs. There was not a tumulus of soil over
this cemetery. The graves were close-packed, and each was marked by
a single row of white stones round it. The local pottery was mainly of
the Boubousti type, and the jug with cut-away neck and the cantharos
were popular. Miss Kouleimane described among others Burial 9, which
had an iron sword of the northern type with remains of ivory on the hilt
and a wooden scabbard tipped with iron, and a Proto-Corinthian aryballos of the eighth century B.C.; and Burial 21 of the same date, with

---

[1] For relations between Epirus and Macedonia in the transitional phase between the
Late Bronze Age and the Early Iron Age see p. 314 above.

[2] Carapanos pls. 54, 4; 57, 2; 58, 1, 3, 5, and 9; pl. 53, 7; pl. 52, 20 hub-junctions, 24, 17;
pl. 50, 9, 11, 12, cf. *Ep. Chron.* 1935. pl. 22*b* and *PAE* 1932. 50 f.; *Ep. Chron.* 1935. 242 and
pl. 22 *b* 2 and 3, armlets with spirals; 242 and pl. 22 *b* 4 and 14; 242 and pl. 22 *b* 25; pl. 22*b*;
237 f. pl. 21 *a* 15 and 16, and pl. 22 *a* 3 (gold leaf).

[3] *AD* 21 (1966 [1968]) B2. 289 f. with pls. 291 and 292.

vessels of the local pottery and a bronze fibula, of which the leaf-shaped back is decorated in the tremolo technique.[1]

A further thirty-three burials have been excavated by Mrs. Vokotopoulou. She has published a preliminary report. Cairns of stones were common. The local hand-made ware provided examples also of the rounded pot with conical neck and everted rim (as at Pateli) and the double-vessel (see p. 366 above).[2] The imported Corinthian pottery gave a date in the eighth century B.C. to certain objects: a large iron knife or hacking-sword, a bronze phalaron with a spike (evidently a shield-boss), and three iron spear-heads (all in one grave).[3] Earlier than these burials were two spiral-headed roll-pins of iron in a woman's grave, a pair of bronze spectacle-fibulae, specimens of the rounded pot with conical neck and everted rim (as in Fig. 16*h*), a pair of iron spectacle-fibulae, a necklace of gilded bronze beads, one bronze and three iron finger-rings found beside a woman's fingers. Three double-vessels, two spiralling bronze finger-rings, and a head-stone or marker 74 cm high.[4] Part of the habitation site was found only 20 m away. The earliest burials are certainly of the earliest Geometric period and may be of the late Proto-Geometric period. Mrs. Vokotopoulou kindly showed me some of her latest finds in the museum at Ioannina in September 1968: these included some long bronze coils (as in Fig. 17*a*), beads of amber, biconical clay beads, and one flat-topped thumb-rest handle from a bowl as in Fig. 16*f*.

The cave site at Tren near Little Prespa Lake probably overlapped the early part of this period, as it has some features in common with Macedonia: jugs with cut-away necks, examples of the *ansa cornuta*, a biconical bronze bead, some pottery of the Boubousti type, and some flat-topped thumb-rests less conically shaped than those at Vergina.[5] One jug with a cut-away neck is a miniature one of unusual shape (Fig. 16*v*); it is exactly like a miniature bronze jug in the Benaki Museum collection.[6] The site at Tren was not occupied again until the late Hellenistic period.

Further north in the region of the lakes it is reported that pottery of the Boubousti type and 'thumb-grip' handles (i.e. with thumb-rests)

---

[1] Illustrated ibidem, pl. 292 *c* (sword) and *d* (fibula); an iron knife and an iron spear-head are shown on the same plate.

[2] *AD* 22 (1967 [1969]) B2. 348 f. and pl. 250 *b* and *d*. Of the double-vessels shown the first resembles one from a Vajzë tumulus burial (*Epirus* fig. 17, 11) and the second one from Vergina (*Vergina* 192 fig. 38 *AZ* 8).

[3] The sword is described as like one in Snodgrass, *EGA* 101 fig. 6, item *g* (from Halus, also eighth century). The phalaron is the boss of a shield laid on the head, as at Chauchitsa (see p. 350 n. 1 above); the live warriors in *Il.* 10. 153 slept head on shield, and here the shield was placed over the head of the dead warrior.

[4] Some of these are illustrated in *AD* 22 figs. 250–4.

[5] *StH* 1967. 142 f. and fig. 3.

[6] Ibid. fig. 3, 17 and *AE* 1937. 2 pl. 1*d*.

connect the area closely with Pelagonia.[1] When I visited the museum at Ochrid there was little of this period on show (only a bronze armlet of six rings with a flattish surface, and bracelets of one turn with thickened ends as in Fig. 17*z*), but V. Lahtov was probably justified in associating the area with the culture of Macedonia in his Phase I, 1150–800 B.C., as well as later.[2]

We shall know much more when all the finds are published, but we may hazard the suggestion that, as in the preceding period, the phenomena at Vaxia and at Vitsa are to be explained by postulating a common source of influence and not any direct relationship between Epirus and Macedonia. At the same time we must remember that in its local pottery central Epirus goes with the large north-western block, which comprises the upper Haliacmon valley, central Albania, and to some extent Pateli and Visoï; this is shown by the so-called 'Boubousti' painted ware with geometric designs and the coarse ware with plastic ornamentation, which persisted from the Late Bronze Age into classical times. These wares are indicative of the settled populations and not of the newcomers at Vaxia and Vitsa.

Central Albania provides a closer parallel to the great cemetery of tumuli at Vergina than northern Epirus does. In the first place the tumuli in the Mati valley, in the Fand valley of Mirditë, and in the Zadrimë plain run into several hundreds (Vergina too having some 300 tumuli), whereas those in the Kseria valley and at Vajzë are numbered rather in tens or less. In the second place the tumuli in and north of the Mati valley were made predominantly in the Early Iron Age,[3] and some tumuli were constructed in the Hellenistic period, whereas the tumuli of northern Epirus which have been excavated were constructed in the Bronze Age or immediately after it. The group of some twenty-five tumuli at Pazhok between the Shkumbi and the Devoli rivers is an intermediate site: the cemetery is larger than the various cemeteries to the south, and all the tumuli so far excavated have been within the Bronze Age.[4] Similarly in their contents the Pazhok group has weapons of bronze only, the northern Epirus group has weapons mainly of bronze, and the Mati valley group has weapons predominantly of iron.

The types of fibula and the pins found in these groups are interesting. Pazhok has none of either. Northern Epirus has many long bronze pins and a few iron versions of the same, with a coverage probably of the centuries *c*. 1200–1000 B.C., and one spectacle-fibula found together with a long bronze pin from a tumulus-burial at Vodhinë.[5] The Mati valley

---

[1] *PM* 94 n. 2, 229; *Zbornik Arheološkog Muzeja* i (1956) 125 with a reference to D. Garašanin in *Muzeji* 7 (1952) 55 f., which I have not seen.

[2] V. Lahtov, *Problem Trebeniske Kulture* (Ochrid, 1965) 200 f.

[3] *SA* 1964. 1. 102. More than twenty-five of the thirty-five tumuli excavated were of the Early Iron Age.   [4] Ibid. 95 f.   [5] *Epirus* 350 and 355 f.

group has neither long pins nor spectacle-fibulae, but it has two violin-bow fibulae of L.B.A. date, a fine arched fibula of the type found near Prilep and dating there *c.* 1200–1150 B.C., a small number of fibulae with a swollen arch and button-topped squarish catch-plate (as in Fig. 20*a*), and most frequently the arched fibula with two springs, a waisted catch-plate sometimes engraved, and two slight buttons on the arch (Fig. 18*q*).[1] Examples of the last two types are in the Benaki Museum collection from Macedonia, one with an engraved, waisted catch-plate coming from Titov Veles.[2] The absence of the spectacle-fibula in the tumuli of central Albania is particularly striking, when we remember its great frequency in Macedonia and especially in the tumuli of Vergina. In addition there are no iron swords in the tumuli of central Albania.

If we may judge from the short summaries of the Mati valley tumuli excavations,[3] the points of resemblance with Macedonia are close but they are limited. They may be described briefly. The tumuli of soil, 12–30 m in diameter, forming groups of 3 to 5 or up to 15 tumuli, and amounting in all to a cemetery numbering hundreds of tumuli. Some tumuli have a peribolos of stones,[4] others do not. The dead were laid sometimes on a floor of pebbles, but usually on the soil; and they were enclosed with a trellis, which has wasted away. Inhumation was usual, but the bones had almost all disappeared. There were some incinerations, and some burials in which the bones were not completely incinerated. Some of the contents resemble those in Macedonia. Iron spear-heads are the most common, some being very large and exceeding 60 or even 70 cm in length; iron knives, often curved; and iron cutlasses some 50–60 cm long.[5] Double-bladed axes of iron, compared by the excavators with Minoan axes, but axes for use and not, as in Macedonia, miniatures.[6] The bronze ornaments include armlets of many spiralling turns and armlets with overlapping ends (as in Fig. 17*e* and *f*, but not of the heaviest kind as in Fig. 17*z*; diadems of bronze plaque; belt-studs or plaques; large biconical beads with projecting knobs at the centre; collared biconical beads; double-shanked hairpins (Fig. 20*b*); tweezers; buttons (as in Fig. 17*dd* and Fig. 18*s*); miniature jug pendants; and long chain-like pendants, which include the solid sphere and the slashed sphere. The top-piece of such a chain-like pendant[7] is shown in Fig. 20*f*, its dotted-circles ornamentation resembling that found at Axioupolis (Fig. 19*c*). One such chain of fourteen units was found attached to the

---

[1] *SA* 1964. 1. 102 f. with pl. xiv, 1–9.   [2] *AE* 1937 2. 519 f. with pl. iv *h* and *i*.
[3] *BUSS* 1955. 1. 110 f.; *SA* 1964. 1. 102 f.
[4] *BUSS* 1955. 1. 112 fig. 1 shows a circular peribolos one stone wide, about 12 m in diameter, within a tumulus some 20 m in diameter.
[5] Ibid. fig. 3, 10–13.   [6] Ibid. fig. 1; *SA* 1964. 1 pl. xi, 1 and 2.
[7] *SA* 1964. 1. pl. xv, 1. Below the top-piece there are four chains, each of ten units. Another is shown *in situ* in *BUSS* 1955. 1. 124 fig. 11.

remains of a leather belt, which had its own bronze ornaments. Pieces of woollen fabric with their bronze buttons survived in some burials. Of the necklaces the beads were mostly of amber; a few were of glass-paste, and a very few of clay; and there were small truncated biconical beads of bronze.

The pottery from the Mati tumuli has a rather limited range of shapes. The cantharos is most common, usually with two upstanding handles, and sometimes with two low-set, rather heavy handles. The former variety is decorated in the Lausitz manner with fluting on the body and often on the handles. A mammiform knob is shown on one such pot.[1] The jug with cut-away neck is also common. Painted and striated geometric designs of the Boubousti type are found on a few cantharoi and jugs. Small cups were also found. Some vessels were covered with a bright metallic black varnish.

One may note here the unimportance or even the absence of some features which are salient in Macedonia and especially at Vergina: the tutuli, the long bronze coils, the torques, and the two classes of bowl, one with the flat-topped thumb-rests[2] and the other with the pinched-out extensions to the rim and two handles. Thus we can again deduce that there are points of similarity and also points of difference between central Albania and Macedonia. As regards points of similarity, the closest links seem to be between central Albania and Axioupolis.

The source of the similarities may lie in one area or the other, or it may be external to both areas. We may take as an example an unusual kind of handle. In his report of the excavations at Chauchitsa[3] Casson drew attention to the *ansa lunata* nature of the lid-handle (Fig. 16q), of the extensions to the handles which Heurtley called 'thumb-grips'[4] (Fig. 16 d and n), and of the horizontal handles sprouting from the rim of a shallow bowl. The last came from the west mound, the others from graves on the tumulus-mound; only one was associated with objects of interest, namely in Grave (9) with a herb-cup and a plain *cothon*-shaped vessel of red ware. The same unusual type of handle occurs sometimes at Vergina on the ritual vessel which is a shallow bowl with two handles and with two pinched-out pieces of the rim (Fig. 16g); for the latter pieces are sometimes of the *ansa lunata* shape.[5] Handles of this kind, whether *lunata* or *cornuta*, have a long history in eastern Italy, the Danube area (including an occasional Lausitz piece), and west Yugoslavia.[6]

---

[1] *BUSS* 1955. 1. pl. xiv, 4.

[2] One such handle is shown in *BUSS* 1955 1. 128 fig. xv, 3.

[3] *BSA* 26. 11, 16 and 17 with fig. 3f, g, i, j, and Fig. 6b.

[4] *PM* 94 n. 2 and 104; but he used the term for a wider range of handles than I do.

[5] Illustrated in *AD* 17. 1 pl. 103 b 2 and c 1 (Tumulus III); pl. 149 d 3 (Tumulus LXV K); pl. 153 d 1 (Tumulus LXV BZ); and in *Vergina* p. 107 and pl. 64 ΑΓ 25, and in a double-vessel AZ 8 p. 112, 191 f., fig. 38 and pl. 72.   [6] Ebert 1. 179.

The nearest neighbours in time and space to the Macedonian examples are those found at Gajtan near Scodra. There they occur in Stratum II and are very characteristic of Stratum III, which includes a long period of the Iron Age.[1] They are so common there that Bep Rebani regards them as a 'purely Illyrian form'. At Gajtan these handles were decorated with grooves and circles. This is not the case at Chauchitsa and Vergina. We may then see a common source for the handles at Chauchitsa, Vergina, and Gajtan, a source definitely in the north-west and perhaps Illyrian in nature.

Among the pots which are illustrated from the tumuli of the Mati valley and attributed to the Early Iron Age is a two-handled pot with extensions, broad and flattened (Fig. 16*r*),[2] as at Chauchitsa. Together with the handles of the *ansa cornuta* type at Gajtan, Rebani shows a type of handle which is a thumb-rest (Fig. 16*f*);[3] it is very similar in shape to that found at Saraj by Visoï and very often at Vergina. The type at Gajtan (Fig. 16*s*) is probably earlier in date, and it is certainly less developed, than those at Vergina; but again a common source may be postulated. The Vergina flat-topped truncated-cone thumb-rest seems to be an imitation of a common metal form, such as we find in bronze pendants in Macedonia especially at Axioupolis (Fig. 19*c*, right; Fig. 17*y* and *aa*; Fig. 18*p*) and many centuries later at Kruje in Albania on silver ear-rings (Fig. 19*g*).[4] An ear-ring (probably in bronze) of a similar shape but lacking the terminals was found in Tumulus III *Δ* at Vergina, and may be regarded as a remote relation of the Kruje ear-rings.[5]

A number of stray finds from north Albania in the general region of Scodra are attributed by Frano Prendi to the Early Iron Age. They include curving-backed one-bladed knives of iron; double-bladed axes of iron; double-shanked pins (as in Fig. 20*b*); a fibula of Blinkenberg's Thessalian type with an engraved zigzag on the long narrow catch-plate; a fibula as in Fig. 18*q*; bronze buttons as in Fig. 18*s*; a large bronze bead of the biconical type with collared ends as in Fig. 19*k*, but with a more massive centre and with four projecting knobs at the widest part of the centre; a bronze bead as in Fig. 17*m*, but with short cylindrical ends instead of collars; a slashed-sphere pendant, with top and foot as in Fig. 18*u*, but with a collar just above the foot; and a miniature bronze vessel (Fig. 20*c*) as a pendant, which is unlike the Macedonian type in shape.[6]

---

[1] B. Rebani, 'Keramika ilire e qytezës së Gajtanit' in *StH* 1966. 1. 52 f. with figs. 5 *b*, *c*, and 11. He concludes on p. 65 'vegje *cornutae* . . . janë përpunim i drejtpërdrejte i formës ilire'.   [2] *SA* 1964. 1. 103 and pl. xvi, 5.

[3] *StH* 1966. 1. 53, fig. 6ç.   [4] *SA* 1964. i. 153 and pl. vii, 3, 4, 6, 7.

[5] *AD* 17. 1. 224 and fig. 10 iii *Δ* 81, granulated like one of the much later ones at Kruje. Grave *Δ* at Vergina was completely undisturbed.

[6] *BUST* 1958. 2. 109 f. with figs. 6–15. The shape of the bronze vessel occurs at Glasinac.

As Prendi points out, these finds fill a gap between the Mati valley tumuli and the Illyrian type-site Glasinac near Sarajevo in north-western Yugoslavia. One line of communication overland between central Albania and Yugoslavia crosses the Drin at Kukës and passes high above the White Drin to Prizren and to Peć. In this area two sites of strategic importance were occupied for the first time in the Early Iron Age: the 'Fortress of Skanderbeg', Qytet i Skanderbegut, 1225 m above sea level, south of the Drin, and a similar height by Rosuje, north of the Drin, near Kukës. It looks as if a new and warlike people came southwards by this route into the Mati valley and kept possession of some high hill-sites.

The famous cemetery of Glasinac is so named after the plateau 'Glasinac', 950 m above sea-level. It has more than 20,000 tumuli, many of which were excavated in the 1890s.[1] The tumuli range in diameter from 5 to 30 m and even to 40 m. They contain usually one burial but not infrequently a considerable number of burials, fifteen or more; the burials of some men are cremations, and those of the rest are inhumations. In the latter case the body was laid on the ground and a cairn of stones was piled on top, as at Chauchitsa. In one instance only were the bones of a skeleton piled up and the skull put on the top,[2] as was done commonly at Pateli. It was noted that on rare occasions an iron double-axe was laid with a dead man, and then apparently as the weapon or the emblem of an outstanding chieftain.[3] The principal weapon was the spear with an iron head, ranging from 12 to 60 cm in length, and with an iron butt; each warrior was buried with several spears, as many sometimes as ten. In the first excavations only one iron sword was found as compared with many spear-heads, six curved cutlasses, and thirteen knives, all of iron.[4] The predominance of the spear and the virtual absence of the sword are paralleled at Chauchitsa. Bronze buttons with a ring on the back and bronze buttons as in Fig. 18s with a bar on the back were very common; one grave contained seventy buttons.[5]

There were several kinds of bronze pendant: the slashed sphere without a foot and with a foot (as Fig. 18f and u), the bird without and with a foot, the bobbin-pendant as in Fig. 19d but probably with two terminals, the miniature jug of a shape like that in the Scodra district shown in Fig. 20c, a variant of Fig. 17v, the miniature four-spoked wheel (as in Fig. 18t), and horse-pendants. There are also pendants hanging on pendants as in the Mati tumuli. One of these, from the Hrastovača group, begins with a ring and a triangular top-piece, from which hang other rings;

---

[1] The early reports are in *WMBH* 1 (1893) 61 f., 113 f., 126 f.; 3 (1895) 1 f.; 6 (1899) 13 f. There is a summary in Ebert 3. 340 f.

[2] *WMBH* 1. 72 f.   [3] *WMBH* 1. 77.   [4] *WMBH* 1. 74 f.

[5] *WMBH* 1. 78 f. and fig. 49, showing a double one (like the triple one from Gevgheli in Ebert 2 pl. 106c).

another has a ring, a bobbin-shaped pendant, and a bell-shaped pendant below it.[1] Both of these types are very reminiscent of the Axioupolis pendants shown in Fig. 19. There are also some examples of what I have called the bronze hub-junction, shown in Fig. 18*m*. At Hrastovača one of them has a bronze plate shaped like the blade of a turf-cutter, of which the shaft fits into the hub-junction; and in the two tumuli of Taline there are both a hub-junction and a turf-cutter pendant (as in Fig. 17*p*) cast complete with a cross at its top.[2]

There are also a number of other objects which are like those found in Macedonia. The two spirals of bronze wire are linked with a high upstanding loop as in Fig. 17*i*. There is a double-axe cast on a hollow rod,[3] which is a variant of the Vergina triple double-axe pendant. There are diadems of bronze plaque; bronze torques (as in Fig. 18*d*); spectacle-fibulae with the eight-shaped join (as in Fig. 17*b*); spectacle-fibulae in bronze and some in iron of the simple kind, in which the wire runs directly from one spiral to the other (as in Fig. 18*e*); an ornamental disc, 3·5 cm in diameter, with hooks for attachment as at Vergina (in burial LXIV *Γ*); a four-spoked wheel forming the centre of a flat round disc, that is to say a miniature of the shield-centres of Chauchitsa (as in Fig. 18*a*); the two-springed arched fibula with a quadrangular catch-plate; the two-springed fibula with a small triangular catch-plate (as in Fig. 18*j*); double-shanked pins (as in Fig. 20*b*); pins with a spiralling top; at Hrastovača, rings with knobs (as in Fig. 18*n*); shield-centres decorated with four large bosses and between each pair of bosses with two rows of four little bosses each, and with a disc-topped ferrule arising from the convex centre-piece; and armlets of various kinds.[4] On the other hand, there is little connection between the pottery of Glasinac and that of Macedonia.[5]

There are many other sites with many tumuli in north-west Yugoslavia which have the Glasinac culture or variations of it. The occupants were very conservative. Thus Sanskimost and Debelo Brdo retained the use of the *ansa cornuta* after 550 B.C., and Sanskimost that of the long bronze pin with several bulbs and discs, the so-called 'Mehrkopfnadel'.[6] Donja

---

[1] *WMBH* I. 100 figs. 165, 166, and 204 (sphere); 100 f. and 124 fig. 30 (birds); fig. 183 (bobbin); figs. 172 f. (jug); fig. 185; fig. 203; and 3. 8 fig. 10 (wheels); Ebert 3. 341 (horses); vi. 13 figs. 6 and 7 (Hrastovača).

[2] *WMBH* 6. 42 figs. 25 and 26; and at Glasinac in *WMBH* I fig. 156 and 102 figs. 192–4.

[3] *WMBH* I fig. 161 and 3. 25 fig. 65 from Tumulus III.

[4] *WMBH* I. 81 and Ebert 3. 341 (diadem); 80 fig. 53 (torque); 81 f. and Ebert 3. 341 (spectacle-fibula); fig. 102 and *AD* 17. 2. 227 fig. 10 top right-hand corner; 91 fig. 105 (disc with four-spoked wheel centre); 83 f. and figs. 60–70 (fibulae); fig. 135 (pins); 6. 38 fig. 8 (ring with knobs); I. 135 fig. 13 (shield centre); Ebert 3. 341 (armlets). The unusual object in I. 135, shown as a 'Zierkopf' of bronze, occurs also at Dodona (Carapanos pl. lii, 18).

[5] *WMBH* I. 103 f. and Ebert 3. 342 (pottery); the use of grooving is a common feature.

[6] *WMBH* 6. 75 f.

Dolina had the hub-junctions, the bronze buttons with a loop behind, and the rings with knobs in the fifth century B.C.; the shield-centre with a spike, the button with slits, and the slashed-sphere pendant in the sixth century B.C.; and both varieties of spectacle-fibula, both varieties of two-springed fibula, and heavy overlapping bronze armlets in the seventh century B.C.[1]

The most important area with this culture for the purpose of chronology is the homeland of the Liburni. A decisive date there is *c.* 900 B.C. when the Liburnian sites were destroyed; for thereafter new sites were adopted and the expansion of the Liburni began. The formation of Liburnian culture preceded 900 B.C. It was marked by the simple form of spectacle-fibula 'with a slanting join' (as in Fig. 18*e*); the large arched fibula with two buttons (as in Fig. 17*w*) and a geometric engraving as at Saraj and elsewhere; and by the ornament with two spirals joined by a wire coil resembling a modern spring; and circular armbands with no opening.[2] These objects are dated by S. Batović some to the latter part of the Bronze Age and others to the beginning of the Iron Age or Hallstatt II. In the latest part of the period before 900 B.C. there appeared the spectacle-fibula with the eight-shaped link; the open-ended arm-band with ribbed surface (as in Fig. 19*m*); bronze torques (as in Fig. 18*d*); and amber and glass beads.[3] In the next period *c.* 900–800 B.C. the same arched fibula was used but without the buttons; the spectacle-fibula was small; the ornament of two spirals of bronze wire linked with a high upstanding loop appeared (as in Fig. 17*i*); and torques and hairpins with a conical head (as in Fig. 20*o*) were in vogue. In Phase III, *c.* 800–600 B.C., which Batović splits into A and B, the spectacle-fibula was larger; arched fibulae were made of twisted wire in A and disappeared thereafter; the ornament of two spirals of bronze wire linked with a high upstanding loop continued in use throughout; bronze arm-bands of several spirals (as in Fig. 17*e*) and miniature four-spoked bronze wheels (as in Fig. 18*t*) came into use, the latter in B. There was much amber *c.* 800–600 B.C., and pendants of flat bronze plaque with two bird- or animal-heads were worn.[4] The conclusions of Batović fit in well with the dating of the Glasinac culture to *c.* 900 B.C. and of its expansion in the ninth century B.C.[5]

We are fortunate in having some literary evidence which bears on

---

[1] Zdravko Maric in *Glasnik* 1964 'Donja Dolina'.
[2] Š. Batović 'Die Eisenzeit auf dem Gebiet des illyrischen Stammes der Liburnen' in *AI* 6.
[3] *AI* 6. figs. 7 and 8 for the fibulae, which are of Blinkenberg's Type II 11*b*.
[4] Most of the objects are illustrated in *AI* 6 in the plates.
[5] For instance R. Vulpe in *BUST* 1957. 2. 172 f. The Liburni inhumed their dead in a contracted position in slab-lined cist-tombs, sometimes under a tumulus of earth, or in a mass grave. Pithoi were used occasionally for children; the graves contained no iron but objects of bronze, amber, ivory, pottery, and later gold and silver.

central Albania. During the Bronze Age this area, we have argued, was held by Greek-speaking peoples, who occupied the coast of the Ionian Gulf and extended inland into Pelagonia, Lyncus, and the Haliacmon valley. The situation was changed by the bearers of the Lausitz civilization who seized control of central Albania and drove southwards until they were defeated by Odysseus in Thesprotia, that is in northern or central Epirus. The foundation myth of Epidamnus, the most important site on the coasting route, is known in outline. Pausanias 6. 19. 8 described the Treasury of the Epidamnians at Olympia as including a representation of Heracles and the apple-tree of the Hesperides, and we may assume that this tradition stems from the foundation of Epidamnus in 627 B.C.[1] Heracles appears again in the summary of the myth which is given by Appian *BC* 2. 39. When he was returning from Erythea, Heracles obtained a share in the territory of Epidamnus by helping the native king. On that account Heracles was regarded as the founder of the city.[2] Later on, the Briges took Epidamnus and the neighbouring territory. These Briges, as we have seen, brought the Lausitz culture to central Albania and occupied the Mati valley; they were of Phrygian stock and spoke a Phrygian language. Next came 'the Taulantii, an Illyrian tribe', says Appian. These Taulantii appear in the genealogical myth of Illyrius (App. *Illyr.* 2), which is itself of early date because some of the tribes were unimportant in classical times.[3] The six sons of Illyrius are Encheleus, Autarieus, Dardanus, Maedus, Taulas, and Perrhaebus, and the first of the daughters was Partho. Thus the Enchelees (near Lake Ochrid), the Dardani (who extended southwards to Lake Ochrid at certain periods), the Taulantii, the Perrhaebi (probably a nomadic tribe of north Pindus), and the Parthini (of the Shkumbi valley) have a leading role. This genealogy was evidently created in what is now south Albania, and created from a Greek view-point, probably that of Epidamnus and Apollonia.

This part of the foundation-myth may be related to the first expansion of the Illyrian peoples. Some of them entered Peucetia *c.* 1000 B.C.; others Picenum later in the tenth century B.C.; and others the territory of Venetia from 1000 B.C. onwards.[4] As Peucetia includes the harbour of Bari, the counterpart of Epidamnus in the crossing of the Ionian Gulf,

---

[1] See *Epirus* 384 f. for the early legends of Apollonia and its territory, as we know them from Paus. 5. 22. 2.

[2] For Heracles obtaining a third part of the Dorian land by helping the Dorian king Aegimius, see *Epirus* 381.

[3] The Illyrii, a small tribe of which Illyrius was the eponymous king, lived later to the north of the Mati river (Pliny *HN* 3. 144 and Pomponius Mela 2. 55). I have suggested in *BSA* 62 (1967) 239 f. that the Greek-speaking peoples, when adjacent to the Illyrii, used that name for this tribe and later for other tribes of the same kind. I see nothing in favour of Heurtley's suggestion that the Lausitz invaders were perhaps Illyrians (*PM* 128).

[4] Randall-MacIver, *The Iron Age in Italy* 241 f. for Peucetia; see *Epirus* 405 f.

we may infer that the Illyrians held Epidamnus by 1000 B.C. at the latest.[1] We shall therefore not be far wrong if we date the Briges' occupation of the Mati valley and Epidamnus c. 1180–1050 B.C. and the first coming of the Taulantii and the Parthini within 1050–1000 B.C.[2] The foundation myth continues with the displacement of the Taulantii from Epidamnus by 'the Liburni, another tribe of Illyrians'. We can place the coming of the Liburni to Epidamnus at some time after 900 B.C. and their capture and control of Corcyra within the period c. 850–733 B.C.[3] Thus we may regard the expansion of the Illyrian peoples as a movement on a very large scale which commenced c. 1050 B.C. and continued into the ninth century. We see archaeological traces of it in the tumuli of the Mati valley and of the plains from there to Scodra, that is in areas taken over by the Taulantii and other Illyrians c. 1050–1000 B.C. In the tumuli we have seen both Lausitz influences and Illyrian influences, and after 900 B.C. the dominance of the Glasinac culture. One route of Illyrian entry was no doubt from Peć and Prizren to Kukës on the Drin, where hill-fortresses were occupied for the first time.

When we consider the approaches from the north-east to the upper Vardar valley, the evidence is much more slender. The north-western-most corner of Bulgaria, namely Vrattsa and Vidin, which faces the Danube, has yielded objects of a similar kind to those found in Macedonia: a bronze sword of Type II with an undeveloped fish-tail top, an olive-leaf-shaped bronze spear-head, two long iron spear-heads, long bronze coils (as in Fig. 17a), heavy bronze armlets with overlapping incised ends (as in Fig. 17z), double-springed fibulae with a triangular or a waisted catch-plate (as in Fig. 18j and q), single-springed fibulae with a button-topped catch-plate (as in Fig. 20a), double-vessels and Knobbed Ware with grooving.[4] On the southern side of the Rhodope range in south-western Bulgaria the heavy bronze armlets with overlapping ends (as in Fig. 17z) are common. K. Popov published some wartime finds from Tefik Bey near Serres, on the east side of the Strymon: a large bronze bead of the biconical type with four collars (as in Fig. 19l), a similar one of medium size (as in Fig. 19i), a smaller one with two collars (as in

---

[1] The Messapian peoples of Calabria and Iapygia spoke an Illyrian language in classical times, and their ancestors may have crossed the Adriatic Sea c. 1000 B.C. The modern population of Calabria also has a trans-Adriatic origin.

[2] This dating accords with the general conclusions of the Albanian archaeologists in *SA* 1964. i. 103 f.

[3] For the Liburni at Corcyra see *Epirus* 414 f.

[4] *Bull. de la soc. archéol. bulgare* 3 (1912–13) 291 f., with long bronze coils on p. 299 fig. 225 (the weapons are reproduced in Ebert 2 pl. 103); Археология 4 (1962) 68 fig. 7 (double-vessel from near Komarevo), 6 (1964) 2. 72 figs. 6–7 (Knobbed Ware), 1 (1959) 3–4. 85 fig. 70, 6 (1964) 3. 53, and 7 (1965) 4. 53 (fibulae); *Starinar* 5–6 (1954–5) 40 f. gives heavy bronze armlets found in Bulgaria at Belenci, Mala Bresnica, Moravica, and Palilula. The last are published in *Godishnik Narodnija Muzei* (Sofia) 1921 figs. 144–6. The miniature jug, here Fig. 20e, is published ibid. fig. 153.

Fig. 19*j*), a bronze armlet of ten turns (as in Fig. 17*e*), a two-springed arched fibula as in Fig. 18*j*, two fibulae as in Fig. 20*a*, an arched fibula with a slightly strengthened arch, an arched fibula with a small catch-plate as in Fig. 17*q*, and two fibulae of a later period.[1]

M. Garašanin has placed these bronzes and their counterparts in Macedonia in Hallstatt C, that is *c.* 700–600 B.C.[2] Although I should date some objects earlier, there is little doubt that western Bulgaria may be regarded as subject to influences from that part of the Illyrian area which is now Yugoslavia, and from Macedonia, and not as being itself a contributor to cultural developments in Macedonia. There is another important consideration in favour of this view. The Bulgarian area is notable for idols and in particular for clay female figurines incised with dot-centred circles, the incising being often filled with white. Such figurines are found in the Macedonian area only at Golivats, which is east of the Vardar river.[3] The conclusion seems to be valid that the culture of the Bulgarian area did not influence Macedonia generally in this period of the Early Iron Age. The only exception we have noted concerns the burial customs at Koundouriotissa in Pieria, which were of a Thracian kind. We may add for the decades around 550 B.C. the mouth-pieces of gold foil, impressed with designs of circles (as in Fig. 18*i*), which were placed on the dead; for many of these have been found in Thrace.[4]

---

[1] *Godishnik Narodnija Muzei* (Sofia) 1921. 152 f. with figs. 133–8.

[2] In general Ebert 2. 207 and M. Garašanin in *Starinar* 5–6 (1954–5) 40 f.

[3] *Spomenik* 78 (1941–8) 270 (Golivats). This Bulgarian type of figurine is found also in the district of Zagreb in northern Yugoslavia (e.g. *Starinar* 3–4 (1952–3) 11, from Dalj). The appearance of such figurines in Proto-Geometric graves of the Ceramicus at Athens may be attributed to soldiers of fortune who had come from Thrace (for illustrations see *JDAI* 77 (1962) 97 fig. 15, 6 and 7, and 98 fig. 16, 13 and 14, and *PPS* 31 (1965) 224 pl. 32).

[4] Ebert 2 pl. 109, 1 and 2, with the holes for attachment; reproduced from *Bull. de la soc. arch. bulgare.* Ebert 2. 207 stresses the strong separation of the north-west Balkans from the north-east Balkans, which is attributed by G. Wilke to ethnic differences.

XV

THE CHRONOLOGICAL FRAMEWORK OF
THE EARLY IRON AGE

WHILE it is generally admitted that most of the objects found in Macedonia were derived ultimately from the northern Balkans and central Europe, the task of co-ordinating central European archaeology and Greek archaeology has hardly been attempted in respect of Greek Macedonia. Archaeologists studying the Greek area have used such generalizations as 'objects of northern type' or 'Hallstatt objects', and they have absolved themselves from closer concern with the central European field. When they have offered a chronology, it has been based on similar objects found sporadically in Greece, where they are *ex hypothesi* an overflow and not a source of origin. Andronikos has made an important advance in his book *Vergina*, but the number of detailed comparisons with areas to the north is small. Moreover, a conspectus of the evidence from all parts of Macedonia and from adjacent regions, such as we have put forward in the preceding section, has not hitherto been attempted. There has also been a serious defect of method. A tumulus has often been dated by a particular burial. As we have shown, this is misleading; for a tumulus at Vergina, as elsewhere, may contain burials which span several centuries. Ideally a complete study of all burial-groups in Macedonia and in adjacent areas should be undertaken, but this is not possible in a work of the present scope. In what follows I hope to draw the general lines of a chronological framework in relation primarily to central European chronology, and here I rely to a great extent on the work of Batović, who starts not from Greek chronology but from that of the northern Balkans and Italy.[1]

---

[1] Of early studies the best is that of Rey in *Albania* 4 (1932). In *Prehistoric Macedonia* (1939) Heurtley did not deal with the bronzes of the period, and he was rather concerned to stress the Aegean connections of Macedonia, as he said in his Preface, p. xvii. A recent study by A. M. Snodgrass, 'Barbarian Europe and Early Iron Age Greece' in *PPS* 31 (1965) 230 f., has the same tendency. The important work of V. R. d'A. Desborough, *The Last Mycenaeans and their Successors* (1964), reinforced by his article in the same number of *PPS*, is least satisfactory for Macedonia (pp. 142–6 in particular), where he lacks geographical knowledge (putting Pateli on the river Cerna which he links with the Haliacmon), argues that 'tomb C' at Vergina (i.e. Tumulus C) contained only bronze objects (in fact it had fragments of an iron sword in the burial CB), and dates the 'disk' handles of a pot in one burial by the bronze sword in another burial. The valuable conclusions of Andronikos are on pp. 274–9 of his book; he proposes dates for the earliest burials in 22 of the tumuli he excavated, but I am not convinced that the burials in question are the earliest in each case or that his dates are all

Period I, c. 1100–950 B.C. For much of our period we have conclusions for three areas which were formed independently of one another: for Epirus by myself and others, for Vergina by Andronikos, and for Liburnia (to coin a convenient abbreviation) by Batović. Thus Andronikos placed among the earliest objects found in his excavations at Vergina (not including those of Petsas, whose bronze sword in C∆ was earlier still) ten bronze pins, 32 to 38 cm long, with a very small head, a swelling lower down and elaborate engraving both on and on either side of the swelling (Fig. 20 *k* and *l*). He dates these in some of his preliminary reports *c.* 1050 B.C. and in his book *c.* 1000 B.C. In Epirus, where some twenty-five to thirty long pins have been found (Fig. 20 *i* and *j*), the engraving is simpler, consisting usually of a zigzag line, and I dated them by their context and by their primitive form to *c.* 1180–*c.* 1075 B.C.[1] Thus we may put the more developed Vergina pins within the period *c.* 1100 to 1000 B.C. Unfortunately, as in Epirus, very few objects were found with these pins in most of the burials (*N* XIII, *AΓ* X, *AE* VI, and the fill of *N* and *AB*): one gold hair-ring, jugs with cut-away neck, one of the distinctive bowls with two handles ending in flat-topped thumb-rests (as in Fig. 16*f*), and a pot with a vertical handle on the cylindrical neck, two handles on the body turning upwards (as in Fig. 16*u*), and two mammiform knobs.[2] The best parallels for the last are from Petilep and Progon near Visoï. In that area the distinctive bowl with such thumb-rests is also at home.

N X, which contains long bronze pins, was much richer.[3] The pots were a rather bulbous jug with cut-away neck, a bowl with the distinctive thumb-rests as in Fig. 16*f*, and a high-handled cantharos. By the head were two sets of long bronze coils, each of four coils and each with a button (as in Fig. 17*a*), and a hair-ring; just to one side a single long bronze coil, three hair-rings, and a miniature four-spoked wheel (as in Fig. 18*t*); underneath the head one long bronze coil, a bronze fitting for the back of the head as in Fig. 20*g*, two hair-rings, and a small bronze object of unknown purpose; two more hair-rings were also beside the head. At the shoulders were the two long pins, heads upwards, and thirty-one carnelian beads, one large bead being of biconical shape. At a considerable distance further down and close to the cantharos,

acceptable. Much evidence was not known to him; for instance, my book *Epirus*, which summarized the reports on tumuli in Albania, came out too late for him to use (see his p. 285 n. 4).

[1] *Vergina* 234 f., 276 f., and pls. 90, 91, 92, 109, 111, 121, and *Epirus* 359 f.

[2] *Vergina* pl. 45 *N* 43 from burial *N* XIII and pl. 63 *AΓ* 13 from burial *AΓ* X. This unusual pot occurred also in *E* I, *N* II, and *N* VII (*Vergina* pl. 37 *E* 24; pl. 43 *N* 8 and *N* 16; and pls. 62 and 63 *A* 13).

[3] *Vergina* 35 f., 92, 124, pls. 44, 45, 90, and 91. For the finger-rings see figs. 80 and 81 on p. 240.

which was apparently by the feet, there were a single-coiled anklet of bronze with overlapping ends and a thirteen-coiled anklet, of which one end was pointed and the other flat. Of these objects the miniature wheel occurs elsewhere with a pot E4 having a mammiform knob, as in Fig. 16*h*, and with a finger-ring of thin bronze wire in *E* VI—which may be an early burial—and with a great many objects in a later rich burial, *AZ* VII, where its presence is probably due to religious conservatism. It has a long history from Malik IIIa as a plastic ornament on pottery (see p. 267 above) down to Olynthus in the Bottiaean period *c.* 650–550 B.C.[1] The combination of this particular type of long bronze pin, miniature wheel-pendant, and bronze anklets is found in the Tumulus culture of central Europe around 1300 B.C.[2] The bronze fitting for the back of the head is paralleled by one in iron at Vitsa in Epirus, dated *c.* 500 B.C. (Fig. 20*g*); on the other hand, Andronikos has noted an analogy at Nezmely in Hungary of Hallstatt period B, i.e. 1000–700 B.C.[3] There is nothing which militates against dating burial *N* X to the eleventh century B.C., together with the other burials which contain such long pins at Vergina.

Andronikos regarded as equally early at Vergina the arched fibula with a large spring, two small buttons and engraving on the arch (the shape as in Fig. 17*w*).[4] Batović dated the examples in Liburnia to his Late Bronze Age, which precedes Hallstatt II, i.e. to within 1200–1000 B.C. The same fibulae from cist-tombs near Prilep were dated by the excavator within Hallstatt A, i.e. within 1200–1000 B.C.[5] and by myself to the earliest part of that period *c.* 1200–1150 B.C. Once again we may take as a safe date for the Vergina examples *c.* 1100 to 1000 B.C. A similar one from Pateli may be of this period. Unfortunately only four of these fibulae were found by Andronikos at Vergina, although others had been collected from tumuli damaged in the past. This time we have a better repertory of objects found in the two burials where fibulae of this kind were present. In E 11 a large number of small shield-shaped bronze buttons, attachable to a belt by a perforated 'teat' (a sort of triangular loop on the back); two bronze finger-rings, and one of thin bronze wire;

[1] It is found also at Glasinac after 900 B.C. (*WMBH* 3 (1895) 8 fig. 10) and in Liburnia in 700–600 B.C. according to Batović's dating. Andronikos comments on the wheel in *Vergina* 255. It is no doubt connected with the bronze shield-centres having a four-spoked or six-spoked centre at Chauchitsa, and with the miniature four-spoked wheel with an extended rim, which looks like a replica of the shield-centre (at Pateli, in the Benaki Museum collection and at Glasinac in *WMBH* 1. 91 fig. 105).

[2] Childe, *Danube* 306 and pl. xi, C3 and C7, for the pins.

[3] *AD* 22 (1967 [1969]) B2. 349 and pl. 254*a*; Andronikos in *Vergina* 258, citing *Act. Arch. Hungarica* 13 (1961) pl. 5, 6.

[4] *Vergina* 230 f., 274 f., pl. 80 *E* II, pl. 81*a*, pl. 124 *γ*. In Blinkenberg's classification these belong to Type II 11*b*.

[5] I adopt here the dates given by M. Gimbutas but not her nomenclature of Urnfield periods. Batović gives absolute dates on the same system.

and a globular pot with cylindrical neck as in Fig. 16*h*.[1] In *AZ* IV the same kind of pot, this time with a mammiform knob; a jug with cut-away neck and twisted handle as in Fig. 16*i*; a small specimen of two long bronze coils, attached to a bronze button at the ends as in Fig. 17*a*; two shield-shaped bronze buttons; nine carnelian beads, one being biconical; and two armlets of very thin flat bronze strip, of two coils and of four coils respectively, which are very unusual at Vergina.[2] A large number of similarly shaped but differently attached bronze buttons, evidently for a belt, came from Vajzë Tumulus A Grave 7, and larger bronze buttons for clothing came from Bodrishtë Tumulus B Graves 9 and 10. The later burials in these and other tumuli in Epirus seem to be early in the Iron Age, probably not later than *c.* 1050 B.C.[3]

Thus the few examples of the long bronze pins and the arched fibulae of the earliest type provide us with important evidence for dating the first comers of the Early Iron Age at Vergina to *c.* 1100–1000 B.C. They already had the long bronze coil and the hair-ring, which were to be typical; the distinctive bowl with the flat-topped thumb-rests, which was to be typical; the bulbous pot with tall cylindrical neck, two handles usually on the belly, and sometimes mammiform knobs, which was to be common;[4] little bronze belt-buttons and bigger bronze buttons, which were to be common; carnelian beads, frequent later; and armlets of bronze strip, which went out of fashion. The analogies from the area of Visoï and Prilep in Pelagonia and the affinities with tumuli in Epirus suggest strongly that these newcomers came from Pelagonia, where they had been in touch with people of Lausitz culture, that is the Briges. And on the way some of them may have occupied Pateli, where a fibula of this, the earliest type, pottery with mammiform knobs of the Lausitz kind, and bulbous pots with cylindrical necks and two or more handles were found.

I include in my list with a question-mark the phalara which G. von Mehrart published as having been found together with two large arched fibulae at Vergina. He dated them to the eleventh century B.C.[5] Andronikos has related these phalara to those which he found at Vergina; the latter were not with any such fibulae, and were undoubtedly of the

---

[1] For these objects see *Vergina* 20; 85 (E18) and pl. 37, 18; 117, *E* II a–e and pl. 80; 236 on buttons.

[2] *Vergina* 74 with fig. 19; 112, *AZ* 10 and 11 with pl. 72; 142 *AZ* IV and pl. 124; 241 for the armlets being unique in the Andronikos excavations and particularly close to Central European examples as in Childe fig. 177, being a Lausitz form.

[3] *Epirus* 346 f.

[4] Andronikos shows 29 of these on his plates in *Vergina*, which is a high proportion; Petsas has only one, in *AD* 17. 1 pl. 103*a*.

[5] *Jahrb. d. röm.-german. Zentralmuseums Mainz* 3 (1956) 59, 98, figs. 11 and 20. He was relying on a report by the villagers. The phalara, four in all, are in the museum at Salonica (*Vergina* 243).

early Geometric period.[1] On the other hand, phalara have a long history. Phalara from a shield have been found at Leucas in Familiengrab S 8, dating to the Middle Helladic, and at Mouliana in Crete in the twelfth century, while phalara were worn on clothing in the early Lausitz culture. Phalara have been found at Scyros, together with arched fibulae, and at the Ceramicus in Athens, which may be of the eleventh century B.C.[2] Thus eleventh-century phalara at Vergina would not be at all surprising.

Two arched fibulae with a strengthened arch, two buttons, and a small catchplate were found in Tumulus LXV burial *AP* at Vergina, which is one of the three earliest burials there (see pp. 331 f. above). They belong to Type II 10 a in Blinkenberg's classification, and he attributed Type II generally to the sub-Mycenaean period, which in his terminology covered the twelfth to tenth centuries.[3] Together with the fibulae there were found a high-handled cantharos painted with a zigzag design below the lip, which is typical of the transitional period from sub-Mycenaean to Proto-Geometric in modern terminology, i.e. on either side of 1050 B.C.; a bulbous jug with cut-away neck; a number of iron and bronze rings with long bronze coils in the position of the head; two bronze finger-rings covered with gold leaf; and some forty beads, probably of carnelian.[4] The fact that the long bronze coils were attached not to buttons (as in Fig. 17*a*) but to rings suggests an early date in the sequence of burials. The probability is that we should date LXV *AP* within the eleventh century.

The next group of objects which we must consider consists of spiralling ornaments. It was observed by Childe that the earliest form was that in which two spiralling coils were linked by a spring-like bridge, as in Fig. 17*h*.[5] Of this form single examples were found in burials, and they were judged by their position to have been worn on the breast. They appeared already in the early Lausitz phase in Hungary. The examples in Liburnia were dated by Batović to his Phase I, anterior to 950 B.C., and their disuse after that date is to some extent supported by their absence from Glasinac, which began *c.* 900 B.C., and from Vitsa in Epirus, which began probably in the latest Proto-Geometric period, say *c.* 950 B.C. We may then propose the date *c.* 1000–950 B.C. for the first appearance of this form in Macedonia. It is rare at Vergina. It is found in two graves in which

---

[1] *Vergina* 246; for the later phalara see p. 392 below.

[2] Desborough, *TLM* 66 f. and Snodgrass, *EGA* 38 f. do not mention the Leucas phalara in their discussion of phalara. For the Lausitz phalara see Schránil pl. 28, 115. On these early phalara see my remarks in *Epirus* 355 f. and for the date of the Leucas tumuli my article in *BSA* 62 (1967) 94. The Scyros finds were published in *Arch. Anz.* 1936, 228–34, and the Ceramicus ones in *JDAI* 77 (1962) 88 and 120.

[3] Blinkenberg p. 67 and p. 24.

[4] *AD* 17. 1. 285 fig. 58 and pl. 152. For the design see V. R. d'A. Desborough, *PGP* pl. 1 G 82 *e* and *f*. One of the fibulae had an iron pin, having perhaps been mended. For an earlier type of this fibula see p. 321 above.   [5] Childe, *Danube* 327 fig. 183.

a priestess or princess was heavily adorned, and in these cases it is to be regarded as a traditional emblem in burials made after this period.[1] In *N* I, which was relatively poor, it was found with a globular pot having a mammiform knob as in Fig. 16*w*, an open bowl as in Fig. 16*b* but with a single perforation of the rim, a jug, individual bronze buttons, a small bit of long bronze coil, and an armlet of bronze wire in three coils.[2] We may perhaps date this burial within 1000–950 B.C. The spiralling ornament with the spring-like bridge is found also at Pateli. And the armlet of bronze wire in three to five coils was the rarest and therefore probably the earliest type of armlet at Chauchitsa.[3]

Period II, c. 950–900 B.C. Batović dated also to his Phase I, anterior to 950 B.C., the fibula of two or three spiralling coils between which the wire slants, as in Fig. 18*e*. This was the commonest form among the so-called spectacle-fibulae at Chauchitsa (nine examples out of twelve at one stage in the reports).[4] Only one has been found at Vergina; they are unknown elsewhere in Macedonia. Alexander in his general study placed this type of fibula in the ninth and eighth centuries B.C. They certainly remained in use for longer in central Yugoslavia than in Liburnia, because they occur at Glasinac, i.e. after 900 B.C. On balance one may put the earliest of them perhaps in 950–900 B.C.

The first appearance of the spectacle-fibula proper, in which the connecting wire forms a figure of eight (as in Fig. 17*b*), is dated by Batović in Liburnia within his Phase II, 950–900 B.C. It is found in the lowest level at Vitsa, that is in 950–900 B.C., and at Vodhinë in a tumulus burial together with a long bronze pin, where it was probably earlier still.[5] They are extremely common at Vergina and at numerous sites in Macedonia, and they remained in use well after 550 B.C. Batović carried the *floruit* of the small spectacle-fibula down to 800 B.C., and introduced the

[1] In *AZ* VII (*Vergina* 75) and LXV *Ξ* (*AD* 17. 1. 274); and in LXV *AΘ* (*AD* 17. 1. 281), which is considerably later in view of the armlets. Others were in the soil of Tumulus III (*AD* 17. 1. 223), and in the soil of Tumulus LXV (ibid. 267).
[2] *Vergina* 32, 90, pl. 42 *N* 1, pl. 72 *N* 15, 16, and 17. This type of armlet is Andronikos's category 4 on p. 241; it is relatively rare at Vergina.
[3] *BSA* 24. 14 and fig. 11*a*.
[4] *BSA* 23. 32 pl. vii*b*; 24. 15 fig. 10; 26. 24; Casson, *Macedonia* fig. 51. While Casson distinguishes the types in his summary, he does not do so in describing his individual burial-groups. Most of the specimens were found during the 1914–18 war and are not necessarily from the mound which Casson excavated. The one example from Vergina is a stray find in the centre of a rifled tumulus, A (*Vergina* 80, 148 and pl. 133). The three-spiral piece from *AZ* II e, as described on p. 142, seems to be something different. I follow Batović rather than J. Alexander, 'The spectacle-fibulae of Southern Europe' in *AJA* 69 (1965) 12 fig. 5 and 17 fig. 9, who places this type of fibula (his Class II a i) in 'the ninth–eighth centuries' B.C.; he is working on a very wide field of distribution and not upon a particular area as Batović has done.
[5] *AD* 22 (1967) B2. 348 and pl. 252*b*; *Epirus* 350 in Grave 12; as J. Alexander puts the life of this kind of spectacle-fibula (his Class I*b*) at 1050–450 B.C., the Vodhinë specimen may be of the eleventh century B.C.

floruit of the large spectacle-fibula after 800 B.C. We may conclude that the earliest appearance of the spectacle-fibula in Macedonia fell within the period 950–900 B.C. and that the vast majority of specimens both small and large are to be dated after 900 B.C.[1] As the bulk of burials at Vergina contained spectacle-fibulae, it follows that the chief period in which the cemetery was used was after 900 B.C.[2]

We turn next to the Proto-Geometric pottery. As this style continued in use in Macedonia until the appearance of orientalizing pottery, its life there was a long one. Only a few pieces can be dated with any precision, and these are all attributed to a later date than most of the objects we have enumerated here. It is to be noted that Proto-Geometric pottery was not found in any of the burials which we have considered so far in this section. An imported skyphos at Vergina, E 26 from *E* VIII, which is an almost rectangular tomb lined with field-stones, can be dated confidently *c.* 900 B.C.[3] This burial contained a bronze finger-ring, a jug, and an open bowl with two handles sprouting from the rim. This is the first datable example of this form of open bowl, which was very common at Vergina, whether with just two handles or with two pinched-out extensions of the rim in addition (as in Fig. 16*g*).[4] Two skyphoi of the same shape as E 26 but locally made are dated by Andronikos to the same time, *N* 15 from burial *N* VII and *Ξ* 2 from the soil of tumulus *Ξ*. The following objects were found in *N* VII. A cup; a bulbous pot with two handles on the belly and one set vertically half-way up the cylindrical neck, as in Fig. 16*u*; long bronze coils, as in Fig. 17*a*; carnelian beads; a bronze ornament of two spiralling coils linked by a high-standing loop, as in Fig. 17*i*; an arched fibula of twisted wire without buttons; two shield-shaped bronze buttons; a bronze finger-ring with overlapping ends; an armlet of seven coils, as in Fig. 17*e*; many nail-less tutuli and three tutuli with nails, evidently from a belt.[5] Among these objects the following have not appeared before. (1) The bronze ornament as in Fig. 17*i*. This is dated by Batović in Liburnia to 900–600 B.C., so that we may reasonably put its introduction at Vergina *c.* 900 B.C. (2) The arched fibula of twisted wire. This is dated by Batović to 800–700 B.C.; but our date of

---

[1] Alexander held that in Macedonia the spectacle-fibulae of Class I*b* 'could date from the Geometric period', i.e. from 900 B.C. Only one fibula of Alexander's Class I*d*, *c.* 850–650 B.C. on his dating, was found at Vergina; it was in *AE* V, the burial of a priestess or princess. Andronikos in *Vergina* 278 puts the large spectacle-fibulae not later than the ninth century B.C.; he has a valuable section on his spectacle-fibulae on 227 f.

[2] Andronikos puts the richest phase at Vergina in the ninth century (*Vergina* 280).

[3] *Vergina* 173 and 209, late tenth or early ninth century; Desborough, *TLM* 266, thought it was 'presumably an import'.

[4] *Vergina* pl. 37, 22. This type of bowl is classed together with a handleless bowl as 'phialo-skhema', and the class is dated generally to the eighth century by Andronikos in *Vergina* 208 f. and 277. I keep the two separate.

[5] *Vergina* 34, 91, 122 f., pl. 36, pl. 88. For his dating of the skyphoi see p. 274.

900 B.C. resting on the skyphos *N* 15 is better at Vergina. It is supported by the fact that at Vergina two such fibulae were found together with a Proto-Geometric amphoriskos *Δ* 23 in burial *Δ* X; for this amphoriskos is dated *c.* 900 B.C. by Andronikos.[1] (3) The armlet of seven or more coils. It is dated by Batović to 800–600 B.C., but at Vergina its introduction should be put *c.* 900 B.C. in view of the burial group in *N* VII. It is quite common at Chauchitsa, where its introduction may be set at the same date.[2] The other Proto-Geometric pots which may be dated *c.* 900 B.C. have no associated objects which would repay consideration.[3]

The dating of the earliest arched fibulae of twisted wire to *c.* 900 B.C. carries back into the tenth century at latest the introduction of the plain arched fibula with no buttons, as in Fig. 17*q*. For the latter precedes the former in Liburnia, and is placed in Batović's Phase III. Plain arched fibulae are rare at Vergina: a pair in C*A*, one in *N* V and one in *AΓ* VI.[4] For the purpose of dating, the only significant find in these three burials was a torque in *AΓ* VI. The torque (as in Fig. 18*d*) in Liburnia is allocated by Batović to Phase II and Phase III, i.e. 950–800 B.C. We may then put the appearance of the plain arched fibula and of the torque in *AΓ* VI *c.* 950–900 B.C. The other examples may be earlier (see p. 316 above). Although the torque remained in use in central Yugoslavia into the sixth century B.C. the nineteen examples at Vergina are dated by other objects in the burials to within the same period as in Liburnia, *c.* 950–800 B.C.[5] This carries with it the implication that torques elsewhere in Macedonia are of this period: a pair in Voïon at Axiokastro, perhaps some at Pateli and one at Axioupolis.

Period III, c. 900–800 B.C. The triangular-topped or cone-headed long bronze pin is attributed to Phase III in Liburnia, i.e. 900–800 B.C. There is one example at Vergina in burial *K* VII (Fig. 20*o*), found together with a single spectacle-fibula worn near the waist and with a finger-ring

---

[1] *Vergina* 17, 178, and 274. The burial was confused, but the connection of the amphoriskos with the fibulae was established. If a pair of these fibulae went with the cup AB 13 (*Vergina* 62), this type of fibula is again within the period 900–700 B.C. (ibid. 181). The same is true of *N* VII and *N* 17 (ibid. 34 and 181).

[2] *BSA* 24. 13 and fig. 10; Andronikos, *Vergina* 241, stresses the Central European origin of these armlets at Vergina.

[3] These are *N* 36, *E* 8, *AΓ* 35, *E* 6, *Δ* 22, and *Φ* 1. See *Vergina* 174 f. The krater *N* 36 was with an iron sword and two iron knives in *N* XIV.

[4] *AD* 17. 1 pl. 145*a*; *Vergina* 63, 230 f., pl. iii.

[5] The torques at Vergina were in *N* II, *N* IV, *AZ* I, *AZ* VII, *AΓ* VI (*Vergina* 247 f.), in LXV *Ξ*, *Π*, *Φ*, *BA*, *BΓ*, and in the fill of LXI (*AD* 17. 1. 262 and 274 f.). They were associated sometimes with arched fibulae either of the plain kind or of twisted wire and with the small spectacle-fibula worn as an ornament, and not as a fastening at the shoulder. Andronikos reckoned that his five torques at Vergina (he does not mention those published by Petsas) belonged within Hallstatt B, i.e. 1000–700 B.C. (*Vergina* 248). There are two types of end in the Macedonian torques, some having a small spiral at each end and others a small spiral at one end and a point at the other end (compare the illustrations in *AD* 17. 1 pl. 136*b* with pl. 135*a*; *Vergina* 247 fig. 86 shows the latter kind).

of bronze wire in four coils; these indicate a similar date to that in Liburnia. There are many of these pins at Chauchitsa, one at least being in a sixth-century burial.[1] It is not possible to determine the date of this pin's introduction at Chauchitsa, except that it was probably after 900 B.C. There is one in the museum of Monastir, from Visoï or the vicinity.

As we inferred from the dating of spectacle-fibulae, much the greatest period of use of the Vergina cemetery was from 900 to 700 B.C., and the ninth century marked the richest time of all in the judgement of Andronikos. We should expect the appearance of new objects at this time. Burial *AZ* VII, a woman's grave, provides some of them. They may be dated within the period 900–850 B.C., because *AZ* VII contained a Proto-Geometric skyphos, *AZ* 16, so dated by Andronikos. They are a ring-pendant (as in Fig. 17*l*, but with an upper part as in Fig. 17*v*), bronze finger-rings with two spiralling coils attached (as in Fig. 17*j*), a hook-shaped ornament, a rectangular iron strip with bronze studs, and several phalara, some being from a belt and others from unknown objects.[2] Another ring-pendant was in LXV*Φ*, which contained a torque (as in Fig. 18*d*), the earliest form of spiralling ornament as in Fig. 17*h*, and a single small spectacle-fibula worn as an ornament on the breast;[3] these support Andronikos's dating of *AZ* VII within 900–850 B.C. The hook-shaped ornament appeared also in *AΔ* I and *AE* IX, and the rectangular iron strip with bronze studs in *AΔ* I.[4] Their rarity suggests that *AΔ* I should be dated, like *AZ* VII, within 900–850 B.C. We shall return to *AΔ* I later.

The phalara in *AZ* VII are dated to the period 900–850 B.C. The phalaron in *N* IV is dated within 900–800 B.C., as the burial contained a torque (within 950–800 B.C.) and an arched fibula of twisted wire (*c.* 900 B.C. onwards). The phalara in *Y* I are dated by a cantharos painted with concentric circles to the vicinity of 900 B.C. Those in *AH* II and in LXV *Γ* were found together with large spectacle-fibulae, which puts them after 900 B.C.[5] In these graves—the only ones with phalara, except

[1] *Vergina* 29, 120 pl. 84; *BSA* 24. 15 and fig. 11; *BSA* 26. 24 and for Graves 13, 16, 17, and 18 pp. 9–12. J. Alexander, 'The Pins of the Jugoslav Early Iron Age', in *PPS* 30 (1964) 169, calling them cone-headed pins, derives the examples in Macedonia from the Hungarian Bronze Age tradition. Those he illustrates in fig. 6, 10–15, are more elaborate than our specimens. The situation as regards roll-pins is similar in that one appears at Vergina in P III, and one from Grave 6 at Chauchitsa (*BSA* 24. 15); at Vitsa in Epirus they are dated to the Geometric period (*AD* 22 (1967) B2. 348).

[2] *Vergina* 75 f., 113, 143, pls. 72, 125–9.

[3] *AD* 17. 1. 276 and fig. 10; compare a ring-pendant at Dodona in Carapanos pl. liv, 5 (upside down).

[4] *Vergina* 67 and 70; the only illustration of the hook-shaped ornament, that on pl. 122, *AE* IXζ (cf. p. 70), appears to be something else (compare p. 141 *AE* IXζ).

[5] *Vergina* pl. 86 (*N* IV); pl. 100–1 (*Y* I); pl. 132 (*AH*); *AD* 17. 1. 270 and *Mak.* 7 pl. 41 (LXV *Γ*), the last showing exactly the same embossed ornamentation as *AZ* VII ρ (*Vergina* 245 fig. 85). For the date of the canthorus see Andronikos in *Vergina* 185. Snodgrass, *EGA* 39, places all the Vergina phalara in the Proto-Geometric period, i.e. before 900 B.C.; Andronikos in *Vergina* 246 in the tenth century or early ninth century.

for those published by G. von Mehrart (see p. 387 above)—there were no objects which required a date later than 800 B.C. These phalara were worn by women on belts and on other articles, but there is no doubt that they were inspired by the male equivalent, the shield-boss, in which the spike had a practical purpose. Shield-bosses of a different design have been found at Chauchitsa and at Axioupolis, where they are probably later in date. A shield-boss of the same design but with a bigger spike has been found at Vitsa in Epirus together with imported Corinthian pottery of the eighth century B.C. Most of the Vergina phalara are decorated in the repoussé technique. On a fine shield-boss at Dodona the tremolo technique is employed; this technique is used on a fibula at Vitsa, which is dated by imported pottery to the eighth century B.C.[1]

Returning to *AΔ* I, which we have dated within 900–850 B.C., we can now attribute the emblem of the three double-axes (Fig. 17*k*) in this burial to the same period. A rectangular iron strip with bronze studs, found in *AE* VII and in *AΔ* I, was also in *AE* V, which may therefore be dated like them within the ninth century. *AE* V contained the emblem of the three double-axes, and on this one alone the tremolo technique was used, as at Vitsa and Dodona.[2] The same emblem was in *AH* II, dated by its phalara probably to the ninth century; in *Φ* III, which is after 900 B.C. as it contains large spectacle-fibulae; and in LXV *Ξ*, which has a single small spectacle-fibula and a torque, so that it might be dated possibly within 950–800 B.C. and probably within 900–800 B.C.[3] Thus it appears that this emblem appeared first around 900 B.C., was in vogue during that century, and may have run on into the eighth century if the tremolo technique should be placed then.

In three of the five burials with the emblem a large number of tutuli showed that a studded chin-strap, connected to some head-gear, had been worn by the dead woman. In burial *Y* III the same studded chin-strap was worn; but this time it was connected with a magnificent bronze diadem with repoussé decoration (Fig. 17*g*), similar to that on the phalara. This diadem, being 7·5 cm wide, was very different from the narrow ribands or diadems, 1·6 cm to 1·2 cm wide, which were found in burials *Z* IV, III *B*, III *Δ*, LXV fill (two), LXV *T*, and LXV *AB*. In describing the head-dress Andronikos, while making no reference to the Bottiaeans and Minoan traditions, commented on the resemblance

---

[1] *AD* 22 (1967 [1969]) B2. pl. 251*b* (Vitsa) ; Carapanos, pl. 54, 4 (Dodona) ; *AD* 21 (1966 [1968]) B2. pl. 292*d* (fibula).

[2] The rectangular iron strip was found only in these three graves (*Vergina* 258) ; the tremolo technique in *Vergina* 249 fig. 87.

[3] *Vergina* 78 and pl. 130 ; 53 f. and pl. 104 ; *AD* 17. 1. 274 ; the emblem in *Mak.* 7 pl. 40*b* is, I imagine, from burial LXV *Ξ* but its resemblance to that from *Φ* III is very close. Andronikos does not offer any date for these emblems in his discussion in *Vergina* 248–51. He rightly rejects the view of Milojčić, in *Jahrb. der röm.-german. Zentralmus. Mainz* 2 (1955) 153 f., that the small double-axes were not religious emblems but razors.

to the head-dress of the Minoan girl-tumbler in the bull-ring, now in Toronto Museum.[1] It seems likely, then, that we should see a Minoan tradition in the head-dress, as in the cult of the double-axe, at this period at Vergina, a tradition which was due not to intruders from central Europe but to the Bottiaei of Lower Macedonia. For the repoussé technique on the diadem Andronikos draws comparisons with objects such as the eleventh-century helmet at Tiryns, belt-ornaments at Olympia, and objects in Italy and Poland, but there are more immediate parallels at Chauchitsa in gold leaf, at Vajzë in gold leaf, and at Kakavi in bronze plaque—the last two being closer in date to the helmet at Tiryns. The technique may well have come from a common source in the north-western Balkans in the latter part of the Mycenaean Bronze Age; for the examples at Vajzë and Kakavi point in that direction. But the diadem in *Y* III is of the ninth century, at the earliest; for the burial has two spectacle-fibulae of medium size, worn at the shoulders. I should attribute it to the ninth century B.C.[2]

One narrow diadem from the fill of Tumulus LXV has a triple row of impressed dots in repoussé technique, a design which occurs on the big diadem, but this diadem and the other examples are probably later in date. The Russians found bronze diadems, one with decoration, at Pateli; as the others were undecorated, one may attribute them to the same period as the narrow diadems at Vergina. The diadems which are reported as a conspicuous feature of the Mati valley tumulus-burials are not illustrated, but it may be assumed that they too are of the narrow variety.[3] Lastly, a pair of iron tweezers in *Φ* I, the central burial of the tumulus, and another pair in LXV *Γ*, which we have dated to the ninth century, should be added to the novelties of 900–800 B.C.[4] It is interesting that they are probably earlier than tweezers in bronze.

We may place within this period the emblem of three double-axes, perforated vertically as in Fig. 17*u* to go on a rod, which were found in the tumulus at Visoï; and also at Pateli.

Period IV, c. 800–650 B.C. Andronikos excavated a group of some thirty tumuli, all within a roughly triangular area, in the northern part of the great cemetery. Petsas dug two tumuli in a separate part by a drainage channel (Tumuli C and CI). He also dug some seventy tumuli along the line of the projected road in the southern part of the cemetery, so that

---

[1] The three burials are *ΑΔ* I, *ΑΕ* V, LXV *Ξ*; for *Y* III see *Vergina* 51 f., 129 f., 252 f., pl. 101, and *Ergon* 1959. 56 fig. 54. Andronikos discusses his two diadems only (*Vergina* 251 f.); his comment is in *Vergina* 51. The woman in *Y* III had the same sort of carnelian bead necklace with a large biconical bead as the woman in *ΑΕ* V.

[2] See *Epirus* 348 f. Andronikos dates it within 900–850 B.C. (*Vergina* 254), but without mentioning the other objects in the burial.

[3] For Pateli see p. 341 above; for the Mati valley *SA* 1964. 1. 103.

[4] *Vergina* 53, 130, and pl. 102; *AD* 17. 1. 269.

they did not form a group like those of Andronikos but a long strip. It is clear from the contents that the most westerly of these tumuli, LXVI–LXXI, were later than those to the east. Andronikos expressed the view that in general his tumuli were earlier in date than those of Petsas. But the exceptions are important ones: C has the earliest burial of all, and LXV, although immediately adjacent to LXVI–LXXI, has some early burials in its unusual total of fifty-nine.[1]

Andronikos observed that in general the latest burials in his tumuli were before 700 B.C. and that some burials in pithoi and those in Tumulus I, which lay at the south-western extremity of his group, were after 700 B.C.[2] Between 800 B.C. and 700 B.C. two shapes of vessel became popular: the open bowl with two or more often four perforations through its flat extended rim (Fig. 16*b*), and the open bowl either with two or four handles sprouting from the rim or with two such handles and two pinched-out extensions of the rim (Fig. 16*g*).[3] One grave, *Z* V, has a later type of spectacle-fibula and a cylindrical bronze bead with three collars. Otherwise there are no developments or novelties until we advance to the later cases, namely *AE* pithos burial 4 with its two biconical beads of bronze, and Tumulus I with a bird-headed slashed-sphere pendant and a miniature double-axe of Minoan shape, which has a horizontal perforation of the waist for suspension as a pendant.[4]

Tumulus LXV provides evidence of the same changes in the pottery. The vessels of the now popular shape which are illustrated from LXV are in seven cases from pithos burials, in six cases from unusually poor burials, and in one case from a burial with a gold ring, a piece of long bronze coil, and a spectacle-fibula. We may put them in the eighth century, if not later. Of bronze ornaments the novelties in LXV were biconical bronze beads in seven burials, within which there were the only pair of bronze tweezers, the only herb-cup pendant, the only turf-cutter pendant, and the only truncated biconical bead with concentric circles (Fig. 17*m*) in the burials of Tumulus LXV.[5] This lot of bronzes may well extend into the seventh century. They are of particular interest because the burials in this presumably familial tumulus are likely to form a chronologically consecutive series.

Of the other tumuli dug by Petsas some have no overlap with the period before 800 B.C. Tumulus III includes in its seventeen burials two

[1] Plans in *Vergina* pl. 2 and *AD* 17. 1. 218; Tumuli LXVI–LXXI are published in *AD* 18. B2. 217 f.; Andronikos's view in *Vergina* 279.

[2] *Vergina* 277 f., arguing partly from the absence of 'Geometric or orientalising and Corinthian imports', which could apply as well to 800 B.C. as to 700 B.C.

[3] I have checked all the examples in *Vergina*; they come from later and often disturbed burials (e.g. pots Z 15 and Z 31). Forerunners occurred with one perforation only and with two sprouting handles only.

[4] *Vergina* 24, 118, 257, 279 fig. 93 (ZV); 141 pl. 123 (*AE* pi. 4); 119, pl. 83 (i γ).

[5] *AD* 17. 1 pls. 149 f.; the bronzes are in burials *A*, *O*, *P*, *AA*, *AΓ*, and *AO*.

with narrow diadems and one-coil armlets of thin wire with overlapping strengthened ends; such armlets occur in two other burials. There are three sickle-shaped iron knives, two whet-stones, a few small bronze beads, and in two burials pieces of bronze plaque nailed originally to a woman's belt. The two richest burials were of women (III *Z* and *I*). Other objects were the traditional ones: spectacle-fibulae, long bronze coils, hair-rings, finger-rings, carnelian beads, bowls with flat-topped thumb-rests, globular pots with cylindrical neck and mammiform knobs, bowls with two handles and two pinched-out extensions of the rim, jugs with cut-away necks, but also some with straight tops.[1] We may place this tumulus in the period 800–700 B.C. on the grounds that it has only a few bronze beads and no pendants.

Tumulus LV had burials of perhaps partly cremated corpses inside urns standing on two feet. There were offerings both inside and outside the urns; those inside included spectacle-fibulae, a bronze bead-pendant (Fig. 17*d*), a biconical bronze bead, iron knives and iron pins, and outside the urns were iron spear-heads, either singly or a pair side by side.[2] Tumulus LXIV had cinerary urns, bead-pendants, pairs of biconical bronze beads, a pair of bronze tweezers, a bronze pin, an iron spear-butt, tutuli, and a bronze disc with two hooks.[3] Tumulus LXVI had biconical bronze beads, as at Glasinac, and two slashed-sphere pendants, one with a bird-headed top and the other with a horse-on-stand top.[4] Tumulus LXVII had biconical bronze beads, bronze tweezers, sickle-shaped knives, bronze armlets with incised decoration, and iron pins with bronze heads.[5] These three tumuli may be taken as typical of the latest group, LXVI–LXXI, among the tumuli which have been excavated so far at Vergina.

The general impression created by this group is that a new element has appeared among the ruling class, more martial in outlook, less cultured, and more masculine; for, whereas Andronikos found more women's graves than men's, the reverse is now the case. Some traditional features survive. Among them is the wearing of the long bronze coils for the hair, but in two undisturbed burials they were worn by men who were buried with their spears, one spear being 2·22 m long, as we can tell from the interval between spear-head and spear-butt.[6]

There are two chronological clues for this last group, comprising LV, LXIV, and LXVI–LXXI. Petsas reported the horse as like that from Pateli, which resembles a mount from Syracuse dated by Sylvia Benton

[1] *AD* 17. 1. 222 f., pls. 102, 103, and 145.   [2] *AD* 17. 1. 260 pls. 145*a*, 147*a*.
[3] *AD* 17. 1. 227 fig. 10, pls. 145*a*, 147*b*. For Glasinac see p. 378 above.
[4] *AD* 18. B2. 217.   [5] Ibid. 219.
[6] Ibid. 222. In calculating the number of women's burials Andronikos assumed that women alone wore these long coils; and the absence of weapons in graves with long coils which he excavated supported his view (*Vergina* 152 f.).

to just before 700 B.C.,[1] and the iron pins with bronze heads as like Jacobsthal's pins nos. 81–2 and nos. 105 *a* and *b*, which belong the former to *c.* 650–575 B.C. and the latter to *c.* 700–650 B.C.[2] Thus we may date this last group tentatively *c.* 700–650 B.C., and regard it as more or less contemporary with the latest burials in Tumulus LXV.

Period V, 650–550 B.C. Vergina has nothing to contribute for this period, unless some objects in Petsas's preliminary report prove in a fuller report to be datable after 650 B.C. The negative evidence is not conclusive; for two-thirds of the cemetery is still unexcavated. But a working hypothesis on present evidence must be that the cemetery went out of use about 650 B.C. or soon after 650 B.C., and that it was not used for burials again until the early Hellenistic period.

The key-site for this period is Olynthus, where there was a remarkable love of bronze beads, usually with two collars, bronze pendants of many kinds, and knobbed rings. This fashion was not confined to the Bottiaeans of Olynthus, but it was followed also by the people of Pateli and by the people of many sites in the Vardar valley. It seems a likely inference from the comparative rarity of these things at Vergina, that the burials excavated there do not come down into this period. Again, a marked feature at many sites in Macedonia is the very heavy bronze armlet of one turn with overlapping ends, often engraved, as in Fig. 17*z*. This armlet does not occur at Vergina, and again we may infer that the excavated tumuli there were not in use when this type of armlet became popular.

I append now a summary of the chronological guide-lines. It must be remembered that for Periods I–IV the first appearance of an object is given and not the length of its life, which in many cases may cover the whole range at Vergina. Where an object is asterisked, the life of the object at Vergina is limited either to that period or to a period which is placed in brackets after it. For Period V I give the objects which were uncommon or lacking at Vergina and were in vogue elsewhere in Macedonia; these objects may well have been in use at places other than Vergina during Period IV.

Transitional Period (see above, pp. 312 ff.).

1150–1050. Sub-Mycenaean pottery* (Mikro Karaburnu, Saratse, Vardarophtsa, Vardina, and Vergina); violin-bow fibulae* (Visoï, Vardina); bronze swords of Type II* (Prilep, Visoï, Vergina C*Δ*); cantharos with incision (Vergina); bronze finger-ring and probably hair-ring (C*Δ* and C*B*); iron sword (C*B*); globular pot with three mammiform knobs; impressed,

---

[1] *AD* 18. B2. 218; *PM* 240 fig. 112*m*.; S. Benton in *JHS* 70 (1950) 21 and pl. V*c*. A horse on a stand reported to be from Chauchitsa is dated *c.* 700 B.C. by S. Benton in *JHS* 72 (1952) 119.

[2] Jacobsthal pp. 21 f. and 33.

stamped, and incised decoration on pottery (Vardina and Vardarophtsa); arched fibulae with buttons and engraving (Prilep); arched fibula with buttons and slight swelling of the arch (Demir Kapu); bronze armlets of five turns (Prilep); heavy armlets with open ends* (Fig. 20*x*); finger-ring of bronze band with ends meeting at an oblique angle (Fig. 20*w*); amber beads; glass-paste beads; red pottery with geometric designs in black paint of Boubousti type; Peschiera-type fibula* (Saraj); circular bronze buttons with loop on back; bronze stud with two points; ribbed armlet of bronze, open-ended (Fig. 19*m*); one-handled cup; bronze armlet with overlapping ends (Demir Kapu); and probably a finger-ring ending in two spiralling coils (Prilep).

1100–1000. Long pins with swelling and engraving*; arched fibulae with buttons and engraving*; arched fibulae with strengthened arch, buttons, and small catch-plate*; bowl with flat-topped thumb-rests; high-handled cantharos; bulbous jug with cut-away neck; jug with cut-away neck and twisted handle; globular pot with cylindrical neck, two or three handles and sometimes mammiform knobs; long bronze coils attached to rings*; ditto attached to buttons; gold hair-rings; bronze hair-rings; belt-buttons; clothing-buttons; finger-rings of thin bronze wire; solid bronze finger-rings; ditto covered in gold-leaf; armlets of thin, flat, bronze strip*; anklet of one coil with overlapping ends*; anklet of thirteen coils*; bronze hair-grip as in Fig. 20*g**; miniature four-spoked wheel; carnelian beads; ? phalara.

1000–950. Two spiralling coils linked by a bridge (Fig. 17*h*); armlet of bronze wire in three coils; open bowl with single perforation of the flat rim.

950–900. Fibula of two spiralling coils connected by a slanting wire (Fig. 18*e*); plain arched fibula in *AΓ* VI*; earliest (small) spectacle-fibula; torque (950–800)*.

c. 900. Two spiralling coils linked by a high-standing loop (Fig. 17*i*); arched fibula of twisted wire; armlet of seven or more coils; open bowl with two handles sprouting from the rim.

900–800. Great majority of spectacle-fibulae;[1] cone-headed pins; phalara*; ring-pendant; hook-shaped ornament*; rectangular iron strip with bronze studs*; studded chin-strap*; emblem of the three double-axes*; large diadem*; iron tweezers; finger-ring with two spiralling coils attached.

800–650. Narrow diadem; preference for large spectacle-fibulae; open bowl with two or four perforations in the flat, extended rim; open bowl with handles sprouting from the rim and pinched-out extensions of the rim; small bronze beads; bronze plaque belt-ornaments; sickle-shaped iron

---

[1] The only burial in which a spectacle-fibula may be earlier is LXV *AΞ* where it is associated with a large urn of Proto-Geometric style. In *Essays in Memory of Karl Lehmann* (New York, 1964) 255 f. Petsas proposed a date within 1000 to 900 B.C., but he mentioned that the use of the multiple brush freehand, as on this urn, has been attributed by J. Boardman to the eighth or seventh century. On the whole the later date seems more likely to be correct.

knives and whet-stones. Probably in the later part of the period pithos-burials; some cremations and cremation-urns: collared cylindrical beads of bronze; biconical bronze beads; truncated biconical bead with concentric-circle ornamentation; bronze tweezers; one-coil armlets of thin wire with overlapping strengthened ends; iron pins; iron pins with bronze heads; two-hooked bronze disc; heavy bronze armlets with incised decoration; and a variety of bronze pendants.

650–550. Dated so at Olynthus but may be earlier at sites other than Vergina. Popularity of bronze beads and pendants of various kinds; knobbed rings of bronze; very heavy bronze armlet of one turn with overlapping ends, often engraved (Fig. 17z).

XVI

MACEDONIA AND HER NEIGHBOURS IN THESSALY IN THE EARLY IRON AGE

I HAVE left the contact of Macedonia with Thessaly in this period to be considered last. In general the overspill is from the north. As the dating of objects in Thessaly is determined by Greek chronology rather than by central European chronology, we shall obtain to some extent a cross-check on our dating so far. Verdelis noted two forms of Macedonian pottery which reached or influenced sites in Thessaly such as Theotokou, Kapakli, Marmariani, and Halus. The first consisted of the jug with sloping neck and the jug with cut-away neck, particularly in the Lausitz style with twisted handle and grooving, and the second was the Boubousti type with geometrical designs painted directly on the surface of the pot, often a two-handled cantharos.[1] He believed the contact was made by sea throughout the period, but it is very likely that the Boubousti type which belongs much more to western Macedonia and to Epirus than to coastal Macedonia was brought rather by a pastoral people who practised the transhumance of sheep, moving as they do today from the plains of Thessaly, Macedonia, Epirus, and Albania to the summer pastures of the Balkan range. Both these forms of pottery had a long life in Macedonia, and their occurrence in Thessaly provides no chronological cross-check. But it is otherwise with the objects found together with such pottery in Thessaly.

Theotokou, situated on the south-eastern tip of the Magnesian peninsula, is on the sea-route from the Gulf of Pagasae to Macedonia. Three cist-tombs were excavated. Tomb C, dated by a locally-made lekythos to c. 1050 B.C., contained a plain arched fibula with diminutive catch, a bronze ring, and an iron ring.[2] At Vergina there were four such fibulae, of which only one was datable, to 950–900 B.C., and the use of rings both in bronze and in iron in the same burial occurred there first c. 1050 B.C. Tomb B, dated by its pottery to 1000–950 B.C., contained six bronze-headed iron pins, three bronze rings and one iron ring, a piece of a curving-backed iron knife, and part of what was probably an iron

---

[1] Verdelis 62 f.

[2] *PTh* 213, fig. 146*f* and fig. 147 *b* and *c*; Desborough, *PGP* 148; Verdelis 52 and 87; Desborough regarded the lekythos as imported, but Verdelis claimed it was made of local clay; in *PPS* 31 (1965) 217 Desborough dates the burial to 1100–1050 B.C., with reference to a fibula and rings at the Ceramicus cemetery in Athens.

fibula.[1] The use of dress-pins began earlier in Macedonia; one iron fibula was also earlier at Vergina; and the only bronze-headed iron pins at Vergina were of *c.* 700–650 B.C. While these tombs were single burials, tomb A had four skeletons and four sets of gifts, to judge from the pottery; it contained nine finger-rings of bronze and four fibulae of bronze, one of which was a plain arched fibula with a slightly strengthened arch and another was of the Geometric period. Desborough dated all the objects by the second fibula, but Verdelis has argued that the pottery spans the last stage of the Proto-Geometric period and the early Geometric period.[2] His argument seems to me convincing. The plain arched fibula with strengthened arch may be dated at Theotokou *c.* 950–900 B.C., as at Vergina.

At Kapakli, close to Volos on the Gulf of Pagasae, a Tholos Tomb contained seventy skeletons and some 300 vases. Among these Verdelis distinguished two groups of Macedonian-type pottery, which he dated, like Tomb A at Theotokou, from *c.* 950 B.C. into the ninth century; Desborough dated the earliest material as going back 'into the ninth century, if not earlier'.[3] As the ninth century is the acme of Vergina's prosperity, it is likely that some close link was established at this time between the ruling classes of Vergina and Kapakli. One group of the pottery is of the Boubousti type. The other consists of jugs with cut-away neck; some specimens have incised decoration and others an unusual plastic line. At Vergina incised decoration occurs on jugs, as well as on cantharoi, and there is one case of the plastic line. In Pelagonia examples of incised decoration from Petilep near Visoï and of the plastic line from Tsiplevets by the river Cerna were on show when I visited the museum at Monastir.[4] In this case too one may see a line of communication by land via the middle Haliacmon valley, as well as one by sea from Vergina to Volos.

Marmariani, at the foot of Mt. Ossa and overlooking the plain of Larissa, is notable for six Tholos Tombs, each of which contained many

---

[1] *PTh* 213 figs. 146 *a–e* and 147 *g, h, i, k, l, m*, and *n*; Desborough, *PGP* 148; Verdelis 87. The bronze-headed pins, mentioned by Jacobsthal 94 f. as belonging to a Proto-Geometric burial, are not of a type illustrated either by him or by Alexander in *PPS* 30. 160 f. for that period. The closest parallels are of the seventh century B.C.

[2] *PTh* 209 f., figs. 145, 146*g*, and 147 *a, d–f*; Desborough, *PGP* 149; Verdelis 87 f. In connection with the sea-route off Theotokou one may note the jug with cut-away neck and mammiform knobs of Lausitz type from Scyros, which Wace and Thompson regarded as being of the same period as Tomb A at Theotokou.

[3] *AE* 1914. 141; Verdelis *passim*, especially 72 f. and pl. 14, 1–3; Desborough, *PGP* 132.

[4] *Vergina* 191 f. (incised decoration); *AD* 17. 1. 258 and pl. 146*b*. The specimens in the Monastir Museum were a one-handled jug with an incised band containing triangles below the rim and pendent triangles below the band, a two-handled mug with a low, collared neck and with incisions suggesting a human face (both from Petilep), and the plastic line running in a large zigzag on a two-handled jar with handles set from rim to shoulder and a suggestion of a face incised above the top of one zigzag (Tsiplevets).

burials and had been in use for a long period. Heurtley and Skeat dated them *c.* 1000–800 B.C. They saw within this period evidence 'of renewed intercourse with Macedonia and probably . . . of a fresh incursion of Macedonians into Thessaly'.[1] This evidence consisted mainly of the jugs with cut-away neck, twisted handle, and sometimes incised decoration, and of the jugs with sloping neck and bowls painted with geometric designs of the Boubousti type. They believed that the line of communication was via the middle Haliacmon valley, because pottery with Marmariani characteristics has been found at Palaiogratsiano, and because the closest analogies to some of the Marmariani pottery are at Pateli and Boubousti. Verdelis wrote of some pottery being 'imported' to Marmariani from Macedonia, and he defined the period of strong Macedonian influence as the transitional phase from Proto-Geometric to Geometric or the early part of the Geometric period.[2] Some of the few metal objects have northern characteristics. One armlet of thin, flat, bronze strip is of a central European type; of which the one and only example at Vergina belongs to the eleventh century B.C. Marmariani has two more armlets of this type, but they are decorated in *tremolierstich*; such decoration on a fibula at Vitsa is dated by Corinthian pottery to the eighth century B.C. This supports the view expressed earlier by Jacobsthal that 'the eighth century would be a likely date for these armlets' at Marmariani.[3]

Three iron spectacle-fibulae have bronze bosses at the centre of each spiral disc, and one boss was covered with gold leaf. These are of a central European type; there are none at Vergina, but the covering of bronze with gold leaf was practised there in the eleventh century and later. The spectacle-fibulae of iron, if brought by northerners, are probably of the eighth century at the earliest; and the bosses suggest that they may be even later.[4] Four gold hair-rings are of a kind not found in Macedonia (Fig. 20 *u* and *v*), while one of thin, twisted, gold wire is of a technique known in Macedonia; these hair-rings were all in Tholos Tomb II, which also contained an armlet decorated in *tremolierstich*. A number of barrel-ended iron pins from four Tholos Tombs are related to pins in Italy.[5] The other objects are less distinctive, but two of them—an arched bronze fibula and a *cothon*-shaped dish—suggest as terminal dates the sub-Mycenaean period and the sixth century respectively for the life of

---

[1] *BSA* 31 (1930–1) 1 ff.; the quotation is from p. 43; the important extract on p. 10 from Dr. Leonardos's report of his excavations makes it clear that many skeletons and many vases were found in Tomb VI, for instance.   [2] Verdelis 62 f., 65 f., and 72.

[3] *BSA* 31. 34 f. and fig. 14, 8, 9, and 10; *AD* 21 (1966) [1968] B2. 290 and pl. 292*d*; Jacobsthal 211.

[4] *BSA* 31. 35 f. and fig. 15; in 36 n. 1 this type of bossed fibula has 'not been found elsewhere in the Aegean'.

[5] *BSA* 31. 33 f. and fig. 14; compare *Vergina* 259; Jacobsthal 124. For the hair-rings see also the Appendix.

this group of Tholos Tombs.[1] We may conclude that there was a continuity of Mycenaean traditions at Marmariani, as elsewhere in Magnesia and also in Perrhaebia,[2] in the use of Tholos Tombs; an inherited and continuing *rapport* with the middle Haliacmon valley; and an intrusion by northerners in or soon after the eighth century B.C. who used the tombs no doubt as rulers of the district.

At Halus in south-east Thessaly, on the coastal route southwards, two cemeteries have been excavated, one of the Late Proto-Geometric period and the other of the Geometric period. The former consisted of cist-tombs with inhumations and few or no offerings. The latter was a tumulus, some 20 m in diameter and some 2 m high, within which there were sixteen cairns, made principally of massive stones; under the cairns a burnt layer of wood ash contained bits of bones, pottery, and accoutrements, and under the burnt layer there was virgin soil, baked hard by the fire. Wace and Thompson are probably correct in deducing that the tumulus was built *after* the sixteen cremations had occurred, because all the pyres were at the same level on virgin soil.[3] The pottery includes jugs with cut-away neck and mammiform knobs, which are likely to have been derived ultimately from Macedonia, but there is no sign of the Boubousti class at all. It appears from the metal objects that some pyres were for men and others for women. From the former came 11 swords, 10 spearheads, and 17 knives, all of iron; the standard equipment for a warrior was a sword, a spear, and one or more knives. There were no spear-butts and no curved knives. Snodgrass and others have dated the weapons to the eighth century B.C.[4] Spits, 42 cm long, two in bronze and two in iron, came from the men's pyres, and they are appropriate to the period; Dodona provides the nearest analogy geographically.[5] The women had bronze fibulae, arched with a large catch-plate, and sometimes the arch was strengthened; and also small iron knives.

There is no parallel to the Halus pyres. Vitsa in Epirus has examples of burial under a cairn of stones without a tumulus and an iron sword similar to some at Halus, both sites being of the eighth century; the eastern mound at Chauchitsa had cairns of heavy stones, all under a tumulus as at Halus, but no cremations and no swords; and Vergina had

---

[1] Other objects are pieces of thin bronze plaque with rivets (perhaps like the plaque in Bodrishtë Tumulus B9 in *Epirus* 350); bronze and iron finger-rings; part of an iron sword with bronze-headed iron rivets on the hilt; iron knives, including a curved one; and probably a bit of a spear-head. The fibula is shown in *BSA* 31. 34 fig. 14, 11 and dated on p. 51; the dish is shown on pl. viii no. 131 and discussed rather unconvincingly on p. 46; Desborough *PGP* 147 mentions the metal objects, but his concern was mainly with the painted pottery of Proto-Geometric type, of which he put the start *c.* 950 B.C., while Verdelis preferred *c.* 975 B.C.

[2] *BSA* 31. 12 lists the Tholos Tombs in the area; for those in Perrhaebia see *PAE* 1914. 168.

[3] *BSA* 18 (1911–12) 11.　　　　　　　　　　　　[4] Snodgrass, *EGA* 96 and 130.

[5] Jacobsthal 14 and 123.

cremations in urns under a tumulus, iron pins, iron knives, and iron spear-heads in Tumulus LV, which is probably of the eighth century. It is probable, then, that the Halus pyres were made by people of northern origin, who settled with their women at Halus and controlled this strategic place for some time in the eighth century B.C. There is no particular reason to suppose that they had come via Macedonia rather than via Epirus.[1]

At the northern extremity of Magnesia, below the strategic site of Homolion, a Tholos Tomb of the Early Iron Age period and six Chamber Tombs have been excavated. The latter contain spectacle-fibulae, pieces of twisted bronze wire, iron pins, and in Chamber Tomb I two pairs of gold hair-rings of two types, which are exactly like the two pairs in Tomb II at Marmariani (Fig. 20 *u* and *v*). These burials probably extend down to the eighth century B.C. The hand-made pottery is of the Macedonian type, if we may judge from the two jugs with cut-away neck and twisted handle which are illustrated in the report.[2]

The excavations at Iolcus itself have shown a remarkable continuity of civilization in the Mycenaean, sub-Mycenaean, and Proto-Geometric periods and a high level of prosperity, with buildings on stone foundations, throughout the Proto-Geometric period.[3] Thus until *c.* 900 B.C. Iolcus flourished apparently in security. The children there were buried in cist-tombs. Graves of adults have not been found, but we have seen elsewhere in Magnesia the survival of Mycenaean customs in the Tholos Tomb and the Chamber Tomb. The prosperity of Iolcus was no doubt due partly to trade with the Aeolian settlements overseas[4] and partly to friendly relations with the people of the middle Haliacmon valley, which continued unbroken from the Mycenaean period. After 800 B.C. northern intruders—not necessarily from Macedonia—took control of Marmariani, and similar intruders appeared at this time at Homolion and at Halus. The stability of the situation from *c.* 1150 B.C., when the palace alone at Iolcus was burnt, down to *c.* 900 B.C. in north-eastern Thessaly shows beyond doubt that no great wave of invaders, such as the Dorians, passed through this sector of northern Greece. The Peraebi and the Magnetes remained in possession of the lands which they had held at the time when their forces were mustered for the Trojan War.

---

[1] Two tumuli of the same size and of the same period as that at Halus were excavated at Chalandritsa in Achaea (*BCH* 85. 682).

[2] *AD* 17. (1961–2) 2. 175 f., pls. 195 and 196a; *BSA* 31 (1930–1) 34 fig. 14, 1–4. The excavator dated the Chamber Tombs to the Proto-Geometric period on the strength of the 'Protogeometric pottery', but such pottery persisted in Thessaly during the Geometric period. He did not notice the analogy with Marmariani in the matter of the gold hair-rings.

[3] *Ergon* 1960 and 1961, being preliminary reports.

[4] It is important to remember that the settlements were planted when north-east Thessaly was strong; this is obviously so in the case of the Ionian settlements which were planted when Athens was strong, as Thucydides emphasizes at 1. 2. 6.

XVII

THE HISTORICAL DEVELOPMENTS OF THE EARLY IRON AGE DOWN TO *c.* 800 B.C.

1. *The Dorian Invasion*

THE Dorian invasion has cast a long shadow over the Early Iron Age. Many scholars have used the term in a vague sense to refer to any northern intruders between 1200 and 800 B.C. Thus 'Dorians' have been seen at Vergina, at Marmariani, and at Halus.[1] But if the term is used precisely, the picture becomes much clearer. 'The Dorian invasion' is meaningful only if we refer to peoples speaking one of the Western dialects of Greek entering south-western Thessaly sixty years after the sack of Troy, occupying the Peloponnese eighty years after the sack of Troy, and promoting and participating in movements from the mainland overseas in the ensuing period. The dates which stem from the sack of Troy are *c.* 1140 B.C. and *c.* 1120 B.C. in my chronology. But whatever chronological system is followed, the Dorian invasion and the breakdown of the Mycenaean world cannot be much postponed. The other point which has become clear is that, just as the literary evidence brings the leading groups of invaders from Epirus, so too does the archaeological evidence. It is of two kinds: the positive evidence in Epirus of cist-tombs, Type II bronze swords, long bronze pins, leaf-shaped spear-heads, javelin-heads and arrow-heads, and shields, and the negative evidence in north-eastern Thessaly which we have just considered.

To the arguments which I adduced in my book on Epirus,[2] we may add the further evidence from Macedonia of cist-tombs, Type II bronze swords, and the long bronze pins—of a later kind than those in Epirus—which were found at Axiokastron and Sianitsi in the middle Haliacmon valley and at Vergina. In writing of the origins of the invasion I included the possibility that the peoples of Western Macedonia played a part. It has now become apparent in Western Macedonia that Pelagonia had very early examples of some of the objects which seem to characterize the invaders; these are in particular cist-tombs, arched fibulae and spiral-ended finger-rings.

Evidence at Mycenae was lacking until recently. In 1964 when Lord

---

[1] *Vergina* 283 f.; J. L. Myres, *Who were the Greeks?* (California, 1930) 456 f. V. Milojčić in *Arch. Anz.* 1948–9. 35 distinguishes between the Dorian wave of invasion and his later wave of the ninth and eighth centuries. See also the article by Andronikos in *Hellenica* 13 (1954) 221 f.

[2] *Epirus* 354 f.; see also my article in *BSA* 32. 131 f. and my chapter in *CAH*² 2. 36. 22 f.

William Taylour was excavating at Mycenae on the inside of the Citadel wall, he found three cist-graves 'cut into the Mycenaean remains'. One of these contained a stirrup-jar, a shape which generally died out before the Proto-Geometric period.[1] This tomb at least is early sub-Mycenaean, and perhaps the others are as well, and it is most probable in view of their position inside the Citadel that they belong to the new rulers who had occupied Mycenae in that generation or in the preceding generation. The first grave contained also four lekythoi, a small jug and a miniature cup; two long bronze pins with a small, almost flat mushroom top and a small swelling lower down, above and below which the pin was engraved with rings (Fig. 20 *m* and *n*); three plain arched fibulae of bronze; and an open-ended finger-ring of bronze band, of which the obliquely cut ends terminated in spiral coils (Fig. 20*t*).[2] The pins are less primitive than those of Vajzë Tumulus A in south Albania (Fig. 20 *i* and *j*) and closer to those of Vergina (Fig. 20 *k* and *l*)—the former dating probably within L.H. III C and the latter *c.* 1100–1000 B.C.[3] Arched fibulae are unknown in Epirus, but they appear in a cist-tomb of the twelfth century near Prilep in Pelagonia, while the simple ones at Mycenae are best paralleled by a pair from the burial CA of the eleventh or tenth century at Vergina (Fig. 17*q*). The ring of bronze band with the spiral ends at Mycenae, a form of ring which is typical of the early Lausitz culture, has an exact parallel in the ring (Fig. 20*w*) and the bit of spiral in the cist-tomb of the twelfth century near Prilep, which contained the arched fibulae.[4]

Another of the cist-tombs at Mycenae had a plain bronze ring, an iron pin with a bulbous swelling in bronze near the head, and a large amphora with a smaller lekythos in its mouth. The ground above a third had been burnt, affecting the skeleton and leaving ash over the area. Work in the two metals is found early in Epirus and in Macedonia, and burning of the ground was noted in some burials within tumuli in Epirus and Albania.[5]

Thus the new occupants of Mycenae's Citadel[6] had clear connections

---

[1] *Arch. Reports* 1964–5. 10; Desborough remarks in *TLM* 11 that there was 'no specifically Granary Class type' of stirrup-jar; and in *PGP* 118 he notes the almost unique and debased specimen of this shape at Athens in the Proto-Geometric period.

[2] Illustrated by Desborough in *PPS* 31 (1965) 225 pl. xxxiii *d* and *e*. I am most grateful to Lord William Taylour for letting me use his own photograph of the pins and the ring.

[3] *BUSS* 1957. 2. 79 (in Albanian) fig. 2 = *Epirus* fig. 25; *Vergina* 234.

[4] For armlets with similar terminals from Kalbaki and Dodona see *Epirus* 401. Rings with such terminals, not open-ended but closed, are common after the Mycenaean and sub-Mycenaean period in the north-east (see *Vergina* 238 f., *AD* 17. 1. 274 and fig. 10. LXV *Ξ*; and *AD* 22 (1967) *Chronica* pl. 249*b* at Elafotopos in Epirus).

[5] *BUSS* 1956. 1. 185 (in Albanian) Graves 15 and 16 are cremations in slab-lined cist-tombs, probably pre-1200 B.C., at Vodhinë (see *Epirus* 203 f.); for signs of cremation, such as burning of the ground, see *Epirus* 229 at Vajzë (M.H. period) and *SA* 1964. 1. 102 in the Mati valley.

[6] The sequence for L.H. III C and the sub-Mycenaean period at Perati, Salamis, and the Ceramicus provides sufficient examples to indicate that the post-invasion finds at Mycenae

with the relatively backward civilization which prevailed during the twelfth century in Western Macedonia, Central Albania, and Central Epirus. That region, as we have seen (p. 290 above), was a reservoir of Greek-speaking peoples and had a 'north-western geometric style' of pottery, which in its artistic principles seems to foreshadow the post-invasion change from Mycenaean to Proto-Geometric style. Let us consider another area of invasion, Western Thessaly, into which invaders came from the west according to the evidence of literature and dialect. There at Hexalophos, west of Trikkala, a new form of burial appeared in the period 1150–1100 B.C.: a tumulus of soil, 27 m in diameter and some 2 m high, containing cist-graves, in which weapons and pottery were found similar to those in tumulus-burials and cist-graves in Central Epirus. In particular there was a spiral-ended finger-ring of bronze which resembles the spiral-ended rings and armlets of twelfth-century cist-graves at Kalbaki, Mazaraki, and Elafotopos in Central Epirus.[1] There is no doubt that the invaders at Hexalophos had come from the north-western area. They were evidently Thessali led by Heracleidae.

Thus the evidence is conclusive, if we take together the data of dialect, literature, and archaeology on the whole broad front, not only for the fact of a great invasion and its effects in the last decades of the twelfth century but also for its origins, its course, and its personnel. No other movement of peoples in the prehistoric period is so well documented and dated. As far as Macedonia is concerned, three points about the Dorian invasion are important. The Briges, who were the bearers of the Lausitz culture in Pelagonia, were a very powerful people. It was their pressure which instigated the great invasion, and in addition some of them followed the invasion through to its success at Mycenae. The great mass of the invaders were speakers of the Western dialect of Greek, and among these there were probably inhabitants of Pelagonia and Lyncus. The invasion passed altogether to the west of the Pindus range; it did not penetrate the Haliacmon valley, Lower Macedonia, and north-eastern Thessaly.

2. *The Phrygians in Macedonia*

We have already discussed the identification of the bearers of the Lausitz culture as the Phrygians, their arrival in Pelagonia soon after 1200 B.C., their expansion westwards into central Albania, and their

are fairly typical: e.g. signs of burnt human bones at Perati (*AD* 19 (1964) 2. 87); arched fibulae at Perati, Salamis, and Ceramicus; long bronze pins at Salamis (Fig. 20*p*); and spiral-ended rings of bronze band at Perati and Ceramicus.

[1] See p. 406 n. 4 and add the reports by I. P. Vokotopoulou on Mazaraki and Elafotopos in *AE* 1969. For the partial excavation of the tumulus at Hexalophos see D. Theochares in *Athens Annals of Archaeology* 1 (1968) 3. 289 f.

pressure upon Epirus before 1150 B.C., and their intrusion southwards into the coastal plain of Macedonia *c.* 1150 B.C. If we are correct in dating burial C Δ at Vergina to *c.* 1140–1120 B.C., the Phrygians reached Vergina at about the same time as they reached Kilindir, Vardarophtsa,

MAP 23. THE PHRYGIAN INVASION AND ITS REPERCUSSIONS.

and Vardina. The distribution of these sites shows that the Phrygians occupied the western part of the plain and some of the eastern part towards the end of the twelfth century B.C. At that time they were certainly in contact with their kindred in the Troad, and they shared with them the working of iron as well as of bronze. By 1080 B.C. or so the Phrygians lost their lands east of the Vardar, but contact by sea especially with Thessaly and the Troad was maintained throughout the sub-Mycenaean period *c.* 1120–1050 B.C.

During this relatively brief period the Phrygians were the most formid-able people in the north Aegean area, and there is little doubt that their services were in demand as soldiers of fortune and as workers of metal. We have seen their influence in north-eastern Thessaly which stood firm for a time against the Thessali of the Dorian invasion. It is therefore interesting to turn to another centre of resistance, Athens, where the Ceramicus or Potters' Quarter was used for the burial of re-fugees or aliens of some importance and standing.[1] In the sub-Mycenaean period at the Ceramicus, cist-graves lined with slabs, and graves cut in the earth, and in one case a grave under a cairn of stones ('Steinschüt-tung') were novelties at Athens but commonplace in the northern areas, such as Pelagonia, northern Epirus, and Vergina. When one looks at the objects from these graves in the Ceramicus, as illustrated by H. Müller-Karpe,[2] it is almost as if one were looking at objects found near Prilep in Pelagonia and at Vergina. The plain arched fibulae found in Cera-micus Grave 2, Grave 46, Grave 24, Grave 27, Grave 42, and Grave 47 are precisely like those in Vergina Grave C*A* (Fig. 17*q*); the long bronze pins with a slight swelling in Ceramicus Grave 41, Grave 70, and Grave 85 are like those from Vergina *АГ* Xa and *N* Xb (Fig. 20 *k* and *l*); the same with a larger, more artistic swelling in Ceramicus Grave 20, Grave 2, Grave 46, Grave 24, Grave 27, and Grave 42 resemble one found at Axiokastron (Fig. 20*s*); bronze finger-rings of six kinds at the Ceramicus are paralleled at Prilep and Vergina, including the ring with spiralling ends (Fig. 17*j*);[3] and arched fibulae of other types—with twisted wire, with strengthened arch, with small buttons—and fibulae of the Peschiera type with incised designs, which all occur in the Cera-micus Graves, are found also at Vergina and at Vitsa in Epirus but generally at a later period.[4] The pottery at the Ceramicus is naturally different when it is of Athenian quality, but two plain and rather crude pots resemble the early Vergina type with cylindrical neck and out-turning rim (Fig. 16*h*).[5] Conversely finger-rings with a convex, triangular plate in Ceramicus Grave 27, Grave 44, Grave 52, Grave 70, and Grave 108 enable one to understand a similar piece from Vergina, BIIa.[6] There was clearly some traffic not so much in objects as in persons be-tween the northern part of the Greek peninsula and Athens in the sub-Mycenaean period.

[1] As I maintained in *HG*[2]. 84 on the basis mainly of Thuc. 1. 2. 6 and 2. 16. 2.

[2] In *JDAI* 77 (1962) 83 f.

[3] Ibid. fig. 2, 7, 10, and 13; fig. 4, 4, 5, and 13; fig. 5, 3 and 16; and *Vergina* 238 f.

[4] Ibid. fig. 3, 9 and 10 (contemporary with the plain arched fibula); fig. 4, 7 and 8; fig. 5, 7–10, 12–13, 17, 19, and 21; fig. 6, 7; *Vergina* 231 f. and *AD* 17. 1 fig. 58 and pl. 145*a*.

[5] Ibid. fig. 4, 6 and fig. 5, 20 with a more artistic base than in the north.

[6] *Vergina* 257 as perhaps a pendant; but the size and the decoration suit my suggestion that it belonged originally to a ring.

From 1050 B.C. onwards the cemetery at Vergina was used on a large scale, and the settlement which it served was undoubtedly the largest centre on the Haliacmon side of the plain from that time until late in the seventh century B.C. Although only one third of the tumuli have been excavated, the evidence is sufficient for us to sketch the history of the site. In the first place Lausitz influences remained strong until *c.* 800 B.C. For instance, fluted pottery has been found in the same burial as a skyphos of Proto-Geometric style, which Andronikos dates within 900–850 B.C.,[1] and in a pithos burial, which on general grounds is likely to be not earlier than the late ninth century B.C. Ornaments in the Lausitz tradition have been found in ninth-century burials of princesses or priestesses, and these show a continuity of religious belief as well as of material culture.[2]

The period of greatest prosperity at Vergina was 900–800 B.C. During it there were some innovations. The most significant was the appearance of the three double-axes as the emblem of some religious cult, and we have argued that it was the emblem of the Bottiaeans, who had originated from Minoan Crete. Other innovations, such as the ring-pendant and iron tweezers, may have been introduced from the north or north-west.

A radical change ensued *c.* 800 B.C. Bronze beads, belt-ornaments, sickle-shaped knives, and different types of pottery came into vogue. A great wave of new practices and ornaments followed, and the objects in the burials showed a growing impoverishment.

The literary tradition gives precision to the picture. Although in classical times Briges or Brygi were living in Illyris inland of Epidamnus and in norther Pelagonia but not in Central Macedonia, the *floruit* of the Phrygians in Europe was firmly located below Mt. Bermium and firmly dated by Herodotus in the period before the foundation of Gordium in Asia (8. 138. 3 and 7. 73; see p. 303 above). An important city below the northern end of Mt. Bermium is Edessa. It was so named from the Phrygian word for water, and it was probably the capital of the Phrygians at that time in Macedonia. The name survived as their memorial in classical times. The well-watered, fertile slopes of the foothills by Edessa and Naoussa were evidently 'the gardens said to be those of Midas, son of Gordias'. A Phrygian state centred on Edessa, like the Macedonian state later centred on Pella, could have been powerful only if it controlled the plain west of the Vardar river. To do so the Phrygians needed to rule over

---

[1] *Vergina* 187 on the two pots *Δ* 15 and *Δ* 24.

[2] I differ here from Andronikos, who believes that the northerners who brought the Lausitz culture had only a brief period of influence (*Vergina* 282 μόνον διὰ μικρὸν διάστημα) and were absorbed by the indigenous population. He mentions the possibility that the northerners were the Phrygians of Herodotus; but, since he dates the beginnings of the cemetery at Vergina to the end of the eleventh century (e.g. on p. 280), he is left with a gap of a century and more between the intrusion of the Lausitz invaders at Vardina and Vardarophtsa, where their culture is related to that of Troy vii B 2, and their arrival at Vergina.

the foothills, where the cultivators of the plain mostly live, because the plain becomes inundated at certain times of the year. On one of those foothills stood the settlement which used the cemetery at Vergina. We have already argued that the early name of this settlement was Edessa, and that it was changed to Aegeae by the Macedones, when they captured it. But in the period *c.* 1140 to *c.* 800 B.C. Vergina–Edessa was one of the centres of Phrygian power.

The wealth of the Phrygians in Macedonia was said by Callisthenes to have come from the mines on Mt. Bermium (*FGrH* 124 F 54). The Brygi inland of Epidamnus are mentioned by Strabo, who adds that somewhere near by were the silver-mines at Damastium.[1] We have seen above (p. 317) that the Phrygians may well have been early exploiters of the mineral wealth of Macedonia. But the prosperity of the Phrygians in Europe was certainly connected with trade, as it was to be later in Asia Minor. With their kinsmen in possession of Pelagonia and of Epidamnus and its hinterland, they were particularly well placed to trade across the Balkan range from the Aegean to the Adriatic on the line of the later Via Egnatia and also northwards through Gostivar and the Kačanik pass along the overland route to central Europe. One factor in the ninth-century flowering of the Phrygian state was the growth of a strong Illyrian culture, that of which Glasinac is the type-site, from 900 B.C. onwards. There are also Phrygian connections which have survived on the Thracian part of the Via Egnatia route: Mygdonia east of the Vardar is a name of Phrygian origin, the 'Thracian Brygi' who attacked the army of Mardonius at night in 492 B.C. were Phrygians still resident in Thrace, that is probably between the Athos peninsula and the Strymon valley (Hdt. 6. 45 and 7. 185. 2), and Phrygian ideas in religion affected parts of Thrace and particularly the cult of the Cabiri in Samothrace. We may then see in the Phrygian state an example of power consolidated in the coastal plain of Central Macedonia, and of exploitation of Macedonia's strategic position for commerce at the cross-roads of the Balkans, at a time when Greece was still weak and backward.

The Phrygians held the plain for some 350 years before they invaded Asia Minor, and the Macedonians in their turn held the plain for a similar length of time from *c.* 650 to 334 B.C., when Alexander led them into Asia Minor. The Phrygians had probably succeeded in integrating some of the neighbouring peoples before they set out. The Bottiaeans in particular may have been raised to a position of co-operation, as the emblem of the three double-axes was held in esteem during the ninth century at Vergina. The Phrygians' neighbours to the south were Thracians, as we know from the burials at Koundouriotissa, and some legends connected Phrygian Midas with Thracian Orpheus.

[1] See *Epirus* 466 for a discussion of this passage in Strabo C 326.

The Macedones of Pieria and the middle Haliacmon valley formulated the account of the Phrygians which came down to the writers of the classical period. Phrygians and Macedones were σύνοικοι, i.e. they lived in the same country (Hdt. 7. 73). There is no mention of war between them. When the Macedones occupied the coastal plain, it was the Bottiaeans who were dispossessed and driven eastwards (Thuc. 2. 99. 3). The so-called gardens of Midas preserved a memory not of that moment but of the past;[1] for the Phrygians had departed about 150 years before the Macedones came. As far as the Macedonian account is concerned, the Macedones remained independent of the Phrygians during the ninth century. The powerful state of which Pateli was the centre may have joined the Phrygians in the ninth century; for the emblem of the double-axes has been found there. Indeed at the zenith of its prosperity the Phrygian state is likely to have incorporated this area, which lies on the direct route from Edessa to Pelagonia. Its influence was felt also at Theotokou on the coast of Magnesia and at Kapakli near Iolcus. Sea-borne trade may have started the connection, but it is likely that settlers came to Kapakli from the north. In addition to the sea-route from Vergina via Theotokou there was overland communication from the middle Haliacmon valley through Perrhaebia.

The Phrygian invasion of Asia Minor was mounted from a position of strength. Its immediate result was the formation of a strong Phrygian state with its capital at Gordium, and a later development was the establishment of a Phrygian empire in north-western Asia Minor in the latter part of the eighth century B.C., when Midas made dedications at Delphi (Hdt. 1. 14. 2).[2] Scholars have been fairly unanimous in dating the formation of this Phrygian state to c. 800 B.C.[3] The American excavations at Gordium have dated 'The Royal Tomb' c. 725–700 B.C., and have found a phase of fortification in the city which is earlier than that of the late eighth century.[4] The excavations at Vergina now throw fresh light on the matter. For the abrupt changes c. 800 B.C. and the rapid impoverishment which followed are fully understandable if the

[1] E. A. Fredericksmeyer, 'Alexander, Midas, and the Oracle at Gordium', in *CP* 56 (1961) 161, is mistaken in supposing Herodotus to say that the gardens still belonged to Midas when the Macedones took possession of them and therefore 'that Midas and the Brigians moved to Asia when they were dislodged from Macedonia by the Argead conqueror'. Gordias and Midas were dynastic names, and the kings of these names who led the migrations to Asia were the predecessors of the Gordias and Midas who turned all things to gold in Asia.

[2] Phrygian dedications of eighth-century date have been identified at Delphi and at other Greek shrines; see R. D. Barnett in *CAH*² 2. 30 (1967) 14.

[3] See How and Wells, *Commentary on Herodotus*, Appendix 1 p. 373, and H. Treidler in *Das Kleine Pauly* s.v. Gordion. They based their views upon the archaeological data in Asia Minor and upon reconstructions of the genealogy of the Phrygian dynasty in Asia Minor.

[4] R. S. Young in *AJA* 62 (1958) 154 (the Royal Tomb) and *AJA* 66 (1962) 167 and 68 (1964) 292 (fortifications of Gordium).

Phrygians moved *en masse* at that time from Macedonia to Asia Minor. On this point the tradition of the Macedones, as retailed by Herodotus (7. 73), is entirely clear: the Briges changed their habitat and their name alike on crossing over into Asia (μεταβάντες δὲ ἐς τὴν Ἀσίην ἅμα τῇ χώρῃ καὶ τὸ οὔνομα μετέβαλον).[1]

A conspicuous sight outside the walls of eighth-century Gordium was the cemetery of the Phrygian kings and nobles, in which some eighty great tumuli are still to be seen. Of these tumuli some contain cist-tombs and others contain cremations, and we thus see the continuity in burial practices which we should expect, if the Briges of Vergina moved to Gordium. The most interesting tumulus at Gordium, Tumulus P, contains a built tomb.[2] Its construction was as follows. A pit was dug in the hardpan; a wooden chamber was built on the floor of the pit; a cairn of large stones was made over the roof of the chamber; a clay dome was made over the cairn; and a very large tumulus of soil was erected over the dome. The analogies with the earlier 'Kurgan' burials are obvious. The development of the built bee-hive tomb from the shaft-grave within a tumulus at Mycenae[3] exactly foreshadows the development at Gordium from the cist-tomb inside a tumulus. The central pit, the wooden chamber, the cairn of stones, the dome sealing off the inner group, and the large tumulus of soil—all this is most closely paralleled by the double tumulus with its dome of stones sealing off the inner group at Pazhok in central Albania, where the original burial was of M.H. date at the latest and the upper tumulus was of L.H. date.[4] It is likely that the Phrygians' leaders were related to the Kurgan group of peoples.

Tradition does not offer any reason for the Phrygian migration from Macedonia to Asia Minor. We may see the expanding power of the Illyrians as a possible factor in the situation. The Taulantii captured Epidamnus from the Phrygian group in central Albania, and the piratical Liburni replaced the Taulantii at Epidamnus sometime after 900 B.C.; the latter event in particular, followed as it was by the capture of Corcyra by the Liburni, is likely to have disrupted any sea-borne trade in the Adriatic with Italy and with central Europe.[5] At the same time we can see that Illyrian pressure was being exerted by land upon a northern part of central Epirus at Vitsa throughout the ninth century B.C. The

---

[1] Conon (*FGrH* 26 F 1) gives the account a little more fully than Herodotus does, and includes the comment that the Briges below Mt. Bermium were an ἔθνος πολυανθρωπότατον ὄν, and that they crossed to Asia by the Hellespont. The dedication of the wagon to Zeus at Gordium suggests a migration overland.

[2] See R. D. Barnett in *CAH*² 2. 30 (1967) 5 and 12, and R. S. Young in *AJA* 71 (1967) 325 f.

[3] I have given reasons for this view in *BSA* 62 (1967) 83 f.

[4] Ibid. 77 f. The great tumulus at Pazhok is some 40 m in diameter, while the one at Gordium is some 35 m in diameter.

[5] For the Liburni see *Epirus* 414 f. and 474 f.

growth of Illyrian power in southern Yugoslavia pressed hard upon the Phrygian group in Pelagonia during the ninth century, and it may have endangered trade overland through the Kačanik pass. If the western terminal and the northern terminal of Phrygian trade had both been cut off, or were in danger of being cut off, a move to the richer territories of Asia Minor may well have seemed politic at the end of the ninth century.

The name of Skudra, a town on the foothills below Edessa, has been discussed recently by Petsas. The ancient Skodra, in Illyris, now Shkodër in northern Albania, is a dialectal variation of the same name. Kudrai, the only town of the Brygi of Pelagonia in Strabo's account, lacks the initial sibilant. Kudrara, mentioned by Hdt. 7. 30. 2 as a town on the border of Phrygia and Lydia, is of the same derivation as Kudrai. The explanation of these names is that they are variants of a Phrygian place-name, and their survival in the vicinity of Gajtan and the Mati valley, in Pelagonia, in the Macedonian plain below Mt. Bermium, and in the Phrygian territory which Midas ruled in Asia Minor gives independent support to our argument, that the literary evidence concerning the Brygi, Briges, and Phryges is worthy of credence.[1]

3. *The Eordi*

At the beginning of the Early Iron Age the kingdom of which Pateli was the centre seems to have been independent of the Phrygians who held Pelagonia and the coastal plain. Its connections in terms of culture and perhaps of trade were rather with the upper Haliacmon valley, Epirus, and southern Albania, where the Boubousti type of pottery was in vogue. It is probable that this kingdom became affiliated to or even subject to the Phrygians of the coastal plain in the course of the ninth century, but it continued as a separate and rich centre of power after the departure of the Phrygians to Asia Minor. Some of the burial practices of its rulers were idiosyncratic: in particular the placing of skulls as a frame around a complete skeleton and the storing of other bones apart. The rulers of this area were named the 'Eordi' by Thucydides (2. 99. 5), when he was describing the expansion of the Macedonian state. Most of them were destroyed by the Macedones. The district continued to be named after them as 'Eordia' or 'Eordaea', but the small remnant which survived departed to Physca in Mygdonia.

---

[1] Petsas in *AE* 1961. 46 f. with bibliographical references. I doubt his connection of Skudra with Skordiskoi, Skirtioi, and Skuthai. For the sibilant in Illyris compare 'Scampis' (above, p. 37 n. 2). In Strabo C 327 Κύδραι δὲ Βρύγων is an emendation of the MS. βυρσων, and this emendation is unavoidable as the 'Brygi' have been mentioned a few lines earlier. St. Byz. mentions both Kudrai, which he allots to the Deuriopes, and Kudrara. For a possible connection with the Persian list of Satrapies see Volume II.

The Eordi were evidently the descendants of a Bronze Age people. Their name survived outside Eordaea in the river Eordaïcus, that is the upper Devoli, on which the important site of Malik was situated; in a place 'Ordaea' in the plain below Naoussa; and in a part of Mygdonia which was called Eordaea.[1] A common feature of the districts in which the name survived is the proximity of a lake; and at Malik and at Gona in southern Mygdonia there were settlements built upon piles.[2] The conjecture is certainly attractive that the original Eordi were the settlers of Malik IIa, who were an unusually gifted and enterprising people and seem to have introduced into Macedonia the practice of building settlements upon piles; that branches of this people lived at various times on the lakes of Ochrid, Prespa, Rudnik, and Kastoria, in the marshy plain below Naoussa, on the marshy estuary of the Vasilikos river at Gona, and perhaps on the lakes of the Langadha basin; and that the pile-dwellers on Lake Prasias were either Eordi or else Paeonians, in which race Herodotus apparently included them, who had learnt this way of life from the Eordi.[3]

4. *Epirotic tribes in Macedonia*

We have maintained above (pp. 271 f.) that the peasant populations of the three cantons Pelagonia, Lyncus, and Orestis spoke a dialect of West Greek and were grouped together with the tribes to the west and south-west as members of what Ephorus called the Epirotic group. This grouping was as old as the time of Hecataeus in the late sixth century, except that he labelled some such tribes as Molossian, others as Chaonian, and others as Thesprotian. In particular he called the Orestae a Molossian tribe and the Dexari (of the later Dassaretis) a Chaonian tribe (*FGrH* I F 107 and 103).[4] This peasant population in Pelagonia and Lyncus was overlaid and ruled by the Phrygian group soon after 1200 B.C. I have included Lyncus—where there is no evidence either way as yet—because a strong power in Pelagonia is certain to dominate the entire plain which forms the catchment area of the river Erigon. The objects from the

[1] St. Byz. s.v. 'Εορδαῖαι . . . Μυγδονίας; Hdt. 7. 185. 2 lists the Eordi between the Paeones and the Bottiaei as providing troops for Xerxes, and these Eordi are evidently those in Mygdonia. It is more likely that the small remnant went to Physca, because their kinsfolk were already there, than that this remnant caused a part of Mygdonia to be renamed.

[2] See pp. 229 f. above.

[3] As the Paeonians did not generally live in such settlements, the particular group at Lake Prasias is likely to have adopted the practice. At 5. 16 Herodotus seems to be distinguishing between those of the Paeonians who were captured by Megabazus and those of the Paeonians who escaped capture. Whether the opening sentence is corrupt or not, it seems that Megabazus' orders (5. 14. 1) were to take the Paeonians only, and it follows that those on Lake Prasias were regarded by Megabazus as Paeonians.

[4] See my discussion of the fragments of Hecataeus in *Epirus* 451 f.

tumuli at and near Visoï indicate that the Phrygian Briges maintained their rule into the ninth century; for example, the double-axes at Visoï may be dated to that period on the analogy of those at Vergina.

The Orestae probably remained independent in the opening period of the Early Iron Age. Their mountainous territory afforded a living for pastoral people, if we may generalize from the shepherd encampment at Boubousti, and it had little to tempt the Phrygians. At this time the contacts of the Orestae were probably more with the Molossian tribes of northern Epirus and north-west Thessaly than with the peoples of central Macedonia. We have already seen that the Haliacmon valley was very closely linked with north-eastern Thessaly.

5. *Thracians in Pieria*

The name Pieria is clearly Greek in origin. It means 'the rich land', and it may be compared with the name Pieros, which was used for instance of a river and of a spring in the Peloponnese.[1] From very early times Pieria was occupied by the Greek-speaking Magnetes (Hes. fr. 7), and Pieria was the scene of many legends about the Olympian gods, especially Apollo and Hermes.[2] There is no doubt that Pieria was a part of the Greek world during the Early and the Middle Bronze Age. But at some time in the Late Bronze Age this ceased to be so. The Teucri and Mysi, crossing from Asia to Europe 'before the Trojan War', conquered 'all the Thracians' and advanced as far as the Peneus river (see p. 297 above). In the Homeric poems Olympus continued to be the home of the Greek gods, and from Olympus the gods descended at times to Pieria and Emathia or Iolcus. But the Magnetes were no longer in Pieria; for the Catalogue of Achaean Ships placed them further south 'by Peneus and leafy Pelion' (*Il.* 2. 756).

In the two catalogues there was a gap between the Peneus and the Axius. The Achaean alliance ended with the Magnetes; and the Trojan alliance reached its western limit with the Paeonians on the east bank of the Axius. There was no mention of the inhabitants of this no-man's land. Yet Homer may provide a clue in a rather unusual entry in the catalogue which concerns the realm of Nestor. There, at Dorion, the Muses maimed 'Thamyris the Thracian as he was on the way from Oechalia, the Oechalia of Eurytus' (*Il.* 2. 595); this Oechalia, as we learn later, lay in northern Thessaly (*Il.* 2. 730). It seems very likely that Thamyris' acquaintance with the Pierian Muses began in Pieria, and that the occupants of Pieria before and at the time of the Trojan War were Thracians. Some traditions

[1] For instance in Paus. 5. 16. 8 and 7. 22. 1.
[2] See the Homeric Hymns, to Apollo 216 and to Hermes 70, 85, and 191.

which seem to have originated in Mycenaean times place Thracians at Daulia in Phocis and Orchomenus in Boeotia, and bring Theseus into conflict with Thracians; and the story recounted by Pausanias, that one 'Pieros Makedon' introduced the cult of the nine Muses to Thespiae in Boeotia but may have learnt of them from 'one of the Thracians', may be a confused memory of a time when Thracians occupied Pieria.[1]

In the Early Iron Age we have archaeological evidence that there were Thracians ruling at Koundouriotissa, north of Dium, in Pieria; for a specifically Thracian method of burial for leading men was used in the graves which have been excavated, each with its own tumulus. Here again we have literary evidence. For example, Str. C 471 remarked that Pieria, Olympus, Pimplea, and Leibethron in early times were 'Thracian places and mountains but are now occupied by Macedones'. Of the 'Thracian' singers Orpheus had the closest connections with Pieria; for a tumulus near Dium was believed to cover his grave.[2] How did these Thracians come to be in Pieria? As the Phrygian Briges held the coastal plain and in particular Vergina, which is the key to Pieria from the north, from *c.* 1150 B.C. to *c.* 800 B.C., we may exclude the possibility within that time of a successful large-scale Thracian invasion, which ended by occupying Pieria. Further, the changes which came about in Macedonia after 800 B.C. seem to have been due not to Thracians but to Illyrians. Thus we are driven back to our belief that the Thracian occupation of Pieria dated from before the Trojan War. It seems that the Thracians held Pieria from *c.* 1300 B.C., let us say, to *c.* 650 B.C., and it was during this long time that Thracian influences in music and in religion percolated into Greece from Pieria and not from what was later known as Thrace.[3]

The Thracians of Pieria took their name from that of the country, being called Pieres by Thucydides (2. 99. 3), and retained it after their expulsion to territories east of the Strymon. The description of them as Thracians has a geographical and linguistic meaning rather than an ethnographic association. As neighbours of the Macedones and the Phrygian Briges, the Pieres were believed to have come from the region known as Thrace, that is from east of the river Axius or perhaps of the Strymon, and they spoke neither Greek nor Phrygian but a language loosely termed Thracian; and when Methone was founded on the coast

[1] Thuc. 2. 29. 3 (Phocis); *FGrH* 4 Hellanicus F 42b (Orchomenus); Isoc. *Paneg.* 68 (Theseus); Paus. 9. 29. 3 ('Pieros Macedon'). Conflict between Thessaloi and Thrakes in Tempe is mentioned in the foundation-legend of Aloïon (St. Byz. s.v.).

[2] Paus. 9. 30. 7 f. I am concerned here not with the historicity of Orpheus, who attracted many fictitious and chronologically incompatible stories, but with the location of Thracians in Pieria.

[3] Traditions of Eumolpus and Eleusis, of Thracians capturing Thebans, of Orpheus teaching the Aeginetans to worship Hecate and the Lacedaemonians to worship Kore Soteira at Sparta become more intelligible, when it is realized that a strong Thracian group was close at hand to invade or influence the east side of the Greek mainland.

the Pieres were no doubt described by the Eretrian settlers as Thracians with the same connotations. It is important to make this definition, because ancient and modern writers tend to include Phrygians, Mysians, Teucrians, Illyrians, and Paeonians under the general umbrella of Thracians'.[1]

6. *The Paeonians in Macedonia*

If we are correct in identifying the Paeonians with the Early Bronze Age invaders of Macedonia, they exercised control over all the coastal plain and much of Upper Macedonia during most of the Bronze Age. A tradition that they had held the coastal plain is found in Polybius 23. 10. 4, τὴν νῦν μὲν Ἠμαθίαν τὸ δὲ παλαιὸν Παιονίαν and in Str. 7 fr. 38, who adds that Paeonia had once extended μέχρι Πελαγονίας καὶ Πιερίας 'up to Pelagonia and Pieria'.[2] This tradition refers to a period before the time of the Trojan War; for in the Trojan Catalogue the Axius river was the western frontier of the Paeonians both in the coastal plain at Amydon and at and above Demir Kapu (see pp. 296 f. above). The eastern frontier of the Paeones is vague in the Trojan Catalogue. From east to west the coast was divided between Thrakes, Cicones, and Paeones. As the Thrakes were contained by the Hellespont and one of their leaders came from Aenus, we may put them between the Propontis and the river Hebrus. Ismarus, the city of the Cicones, which Odysseus sacked, is usually identified with Maroneia, since the Ciconian priest of Apollo was called Maron; in that case we may put the Cicones between the Hebrus and the Strymon, including Lake Bistonis near the mouth of the river Nestus within their realm, as Biston was reputed to be the son of Cicon.[3] The Paeones, then, held the country between the Strymon and the Axius. Inland they are likely to have occupied the territory between the two rivers, as some traditional rites of the Paeonian kings were enacted at Astibus (above, p. 202 n. 5).

In the decades after the fall of Troy the Paeones were pushed eastwards from the middle and lower Axius by the advance of the Phrygian Briges. There are traces of the Briges at Demir Kapu. It is probable that the

---

[1] Str. C 295. On this subject see J. Wiesner, *Die Thraker* (Stuttgart, 1963) 13 f.; he uses such terms as 'paionisch-thrakische Mischstämme', 'thrakophrygisch' and 'thrako-kimmerisch', but it is doubtful whether the 'thrako' element is more than geographical in this context.

[2] I take the expression to mean that Pelagonia and Pieria had lain outside the Paeonian empire; this is correct, as Pelagonia lay rather in the sphere of Bubanj-Hum influences, and Pieria was held first by the Magnetes and then by Thracians.

[3] *Il.* 2. 846 f.; 4. 520 (Aenus); *Od.* 9. 40 and 198. See T. W. Allen, *The Homeric Catalogue of Ships* 154 f. Herodotus placed Doriscus (just west of the river Hebrus) in the territory of the Cicones (Hdt. 7. 59. 2). Strabo 7 fr. 57 discusses the problem. Wiesner, op. cit. 17 puts the Cicones between the Nestus and the Hebrus, but he does not distinguish the period of the Homeric poems from later times in his allocation of tribes to districts.

Briges were the destroyers of Kilindir and Chauchitsa, and they held Vardina and Vardarophtsa from *c.* 1150 B.C. to *c.* 1080 B.C. We do not know whether the Paeones gained any territory at the expense of the Cicones. At some period during the Early Iron Age the Cicones disappeared under the impact probably of the Paeones from the west and the Thrakes from the east.

The Paeones have left very few traces for the archaeologist. Unenterprising and not distinguished by any object except for the anchor-shaped hooks of clay in the Bronze Age, they cannot be identified by any particular object in the Early Iron Age. It is possible to attribute to them the continuity of the pottery styles of Central Macedonia between the Bronze Age and the Early Iron Age, but this may well have been due to earlier subjugated strata of the population. The maintaining of contact by sea with Thessaly during the sub-Mycenaean period and the Proto-Geometric period was due to the Crousaei or the Mygdones rather than to the Paeones, who were an inland people with the tough qualities of the highlander, which enabled them to outlast many of their attackers.

XVIII

THE HISTORICAL EVENTS OF THE PERIOD *c.* 800–550 B.C.

1. *The Illyrian expansion* C. *800–650 B.C.*

WHEN the Phrygian Briges departed from the coastal plain of Macedonia *c.* 800 B.C., the prosperity of Vergina began to decline. New objects made an appearance in the burials—narrow diadems, small bronze beads, belt-ornaments of bronze plaque, sickle-shaped iron knives, and whet-stones—and there was a marked preference for large rather than small spectacle-fibulae. Taste in pottery changed. The open bowl developed two pinched-out extensions of the rim in addition to the two handles; and the open bowl with the flat, extended rim and two or four perforations through the rim came into fashion. Both forms of bowl appear to copy wooden bowls, such as are still made by Vlach shepherds in northern Greece. At the same time there was much continuity of tradition. We may then infer some changes in the ruling class but also a continuity in the basic population at Vergina and in the adjacent part of the plain. This initial stage was one of gradual change or transition at Vergina. It was followed by a period of much more radical innovations in burial customs, such as cremations, sometimes in urns, and many more burials in pithoi, and in the objects placed with the dead. During this period those parts of the cemetery at Vergina which have been excavated so far were ceasing or had ceased to be in use.

Discoveries at other sites add to the evidence from Vergina and enable us to see more fully what the new objects were: a great variety of large bronze beads, heavy bronze armlets with overlapping ends often incised, bronze tweezers, iron pins, and an astonishing range of bronze pendants. There was a great love of engraved ornamentation in the form of two concentric circles or a dot-centred circle. In this second stage there were more graves of warriors, armed with knives and spears, and fewer graves of women at Vergina than in the past. We gain the impression that new rulers of a militaristic type have taken control of Vergina, and that in this ruling class the women held a lowly position.

In other parts of Macedonia the evidence does not admit of a distinction between a phase of transition and a period of radical change. We see only the extent of the change and its radical nature throughout most of Macedonia. The new features occur at Visoï and at Petilep in

Pelagonia; they are very marked at Pateli in Eordaea; they occur at
Kozani; and they appear at a large number of small sites in the middle
Haliacmon valley. The strongest impact of the new features is in the lower
Vardar valley at Axioupolis, Chauchitsa, and Gevgheli—three sites of the
greatest strategic value on the route from the coast to the interior. Inland
up the Vardar valley there are similar innovations at places of strategic
importance: for example, at Titov Veles, at Radanja near Štip, at Vučedol
near Skopje, and at Kumanovo. Eastwards of the Vardar valley there
is scattered evidence of similar objects from the area of Doiran to the
vicinity of the Strymon valley, and there are the collections of such
objects in the Benaki Museum and in the British Museum which, coupled
with the objects found later at Olynthus, indicate that the new influences
permeated the eastern side of the coastal plain and reached into Crousis
and perhaps into the hinterland of Chalcidice.

The meaning of these radical changes is not in doubt. They represent
an expansion of the culture of central Yugoslavia, of which Glasinac is
the typical site. In ethnological terms it was an expansion of the Illyrian
peoples; and since the objects come mainly (indeed probably entirely)
from burials, there can be little doubt that the expansion was not in
terms of articles of trade alone but in terms of actual rulers. The expansion may have been gradual at the start, but it was continuous and it
became complete within the period 800–650 B.C.

A memory of this event survives in our literary sources. A fragment of
Strabo from the Vatican Epitome, C 329 fr. 11, begins an account of
Ἠμαθία ἡ νῦν Μακεδονία as follows: κατεῖχον δὲ τὴν χώραν ταύτην Ἠπειρωτῶν τινες καὶ Ἰλλυριῶν, τὸ δὲ πλεῖστον Βοττιαῖοι καὶ Θρᾷκες. The omission of the Macedones and the presence of the Bottiaei show that Strabo
was dealing with the coastal areas and with the period before c. 650 B.C.
The fragment enumerates the Thracians, who include the Paeonians,
and says no more of the Epirotes and Illyrians, but by defining the
habitat of the others it reveals that the Epirotes and Illyrians held the
western part of the plain between southern Pieria and Bottiaea itself.
This is precisely where Vergina lies. In considering the archaeological
evidence we saw in the first stage of gradual transition at Vergina the
influence of the north-western area, including central Albania, where
pithos-burial has a long history. This influence accounts for the juxtaposition of Epirotes and Illyrians. For the peoples of Pelagonia and
Lyncus rank as 'Epirotic' in Strabo, and the newcomers to Vergina came
most probably either from or via Pelagonia and Lyncus. But in the second
(and final) stage of the burials at Vergina the Illyrian element was in
the ascendant. This element was marked here and elsewhere in Macedonia by its militaristic qualities; for the Illyrian warriors were heavily
armed with iron weapons and had some defensive armour, including the

metal-centred shield. Small, tightly-knit groups of warriors seem to have formed the élite of this Illyrian culture, as we see for instance at Halus.

The names of some at least of the Illyrian tribes which led the movement of expansion may be inferred from a genealogy, preserved in Appian *Illyr.* i, which is likely to have originated in the period of Greek colonization.[1] From the Adriatic coast eastwards these tribes were the Illyrii proper, the Taulantii, the Parthini, the Enchelees, the Dardanii, and the Maedi.[2] The first three may represent the first large-scale penetration from the north, because they acquired the rich coastal plain and the Shkumbi valley. Their advance caused the Phrygian Briges to withdraw into the mountainous interior. The Enchelees had an earlier history (Str. C 326), but Illyrians evidently occupied their strategic and rich territory at this time and adopted their name. The Dardanii broke into Pelagonia probably via Tetovo and Gostivar, and pushed the Phrygian Briges there into the northern hills. It is probable that they overran Lyncus, Eordaea, and Edessa and occupied the southern part of the coastal plain, where they buried some of their dead in the cemetery of Vergina. They seem to have filled the vacuum left by the Briges on their departure to Asia. The Maedi probably led the latest large breakthrough of Illyrians. They took possession of the Vardar valley itself, together with the lower valleys of its eastern tributaries, and they gained control of the eastern part of the Macedonian coastal plain. Some of the Maedi pushed on into the valley of the middle Strymon, where Sitalces found them in 429 B.C. (Thuc. 2. 98. 2).

The latest conquests were made at the expense of the Paeonians, who seem to have withdrawn somewhat eastwards. After 700 B.C. the main centres of Paeonian power were in the upper Strymon valley, where the Agrianes and the Laeaei held their ground, and in the valleys of the Strumitsa and the lower Strymon, the latter being the territory of the Siropaeones.

The extent of the Illyrians' expansion should not be underestimated. They occupied parts of eastern Italy round the head of the Adriatic Sea, in Peucetia, and in Picenum. The Liburni and other seagoing tribes controlled the Adriatic Sea. The Liburni acquired Epidamnus and then Corcyra, which enabled them to block the coasting route leading from the eastern Mediterranean to Sicily and Italy. They are likely to have raided further south and made settlements, as their predecessors had

---

[1] The omission of the Liburni is particularly interesting. It is understandable if the Greek settlers of Epidamnus created this genealogy; for they were invoked by the Taulantii and ejected the Liburni from Epidamnus.

[2] The other tribes are the Autarienses, the Dassaretii (not those on the western border of Macedonia) and the Daorsi—all further north—and the Perrhaebi. The last are unknown; they cannot be the Greek Perrhaebi who were enshrined as Greek in Homer and in Strabo C 441.

done in the Bronze Age, and as their successors were to do in the Hellenistic period. For example, two tumuli containing burials of the Geometric period at Chalandritsa in Achaea are best explained as the work of Illyrians, who had come by sea to Achaea, perhaps to serve as mercenaries.[1]

On the western side of the Balkan peninsula they pressed down into Albania, occupying the entire coastal plain as far as the lower Aous valley, where the Greek settlers of Apollonia found Illyrians in possession. Inland the Parthini held the Shkumbi valley in central Albania. Nor was this the limit of their influence. The excavations at Vitsa in northern Epirus show an admixture at least of Illyrian elements from *c.* 950–900 B.C. onwards,[2] and objects found at Vaxia on the south side of the plateau of Ioannina suggest some Illyrian penetration *c.* 700 B.C. The dedications at Dodona within this period include Illyrian offerings, and much of north-western Greece was affected by the proximity of the Illyrians.[3]

On the eastern side of the Balkan range there is evidence of Illyrian conquests in the Bulgarian provinces of Vidin and Vrattsa between the Danube and Sofia, and as far as the river Strymon. In the south the Maedi carried their sway beyond the Vardar valley and occupied the western part of the middle Strymon valley somewhat above the Rupel pass. They must have forced their way through the Paeonians, who remained their neighbours (e.g. in Athenaeus 45 c). Further south in the district of Doiran, and in the rift which leads towards the lower Strymon valley, there are sporadic signs of Illyrian penetration. At the height of their success they held almost all Macedonia except southern Pieria. Further south their influence is seen in dedications at Pherae, and some bands of Illyrian warriors marauded southwards even as far as Halus in south-eastern Thessaly.

A constant feature of Illyrian life was the particularism of the tribe. This is seen even in the archaeological remains. If we compare adjacent sites, such as Axioupolis and Chauchitsa in the Vardar valley, we must deduce that they were occupied by different Illyrian tribes. The Taulantii, the Dardanii, and the Maedi were each a combination of related tribes under a common name. The combinations fell apart as easily as they had been formed. When the tide of Illyrian power turned shortly before 650 B.C., the ebb was very rapid. Little was left to indicate its high-water mark except the graves of its warriors.

[1] *BCH* 85. 682.
[2] In *Epirus* 273 I noted some unusual rock-cut graves at Palia Goritsa near Konitsa. Since then I have seen illustrations of such graves at Treskavtsa in western Yugoslavia (*Spomenik* 98. 193 f.), and the probability is that the graves were those of Illyrian chieftains. Vitsa, south of Konitsa, is approached from the north via Palia Goritsa.
[3] See *Epirus* 428 f.

2. *Relations with the Greek city-states*

During the period of Illyrian expansion from 900 B.C. onwards Glasinac was the main centre of exchange in the north-western Balkan area. Its contacts overseas were principally with the Etruscan area and with south Italy on the one hand, and with Ionia on the other.[1] The former were conducted across and up the Adriatic Sea by traders, including the Liburni, and the latter probably down the Danube valley and through Black Sea ports. Objects from mainland Greece came to Glasinac later, from *c.* 700 B.C. onwards, and were not many until after *c.* 550 B.C. The situation was very different in northern Epirus. At Vitsa, a remote inland place, there were Greek imports in the graves from 800 B.C. onwards, and they were common already during the eighth century. It is probable that these imports came to Vitsa via ports on the coast of Epirus such as Oricum and Buthrotum, which were themselves trading with Corcyra. The Liburni were the masters of Corcyra at the beginning of the eighth century, and it is probable that the Eretrians established themselves alongside the Liburni about 750 B.C.[2] At that time the Chalcidians and Eretrians of Euboea were planting colonies in Italy and Sicily, and Corcyra was an important port of call on the coastal route from the eastern Mediterranean to the west and also into the Adriatic Sea. Thus Corcyra is a likely source for the Greek imports at Vitsa.

In 733 B.C. an expedition from Corinth expelled the Eretrians and the Liburni, and founded a powerful colony at Corcyra. From now on the imports at Vitsa were of Corinthian type. This was the first success known to us of a Greek city-state at the expense of an Illyrian naval power. The second was a century later, *c.* 626 B.C., when Corcyraean settlers, led by a Corinthian, and local Illyrians, the Taulantii, expelled the Liburni from Epidamnus. They founded a colony which was mixed at first but soon became dominated by the Greek element. The interest of Corcyra and Corinth in Central Albania, which was by this time being called Illyris, was undoubtedly in commerce, and it follows that the Illyrians of this area had goods to offer.

In the matter of imported Greek wares Macedonia has no site to compare with Vitsa in Epirus. There are only a few scattered objects of the Geometric period: a pin of Corinthian manufacture made *c.* 750 B.C. and found at Titov Veles on the Vardar (Fig. 20r), a *crater* of Late Geometric type at Saraj on the Cerna Reka in Pelagonia, an example of the multiple brush used freehand at Vergina, a (probably) imported pot at Boubousti, and a sherd of an imported pot near Tsotyli in

[1] Maja Parović-Pešikan, *Bull. de l'Ac. Serbe d. sciences et d. arts* 28. N.S. no. 8 (1961) 1–5 and *AI* 5 (1964) 62.
[2] See *Epirus* 414 f. for the evidence of Eretrians and Liburni at Corcyra.

Voïon.[1] The last two instances indicate that contacts were still being maintained between north-eastern Thessaly and the middle Haliacmon valley, but the others suggest the first beginnings of commerce from the south along two routes, one via the western part of the coastal plain to Pelagonia and the other up the Vardar valley towards the north.

The very paucity of objects travelling from the south is important. It shows, for instance, that the spectacle-fibula was not introduced into Macedonia from Greece; indeed for a century and more before it appeared in Greece it had been an article of wear in lands to the north of Greece. The truth about the spectacle-fibula is that it was adopted late in Greece, most examples south of Thessaly being later than 750 B.C.,[2] and that it was adopted as a result of contacts with northern lands, both in the lower Adriatic Sea and on the north Aegean coast, and no doubt with northerners who came into Greece as mercenaries or workers. The same is true of bronze diadems.

The first stirrings of commercial activity between the city-states of Greece and Macedonia attracted those pioneers of colonization, the Eretrians, and among them the very Eretrians who had been expelled from Corcyra. About 730 B.C. they founded their new colony at Methone, probably at the then mouth of the Toponitsa, where the most northerly outlier of the Pierian range comes down to the sea (see p. 129 above). The site was at the extreme edge of Pierian territory, and at the same time it was close to the navigable river, the Haliacmon, beside which lay Vergina, still the leading city on that side of the plain.

The tradition of Methone's foundation is preserved in Plut. *Greek Questions* 11, 'Who were the men driven-away-by-the-sling?' The answer is that they were Eretrians who had held Corcyra, been ejected by Charicrates of Corinth, and had sailed home. There they were repelled by the slings of the citizens. Unable to win an entry by force or persuasion, 'they sailed for Thrace, seized a place which they relate had at an earlier date been occupied by Methon, an ancestor of Orpheus, called it Methone, and were nicknamed by their neighbours "the men driven-away-by-the-sling"'. That the ultimate source is very early may be inferred from the story itself, analogous as it is to the oath of the Theraeans not to return, when they went to Cyrene; from the naming

---

[1] *AE* 1937. 2. 520 pl. 5*e*; *Starinar* 11 (1960) 201 fig. 5; *Essays in Memory of K. Lehmann* 255 f.; *PM* 43 = *BSA* 28 fig. 29, 8; *PAE* 1935. 49.

[2] Sylvia Benton argued in *JHS* 70 (1950) 17 ff. that all examples at five sites—namely Artemis Orthia at Sparta, Thera, Chauchitsa, Delphi, and Marmariani—were after 750 B.C. Later evidence, e.g. at Vergina, has shown that Macedonia and (I should add) Marmariani are to be excluded from her generalization, which remains true enough for the other sites. See Snodgrass in *PPS* 31 (1965) 236, who agrees with her dating for the area south of Thessaly, and my remarks in *Epirus* 355 f.

of the district as Thrace, which precedes the expansion of the Macedones in *c.* 650 B.C.;[1] and from the local Thracian genealogy of Orpheus, which probably lapsed after the ejection of the Thracians from Pieria. The name Charicrates is peculiar to this passage, as is the mention of Eretrians holding Corcyra. I conclude, then, that the tradition is acceptable, and in particular that the date is correct.[2]

The Eretrians planted another colony in the Thermaic Gulf, Dicaea, which is named as such in the entries in the Athenian Tribute Lists Δίκαια ’Ερετρι[ὂν] and Δικαιοπολῖται ’Ερετριῶν ἄποικοι. It was certainly on the eastern side of the Gulf and probably on the coast of Crousis. The date of its foundation is not known.[3] The Eretrians planted also a colony, Mende, on the south-western promontory of Pallene, which is the westernmost prong of Chalcidice. This site overlooks the entry into the Gulf.

Methone and Mende, both founded *c.* 730 B.C., were the earliest colonies in the north-western Aegean. Next in Chalcidice came Torone, founded by Chalcis *c.* 710 B.C., and Scione, founded by Achaea *c.* 700 B.C. The choice made by the Eretrians, when they were first in the field, shows that Macedonia had much to offer to the maritime trader. From this time onwards there was a gradual increase in the importation of Greek wares. One example is the bronze horse on a stand, a product of Greek bronze-working, which has been found in many parts of the Greek world *c.* 725–700 B.C.[4] Such horses at Vergina, Pateli, Visoï, and Chauchitsa, adapted sometimes to fit an Illyrian type of pendant, may be regarded as objects made by Eretrian craftsmen and sent from Methone and perhaps Dicaea to the Macedonian market.

Traffic on a small scale between northern Thessaly and the middle Haliacmon valley had probably been continuous since the Late Bronze Age, when the two areas had had more in common with one another than either had had with Central Macedonia. The quickening of commercial interest in Macedonia, of which the foundation of Methone was symptomatic, must have led to an increase also in the traffic between

---

[1] St. Byz. has Μεθώνη, πόλις Θράκης, . . . ἔστι καὶ Μακεδονίας, which is probably a confusion due to an early and a late source. Str. C 330 fr. 20 names this and other cities in ἡ κάτω Μακεδονία, and C 374 ἡ Μακεδονικὴ (Μεθώνη), and this must have been the usual way of describing it in classical times; however, at C 436 in a brief reference to the 'Methone destroyed by Philip' he calls it 'Thracian Methone'.

[2] I differ here from W. R. Halliday in his commentary on Plutarch's *Greek Questions* 63 f. He supposed the immediate source to be Aristotle, *Constitution of the Methonaeans*, which is reasonable, but he denied that the ultimate source was early, despite Cary in *CQ* 40. 148 f. He did not believe in an Eretrian phase at Corcyra (but see my remarks in *Epirus* 414 f.).

[3] *ATL* 1. 482; St. Byz. Δίκαια, πόλις Θράκης, ἀπὸ Δικαίου τοῦ Ποσειδῶνος υἱοῦ. τὸ ἐθνικὸν Δικαιοπολίτης, where the genealogy is of no local interest; Pliny *HN* 4. 36; *IG* iv². 1. 94. 1*b*, line 11.

[4] Sylvia Benton in *JHS* 70 (1950) 21 illustrates examples from Bari, Syracuse, and Ithaca; she published one from Chauchitsa in *JHS* 72 (1952) 119 fig. 1.

Thessaly and the middle Haliacmon valley. Such a traffic may have attracted the northerners who appeared in the eighth century at Homolion, Marmariani, and Halus.

3. *The Cimmerian migrations and their effects c. 700–650* B.C.

During the years 700 to 650 B.C. the situation in Asia Minor and in Thrace was entirely altered by a series of raids and migrations, led by the Cimmerians, who were themselves driven on by the Scythians of southern Russia (e.g. Hdt. 4. 12 and 7. 20). In both areas the Cimmerians found allies. In Thrace they joined forces with the Treres and the Edoni. All three peoples took part in the invasion and settlement of Asia Minor (Str. C 61 and C 627, and St. Byz. s.v. *Antandros*). There the Phrygian empire was destroyed, and in 652 B.C. the Lydian kingdom of Gyges was overrun. Meanwhile on the European side of the straits there was a general upheaval and movement of tribes throughout the Balkans. The literary traditions are supported by the archaeological finds.[1] Signs of the Cimmerians' presence are seen, for instance, in the characteristic horse-trappings and in hoards of gold and bronze objects.[2] A number of these horse-trappings at Dodona and a few specimens in Macedonia, such as the side-pieces of bits at Titov Veles, leave us in no doubt that Cimmerian raiders overran parts of Macedonia and struck down into central Epirus.[3]

The consequences in Macedonia were far-reaching. The power of the Illyrians was shattered. Very few traces of the Illyrian occupation survived into classical times. While the Maedi remained intact in the mountainous district on the west side of the middle Strymon valley, the Dardanii were found only in lands north or west of Pelagonia. The field was now open for new conquerors. Three peoples took advantage of the opportunities which offered: the Thracians, the Paeonians, and the Macedones.

There was certainly a general shift westwards of Thracian tribes. The clearest evidence of this is in the southern area. The Edoni, fortunate in their alliance with the Cimmerians, took possession of the fertile lands of Mygdonia and advanced their realm up to the river Axius. The leading tribes in this particular Edonic group were the Edones, the Mygdones,

---

[1] For a general account see J. Wiesner, *Die Thraker* 73 f. and esp. 77: 'Schriftquellen und archäologische Funde stimmen also darin überein, dass von der Kimmerischen Bewegung Thrakerstämme an der unteren Donau und im östlichen Strymongebiet betroffen worden sind.'

[2] For an example see Reinecke in *Germania* 7 (1923) 50 f.

[3] See *Epirus* 428, where I cite parallels to the objects which have been found at Dodona: Carapanos pl. 54 no. 5, a ring-disc with a pierced tongue (to the parallels should be added 42 examples from the Vidin district; one is shown in Fig. 20d); pl. 52 nos. 18, 19, and 22; and pl. 53 nos. 21 and 23.

and the Sithones (Str. C 329 fr. 11). There were many other Edonic tribes east of the Strymon, and among them were the Odomantes and the Bistones, who held the territory between the Strymon and the Nestus. Their interrelationship is indicated in the genealogy of their patronymic ancestors, in which Edonus, Mygdon, Biston, and Odomas were brothers.[1] This genealogy may have been grafted on to an earlier one, because the name Mygdon had been a local one in the time of the Phrygian domination; for Mygdon was credited with two sons, Grastus and Crousis.[2]

It seems then that a solid enclave of Thracian tribes was formed in the course of the seventh century. It extended westwards to the Axius river, and it had under its control Crestonia to the north, Crousis to the south, and the central peninsula of Chalcidice which took the name Sithonia. It was probably from this time that the coast east of the Axius delta received the general name 'Thrace', which we find in the geographical descriptions of Hecataeus and Herodotus. The extent of a westwards shift of Thracian tribes in districts north of this enclave is uncertain. The Paeonians retained their grip on the Strymon basin by Serres, where the local tribe was called the Siriopaeones. Between them and the Illyrian Maedi a Thracian tribe, the Sinti,[3] occupied the lower valley of the Strumitsa. Further north two Paeonian tribes, the Agrianes and the Laeaei, continued to hold the upper valley of the Strymon.

The pressure of the Thracian movement seems to have pushed the other Paeonians westwards, and it was they who took advantage of the collapse of Illyrian power in the Vardar valley. When the classical period began, the Paeonians were in possession of the eastern side of the upper and middle Vardar valley, and the centre of their realm was near Astibus, the modern Štip. In the seventh century, during which this advance took place, Paeonians occupied some lands below the Demir Kapu gorge on both sides of the river; for Str. C 329 fr. 11 mentions their possession of Amphaxitis, and Thuc. 2. 99 attributes to 'Paeonia' the narrow strip of land which comes down to Pella and the sea, both alluding to the period just before the expansion of the Macedones. They held also Doberus in the upper Strumitsa valley (Thuc. 2. 98. 2).

One archaeological token of the Thracians' presence in the area east of the Axius is the gold plaque which was laid as a mouth-piece upon the

---

[1] In St. Byz. s.vv. *Bistonia, Edonos, Parthenopolis* (cf. *Grestonia*), and *Krousis*. There is no need to athetize the word Edones in Str. 329 fr. 11, because the Edones were evidently the royal tribe in this Edonic group. A tribe such as the Edones was itself a cluster of tribes, one of which was the Panaei (St. Byz. s.v.). Reference may be made to the individual tribe rather than to the name of the cluster; this is done, for instance, by Thucydides at 2. 101. 3, when he mentions the Panaei's fear of Sitalces.

[2] St. Byz. s.vv. *Parthenopolis* (cf. *Grestonia*) and *Krousis*.

[3] Str. 331 fr. 36; for another branch of this tribe see Str. 457 and 549. Thucydides, 2. 98. 1–2, differentiates the Sinti from the Paeonians.

dead. One was found in the second cist-tomb at Ayios Vasilios in Mygdonia (above, pp. 348 and 352 f. and Fig. 18*i*); the other objects in the tomb included a gold bead and an amber amulet, both unparalleled for instance at Vergina, and a *cothon* of *c.* 550 B.C. Seven were found at Chauchitsa. Two came from simple earth-graves, which were probably not on the mound covered with a tumulus. Of these Grave B contained a small bronze bird-pendant, which may be dated after 650 B.C. because none have been found in the Vergina burials, and Grave C contained a spiral of gold, a light bronze armlet with pointed ends, and a bronze bar probably from a shield, all unusual objects in Macedonia. The other five mouth-pieces came from burials on the mound with the tumulus: from burial 8, from burial (2) which had a skyphos with concentric circles among its contents, from burial (3) which had small bronze ringlets, from burial (20) which had a shield-centre of a design peculiar to Chauchitsa (Fig. 18*b*) and a pair of heavy bronze armlets of one turn, rectangular in section, and from burial (22) which had pieces of a *cothon* and a hollow bean-shaped ornament of bronze with a ring for suspension.[1] Other objects in these burials were such as have been found either at sites of the Illyrian period or in the subsequent period at Olynthus.

Of the objects I have mentioned the bronze ones are novel or unusual in Macedonia, the *cothon* gives a date around 550 B.C. and the skyphos is a very late example of the Proto-Geometric style, which may have been made locally *c.* 700 B.C. and placed some decades later in a burial.[2] There is the intriguing point to be noted that burials (2) and (3) are together towards the northern end of the mound, (20) and (22) are together on the eastern edge of the mound, and 8 is below the mound on its western slope. Thus all the burials are likely to have been late in the history of the burial ground.[3] Four pieces of similar gold plaque, but about twice as large, were found at Zeitenlik, some 5 km north of Salonica. They may have been used for some other purpose, but they too were worn probably by Thracians. Such gold plaques have not been found west of the Axius, nor higher up the river than Chauchitsa, but they are quite common in Thrace. If we are correct in associating them with the presence of Thracians, it follows that *c.* 550 B.C. the Paeonian occupation of Amphaxitis stopped short of Chauchitsa, and the Macedones were not yet in possession of this site east of the river Axius.

---

[1] See p. 351 above. Another such bean-shaped ornament was in burial (10); it is shown in *BSA* 26 pl. v, 1 f.

[2] Andronikos discusses the skyphoi of Chauchitsa in *Vergina* 173 and puts them later than those at Vergina, which he dates to not later than 750 B.C. The lack of Geometric objects inland in Macedonia, e.g. at Chauchitsa, means that the Proto-Geometric style lingered late.

[3] See the plan of the mound in *BSA* 26. 2 fig. 2.

4. *The expansion of the Macedones, c. 650–550 B.C.*

We must first consider the background to the Macedonian expansion. Hesiod (fr. 7) made Magnes and Macedon sons of Zeus and Thyia,[1] and located them 'round Pieria and Olympus'. The location was correct of a period some time before the Trojan War, because in the Homeric Catalogue of Ships the Magnetes had left Pieria and were living south of the Peneus river. There is no reason to suppose that the Macedones had been driven out of their habitat. In what sense were they 'around Olympus'? On the south-western side of Mt. Olympus the Peraebi were firmly established by the time of the Trojan War, and they stayed there in classical times, as we see for instance from the march of Brasidas (Thuc. 4. 78. 5–6). To the south and the east of Mt. Olympus the district of Lower Olympus and the narrow coastal strip were closely associated with the legends of Orpheus and the Thracians, and we have seen reason to believe that it was the Thracians who had ousted the Magnetes from Pieria by the time of the Trojan War. These territories alone were not enough to support a powerful people such as the Pierian Thracians then were. They must therefore have held the rich plain of Dium and the lowlands northwards along the coast. The tradition that the site of Methone had once been occupied by an ancestor of Orpheus (Plu. *GQ* 11) should be referred to a Thracian period of occupation, which in 730 B.C. was relatively remote. Thus we have only one side of Olympus left for the Macedones 'around Olympus', and that is the northward extension of the Olympus massif, which went under the more specific names of Mt. Titarium and the Pierian Mountains (above, pp. 123 ff.).

The conclusion that the homeland of the Macedones from the latter part of the Bronze Age onwards was the northern part of the Olympus massif may be supported by turning to Herodotus and Thucydides. When Xerxes was in Pieria, a third of his forces was engaged in clearing a road through τὸ ὄρος τὸ Μακεδονικόν, in order to pass into Perrhaebia. This mountain is certainly the northern extension of Mt. Olympus,[2] and it was called the Macedonian mountain, because it was the mountain of the Macedones proper. At 7. 127. 1 the joint waters of the Ludias and the Haliacmon are described by Herodotus as forming the boundary between Bottiaeis and Μακεδονίς. The term 'Macedonis' must refer in

---

[1] Hesiod fr. 7 is to be preferred to *FGrH* 4 (Hellanicus) F 74 = St. Byz. s.v. *Makedonia* and St. Byz. s.v. *Oropos*, where Macedon is son of Aeolus and of Lycaon.

[2] This needs stressing perhaps because as good a topographer as A. W. Gomme wrote in his *Commentary on Thucydides*, 3. 545, that Xerxes went 'up the Haliakmon valley and then south, by the pass now called Servia, or Sarandopotamo, to Oloosson'. This reveals a complete misunderstanding. The Haliacmon valley between the plain and Servia is a great gorge, difficult on foot and impassable for wheeled vehicles. The route suggested by Gomme by-passes Pieria entirely, whereas Herodotus says that Xerxes spent several days waiting in Pieria while the operations were being conducted (7. 131. 1).

a restricted sense to the land of the Macedones proper. The boundary
was a real one at a time when the Macedones were an independent
people south of the lowest reach of the Haliacmon river and the Bottiaei
were an independent people north of it. Such a time would occur when
the Thracians left the district of Methone and the Macedones took their
place. Indeed we may conjecture with probability that it was the Macedones proper who ejected the Thracians and who advanced their frontier
to the lowest reach of the Haliacmon river, not necessarily making both
steps at the same time.

The placing of the Macedones proper to the north of Mt. Olympus
is also a necessary inference from the account of the Macedonian expansion which Thucydides gives at 2. 99. The extraordinary thing about
this account is that Thucydides does not tell us where the Macedones
started from on their career of conquest. Yet, if we exclude areas which
he does describe as independent of the Macedones at one time or another
and in one way or another—namely the Perrhaebi (4. 78. 6), the Pieres
in Pieria (2. 99. 3), the Elimiotae (2. 99. 2), and the Bottiaei (2. 99. 3)—
we have no option but to place the Macedones before the expansion in
what we now call northern Pieria but what was once called simply
'Macedonia'.[1]

If the northern part of the Olympus massif gives us the eastern part
of the Macedonian homeland, what of the interior? Appian, *Syr.* 63,
writes Ἄργος τὸ ἐν Ὀρεστείᾳ ὅθεν οἱ Ἀργεάδαι Μακεδόνες. These Argeadae
were a tribe of Macedonians who claimed descent from Argeas a son of
Macedon (St. Byz. s.v. *Argeou*: Ἀργέου τοῦ Μακεδόνος, ἀφ' οὗ Ἀργεάδαι).
This tribe lived at one time in the upper valley of the Haliacmon, which
was held in classical times by the Orestae. Where then were the Orestae
when the Argeadae Macedones lived in the upper valley of the Haliacmon? Str. 331 fr. 38 may be thought to supply the answer: 'they say
that Paeonia had extended as far as Pelagonia and Pieria, and that before then Pelagonia was called Orgestia'. If one emends Orgestia to
Orestia, as Kramer and later editors have done, the Orestae lived once
in what became Pelagonia and at a subsequent time moved south and displaced the Argeadae Macedones from the upper Haliacmon valley.[2]
However, I do not accept the emendation to Orestia. The characteristic

---

[1] A confusion is introduced by the modern meaning of 'Pieria' and indeed the meaning it
had when the greater Macedonia was fully established. I have not discussed here the idea
in How and Wells, *Commentary on Herodotus* 2. 284, that the homeland of the Macedones,
'Macedonis', was round the modern Edessa below Mt. Bermium. For the Macedones were
associated in early traditions with Mt. Olympus, not Mt. Bermium, and with what we call
northern Pieria and not with Bottiaeis and the exit from Eordaea. The statement of Herodotus
is treated below, p. 434.

[2] If we are correct in identifying the Early Bronze Age invaders of Macedonia as the
Paeonians, then the Paeonian penetration as far as Pelagonia is to be dated to the Middle
Bronze Age.

of Pelagonia is not mountain but plain, and 'Orestia', being a mountainous area, is very inappropriate as a name for Pelagonia. I suggest
'Argestia' as a much more likely emendation, because Argos means a
plain, and because the Argestaei lived in classical times on the neighbouring slopes of Mt. Babuna.[1] But in any case we can see that the
repeated pressures from the north must have driven the Greek-speaking
tribes southwards, bringing into Orestia its tribe of Orestae and pushing
the Argeadae Macedones down the Haliacmon valley into Voïon.

Now it was probably in Voïon that the 'Dorians-to-be' of Hdt. 1. 56
'lived on Pindus and were called, as an ethnos, Μακεδνόν'. At that time,
which preceded the sack of Thebes by the Epigoni, the 'Dorians-to-be'
and the Argeadae Macedones were either neighbours of one another or
more probably were intermingled, so that the former adopted a variant
of the latter's name, 'Makednoi'. But other tribes pressed forward. The
Tymphaei occupied Voïon and the Elimiotae occupied Elimia. Thus the
Argeadae Macedones were driven finally into the arms of their cousins,
who claimed descent from Makedon but, one supposes, by sons other
than Argeas. This final stage in the movements of the Argeadae Macedones was probably completed very early in the Iron Age.

The movement of the Argeadae Macedones from the upper Haliacmon
valley to the region of Olympus was probably part of a general movement
of related tribes of Macedones which led to a concentration in northern
Pieria. The names of the other tribes are lost, whereas the names of the
tribes of the Molossi have survived in inscriptions. The reason why the
Argeadae Macedones were remembered was that they led the Macedones
in the conquest of the plain. Two fragments of Strabo (329 fr. 11 and fr.
20 fin.) describe their achievement: τούτων δὲ πάντων οἱ Ἀργεάδαι
καλούμενοι κατέστησαν κύριοι καὶ Χαλκιδεῖς οἱ ἐν Εὐβοίᾳ,[2] and, of the
destruction of Amydon, κατεσκάφη δὲ ὑπὸ τῶν Ἀργεαδῶν. The ultimate
source is probably Hecataeus.[3] The history of the Argeadae Macedones
since the Middle Bronze Age at least had been one of struggle with other
Greek-speaking tribes in mountainous country, and they had been
remote from the main streams of invading Phrygians and Illyrians. When
they reached what we call northern Pieria, they were at last close to
the great plain of coastal Macedonia and they came into contact with
more civilized people in the Pieres of southern Pieria, the Eretrians of
Methone who appeared c. 730 B.C., and the unnamed citizens of Vergina.

An event of crucial importance which preceded the Macedonian expansion was the coming of a new dynasty to rule over the Argeadae

---

[1] I have not come across the suggestion elsewhere.

[2] Strabo goes on to mention the thirty colonies of Chalcis, which were mainly planted
c. 650 B.C.; that was more or less when the Macedonian expansion took place.

[3] Hecataeus recorded several otherwise unknown tribes, e.g. the Ἰμφέες Περραιβοί (*FGrH*
1 F 137).

Macedones. The newcomers became the Argead kings, and the line appeared as such in an archaizing Sibylline oracle αὐχοῦντες βασιλεῦσι Μακεδόνες Ἀργεάδῃσιν (Paus. 7. 8. 9 and App. *Mac.* 2). But the dynasty was a foreign one. It claimed descent from the Temenidae of Peloponnesian Argos, and the fact that the claim was accepted without question by Herodotus and Thucydides alike makes its authenticity practically certain (Hdt. 8. 137. 1; Thuc. 2. 99. 3; 5. 80. 2). The date of its coming was well within the Greek historical period; for Hdt. 8. 139 gives the names of seven kings down to Alexander, and Thuc. 2. 100. 1 has eight kings down to Perdiccas, son of Alexander and father of Archelaus. In other words, the dynasty established itself about 650 B.C. The royal house spoke seventh-century Doric Greek and not the relatively primitive dialect of Greek which had been spoken now for a thousand years and more in the Haliacmon valley by their immediate subjects, the Argeadae Macedones.

The route by which the founders of the dynasty reached northern Pieria was a devious one; for as refugees from Peloponnesian Argos, says Herodotus, Perdiccas and his brothers had gone ἐς Ἰλλυριούς and from there had crossed over (the Balkan range) into Upper Macedonia, that is from Central Albania into a canton of Western Macedonia (8. 137. 1 ὑπερβαλόντες ἐς τὴν ἄνω Μακεδονίην). No doubt Herodotus had this from the Macedones themselves, whose traditions he cites on other matters (7. 73), and we have no reason to dispute its truth. Indeed we have a later instance of a similar event and a similar route; for about the middle of the fifth century B.C., members of the Bacchiad clan, whose descent was from Corinth, crossed over from Illyris and established themselves as kings of the Lyncestae in Lyncus.

The story which Herodotus tells of the boy Perdiccas cutting out the patch of sunlight is a well-known folk-story and has no claims to be taken for anything else in relation to the establishment of the monarchy among the Argeadae Macedones. But it was presumably told to Herodotus by his Macedonian informants in order to cover up the true story. Although one cannot be sure, it is most probable that those who put Perdiccas and his family in power were the Illyrians from whose territory he came; for from 800 to 650 B.C. or thereabouts the Illyrians were the rulers of Western Macedonia and of Vergina on the edge of the central plain, where they were on the border of the Macedonian territory, ἡ Μακεδονὶς γῆ. If this is so, the royalist circles had good reason to fob Herodotus off with a bit of folk-lore. There is a further reason for supposing that Perdiccas and his two brothers were not just poor, clever lads who made good; for the tradition is that the conquests began under the new arrival, Perdiccas, and this tradition is pretty well confirmed by the dating of the Olynthus finds, which began with the arrival of Bottiaeans expelled by the Macedones *c.* 650 B.C. It is probable that Perdiccas brought some accession of strength with him, perhaps allies or adventurers from Illyris, and that this enabled him both to win the throne by force and to confirm it by successful conquests.

The piece of folk-lore is rather awkwardly attached to the mention of the conquest in Hdt. 8. 138. 2–3. The three lads, having reached the humble court of the king who ruled over the Macedones, served as his labourers at the city Lebaea, which was presumably the then capital. Turned out of the realm and hotly pursued by horsemen they were saved by a river in flood and got away. 'So they came to another land in Macedonia and dwelt near the gardens which are said to be those of Midas, son of Gordias.' Thus the lads are no longer in ἡ Μακεδονὶς γῆ; indeed it is the one place in which they must not be. But Herodotus is in a hurry to end the digression. So he writes ἐνθεῦτεν δὲ ὁρμώμενοι ὡς ταύτην ἔσχον κατεστρέφοντο καὶ τὴν ἄλλην Μακεδονίην. What we have to supply is the fulfilment of the magic involved in cutting out the patch of sunlight, the winning of the throne back at Lebaea in ἡ Μακεδονὶς γῆ, the conquest of the area containing Midas' garden outside ἡ Μακεδονὶς γῆ, and then the further advance from there to conquer all Macedonia. Herodotus limits himself to the penultimate stage in the words ὡς ταύτην ἔσχον, where ταύτην refers vaguely to the country under Mt. Bermium. 'When they acquired this land, setting out from it they began to subjugate the rest of Macedonia too.'

All we can deduce is that the area round Naoussa was not the homeland of the Macedones, and that it was either the first area or one of the first areas which the Macedones conquered in their expansion. One geographical clue is provided in the story, when Herodotus adds that the descendants of the Temenid founder-kings worshipped the river as their saviour. We happen to know of one river which was incorporated into a Macedonian genealogy, the river Beres, who was son of Macedon and father of Mieza, Beroea, and Olganus.[1] This river would fit well geographically. For the lads presumably left Pieria by crossing the Haliacmon and the king then sent his horsemen, who caught up with them near the next river in the plain, the Beres.

As a hill-people of northern Pieria the Macedones were unlikely to be of any importance, until they acquired the rich plain which runs from Methone to Katerini. This they seem to have done at some time before the foundation of the Eretrian colony at Methone *c.* 730 B.C. The dispossessed Thracians, the 'Pieres', were thus confined to the narrow coastal plain south of Katerini and to the region of Lower Olympus, and it was there that the scene of stories about Orpheus and the Thracians was usually set. The path to power for the Macedones now ran inevitably

---

[1] St. Byz. s.v. *Mieza.*

through Vergina, the largest city on the south side of the central plain. Once captured it could easily be defended; for the deep-flowing Haliacmon provided a defensible line. I have argued above (p. 158) that evidence of the classical and Hellenistic periods indicates that the classical name of the site at Palatitsa–Vergina was Aegeae. Now it happens that Aegeae was the capital city of the Argeadae Macedones and their Temenid kings (for many generations), and it was there that members of the royal family were buried. We should then regard Aegeae as one of the earliest conquests made by the new dynasty. They probably dispossessed the Illyrians, if we may judge from the evidence of the excavations at Vergina up to the present time. The Macedones were now on the edge of the Emathian plain. Beyond the Haliacmon lay Bottiaea to the north and the rich gardens of Midas to the north-west.

The conquest of Aegeae and the adoption of Aegeae as the capital of the Temenid kings were blessed after the event by the oracle at Delphi, which issued an utterance of the Pythian priestess, supposedly a response to an inquiry made by Perdiccas before the event. It was linked with the Macedonian expansion, in that it was supposedly uttered when Perdiccas 'wished to increase his kingdom'. This is the account of it, as it is preserved in a fragment of Diodorus Siculus (7. 16). We may translate the 'oracle' as follows. 'The illustrious Temenidae have royal authority over a wealth-producing land, the gift of aegis-bearing Zeus. But go urgently to Bouteïs,[1] rich in flocks, and where you see goats with gleaming horns and snowy fleece reclining at dawn, make sacrifice to the blessed gods on the level ground of that country and found the city of your state.' The allusion in the epithet αἰγίοχος and in the goats αἶγας is to the name of the new capital 'Aegeae'. We shall discuss the traditions of the Macedones more fully in the next volume. It is enough here to show that Aegeae at Palatitsa–Vergina fits into the first stage of the conquests which the Argeadae Macedones made. The next stage may be inferred from Hdt. 8. 138. 3. They captured the region 'under Mt. Bermium', that is from Beroea to Edessa, including the gardens of Midas; and it was after this that they went on to conquer 'the rest of Macedonia'.

We turn now to the fullest account we possess of the Macedonian expansion. It is attached by Thucydides to the invasion of Sitalces in 429 B.C. I quote it in full, because a detailed commentary is needed. We may note in advance that it serves two purposes. It provides a historical geography

---

[1] The manuscripts have Βουτηΐδα, which is probably correct. St. Byz. s.v. Πέλλα, the successor of Aegeae as a capital city, records that in Syria Pella was called ἡ Βοῦτις. This shows Βοῦτις to have been a traditional name associated with the capital, and Βουτηΐς is 'the land of Boutis'. Most editors follow Dindorf in emending to Βοττηΐδα which they suppose rather improbably to be a form of Βοττία or Βοττιαία; so H. W. Parke, *The Delphic Oracle* (Oxford, 1939) 65. I deal in the next volume with the oracle to Caranus, which Parke discusses.

of the areas under the control or quasi-control of Perdiccas, and an account of the growth of the kingdom over which Perdiccas was ruling. Thuc. 2. 99:

ξυνηθροίζοντο οὖν ἐν τῇ Δοβήρῳ καὶ παρεσκευάζοντο, ὅπως κατὰ κορυφὴν ἐσβαλοῦσιν ἐς τὴν κάτω Μακεδονίαν, ἧς ὁ Περδίκκας ἦρχεν. τῶν γὰρ Μακεδόνων εἰσὶ καὶ Λυγκησταὶ καὶ Ἐλιμιῶται καὶ ἄλλα ἔθνη ἐπάνωθεν, ἃ ξύμμαχα μέν ἐστι τούτοις καὶ ὑπήκοα, βασιλείας δ᾽ ἔχει καθ᾽ αὑτά. τὴν δὲ παρὰ θάλασσαν νῦν Μακεδονίαν Ἀλέξανδρος ὁ Περδίκκου πατὴρ καὶ οἱ πρόγονοι αὐτοῦ, Τημενίδαι τὸ ἀρχαῖον ὄντες ἐξ Ἄργους, πρῶτοι ἐκτήσαντο καὶ ἐβασίλευσαν ἀναστήσαντες μάχῃ ἐκ μὲν Πιερίας Πίερας, οἳ ὕστερον ὑπὸ τὸ Πάγγαιον πέραν Στρυμόνος ᾤκησαν Φάγρητα καὶ ἄλλα χωρία (καὶ ἔτι καὶ νῦν Πιερικὸς κόλπος καλεῖται ἡ ὑπὸ τῷ Παγγαίῳ πρὸς θάλασσαν γῆ), ἐκ δὲ τῆς Βοττίας καλουμένης Βοττιαίους, οἳ νῦν ὅμοροι Χαλκιδέων οἰκοῦσιν· τῆς δὲ Παιονίας παρὰ τὸν Ἀξιὸν ποταμὸν στενήν τινα καθήκουσαν ἄνωθεν μέχρι Πέλλης καὶ θαλάσσης ἐκτήσαντο, καὶ πέραν Ἀξιοῦ μέχρι Στρυμόνος τὴν Μυγδονίαν καλουμένην Ἠδῶνας ἐξελάσαντες νέμονται. ἀνέστησαν δὲ καὶ ἐκ τῆς νῦν Ἐορδίας καλουμένης Ἐορδούς, ὧν οἱ μὲν πολλοὶ ἐφθάρησαν, βραχὺ δέ τι αὐτῶν περὶ Φύσκαν κατῴκηται, καὶ ἐξ Ἀλμωπίας Ἄλμωπας. ἐκράτησαν δὲ καὶ τῶν ἄλλων ἐθνῶν οἱ Μακεδόνες οὗτοι, ἃ καὶ νῦν ἔτι ἔχουσι, τόν τε Ἀνθεμοῦντα καὶ Γρηστωνίαν καὶ Βισαλτίαν καὶ Μακεδόνων αὐτῶν πολλήν. τὸ δὲ ξύμπαν Μακεδονία καλεῖται, καὶ Περδίκκας Ἀλεξάνδρου βασιλεὺς αὐτῶν ἦν ὅτε Σιτάλκης ἐπῄει.

If we take the historical geography first, we see that Thucydides uses three terms of definition: 'Lower Macedonia over which Perdiccas was ruling', 'the present coastal Macedonia . . . first won and ruled over by Alexander and his ancestors', and 'Upper Macedonia where Macedonian tribes owed allegiance but had their own monarchies'. It would appear that the first two terms are used of the same area, although that area includes inland and elevated cantons such as Almopia, Eordaea, and Crestonia. The third term is extremely vague. We may add Orestae, Pelagones, Deuriopes, or Argestaei so as to include the catchment-areas of the Haliacmon or the Erigon rivers, but we do so at our own risk. Thucydides has left his phrase ἄλλα ἔθνη ἐπάνωθεν undefined; for he did not consider that the tribes of Upper Macedonia were in the area under the direct rule of Perdiccas at that time. This point is clear at 4. 83. 1, where Arrhabaeus, king of the 'Lyncestae Macedones', is described not as a rebellious subject but as a neighbouring king. The term 'Upper Macedonia' was not invented by Thucydides; for Herodotus used it to define the high country east of the passes from Illyris (8. 137. 1 ἐς τὴν ἄνω Μακεδονίην).

The order in which Thucydides mentions the parts of Perdiccas' kingdom is consistent in itself. First, he deals cursorily with the Macedones in Upper Macedonia. Then he takes 'coastal Macedonia' from south-west to north-east, viz. Pieria, Bottia, a bit of Paeonia by the Axius, and

Mygdonia between the Axius and the Strymon (although not 'coastal', Mygdonia has coastal finials in the Thermaic and Strymonian Gulfs). Then he goes back and gives additional areas roughly from north to south (or west to east), viz. Eordia, Almopia, Anthemus, Crestonia, and Bisaltia. These areas are not coastal at all, but they seem to be included under the ambivalent term 'the present coastal Macedonia'. It is at any rate clear that all of them had been conquered by the Temenid kings and were still in the possession of the king at the time when Thucydides wrote the words ἃ καὶ νῦν ἔτι ἔχουσιν. Lastly we have the odd addition to this last category καὶ Μακεδόνων αὐτῶν πολλὴν (sc. γῆν). Who are these Macedones, of whose territories only a part had been acquired? They can hardly be tribes of Macedones, other than the Argeadae Macedones, living in their homeland in northern Pieria; for it is inconceivable that the homeland was not entirely under Temenid rule. Accordingly they must be the Macedones of Upper Macedonia, that is the Macedones of 2. 99. 2.

That this is so may be shown also by a consideration of Thucydides arrangement of the thought in this excursus. If we begin at 2. 98 the order is Sitalces, Perdiccas' Macedonia, the Macedones of Upper Macedonia, and coastal Macedonia; and then when he has finished his description of coastal Macedonia in its extended sense, he winds up in the order 'the Macedones' (i.e. of Upper Macedonia), Macedonia, Perdiccas, and Sitalces. This arrangement of thought, which may be summarized in symbols as ABCDDCBA, is typical of Thucydides' earliest writing, as I have pointed out with special reference to the Archaeologia of Book I.[1] Its use here indicates that the passage was written during the Archidamian War, and perhaps before Thucydides went into exile.[2]

It is important to notice that the order in which Thucydides mentions the parts of Perdiccas' kingdom is consistent in itself, being organized on an intelligible geographical system and obeying a stylistic canon of formal arrangement. There are no instances of πρῶτον μέν . . . ἔπειτα δέ. Rather we have simply the use of καί as 'also' (e.g. ἀνέστησαν δὲ καὶ and ἐκράτησαν δὲ καί). In other words, the order does not give and was not intended to give a chronological sequence of conquests. This is readily understandable. The main aim of Thucydides was to describe not the rise of Macedon but the kingdom of Perdiccas as it was in the year 429 B.C.

As so often in an excursus, Thucydides adds interesting information for its own sake. Thus this was the first dynasty of the Macedones to acquire and to rule this amount of Macedonia; the Macedones had to fight (μάχη) to oust the Pieres from Pieria and the Bottiaei from Bottia, and the new habitat of each is defined; the strip of Paeonia down to Pella and the sea was narrow (so too Hdt. 7. 123. 3 στεινὸν χωρίον); they expelled the Edones from Mygdonia; they killed most of the Eordi, and expelled the small remainder who settled at Physca in Mygdonia; and they expelled the Almopes from Almopia. If we put these pieces of information together, we may conjecture that the greatest military feats were in the first stage of the conquest, that is against the Pieres and the Bottiaei, and that the policy of destruction and deportation was practised in the first and second stages, that is in Pieria, Bottiaea, Almopia, and Eordaea. In other words, the Macedones expunged the existing population or at least the warlike elements of the existing population from a large and integrated area, for which Aegeae at Palatitsa–Vergina was a well-placed capital.

Of those who escaped, the Bottiaei and the Eordi presumably thought they would be safe when they crossed the Axius river. That is why they settled where they did; for they were among people who were still independent of the Macedones. In the third stage of the conquest the only deportation was that of the Edones, the strongest of the tribes in the Edonic group; some of these found a refuge in the Athos peninsula (Thuc. 4. 109. 4). We may assume from Thucydides' silence that otherwise the existing populations (which included the remnant of the Eordi in Mygdonia) remained on the ground, and that the Macedones came in as overlords in the narrow strip of Paeonia, in Anthemus, Crestonia, and Bisaltia, and in most of Mygdonia. The escape of the defeated Pieres to the region of Pangaeum is an unexplained puzzle; they may have gone by sea and joined some related tribe near Mt. Pangaeum, because by origin they were Cicones and in the Trojan Catalogue Cicones had held the lands by Mt. Pangaeum.

The third stage occurred at some time after 550 B.C., because the archaeological evidence at Ayios Vasilios in Mygdonia and at Chauchitsa indicates that Thracians were in possession of these places c. 550 B.C. There was also a time of Paeonian power during the sixth century, when they attacked and almost destroyed Perinthus by the Bosporus, a colony planted by Samos c. 600 B.C. (Hdt. 5. 1 and Str. 331 fr. 41). On the other hand, it is probable that the first two stages were completed by 550 B.C. (the date to which this volume extends), because they provided a strong and defensible kingdom with Eordaea as an advanced redoubt against the tribes of Upper Macedonia. These tribes and the Illyrians behind them were the chief threat to the young kingdom. I call them 'tribes', because Thucydides does. He speaks of 'tribes' too when he mentions the conquest of Anthemus, Crestonia, and Bisaltia, and in the words τῶν ἄλλων ἐθνῶν he implies that the Pieres, the Bottiaei, the Edones, the Eordi, and the Almopes had been tribes when the Macedones set upon them. There is, however, an important distinction between the tribes of

Upper Macedonia and those east of the Axius. The former are called
'Macedones' twice; the latter are not so called, pointedly indeed in the
last sentence but one of the passage which I have quoted.

In what sense were the Lyncestae, the Elimiotae, and the other tribes
ἐπάνωθεν 'Macedones'? At 4. 83. 1 we have Λυγκησταὶ Μακεδόνες; we
might equally well have had Ἐλιμιῶται Μακεδόνες or another tribal
ethnic with 'Macedones' appended. The meaning becomes clear when
we notice in Str. 434 that the Orestae, the Pelagones, and the Elimiotae
were τῶν Ἠπειρωτῶν and become, 'some willingly, some unwillingly'
μέρη Μακεδόνων. As I suggested in my book on Epirus,[1] the ultimate
source for the ethnography and geography of Epirus, Illyris, and Macedonia was Hecataeus, and in many cases the time base was that of Hecataeus, i.e. c. 500 B.C. Now the term Ἠπειρῶται in Strabo was probably
a term introduced by Ephorus into the ethnography of Epirus,[2] and a
term used by Hecataeus was 'Molossian'. Thus of the Orestae themselves
Hecataeus (*FGrH* 1 F 107) wrote Ὀρέσται· Μολοσσικὸν ἔθνος. We see then
that the Orestae, the Pelagones, and the Elimiotae certainly, and the
Lyncestae most probably, were described as 'Molossoi' in the time of
Hecataeus and as 'Macedones' in the time of Thucydides. The reason
for the change was no doubt political.

The great era of Molossian expansion is mentioned by Str. C. 324 init.
as coming after the great era of Chaonian power. On the other hand, it
came before the era of Macedonian expansion. The Molossian acme
may have been in the eighth and seventh centuries B.C.; for the statement
in Str. 329 fr. 11 that Emathia was held by Ἠπειρωτῶν τινες καὶ Ἰλλυριῶν is best dated to those centuries in which bronze objects of Illyrian
type are most common. The Macedonian expansion into what came to
be called 'Upper Macedonia' occurred after 500 B.C., and it may be
placed tentatively in the reign of Alexander I, whom Thucydides named
alone among the seven predecessors of Perdiccas. If it seems strange to
modern scholars that the collective names given to such a cluster of tribes
were purely political, they should note the early fourth-century inscriptions of the Molossian state in which some tribes hitherto 'Thesprotian'
were described as 'Molossian'.[3]

There was clearly expansion at some times and contraction at other
times in the cluster which formed the actual Molossian state or the actual
Macedonian state. In 429 B.C. the Macedonian state was contracted,
because the Lyncestae, the Elimiotae, and other tribes had their own
monarchies and behaved at times independently, as in the case of the
Lyncestae. Nevertheless, Thucydides recognized the claim of the Macedonian state to the territories of Upper Macedonia. That claim was based
upon a time when the Macedonians had conquered much of the land of

[1] *Epirus* 447 f. [2] *Ibid.* 461 f. [3] *Ibid.* 531.

Upper Macedonia (Μακεδόνων αὐτῶν πολλήν) and had compelled the tribes there to enter the political state known as οἱ Μακεδόνες. Race, dialect, and customs were another matter. In fact, as archaeological remains over a long period of time and geographical considerations indicate, the tribes of Upper Macedonia were in many respects much closer to the Epirotes than to the Macedonians. But the Macedonian state had in fact come to stay. It brought such changes in its train that 'some even call the whole territory as far as Corcyra "Macedonia" because the peoples are similar in hair-style, dialect, and the wearing of the chlamys' (Str. C 326 fin.).

5. *The Macedonians and the Greeks, c. 650–550 B.C.*

Although the southern Greeks in the world of city-states were unaware of the fact, the Macedones were themselves an example of that Greek-speaking expansion which planted colonies at many places on the Mediterranean coasts. It began, as in Greece proper, after a time of migratory movements and when the Macedones themselves were in secure possession of their own homeland in northern Pieria.[1] They had learnt much from their neighbours—Thracian, Phrygian, and Illyrian—and in 650 B.C. or so they put their lessons to good purpose under the leadership of a new dynasty. By expropriating and in some cases by destroying the previous inhabitants they created a solid block of Greek-speaking Macedonians in Pieria, Eordaea, Almopia, and Bottiaea, which was the kernel of the greater Macedonian state, and which in times of trouble was to be the almost irreducible minimum of Macedonian strength.

The displaced Bottiaeans acquired new territory on the base of the three prongs of Chalcidice, driving out the previous inhabitants who took refuge probably in the eastern prong, which ends in Mt. Athos. In this period of turmoil Andros planted Acanthus, Argilus, Sane, and Stagirus on the eastern side of Chalcidice c. 655–654 B.C., and Chalcis increased the number of her small colonies on the prongs of the Chalcidic peninsula. Corinth planted the strongest colony of all at Potidaea c. 600 B.C. The most remarkable thing at Bottiaean Olynthus is the complete exclusion of objects which were made by the nearby Greek colonies. In the first hundred years, from 650 to 550 B.C., the Crousaei and the Bottiaeans were remarkably resistant to the influences of Greek city-state culture. So too were the Macedones, as far as we can tell from the scanty evidence. Trade was more lively between the Thracians of the eastern coast of the inner Thermaic Gulf and the Greek cities or the Thessalian

[1]   Thucydides 1. 12. 4 gives the conditions which preceded the expansion of the city-states.

ports. From these Thracians the *cothon* spread far inland.[1] In 627 B.C. Corcyra founded Epidamnus, and *c.* 600 B.C. Corinth founded Apollonia in Illyris. These two colonies were well placed to trade inland along the route used later by the Via Egnatia, while Potidaea had the same advantages for trading up the Vardar valley or north-westwards towards Monastir. Their trade-routes might meet, for instance, at such places as Trebenishte, but the old overland trade-route linking the Aegean to the Adriatic was only of local importance. For the Greeks were now more conversant with the sea, and merchandise crossed the peninsula more easily at the Isthmus of Corinth.[2]

In the eyes of the Greek colonists the Macedones were as barbaric as the Bottiaeans and the Thracians, or as the Chaones and the Molossi of Epirus. This is not surprising; for the Macedones were different in political institutions, in manner of life, in dress, and in many aspects of religious and cultural outlook. Moreover, the gulf widened rapidly, as Greek life became more sophisticated and Greek idiosyncrasies became more pronounced. The Macedones had their own grounds for confidence. They had created a stable and growing state. They owned fertile lands and commanded great natural resources. A Greek colony or two on the coast of the Thermaic Gulf had value as a market of exchange, but experience soon showed that the Greeks were better kept at arm's length. The Macedonians had no reason and presumably no wish to align themselves with the Greek states either as promoters of Greek culture or as speakers of a common language. Each people had its own culture, and each people was destined to develop on its own lines in accordance with its own genius and its own situation. Hostility between the two was to be expected. A slender bridge between them was represented by the Greek language, spoken as contemporary Doric by the royal house and in the form of an ancient patois by the Macedones, but a means of communication is very far from assuring peaceful relations between two peoples, as we know from our experience of the modern world.

[1] For instance to Saraj in Pelagonia (*Starinar* 11 (1960) 206 fig. 33 in Tomb 16).
[2] Thuc. 1. 13. 5 emphasizes the general change in Greek methods of trading.

APPENDIX

In 1970 I had the good fortune to be the guest of the Bulgarian Academy of Sciences and visited the Museums of central and south-western Bulgaria. The points of contact between Macedonia and these areas of Bulgaria are of some importance, particularly for chronology. I list them under the chronological headings given to me in Bulgaria by scholars who were most generous in helping me.

Middle Neolithic Age. Human face moulded on a pot, as at Porodin (Fig. I*f*) in the Stara Zagora Museum; female figurine with large buttocks and stylized head, as at Porodin (cf. Grbić, *Porodin* fig. 40, I), in the Kazanluk Museum.

Late Neolithic Age. Phalli vertically pierced, as at Malik IIa (Fig. 3*c* I), from Karanovo; altar-tables, as at Porodin and Malik IIa (Fig. 3*e* I), in the Plovdiv Museum.

"Eneolithic" Period. Copper celts and copper fish-hooks, both as at Malik IIa (Fig. 3*a*), from Salmanovo in N.E. Bulgaria, now in the Sofia Museum. Human figure in adoration, as at Malik IIa (Fig. 3*d*), from Karanovo where it is moulded on the inside of a plate, in the Stara Zagora Museum. Pintaderas, as at Malik IIa (Fig 3*b*, first and second lines), from Karanovo; and drilled plaques of clay or bone, as at Malik IIa (*SA* 1966. I. Pl. III*f*), from Karanovo in the Stara Zagora Museum. Bird-figurine, perhaps of a swan, as at Malik IIa (Fig. 3*f* 3), from Karanovo in the Stara Zagora Museum. Curving plastic line on pottery, as at Tsiplevets and Malik IIIa (Fig. 9*a–f*), from Ashmaschka Mogila, in the store of finds at Alkavarea; and a wheel of clay, similar to one on pottery at Malik IIIa (Fig. 9*k*), in the Plovdiv Museum.

Bronze Age. Stone hammer-axes, as at Kravari (Fig. 13*l*), in the Museums of Plovdiv and Stara Zagora, where dated to the E.B.A. Axes in copper of the shape shown in Fig. 13*b* (from Petralona) and a mould for casting them come from Nova Nadežda in the Haskovo region, where they are attributed to the second millennium (see *Bull. de l'Inst. arch.* 22 (1959) 333 and Археолог. 1969. 4. 66). Axes in bronze of this shape come from Karanovo VII and from the Vidin area, the latter in the Sofia Museum being dated to L.B.A.; others in the Museums of Plovdiv, Stara Zagora, and Kjustendil are undated. For the dating of these axes see p. 299 with note 4.

Knobbed Ware (Buckelkeramik), which I saw in the Museums of Plovdiv, Stara Zagora and Kazanluk, seemed to belong to two periods: one around the late twelfth century, and the other mainly in the ninth century; for this pottery see pp. 319 and 382 above. Incised and stamped decoration, as in Fig. 15, occurs on pottery in the Stara Zagora Museum, and ear-like handles as in Fig. 15*aa* occur on L.B.A. pots from Dipsis.

Miniature pierced double-axes, as at Vergina, Visoï and Olynthus (Figs. 17*u* and 19*h*), are in the Sofia Museum: six from Srebenro near Kazanluk of the Bulgarian L.B.A., almost rectangular in shape, and one of a Minoan shape (as in Fig. 19*h*) from Pazardzik. See p. 336 above for the spread of the cult of the double-axe.

Early Iron Age. Certain objects which I associated with the Illyrian expansion of the eighth and early seventh centuries (p. 420 above) have been found in a burial at Gradec in the Vidin district, where they are dated to these centuries: heavy bracelets with thickened ends (as in Fig. 17*z*), long hair-coils (as in Fig. 17*a*), a button-topped fibula (as in Fig. 20*a*), a necklace of amber beads, and an elaborate pendant (Археолог 1965. 3. 53f.). Heavy bracelets and long hair-coils from a seventh-century tumulus are in the Stara Zagora Museum. The unusual hair-rings of gold and silver at Marmariani (Fig. 20*u–v*) are paralleled exactly by numerous hair-rings of gold and silver of the same shapes from tumulus-burials at Kamena Mogila near Troyan in Central Bulgaria (Археолог 1964. 4. 65).

Bronzes from Amphipolis were shown in Case no. 48 in the Vienna Archaeological Museum in 1970. They were a pierced double-axe (as in Fig. 19*h*), pendants as in Fig. 17*o*, 17*aa*, 19*a* and 19*b*, miniature jugs as in Fig. 17*n*, bronze beads as in Fig. 19*l*, buttons as in Fig. 18*l* and *s*, a spectacle-fibula as in Fig. 17*b*, heavy armlets as in Fig. 17*z*, and a horse on a stand. These bronzes suggest that the Illyrians held Amphipolis during their period of expansion.

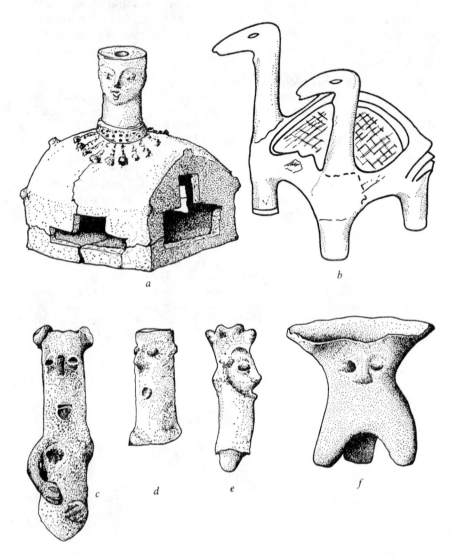

FIG. I. HOUSE MODEL, ALTAR TABLES, AND HUMAN FIGURINES FROM PORODIN. See p. 224.

a. House model, reconstructed from fragments.   *b*. Four-legged altar table with heads of aquatic reptiles, reconstructed from fragments.   *c–e*. Human figurines.   *f*. Three-legged altar table with a moulded human face.

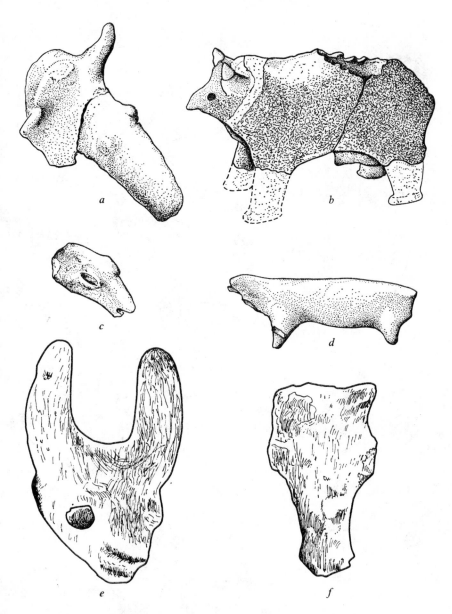

Fig. 2. Animal Figurines from Porodin. See p. 224.

a. Sheep.   b. Bull, perhaps with a hole in the back for use as a vessel.   c. Snake.
d. Pig.   e. Lynx.   f. Horse.

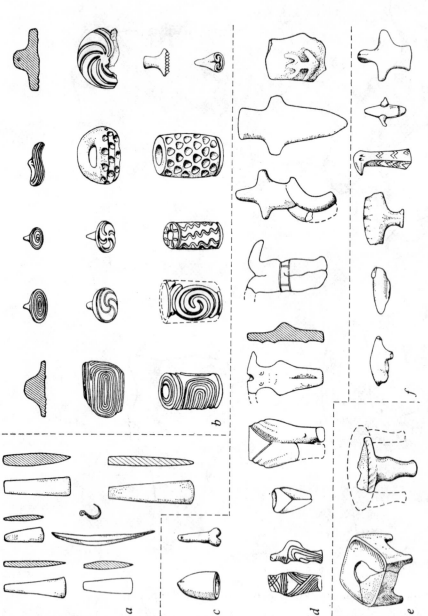

FIG. 3. COPPER TOOLS, PINTADERAS, CYLINDER SEALS, FIGURINES, AND ALTAR TABLES FROM MALIK IIA
See pp. 229 f.

a. Copper celts and copper fish-hook.   *b.* Pintaderas and cylinder seals.   *c.* Vertically pierced phallus, and phallus with testicles.   *d.* Human figurines, and on a sherd a plastic representation of a figure doing obeisance.   *e.* Four-legged and three-legged altar tables   *f.* Animal and bird figurines.

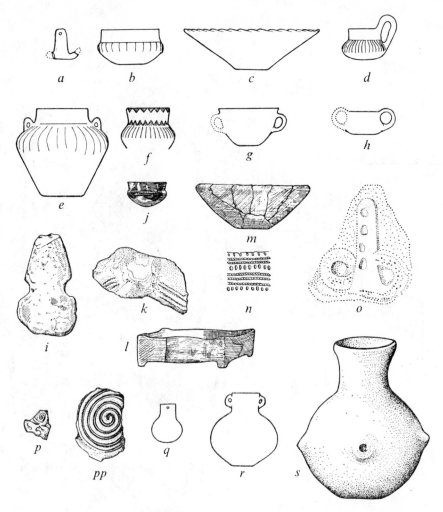

FIG. 4. POTTERY FROM MALIK, GAJTAN, AND SITES IN MACEDONIA.

For *a–h* see pp. 241–2; *i–m*, pp. 244–5; *n, o*, pp. 249–50; *p, pp*, p. 264; *q–s*, p. 265.

a. Anchor-shaped hook of clay, pierced for suspension as an amulet, from Malik IIb. *b.* Wide bowl with vertical collar and with fluting, from Malik IIb. *c.* Basin with thick inturning grooved rim from Malik IIb. *d.* One-handled cup with fluting from Malik IIb. *e.* Large jar with dwarf handles high on the shoulders, almost vertical collar and fluting, from Malik IIb. *f.* Bowl with high collar, the incised triangles containing parallel incised lines and fluting, from Malik IIb. *g, h.* Two-handled tankards from the last stage of Malik IIb. *i.* Waisted pebble-axe from Servia II. *j.* Bowl with almost vertical collar and a line of oblique stripes on the shoulder, from the burial-pit in Servia II. *k.* Piece of zoomorphic vase with white-filled incisions from the burial-pit in Servia II. *l.* Vase in the shape of a four-legged altar table from the burial-pit in Servia II. *m.* Basin with inturning rim from the burial-pit in Servia II. *n.* 'Corded ware' ornamentation and rows of punctures and jabs on pottery from Gajtan I. *o.* Plastic representation of the anchor-shaped hook (as in *a*) with holes for suspension, on a sherd from Gajtan II. *p, pp.* Sherds with deep incised continuous lines in a spiral, *pp* having signs of white filling, from Servia II. *q, r.* Flask-like pots from Malik IIa. *s.* Flask-like pot of miniature size with four small pierced lugs from Porodin.

NOTE: *k* and *pp* have white filling between the narrow parallel lines; the surface is black.

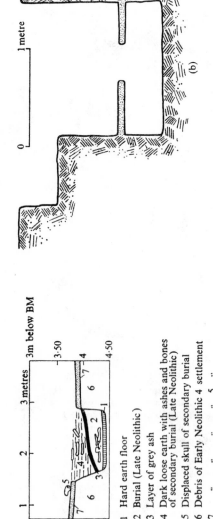

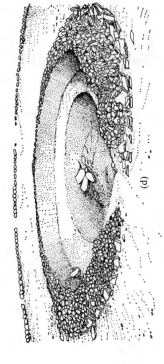

1 Hard earth floor
2 Burial (Late Neolithic)
3 Layer of grey ash
4 Dark loose earth with ashes and bones
  of secondary burial (Late Neolithic)
5 Displaced skull of secondary burial
6 Debris of Early Neolithic 4 settlement
7 ,,   ,,   ,,   5   ,,

(a)

3m below BM

3·50

4
7
6

4·50

TUMULUS

Dörpfeld reported a secondary
burial just above the pithos-burial

(c)

Fig. 5. Burial-pits at Servia, Vergina, Leucas, and Pazhok.   See pp. 243–7.

a. Section of burial-pit at Servia II.   b. Section of burial-pit in tumulus Γ at Vergina.   c. Section of burial-pit R I under a
tumulus in Leucas.   d. Burial-pit in the inner tumulus of a double tumulus at Pazhok.

Note: in (d) the orthostatic stones, being of a different colour and shape from the other stones, are conspicuous in the original
photograph.

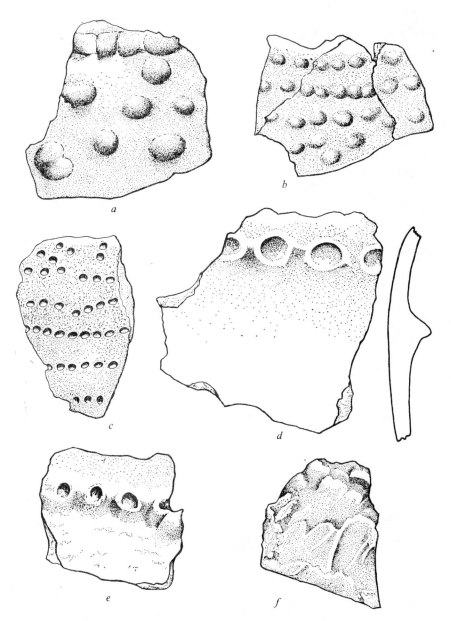

FIG. 6. COARSE WARE FROM PORODIN (1). See p. 253.

The decoration is in *a* with large lumps, in *b* with small blobs, in *c* with impressed round holes, in *d* with round pock-marks on a plastic band, in *e* with round holes punched on a plastic band, and in *f* with rough rippling of the surface.

G g

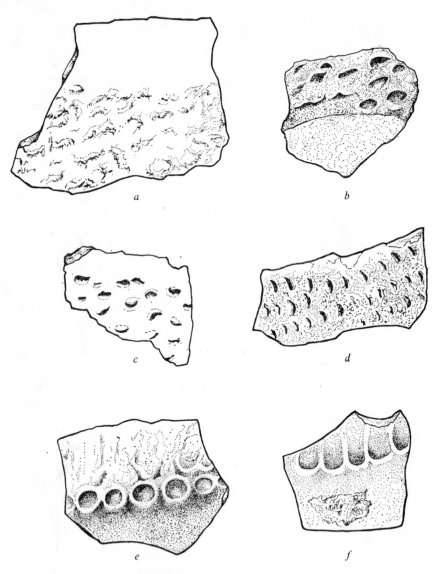

FIG. 7. COARSE WARE FROM PORODIN (2). See p. 253.

The decoration is in *a* and *b* with broken rippling, in *c* and *d* with jags and commas, in *e* with rough rippling and a pock-marked raised band, and in *f* with moulded arcading.

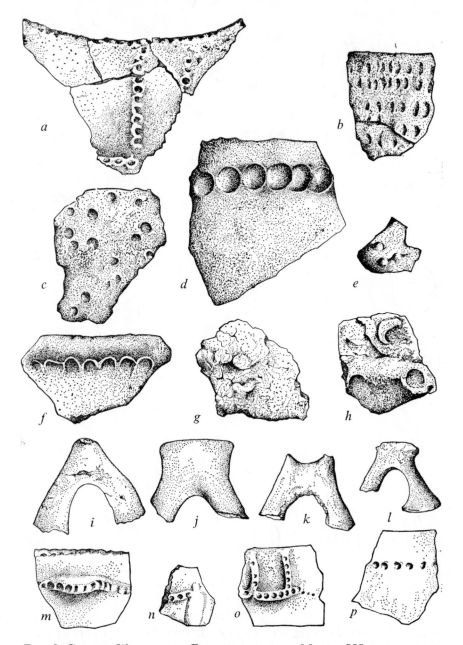

FIG. 8. COARSE WARE FROM EPIRUS AND FROM MALIK IIIA, AND WISH-
BONE HANDLES FROM MACEDONIA. See pp. 253–4.

The decoration in *a* (from Dodona) is with pock-marked raised bands, in *b* with jags and
commas, in *c* with impressed round holes, in *d* with a line of impressed pock-marks below the
rim (*b–d* from Kastritsa), in *e* with small blobs (from Koutsoulio), in *f* with arcading below
the rim (from Terovo), in *g* with large lumps (from Terovo), and in *h* with rough rippling and
pock-marks on a raised band (from Koutsoulio).

The wish-bone handles are *i* and *j* from Vardarophtsa in E.B.A. and *k* and *l* from Molyvopyrgo in M.B.A.

The decoration in *m* is with impressed dimples on the rim and pock-marking on a raised
plastic band, in *n* with impressed round holes on a raised plastic band and plastic loop, in *o*
with pock-marking on raised plastic bands arranged as at Dodona in *a*, and in *p* with impressed holes. These sherds are from Malik IIIa.

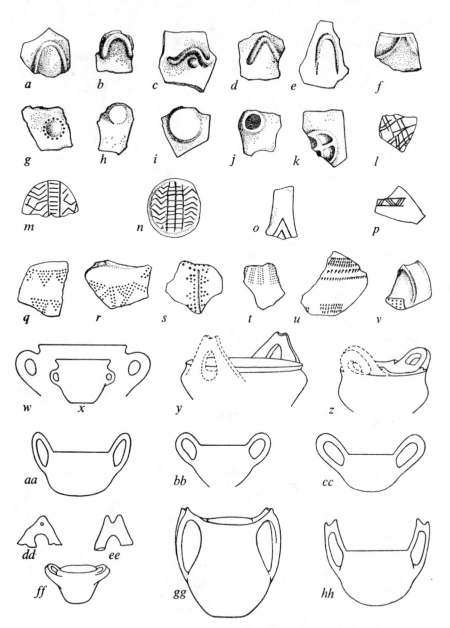

FIG. 9. PLASTIC, INCISED, AND PRICKED DECORATION ON POTTERY FROM
MALIK IIIA(*a–v*), AND POTTERY AND HANDLES FROM MALIK IIIB (*w–z*)
AND IIIC (*aa–hh*). See pp. 255–6.

a–f. Plastic coils.   *g–k.* Plastic nipple, knobs, and four-spoked wheel.   *l–n.* Incised
decoration on the bases of pots.   *o, p.* Incised decoration.   *q–v.* Pricked decoration.
w–z. Two-handled bowls with handles of different types.   *aa–cc.* High-handled cantharoi of
'Minyan' type.   *dd, ee.* Wish-bone handles (and in *y*).   *ff.* Two-handled cup.   *gg.* Pear-
shaped vase with long tipped handles.   *hh.* Bowl with two high, horned handles of the *ansa
cornuta* class.

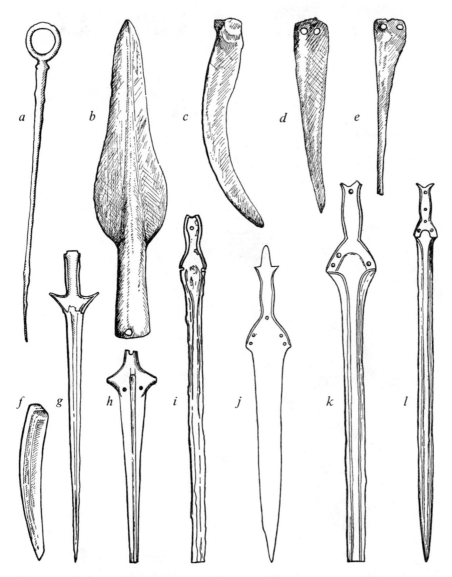

FIG. 10. BRONZE RING-PIN AND BRONZE WEAPONS FROM MACEDONIA, MALIK, AND THE MATI VALLEY.

For *a–e* see p. 254; *f*, p. 300; *g–l*, pp. 292–4 and 315–22.

a. Ring-pin, *c*. 21 cm long, from Malik IIIc.   *b*. Spear-head, 21 cm long, from Malik IIIc. *c*. One-bladed, curving-backed knife, 14 cm long, from Malik.   *d*. Knife, *c*. 12 cm long, with two rivet-holes, from Malik IIIc.   *e*. Knife, *c*. 11 cm long, with a rivet and a rivet-hole, from Malik IIIc.   *f*. Sickle-blade, 13 cm long, curving-backed, from Kilindir (L.B.A.).   *g*. Sword, 56 cm long, from Grevena.   *h*. Sword, 37·5 cm long, from Grevena. *i*. Sword, 76 cm long, from Prilep.   *j*. Sword, *c*. 65 cm long, from a tumulus at Visoï. *k*. Sword, 68 cm long, from a tumulus in the Mati valley.   *l*. Sword, 72 cm long, from tumulus burial C*Δ* at Vergina (see Fig. 13, *a*).

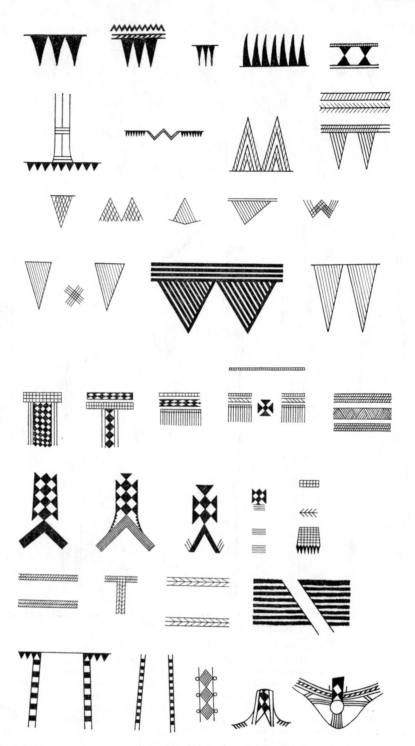

FIG. 11. DESIGNS ON THE MATT-PAINTED POTTERY FROM MALIK AND
TREN.
See pp. 282 and 285.

The last two designs are on handles from pots at Tren.

FIG. 12. SHAPES OF THE MATT-PAINTED POTTERY FROM MALIK.

See pp. 281 f.

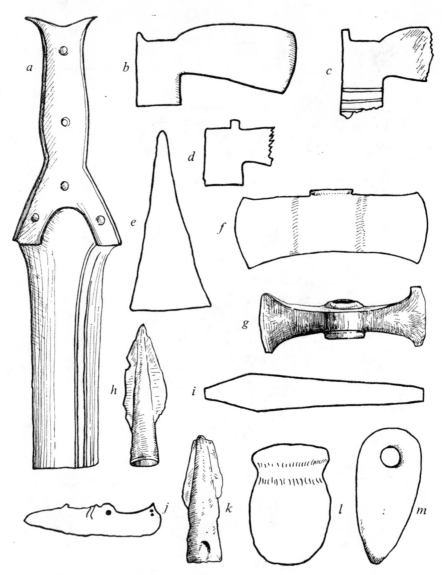

FIG. 13. BRONZE AND STONE OBJECTS FROM MACEDONIA.

a. Part of a bronze sword from tumulus burial C*Δ* at Vergina. See Fig. 10*l* and p. 315.
b–d. Bronze axes from Petralona.   *e.* Bronze celt from Petralona.   *f.* Bronze axe
with collar above the bore-hole, from Kravari.   *g.* Bronze axe, 11 cm long, with
collar above and below the bore-hole, from Kilindir. (*b–g.*) see p. 299.   *h.* Bronze javelin-
head, 12 cm long, from Prilep. See p. 293.   *i.* Bronze cold chisel from Petralona. See p. 299.
j. Stone 'horse' from Tsiplevets. See p. 240.   *k.* Bronze javelin-head, 8·5 cm long, with two
rivets, from Vardina. See p. 292.   *l.* Stone hand-axe, waisted and grooved, from Kravari.
See p. 254.   *m.* Stone hammer-axe from Kravari. See p. 240 n. 1.

FIG. 14. MATT-PAINTED POTTERY, FLUTED WARE, AND AN ARYBALLOS.

a. Shallow bowl with thumb-grip handles, from Kilindir. See p. 277.   *b*. Jug with sloping neck, from Boubousti. (*b–d*.) see p. 283.   *c*. Bowl with horizontal lugs, from Boubousti. *d*. Tankard with two ribbon-handles, from Boubousti.   *e*. Jar with cylindrical neck, everted rim, and two pierced lugs, from Pateli. See p. 280.   *f* and *j*. Matt-painted designs on sherds from Tren. See p. 285.   *g*. Two-handled tankard from Kastritsa. See p. 287. *h*. Handleless bowl, with almost vertical collar and fluting on the shoulder, from Gajtan. See p. 308.   *i*. Two-handled tankard from a tumulus burial at Vodhinë. See p. 286. *k*. Fluted rim from Gajtan. See p. 308.   *l*. Matt-painted tankard from Lianokladhi. See p. 287.   *m*. Matt-painted bowl from a tumulus burial at Aphidna. See p. 288.   *n*. An aryballos of closed angular-cylindrical shape, from Vergina. See p. 292.

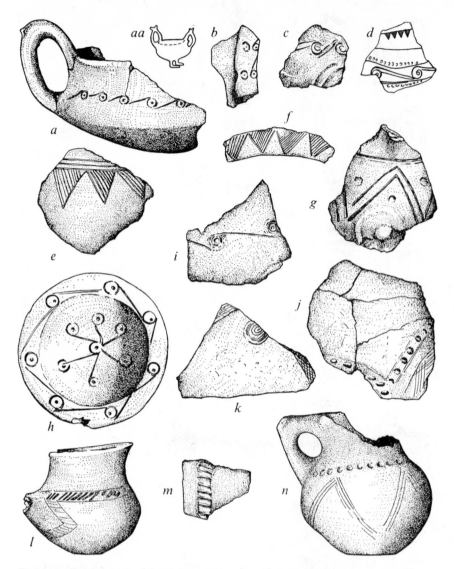

FIG. 15. INCISED AND STAMPED DECORATION ON POTTERY FROM TROY
VII b 2 AND FROM EAST CENTRAL MACEDONIA. See p. 321.

a from Troy; *b* from Vardarophtsa; *c* from Troy; *d* from Saratse; *e* from Troy; *f* from
Vardarophtsa; *g* from Troy; *h* from Vardina; *i* from Troy; *j* from Vardarophtsa; *k* from
Vardarophtsa; *l* from Troy; *m* from Vardarophtsa; and *n* from Troy.

aa. Rippled drinking bowl with two handles of the *ansa lunata* type and with two little feet,
shaped like human feet, of the Lausitz culture in Hungary. See p. 320.

(In *g, j,* and *n* the circles represent 'punctuated round impressions', as Blegen calls them.)

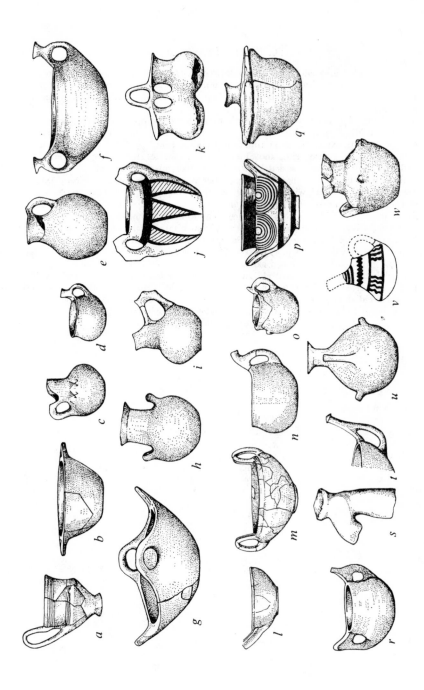

Fig. 16. Early Iron Age Pottery.

a. High-handled grey cup, with horizontal parallel grooves in groups, from Vardarophtsa. See p. 327.   *b.* Bowl with extended flat rim, pierced for two strings, from Vardarophtsa. Ibid.   *c.* Jug with cut-away neck, from Chauchitsa. Ibid.   *d.* Cup with trigger handle, from Chauchitsa. Ibid.   *e.* Jug with straight rim, from Vergina. See p. 333.   *f.* Two-handled drinking bowl, with rounded bottom and flat-topped conical thumb-rests, from Vergina. Ibid.   *g.* Shallow bowl, with rounded bottom, and with two loop-handles and two pinched-out extensions of the rim, from Vergina. Ibid.   *h.* Pot with rounded bottom, cylindrical neck, everted rim, and almost vertical handles, from Vergina. Ibid.   *i.* Jug with cut-away neck and twisted handle, from Chauchitsa. See p. 351.   *j.* Matt-painted tankard with twisted handles, from Saraj. See p. 338.   *k.* Twin vase from Axiokastron. See p. 346.   *l.* Bowl, with one ribbon handle set obliquely, from Chauchitsa. See p. 352. *m.* Cantharos with two triple handles, from Chauchitsa. Ibid.   *n.* Cup with trigger handle, from Chauchitsa. Ibid.   *o.* Cup with trigger handle and a mammiform knob, from Chauchitsa. Ibid.   *p.* Skyphos with concentric circles, from Chauchitsa. Ibid.   *q.* Lidded pot with handle of the *ansa lunata* type, from Chauchitsa. Ibid.   *r.* Cantharos with prolonged handles, from the Mati valley. See p. 377.   *s.* Flat-topped thumb-rest handle, from Gajtan. See p. 377.   *t.* Mushroom-topped extension of handle, from Olynthus. See p. 359.   *u.* Pot with globular body, two small almost horizontal handles, one vertical handle, cylindrical neck and everted rim, from Petilep. See p. 338.   *v.* Miniature jug, with cut-away neck and matt-painted decoration, from Tren. See p. 373.   *w.* Globular flat-bottomed pot, with mammiform knob, two almost vertical handles, cylindrical neck and everted rim, from Vergina. See p. 389.

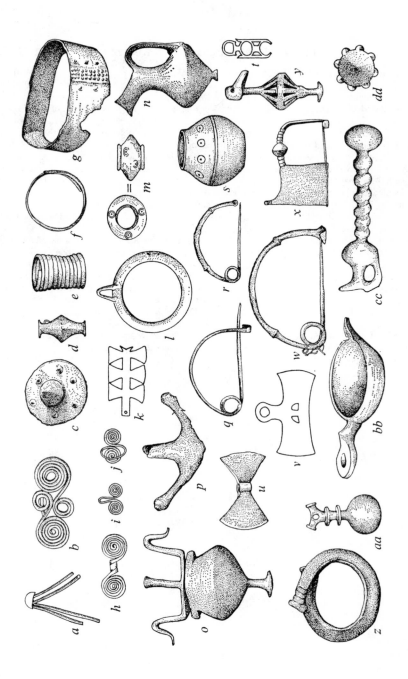

a b c d e f g h i j k l m n o p q r s t u v w x y z aa bb cc dd

FIG. 17. EARLY IRON AGE BRONZES (1).

a. Four long hair coils attached to a button, from Vergina. See p. 331.   *b.* Spectacle-fibula with eight-shaped centre, from Vergina. Ibid.   *c.* Phalaron from Vergina (the small rings indicate small bosses, and in the centre of the central boss there is a protuberance). Ibid. *d.* Collared biconical bead pendant, from Vergina. See p. 396.   *e.* Armlet of twelve coils, from Vergina, *O*1. See p. 390.   *f.* Single-coil armlet of bronze wire, with overlapping ends, from Vergina. See p. 332.   *g.* Large diadem with impressed decoration, from Vergina. Ibid. *h.* Two spirals, joined by a bridge of flattened bronze wire, from Vergina. Ibid.   *i.* Two spirals, with an upstanding extension between them, from Vergina. Ibid.   *j.* Ring terminating in two spirals of bronze wire, from Vergina. Ibid.   *k.* Rod with three double-axes pierced for suspension, from Vergina. Ibid.   *l.* Ring pendant, from Vergina. Ibid.   *m.* Biconical bead engraved with dot-centred concentric circles, from Vergina. Ibid.   *n.* Miniature jug from Pateli. See p. 343.   *o.* Herb-cup with detachable lid, which has duck-headed terminals, from Chauchitsa. See p. 349.   *p.* Turf-cutter pendant, with hollow socket and thin blade, from Chauchitsa. See p. 349.   *q.* Plain arched fibula, from Vergina. See p. 315. *r.* Arched fibula with two buttons and slight swelling of the arch, from Vergina. See p. 333. *s.* Large bead of curving biconical form, engraved with dot-centred circles, from Gajtan. See p. 334.   *t.* Caduceus-like pendant, from Vergina. See p. 335.   *u.* Double-axe with thin blades and stronger pierced centre, from Visoï. See p. 337.   *v.* Double-axe pendant of bronze sheet with two apertures, from Visoï. Ibid.   *w.* Large arched fibula, with large spring, two buttons, and small catch-plate, from Pateli. See p. 386.   *x.* Arched fibula with large catch-plate, from Pateli. See p. 343.   *y.* Distaff-shaped pendant with bird-headed top, from Pateli. See p. 343.   *z.* Heavy armlet of one turn with overlapping ends, engraved with parallel lines, from Pateli. Ibid.   *aa.* Pendant with collared triangular top, two rings, and ball foot, from Pateli. Ibid.   *bb.* Spoon-shaped pendant, from Pateli. Ibid.   *cc.* Jug-on-knobbly-stick pendant, from Pateli. Ibid.   *dd.* Button with eight petals, from Pateli. Ibid.

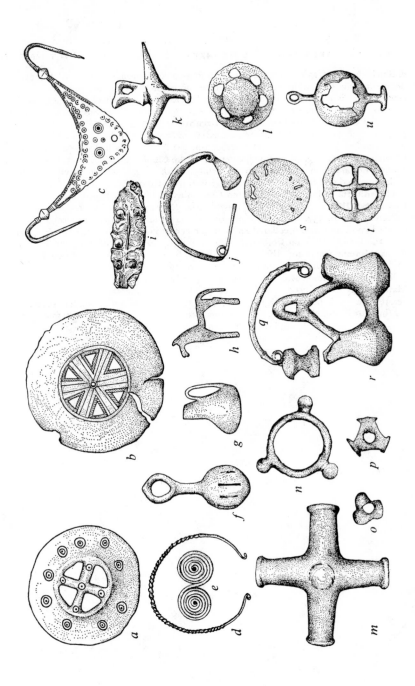

FIG. 18. EARLY IRON AGE BRONZES (2) AND A GOLD MOUTH-PIECE.

a. Shield-centre, *c.* 15 cm in diameter, with four-spoked wheel as centre and engraved with dot-centred circles and dot-centred concentric circles, from Pateli. See p. 343. *b.* Shield centre, 18·6 cm in diameter, with six-spoked wheel as centre, engraved with lines, and having a knob in the centre, from Chauchitsa. See p. 350. *c.* Two-pinned triangular fibula, decorated with dot-centred circles and dot-centred concentric circles, from Axiokastron. See p. 346. *d.* Torque with both ends curled, from Axiokastron. Ibid. *e.* Spectacle-fibula with slanting join, from Chauchitsa. See pp. 348 f. *f.* Slashed-sphere pendant, from Chauchitsa. Ibid. *g.* Miniature jug pendant, from Chauchitsa. Ibid. *h.* Horse of bronze plaque, originally on a stand, from Chauchitsa. Ibid. *i.* Gold mouth-piece, 8 cm long, with impressed decoration of dot-centred circles, from Chauchitsa. Ibid. *j.* Two-springed fibula with triangular catch-plate, from Chauchitsa. Ibid. *k.* Jug-on-bird pendant, from Chauchitsa. Ibid. *l.* Button with roughly triangular apertures, from the Benaki Museum collection. See p. 357. *m.* Hub-junction (or cross-shaped junction piece), hollow with collared ends, and with a collared knob on the centre facing an aperture on the other side, from the Benaki Museum Collection. See p. 356. *n.* Ring with three knobs, from the Benaki Museum Collection. Ibid. *o.* Trilobate bead, from the Benaki Museum Collection. Ibid. *p.* Triangular bead with discs at the ends, from the Benaki Museum Collection. Ibid. *q.* Two-springed fibula with two buttons and waisted quadrangular catch-plate, from the Mati valley. See p. 375. *r.* Twin-jug pendant, from the Benaki Museum Collection. See p. 356. *s.* Button with slit holes, from the Benaki Museum Collection. See p. 357. *t.* Miniature four-spoked wheel, from Vergina. See p. 334. *u.* Pendant with spherical centre and disc foot, from Dodona. See p. 356.

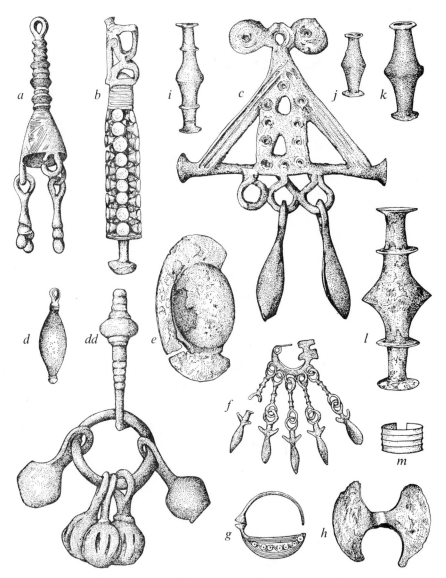

FIG. 19. EARLY IRON AGE BRONZES (3) AND A SILVER EAR-RING.

a. Bell-and-clappers pendant with linear engraving, from Axioupolis. See p. 353.   *b.* Pendant with fretted open work, disc foot, and stylized sitting man on top, from Axioupolis. Ibid.   *c.* Triangular pendant, with apertures and engraved with concentric circles, from Axioupolis. Ibid.   *d.* Bobbin-shaped pendant, from Kozani. See p. 345.   *dd.* Ring with pendants, from Axioupolis. See p. 353.   *e.* Phalaron from Axioupolis. See p. 354. *f.* fibula with pendants, from the Mati valley. Ibid.   *g.* Silver ear-ring with conical, flat-topped terminals, from Kruje. See p. 377.   *h.* Miniature double-axe with thin blades and stronger pierced centre, from Olynthus. See p. 359.   *i-l.* Biconical beads. See p. 357. *m.* Armband from Saraj. See p. 322.

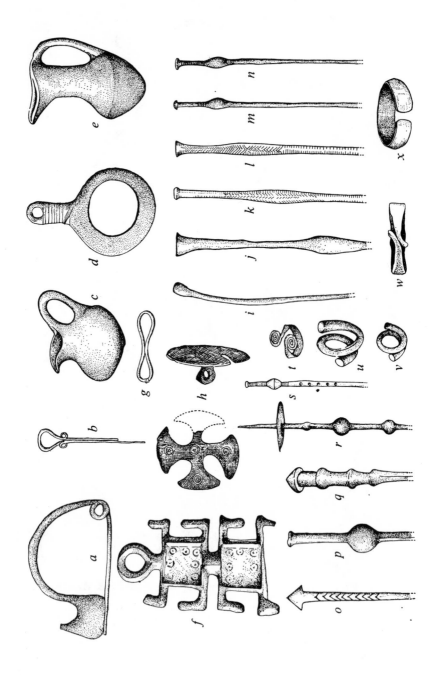

FIG. 20. EARLY IRON AGE BRONZES (4) AND IRON AND GOLD HAIR-GRIPS.

a. Arched fibula with broad button-topped catch-plate, from the Benaki Museum Collection. See p. 357. *b*. Double-shanked pin from the Mati valley. See p. 375. *c*. Miniature jug pendant, from North Albania. See p. 377. *d*. Horse-trapping engraved with parallel lines, from the Vidin district. See p. 427 n. 3. *e*. Miniature jug. See p. 382 n. 4. *f*. Top-piece of chain of pendants, engraved with dotted circles, from the Mati valley. See p. 375. *g*. Hair-grip of iron, from Vitsa. See p. 386. *h*. Button engraved with concentric circles, from Kozlu Dere. See p. 355. *i, j*. Pins from Vajzë. See p. 385. *k, l*. Pins from Vergina. Ibid. *m, n*. Pins from Mycenae. See p. 406. *o*. Cone-headed pin from Vergina. See p. 391. *p*. Pin from Salamis. See p. 407 n. 1. *q*. Mushroom-headed pin with three swellings, from Pateli. See p. 343. *r*. Pin from Titov Veles. See p. 355. *s*. Pin from Axiokastron. See p. 346. *t*. Ring of bronze band ending in two spirals, from Mycenae. See p. 406. *u, v*. Gold hair-rings from Marmariani. See p. 402. *w*. Ring of bronze band with obliquely cut ends, which probably had spiral terminals, from Prilep. See p. 321. *x*. Open-ended plain armlet, from Prilep. See p. 321.

INDEX

When a figure is in italics, it is the main reference.
The names in the Appendix are not included in this Index.

Ossa, Mt., Maps 12 and 19; vii, 9, 11, 137 n. 2, 233, 273, 401

Ostrovo, L., Maps 1 and 19; 8 f., 11, *51 f.*, 54, 266, 340, 369

Ostrovo, town, Map 7; *51 f.*, 106, 108, 207

Osum, R., Maps 10 and 19; 36 f., 95, 97

Othrys, Mt., 238

Ottolobus, Maps 6 and 10; 61, *64*, 65 n. 2, 71

Ouallai, 154

Ovče Polje, Map 1; 8 f.

Ovens, 280

Ovovo, 173

Ox, wild, *see* Aurochs

Pactolus, 147

Paeones *and* Paeonia, Maps 9, 17, and 23; 16 f., 47 n. 4, 69, 75 n. 4, 76, *78* f., 81 f., 88, 100, 109, 143, 153, 167 f., 171 f., 174, 176, 179 n. 3, 181, 192 n. 2, 194, 199 n. 1, 200, *204*, 209 f., 218, 231; in Homer, 296 f.; 301, 303; metal-working, 313; 327, 370, 415 f.; in Macedonia, *418 f.*; 421 f., 423, 427; move westwards, 428 f.; 431, 436 f., 438

Pagasae, 5, 267, 400

Paiko, Mt., Maps 1, 14, and 19; 13, 153, *167*, 206

Palaiogratsiano, Maps 11 and 21; *120*, 155 n. 1, 159, 302, 345 f., 402

Palaiokastron, Map 19; 215

Palaion, 160

Palatianon, Map 14; viii, *181 f.*, 195, 207

Palatitsa, Maps 12 and 22; viii, 13, 129, 133, *155 f.*, 157, 207, 329, 435, 438

Paleokastro, 159

Paleokhora, 133 n. 2

Palia Goritsa, 423 n. 2

Palilula, 382 n. 4

Palio-Sotira, 163

Pallene, C., Maps 1 and 17; 4 n. 1, 9, 132, *186 f.*, 188, 189 n. 2, 301, 426

Pan, 77

Panaei, 428 n. 1

Pandanassa, 217

Pangaeum, Mt., Map 1; 14, 16, 193, 209, 438

Panther, 209

Papoulia, 259, 344

Paradimi, 225 n. 7, 238 n. 3

Paramythia, 293 n. 2

Parauaei, Map 11; 5 f., *74*, 91, 95, 97 n. 3, 102, 109 n. 2, 111, 122 n. 1, 310 n. 2

Paraxia, 179

Paraxiaei, 109

Parembole, Map 6; 39, *42*, 60 f.

Parnassus, Mt., 116

Paroikopolis, 197

Parorbelia, Map 17; 169, *199*, 203

Paroreia, Map 17; 199 n. 2

Parthenopolis, 183

Parthikopolis, *see* Paroikopolis

Parthini, Map 23; 23 n. 3, 33 n. 5, *36*, 74, 91, 95 n. 3, 96, 97 n. 3, 381 f., 422 f.

Partho, 381

Parthos, Map 10; 33 n. 5, 96

Pasikrata, 70

Pateli, *see* Ayios Pandeleëmon

Patrae, Map 4; 29, 32 f.

Patraüs, 181

Patroclus, 297

Paulus, Aemilius, 84, 122 n. 1, 138, 272

Pausanias, 183, 190

Pautalia, Maps 5 and 17; 179 n. 3, 199 n. 1, 202, 204, 210

Pazhok, Map 20; *247 f.*, 257 f., 259 n. 7, 260 nn. 1, 2, 4, and 6, 265, 281 f., 285, 287, 289 f., 293 n. 1, 294, 329, 337, 340, 349 n. 4, 351, 374, 413

Pebble-axe, 233 n. 1, 244, 247 n. 1

Peć, 6, 10, 83, 378, 382

Pecinj, R., Map 1; 4, 8, 10, 12 f., 82 f.

Pegasus, 196

Peierion, 139 n. 1

Pelagones *and* Pelagonia, Maps 9 and 17; 6, 9 f., 13 f., 16 f., 44, 46, *59 f.*, 65, 72, 74, 75 n. 4, 77–83, 88, 90 f., 102 f., 109, 111, 120 f., 143, 153, 166, 173, 175 n. 1, 201, 207, 209, 215, 218 f., 222–7, 232, 238 f.; Minyan ware in, 241, 252; 254, 272, 280, 290, 292 f., 294 n. 3, 295 n. 4; and Troy, 296 f.; axes in, 299; Briges in, 303, 305; metal-working in, 313; 317, 319, 347, 368, 370, 381, 387, 401, 405–12, 414 f., 418, 421, 424, 431, 436, 439, 441 n. 1

'Pelagoniae fauces', Maps 6 and 9; *60*, 65, 68

Pelagonian massif, 10 f.

Pelasgians, 274

Pelegon, 297

Peleus, 301 n. 1

Pelikata, 281

Pelinna, Map 11; 109 f., 118

Pelion, Mt., Map 19; 9, 11, 276, 416

Pelium, 100 f., 109, 118, 209

Pella, Maps 14, 15, 16, and 19; viii, 13, 17, 19, 48 f., 51, 54 f., 57, 74, 75 n. 4, 108 f., 122, 131 f., 138, 143, 146 f., *152 f.*, 159 f., 167 f., 171, 183 f., 190, 192, 203, 206, 410, 428, 435 n. 1, 437

Pellas, 152

Pelops, 304

Pendalofon, Map 11; 5, 116

Pendants (*see* Table on pp. 363–4 and p. 420): anchor, 347, 351; ball, 355 f., 357, 360, 367; bead, 356, 396; bean, 351; bell and

Proto-Geometric pottery (*see* Table on p. 365), 312, 323, 326 f., 346 n. 6, 347, 367, 369, 388, *390 f.*, 398 n. 1, 403 n. 1, 404 n. 2, 407, 410, 429 with n. 2

Protopapa, Map 10; 99

Proto-Sesklo period, 219

Ptolemaïdha, Map 8; 13, *106*

Ptolemy, 116 n. 3

Pudaea, Map 12; 126 n. 2

Pydna, Map 12; 108 f., 126 n. 2, *128 f.*, 132 f.. 138, 146, 154, 158, 183, 186, 188, 192, 206 f.; battle of, 129, 158

Pylon, 27, 33 n. 4, 39, *41*, 54, 78 n. 2, 97

Pylos in Elis, 259, 263, 276

Pylos in Messenia, 259, 263, 265, 269 n. 1, 273, 276 n. 1, 344

Pyraechmes, 176, 296

Pyrites, 14

Pyrrhus, 157, 159

Pythion *and* Pythoüs, Maps 11 and 12; *117 f.*, 123, 137 n. 3, 155, 158

Qadrishtë, 97

Qarrë, 102

Qukës, Maps 4, 10, and 18; 33, 35

Qytet i Skanderbegut, 378

Radanja, Map 22; 356, 421

Radika, R., 43 f.

Radovište, Maps 1, 8, and 10

Rainfall, 4 f., 10

Rajetz, R., Maps 1 and 9; 9, 59, *66*, 72, 79, 209

Rakhmani, Map 19; 225, 233, 264 n. 7

Raleica, 94

Ramniste, 174

Ramphias, 138

Rapsani, Map 12; 137 f.

Ravenna Geographer, 24 f., 42, 67, 78, 108 n. 5, 131, 169, 178 f., 197 n. 3

Razmo, St., *see* Erasmus, St.

Regulus, P. Memmius, 170

Rendina, Map 17; 182, 184, *186*, 193 with n. 2, 194 f., 207

Resava, Maps 9 and 14; *65*, 173

Resen, Maps 1, 6, 9, and 18; 9, 13, *41 f.*, 45, 59, 61, 86 n. 3, 93 n. 4, 103

Rhaecalus, *188*, 190, 302

Rhekhias, R., 152

Rhesus, 203

Rhine, R., 270 n. 1

Rhodokhori, cave, Maps 14 and 19; 220, 228 n. 2, 229

Rhodokhori, village, Map 11

Rhodope, Mt., 8 n. 2, 81, 198, 382

Rhoedias, R., *see* Ludias, R., 167 n. 1

Rhyton, 355

Rila, Mt., Map 17; 8 n. 2

Rings (*see* Table on p. 364), 260 n. 4, 261, 265, 328, 331 f., 341, 353, 356 f., 359 n. 5, 360, 372, 379 f., 388, 395, 397, 399 f., *406;* ring-disc, 427 n. 3; 429. *See also* Pendants

Rizari, *see* Rizo

Rizo, 164 n. 3

Roads, Macedonian, 52, 56 f., 109, 138, 156, 158, 170

Roads, Roman, 41, 52, 67 f., 123 n. 5, 127, 131, 161, 170, 174, 178, 198, 202 with n. 6, 204

Rogozhinë, Map 3; 21 n. 4, 26 n. 1, 35 n. 1

Rome *and* Romans, **96**

Rosna, *see* Sitaria

Rosuje, 378

Rotska, R., 42

Roupaki, 259 n. 2, 273

Rudnik, L., Maps 8 and 19; 230, 415

Rufus, M. Minucius, 168

Rumania, 222

Rungaj, Map 3; 26

Rupel Gorge, Map 17; 18, 193, 197, 199 n. 1, 200, 210, 423

Sabatium, Map 5; 131 f., 135, 138 n. 1

Sabattaras, 168

Sabazius, 138 n. 1

Sabina, 179

Sabinianus, 34 f.

Sadevi, 173

Saint Erasmus, monastery, *see* Erasmus, St.

Saint John, *see* Shenjan

Salamis, 407 n. 2

Salcuta, 222

Saletska, R., Map 6; 13, *43*, 45 n. 1, 59 f., 76, 243

Salmanovo, 231 n. 6

Salmone, Salmoneus, 275

Salonica, *see* Thessalonica, Map 19; 3 f., 7, 9, 11 f., 17 f., 49; Museum at, 231 n. 9, 267 n. 7, 299, 339, 343 n. 1, 387 n. 5

Salt, 47, 144, 160, 187, 206 f.

Same, 259

Samikon, 259, 263, 273

Samos, 438

Samothrace, 411

Sandanus, R., 129; *see also* Sardon, R.

Sane, 440

San Naum, Map 6; 45

Sanskimost, 379

Saraïli, *see* Palatianon

Saraj, Map 21; 319, 322, *338 f.*, 366, 371, 377, 380, 398, 424, 441 n. 1

Sarajevo, 378

Sarandaporos, R., in Perrhaebia, 117 f., 295 n. 3

Index